MW00768263

# Curses and Blessings

## Life and Evolution
## in the 20th Century South

*by*

*Andrew M<sup>c</sup>Dowd Secrest*

Andrew McDowd Secrest

Bob + Jane Parr

(Mac)

To good friends and
good bridge players.
Best wishes

AmS

11/17/04

authorHOUSE™

1663 LIBERTY DRIVE, SUITE 200
BLOOMINGTON, INDIANA 47403
(800) 839-8640
WWW.AUTHORHOUSE.COM

© 2004 Andrew M. Secrest
All Rights Reserved.

No part of this book may be reproduced, stored in a retrieval system, or transmitted by any
means without the written permission of the author.

First published by AuthorHouse 10/20/04

ISBN: 1-4184-5945-3 (e)
ISBN: 1-4184-5946-1 (sc)


Library of Congress Control Number: 2004097020


Printed in the United States of America
Bloomington, Indiana

This book is printed on acid-free paper.

# *Acknowledgements*

Appreciation is due to many people who made this book possible, of whom I can name only a few:

Molly Katz, my daughter, who converted illegible handwriting into readable form by computer voice legerdemain;

David Secrest, my son, who offered editing skills;

Lil Buie, my sister, and her daughter Ann Loomis, who lent encouragement rather than caution;

Elizabeth and Calvin Kytle, friends who not only read the story while it was a work in progress, offering useful advice free of charge, but also urged me to complete it whenever I was tempted to consign the entire project to flames;

The Writers' Group at Carolina Meadows, frank but friendly critics;

Bea Witten, who took up where Molly left off and whipped me and the book into final shape;

Ann Secrest, my wife, who has shared fifty-six of my eighty years, read each chapter as it reached completion, and never got cross when I ignored her advice to omit something. Her bluntly supportive final comment: "It's your life and your book. Say whatever you want." And so I have.

# *Dedication*

This book is for family, nuclear and extended; friends, near and far; readers here and there interested in memoir as history, and is dedicated to the memory of times, places and people who are gone but not forgotten.

# Table of Contents

# *Partial Cast of Relatives*

SECREST, Andrew Jackson, my great grandfather (1830-63)
Ambrose Arminius (Pa) (1859-1929) m. Lydia Asbury Price (Ma) (1860-1939)

        Andrew McDowd (Dowd) (1884-1946) m. Celeste Lillian
                Covington (Lessie) (1892-1982)
          Mary Covington (1915-2001) m. William English
          Lillian Asbury (b. 1920) m. John Buie
          Andrew McDowd (b. 1923) m. Ann Louise Eastman
                (b. 1919)
      Bertha m. Charles Hamilton.
          Martha m. Wriston Helms
                Jesse (daughter)
      Martha (Aunt Matt), m. Tip Helms
          G.W. Helms
      Essie m. Claude A. Loflin
          Lucy
          Claude Jr.

      Lydia Asbury (Aunt Lid), m. H.D. McKaughan (Mack).
          Ruth McKaughan Carter
      Edgar Lee (Uncle Ed) m. Evelyn Pratt.
      John m. Olive, divorced.
      Vann V. (Uncle Vann) m. Mary Gordon.
          Vann Jr.
          Sara
      Ruth m. Ad Benton.

Mary m. Henry Hinson, divorced.
Isabel m. Hilliard H. Wolfe.
     Hill Jr.
     Lee
Willis Ambrose m. Marion Schallert.


**COVINGTON**, David Anderson I, my great grandfather, (1809-1870)
m. Susannah Ann Gathings
  David Jr. died age 9
  David Anderson II (1853-98) m. Mary Foote Simmons (Molly)
     Katherine m. James Braxton Craven (Uncle Jim)
        Katherine (died at age 13)
        James Braxton Jr. (Brack).
     David Anderson III (Brother)
     Mary Simmons (Aunt May)
     Susan m. Dr. Earle B. Fowler
        Earle Jr.
        David
        William
        Caroline
     Evabelle Simmons (Aunt Eve)
     Celeste Lillian (Lessie) m. Dowd Secrest
     Miz Thompson, illegitimate but recognized daughter
     of D.A. Covington II
  James G. m. Elizabeth Andrews (Aunt Lizzie)
  Mary Ann m. Dr. Thomas Bickett
     Walter
     Anna Laura m. Frank Ashcraft (Cuz Nannie)
     Lillian m. Richard Lewis Brewer (Cousin Lillian)
  Martha Wall, m. Charles Lockhart
     Jesse & William Lockhart, their grandsons
  Susan Sophia m. Hugh Houston.
     Rosa Blakeney Parker & Martha Blakeney
        Hodges, their granddaughters
  Celestia m. Robert Virgil Houston
     Clarence Eustace m. Miriam Stamps
        Midge
        Clarence Jr.
        Edward Roe
        Stamps


**SIMMON**S, Benjamin, my great, great, great grandfather

(1751-1836) m. Nancy Alexander (1767-1846)
Lockey (1796-1880) m. Mary Lundy Pennington (1809-34)
Gaston (1830-1889) m. Mary Elizabeth Foote (1833-1918)
    Nancy (Sis Nannie) m. Henry Trantham
    Ada m. Edgar Timberlake
        Edgar
        Ada Lee
    Mary Alexander (Molly) (1859-1917), my grandmother, m. D.A.
        Covington II
    Henry, m. Lillian (Lily) White
        Henry Jr.
        Tom
        Gaston
        Kate
        Lillian
        Mary Foote
        Lessie
    Thomas, m. Lessie Southgate
    Evabelle
    Willie m. Edwin Yates Webb
        Betty m. Roy Veatch
        Edwin
        William

**A few other connections:**
Mary E. Foote's sister, Ella Lillian Foote, m. U.S. Rep. John H. Kerr
Faye Webb, Betty Webb's paternal aunt, m. Governor O. Max Gardner.
Max Gardner's sister m. Governor Clyde R. Hoey.
Dr. G. Marvin Smith (Dowd's first cousin through the Monseur Price line not traced here) m. Betty Howie
    Peggy
    Kelly Ann
    George Jr. (Spud)
Rachel Howie, Betty Howie's sister

*For descendants in later generations, see Chapter 50, "New Branches on the Family Tree."*

# *Introduction*

This book is unlike any other I have ever read. It started as a conventional family memoir, but it moves out in all directions, from a small North Carolina town to a Southern perspective on the nation and world at large in the twentieth century.

Mac Secrest is the son of an affluent and prominent family, and his chronicle of their connections near and far includes a huge cast of characters. He spares no one and paints portraits of each one with "warts and all." He mines his memories with remarkable clarity from earliest childhood until well beyond his promised three score years and ten.

Family relationships have always had great importance in the American South. Everyone seems to be kin to everyone else. Cousins abound. For example, when he writes about being born in the same town as Jesse Helms, he notes a close relative who was "first cousin to Jesse's sister-in-law." Indeed, this book gives credence to the claim that there are only "six degrees of separation" from any of us to all others. Although the book also demonstrates that "everybody has a story," this is primarily the story of Mac Secrest who, with a "stream of consciousness"-like style, shares his every thought and insight with the reader.

Secrest's contacts with famous North Carolinians include Luther Hodges, "Skipper" Bowles, Terry Sanford, "Choo Choo" Justice, Harvey Gantt, and W.W. Finlator. Nationally, people whose paths he crossed include Richard Nixon during Nixon's student years at Duke, Dizzy

Gillespie, James Reston, Martin Luther King, Jr., Mohammed Ali, and John Kennedy, whom he met after requesting an invitation to a White House dinner!

A major sub-theme of the book is mental illness, which Secrest calls "the Simmons Curse." He remembers his mother as a victim of what people called "a nervous breakdown." For her and other family members this led to long absences in far away institutions. The family is properly described as dysfunctional, but Mac himself functioned remarkably well in a self-assured and sometimes aggressive way. Even so, a fear that he too would someday suffer a similar fate hovered over him like a dark cloud.

He confesses an underlying agnosticism in response to the intense religious environment that is so typical of small Southern towns. Yet, even as a "Doubting Thomas," he maintained an optimistic attitude that sustained him as he revealed a faith in a Providence that works things out. He is skeptical but never cynical.

The book is a remarkable sociological illustration of how the racial issue played out in two small Southern communities. It illustrates the reality that there is no such thing as the South; there are many Souths. There was exceptional acceptance of multiculturalism in Monroe, North Carolina, even though black people were seldom seen as anything more than a servant class. Later, when Secrest became the owner and publisher of the local newspaper in Cheraw, South Carolina, he found it possible to address the injustices highlighted in the Civil Rights Movement without the furor that often accompanied such courage in other Southern towns.

Indeed Secrest, himself a product of the South, spent two years employed by the federal government in the Community Relations Service which led to his becoming a mediator in the racial impasse in Selma, Alabama. He helped broker an agreement between protesters and law enforcement agencies that prevented certain further bloodshed. Secrest is one of many Southerners who have lived through the Second Reconstruction of the American South and who now see it as emerging from its traditional role as a scapegoat of the nation to the nation's showplace. Today the region seems light years removed from the segregated fortress of its past, despite evidence of resegregation in some urban public schools due to white flight.

As a precocious child, Secrest was interested in politics and in what was happening far beyond Monroe. His book serves as a running commentary on national and world events as seen through the eyes of a maturing adult. No doubt it was this interest that led him first to a career in journalism and later in education as a faculty member in the School of Journalism at the University of North Carolina in Chapel Hill and then at North Carolina Central University in Durham.

Mac's journalistic talents are evident throughout this lengthy volume. Some of the chapters read like feature stories, covering a wide range of topics, while others reveal a reportorial and an editorial style. Anyone interested in the American South will get a good taste of its flavor by reading this book. Faithful to its title, it recounts "Curses and Blessings" and offers a genuine perspective on "Life in the 20th Century South."


Robert E. Seymour, Minister Emeritus, the Olin T. Binkley Memorial Baptist Church, Chapel Hill, North Carolina

July 2004

# *Preface*

This book is a literary hybrid. It is not an autobiography, although it is much about me. It is not exactly a memoir, although it deals with people who shaped the way I came to look at things and deeply affected my life. It is neither history nor fiction, although it deals with factual events in a narrative style. One editor called it a "life and times book," revealing a personal story that sometimes reads like a diary or a private letter. I intrude upon the lives of many individuals as my life unfolds (and occasionally unravels), from parents and sisters to other relatives and friends, classmates and teachers, enemies and allies, as well as a miscellany of characters who enlivened, enriched, informed and otherwise influenced me.

I have sought to bring these people, largely lost in the shadows of the past, back into the sunlight of the present. As a writer I value the chance to extend memory and provide a prolonged life to people among the pages of a book. Neglected, they recede like Alice's Cheshire cat, growing dimmer and dimmer until all memory of their ever having lived disappears.

It should come as no surprise that as a child of the South I concentrate on family. While intimacy generates anger as well as affection, I have sought to strike a balance. Life, like Greek drama, dons masks of both comedy and tragedy, but I have chosen usually to laugh rather than to cry. Life in Southern places, I have found, is crowded with people like me whose families occasionally become dysfunctional, yet who typify their time and place. I have lived through four-fifths of the twentieth century. The one-fifth that came before my time I have learned about through research and reading, and from songs and stories my mother taught me.

Although a memoir is usually told chronologically, it requires some organization around themes. I have found parallels between my personal life and broader matters: race and religion, politics (foreign and domestic), sex and gender, sectionalism and federalism, class and ethnic conflict, mental illness and its treatment, war and peace.

In discussing these issues, I found it necessary occasionally to abandon the time line and fastforward the projector of life, foreshadowing or jumping ahead thirty or so years, only to reverse the process later and flash back a generation or two. My life and times in the twentieth century had its origins in the nineteenth and extends into the twenty-first, so the account cannot be consistently chronological.

As a writer I learned early on not to allow mere fact to get in the way of a good story, so long as I did not confuse fact with fiction. While the book is not designed to be instructive, it does contain commentary and conclusion that may provide insight into the human experience. You are free to draw your own conclusions.

I accept the opinion of Socrates that "an unexamined life is not worth living," and I've tried to follow Apollo's advice to "know thyself." This book has been an exercise toward that purpose. But I feel that a corollary may be equally important: to "forget thyself" and to merge one's self-consciousness into a broader awareness of the value of all things.


Andrew M. Secrest

Chapel Hill, North Carolina

July 2004

# *Prologue*

In October 1982 Locke Everette, perennial bachelor and best man at Dowd and Lessie Secrest's marriage in 1914, stopped by Wagram, North Carolina to pay his respects. Lessie at 90 had died peacefully in her sleep at her daughter Lil Buie's home, not far from his own in Bennettsville, South Carolina.

Locke carried his 97 years lightly, his mind as sharp as ever, his step lively. His thick hair was snow white, nose rose red, eyes a fading blue. Locke was in a reminiscent mood.

"Lil, your mother was a remarkable woman but, you know, I never thought that she and Dowd would be so well-suited. They came from such different backgrounds. Lessie was gentle and genteel. Dowd, rough and ready."

Dowd had died in 1946. Lil made a noncommittal reply. "Well, they gave all the years they had to each other. I guess that says a lot."

" I know, girl! " Locke replied. "That's what is so surprising. Here I was thinking this will never do, and look how well everything turned out. They complemented and supplemented each other perfectly. Three fine children, 13 grandchildren, and a happy, compatible life together. That just shows what an old bachelor like me knows."

Lil's mind flashed back to events over the years—some good, some not. She wondered how much Locke really knew. Her face bore an enigmatic smile, concealing contradictory and ironic memories. She thought to herself, "I wonder what Mary C. would say, and Mac, were they to hear Locke's Final Judgment?"

# Part I

# Childhood

# 1923-1935

# 1. When Mom's Away

A boy set apart. That is how early on I looked upon myself. It has been a feeling I've experienced intermittently ever since. I was literally set apart, or at least set aside, the day I was born on an early Saturday evening, September 15, 1923. Dr. G. M. Smith, my father's first cousin, had come around to Broadacre at 809 South Hayne St. in Monroe, N.C., to answer Dowd Secrest's insistent call for help.

"Hurry up, Marvin," Dowd ordered the young doctor, "Come along now without delay. Lessie is having a lot of pain." Daddy, a pharmacist, thought he knew a lot about medicine. He sensed that as the contractions increased, all did not bode well. Lessie Covington Secrest, to become 31 years old the next day, was preparing to present her husband, Andrew McDowd Secrest, 39, with a birthday surprise. Mother, I've been told, was stoical when dealing with physical pain and outwardly composed when faced with medical emergencies. But she too felt apprehension that afternoon.

"Yes, Mr. Secrest," she said to her husband, "Tell him to hurry. Something isn't right." Lessie, having already given birth to two girls, Mary Covington eight years earlier, and Lillian Asbury four years later, wasn't a novice at giving birth. The first two pregnancies had been normal and relatively easy. By the time Dr. Smith arrived at Broadacre, a sprawling two-story frame house my grandfather had built for his wife in 1889, I was already on my way out. Having babies at home was no novelty in Monroe in the early 1920s, the Ellen Fitzgerald Hospital a few blocks up the street having been completed only two years before. Mother herself had been born at Broadacre on September 16, 1892.

"All right, Lessie," Big Doc said. "Let's go to work. Give us a big push. This little baby is just about here." Soon the baby boy, full-term and weighing nearly nine pounds, was pulled out, wiped off, and patted firmly on the back, after which he let out a lusty yell.

But all was not over. Another baby, a replica of the first, was unexpectedly on its way. Unlike the first, he didn't come quite so quickly or easily. Something first had to be uncoiled from around his neck. The first baby, still yelling, red-faced, wrinkled and apparently furious, was hurriedly set apart. Attention had to be given to this unannounced second arrival.

After what seemed like a long interval but probably lasted only a few minutes, Dr. Smith turned to his cousin. "I'm sorry, Dowd. I did the best I could, but the cord was just bound too tightly. There wasn't sufficient oxygen and I couldn't keep him breathing."

So the surviving bawling baby boy, later christened Andrew McDowd Secrest Jr., so quickly set apart from his dead identical twin brother, was picked back up and placed with his mother, and David Covington Secrest, whose spark of life had briefly flickered, then faded, was taken away. The clock on the mantel read 7:00 o'clock.

Lil, not yet four, remembered the funeral for my twin and later penned these lines which presaged the bond between us that has lasted a lifetime:

> That special September Day
> Etched in memory far away
> Mother in bed
> A lacy cap upon her head.
>
> A nurse sterilizing Mother's kiss
> Making me feel something must be amiss.
> My pink bassinet now trimmed in blue,
> And Daddy's saying,
> "See what the stork has brought to you!"
>
> And then a trip to the freshly dug grave
> And my feeling—I must be brave.-
> I imitated my sister as she
> Bowed her head in prayer,
> All the while restless
> As we were kneeling there.

In tightly fisted hand I held the button mums
Gold in the September sun.
Daddy explained that this little brother
Had decided to stay with God on high
And that we had come to bless him
And then to say goodbye.

Mary C., aware of her advancing age,
Smiled as wisely as a sage.
But I shook my head and firmly said
"This one can be yours.
Mine is the stork baby
Asleep by Mother's bed."

Although I was the prized heir apparent, thoroughly loved and cosseted from the day I was born, I also was set apart—or set aside—not only on that occasion but several others as well. I was just four years old when another separation occurred. One day in mid-September, 1927, a loving mother was there as usual, providing all the care and maternal support a young child needs. The next day she was gone. No goodbyes. No explanations. No reassurances. Just gone. In her place appeared a gray-haired, angular, severe-looking woman, Miss Julia, who was to be my caregiver and substitute mother. The first night I slept in the bed with her I yowled, probably as lustily and loudly as I had four years earlier. I can't remember the events of 1923, but those on my fourth birthday I recall as vividly as if they had happened yesterday.

Apparently I accepted Miss Julia fairly quickly. She wasn't a demonstrative woman like my real mother, and she wasn't much fun. She never told stories, played games, or read aloud to me. But she was kind enough in her own brusque country way, keeping me clean, well fed and properly dressed. I can still recall the sense of loneliness I felt at night, though. I missed my mama. My older sisters were attentive and patient, sometimes too much so, but they couldn't take a mother's place. And no doubt they were lonely, too.

I don't know why I started sleeping with my elderly caregiver in the first place, but it had something to do with my becoming afraid of the dark. One night I awoke to find myself cuddled up to Miss Julia, who was sound asleep, her head covered in an old nightcap. I can remember putting my head on her bony chest and none too ample bosom, then feeling for her breasts.

5

The next morning I heard voices in the sun parlor as the adults prepared breakfast. A flustered Miss Julia was trying to explain to Daddy that her four-year-old charge had groped her during the night. "Mr. Secrest, I think I'd better let you know," and her voice dropped to a whisper. I knew I was in trouble but I wasn't quite sure why. When I looked in, there gathered around the table were, in addition to Daddy and Miss Julia, my two maiden aunts, May and Eve, as well as sisters Mary C. and Lil, both looking big-eyed and serious. Nothing was said to me, but I understood that I was the topic of the breakfast conversation.

That night I slept alone and lonely upstairs in a huge feather bed, plenty big enough I thought for me and Mother and even Miss Julia. Dark shadows cast strange patterns on the walls and in dark corners. Who knew what lurked there? I was by turns shivering with fear and sweating with anxiety. I surely felt set apart and adrift from all those I loved.

I awoke to blue sky and the sound of birds singing and pigeons cooing. And the sound of two men laughing loudly. Daddy was talking to Locke Everette, his old friend, business associate, and best man.

"You should have seen the expression on that old maid's face," Daddy said to Locke. "You'd have thought the sun had set in the East." And they laughed again. "I bet it was the first time anyone had ever grabbed hold of her titties." Both men, seeing me at the door, welcomed me in, and as I sat down, still in pajamas, Daddy regaled Locke with my investigation of Miss Julia's mammary glands, such as they were. Neither man reproached me for my behavior, but neither showed any inclination to disregard the matter in my presence. For many months thereafter, my midnight amorous turn with Miss Julia was the source of much teasing, storytelling and exaggeration, especially during family gatherings every Saturday night at Ma's —my paternal grandmother.

It was no joke to me—more a source of embarrassment and shame. With so much openly made of it, how could I forget? But I didn't dwell on it. Instead, I put the memories aside until enough time had passed for them to be safely brought back out into the light for examination from a different perspective.

While Mother was away that year, Daddy had to be "mother and father both," as he would often say. He wasn't cut out for the role, preoccupied with business interests and lacking patience with or much understanding of prepubescent children. Mary C., now 12, was becoming more self-assertive, often trying to provoke a row with the authority figure. She probably was also seeking Daddy's attention, not having gotten over being pre-empted from the number one spot when Lil came along and later me.

I had nursemaids, first Vancy, then Mary, both nice young black women who doubtless had personal lives of their own, about which we neither knew nor cared. They were paid two dollars a week and provided food and a room of their own. Their responsibility was to look after and keep me out of harm's way. One day Daddy, at home for a nap after an early midday dinner, was awakened by screams in the backyard. Up he jumped to find Vancy carrying me by my right arm while I writhed around and bellowed loudly.

"What's the matter? What's happened to Mac?" Daddy shouted.

"I dunno, suh," Vancy replied. "I jest jerked him up off the ground to keep him from getting dirty, and he starts to throw a fit." Daddy took me from Vancy and examined me, noting my right arm hung limply from the shoulder. I can still remember the searing pain. As my right cheek pressed heavily against his rough wool coat, scratching and burning my face, I began to howl anew.

"How did you pick him up, Vancy?" Daddy asked, his voice rising in suspicious anger. "What did you do?"

"Why, I just jerked him up by his right arm and pulled him up off the ground where he was rolling around, gittin' all dirty," the girl replied, "and he started hollerin'. That's all I knows about it."

"Well, you damn fool, you probably pulled his arm out of the socket. Don't you know any better than that? That's no way to pick up a child," and Daddy, quick to anger, and quick to repent, rolled up the morning newspaper lying nearby and struck Vancy across the head with it —a glancing blow that could have caused no real pain but carried with it a menacing message and a sense of humiliation. Vancy cringed to ward off the blow and then burst into tears, saying she'd meant no harm to little Macky.

Mary C. and Lil, alerted by all the noise, came in just as the blow was struck. Mary C., scandalized, shouted, " Daddy, how dare you treat Vancy like that?"

Daddy's reply, "Vancy, you're fired. Pack your stuff and get out of here."

Whereupon Lil, also siding with the nursemaid, declared, " Daddy, Vancy didn't mean anything by it. Fire Vancy? Oh, I'll never be happy again!" and she burst into tears.

By now I had stopped crying but when I saw Lil, soon to be joined by Vancy, I started to cry in protest as well, while Mary C. continued to berate Daddy for his unkind treatment of Vancy. Daddy was in the doghouse. But harassed, uncontrolled and uncontrollable Dowd had been right. My arm had been pulled from the socket, requiring yet another unwanted visit from Dr. Smith. My shoulder hurt when he snapped it back into place and put it in a sling.

Mary C. and Lil soon got over Vancy's loss, as she'd not been in our employ very long nor was ever a beloved companion. I soon forgot about her as well. My older sisters now turned all their attention to me, who enjoyed again being the center of attention. Soon Aunt Eve and Aunt May were on hand to see what could and should be done as well as cousin Annie Ashcraft, Aunt Kathryn Huntley, and Miss Ann Redwine, as well as the neighborhood friends of Lil and Mary C. Daddy, forgiven for his abuse of Vancy and approved for properly protecting his son from further unintentional damage, was no doubt glad to leave home for his beloved tenant farmers, who gave him a whole lot less grief.

Such excitable scenes were not unusual in Broadacre during Mother's year-long sabbatical. One night just before bedtime Lil, Mary C. and I were playing a game. Mary Cov had earlier ragged and teased me till I was about to cry. I remember a feeling of anger but not the specific cause. Knowing her ability to get my goat, I'm sure it was something she had done. In any event, as we were playing some parlor game and I was passing along in front of my seated sisters to deliver some surprise in their hands, I lashed out at Mary C. and slapped her as hard as I could in the face with my open palm.

Stung by anger and surprise, she struck back, whereupon I started to yell bloody murder. In charged Daddy, looking both menacing and harassed, to demand what had happened. Knowing only that I had been slapped by my older sister and not knowing about my earlier misdeed, he blamed Mary Cov, verbally berating her. Then out came the rolled up newspaper, just like the one used not long before on Vancy. He struck Mary C. on the head. It was a blow that, if not heard around the world, was heard all around the family forever after. Mary C. never stopped talking about that injustice and indignity, nor did Lil or I let Daddy forget about it. All three children now were united against the authority figure who was in turn bawling Mary C. out for mistreating her pesky four-year-old brother. Mary C. forgot, when retelling this tale, to add that she had replied "Oh, bull!" to every one of Daddy's reprimands.

No, without Mother on hand, Broadacre was not a very peaceful place, not that it improved much when she did return. While Daddy may not have approved of an older sister inflicting bodily harm on her much younger brother, he wasn't above misbehaving himself if he were seriously provoked.

Some months later, I was in the living room, playing some solitary game, while Mary C. and Lil were doing homework. My dog, a mixture of hound and bulldog called Joe that had just come up one day to the front porch and been allowed to stay, was lying nearby. Joe thrived on the good indoor life, sleeping on the best beds and chairs, but he had never been vaccinated for rabies. In the poverty-ridden South of the 1920s, people didn't provide that kind of protection for their animals or themselves. Pets didn't get other vaccinations for respiratory infections or medication for deworming either, and were thus subject to occasional running fits.

One minute Joe would be resting and snoozing happily, the next he'd jump up, tremble and shake and then take off—running in great round circles until he collapsed on the floor, jerking, panting, breathing heavily, his eyes rolled up into his head. Then he'd come to, trot over and lick my hand and face.

Daddy often could reveal a mean sense of humor. He sometimes would spray "High Life," that smelled like ether and stung the skin, on one of our hounds, causing him to run in circles just as if he really did have a running fit. As this practice received universal condemnation from the rest of the family, Daddy would often find himself condemned and in the psychological doghouse himself, so he eventually gave up that little game.

On this particular evening Joe, blissfully happy and sound asleep, began to break wind, as many bulldog-type dogs are prone to do. "Joe," Mary C. snapped. "You stink!" Joe flattened his ears, pinched in his bobbed tail, looked guilty and ashamed, and then did it again. But Joe was not the only guilty party. I had felt the need to go to the bathroom for a long time but had put it off to play. Soon I was joining Joe in breaking wind, a fact which Lil suspected and then accused me of but which I denied.

"No, it's not me," I lied.

"It is too," Lil insisted. "I can tell the difference."

The dispute continued until both girls finally left Joe and me to our own foul odors. As time passed, the need to go left me also, but now I had the urge to relieve my bladder. I had postponed that task, being both lazy and preoccupied with play, but soon the need was too great. I hid behind the big green chair, alone and ashamed and soaking wet, leaving behind a considerable puddle.

Knowing that I'd done wrong and feeling guilt and dread of uncertain consequences, I just stayed hidden behind the chair, ignoring calls from Daddy to come get ready for bed. Miss Julia finally found me sitting behind the chair and discovered the puddle. Finding my shorts soaked, she declined to believe my excuse that the puddle was Joe's fault.

9

"Mr. Secrest, please come in here," Miss Julia called. "I think Mac needs you." She wasn't about to clean up after a boy four years old. Daddy came on a trot, relieved that I'd been found. But relief soon turned by way of indignation and disgust to rage as he discovered I'd wet my pants.

"Well, Joe certainly did not do this," Daddy shouted. "He is housebroken. And you should be toilet-trained." Dog owners often taught their puppies not to wet by rubbing their noses into the rug where the mess was made, popping their rear ends and setting them outside along with cries of "Shame! Bad dog!" Daddy, lacking self-control at home (though seldom elsewhere), dragged me kicking and screaming from behind the green chair by one leg. He roughly pulled down my shorts, stripped them off, rolled them up into a urine-sodden ball and started washing my face with it. I howled and yelled, but Daddy, apparently believing what was good for a puppy was good for a boy, rubbed my nose in it thoroughly. Then he gave me a slap on my rear, picked me up and set me outside.

That year of 1927-28 was a lonely one. I can remember being walked down to a local playground, Lake Tondawanda, with swings, merry-go-round and other rides, by my colored nurse Mary Garrison and feeling alone, empty, restless, even sad. I had become left-handed, well before I could write, and Mary had taken it upon herself to correct that. Every time I'd start to use my left hand, Mary was there to shift me to the right. Before the year was out, I had begun to stutter. For years there were certain words I would stumble over. Like a lot of other things later on, I got over this on my own. And I remained left-handed.

My paternal grandfather, whom we called "Pa," died that same year. I remember him remotely as a kind, gentle figure. He just keeled over and died one Sunday morning in Central Methodist Church, which he had faithfully attended and generously supported all his adult life. I sat in the backseat of the car as Daddy drove Mary C., Lil and me to the funeral and could see in the rearview mirror tears forming in Daddy's eyes and gradually rolling down his face.

"Ma" once said to Mother, " Oh, I know you like Ambrose better than you do me. You think he's just about perfect, don't you? Well, do you know what he said to me one day when I was trying to help him fix the stove?"

"No, Ma, I don't, but I'm sure it was something very kind and gentle," Lessie replied.

"Oh, you are, are you? Well, let me set that straight. He turned to me as quick as you please and said—I remember his exact words— 'I wish you'd hush.' Can you beat that?"

Well, yes, Mother could, since Ambrose's son, Dowd, had a colorful vocabulary and, like his mother, could become sulfurous when angered. I recall some pretty rough name-calling and personal insults being hurled about, including his calling Mother "fat-assed" for something that she had done to displease him.

But Mother had learned to accept earthy language after many years of marriage and took such oral abuse in stride. On that occasion, she unexpectedly laughed heartily, named herself "Fatatia of the Veils" and performed a spontaneous belly dance, after which everyone, including Daddy, relaxed in laughter.

# 2. Little Gladiators and Dominating Dads

Uncle Vann Secrest and Vann's children, Vann Jr. and Sara, were in and out of my life for as long as I can remember. Uncle Vann was nine years younger than his brother Dowd but they were very close. Cousin Vann is two months older than I. Today Vann Jr. is a happily married father of four and grandfather of eight, richer than God, and a revered elder statesman of Monroe.

Vann and I graduated from Walter Bickett High School together at 16, for all practical purposes completed our education at Duke University by 19, where we were fraternity brothers, then joined the U.S. Navy together. We were assigned to temporary duty at Willow Grove Naval Air Station in Pennsylvania and received our U.S.N.R. commissions as ensigns from Harvard University, still shy of our 21st birthdays.

We were fast friends as well as first cousins, but my earliest memory of Vann was not a happy one. From our first encounter at age four, I came away feeling defeated, ashamed, rejected, and guilty—and none of that was either Vann's fault or mine. The culprits were our fathers, Dowd and Vann. Vann was the only brother of the four Dowd had whose company he really enjoyed and whose opinions he valued. I can recall one dressing down the younger brother gave the older one in the fall of 1938 which Dowd accepted with uncharacteristic humility. He knew Uncle Vann was right and he wrong, something Dowd could seldom recognize, let alone admit.

In late July 1928, Daddy took me to visit Uncle Vann and their older sister Aunt Matt and her husband Uncle Tip Helms, their retarded son, G.W., whose mental age was about two, and Vann's children, Vann Jr., just turned five, and Sara, three. Already on hand were Daddy's younger brothers John and Willis and two sisters, Lydia and Mary. Vann lived in a big brick house in Benton Heights, a little settlement just outside Monroe on the Charlotte highway. Uncle Vann's wife, Mary Gordon, was not present. She had been over earlier for Sunday dinner but had returned to her mother's home on West Franklin Street in Monroe, which was her permanent residence.

Mary had been stricken with encephalitis shortly after Sara's birth. Her life hung in the balance for months and when she regained consciousness, her motor skills were damaged, her vocal cords adversely affected, and her emotions deeply scarred. Her appearance was also ravaged—eyes sunk deep in their sockets, long in the tooth as her gums receded, her once fair skin loose and mottled, her thick, dark hair, formerly her crowning glory, thin and brittle. As she walked assisted, she lurched along as in a bad dream. More like a nightmare.

Her brain, however, was not affected. She understood her condition. I once saw Aunt Mary look into a mirror, then shake her head and cover her eyes with palsied hands and sob as if her heart were breaking. It probably was.

On this particular day we were gathered in the front parlor when the two brothers decided it would be fun to see which son could best the other in a wrestling match. I didn't want to fight. I doubt that Vann did. We weren't mad at each other. I felt first apprehension and then was downright scared. Vann probably felt the same way. But soon Vann Jr. and I were shoved against each other, and amid shouts of encouragement and competitive urging, we were writhing, hitting and rolling over each other on the hardwood floor. It was as if we were two tiny gladiators, each with some kind of personal honor to uphold. First Vann was on top, then I, then Vann again, as the battle swirled this way and that, along with shouts of encouragement to pin the adversary down.

Suddenly I realized I was losing, that Vann was holding me down, his shirt pressing against my face, making it difficult for me to catch my breath. I began to feel smothered and panicked—lest I let my cheering section down. With growing desperation I opened my mouth and bit down hard. Vann let out a startled cry and drew back. Then adult hands reached down to pull him off me, along with reproving comments.

"Mac, no fair! No biting. You can't fight like that," someone said.

"What a thing to do," declared another voice. "What a bad sport. Only babies bite."

Big hands lifted me up with an impatient shake, placed me on my feet, and hustled me out in general disapproval from Vann's house. There was no sympathy and no mother to wipe my tears away or to console my battered ego, only a feeling of humiliation for having lost a fight with an evenly matched opponent and a sense of shame for having used babyish tactics in an effort to avoid defeat.

About five years later, I got even with Vann, although I didn't connect my deception then with the earlier fight. By age nine I had started collecting pigeons and must have had hundreds in cages. Daddy suggested I give a few to Vann. Aunt Matt reluctantly agreed to help Vann tend to them.

I didn't want to part with any but acquiesced as several were placed in containers and we drove over to Benton Heights to deliver them. With the pigeons safely cooped up and as we were about to leave, I whispered to Vann, "After a couple of days, let 'em loose. They're used to flying free," I lied. "They won't live long in cages, and they're not homing pigeons. They'll stick around."

Presumably Vann Jr., Aunt Matt and G.W. believed that, for within two or three days, I spied the pigeons flying around the corn crib. Soon Doll Jr., my black best friend, and I had successfully trapped them and once all were accounted for had placed them back in their pens. This loss didn't disappoint Vann or Sara. They hadn't shown much enthusiasm for the gift in the first place, and they had plenty of chickens, ducks, kittens, and other little creatures that Aunt Matt lovingly tended to.

Vann Jr. led a happy life with Uncle Vann, Sara, Aunt Matt and G.W. It was a part of southern small-town life to accept one's family as one found it, "including the least of these." Everyone not only accepted G.W., this two-year-old child in a man's body, but loved him, even enjoyed his company. He certainly was not shut away with any sort of secret shame. G.W. was included in extended family gatherings. He belonged in the Secrest family and somehow he knew it.

Neither was Aunt Mary Gordon set aside, or, like some crazy aunt, hidden away in the attic. Nearly every week she came for Sunday dinner and was included, insofar as it was possible, in the life of her husband and children. This situation continued until her death in early 1940, when Vann Jr. and I were seniors in high school.

Uncle Vann was similar in temperament, personality and character to my father. He could be bossy and domineering, sometimes controlling. But, as he later told me, "Life and necessity taught me lessons about self-control and acceptance that Dowd somehow never learned." Perhaps this was due to Uncle Vann's having to be "mother and father both" all the time, whereas Daddy had to play that role only intermittently and relatively briefly. Uncle Vann had a lot of help from Aunt Matt, too, who loved Vann Jr. and Sara as the normal children she never had. Between the two of them, plus plenty of hired help, they provided Vann and Sara security and a happy childhood, although they both were also surely children "set apart."

Aunt Matt did well by her young charges, though she did a better job with Vann than with Sara. She favored Vann at Sara's expense, perhaps overcompensating for G.W. And Sara seemed star-crossed from birth. Her mother was taken ill not long after her birth and came to believe that her condition was somehow related to Sara's arrival. Mary soon couldn't be left alone with her daughter, whom she would pinch and possibly mistreat more seriously if the opportunity arose. Aunt Matt and Vann Sr. both felt a special obligation to see to it that Sara was not only well protected but also trained and taught moral lessons befitting a young girl of her background and social station. Whatever the cause, Sara grew up feeling, as she once told me, that she'd been raised like a Puritan, socially and morally inhibited, developing in the process an inferiority complex.

Who really knows how and why people turn out as they do? The proof of the pudding, however, lies in the ultimate result, and Vann turned out to be a strong, well-balanced, successful man, and Sara, married twice, both times unhappily, died early, childless, and an emotional basket case.

A veteran of World War II, Vann Jr. spent some time in Shanghai, China, where he detected a counterfeit ring. While in Okinawa later he injured his knee when the vehicle in which he was riding ran over a mine. When the war was over Vann had had enough of foreign lands. He became more like his uncle Dowd than his father Vann when it came to travel. After receiving his degree in pharmacy at UNC, like Dowd, he settled down to marriage, family and work in Monroe and, like Dowd, believed he'd never lost anything outside Union County that he needed to go look for.

Uncle Vann took parental obligations and marital vows seriously. Although he was in his early thirties when his wife became afflicted, he never had anything to do romantically with another woman until after Mary's death some fifteen years later, in January, 1940. Then he started courting Mary Douglas, widowed years earlier. Mary had been named Miss North Carolina as a young woman and had proudly worn the crown and trod the boardwalk in Atlantic City as a Miss America contestant. Uncle Vann and Mary's courtship lasted twenty years. They finally tied the knot on his sixty-eighth birthday, December 25, 1962. He built his bride a fine new house just behind his son Vann and wife Jane's even finer house on Lakewood Drive. From there Uncle Vann could monitor his son's activities. Not infrequently Vann's phone would ring at seven o'clock in the morning.

"Vann, Jane left the light on again all night on your back porch. You all have to be more careful. There's no point in feeding the power and light company."

Both Cousin Vann and I had to put up with bossy, dominating fathers. Dowd died early, though, when I was only twenty-three and had already left Monroe. Vann had to put up with it until he was nearly sixty years old. But Vann accepted his father with love and understanding, even if such emotions were occasionally tinged with irritation. I had to seek psychiatric consultation to handle parental conflicts.

Both Vanns—father and son—played continuing, prominent, and positive roles in the life of our family, individually and collectively. I don't know how we could at times have managed without them both. Uncle Vann stayed young a long time. At 78 he served as president of the Duke University Alumni Assn. He was also chosen N.C. Seedman of the Year.

Vann and I had two Monroe first cousins, however, who found life a difficult road to travel. Hill Wolfe, his five children and his multiple wives, some lovely and highborn, others not, and brother Lee, were prominent players in the lives of those who lived at Broadacre. Both boys were also somehow "set apart." It's always comforting to blame the in-laws—as I do blame Grandma Wolfe to some degree for Hill's and Lee's troubles—but the explanation lay closer to home.

# 3. Circumcision and Black Satin Shorts

Mother and Daddy were entirely different in their temperament, personality, disposition, and interests. Daddy was one of twelve children and the eldest son, sandwiched between two older and two younger sisters. He had four brothers and seven sisters. The family owned their farm in Unionville about 10 miles from Monroe, the county seat of Union County.

The Secrests were yeoman farmers. Neither of my father's parents had finished high school, but all twelve children graduated from high school and college or university to become successful business and professional people and community leaders. In the post-Reconstruction Era in North Carolina there was no public school system and few private schools beyond middle school. My grandfather, Ambrose Arminius Secrest, whose own father Andrew Jackson Secrest had been killed in the Civil War, was a man of strong character and gentle disposition. His wife, Lydia Asbury Price Secrest, was a strong character as well and a hard worker but possessed a sharp tongue and an uneven disposition.

Daddy preferred the company of women to that of men. Close to all of his seven sisters, he was really close to only one of his brothers, Vann. They were involved in business together and both became their own bosses, and eventually millionaires, while many of their friends were barely breaking even in the rural, poverty-ridden South of the 1920s and '30s. Daddy ridiculed brother Ed as an over-educated theologian. Ed had earned a doctorate in theology from Yale University and spent his career at the University of Georgia in Athens. Mother loved Ed and his wife Evelyn. Instead of appreciating Lessie's fondness for his brother, Dowd made it another bone of contention between them. Uncles John and Willis became dentists in Winston-Salem. They didn't much like Dowd because he had lent them money to attend school and expected them to repay it, without interest. They resented his generosity.

Daddy had made a million dollars during the Roaring Twenties, having established a drugstore in 1909 and a General Motors dealership in 1917, and having acquired a lot of farm acreage out in the country around Indian Trail, Goose Creek, Weddington and Houston Crossroads. He was also a bank officer, a major shareholder in a Savings and Loan Association, and active in the seed and feed business, among other enterprises. Daddy may have been a pharmacist, having graduated from UNC in 1907, but he remained a farmer at heart. Having lost most of his wealth between 1929-1933, he managed to recoup much of his fortune and die, once again a millionaire, at age 62 in 1946. But with inheritance taxes being what they were at the end of World War II, there wasn't a lot to show for it after Uncle Sam got his share.

During the 1930s Daddy operated several farms that supported, and were supported by, a dozen or so tenant farm families, all of whom were white and of Anglo-Saxon and Scotch-Irish ancestry, with such old established names as McAteer, Hartis, Fincher, Furr, Parker and Griffin. These families produced large numbers of children to help them work the land, and the babies, whom Lil adored and often would go out to the farms to care for, were invariably beautiful, healthy and normal, despite deficient diet and no medical attention.

A Democrat and a Populist, Daddy believed in helping his tenant farmers work themselves out of what he recognized was a feudal and futile economic system that handicapped the many for the benefit of the few. Mother, a social worker at heart, at least agreed with him on that. One day Mother, distressed by the scene of flies swarming around infants in the tenant farm cabins, arranged to have screens installed in all the windows and doors. She was no less distressed to find out a few days later that all the screens had been removed as the occupants thought they "filtered out the fresh air."

While both my parents were of English, Scotch-Irish, Welsh and German-Swiss descent, their ancestors having settled in the foothills of North Carolina several generations before—among them veterans of the Revolutionary and Civil wars—Dowd and Lessie were never Confederate partisans or race-conscious and didn't raise their children to be. Mother's ancestors were slaveholders; Daddy's were not. Mother's people were planters, landowners, and educated professional folk who lived a life patterned after the rural Tory ideal. Daddy's folks were independent yeoman farmers who owned their own land but benefited only from their own labor. While plain country people, they highly valued education and were leaders in establishing public schools in Union County. My paternal grandfather served as chairman of both the Union County Board of Education and the Union County commissioners.

Mother's father and only brother died early. She was six when David Anderson Covington II died and 16 when her brother, David Anderson Covington III, a scholar of the classics at the University of Chicago, succumbed. She was the youngest of five girls, a liberal arts graduate from Brenau College in Gainesville, Georgia, which two of her maternal uncles—Tom and Henry Simmons—owned along with Shorter College in Rome, Georgia. When she married, as her mother warned her future husband, she knew nothing about men.

"Why do you want to marry Lessie?" Grandmother Mary Foote Simmons Covington asked Andrew McDowd Secrest, when he asked Mrs. Covington for her daughter's hand. "She doesn't really know anything and she can't do anything."

My father replied, "She can learn."

"She can't cook. She can't sew. She doesn't know anything about babies," Mrs. Covington continued.

"She can learn," Mr. Secrest replied.

"Well, all she knows she's learned from books," her mother argued. "She's done the Continental and Holy Land tours. So she thinks she understands life and religion, but she really doesn't know anything at all about either. And she doesn't know one thing about men," she added darkly.

"I can teach her," was Dowd's stubborn reply.

"She's too young and immature and you're too old for her," argued his mother-in-law-to-be. Lessie was then 21 and Dowd 30. "And neither of you is a bit alike, and, frankly the Secrests and Covingtons don't have backgrounds in common." Daddy, who had been known to say when he first saw Lessie Covington walk past his store at age 16, "That's the girl I'm going to marry someday," insisted that Mrs. Covington give the marriage her blessing.

She did so reluctantly, and it may be that they all came to regret it.

When Lessie told her mother of Dowd's proposal and her acceptance, Mrs. David A. Covington II said, "Secrest! Oh, my, no! That was one of your father's most notorious murder cases." What that was all about, and of what if any significance it held for anyone, I wasn't to learn until some sixty years later.

She was referring to Hoke Secrest, a collateral kinsman who had killed his wife and children in the late 1880s. Grandfather Covington had successfully prosecuted the case, and Hoke was executed later in Raleigh. Hoke's father had married a Medlin and the Secrests, quick to criticize the in-laws and eager to place the blame and the shame elsewhere, put it on them.

Mother was of an independent nature, attuned to the feminist movement and not inclined to take any vow that included the word "obey." So she had it removed on her wedding day, December 9, 1914. Daddy was a devoted and loving husband, at least for a while, but like his mother, inclined to be domineering. It was not a marriage made in heaven—not at least any part that I can remember.

Yet who can say what any marriage is really like, least of all that of one's own parents? They had  good and bad times; they supported each other through thick and thin. Outwardly they presented a united front. Their marriage was recognized as a stable and enduring one. They remained committed. Mother once told my wife many years after his death that Dowd Secrest was the only man she'd ever loved or could have been married to. Daddy never said the same about her to anyone that I know of, but he wasn't a demonstrative man. He was a loyal one and at times seriously put upon, but he was never long-suffering. He had an uneven disposition, was not easily pleased, never paid compliments, and wasn't inclined to suffer fools gladly.

My grandmother was both right and wrong about her youngest daughter. Lessie was both brilliant and foolish. Dowd could also be both brilliant (in business) and foolish (in close personal relationships).

Both my sisters, Mary Covington and Lillian Asbury, and I were unduly influenced at vulnerable ages equally by Mother and Daddy—parents who sought to fight and win their battles with each other through their children. Yet I don't want to seem ungrateful. Here I am, at age 80, still financially benefiting somewhat from parental inheritance. And if I possess strength of character, or have attained personal standards that have allowed me to live a decent, successful life, or have strived to be a kind and giving member of the human race, some of that I owe to them.

The Covingtons of Monroe set out to live an English-style country life. Broadacre itself was modeled after an English estate. Daddy, while of a different heritage, paid the Covingtons the sincerest form of flattery, that of imitation. When D. A. Covington died in 1898 at age 45, leaving his widow with six children to rear and educate, family fortunes changed. Dowd Secrest, yeoman farmer, came to the rescue when he married Lessie Covington in 1914 and some years later bought the Covington home place, restoring it on the one hand to its proper place and changing it, on the other, by converting it into a working farm with every kind of domestic animal known to man placed thereon.

Mother tolerated the changes as long as she could preserve her English ideal, having portraits painted of Lil as *The Age of Innocence* and me as *Little Boy Blue.* She also dressed me up as *Little Lord Fauntleroy,* complete with black satin shorts and silk shirt. Not content with that, she sent me off to First Grade in Monroe Primary School dressed like that.

One might imagine what kind of reception I received from the tough little boys and girls from families of farmers or cotton mill workers. The reception I got my first years in public school certainly made me feel like the boy who was "set apart" from other school boys in Booth Tarkington's *"Penrod and Sam."* The ridicule, taunting and teasing may have been understandable, but I felt picked on and rejected.

In those days, teachers didn't concern themselves about classroom or schoolyard bullying or a student's self-esteem. I was left alone to endure the torment. I was a logical target, not only because of the way I was dressed but also because of my obvious privilege. I was taken to school by a nursemaid or chauffeur. Some children perhaps had heard their parents make negative comments about the Secrests and Covingtons and their sense of lordship. But I suspect most of my suffering was my own fault.

I had heard that Grandmother Covington was proud of her education and extensive vocabulary. One day when I was being heckled because of my English schoolboy attire and for using such a big word as "impossible," I replied, "How can you accuse me of being verbose, when I am only employing my ordinary vernacular?" My grandmother was often quoted as having once said that as witty repartee, and I thought it appropriate to quote it, without attribution, on this occasion. That really set my tormentors off. I was the butt of many a joke and harassed by many a bully from age six to eight, earning the nickname "Impossible."

Mother also enrolled me in violin classes and ballroom dancing. It was obvious that she considered me set apart and because I assumed a defensive air of superiority, my early school classmates considered me arrogant and set apart as well. I internalized the differences and conflicts of my mother and father, pulled first one way, then another, a composite of an irresistible force and an immovable object.

If my first years of life weren't easy, they weren't all bad either. My immediate family met most of my emotional needs. I was indulged, I did pretty much as I pleased, and life at Broadacre, especially among the animals, was exciting and fun. If I were a boy set apart at school, I was the center of attention at home.

Mother wasn't the only foolish parent. Daddy was equally, and more egregiously so, in a decision about circumcision. Not everyone in small southern towns in the early 1920s knew much about Sigmund Freud. And not many thought much about childhood sexuality, and had they done so, would probably have denied that it even existed. Who had heard of an Oedipus Complex, subconscious incestuous desires, or the psychological implications of male intimidation and appeasement as a consequence of a Castration Complex?

My introspective, intellectual mother might have but would not have applied such ideas to herself or anyone else she knew. That was the stuff of mythology, modern literature and new psychology. Her religious faith would have caused rejection and denial. My practical, down-to-earth father—too busy to listen to any far-out theories and influenced by a strong Wesleyan faith—would have dismissed such notions as nonsense or simply crazy.

Apparently Dr. Marvin Smith and Dr. Robert Payne, family physicians, were not much more sophisticated. Old Testament beliefs influenced America, in contrast to Europe, in accepting the Jewish practice of circumcision. It was almost a universal practice throughout the United States during most of the nineteenth and twentieth centuries. Muslims also practice it but select age 13 to perform it. The more learned circles by 1927 understood that if circumcision were to be performed, it was to be done within days of birth or much later, at the age of puberty.

Daddy and Dr. Smith apparently were not privy to this latest information, for at age four I found myself in a Charlotte Hospital confronted by a surgeon with a knife. I can clearly remember the pain and the anxiety associated with it and later standing on the bed, fighting and kicking at Dr. Smith whenever he came around home to dress the wound. Once again, I felt set apart, if not wrought asunder.

Apparently children are pretty tough customers, as I managed to survive this mistake, and others to come, and in many respects to thrive. In my first six years, I was overly loved and praised by the female members of the family. I was Mary Cov's toy, Lil's doll and Mother's adored baby boy. Aunt Mary Covington, an unmarried sister of Lessie, seven years her senior and a practicing criminal attorney in Monroe as early as 1917, treated me as the child she never had. Aunt Eve, a professor of sociology and economics at several North Carolina colleges, spoiled me outrageously, although she often quoted me as saying, "Aunt Eve is the one who doesn't believe in spoiling children."

On my fourth birthday she and Aunt May gave me a party, complete with cake and ice cream. For a present Aunt Eve gave me an expensive sailor's cap. Disappointed and sulky, I accepted the cap with ill grace. Aunt Eve then produced a balloon to appease me, which I blew up until it exploded with an enormous pop! First startled, then scared, next enraged, I threw myself on the floor stiff as a board, screamed loudly and beat my fists in the air, on the rug and upon anyone who dared come near.

Three years later I was taken to see a film, "East Lynn," starring Ann Harding, and, disconsolate at the sad turn of events, began to scream and holler and had to be carried out of the theater. Even at age seven I had not learned the value of self- control.

My father and I were usually at cross purposes. He was ambivalent and unpredictable. If in a sentimental, paternal mood, he would cradle me in his lap or toss me high in the air to hear me laugh, even become tearful when he heard Al Jolson singing "Sonny Boy" on the radio. But something usually went awry.

One evening in such a mood, he picked me up to show off to some friends over for dinner. As he started to toss me up in the air, my cheek grazed the side of his lapel where his Shriner pin was placed. The open pin scratched my face on the upward spiral and out splashed some blood along with shrieks of protest and anger from me. I reached for my mama for comfort, to the irritation of Daddy who thought I had over-reacted to the minor episode. But the picture perfect moment of Father with Son that Daddy had wanted to project to his friends was ruined.

Daddy wasn't above manipulating his children for his own advantage. He treated his elder daughter sometimes in this way. When an important business associate came to dinner one evening and Daddy wanted to impress him, he put Mary C. up to bringing him a copy of *Who's Who in North Carolina,* turned to the page on which Dowd Secrest was featured. Receiving the book in feigned surprise, he turned to his daughter and asked innocently, "Why, what's this, honey, a picture of Daddy?" as if Mary C. at age 12 would have cared anything at all about his listing in *Who's Who.* When she obediently nodded yes and gave him a practiced hug around the neck, he then shared the book with his prominent guest, who may - or may not- have been gulled by such a sham. Later on, we often reminded Daddy of that little scene.

The blame for this conflict between father and son wasn't on just one side. I was spoiled and undisciplined. Whenever Daddy was in a good mood and decided to take the family over to Charlotte, twenty-five miles away, for dinner, I usually managed to spoil the occasion.

23

The problem as usual would arise over women. Daddy, acting expansive and benevolent, would become friendly with the waitress, especially if she were young and pretty. He'd ask her personal questions, josh and joke with her and generally behave in a forward and flirtatious way. Then I would pout and complain, cry and generally seek to create tension at the table.

I should not have been allowed to get away with it. Mother, not wanting to clip Daddy's wings herself, perhaps was glad to have me do it for her. But I doubt it. I think they just found it easier to give in than to provide a firm but loving discipline. Or maybe they were just "foolish" where child-rearing was concerned. Lil, an anti-social child herself, didn't care. In fact, she was often a partner in crime and always an ally. Mary C., eight years older, often disapproved of my behavior, but then she too was sometimes part of the problem.

My older sister had a cutting sense of humor. She found it great fun to get the better of me by some psychological manipulation. Mary C. was the leader of the pack. Lil was her adoring slave. Young friend Helen and cousins Jane, Martha and Lillian fell in step behind her. Children in the 1920s made up their own games. Outside we played croquet, tennis and basketball and had thirty-five acres of yard to play in. Indoors, Mary C.'s fertile and febrile brain thought up all kinds of games to play or plays to enact. One day she suggested the game of "Superlatives," in which each girl performed and awards were presented to the cutest, the cleverest, the smartest, the prettiest, the most original, among many others. It could be an active event or silent tableau.

The plan was to get all the players to agree behind my back to vote me in as the number one winner in category after category, along with lavish praise—darling, adorable, handsome, smart—a cornucopia of loving approval. I must have cut quite a figure at age five or six pretending to be a sheik, as played by film star Ramon Novarro, or posing as a femme fatale like Pola Negri, or racing around the room, stopping before the grate to "pop the fire" as I did an interpretive dance to the tune of Stravinsky's Fire Bird.

Then, with head thoroughly swollen and heart filled with gratitude and appreciation and with self-esteem at its highest possible point, the pendulum would swing. Suddenly the votes went the other way. Nothing I did was smart, cute or clever. Everything was horrible, terrible, tacky, disgusting and wrong... wrong ... wrong! I was voted last in every category, time after time.

My heart sank. I couldn't believe how far I'd fallen from grace or why. My harem had deserted me. Finally, bafflement changed to disappointment, then to pain, next anger and finally to rage. "I am too the cutest," I screamed in impotent anger. " I am too the smartest," and I would run from one older girl to the next, hitting and crying while they held me off, laughing till they too almost cried. Then I'd go crying to Mother to be comforted and to be reassured that I was indeed the cream of the crop and the apple of her eye.

But Mary C. could be attentive and affectionate as well. She invented a game, modeled after some silent film, in which we would play lovers, named of all things, "Gay and Rudolph." Today, one's eyebrows might rise at such names—Freudian indeed—but in the 1920s such notions would never have occurred to anybody, just a frolicking, good-natured, affectionate game, really meaning nothing to a 13-year-old girl. But what was a boy of five to make of it?

Lil and Mary C. during their adolescence were interested in the opposite sex and feminine pursuits, leaving me in my prepubescent years to handle that as best I could, largely bereft of suitable male role models. This problem was especially noticeable in the popular culture of the day, particularly film and radio.

The movie sirens were secretly admired by my sisters but virtuously condemned for their overt sexuality: Pola Negri, Bebe Daniels, Joan Crawford, Clara Bow, Marlene Dietrich, Mae West and other early vamps. The heroes were raved over but whenever I dared express an opinion over some female star, my preferences were immediately overridden, ridiculed or dismissed summarily.

One radio mystery-drama at 9:00 o'clock each Monday night was An Evening in Paris, sponsored by a perfume of the same name and featuring two actors. The male lead, whose name I can't even remember, was in the girls' eyes "cute, darling, adorable" while the female star—I do remember her name, Patti—was dismissed as silly, vapid, dumb and ugly, although none of us had actually seen her in the flesh.

Lil, Martha and Helen wrote off to the program, carried by the CBS network, for an autographed photo of the male star, which in time arrived to the squeals of excitement and approval by the girls. I was not permitted to have a picture of Patti, whom I secretly had a crush on. An Evening in Paris was considered to be the epitome of continental class and sophistication for provincial kids in Monroe. It was years later that I learned the perfume itself was a cheap, lower middle-class concoction, available in any Rexall Drugstore and a far cry indeed from Chanel Number Five, of which I'd never even heard.

Male sexual attraction can be a stubborn thing, however, and I continued to prefer Jean Harlow to Clark Gable, Olivia de Havilland to Errol Flynn, Anita Louise to Ian Hunter and Bette Davis to Leslie Howard, no matter how much fun the older girls in the house and in the neighborhood made of my choices or how disdainful they were of my preferences.

I liked the male performers as role models with whom to identify and to imitate but found the female stars far more beautiful and exciting. I must have been well past puberty before the women in my life gave up trying to determine my tastes in such matters and allowed me to decide for myself whom I did and did not like. And by that time I wasn't always so sure myself.

# 4. Too Much, Too Soon

Mother and Daddy were contradictory parents. Both firm in their Christian faith, they inclined toward a puritanical view of sin and sex, at least as it existed outside the bonds of holy or unholy matrimony. They were natural products of their time, raised themselves by parents in a Victorian age.

One might expect modesty from Mother, reared in a female environment, this woman who knew "nothing about men." Daddy may not have been brought up so carefully. Grandmother Covington is reported to have told all her daughters that she'd rather see them dead in their coffins than to be deflowered before marriage. Perhaps as a consequence, Aunt May and Aunt Eve, although both once engaged to eligible suitors, could never bring themselves to marriage and all the physical intimacy that such a commitment implied.

Mother, Aunt Susan Covington Fowler and Aunt Katherine Covington Craven managed to free themselves from such taboos, but Mother, feeling herself to be an emancipated woman, suffragette and feminist, wasn't as free as she thought. If she were, why was she always preaching and teaching about sex and its dangers and pitfalls?

There was an educational movement abroad in the 1920s and 1930s to lift an earlier repression and hypocrisy and to teach the emerging generation about the proper relationship between men and women. There was also a lifting of the taboo about and discussion of venereal diseases. Even movies were made later about "Dr. Ehrlich and His Magic Bullet." Mother believed passionately in sex education, but, her mother's daughter, she couldn't resist preaching about the evils and dangers of premarital relations, so much so that the part about the beauty and sanctity of sex within marriage somehow got lost in the presentation. There were also movies about sex, venereal diseases and drug use, especially marijuana, that did have the effect of making impressionable kids scared straight. "Reefer madness," a cult favorite today, was one such film. It was enough to take the joy if not the temptation out of sin, so the only alternative was to go around feeling guilty and scared a lot of the time.

Mother did not recognize any differences between boys and girls. She deplored the double standard regulating the relations between the sexes, yet she accepted the practice. Lessie felt compelled to prevent anything untoward happening by talking about and warning against premarital sex to her children at ages when no such ideas would otherwise have entered their heads and who really had little conscious interest in such things. Instead of "too little too late," it became "too much too soon."

To Mother words were everything, action something else entirely. One day Lil came home from grade school to announce that she'd been invited to join an all-girl sex club to find out what it was all about. She had proudly told her classmates that she already knew all about it because her mother had told her. Whereupon the girls elected Lil president of the club, an honor she turned down, smugly reporting the episode to Mother like a good girl and dutiful daughter.

Mother didn't, however, practice what she preached about modesty. She was careless about feminine hygiene, and Mary C. and Lil when they became older were none too careful either. They all made a big deal about monthly periods, speaking in hushed tones about the mysteries of menstruation and becoming periodically "unwell." Later the girls were not permitted to swim in Helms Pond on certain days. Mary Cov and friends spoke openly—and proudly—about "getting the pip."

"Why can't they swim today?" I wondered. "What's the matter with them?" I never received any explicit explanation, just mysterious murmurs about female functions. Occasionally Mother or one of my sisters left used pads, delicately referred to as sanitary napkins, poorly wrapped and lying around.

Once they were embarrassed when Joe, my dog, found one such parcel flung carelessly into the corner of the bathroom and came trotting out with it, placing it at the feet of Mary C.'s date. "Good for Joe," I thought. "Serves her right." Young males before the age of puberty don't need this kind of immersion into female physiology. Some aspects of the feminine mystique should be maintained.

28

Neither Mother nor Daddy ever dreamed that they could be sexually provocative to their children. So they ran around the house naked, or half so, seldom closing doors, dressing and undressing as the occasion demanded without requiring  privacy from prying young eyes. I cannot speak for Lil, as she never subsequently talked about it, but as we grew older, Mary C. and I, submerged in Freudian psychology, compared notes and talked about it a lot.

When Mother recovered from her first depression and returned home in August 1928, Miss Julia vanished immediately. Mother was now back in the kitchen cooking, cleaning house, playing the piano, and also back in bed at night with Daddy. Soon I began to be afraid of the dark again.

I couldn't get to sleep. I had bad dreams. I was hungry or thirsty. I was scared the Boogey Man would get me. Couldn't I come and sleep with them for a little while? And so I was permitted to manipulate my parents, both of them blissfully unaware that children up to and sometimes beyond age six do have sexual curiosity and can be stimulated and that some intelligent, educated people, even in the rural South, knew that, some instinctively.

Neither of my parents apparently had a clue. They shared their bed with me as casually as some fourteenth-century Sardinian peasants might. Feigning sleep, I became aware of occasional intimate acts between a man and woman. And I felt betrayed.

That year was a happy one for me, despite my occasional nighttime disappointments. There were plenty of females quite willing to share their beds with me. I'd play with Mother, lying on her legs and stomach as she lifted me up high and then swung me down, as if I were on a rollercoaster. And I'd tell her all the things I was going to do when I became a big boy on my sixth birthday. My list of achievements grew longer every day. I'd tie my own shoes. I'd brush my own teeth. I'd dress myself, including all the buttons. And I'd stop being afraid and always stay in my own bed in my own room at night.

When Aunt May came to visit, she'd let me join her in bed if I woke up early. One morning as the rain beat down on the roof and lashed against the window panes, she said, "Oh isn't that a wonderful sound? It's saying 'I can't get to you, because you are safe and sound in this nice big house.' Mac, when I'm old and gray and wrinkled and all alone in the world, with no one to look after me, will you take care of me?" And adoring Aunt May, as I adored in turn all the women in my extended harem, I'd promise her solemnly. "Yes, Aunt May, I love you and I'll always look after you."

Years later, when that need arose, I was as good as my word. I always helped to look after Aunt May, as much as I could and she'd allow, and I always loved her till the day she died, even though she was no longer the woman I had earlier known. Lil was an equally devoted niece who years later always kept a welcome mat out for Aunt May.

Sister Lil, born on January 31, 1920, had not been an easy baby, I've been told. She was sickly, puny, bald as an onion, and for months didn't thrive at all. Mother's own nursemaid, Hattie, and Lil's new one, Mary Simmons, whose family had taken my grandmother's maiden name as their own, were credited with saving Lil's life. Cream of Wheat and coffee did the trick, and by the time Lil was 18 months old, she was pretty and chubby, her head covered with golden ringlets.

By the time she was seven or so, however, she had become difficult, this time a loner, anti-social, a child who hated school and authority and would defy adults, including her parents, if they tried to get her to leave the cemetery next to the school yard and go to class. Her resistance technique? To throw rocks at anyone who came near. Eventually she got straightened out, and thereafter was Mother's doting daughter, taking to heart all the sex education and preaching that Mother thought it better for her to learn at home than from her classmates' sex club.

I wasn't so sure but what it would have been better to let Lil learn things her way in her own time. In any event, before I reached the age of six, Lil and two or three cousins and friends from the neighborhood formed a little sex club of their own, and I was promptly initiated as a charter member. There was a lot of play acting and Shakespearean drama mixed up with the sexual explorations, including claims that Lil and her friends had once been endowed with the same sexual attachments that boys had but that some wicked witch had cut them off.

At the ages of six and nine, there wasn't any adult sexual activity going on but a great deal of looking and examining and playing doctor. Given the fact that my circumcision had come only two years earlier, the stories about the witch and her acquisitions might be expected to arouse in me a castration complex, as well as reveal in Lil and her friends a penis envy, but I never felt the slightest anxiety or guilt about any of that intimate play and never asked Lil if she ever felt envious.

But that she did feel guilty was proven one miserable Saturday morning when Mother discovered me playing paper dolls from Lil's collection. She had both boy and girl paper dolls, and I had placed the girl dolls' faces down on the boys' pelvic areas. If that didn't wake Mother up to why I'd been so afraid of the dark and had asked and been granted the privilege of sleeping with and sometimes between her and Daddy, what would?

"Mac, what on earth are you doing?" Mother inquired, sounding distressed.

"Playing paper dolls," was the nonchalant reply.

"Well, I know, but what are your dolls doing?"

As the inquisition proceeded, I 'fessed up to my little game, which was bad enough, but Lil had to make matters worse by confessing, between deep sobs, to what she and I and some of her friends had been up to as well. Poor Mother didn't know what on earth to do about that. And were Daddy to have known, he'd have been even more at sea. Lil, I suppose, genuinely felt remorseful. She felt she had committed a sin, and Mother didn't help matters much by saying how surprised and disappointed in us she was, and how much this had hurt her and made her feel as if she had failed as a mother and in her responsibility to us, and what on earth do you suppose God and Baby Jesus thought about all this.

I didn't feel any guilt or remorse, but I was sorry that Mother was unhappy and still sorrier when finally she told Daddy who, as shocked as she, told her she should spank both of us soundly, which she did very effectively. I wasn't even angry with Lil for such a betrayal, although I did think she ought to have known better than to tell Mother. What did she expect—parental approval? Now our little games would have to end, and that didn't please me at all.

That ended all the incest—if one can call it that—in the Secrest family. But that parental intimacy continued—running around half clothed, failing to close bedroom and bathroom doors, carrying me along to department store fitting rooms while Mother tried on girdles and dresses, Daddy taking Lil into the men's shower room at the beach bathhouse with a lot of naked men showering and engaging in locker room banter—-because he didn't know where else to put her as he changed from bathing suit to street clothes.

# 5. Doll, Jr. and Cross Dressing

Mother came back into my life before I was five years old. How glad I was to see her—vibrant, alive, beautiful, loving. Now I had someone to read to me again and to tell stories of a world far away, to paint mental pictures of mythological creatures, beautiful goddesses and handsome warrior gods—Greek, Roman, Norse. And again I heard the beautiful music which reawakened in me an appreciation of melodies I still associate with light, love and laughter.

As suddenly as she had disappeared, she as unexpectedly returned—looking exactly as I had remembered her from nearly a year earlier. Where she had been, why she had gone, what had happened remained a mystery, but I was glad to see her back, although initially somewhat shy and reserved. I later learned she had spent much of the time first down the street at Aunt Eve and Aunt May's and later with Miss Olive, a paid caregiver, at Bat Cave, near Chimney Rock. I finally met Miss Olive, a likable, attractive young woman quite in contrast to Miss Julia. She would've been a much more interesting bedtime companion.

My life was now one filled with women... Mother, aunts, sisters, cousins, family friends, cooks, caregivers and nursemaids. Broadacre itself, on the edge of town, was in a neighborhood in which only girls seemed to come in ample supply-all older than I. Helen next door, Martha across one street, Margaret and Lillian across another. I became a man basically raised by women.

There were of course men in my life as well: my father, an uncle or two, an occasional cousin, a couple of hired men. But the moral tone, the ethical standards, the religious beliefs, the manners and the moral teaching and preaching were preponderantly feminine, and I was an avid and willing listener. This attitude created tension between Daddy and me, as he felt I needed a strong male role model, a role he was usually too busy or impatient to play. And I felt he was an increasingly unnecessary and unwanted presence in the house, someone who took away from me quality time from my harem, all these women, including sisters Mary C. and Lil, Aunt May and Aunt Eve, and all of their female friends, but especially, above all my beautiful, adoring and adored mother.

After a couple of years of this, Daddy decided to bring a playmate of my own age into my life. "He's surrounded by girls," Daddy announced to anyone who'd listen, including me. "You're making a sissy out of him. He needs some boys his own age to play with."

So Daddy brought Darling Baker, Jr. into Broadacre, from the boy's little shack across Church Street extension, a black neighborhood just across the road and beyond the orchard from us, similar to another called Quality Hill west of town. Doll, as I came to call him—Darling seemed so inappropriate—was the son of a preacher and part-time farmer and handyman. Doll had a complexion so black as to be almost purple, about the color of an eggplant. He had sisters too, and Darling Baker, Sr. and Andrew M. Secrest, Sr. both thought there were too many women in their boys' lives. Concern for their sons trumped race and segregation.

So Doll and I became acquainted: first a little gingerly, but soon close buddies and before long, alter egos. While not my identical twin, Doll became for me the reincarnation of David Covington Secrest. About the same time that Doll joined Mother and all my maternal-surrogates at Broadacre, Heath, a semiliterate, tongue-tied white man about 21 years old, also took up with us as hired man and general serf. Whatever part of the bill Doll Jr. didn't fill, Heath did. Between these two I had all the male companionship I needed or wanted, although Lindsay, black, and Murray, white, soon joined the growing crowd.

A few years after that, young men from the Northeast, mostly Puerto Ricans from New York's Spanish Harlem, came to town with the New Deal's Civilian Conservation Corps (CCC). Their camp was within short walking distance of Broadacre, the school and the cemetery, the land for which my maternal great-grandfather David Covington the First had given the town of Monroe a hundred years earlier.

My new male acquaintances may not have known much about mythology, classical music, poetry or Shakespearean drama, but they knew a lot about boxing, wrestling, rodeos, animals, and hard work, and something about sex, too, and again, I was an avid learner.

If Daddy thought, however, he could break Lil's firm hold on me, as her living doll, he had another thought coming. Instead of Doll's making more of a boy out of me, Lil, Helen, Martha and their coterie of friends managed to make more of a sissy out of Doll.

Daddy was at first irritated but later more amused as he told the story of coming home one afternoon, expecting to find Doll and me rough housing it up somewhere outdoors, only to discover Doll standing at the top of the stairs, dressed resplendently in a frilly, blindingly white dress, starkly contrasting with his ebony skin, and wearing one of Mother's broad-brimmed picture hats. Next to Doll Daddy found me, wearing one of Mother's chestnut brown wigs, made many years earlier from her real hair, and a fur stole.

"Lil," roared Daddy, his balding scalp turning red, "What in the devil do you and Martha think you're doing? And where's your mother?" Martha, startled at the tone, darted down the stairs and across the yard, jumped the fence and ran home to Aunt Bertha, Daddy's oldest and favorite sister.

Mother asked not to be disturbed, please, as she was composing the minutes of her garden club meeting, which were to be a close parody of Edgar Allan Poe's "The Raven." The poet's muse must not be upset and the spell broken. Doll and I were sorry to have the game ended. At that age, cross-dressing didn't give us any pause. In fact, the role-playing in the cool of the upstairs, punctuated by lemonade and cookies, was a lot more appealing than doing farm chores outside amid the heat and gnats with hired man Heath.

But being the goat of a joke, which Daddy would tell and retell to the raucous laughter of uncles, aunts and first cousins on Family Saturday Night Live at Ma's, got cold in a hurry. Once again, I felt embarrassed, self-conscious, guilty and ashamed, as if I'd let Daddy down. Again I felt set apart and some resentment smoldered.

If in our early years Lil was Mary C.'s willing slave, Doll Jr. and I were Lil's and if not slaves, surely serfs and vassals of Lil's friends as well, especially Helen, Martha and Catherine. Catherine had a younger brother Livingston whom she, however, could not tolerate. Even as adults they were never close.

"Lil," she would complain, "Do we have to have Mac come with us to the theater?" or, "Why on earth do you let him come to the playground? You'll just have to look out for him." Catherine made it clear I was a pain and a nuisance and an unnecessary and unwanted presence.

Lil's reply was unexpected. "Mother doesn't make me take care of Mac. I love my little brother and want him to come along. You'll see, he's not so bad." Catherine was a year older than Lil but just as clannish and no more socially mature.

But I soon came to love and adore Catherine along with Helen and Martha, although I didn't see her as often. Catherine lived in Winston-Salem, where her father was a prominent doctor. Aunt Eve, a friend of Catherine's parents, sensed that Catherine, like Lil, was inclined to be a loner and needed a friend. She arranged to have Catherine visit Monroe every summer for weeks on end, as Lil later visited Catherine, both in Winston-Salem and at the Johnsons' summer place in Riverton on the Lumbee River in Scotland County.

Riverton, near Wagram, N.C., was the home of North Carolina's best known poet laureate, and Catherine was somehow connected to John Charles McNeil and his "sunburnt boys of summer." As usual, Aunt Eve was right. Lil and Catherine became life-long friends through both happy and difficult times, even after their personalities developed in divergent ways: Catherine becoming more narrow, negative, rigid and self righteous, Lil more tolerant, liberal, gregarious, open and permissive.

Indeed, Aunt Eve's arrangement for Catherine and Lil led indirectly to Lil's meeting and marrying John Buie of Wagram. Later on Lil was to have second thoughts about this marriage, as her mother earlier must have had about her own.

Being slaves and vassals to girls four to six years older can come at a high price. Doll and I paid such a price one hot summer afternoon. Our parents had built a playhouse several hundred yards behind Broadacre. The exterior was a miniature replica of the house itself, complete with portico, bay windows, and front porch. It even had the same stained-glass windows that adorned the main hall. The playhouse had two large rooms and a screen and wooden door, exactly like the ones in Broadacre too, and both doors came with latch, lock and key.

On an early afternoon in the dog days of August, when it isn't unusual for the heat to rise to 100°, Lil, her friends, and Doll Jr. and I were playing some game among the high mounds of cotton waiting there for delivery to Broom's Store and Gin just down the street. Mary C. was entertaining her older friends on the side porch, talking, playing records, dancing and innocently flirting with Tommy, William, Percy, and Jesse. Irritated by the silly games and the noise her younger siblings and friends were making, Mary C. came out to order us to be quiet, indeed to leave the playhouse area altogether.

This didn't sit well with Lil, who knew one way to get even with her older sister. Catherine thought Lil's plan was an equally good way to get rid of Doll Jr. and me. Sam, our evil-tempered, foul-smelling ram, was another of our adored pets, who at times would actually obey his lords and masters. Lil, upon receiving Mary C.'s reprimand, went over to the nearby pen, unlatched the gate and turned the ram in the direction of her sister. After waving something in front of his face to irritate the beast, which wasn't hard to do, Lil sicced Sam on Mary C.

Sam, now aroused, charged straight toward the nearest possible victim, Mary C. She crossed the yard as fast as her legs would carry her while her friends shouted, "Run, Mary Cov, run! Hurry up, Sam's gaining on you!" The girls' alarm turned to relief when Mary C. escaped one jump up the stairs ahead of the ram, but the boys fell on the floor laughing at her predicament.

Sam, however, was not to be denied. Snorting and pawing the ground, he quickly turned around and aimed his ire at Lil, Catherine, Martha and Helen, who, seeing it was now their turn, fled toward the playhouse. They flung open the door, and all four girls rushed through, slamming shut and locking the door just before Sam banged his head against it.

Frustrated once more, Sam looked around and spied Doll Jr. and me, who had trailed behind the four girls dashing for the door. We had been handicapped by the long dresses which Lil and friends had again dressed us in, complete with big bows and sashes. I was further hobbled by Mother's high heeled shoes and her Hudson seal coat.

Doll Jr. and I ran for the playhouse door, too, just as a bolt of lightning flashed, thunder roared and rain and hail fell heavily from the passing storm cloud. The rain cooled Sam's anger too, but not before he delivered a couple of good head butts to our rear ends, knocking us against the barred door. The girls, safe inside, and afraid to open the door either because of Sam or the storm or both, and indifferent to Doll's and my fate, kept the door locked despite our cries. Soon Sam, sheared for the summer, was soaked to the skin. Doll Jr. and I were equally sodden in all of Mother's castoff finery, and nothing was hurt but our feelings and our pride.

Mother and Daddy certainly heard about that—from Mary C. in her humiliation and from Doll and me with our sense of subverted justice. I don't recall Lil and her coterie receiving any punishment, but I do remember the story being told repeatedly at our large family gatherings, another story of which I was the butt and the goat. I didn't get it. What was so funny?. But I'd learned what it meant to be a good sport; you had to grin and bear it.

For the most part, though, Doll Jr. and I did spend a lot of time away from the girls and with Heath, Murray and Lindsay—the field hands so to speak—and especially among the barnyard menagerie. For some reason Broadacre generations earlier had become a haven for street pigeons. There were literally hundreds of them nesting in the trees and eaves of the house. They came in many colors, from pure white to dark gray to a variety of multicolors. They flew regularly in and out of the crib to eat the corn and other grain stored there. Partly to please me, partly to protect his grain, Daddy agreed to build a series of large pens, complete with roosting perches and nesting sites. Doll's and my job was to capture these wild and wily birds.

In this contest between boy and nature, the boy finally won. Doll and I built a trap door across the top of the crib, with a string attached that would snap the door shut when yanked. We'd watch the crib by the hour and when several pigeons had flown in, we'd pull the string to trap the quarry, then go inside and chase them down. When caught, the pigeons were transferred to the pens, where they were given all the advantages of total care—food, water, shelter, warmth, mates, a cradle-to-grave security—everything except their freedom.

I soon had learned "pigeon English," and could not only translate but also imitate the sounds so accurately that the birds themselves couldn't tell the difference. They'd come when called, perch on my shoulder, coo and bill in my hair. I also observed their courting and mating habits and watched them as they laid eggs and hatched and fed their young. Both mother and father assumed responsibility for the care and feeding of their offspring.

Before long, there were four rather than three children in the house. Despite economic hard times, whatever I had, Doll had to have as well. If I got a new suit, so did Doll. When Santa Claus left me a bicycle beneath the Christmas tree, an exact replica was found under Doll's tree at his house. If I had an extra piece of cake, Doll had one too, even if it meant on occasion Mary C. and Lil did without.

On some evenings Mary C. would make fudge or truffles, although Dowd and Lessie insisted we now had to be careful due to hard economic times. Doll was of course with us in the kitchen. Mother was out doing good somewhere, Daddy was as usual out working, as he would say, "my ass off for you all," implying, accurately, that we weren't doing much to help.

Our kitchen was old-fashioned, though equipped also with the latest model electric range and refrigerator. We had an old wood-burning stove that heated water in a free-standing boiler that would literally turn bright red with heat. Why it never exploded or set fire to the house, or why we didn't burn ourselves against it, I'll never know. The kitchen, originally detached from the house for fire safety's sake, was now co-joined by a back bedroom and a sun parlor. It was lit by a bare light bulb dangling from a wire overhead, turned on and off by a piece of string.

One evening Doll, temporarily alone in the kitchen to watch the boiling chocolate to be sure it didn't burn or boil over, called out anxiously to Mary C. and Lil.

"Mary Cov, Lil, come quick—a roach has done fallen into the fudge." Well, sure enough, one had, so Mary C. fished it out with a spoon and flung it out, along with grunts of disgust—"yuck, gross, horrible." But the fudge proved to be creamy and delicious. Such intrusions into our food in those days were not at all uncommon. Mother was a casual cook and housekeeper, and the hired help followed her lead. I recall weevils in the flour and grits, insect wings and "mother" in the bottom of the vinegar cruet, and occasionally little mice and baby bats would drop down from fissures in the kitchen ceiling and plop into whatever might be simmering on the stove uncovered. It didn't bother any of us much, nor harm our health.

Another blessing in these days at Broadacre was the household black fly. With the barn only two hundred yards away and horses and cows leaving large and numerous pies nearby, the flies came in droves. These insects inevitably found their way into the house, joining the other little creatures in the kitchen and elsewhere.

This blessing, which was, of course, more like a curse, was ubiquitous throughout houses in the South prior to World War II. Every room at Broadacre displayed its quota of flypaper, long strips of sticky tape. A typical piece at day's end would be black with dozens of the dead.

Other weapons were wood-handled fly swatters and various chemical compounds. The best known chemical was commercially sold as Flit. A frequent advertisement on the radio and in newspapers and magazines showed a well-upholstered woman calling to her husband, "Quick, Henry, the Flit!" as flies swarmed around her. Flit was a spray placed in a little canister in the front of a cylinder about a foot long and pumped by a handle that one pushed and pulled. It had a pungent odor and was lethal to flies initially, though they became gradually resistant and eventually immune to it.

We fought a losing battle with flies, as there were always little tears in the window screens, despite balls of cotton sprayed with Flit that were stuck into the holes. Also Lil and I, it must be said, kept at least one door and screen propped open so Queenie, Joe, Betty Boop, Wimpy, Smokey, Jim and other pets could come and go freely.

I don't know what happened to household flies after 1950. They are still around, of course, everywhere, but not like before. Fewer farms, better screens, air-conditioning, improved sanitation and more effective chemical control are among the reasons for the Southern household fly's decline and fall.

On Lil's next birthday Mother had promised to make Lil's favorite dessert—a yellow cake with coffee chocolate frosting. Doll Jr. and I had a better idea. To surprise Lil and do something nice for Mother as well, we decided to bake the cake ourselves. Following the recipe, we mixed the ingredients carefully: eggs, butter, flour, cream, sugar—most produced at Broadacre itself. We then placed the mixture in cake tins into the oven.

Mother and Lil came home just as the cake, rising above the rims of the pans, was brought out. Doll Jr. and I proudly displayed our work of culinary art. Lil, anxious to taste it, suggested we cut a piece while it was still hot and before icing it. When Mother cut the cake, however, out poured the batter, barely cooked and hardly hot at all. Apparently Doll and I didn't know about preheated ovens or proper baking temperatures. Down the drain went Lil's cake for her thirteenth birthday. She tried to hide her disappointment, but her face crumpled with tears which soon turned to heartbreaking sobs as Mother murmured, "I don't see how we can afford another one. The expense. Mr. Secrest just won't hear of it."

Well, he heard of it, plenty of it, and so did Doll and I, who were once again dismissed in disgrace. But despite a lack of money, somehow enough was found for Mother to bake Lil a proper cake, complete with frosting, even if it did, as usual, have lumps in it.

Mary Cov on her thirteenth birthday had received a huge surprise too, one that Doll Jr. and I had nothing to do with. On that cold early morning of December 23, 1928, all of us were in for a shock. The sun had yet to rise when in burst Heath, followed by Gene Watts and John Teal, a young black man who divided his time between the Saleeby Kandy Kitchen and Secrest Drug Store. Each of them carried toiletries and boxes of partly melted chocolates from Whitman's Samplers. Mary C. got more candy that day than she did probably for the rest her life and better too than our roach fudge.

Excitement, mixed with anxiety, permeated the atmosphere. I had turned five the preceding September. Mary Garrison helped me hurriedly to get dressed and led me out to the front porch. Looking north, I saw a horizon bright red and orange, with plumes of smoke billowing out of the roof of the red brick building.

The Secrest Drug Store, the Seed Store and adjacent buildings in the heart of town, were ablaze. Despite the best efforts of the fire department, directed by Chief Jesse Helms, assisted by police chief Spoon, the fire raged out of control the better part of that day, leaving only the outer walls standing.

The professional offices upstairs, the barber shop in the basement, Ethel Blackwell's beauty parlor, and all the stores' inventory were destroyed—everything but a few bottles of Evening in Paris perfume and boxes of melting Whitman's Sampler chocolates. The fire was a financial disaster for the family, even though the building and contents were partly covered by insurance. But the experience was exhilarating for me. The excitement was contagious. The mighty sweep of the flames, the crackling sounds of the fire, the heat I could feel on my face, even all the way across the street and down the block, were intense. The crimson and orange glow, mixed with gray and black smoke, was awesome, even beautiful in a dreadful kind of way.

That memory lingered and helped me understand twelve to seventeen years later what the children first of London, later Hamburg and Berlin, and finally Tokyo must have seen and felt (many times over) as their homes and family businesses fell victim to the winds of war.

# 6. A Gun to Dowd's Head

"Good Golly, Miss Molly," didn't our household and everyday lives ever concern themselves with ordinary things? Of course they did. These accounts have been about the unusual and rare occurrences. Most of our time was spent in a carefree, happy, bucolic life on our English-estate-turned-American-farm: Broadacre, mecca of all domestic animal life and full of games, sports and parties. Although we mostly made up our own games, we also played basketball, tennis, and croquet. We attended school, had beach vacations and, above all, enjoyed life on real farms, among our tenant families.

On Friday nights during corn shucking time Mother and Daddy, Mary C., Lil and I would join the Hartis family in their little farm cabin to help. Between chores, someone would play the fiddle as others sang and danced around, "hillbilly" style. It was a friendly, cozy scene, with a roaring fire in the chimney grate, especially on early winter evenings when the cold wind blew through the cabin's cracks and sleet pinged against the window panes. We ate apples and drank cider (some pretty old and hard for the adults), played parlor games, and tended to the newest baby.

I spent many Saturdays with white tenant youths at one of the farms to explore abandoned wells and learn how to handle the animals, climb trees, swim in a local pond or the abandoned rock quarry. My farm friends and I explored, hunted, fished and fought, friendly style, from early morning till sunset.

We attended Sunday school, church, camp meetings, sleepovers, and did all the things one associates with growing up in a small Southern town in the earlier part of the Twentieth Century. Helms Pond was a

41

favorite swimming hole for Monroe. Daddy bought the pond—originally commercially run—in 1934 and built cabins on it. We used it as a vacation spot, a respite from Monroe's summer heat, and townsfolk were welcome to swim, now free of charge.

Mother was a role-model housewife and small-town society matron. She had always looked matronly to me, although she was then still young. She was a member and eventually president of her book club, the Methodist Women's Circle, and the Women's Business and Professional Club. She was an avid bridge player, another bone of contention between her and Daddy. One person once described her as the prettiest, smartest, and most intellectual woman in Monroe; the speaker, unsurprisingly, was not her husband.

Daddy was one of the leading businessmen in Monroe, a pillar of both church and community—chairman of this board and that. Mary C. was a popular member of her class at school, a girl who unconsciously drew boys around her as bees to honey but basically unaware of it and as innocent and virginal as people expected and the times demanded. Although she liked to shock people, she was actually easily shocked herself. Lil was an excellent student, content with her close circle of girlfriends and my staunchest ally.

But good times never lasted long uninterrupted, and good and bad things happened simultaneously, often out of our control. Mother had recovered and returned home in the summer of 1928. Lil's and my indiscretions had been set aside and atoned for by 1929. My intrusions into my parents' bedtime activities had been brought to a halt at the same time.

Soon Doll, Jr. and Heath were to enter my life. Family life gained an even keel. We loved our parents, even as we showed them good-natured disrespect. I can remember coming across a cache of love letters from my parents to each other. Mary C., Lil and I would grab them and, running fast out of reach of Mother and Daddy's hands, read aloud in mocking tone some of the more romantic parts. Personal privacy was not something that we learned to respect as we were growing up. Both Mother and Daddy were good-natured and permissive about that kind of teasing by their children.

In 1929 the great economic Depression descended upon the entire land. It hit the South very hard. It struck upper-middle-class people in small towns heavily. And my father, now in business up over his head, a huge landowner, and involved in banking and lending, had his work cut out for him.

He made it work. He survived. He recovered but at great cost. I think he himself had a nervous collapse, or at least a personality change, and as soon as he was in the process of recovering, depression once again took Mother out of the home and Daddy felt once more that he had to become "mother and daddy both." And again, he complained about it loud and clear to all who would listen.

But Mary C., Lil and I were not particularly concerned about the stock market crash of October, 1929. I had barely turned six and was more anxious about my Little Lord Fauntleroy attire. And even more intrigued with my new best friend, Doll Jr. In the fall of 1932, the economic depression deepened. Our tenant farm families didn't seem to feel it much, however, as they had learned to be self-sufficient. Besides, a farm depression in the Roaring Twenties had already presaged the larger downturn ahead. Daddy still managed to find the wherewithal to provide the open flatbed GM trucks and the gas and oil to take these families and all their children down to Myrtle Beach for the annual outing in September.

We'd camp out on the beach, joined by Locke Everette who, thanks to inherited family wealth, had already left the material world to become a beachcomber. The adults would cook on charcoal grills and over homemade fire pits and roast beef and pork and cook vegetables and drink ginger ale and Coca-Cola. The kids would run and splash in the water, finally getting the nerve to go out beyond the breakers accompanied by adults who couldn't swim either. There were no lifeguards, but no one ever drowned.

We'd stay out in the sun and surf all day Saturday, get thoroughly burned through several layers of skin, eat and drink too much, finally get sick and throw up and, next morning, all burned up, ride home in great discomfort, often in real pain, to look forward to another great outing next year.

Mother wisely chose to stay home. Mary C. was in summer school at UNC-Chapel Hill or at Mars Hill College up in the mountains. Here Daddy's cousins, the very prim and proper maiden sisters Miss Caroline and Miss Martha Biggers, were academic dean and teacher respectively. Many coeds probably still remember the Biggers women ringing their little bells while searching for errant girls after hours among the hills and valleys of the college campus.

But Lil and I joined Daddy and Locke on this and several other weekend jaunts to Myrtle or Wrightsville Beach. It was on such occasions that Lil got her first look at naked men in mass, showering off sand and sunburn lotion and snapping each other sharply with wet towels in high-spirited horseplay.

Locke, who had quit his job in Monroe disillusioned with the capitalistic system to retire to the coast, seldom again put on a coat and tie or a pair of shoes. He dressed in shorts, sandals and tank top and raised bees. A shrewd man, he realized the potential value of beach-front property and bought thousands of yards of it at one dollar per foot. He wound up owning a lot of South Carolina's golden strand by the mid-1930s.

He urged Dowd Secrest to invest with him but Daddy's reply was, "Who would ever want to live in a sandy wasteland like this?" Daddy, the farmer, liked fertile soil and to see things grow. Locke later ran a free boys' camp and had Monroe youths down for weeks at a time. He cut their hair, fed and housed them and taught them values of work. Among his most devoted charges were John and Hargrove (Skipper) Bowles. Locke had a sister with five daughters who lived in Charleston, South Carolina. They were part of old Charleston society. The girls became very attractive young women whom I got to know years later when I was in the Navy during World War II.

Later in that autumn of 1932, as the leaves began to lose their color, dry up and blow away along with the checking and savings accounts of many of the depositors in the banks and savings and loan associations, an incident occurred which was seared deeply in my mind.

Daddy and I were in the office of the Secrest Motor Company after supper. The sun had long since set. Miss Wilma Joyner, parts department worker, had closed up. Gene Watts, our black family chauffeur and full-time mechanic, along with Bright Benton, a distant cousin, were getting ready to leave when in staggered a red-faced Jim Fowler. He was a family friend who lived across a slow creek which separated our back yard from the Fowler homestead. That little ditch became a roaring river after a hard rain and was a favorite place for neighborhood children to play. Luckily none of us was ever caught in the storm drain and swept away, although sometimes it was a close-run thing.

Ersel Fowler, Jim's niece, was a friend of Mary C. and Lil, though not a close one, as Ersel had a way of saying nice things with a sharp edge at the end like, "Gee Lil, what a pretty dress. It goes so well with your eyes. What a shame it doesn't fit you across the chest and leaves your slip showing." Such remarks came to be known as the "Ersel Compliment."

Jim's son Horace, not at all like his father, had a fine-chiseled face, a high forehead and intellectual tastes. He was also an accomplished horseback rider. He and Mother used to go riding in the country. They loved to discuss religion and literature and horses. Horace was sixteen years Mother's junior, and while Mother would never admit it to herself or anyone else, I thought she had a crush on him. She was also a friend and bridge-playing partner of Mrs. Fowler. Horace had a much younger brother we called Pap, whom I never liked much, but that was not necessarily a reflection on him as I was, like Lil, on occasion anti-social and overly critical. But I didn't like Pap, like the guy who didn't like Dr. Fell, and well I knew it.

"Where's Dowd?" Jim Fowler shouted. Fowler was over six feet tall and weighed about 250 pounds, to my father's five foot, ten inch frame and 180 pounds, but Daddy was muscular and taut, and no coward. If a fight were brewing, I was not so sure Daddy would lose.

"Oh, there you are, you no-good, thieving, lying son of a bitch," Fowler roared as he saw Daddy standing over by the desk. "So you think you're going to take my house away, do you? And leave me and the missus homeless, and my kids, too? Well, we'll see about that." And Mr. Jim, who'd served on the Board of Trustees of Central Methodist Church with Dowd and who had, with Mrs. Fowler, played "42" with Mother and Daddy all night before Mary C. had been born the next day, pulled out a pistol and held it next to Daddy's head.

"Well, I'll blow your God-damned head off first," and with that, Jim threw off the safety lock and cocked the pistol. Daddy first turned bright red, then deathly white as a hush fell on the few of us remaining in the office. He started to speak but was silenced by Fowler who warned him if he said a word, he'd kill him. And out poured a stream of invective as well as a story of profound anger, grief, and frustration—feelings that millions of other Americans must have felt as the nation faced its most dangerous domestic crisis since the Civil War. At stake were capitalism and the democratic political system upon which it depended.

For what seemed like forever no one said anything. One could, however, hear Fowler breathing heavily and smell the whiskey on his breath and see his trembling fingers playing over the pistol's trigger. Then Gene Watts said in a low voice, "Now, Mr. Jim, I wouldn't do that. No, just think, Mr. Jim. No, I wouldn't do that." I was no means sure Mr. Jim wouldn't. I don't recall being scared. Only curious. Would he really pull the trigger? If so, what would that look like? For a change, I kept quiet.

Then I heard the familiar voice of Bright Benton: "Mr. Fowler, why in the fuck don't you put that God-damned gun down and go home? Dowd ain't done nothing to you yet, and you ain't gonna lose your house. But if you keep this shit up, you're sure as hell gonna lose your life." Bright and Gene, supported now by some boys from the back, moved closer to Jim Fowler. I could feel the tension break. After a moment's hesitation, he put the gun down on Dowd's desk, turned on his heels and left without another word.

Daddy and I went on back home, and I was quickly put to bed, but as I fell asleep, I could hear Mother and Daddy talking quietly in the dark, broken only occasionally by the fireflies. I wonder what will happen in the morning, I thought to myself as I drifted off to sleep. Who could tell? Every day at Broadacre seemed larger than life. It was like Grand Opera, only the people were thinner, to borrow from a review of *"Deception,"* the Bette Davis-Claude Raines movie released fourteen years later.

The next day Mother suggested to Lil and Mary C. that they ask Ersel over for lunch and to shoot some hoops in the back yard. Ersel loved to play basketball at our house because she could always beat Lil and sometimes even best Mary C.

Mother then directed me to ask Pap to go horseback riding and "don't you dare give him Ben. You know that horse is mean and Pap can't handle him." That afternoon Mother asked Mrs. Jim Fowler over for early tea, later to be joined by mutual friends Ora Lee Duncan and Margie Henderson to play bridge. Daddy was back at work in the motor company. I don't know about Mr. Jim. That's the way people handled personal crises that inevitably flared up among friends and relatives in the close-knit society that comprised Monroe's ruling class in the early 1930s.

# 7. Pets and Guns

Animals were almost as important as people at Broadacre. To Lil and me they seemed more so at times. Pets and guns were things we all understood, but while I loved the former, I grew to fear the latter.

In many ways, despite occasional family dysfunction, Broadacre and the farms it sponsored were wonderful places for children to play, grow up and learn about nature: animal and human. Our animals were just more fun—and seemed more human—than other people's pets. Mary C. had a five-gaited horse named Tom, whom she loved to ride, as she once penned in a poem, "down lovers' lane with my favorite swain," Percy Laney, a high-school sweetheart who couldn't decide between her and rival Jo Neal Caldwell.

Jo Neal was a beautiful young woman whom Mary C. disliked intensely and called self-centered, self-conscious, shallow and vain, none of which was true. But neither Jo Neal nor Mary C. was ever to find out what kind of man Percy would become because within a few years, he lay dead on some World War II battlefield on some godforsaken island he'd never even heard of in 1934. His twin sister Margaret remained a lifetime friend of both Mary C. and Jo Neal, who, however, never learned to like each other.

Daddy bought a Shetland pony for me and a larger white one for Lil. Lil's was sweet-natured and gentle. My little pony, however, had a mean disposition, disliked me on sight, flattening his ears and flaring his nostrils to register disapproval. He tried to kick or bite me as I saddled him, and once astride him I had to be careful as he would try to throw me off, either by bucking or walking along the sides of the barn to scrape me off. But nothing worked. I broke him in and rode him, but he never liked it.

Soon I abandoned the Shetland for a white five-gaited mare named Lady. We loved each other, and I rode her all over Monroe and Union County. One of the last times Daddy gave me a whipping was over Lady and my inability to hitch her up to a buggy to ride in Monroe's July 4th parade.

Daddy had told Heath to show me how to harness and saddle the horse, to hitch it to a plow and now to a buggy, but somehow I couldn't learn the buggy part. When Daddy came home for lunch to discover I hadn't done it, he required an explanation.

Heath, whose voice only his parents, Daddy, Lil and I could translate into English, said, in effect:

"I dunno, Mr. Secrest, he just can't do it."

"You mean 'won't do it'," Daddy replied.

"Well, he can't get the bit into her mouth, and he gets the reins all mixed up, and I dunno, I can't seem to teach him how," Heath explained.

"Now, when I come home at four o'clock, you'd better have Lady hitched up to that buggy, or I'm going to wear you out," Daddy threatened. I didn't reply. I sulked. I complained to Heath. I reported to Mother. Then I dismissed it from my mind. Doll Jr. and I caught a few more pigeons and then went down the street to fish in Mrs. Carpenter's goldfish pond. Doll had gone home, and I was home alone when Daddy pulled up in the driveway and came around back to find Lady free and the buggy unattached, and me still in my pajamas.

"Mac, come in here," Daddy called from the kitchen. I knew I was in for it. I was angry, defiant, balky—perhaps a little apprehensive—not really scared, as Daddy took off his belt and told me to bend over. I decided not to. I knew I was in for a licking, but I thought I'd get in the first blow. Instead of obediently bending over, I suddenly lowered my head and charged Daddy like a young bull, aiming for the solar plexus.

"Ugh!" Daddy exclaimed, the breath momentarily knocked out of him as he reeled backward. But my moment of triumph was short-lived. At nine years of age, I was no match for my 47-year-old father who, though he'd long since given up exercise, was still plenty muscular and strong.

To sum up, I got the licking of my life and was told to go out and hitch Lady up to the buggy and have her ready for Daddy's inspection when he came home for supper. If I didn't, I could expect to get another whipping and this time it wouldn't be so easy. To paraphrase Dr. Johnson, you can depend upon it. Such a threat can concentrate a boy's mind wonderfully. I was surprised to discover how easily and quickly I could hitch Lady up. It took almost no time at all. It was even fun. I felt proud and accomplished. I believed I had really earned Daddy's approval. I had to admit to myself that I had deserved that whipping, especially as I had struck the first blow.

When they heard about it, Mother didn't like it, Lil didn't like it, Cousin Annie and Miss Ann Redwine didn't approve. Mary C. wasn't on hand to register her opinion, but when Daddy got home right at six o'clock, he did like it.

"That's a good job, son," he said, putting an arm around my shoulder. "I knew you could do it. But you should have done it long before this." It was a rare moment of parental male bonding, and it didn't last long.

Daddy wasn't much of a hunter, but he kept a shotgun and a pistol in the house, both loaded and neither kept safely locked away. Heath also had a shotgun with which to shoot snakes if need be as we went out to work on the farm together.

Hunting was a way of life in the rural South in the 1930s. No one had ever heard of gun-control laws or felt the need for a National Rifle Association to protect our Second Amendment rights, or a Charlton Heston to declare that no federal official would ever "pry my cold dead fingers" from the trigger.

But I learned early not to trust guns. People often lack the judgment or caution to guard against accidents. My concern was justified on two occasions and came close on two others. Mother also was always warning about the danger of firearms and reading from newspapers horrific stories— both accidental and homicidal. One day when Heath and I were walking through a field, he stumbled over a stump. The safety catch was off and the gun fired, blasting away two of his toes and requiring the amputation of another. I was unscathed but unnerved.

A few years earlier a much more deadly accident occurred right in our circular drive at Broadacre. Mr. and Mrs. Cox lived down the driveway and across Hayne Street. Since our front yard was so large, it didn't seem as if we were near neighbors. Cox is a fine old English name. I guess there are highbrow and lowbrow Coxes, just as there were silk-glove and hoe-hand Covingtons. Our neighbors were described by Mother as "good, plain people," hard-working and honest but not noticeably successful.

Their son Tommy was the pride of the family and properly so. He was exquisitely handsome, and all the girls chased him, even if he wasn't from a good family. He was popular, self-possessed, a good student, and just naturally cool. He was about a year older than Mary C., a close friend. His best friend was our cousin William Lockhart, who lived on the other side of the circular driveway but a world away from the Cox home.

One summer morning shortly after their high school graduation, Tommy and William had gone for a ride in one of Daddy's demonstrator Chevrolets, taking Mary C. along and Hilda Outen, a friend who lived nearby. Around noon they returned the car to Broadacre and Mary C. and Hilda got out. The usual neighborhood crowd was hanging around talking, playing ball, doing what teenagers did. As usual, Lil and I were the tag-alongs.

William's grandfather Lockhart had married my great aunt, Martha Covington. That man's early promise had never been realized, as he proved to be both a non-provider and a wife-abuser. His grandson had that day brought along a pistol which his father, my mother's first cousin, had recently purchased. Out came the pistol, and after brief examination, a shot rang out. Tommy slumped over in the front seat, blood gushing from his head.

Dr. Smith was called. An ambulance came. So did the police. Off went the whole crowd, but not before I got a quick glimpse of Tommy, that promising, bright, handsome young man, with his head half blown away. William was penitent. He was sorry. As Daddy later uncharitably observed to Mother, "Hell, your little cousin was always sorry."

In any event it was a double tragedy, for whereas Tommy, the light and hope of the Cox family, lay dead, his lowbrowed, half-witted brother continued to live, slouching his way home from work at the cotton gin, barely aware and hardly caring what had become of his younger brother. That was no fault of the older brother, but again I was reminded of the bitter irony life can hold. There was no investigation. No inquest. No charges. No criminal or civil lawsuit. No insurance or recompense. And no justice. The favored family from the right set, while temporarily upset and sorry about the incident, soon forgot about it.

But not Lessie, who grieved over such matters and even assumed some responsibility for them where there was none to bear. And not Mary C., nor Lil, nor I. We all felt guilty and sensed the sadness that transcended this one episode which served as a metaphor for the tragic side of ordinary life.

No wonder Mother had a fit when Bobby Dobson, another Lockhart relative, later came to play with me, found Daddy's loaded pistol in a bedroom drawer, and brought it out to examine. I wonder if Bobby ever forgave me for running to get Mother and tattling on him. She removed both Bobby and me from the room and quickly returned the pistol to its place in the drawer, still fully loaded and unsecured. And the shotgun still stood on its stock, both barrels loaded, in the corner, waiting for goodness knows what to happen next.

The summer after my third year in primary school, when I was eight years old going on nine, Daddy decided Doll Jr. and I both were to be farmed out to Heath. He figured we needed to be removed from the excessive attention of my sisters and their friends and all that dressing up and paper doll playing. We would spend the summer cutting sugar cane, shocking wheat, helping build hog pens and wallows, butchering and cleaning pigs and calves, breeding horses and midwifing cows. It was tough, raw, hard and at times dangerous work; I can't imagine Mother allowing it.

But I thrived on it. I was almost never home. I spent as many nights at Heath's house on the wrong side of the tracks as in my own. I became thin, hard, tough, wiry, and, for my naturally light complexion, deeply tanned. I went barefoot all summer long, my feet so tough that by early frost I still wore no shoes to school. Miss Ollie Alexander, my teacher and one of Mother's closest friends, called to complain. She reported that Ray House, the new principal, said there had to be some minimal dress code.

What baths I took were in Richardson's Creek or some such rural stream, where Heath, Murray, and Lindsay would skinny dip after work. I joined them, admiring and also envying their well-developed, muscular bodies made hard from physical labor; perhaps also with an artistic appreciation, much as Michelangelo's patron may have admired the artist's masterpiece, "David," the model for which also posed without a fig leaf. I wasn't aware of any sexual curiosity then and don't recall any now, but who knows? Maybe there was a component of that as well.

My new persona was appreciated in school and was openly acknowledged one day when I duked it out with John Futch over the hand of Margaret Hamilton, my first childhood sweetheart. John—a much admired, cool kid—and I both developed a crush on Margaret that fall of 1932. So we got into a fight and a crowd gathered on the school ground, betting on and rooting for John to clean "Impossible's" clock. But it came out the other way. And, fickle as school kids can be, I now became the acclaimed hero. No bully or any prior tormentor was willing to challenge me now. Over the summer I'd become tough, in body and in spirit.

I came to remember that fight with sadness too. John was a nice boy, likable, unaffected and musically talented. He was born twenty years too soon. He had a mop of unruly hair and looked like Ringo Starr. In 1940 he was a big band musician. In the 1960s he may well have become a rock-and-roll star. But fate intervened and John never lived to fulfill any potential. He died an army private on a Philippine island in late 1944, another Union County kid who had never heard of Mindanao until shortly before a Japanese sharpshooter bagged him there.

One can't help but wonder about who and why, and ask "What if?" Is there a purpose, a design, a plan? If so, what is it and why? Is it all accidental, or pre-designed, who'll live, who'll die? Thornton Wilder asked the question in "The Bridge of San Luis Rey," but he never provided any answers that satisfied me.

A few years later I experienced an emotional crisis over this question of life and death, the Biblical age of three score and ten and the promise of everlasting life. Did I really believe this? What was seventy years, even if one were to attain it, in comparison to the everlasting and expanding universe and its enormity, measured in light years. Imagine! Stars we see still brilliantly shining have long since disappeared. What if Doubting Thomas were right? Seventy years. Is that all there is? One might as well be dead right now.

Such thoughts were rare and transient, however. I was much more preoccupied with my horses, dogs, pigs, cats, and pigeons. I was as much at home in the saddle as on my own two feet. By the time I was ten and had left my Little Lord Fauntleroy image behind, I was a movie cowboy fan. My favorite was Ken Maynard. I learned after many a fall to take a running jump and leapfrog my way from the horse's rump onto the saddle and gallop away.

Every year a professional rodeo troupe would visit Monroe and stay several weeks. I'd hang around their encampment and talk to the male and female performers, who could ride hanging half out of their saddles and do other amazing feats. I also became enamored of boxing and wrestling, both amateur in Monroe and professional in Charlotte. Daddy would often take me and Doll Jr. to these evening attractions.

Mother found all this to be uncouth and common, and there commenced a struggle between my parents; one to see to it that I was exposed to the more refined things in life, the other to expose me to what he considered the more manly arts. I liked both, but did not enjoy the parental tug of war which became another subject of discussion at Ma's on Family Saturday Night Live.

Neither parent objected to my being exposed to whatever Hollywood had to offer, and the silent films and early talking pictures, before the Hayes Office was established to self-censor content, offered some pretty steamy stuff, as well as some creepy horror shows. The Kentucky Fowler kids, Aunt Susie's children, loved to visit Broadacre and the permissive Secrests. David and I preferred the early Warner Brothers gangster pictures, especially those with Paul Muni, Jimmy Cagney and Edward G. Robinson.

In the horror film genre, Boris Karloff and Bela Lugosi, as the monster in Frankenstein and as Dracula, the original vampire—and earlier, Lon Chaney, senior and junior—were delightfully frightening. Early on I decided that film was the future in the entertainment field, far preferable to live Chatauqua or touring Broadway shows which annually visited Monroe.

Mrs. Earle (Rowena) Shute owned the Pastime Theater on North Hayne Street right across from the courthouse. Rowena was a queer little old lady, always dressed in mourning black. Her helper, and presumed lover, with a shadowy past, was just called Pickett. He was a heavy drinker. I never knew for sure, but somehow, in comments overheard, and observing the easy banter between Rowena and Daddy, I was led to believe that they too may have been close friends themselves many years earlier. Mrs. Shute also owned the recreation park "Lake Tondawanda," where Mary Garrison had taken me when I was four years old.

The Pastime Theater was unique in that you walked into the theater facing the projection booth, with the screen to your back. You had to turn around to sit down and see the movie. The theater carried feature films from Columbia, Paramount, and 20th Century Fox studios. The Strand Theater, owned by Mr. and Mrs. Hamilton on Main Street, on the other side of the courthouse, carried movies produced by MGM, Warner's, Universal, RKO, and United Artists. Friday night was cash night, when people won prizes, usually a set of dinner dishes.

The Hamiltons were the parents of Margaret and Virginia. I had an on-again, off-again crush on Margaret throughout high school. My first cousin Lee Wolfe and Virginia really were sweethearts, however, and much later were engaged to be married. But their wedding was never to take place, as Lee, bedeviled by God only knows what, killed himself one spring evening in Hawaii where he was on duty as a military policeman barely 20 years old. As luck would have it, my ship weighed anchor in Honolulu a few months after Lee's suicide. I went by his army unit and spoke with his commanding officer and many of his buddies and then paid a visit to his temporary burial site.

Margaret's parents both died early, leaving her and Virginia orphaned by ages 11 and 13. They went to live with relatives on Long Island, New York, for a couple of years, only to return to Monroe for the last two years of high school, bringing with them a cool new vocabulary where everything was "neat" and "keen." The self-appointed in-crowd welcomed them into the high school social club, a haven for the hip kids whose older siblings some years earlier had founded the sex club that Lil had disdained.

Rowena Shute lived to a ripe old age, never changing habit or appearance, and taking Pickett back as her consort after he had been released from jail; he had received a brief sentence for "committing a crime against nature" with a cell mate (himself a respectable family man and father of one of my friends) while they were either drunk or high on drugs or both.

That friend, who fought in World War II as a Marine, and a decorated one to boot, returned home a hero, only to be killed late one night years later in an auto accident on his way home from an evening with his fiancée. Our world has always been an unsafe place. Nothing comes with a guarantee, and Providence moves with an unpredictable whimsy. But most of us, exposed to the same hazards and often taking far greater risks and who, by any just standards don't even deserve to make it, not only survive but thrive, and grow old enough to learn better and even to write about it.

# 8. Barking and Biting

While one may never know what fate holds in store, neither Lessie nor Dowd made much effort to find out or to change its course. Mother delivered dire warnings but never really followed up with any enforcement or measures of prevention. To her, words were the equivalent of action. Mother usually said, "Yes, but be careful." Daddy usually said "No," but we often disregarded him.

When I was not yet six years old, I was bitten by a mangy-looking stray dog while I was climbing around under an abandoned house some blocks from home. The bite on my left hand just below the thumb was deep, the wound jagged. I ran home crying. Mother soothed my fears, kissed away my tears, and then casually instructed Mary Garrison to put me in the tub and wash my hands with soap and water. That was all. No effort was made to find the dog to discover if he may have been rabid; I didn't even get a tetanus shot. Mother put her faith in God, where He "is in heaven and all's right with the world."

Most animal diseases are species-specific and for those that aren't, Lil and I must have developed immunity. We certainly lived in a sea of animals: horses, goats, cows, pigs, sheep, pigeons, crows and bats, not to mention the more mundane cats and dogs. Most of these at one time or another also became household pets.

Queenie, our Black and Tan hunting hound, was converted into a house pet, no longer allowed to hunt. She was permitted one litter of puppies a year so she wouldn't become depressed. She was a natural mother and caregiver. She always had twelve puppies; she knew how many; you could see her count them. One day she lost one and was disconsolate.

We also had a sow who that same day gave birth, but she wasn't stable like Queenie. Apparently she suffered from postpartum depression, for I discovered one morning when I went to feed her that she had devoured her young—all except one little runt that had already been kicked out and lay some feet away, its breath of life so feeble as barely to sustain it.

I called Heath to take care of the distraught sow, whom we named Medea, and Lil to come help with the baby pig. We decided that Queenie, still sad over having lost one of her puppies, should nurture the pig. It was love at first sight. Queenie quickly accepted the piglet, which immediately found a feeding station, dislodging several pups in the process. Queenie, after counting noses and finding twelve, put her head protectively over her brood and sighed happily.

All twelve survived and the pig, named Princess, raised as a dog, always thought she was one. She did everything a dog did except wag her tail. She continued to twirl and twitch it pig-fashion and to go "Oink, oink," rather than "Arf, arf," which caused Queenie to cock her head and look quizzically upon her twelfth child.

Princess didn't remain a runt for long. Soon she became an imposing porker, ultimately topping 300 pounds. But she had become one of our house pets, toilet-trained and taught to come when called. She also sat down, spoke and rolled over on command. She was fastidiously clean and very affectionate. But she couldn't be allowed out much due to her short hair and thin skin, and of course was denied her mud bath, which is a pig's protection against sunburn. The day she broke down Mother's prized antique sofa was the last day she lived at Broadacre.

"Mr. Secrest, you've got to do something about Princess," Mother informed Daddy. "She's badly damaged Mama's Empire sofa." Lil and I protested the move, but in vain. Princess was taken out to the Hartises where she could live in a pigsty, wallow in mud and live as a pig should, but she could never be slaughtered for food. The Hartis children were thrilled; the Secrest children grieved. Daddy said he'd provided financially for Princess's future, so Mr. Hartis wouldn't be tempted to eat her. But I never was absolutely sure and sometimes envisioned Princess's head on a platter with an apple in her mouth.

Betty Boop, whom we raised as a tiny kitten, first with an eyedropper and later with a doll's bottle, was equally exceptional. Largely black with some white here and there, Betty Boop was an indoor-outdoor cat. Like Queenie, she had frequent litters and, like the dog, was a superb parent. Like my mother, however, Betty Boop may have loved not always wisely but too well. And like my father, she was often ambivalent and contradictory in her behavior to her offspring. She had favorites and was much too permissive with her oldest son. We named him Wimpy because he was lazy and no-account, like his namesake in the comic strip Popeye.

Betty Boop, long since abandoned by her mate, had to raise her brood as a single mom. That didn't bother her, as she was bossy and domineering, like my grandmother Ma. By the time the kittens were old enough to be weaned, Betty would begin to teach them to hunt. They started off with moles and mice and other little rodents, but they soon graduated to birds, their preferred meat. Betty was an amazing athlete and easily jumped up, fast and high, to catch a bird on the wing. When she did that, she summoned her kittens with a distinctive come-and-get-it call which brought them to her on the trot. Lil and I learned to mimic that mealtime call so well that any set of kittens would come when we used it.

Betty showed them how to tear into the bird and eat it properly. She shared generously with them and made them share with each other, punishing the more aggressive and greedy kittens with a sound slap. One day Betty would share her catch. The next she'd call her kittens and when they appeared, eager to share in the feast, she'd hiss and growl and, if they came too close, slap them soundly and send them scurrying for cover. Then she'd call them back and make them watch her as she ate the whole thing. It was time, she was saying, to catch your own dinner. Then she'd go over to them, wash their faces affectionately, letting them in turn lick some of the food off her face, as everybody in the family started to purr.

Late one spring evening in 1934, after the family had finished supper in the sun parlor and set out Daddy's for him to eat when he got home from work, Lil and I heard that familiar come-and-get-it call from Betty Boop. At the same time, we heard Daddy's car drive up. Daddy quickly went to the bathroom, presumably washed his hands, swallowed a large slug of bootleg whiskey, and came out to the breakfast room to eat supper, only to find Betty Boop and three kittens up on the table, enjoying the country fried steak, buttered rolls and cream. Lil and I, having heard the call, arrived too late to prevent the raid. But now seeing it, we exclaimed over Betty Boop's cleverness and the adorable antics of the kittens, who seemed to enjoy the cooked beef even more than raw bird.

Daddy didn't see it our way. "God damn!" he shouted. "Look at what Betty Boop has done to my supper." And after aiming a blow in her direction, which missed by a country mile, he snatched up the three kittens and ordered Lil and me to go get a sack, as he was going to get rid of those cats once and for all. There was a great clamor. Mother was called. Mary C. appeared. Glennie, the cook cleaning up in the kitchen, was enlisted, along with Heath and Doll Jr. Only Betty Boop was missing.

The kittens, lying in the bottom of the cloth sack, were still. No sound from them. "Mac, go put these kittens in the car. Lil, you go, too." Daddy ordered. Mary C. had lost interest and gone back to her phone conversation with Margie McRorie. Mother began, "Mr. Secrest, don't you think that..."

"No, I don't think anything," Daddy snapped back. "I know I've worked all day and I'm tired and hungry, and I deserve a little consideration."

"I thought Betty Boop and her kittens were outdoors," Mother started to explain, but Daddy interrupted, "Well, you know what Parker's puppies thought, don't you? That horse turds were biscuits." And with that insult still ringing in Mother's ears, out came Daddy to join Lil and me to take a ride into the country.

A few miles out on the old Charlotte highway, Daddy pulled into a driveway to be greeted by a man in overalls who called from the lighted porch, "Howdy, yu'enzes, git out and light." The three of us lit and Daddy started talking.

"I want to show you something," Daddy said confidentially. "We've got something here that will make that little girl of yours mighty happy." And he opened the sack and pulled out one of the kittens. "This is a fine gray tabby," Daddy confided. "His mother is the best mouser in the world. Just what you need to keep mice out of your house. And barn too. This kitten's mother is the smartest cat you'll ever see and he is just like her."

The more Daddy talked, the greater became the virtues of Betty Boop. Lil and I had had no idea how much Daddy appreciated her true value. One would never have guessed that he had been ready to kill her less than an hour earlier and drown her three offspring. The discussion went on for a long time, with talk about weather, crops, prices and family health co-mingling with further praise of the kitten. Whenever opposition to the adoption arose, Daddy's sales pitch expanded.

"Well, I'll tell you what I'll do," Dowd finally said. "You can have the little fellow for nothing—and because I hate to separate them, you can have all three, one each for your three youngest children."

"Can't take ' em. Can't afford 'em. Got enough cats already." But when Daddy urged him to let the children see them, the farmer relented a little. Finally, after much discussion, in which the farmer's wife got into the argument long enough to say that if the children accepted another kitten, they'd have to care for it, the deal was closed. They'd take one, not three, but they promised it a good home. Daddy handed each child a dollar bill. Lil and I cried as we parted with the tabby, and off we drove.

This time back to Monroe and out to Houston township, where the scene was repeated. Again opposition was overcome, a grudging agreement reached, and Daddy, having agreed not to charge anything, ended up paying the little boy $5 for taking the kitten. Again Lil and I wept over the separation but were relieved that at least the kittens were not to be drowned.

The last stop was in town. Daddy parked the car in front of Secrest Drug Store and Feed and Seed Store, carried the remaining kitten in his arms, and accompanied by Lil and me, made his way to the Pastime Theater. "Rowena, got a kitten for you." Rowena was a kind soul and a fool about animals. "Really? Dowd, you're just too good to me." Taking the kitten and scratching it beneath its chin, she was rewarded by the start of a motor which vibrated through the small body.

"Rowena, this kitten will become an exceptional cat. Its mother is a wonder. You won't have any mice running around the feet of your customers with him on duty. And," he added slyly, "he will be worth a hell of a lot more to you than Pickett." Rowena, no fool, accepted the cat with no illusions but with great good humor. "Give my love to Lessie, Dahlin," she said as she ushered us out.

Daddy's bark was worse than his bite. Sometimes he really wasn't so bad; but sometimes he was. Later that year Betty Boop had still not weaned Wimpy, eldest of an earlier litter. Wimpy, a grown tom cat, still nursed his mother. He was also sly about it, polite toward the kittens while humans were watching, but hissing and spitting and driving them away from their mother as soon as the coast seemed clear so he could have her and her milk all to himself. He was such a mama's boy. She even still caught birds for him and summoned him with that special call.

Comedy and tragedy, like theater masks, were often co-mingled at Broadacre. One cold November night in 1933, I was at home with my parents. I was ten years old and in the fifth grade. Lil, now thirteen and a sophomore in high school, had gone to the movies with Helen. Mary C. was a sophomore at Meredith College.

59

I was doing homework when I heard rising voices from the living room. Mother sounded distressed and tense, Daddy angry and ill-tempered. He was not an alcoholic. He didn't drink a lot or steadily, but he didn't hold liquor well and metabolized it slowly. And sometimes it left him angry, hateful and depressed; tonight it sounded like all three.

"I can't account for every penny we spend, Mr. Secrest," Mother told her husband as he demanded to know where all the household money had gone.

"Well, why can't you?" Daddy asked. "You know as well as I do we have to budget." And he started to talk about how slow business was, how he couldn't sell any cars, except to some old maid friends of hers, and to do that, he had to teach them to drive and spend hours demonstrating the automobiles. "Who's got $900 to buy a Chevrolet?" Daddy wanted to know.

"Dowd," Mother replied—unusual use of his first name, bad sign, I thought—"Why do you get so worked up by everything? You're no pleasure to be around."

"You don't seem to realize or even care that we can hardly keep ourselves out of personal bankruptcy, do you?" Daddy observed, adding that Mother had no business sense, couldn't even keep the checkbook balanced, and was no help at all to him or to anyone else.

Mother denied the charge, declaring it a hateful thing to say. Daddy raised the ante, threatening to take Mary Cov out of college, and adding that they might have to sell Broadacre and lose their home, just as Jim Fowler nearly had. At this point the row became personal. Mother said he didn't love her and never had, suggesting Rowena Shute or Mrs. Warren might have been better suited to him. He reminded her that she was like her own mother, having once been gone a whole year when he had to be mother and daddy both to Mary C., Lil and me.

Voices rose to a higher pitch. Daddy cast aspersions upon the Covingtons, implying that Mother's father had died not from Bright's Disease, but from some long-working social disease he may have contracted as a younger man, a condition that might explain Lessie's mother's health and her own earlier breakdown.

Things escalated from there, neither apparently concerned about where I was or what I might have heard. I got up and went into the living room just as Daddy picked up that fully loaded double-barreled shotgun standing in the corner. I remember a tussle over the gun as Mother sought to take it from Daddy's grasp, and my beating my fists on his back shouting, "No, Daddy, no!"

The struggle lasted only seconds. Daddy never had any real intention of firing the weapon, unless to train it on himself. He never meant to harm Mother, and as I later told Lil, I thought it was just a desperate gesture, to act out how worried he was about everything. Things were tough in 1933. They got worse in 1935. I really didn't then, and can't now, blame anybody.

But Betty Boop did. She sensed the tension, and worse yet, possible danger to her adored Wimpy. As soon as she saw Dowd grab the gun and Lessie wrestle for it, down she jumped from the sofa, jerking Wimpy away from her teats; both fell to the floor, knocking the table lamp over with a great crash. The only explosion that night was the popping of the light bulb, which seemed to snap everybody back to their senses.

Lil and Helen came in just as the drama played out. That weekend, Aunt Eve came in from Salem College. Aunt May arrived shortly thereafter from Duke University. Uncle Jim and Aunt Katherine Craven drove over from Charlotte for Sunday dinner. Mary C., summoned by Lil and me, came home from Raleigh by bus Friday night. Miss Ann Redwine, Aunt Kathryn Huntley, Cousin Annie Ashcraft—all the usual suspects—were in and out of the house as they talked, debated, agreed, discussed, quarreled, fussed, laughed and cried over what to do about Mother and Daddy.

# 9. Cat with an Oedipus Complex

By Monday morning everything was back to normal. Broadacre wasn't to be sold. Mary C. wasn't to be yanked out of Meredith and put to work at the Five and Dime. Daddy was back at work. Lil and I were back in school. Lessie was back playing bridge with two of Dowd's younger sisters, Aunt Mary Hinson and Aunt Isabel Wolfe. Everyone else had returned to their places. Betty Boop was nursing her latest litter, with Wimpy back at the trough whenever Lil and I weren't around to drive him away. But Daddy was still unsettled, and so it was Wimpy's turn to pay.

In late spring of the next year, Daddy came home one evening, late for supper as usual, to find the house in its normal state of physical and emotional disarray. He was cross and went to the bathroom for his customary slug of white lightning. Lessie failed to answer an imperious call. Lil and I were in the back room, the door open to the back steps, playing with the snow-white Spitz pup we'd just received from Dr. Sam Alexander, the town veterinarian. We were already surrounded by our two pet goats; Lil had taught Smokey to jump into her lap. Sam, our ram with the evil disposition, was hitting a tree, practicing for his next victim.

No one heard Daddy calling, or else paid no attention. I had forgotten that the new pup had left his most recent deposit near the door sill. I remembered as Daddy growled, "Shit!" under his breath and pushed his soiled shoe in my rear to shove me down the steps. As I fell, yelling in protest, I looked up in time to see him falling down right behind me. We both looked up to see Lil standing there cuddling the puppy and staring down at us.

"Lil, what in the devil did you do that for?" Daddy asked, more at first in bewilderment than in anger.

"Well, I thought you might like to know how it feels to be kicked downstairs," was her self-possessed reply. "Did it hurt? Why don't you ask Mac?" And with that she went back inside, latching the screen and bolting the door.

Sam, having seen all this and now presented with an inviting target—Daddy and me still bent over as we were getting to our feet—charged, butting both of us back onto the ground. We raced around the corner of the house onto the side porch, and escaped through the sun parlor door just ahead of that practiced, snorting ram.

"Lil!" Daddy roared, "come back in here." She obeyed at once, now contrite and prepared to accept the consequences for her ill-considered action. At 14, she knew she was well beyond any danger of corporal punishment, but she was apprehensive nonetheless.

"Go get Wimpy," Daddy ordered. "That sorry cat has got to go. And you can't continue to collect puppies and kittens like this. For each new one added, an old one must be subtracted."

Tears and protests and promises of reform fell on deaf ears. "Now listen," Daddy tried to explain. "Wimpy needs to learn to take care of himself. And Betty Boop needs to break that bond." That makes sense, I thought to myself, identifying my own earlier days with Wimpy's fixation.

"All we're going to do is take him down to the seed store and let him earn his keep," Daddy continued. "That place has rats half again as big as he is, and he can help us control them." Well, yes, Lil guessed she could see the reason to that.

So Daddy, again foregoing a cold supper, drove Lil, Wimpy and me down to the seed store where Mr. Starnes, the manager, took Wimpy, looking big-eyed and frightened, down to the basement where sacks of seed and feed were stored.

Wimpy fled beneath some shelves and hid behind the sacks as Lil and I, heavy of heart but resigned to the separation, returned to the car. After all, it wasn't as if we'd never see him again. Why, we were in the drugstore right next to the seed store practically every day. We expected to find Wimpy happy and secure in his new home and probably an entirely new tomcat, full of feline pride and male self-esteem at his emancipation from a dominating if doting mother.

Within days Mr. Starnes reported to Daddy that the mouse population had not dropped. Wimpy was not doing his job; in fact, he was scared of mice. He yowled all day long and wouldn't come out of hiding. He drank some water but had nothing to eat until finally Mr. Starnes began to feed him canned cat food.

"No, indeed," Dowd ordered. "Wimpy must earn his own keep. Don't feed him anything. There's plenty for him to eat here, including scraps in the alleyway from the restaurant next door." Wimpy's misery continued, however, harassing poor Mr. Starnes, who liked cats and had a kind heart. Wimpy grew leaner, more timid, and one day, just disappeared altogether.

One Monday night some weeks later, Daddy, then chairman of the Board of County Commissioners, was meeting with its members in the board room of the courthouse. The red brick Union County Courthouse was and remains a gem of mid-Victorian architecture, dominating the town square and the major streets running out from it north, south, east and west. Surrounding it stood huge oak, maple, elm and magnolia trees, all pre-dating the courthouse itself, built in 1886. Among the trees loomed the inevitable monument honoring the fallen in both the Revolutionary and Civil wars. In 1935 Monroe still recognized Confederate Memorial Day on May 10th, while largely ignoring the national holiday of May 30th.

The courthouse was the hub of Union County legal activities, housing several courtrooms and many offices that conducted official county and municipal affairs, as well as the public library. That night in mid-May was unusually hot, and all the windows were open to allow what little breeze that stirred to blow on in. The meeting was nearing its end, toward eleven o'clock, when an eerie, plaintive cry wafted in from outside.

"Did you hear that?" Daddy asked his fellow commissioners. Business resumed, but the sad, sorrowful sounds, like a crying child, continued intermittently. Then it dawned on Dowd.

"That sounds like Wimpy," Daddy exclaimed, though his colleagues had no idea who that might be. "It's our old tomcat from home. I brought him down to the seed store to catch mice, but he disappeared weeks ago. I bet you that's him, stuck up there in a tree." But no, Wimpy was not up a tree; he was perched atop the Memorial Day monument, nearly as high as a tree but pretty far from one, and it had no branches by which to descend. Wimpy was stuck, and he was unhappy.

"Let's adjourn, gentleman," Dowd suggested. "We're about finished anyhow." And he who had snatched Wimpy away from Betty Boop in anger now had to pay the price. The fire department was called, extension ladders were raised, and a frightened, clawing cat was pulled to safety.

But his fate was yet to be sealed. Wimpy was not allowed to return to Broadacre. He was taken instead to the McAteer farm, where he was turned loose in the barn to fend for himself. McAteer was no Mr. Starnes. There were no small children around any more, just hardened older folk and tough younger men and callous teenagers who loved to hunt and fish and fight when they weren't working, and who had little feeling for a spoiled, pampered tomcat with an Oedipus complex.

Wimpy had to adjust, and he did so in his own strange way. He first became anti-social, then turned wild, and finally became a predator—an outlaw and a killer.

McAteer came to see Daddy. Now a huge, rangy cat, Wimpy survived on the farmer's chickens and rabbits and anything else he could get his bloody claws and teeth into. He avoided people, hiding out by day, to stalk and hunt by stealth at night.

One early morning several months later, I had gone with Heath to the McAteer place to work. There we found a posse had been formed, amid cries of great excitement. "The cat's been sighted!" some young fellow called out. "C'mon, I think he's run into the barn." Soon half a dozen men with hoes, shovels, picks and ax handles, were running through the barn, connecting cribs and sheds, all of which offered hiding places for a predatory cat.

"Call the hounds," ordered McAteer, determined to rid his farm of the curse Dowd Secrest had thrust upon him. I trailed behind the hunters, excited by the chase but secretly hoping that Wimpy would escape. The hounds were baying with excitement, tails stiff and straight out.

"I think he run over here," shouted one boy. Another cried out, "There he is. I seen him!" Between the shouts and barking, I could hear an occasional guttural growl and weird caterwauling. The sounds were leading the pursuers ever closer to their quarry. Now close enough to follow the action, I spied a streak of gray and white as it darted this way and that, always just out of the reach of the slashing hoes and shovels.

"We've trapped him!" called out the lead huntsman. "He run under that shed," and he pointed to a spot near my left shoulder. And I could hear sounds—snarling, hissing, short heavy panting, punctuated by piercing screams. I moved closer, suddenly to see Wimpy's face, even his long white whiskers. His pupils were dilated, huge and black, swallowing the placid green eyes that once had regarded me lazily but trustingly, even lovingly.

I remember seeing for a second a look of recognition, some memory in Wimpy's eyes. He hesitated, took a tentative step toward me, emitting a plaintive "meow." This cry for help was followed by another image of frothing mouth and huge slashing tail.

Wimpy scurried beneath the wooden floor and emerged on the far side to leap up onto the support beam leading to the roof. As he did so, one of McAteer's men swung at the cat and knocked him back down on the open floor, fully exposed. Men and dogs rushed in. Blows from hoes, rakes, and shovels rained down. Terrible screams rent the air. And Wimpy's head was bashed in as his sides were opened up. The dogs rushed in at fever pitch to finish him off.

What a terrible end to an old friend. What a terrible commentary on all living things and the brutal gratification man can take from the savage hunt. And what a terrible price to pay for a mama's overindulgence. In the back of my mind memories stirred. I identified with Wimpy.

I went back to the truck and cried my heart out. It was really nobody's fault and everybody's fault, and I hated everybody for it. The experience was not a happy one for a child of eleven, but I didn't dwell on it much.

Soon after Wimpy' cruel demise, I was harvesting sugarcane with Heath. We had a new harvester with low, sharp, horizontal blades that cut near the bottom of the stalk. My dog at that time was a small but very hardy, aggressive terrier. Skippy went everywhere with Heath and me. Once a rattlesnake struck him just below the ear. The venom caused his head to swell and his little body to become first hard as stone, then gradually over hours to soften, leaving him limp and weak, unable to move, even to lift his head.

Heath took quick action. As translated, he gave orders. "Quick, Mac, hold him up while I cut the bite." And he pulled out his sharp all-purpose pocketknife and cut straight into Skippy's jaw. The little dog, quivering and in shock, didn't move as I held onto him. Then Heath squeezed, gradually expressing some of the poison from Skippy's head.

"Take some of this black earth, down from beneath the root, and rub it in the side there," Heath continued, as our little friend became more comatose. We used water, mudpack, and cut one more time, then lay his inert body over in the shade, climbed up on the combine, and went back to work.

Some hours later we returned to find Skippy holding up a wobbly head, now three times its normal size, but wagging his tail. As I moved to pet him, he licked my hand.

"Do you think he's going to be all right?" I asked Heath, the primitive oracle. Heath, in his mumbled and garbled way, assured me yes. "Hell, Mac, you can't kill that little dog. He'll be fine. All the swelling will go down and the big crusty sores will slough off. You'll see." And as usual where animals were concerned, Heath proved to be right. Skippy did recover, but it took weeks and caused a lot of anxiety.

All was not to remain well, however. Several weeks after the snake bite, with Skippy running along the combine again, occasionally darting and biting at its wicked blades, Heath suddenly turned the machine to the right. Skippy had not anticipated that and his rear left paw got caught in those horizontal blades.

A shriek of pain and surprise. I jumped off the machine and ran over to him. He still had all four legs, thank God, I thought, but the pad on his hind left paw had been cut clean away, leaving no skin, flesh, or padding at all. Blood spurted everywhere, covering his entire body and half of mine, it seemed. This time no home remedy would do. Heath and I rushed him to Dr. Sam Alexander's office, having first wrapped the bleeding paw with my shirt.

No, Skippy didn't die. He was as I said a tough little dog. He lost the bottom part of his left leg to amputation, but true to form, as soon as I saw him after the procedure, he wagged his tail and licked my face.

Neither of those two accidents discouraged Skippy from living the good farm life with its open fields of harvest. He quickly compensated for the lost lower leg and for a number of years, after I had given it up, Skippy still went with Heath to hunt, catch rats, and run around as Heath and his helpers shocked wheat or baled cotton. He even acquired another snakebite or two. Skippy was never a household pet. He was a field hand.

Lil, Doll Jr. and I continued to observe the habits of our barnyard menagerie, which taught us a lesson I've retained throughout life. Animals are not so one-dimensional as humans think, and beyond instinct, they move with an individual intelligence that varies just as abilities do among people.

There was usually a lot of drama with our pets. One duckling's back was broken when Lady inadvertently stepped on it. Lil and I took it down to Dolan Jones, a pharmacist in the drugstore who could fix almost anything. Mr. Jones rigged up some contraption that lifted the duck's body weight off its legs, pinned its wings together, and gave the little thing, bound up so tightly it could hardly move, back to us to care for. We fed and watered it every day. As days melted into weeks, the little duck gained in strength. It never did waddle quite right after its accident, but it survived, and managed to rejoin its mates and even to swim again.

Our pet crow had a more sorrowful end. Having lost its parents through a shooting by an irate neighbor who grew tired of their eating his grain, the baby crow, almost featherless, was raised by Lil, me, Doll Jr. and Heath. He was an indoor-outdoor crow, fully free to fly throughout the house as he called out to us, "Caw! Caw!" He had other sounds to indicate other needs to gain our attention. We soon learned his language about as well as we had Heath's.

The crow, now fully grown, loved to land on Mother's shoulder whenever she was stooped over weeding in the flower beds and pick the silver hair pins out of her graying hair. I think Mother was flattered by the attention, as, I further suspect, Daddy had long since lost interest in loosing her hair, which Mother always wore in a bun on her neck, seldom letting it cascade down to her waist. But Jim—with his politically incorrect name—never tired of it.

The crow was impartial, however, and paid attention to Daddy as well. Sometimes after mid-day dinner, Daddy would lie down and fall fast asleep on the living room sofa. As he turned from one side to the other loose silver change would fall out of his pockets: nickels, dimes, pennies, quarters, sometimes even fifty-cent pieces.

As soon as the crow observed Daddy asleep, he'd light very gently on Daddy's bald head and wait. Soon the change would begin to slide out, and the crow would collect some coins in his beak, fly out the window to a nearby sand box, and bury his loot. Often Jim would have to make several trips until he'd collected everything and buried it beneath the sand, along with some of Mother's hair pins.

Daddy never seemed to notice the disappearance of his change, and we children certainly never told him. After he'd driven off to work, Lil and I would go out to the sand box, dig down and collect the fortune. Jim would circle overhead, crying out "Caw! Caw!" sometimes swooping down close enough to be caught. I never knew if he were protesting our theft of his earlier one, or if he approved of it. Jim also would steal Daddy's eyeglasses, attracted by the glitter of the steel rims and reflection in the glass. He would bury the glasses in the sand box along with the change. Daddy always offered a cash reward to anyone who could find his glasses. So Jim increased our income in two ways.

Jim was a loner. Raised by humans, he was an outcast among the other crows, and the mockingbirds hated him. I still don't know why, but several of these smaller birds would gang up on him as he flew around the yard, harrying and harassing him, cutting him off, bumping into him, and delivering sharp pecks on his head. There seemed no way to protect Jim against this barnyard bullying, although we tried. One day we found him dead on the ground near the crib, his eyes pecked out.

# 10. Questions and Contradictions

Despite the bumpy road to love that my parents trod and the disparity of their backgrounds, Lessie Covington proved to be an adaptable and flexible woman, quite content to take the Secrest name and embrace the Secrest family. Despite her ignorance of mundane things, as her mother had warned Dowd, Lessie quickly and willingly learned how to cook and clean and run a household and a growing family. She embraced the ritual of spring cleaning, dragging out Persian rugs and, with the hired help of Alice Bowell, hanging them over heavy rope lines strung between trees and beating the dust out of them. And scrubbing down walls, washing and waxing hardwood floors, and washing curtains and draperies in boiling water with special soap in huge black cast-iron kettles out in the backyard.

She even learned on occasion to prepare chittlins, filling the kitchen with that peculiarly foul odor associated with cleaning hog intestines, all this to please her husband and to prove she could do anything the Secrests expected and that her own mother said she'd never learn.

All of this Dowd secretly approved and was proud of, although the most praise Lessie ever received for all her efforts, despite broad hints and many self-paid compliments, was a non-committal, "I'm eating it, ain't I?"

And eat well we did, even though Mother wasn't especially interested in cooking or very good at it. We produced our own milk, with cream several inches thick on top. We churned our own butter, skimming off the top and using the skimmed milk, called "blue John," to slop the hogs. We made our own delicacies such as andouettes (chittlins), sweetbreads, pig knuckles and feet, brains and eggs, and poached squab, which Lil and I refused to eat lest one turn out to be "Pidgy-Widgy".

Mother's close friend, Kathryn Huntley, introduced her to Alice Bowell, a hard-working, chain-smoking, loud, foul-mouthed woman about 45 years old. Almost as white as she was black, Alice feared no man or woman, regardless of race or position, any more than she feared work. She tackled dust and dirt as if they were the devil himself. Alice was skinny but had a wiry strength. She had a pockmarked, sallow, light tan complexion, and hazel eyes. Her woolly, kinky hair was sparse. Two deep scars ran parallel down her neck. She wore the same old skirt, down to her thin, sinewy legs and white cotton stockings, knotted just below the knee.

Despite differences in race, background and education, Aunt Kathryn and Alice were in a way sisters under the skin. They loved to fuss and quarrel. Aunt Kathryn was as determined to boss Alice and tell her what to do as Alice was not to be told.

Mother was made of gentler stuff, a fact Alice recognized and appreciated. Lessie never raised her voice to Alice, who accepted tactful suggestions willingly. I think Alice really liked Lessie and Kathryn equally, each for different reasons. And they liked Alice and respected her ability to work, although during spring cleaning Aunt Kathryn would come by and begin the conversation with, "That Alice Bowell made me so mad today." Alice and I were great buddies.

Alice had no political position. She wasn't a racist and she didn't consider herself a victim, though in many ways she was. She lived life without self-pity and dealt with it pretty much on her own terms. She never paid much attention to segregation and considered herself the equal of Lessie Secrest and Kathryn Huntley.

Mother, given to bouts of depression which sometimes disguised itself as back pain, would enlist help from Alice. The cleaning woman became a masseuse, rubbing and pounding Lessie's back with almost as much vigor as she used on those Persian rugs. At the end of one session, Alice viewed Mother's naked body favorably, "I declare, Miss Lessie, you've got the most beautiful body I've ever seen—a tiny wasp-like waist and hips as big as all outdoors!"

Mother was moved as well as amused at Alice's observation. Snapped out of her depressed feeling, she enjoyed telling her friends over the card table of Alice's opinions, all the while acknowledging ruefully that they were all too true. Well, yes, wide hips did run in the Covington family.

Big hips in women weren't then, and aren't now, big news or some foreign idea, are they? Isn't that why women are called "broads?" And don't some women learn to hate their bodies for just this reason, swallowing the line that "a woman can never be too rich or too thin?" And isn't this dissatisfaction one of the causes of eating disorders, especially anorexia and bulimia among some young women, and an addiction to yo-yo dieting in others? Why would any woman really, to borrow from Professor Higgins, want "to look more like a man?" Why aren't they satisfied with their own bodies? It certainly can't be that they think men aren't interested in them.

Monroe had some good doctors and dentists. At an early age I must have been the bane of their existence. I never accepted treatment easily, resisting every move they made and screaming and hollering at the top of my lungs at their approach. I was equally difficult in the barber's chair. Poor Barber Rogers used to dread to see me coming, dragged in by Alice, to get my little Dutch boy haircut.

I made life especially difficult for Dr. Ingram, a new young dentist who rented an office above the Secrest Drugstore, with a good view of the Courthouse just across Franklin Street.

As a child I was told I had soft teeth which were subject to lots of cavities. Dentistry in the late 1920s was not like dentistry today. The drills were thick, large, and slow. To me their grinding sounds were terrifying, and when they hit a nerve, the pain was excruciating.

"There's a surprise for you today," my parents informed me one day when I was about six years old. "You're going to see Dr. Ingram, a fine young dentist, and he's going to make some ice cream in your mouth. Alice will take you and see that everything is all right. Now be good."

What a lie, and what imagination. Ice cream, indeed. I went willingly enough, despite trepidation. The Novacaine admittedly froze my mouth, but it turned my trepidation first to terror and then to outrage.

I kicked and screamed and nearly pushed poor Dr. Ingram out of his second story window. Dr. Ingram suggested that Alice leave, as he and I could work together better alone. After a few more minutes of struggle, Dr. Ingram, no doubt driven to desperation, gave me a sharp, stinging slap on my leg, just above the knee. Startled, I looked down to see a bright red mark and partial outline of his hand.

Somehow or other, Dr. Ingram managed to drill out the teeth, tap in the filling and called the family to come get me. I never mentioned the slap, thinking I deserved it, and I always rather liked and respected Dr. Ingram himself. But that experience instilled in me an unreasonable, long-lasting fear of dentistry. I overcame it on my own, by willing myself into an acceptance of the inevitable. Today my fear is not one of dental procedure but of dental cost, all of which is uninsured. I carry about $8,000.00 worth of crowns in my mouth. Dr. and Mrs. Ingram never had any children, and I always wondered if the dentist's experience with me had anything to do with that.

While most doctors were pretty good, there was one who wasn't; at least that was the impression I got of Dr. G. He had one daughter approaching "old maid" status and a wife who was reclusive; at least, I never saw her. The daughter was not unattractive, but she had a tentative, hesitant manner, seemingly uncomfortable and uncertain. I was told later that Mrs. G. had taken her own life.

When he was eight my cousin Lee Wolfe, a year younger than I, went to see Dr. G. and left in a state of panic. What had gone wrong? Uncle Hill and Aunt Isabel were upset. Hushed conversations were overheard, then stopped abruptly if I came near. Mother and Daddy were consulted.

I learned later that Lee claimed the doctor had let his hands wander into an inappropriate area and that Lee, uncomprehending but sensing something wrong, had gone home and told his parents. Dr. G. was suspected of being a quasi-pedophile. Although Uncle Hill was furious and wanted to beat the doctor up or bring charges, nothing was ever done. He continued his practice in offices, along with all the other doctors, above the Secrest Drugstore. Apparently the problem isn't limited to Catholic priests or the bishops who cover up for them, Boy Scout masters or schoolteachers.

As a prepubescent youth, I frequently indulged in unanswerable and unsolvable internal debates, such as personal immortality or gender preference, as if one could have done anything about either one.

Which would I rather be, a man or woman? Given my role models and nature's choice, it was a toss-up to me. I had no desire to be a girl, much less a grown woman, and the idea of having a baby scared me to death. What if I had been born a girl, someday got married and had a baby? The notion that anything so big could come out of a female body fissure so small boggled the imagination. Prolonged labor and birth pangs? What if one had multiple births, as Mother did? What if the mother were to die, as lots of women did? No, best to remain a boy and become a man.

But what if I were to grow into a man only to have to go to war? Lots of men died in war. My own great-grandfather had been killed in the Civil war. The country had fought in lots of wars, one barely fifteen years before, and war clouds were gathering again on the distant horizon.

Daddy and Locke were already saying that another European war was likely. If I were nine, would war come in time to swallow me up? Could I shoot someone's head off, or charge out of the trenches and across no-man's-land in the face of steel bayonets and barbed wire? Or worse yet, have my own head shot off or intestines laid bare? No, better to suffer the pangs of childbirth and stay home safe from hostile fire in foreign lands.

In the 21st century these concerns may seem irrelevant. Now you can do something about them. Today if one wants to become a woman, just go to a medical specialist, trim off some genitalia, have some cosmetic surgery to fashion some faux female organs, receive some hormone replacement therapy and voila! You can palm yourself off as a woman. And if you happen to be woman who wants to become a man, just reverse the procedure.

Childbirth is much easier. C-sections and saddle blocks can make it practically painless. The maternal and infant mortality rates everywhere, except in Third World nations, have been reduced dramatically. With fertility drugs women can give birth to litters nowadays, largely without pain or risk. Little reason to worry about that.

Immortality is stickier stuff. But with the decoding of the chromosome chain, the introduction of human interchangeable parts, the promise of cloning and stem cell research, further uses of RNA and DNA, and, finally, cybernetics and freezing of human tissue for future thawing, who knows? In the future my pre-teen angst about sex, war and death may become irrelevant.

My anxiety about war, however, was right on the money. Only eight years later, Pearl Harbor was attacked and we were in a shooting war, and I was at the vulnerable age of eighteen, in time to participate in the re-introduction of allied troops into Western Europe. Time took care of my internal dilemma. Best to grow up and become a man.

I freely shared these ideas with anyone who would listen, but most of my friends didn't think about such things and when forced to didn't much like it. So I felt set apart once more, left alone to debate imponderables in Hamlet-like indecision.

Between the ages of nine and eleven I developed a keen interest in ancient, medieval and Renaissance history, another preoccupation I found it difficult to share with boys and girls my own age. The Roman Empire and its conquests fascinated me. Hannibal's excursion from Carthage, with elephants yet, across the Mediterranean Sea and the Alps during the Punic wars held me spellbound, as did the Peloponnesian War and the tragic conquest of the glorious Athenian Empire by the savage Spartans.

Equally interesting was the rise of the Catholic Church and its effort to keep burning the lamps of learning during the Dark Ages; the rise of the nation state and the conflicts of sovereignty between the monarchs of church and state. I could picture vividly a western potentate crawling on his hands and knees to pay homage to the Holy See in Rome but could not fathom why, with all the power at his command, he would do such a thing.

This interest led me to haunt the stacks of Perkins Library at Duke University during occasional weekends I spent with Aunt May. A nice old gentleman befriended me, once retrieving a volume with illuminated pictures, brilliantly illustrating the narratives, and generally serving as my mentor. Dr. Reid was a white-haired old man who sported a neatly trimmed Van Dyke beard, spoke with a hint of English accent, and always dressed in coat and tie. To me he was ageless.

"Young man," he asked me one day, "Is that young lady who sometimes comes in here related to you?"

"Yes sir," I replied respectfully, "She's my sister."

"Is she a student here?"

"Yes, she's a junior, transferred this year from Meredith."

"Well, she is certainly a pretty girl and if she's your sister, she must be smart as well," the man with the professorial air added. "What her name?"

Following this detailed inquiry, Dr. Reid had all he needed—name, address and telephone number. I didn't see him much after that, but several months later I overheard Mary C. complaining to Aunt May.

"That Dr. Reid is bugging me to death. Every time I go over to West Campus, there he is. He's even called me at Brown House. He said Mac gave him my name and number." Mary C. seemed both irked and pleased by the attention.

A little later she was somewhat less so. Both visiting Broadacre for the weekend, Mary C. told Aunt May and Mother that Dr. Reid, who couldn't maneuver Mary C. into a date, had outmaneuvered her one afternoon in the stacks and bestowed a French kiss upon her.

"Good grief!" Mary C. exclaimed. "What's the matter with the man? He's old enough to be my father." Grandfather, I thought to myself.

Aunt May, who believed any professor was beyond reproach and probably lived in monk-like chastity among the ivory towers of academia, was properly shocked. Mother, less so, was titillated. Mary C., interested in students nearer her own age over at Chapel Hill, Wake Forest, and Davidson, not to mention Duke, was more annoyed and disgusted.

I felt somewhat disloyal. I knew I should have been disapproving— and at some level I suppose I was, but Dr. Reid had always been nice and helpful to me. I did wonder though, "Why on earth would he want to kiss Mary C. anyhow? What did he see in her? Why didn't he act his age?"

And what was that? I never found out whether Dr. Reid was a member of the faculty, a visitor, or retired. He could have been forty or seventy; it was all the same to me. And it certainly seemed that at either age he was over the hill as far as having any interest in a girl of twenty. That was at age eleven. Now I understand that at any age, it is "L'amour, l'amour, toujours l'amour."

Despite Aunt May's legal sophistication, she remained emotionally inhibited and could be incredibly naïve, especially when sexuality was involved. Given the frequency and comfortable duration of her visits to Broadacre after she moved to Durham, and her exposure to all of our animals, her ignorance of barnyard behavior defies reason.

The evening after Mary Cov had complained about Dr. Reid's harassment, Aunt May strolled into the back yard and on out to the hen house to gather a few eggs. Soon I heard a scream and then a frantic call. "Mr. Secrest, come quickly! A rooster is abusing one of your hens!" Daddy, Mary Cov, Lil and I came on the run to find the rooster perched precariously on the hen's back and balancing himself by holding her head in his beak. There was a fluttering of wings and some ruffled feathers, but the hen didn't seem perturbed. She occasionally pecked at some kernels of corn on the ground nearby as the rooster hung on.

"Shoo! Go 'way!" Aunt May, careful to keep her distance, shouted at the chicken. "Leave her alone! Mean old thing! Mr. Secrest, you've got to make him stop hurting her." Using his foot, Daddy pushed the aroused rooster off the hen, then took Aunt May by the arm. "Come on, Miss Mary, let's go on back to the house. The hen will be all right." He didn't try to explain. Neither did anyone else.

Some months earlier Aunt May had sounded a similar alarm when a stray bitch in heat wandered into the front yard. One of our hounds picked up the scent and made contact just as Aunt May arrived on the scene. "Mac, Lil, come here at once! One of Mr. Secrest's hunting hounds is in trouble. Look at the way he's caught up with that other dog. They've gotten stuck together somehow and can't break apart. Call Heath!" Lil and I tried to explain the mating habits of dogs, but she wouldn't really listen. When it came to such matters Aunt May, a brilliant woman, was a slow learner.

By 1932 my fascination with France and my indignation with England for always defeating the French, "losing every battle but the last one," had been replaced by admiration for anything Italian. The Glory that was Rome was surpassed only by the Italian Renaissance and all of its artistic and cultural splendor. The city states of Florence, with its Medicis and Macchiavelli, not to mention Michelangelo; Rome with its papal princes and Borgias; Venice with its Doges and Marco Polo—what romance and adventure to excite the youthful imagination.

How I longed for a restoration of the Roman Empire! The story of the Kingdom of the two Sicilies, the alliance of Lombardy with Sardinia, later joined by Tuscany and other provinces, was inspiring. And then Garibaldi and his March on Rome, and the unification of Italy in 1871.

The decision of Italy to join the Allies in 1915, the brave and costly fight the Italians put up against the forces of the Austro-Hungarian Empire, inspired me further as I re-read history and Ernest Hemingway's novel, "A Farewell to Arms," soon to be made into a movie shown at Miss Rowena Shute's Pastime Theater.

By age ten I was an ardent fascist and admirer of Benito Mussolini—a "fascist with a human face." I knew nothing of the darker side of events unfolding in Italy. I only knew that Mussolini, who "made the trains run on time" also was seeking to restore Italy's "rightful place in the sun" among the major states of the world. At the same time that I loved Mussolini, I hated Adolf Hitler and his Nazi movement, instinctively associating it with German militarism and authoritarianism which the Allies, including the U.S.A., had defeated in 1918.

When I wasn't preoccupied with our animals and pigeons at Broadacre, busy with homework from school, or monopolized by one family crisis or another, I spent my time reading military history, especially that of the Great War. Despite our good neighbors across the street, all of whom I liked tremendously but who were half German, I was very anti-German.

Jack Hernig had immigrated to the U.S. before the War, moved to Monroe as a young man and married a Miss Starnes from Van Wyke near Union County. They produced three children: Elsa, Margaret and Jackie, who corresponded in age to the three Secrest children. We were close friends, in and out of each other's homes constantly. I never associated the Hernigs with anything Teutonic; neither did anyone else in Monroe. Mr. Hernig established Monroe's bakery, soon a municipal fixture. I don't remember much about the man himself, as he died early.

The Great War, however, was still very much in the minds of people in the early 1930s. In school assembly every November 11th we observed a moment's silence in memory of the cease-fire on the Western Front at the eleventh minute past the eleventh hour on the eleventh day of the eleventh month of the year. My first-grade teacher had gone to France to serve with the Salvation Army, as had my subsequent eleventh-grade English teacher. Student heads were filled with stories of battles on Flanders Fields. I memorized the works of American and English poets, many of whom were casualties of that war. Among Miss Lura Heath and Miss Annie Lee who represented the Great War of 1914-18, and Mrs. Vernon Austin, my third-grade teacher whose grandfather had fought in the U.S. Civil War, I had no inclination "to study war no more."

In Monroe I had the perfect companion to encourage my interest in Italy. He was an Italian immigrant—the only one in town—named Pedro. I don't know how Pedro wound up in Monroe. Uncle Vann had met him in 1918 when Vann was stationed at a New Jersey army base; perhaps that was how Pedro came to North Carolina.

Pedro operated a fruit stand and played an organ grinder, featuring water boat music and street songs the world associates with popular Italian music, while a real live monkey played around on his back. His fruit stand was the only place one could buy Italian plums, apricots, grapes, olives and special bread, pastries and olive oil. I would spend many a late afternoon and early evening talking with Pedro about Italian life, customs and history, but most particularly, about Mussolini and fascism.

In the summer of 1934 when Hitler was making threatening moves toward Austria after Austrian Nazis had assassinated Chancellor Engelbert Dollfus to set the stage for an early anschluss, my heart was thrilled when Mussolini dispatched Italian troops to the Brenner Pass to prevent a German takeover.

The following year I was equally disgusted with France, Britain and the League of Nations for voting sanctions against Italy in a collective if futile effort to stop her conquest of Ethiopia. Despite my friendship with Doll Jr. and my affection for the many black people in my life, my enthusiasm for Italian imperialism was undiluted. That fall in seventh grade, I debated the Italian position against my friend Bob Houston, extolling the power of Italian tanks and bombers against the fierce resistance of the lions and elephants that Bob's youthful imagination envisioned as coming to the aid of Haile Selassi—the Lion of Judea—and his native army, still largely dependent upon spears and primitive weapons.

Thankfully my Fascist period didn't last long. My main satisfaction from Pedro derived from those big plums, which I preferred slightly green and sour and consumed by the dozen until I got sick and threw up. To Mother's chagrin, I proved a slow learner and continued to abuse my stomach and get sick, reminiscent of earlier beach weekends with the tenant farmers.

Sometime in 1936, Pedro left Monroe. But among Pedro, the CCC Puerto Ricans and all my black companions, I was exposed to a good deal of ethnic, racial, and cultural diversity in rural North Carolina, despite the boast by the Chamber of Commerce that the state's people were ninety-eight percent of Anglo-Saxon stock.

By early 1936, I had abandoned Fascism, re-embraced the French heroes of the first and second battles of the Marne in the Great War, and the English, who had successfully sealed up the German battle fleet at Jutland and had suffered such enormous casualties in the battles along the Somme and Paschendale. I agreed with President Woodrow Wilson's 1916 assessment: the U.S. could never allow the triumph of Prussian militarism and German authoritarianism over Western European democratic institutions. That concern was the real reason the U.S. entered World War I, not the usual explanation about the freedom of the seas and German U-Boat attacks on American shipping.

By the time I was twelve, however, family pressures once again dominated my life. History temporarily took a back seat, although in my mid-teens I evolved further politically, into and out of a fascination for the Communist experiment in the Soviet Union and confronting the confusing and conflicting ideologies of the Spanish Civil War. Above all there was a mounting realization of Nazi tyranny in Germany and Hitler's growing threats abroad.

# 11. Wrecks on the Highway

One recurring cause of family conflict, which continues to this day in many American homes, was motor cars. When Mary C. reached the legal driving age of 16 in December 1931, the pressure was strong to let her have a car. This scene was repeated as Lil in 1936 and I in 1939 also hit sweet sixteen. Daddy's answer was always no, and we would cajole, nag and complain to Mother, who sided with her husband.

"I wish you children would try to understand your father better. He runs a motor company. He sees the results of young people driving too fast and without sufficient experience. Every Saturday night it seems some young people—their whole lives ahead of them—are killed in auto accidents or suffer horrible injuries that ruin their lives." It was because Daddy understood such dangers better than we possibly could and because he loved us that his answer was always no, she insisted.

When we countered that Daddy just liked to say no, Mother reminded us of what had happened to cousin Miriam, who was Mary Cov's age. Midge, as she was called, was the only daughter of Clarence Houston, Mother's first cousin, and his wife Miriam, who was a close friend of Mother's and my second-grade teacher.

Petite, pretty, flirtatious and fourteen, Midge was popular with boys and rebellious over the restrictive, protective discipline of her elderly parents. So out she skipped one dark rainy night in the early spring of 1930 to go joy-riding in an old jalopy that Dowd had recently sold to a friend with two sons.

With three teenagers squeezed into the front seat, two into the back, and two more into the rumble seat, the driver scratched off and headed down Franklin Street. Two miles out of town, near the old county poor house next to Major Heath's, they approached the unmarked railroad crossing.

The teenagers were oblivious to the whistle and bright lights of the approaching freight train. Then, as the old car approached the tracks, the engine stalled. The sound of rent metal, the smell of gasoline, a muffled explosion reached Miss Lura Heath and her younger sister, who rushed out to find the crushed automobile and seven bodies flung around the bloody scene like rag dolls.

Midge was the only survivor. She lay in a coma for weeks in a Charlotte hospital. Ultimately she did recover from her multiple bone fractures and burns, but her personality had changed. No longer high spirited or interested in boys, she became subdued and dependent upon her mother. Mercifully she had no memory of the accident.

Midge went to secretarial school, later became a librarian, commuting to Charlotte, and regained her independence. To me she was always pretty, with occasional flashes of the witty, high-spirited girl she once had been. But for the rest of her days, she slept in the bed with her mother. When Miriam became old, frail and finally terminally ill, Midge took the same good care of her in their rotting, decaying house of onetime splendor on Church Street as her mother had of Midge forty years earlier.

Trouble seldom travels alone. Three years before that awful accident, which Mary C. barely missed as Midge had secretly importuned her to run off too, tragedy had already struck the Houston family. Coming home early from school one afternoon, before his mother got home, Midge's brother had stumbled upon the body of his father in the dining room—dead from a self-inflicted shotgun blast to his head, blood scattered over the faded blue carpet.

Midge's three older brothers were all bright. Edrow studied law at Columbia University and was editor of the Law Review. Despite a promising legal career in New York City, he wound up years later a victim of drink and drugs, as a night clerk at a rundown Charlotte hotel—unmarried and alienated from all those he had once known and loved. Clarence Jr., who had discovered the body of his father in 1927, also died at his own hand. Stamps lived up to his promise, a resounding success in business and finance in New York City and a family man who always found time for his mother and sister Midge in Monroe.

As for the six young boys and girls who died in that accident, hardly a family in Monroe escaped its imprint, as the town's close-knit families were all in some way interrelated. With such grim reminders, Mother quelled our protests over Daddy's meanness about his cars.

Mary C. did receive a car at age 20 upon graduation from college, with disastrous results. Mother and Daddy were also prevailed upon to allow me at age 16 in 1940 to drive Lil to Wilson, North Carolina, and back, hundreds of miles, with almost no experience under my belt. As I look back upon it, it's a miracle we made it. In those days even federal highways were only two-lane roads, many poorly engineered. Seatbelts and airbags were decades in the future.

God must indeed "look after fools and children," but don't count on it. A short time after the tragedy involving Midge, Cousin Claude Loflin, Aunt Essie's son from Savannah, came to Monroe with his parents for a visit. One night he and Mary C. slipped off from Broadacre to take an unauthorized spin around Monroe with Paul Hudson and "Bat-eye" Bailey and their girlfriends in one of Daddy's old Chevrolets "borrowed" for the occasion.

"Oh, sure, you can take it," Mary C. told Bat-eye. "Daddy won't care," she added, knowing better. They left by stealth just after dark—all under age and none really knowing how to drive. With Bat-eye behind the wheel, they veered uncertainly around the courthouse square, then swerved south down Main Street, back west to Windsor Street and across to the old Charlotte highway. Bat-eye turned right up the Franklin Street hill, stalling just as he passed the Monroe Hotel on his left. Try as he might, he couldn't coordinate the clutch and pedal as the car kept sliding down the hill, while motorists dodged past him right and left.

Finally he put the pedal to the metal and the car jumped ahead and ran the traffic light, as the frantic teenager tried to regain control. He took a sharp right back to Main Street at high speed on two wheels, overcompensated, and hurtled headlong through the plate glass window of the J.C. Penney store, coming to rest on the broad display counter.

Police cars appeared. Parents were called and family conferences held. Uncle Charlie Hamilton, a county judge, condemned Claude's and Mary C.'s "dastardly deed." Mother and Aunt Essie condemned Uncle Charlie—the in-law—as overly judgmental, with children who "were far from perfect themselves." Daddy was initially tight-lipped but, swayed by Mother, declined to press charges against Bat-eye.

Mary C. was tearfully defiant, her only injury a minor cut on the mouth, until she learned of her parents' unexpected indulgence. Aunt Essie and Uncle Claude didn't have much to say. The next day the teenagers, feeling immortal, were heard laughing and joking about it all. Lil and I thought Uncle Charlie was mean, taking a cue from Mother and Daddy. Aunt Bertha, always kind, expressed only concern for the welfare of all the youngsters, relieved no one was really hurt and sure they had all "learned their lesson" from an experience that may have been "a blessing in disguise."

Daddy, after consultation with Uncle Vann, paid for store damages, and arrangements were made with the police so that no charges were brought and the whole matter was dropped.

Mary C. kept up with Cousin Claude. Years later, when she was a student at Case Western Reserve in Cleveland, Ohio, she introduced her roommate from Shaker Heights, Mary Lou, to Claude, now a young Georgia Tech engineer working nearby. An avid matchmaker, Mary C. was delighted when, for once, her efforts bore fruit. Mary Lou and Claude married, had several children, and, as far as I know, lived happily ever after. Well, as long as "ever after" lasted; Claude succumbed to cancer at an early age. His sister Lucy remained unmarried until her mid-fifties, when she married an older man named Winkle; they enjoyed a happy union for several years.

Mary C. and Lucy were near in age but not close; the same was true of another first cousin, Ruth McCaughan, who lived in Salisbury. Ruth's mother Aunt Lydia, Daddy's sister, was a difficult woman by anyone's standards. Aunt Lid and Ruth fought all the time, and Lid of course didn't approve of Ruth's choice of a husband, whom she may have married as much to spite her mother as out of love for Bryan Carter.

When Aunt Lid uncharacteristically decided to do something generous and loving for her niece Martha Hamilton, Ruth deeply resented it. In 1941 Martha had finally succumbed to Wriston Helms' blandishments and agreed to marry him. Her mother had died in 1938, so where were they to be married? Aunt Lid decided she would have the wedding in her home and bear all the expense for the sake of her older sister Bertha.

"Why are you doing this?" Ruth demanded of her mother. "You didn't do a thing for me when I wanted to marry Bryan; in fact, you literally drove us away—we had to elope."

Her mother denied the charge, adding that Ruth had always been "a jealous, unloving child," entirely different from her appreciative, sweet cousin Martha. Ruth sulked and pouted and made pointed remarks to

Martha and Wriston and tried to make the nuptials uncomfortable for everyone. But in this she failed, for Martha, inheriting her mother's equitable disposition, remained in happy repose throughout. But Lid and Ruth were cut from the same cloth and, while loving each other and mutually dependent, never got along.

Aunt Lid may have been a bit too much even for her husband, H. D. McCaughan. She had grown fat and dowdy as her disposition became thornier. Of course, "Uncle Mack" wasn't any prize himself: tall, gaunt, skinny, with a hawk's beak, sallow complexion and enormous flat feet. Upon arrival for Martha's wedding, Lil reached way up to give him a dutiful hug around the neck, and his response was to grab hold of her backside, give it a squeeze and run his tongue down her throat. "Yuck!" Lil said later. "What a thing to do. I spent the rest of the weekend avoiding him."

While no one else seemed to like Ruth or to be able to get along with her, Lucy did. Later in life as widows living alone, one in Wilmington, the other Asheville, they would call each other every night, taking turns, to be sure everything was all right. And it was, until one evening Lucy learned that Ruth had just been taken to Mission Memorial Hospital for third degree burns and smoke inhalation. A cigarette had ignited her filmy negligee, enveloping Ruth in flames. She died the next morning.

# 12. Besa Mi Culo

Despite all of the melodramatics at Broadacre, our household was probably not so different from those of our friends. Our lives were punctuated with happy times, tolerance and good humor. Cruelty and kindness, wisdom and folly, tolerance and bigotry, education and ignorance were often the strange fruit consumed in Monroe. So was a solemn and fundamental religion, often mixed with a sense of fun, mischief, and earthy, irreverent humor.

The Saleeby family provides a good example. Helen, Lil's closest friend, was asked one day in school by Miss Anna Bernard Benson, her English teacher, to tell the class a joke as part of her lesson in humor in literature. Helen told the tale of the tongue-tied preacher, who had hit the sawdust trail to a Union County camp meeting, prepared to deliver a hell-fire and damnation sermon. Urging his audience to repent of their sins and to come forward to confess, he shouted in his rousing finale:

> "So, come, all ye shaints and shinners,
> Shitting on the back sheat,
> Come, shit on the front sheat and be shaved!
> Now, shine like that shitty—
> Shittin' on a hill!"

Miss Benson, a dark-haired, brown-eyed woman in her late thirties, projected a dignified, refined image to her students. Assured and self-possessed, nothing much flustered her. But Helen apparently had. "Why, Helen," she asked, more in bewilderment than in anger, "Where on earth did you learn that?" The other students, first sitting in stunned silence, had begun to laugh. "I know you didn't hear that in the Saleeby household, did you?"

Helen, puzzled by the commotion but aware now that something hadn't gone according to plan, replied, "No, ma'am, but I know the joke is all right because I heard Mrs. Lessie Secrest tell it to her bridge club."

Well, yes, Mother had, having heard Daddy tell it to Locke Everette. And later I learned Miss Benson wasn't all that shocked either, as Locke, perennial bachelor, whom Lessie and Dowd were always trying to fix up with Miss Annie Lee, perennial spinster and senior English teacher, had already shared the joke with his friend. And later in the teacher's lounge, Miss Lee had told it to Miss Benson.

Miss Lee, despite her air of intellectual elegance, wasn't so inexperienced as she seemed either, having served in France in 1918 with the Salvation Army near the western front, along with her closest friend, Miss Lura Heath, my first grade school teacher, who several years earlier had explained to Miss Lessie why Little Lord Fauntleroy pants didn't constitute proper schoolboy attire in Monroe.

Some years after Helen had inadvertently surprised her English teacher with dirty jokes, I unintentionally insulted mine in Spanish. Some of the Spanish Harlem enrollees of the Civilian Conservation Corps encamped near Broadacre had befriended me. I often hung around the camp to talk with these young men, mostly between 18 and 21 years old, who had unusual accents and some tall tales to tell about New York City life.

Bronzed by the South's hot late spring sun and hardened by tough work on area dams and parks, these guys were role models of a kind. They knew a lot of stuff I didn't, and they obviously enjoyed telling this little Southern country boy things about life in the big fabled city that O. Henry once described as "Baghdad on the Hudson." Some seven to twelve years older than I, they were heroic figures, even though I knew somehow that they were different and not socially acceptable in the big houses on Church, Hayne, Washington, Windsor, Houston, and Franklin streets.

One day one of my CCC friends suggested that I help him out with English and he'd teach me a little Spanish. For several weeks I met him and some of his buddies in Monroe's cemetery, between Broadacre and the high school, and we conversed first in English, then in Spanish.

My friend Juan one day asked, "Mac, would you like to make a big impression on your teacher?"

"Sure, I guess so," I replied.

"Do you like her?" he asked.

"Yes I do. She's real nice."

86

"Is she pretty? How old is she?"

Since all teachers were symbols of authority and hence old, I replied, "I don't know, but pretty old. I think she must be thirty."

"Does she like you? Are you the teacher's pet?"

"No!" I almost shouted, for who wants to be considered that? "But," I admitted, "she does kind of favor me. I think we're related somehow."

"Well, when you see her in school Monday, instead of saying, ' Good Morning ' in English, greet her with, "Besa mi culo," and see what she says."

So Monday morning, on arriving for Florence Redwine's sixth grade grammar class, I said, "Besa mi culo," Miss Redwine." Florence paused a moment, then asked me to repeat what I just said.

"Who taught you to say that?" the teacher asked.

"Juan, my friend at the CCC camp," I replied. Miss Redwine, whom the students called Flossie behind her back because of the way her tight curls bounced around her head, looked both grim and thoughtful but said nothing more. But that evening she came by the house and met with Mother behind closed doors. Later I was called in and told that I couldn't go down to the CCC camp anymore; it was off-limits. And I couldn't see Juan anymore. "And by the way," Mother asked anxiously, "Who is Juan?

I didn't learn at home what mistake I'd made or why Juan had become persona non grata, but later in the week an older boy who'd heard about the gaffe told me, to my shock and embarrassment, that I'd just told Flossie Redwine "to kiss my ass." Still later I overheard Daddy tell Uncle Jim Craven about it. They both laughed.

Florence had a personal story of her own to tell, and like that of so many other people, hers was a "song sung blue..." She was one of the younger children of R.B. Redwine, who had been in law practice in the late 1800s with my grandfather. Her mother was a sweet and gentle woman who was like a foster mother to my own mother. And that family was struck twice by tragedy, first when Florence's twin brother developed paranoid schizophrenia—which doctors then called dementia precox

The twins were 20 years old when John first suspected that Florence wanted to poison him. Figuring he'd better get her first, he planned to shoot her one weekend as she returned home from college, but decided later a knife would be better. Somehow he was not sufficiently coherent to keep his plans secret, and the murder was prevented by parental intervention.

Poor John was hauled off to the State Hospital in Morganton, where he spent the rest of his life a living reminder of the hell he had put his family and his adoring sister through.

Not long after that an older sister, a registered nurse, developed lymphoma and died. Her name was Catherine, and she was another female I'd early attached myself to and loved devotedly. My nickname for her— reason unknown—was "Vinegar." I still remember the viewing of the body and just how she looked, which was pretty good after the morticians had laid her out.

The Redwine parents were now elderly, their income reduced, investments ruined; all that was left for Florence was to teach school in her hometown and gradually become everyone's favorite old-maid aunt. Years later Mary C. and I, deep into abnormal psychology, decided that John had had an unnatural affection for his twin, and that this emotion, once frustrated, turned from love to hate. Florence represented to him a temptation that must be rationalized, then rejected. All very Freudian. His illness was probably biological and biochemical. Today it can often be effectively controlled by medication. Freudian theory is irrelevant in the treatment of a psychosis.

Knowledge of such things, even if I didn't dwell on them, would later escape my mental censor at times and leave me again feeling frightened and puzzled. I too had once been overly attached to my sisters and mother. Did that mean I would one day go crazy like John? It was a frightening thought but then, after all, there had been no secretive repression on my part; it had all been openly acknowledged and acted out early on, by age four, so there was no latter day need to deny, project, or rationalize anything. I usually felt comfortable with my family, even with Daddy, especially when Mother wasn't around. But when beset by typical adolescent worries in my mid-teens, memories of Flossie and John would sometimes resurface and haunt my dreams.

With Mary C. out of the house and in college by the time I was eight years old, my attachment and dependency turned more to Lil, who was my chief caregiver and protector now. I thought she was the fount of all wisdom, a belief validated on March 9, 1933.

By then I had begun to develop symptoms of an obsessive-compulsive disorder (OCD). Having watched scenes in newsreels in Miss Rowena Shute's movie theater, I became possessed by the beauty of snow and the thrill of winter sports.

"When do you think it'll snow, Lil?" was always a question on my lips. With the temperatures often in the high 90s in the dog days of late July and early August, I would dash out—to Daddy's growing disgust—to get the Charlotte News to see if Jo Jo, the black cartoon character who foretold the weather, had forecast snow. I did this all summer long, always badgering Lil, "When is it going to snow? How soon?" Even Lil became annoyed. One hot afternoon in September 1932, she snapped, "Next March 9th. Now don't mention snow again or it won't happen then."

I made a bargain with God: make Lil's prediction come true, and I won't mention snow a single time. The seasons hardly showed change: a warm fall, a warm winter. December, January, February passed and all we got was rain. But in the first week of March the weather turned colder, the northern jet stream dropped farther south. Then as soon as the temperatures dropped, the clouds disappeared and a cold blue sky prevailed.

I went to bed on the night of March 8 resigned to my disappointment. But the next morning my window showed a winter wonderland. The ground was covered with snow and the big thick flakes still fell heavily. No school that day. "Lil! Lil!" I shouted. "Look out the window. It's snowing! It's snowing!" Lil looked and then walked away, dryly remarking, "I told you so." After that I believed that everything Lil said had to be so.

# 13. Political Icons and Family Feminism

Later that month President-elect Franklin Delano Roosevelt took the oath of office and the next hundred days that shook the country if not the world whirled by, incorporating into law most of what became the first New Deal. Equally significant but not yet fully realized, Hitler and his Nazi Party took control that same month in Germany.

Mother forced me to listen on the radio to FDR's inaugural address. I didn't fully appreciate the message, as I was sulking. The network had bumped the early soap opera Myrt and Marge, wildly popular at the time, to broadcast the President's address, a public-service gesture my nine years did not fully appreciate. "We have nothing to fear but fear itself" was, I must admit, lost on me.

Mother and Daddy were enthusiastic New Dealers. I remember during the 1932 campaign seeing FDR drive past us in a crowd in Charlotte. Daddy later proudly displayed the NRA Eagle in the window of his various enterprises. Both my parents believed that the New Deal bank holiday and the subsequent insurance on bank deposits had saved our family and the country.

No one who didn't live through it can understand the panic that gripped the country in 1930 and deepened dangerously with every passing month, or describe the paralysis that held President Herbert Hoover and his administration in such a grip. Of course Hoover wasn't responsible for the stock market crash in 1929, having been in office only a few months when it occurred. Not many people believe anymore that there was a close connection between Black Tuesday, October 1929, on Wall Street and the world-wide Depression that followed closely on its heels. But in 1933 everybody in our family blamed Hoover and his failure to lead and to lend hope to the land, and that strengthened our conviction as "Yellow Dog Democrats" that salvation lay only with our ancestral party.

Roosevelt became an immediate icon, and his stature grew in my family's eyes with each passing month. I identified with this new president as another person set apart—and look what he achieved. A mama's boy, he was bathed and dominated by that strong-willed Delano woman until he was a teenager. An only child, Franklin's elderly father was a figure with whom he never identified. He was spoiled, indulged, with few pals his own age.

Scion of an established Hudson River family with Dutch and English antecedents, Roosevelt was a descendant of men who had been Hyde Park squires for generations. Earlier Roosevelts had looked down their patrician noses at such nouveau riche neighbors as the Vanderbilts. FDR, I learned later, was also set apart in other ways. He was a Democrat in a Republican era and area. And, no matter what popular opinion may claim 75 years later, it was a nationally known fact that the polio that struck him as a young man left him paralyzed from the waist down. How could we not know that the founder of the polio clinic at Warm Springs, Georgia, and also of the March of Dimes, was a polio victim himself? Indeed, why do you suppose that you see the face of FDR on the ten cent coin of the realm?

Of course voters knew in 1932, 1936, 1940 and 1944 that Roosevelt, the only president many people could even remember when he died in 1945, was a cripple—and they loved and admired him the more for it. The fact that he didn't speak about his disability and preferred not to be photographed propped up by the Secret Service or being pushed around in a wheelchair in no way meant that people didn't know.

And, finally, Roosevelt was set apart from his natural friends and his social set by his pragmatic political views. He was "that man in the White House" and "that traitor to his class." He thundered against the "malefactors of great wealth." He relished their hostility and was a self-proclaimed "tough-guy" who "loved a good fight" against the self-appointed "in-crowd" on behalf of "the little man."

Yes, from an early age I identified with FDR, far more than I did with Eleanor, another person set apart, but for a welcome change, a woman with whom I didn't identify and who was not a congenial role model. Yet Eleanor, only child of an alcoholic father and orphaned early, had much to overcome herself. Painfully shy, reserved, unhappy as a girl, she overcame her feelings of inadequacy to emerge from an ugly duckling into a glorious political swan and a national role model. Eleanor's political ancestry, however, was more impressive than her husband's. Franklin was President Theodore Roosevelt's fifth cousin, whereas Eleanor was Teddy's niece.

Today I understand that Roosevelt made mistakes. One of his least perceptive remarks came early, perhaps during the first campaign in 1932 in a speech delivered in San Francisco. "America's industrial establishment has been built," he proclaimed. The task now was not further growth and development but more government control and regulation; less free enterprise and venture capital and wider distribution of wealth. The nation needed in 1932, in the desperate plight of the Great Depression, first relief, next economic recovery and finally, reform. In the second New Deal came structural changes, including Social Security and labor laws to protect working men, women and children, including minimum-wage and hour laws and strengthening the right of collective bargaining.

In retrospect a friendlier business climate, accompanied by even stronger Keynesian economic policies—that is, more massive deficit spending—may have spurred economic recovery more quickly. As it turned out, the U.S. had to endure prolonged economic dislocation, the recession of 1938 and the defeat of Roosevelt's Court-packing scheme before world conflict intervened to bring about permanent change. By 1940 as the third term election loomed, Roosevelt had abandoned his keen partisanship and considered his earlier political and social programs completed. In his own words somewhat later, "Dr. New Deal (has been) replaced by Dr. Win-the-War."

A more perceptive Roosevelt voiced an early warning against American isolationism when he told his radio audience in 1937 that "this generation has a rendezvous with destiny." What did that mean? many people, including historians, have asked. Given the date—before Hitler's move into Austria, before Munich, before "Kristallnacht," before the occupation of all the rest of Czechoslovakia, what was the president talking about? It seemed pretty obvious to me, a boy of fourteen at the time. Roosevelt clearly saw war clouds on the horizon and sought to alert his countrymen.

There was no Midwestern and New England isolationism around Broadacre. Daddy knew, Mother knew, and I knew. Within three years of FDR's rendezvous speech, Hitler had conquered Western Europe, leaving only Great Britain and the Commonwealth and Empire to fend off an invasion and to defend the world cause.

No matter what anyone else thought, the family at Broadacre refused to believe that Nazism was "the wave of the future," in Anne Lindbergh's unfortunate phrase. With the fate of freedom (and national security) at stake, the struggle between isolationism and intervention had begun, and the South, including North Carolina, so often opposed to the New Deal despite always voting Democratic, was behind Franklin D. Roosevelt, not only political chief but also now the nation's Commander-in-Chief. And the residents at Broadacre —including the extended Foote-Simmons; Gathings-Covington; Price-Secrest families—continued to be dedicated Democrats and Franklin Roosevelt partisans.

That loyalty was well placed. For it is generally accepted today by Democrats and Republicans alike, liberals and conservatives, right and left wings, that FDR and his various programs and administrations—based more on pragmatism than ideology—did a great deal to strengthen the American free enterprise system, our republican form of government, and our democratic society—all of which he was charged by his opponents during his lifetime with trying to destroy.

His sure hand that helped guide the nation away from isolationism and into the international fight against Fascism and Nazism helped save the world from that totalitarian threat and indeed set the stage for American pre-eminence in the twentieth century. No less than our first President George Washington, this set apart squire from Hyde Park would rank as "first in peace, first in war and first in the hearts of his countrymen." I've always been proud to be his partisan and grateful to my family for influencing me in that direction while I was still of an impressionable age.

Another politician turned world statesman was also a boy set apart. And he too was a man whom I admired from my early teenage years. Winston Churchill was a lonely youth. Like his latter-day friend, FDR, Churchill—half American himself—was a high-born child of privilege. But unlike Roosevelt, he wasn't a mama's boy. Indeed he was rejected and maligned by his father and neglected by his mother, loved only by his nanny. At Harrow, he was neither a good nor a popular student. He lived in his imagination and played largely alone.

And look what he achieved. Without the leadership provided by Churchill and Roosevelt, the second half of the twentieth century and the first part of the twenty-first would not have become a time of triumph for the ideals of freedom we've come to take for granted. As if it had to have turned out that way.

Aunt May, like her sisters, as well as all the women of an earlier generation on the Simmons side, was a Yellow Dawg Democrat and a feminist. Her ideal was Eleanor Roosevelt, with whom she could identify as a former "ugly duckling." She was determined to make her own way in a man's profession (and also her father's) without the help of any husband.

Aunt May, twenty-eight years old, left her job as a primary-school teacher in Monroe in 1914 to earn a law degree at George Washington University. She worked in the Department of Justice at night to finance her education and lived in Washington with her Aunt Willie Simmons Webb and her husband Congressman E.Y. Webb, and their three children Betty, William and Edwin. She graduated first in her class.

Being a woman, she was not eligible to be named editor of the Law Review. To protest this injustice, her fellow all-male students collected money to buy her a diamond brooch to signify her achievement. The gesture was approved by the School of Law and the pin awarded to her at graduation in 1917.

The law school boys' action on behalf of their female classmate is reminiscent of what the graduating class at Wake Forest College had done for May's Aunt Evabelle Simmons a generation earlier. Great-grandfather William Gaston Simmons was a professor at Wake Forest for nearly forty years, and his father had served on the Board that established the college in 1834. Simmons was acting president of the school during the Civil War and was said to be the only member of the faculty who was qualified to teach every subject in the curriculum. A practicing attorney and once mayor of the village, Great Grandfather Gaston's real passion lay with the physical sciences, especially physics and chemistry. It was a talent he passed on to some subsequent members of the Simmons clan, particularly Betty Webb's brother.

Edwin Webb, an inventor and owner of numerous patents, once wrote a letter to Albert Einstein, pointing out what he perceived to be an error in the theory of relativity. Edwin claimed a letter from Professor Einstein, dismissing Edwin's argument but adding that it was a pleasure to receive communication from a layman who could at least comprehend the implications of the theory. Edwin, married three times, was an habitual problem for his sister Betty and brother William. A heavy drinker, he suffered from recurrent depressions, neglected his family, was often involved in lawsuits with corporations contesting his patent applications, and retreated to Betty's house for help.

Great Grandpa Gaston's daughter Evabelle Simmons was the only female member of her graduation class at Wake Forest in the 1890s. She too finished with highest academic honors. The admissions policy excluded women, but an exception was made for Evabelle because of her father's association with the school. She would not be permitted, however, to graduate with the class or receive any public recognition. The male students struck in protest, refusing on graduation day to walk across the stage to accept their diplomas if Evabelle, who had bested them all, could not publicly receive hers. College administrators bowed, and Great Aunt Evabelle became the first woman graduate of Wake Forest College. Her portrait, the last time I checked, still hung in the university library alongside that of her father.

After graduation from George Washington University, Aunt May moved back to Monroe to open her law practice with W.B. Love. The family scrapbook contains a picture of her in the mid-1920s in the Union County courtroom, holding a gun as her black defendant, charged with murder, looks on. The story, from the Monroe Journal, details how Miss Covington won acquittal for her client, at first presumed guilty, by demonstrating that the trajectory of the bullet made it impossible for him to have fired the weapon.

Aunt May, then thirty-two, continued a successful, if spotty, practice of law until 1929. That year she received an invitation from William Preston Few, first president of Duke University, and Law School Dean Horrack, to join the faculty and develop a library for the new law school. Part of their search involved asking other schools to suggest candidates, and from George Washington University they received this reply: "You cannot possibly find a better qualified person than Miss Mary Covington in your own state, in Monroe, North Carolina." Aunt May served as head librarian at the Duke Law School until her retirement in 1948.

The year 1929 was also the year of the Gastonia textile strike that many people believed was communist-inspired and that resulted in at least one death and many arrests. Aunt May's uncle Edwin Yates Webb, now living in Shelby, N.C., presided over one of the several trials in Gastonia associated with the strike, while his daughter Betty actively supported the strikers.

When many of the strikers and their sympathizers were charged with inciting to riot, disorderly conduct and refusal to obey court orders, Judge Webb dealt out evenhanded justice.

"Next," the court bailiff called out, and up stepped Betty.

"What's the charge?" inquired Judge Webb.

"Disorderly conduct, among other things," replied his defiant daughter.

"Do you have an attorney?"

"No, your honor."

"Do you want one?"

"No, your honor."

"How do you plead?" a stern and somewhat despairing voice inquired.

"Guilty, and proud of it, your honor," came the insolent reply.

"Ten days," came back the decisive verdict and sharp sound from the gavel, followed by "Next." Whether Judge Webb actually sat in judgment of his daughter and whether she went to jail I cannot say for certain, but it's a family story I've heard all my life.

The strike and subsequent trials received international attention. Appeals found their way up to and beyond the Fourth Circuit Court of Appeals in Richmond, where John J. Parker of Monroe presided as chief judge. It may be that rulings there later adversely affected President Hoover's nomination of Parker, a close friend of Aunt May's, to the U.S. Supreme Court.

Judge Webb was part of North Carolina's political establishment. His sister Faye was the wife of O. Max Gardner of Shelby, a textile magnate soon to become governor and in 1948 appointed by President Truman Ambassador to the Court of St. James. Mr. and Mrs. Gardner, head of the "Shelby political gang," were Betty's aunt and uncle. Betty herself had grown up in Washington, D.C. when her father served in Congress.

So well-connected Betty was soon out of jail if indeed she was actually sent there. A graduate of Vassar, she later earned her Ph.D. from Johns Hopkins University and worked as a researcher on political and social issues at the Brookings Institute. She married a man from Oregon without changing her name. A product of the Roaring Twenties, Betty would say at cocktail parties, "No, no, I'm Betty Webb. He's Roy Veatch. We just live together."

Another female family member I greatly admired, she was also definitely set apart. Betty was an alpha woman. She bossed and dominated her husband, who waited on her hand and foot and treated her like a queen. "No children," Betty decreed, but she was still a maternal soul who mothered her younger brothers, nephews and young cousins like me.

Betty and Roy lived in a renovated antebellum mansion in the heart of Georgetown that had served as a hospital during the Civil War; here Betty, between research assignments, and Roy, an early New Deal braintruster, presided over a lively political and social salon. Thirty plus years later when Ann and I were living for a couple of years in McLean, Virginia, and for some years thereafter, Betty and Roy were the souls of kindness and consideration in a period of testing for us. They made their home in Georgetown and their place in Upperville, Virginia, our home whenever needed.

Another first cousin of the Monroe Covington sisters was Ada Briggs, whose husband, a native of McLean, Virginia, owned farmland that came to comprise much of today's downtown McLean. In the late 19th and early 20th centuries, McLean was just a country hamlet, a far cry indeed from the northern Virginia city that is an upscale bedroom community for Washington today.

During the Wilson Administration, when women were demonstrating for the right to vote, Ada was among those protesting. One summer, when Mother, Aunt May, and their first cousin Nan Trantham Poe were visiting Ada, she urged them to join a demonstration in the nation's capital.

"You must come," Ada urged. "This is history in the making. You owe it to our sisters, those who struggled so valiantly in the past and our leaders today. Come on, women, let's go!" The women went.

They soon met helmeted policemen armed with night sticks and, like Betty fifteen years later, were in jail. But not many years passed before the Nineteenth Amendment was approved in 1920, giving women the right to vote.

# 14. Political Faces and Bragging Rights

The political stalemate that followed the 1930 midterm elections did not help the nation's economic recovery. Democrats, hungry for power, and Republicans, eager to retain it, blocked President Hoover's plans and leadership, however feeble and uninspiring. His administration did provide the Reconstruction Finance Corporation, however, and later Hoover expressed regret that his program had not included the principle: "Forgive all debt." One victim of this 1930 political deadlock hit close to home.

Judge John J. Parker of Monroe was a schoolboy sweetheart of Aunt May. His mother was a penniless aristocrat from Edenton, a direct descendant of the earliest settlers and perhaps of the colonial Lord Proprietors. How she came to meet his father, a Monroe butcher, and to raise his family on run-down Parker Street, I never learned. Both John Parker and his brother Seth were self-made men. Seth was awarded the Congressional Medal of Honor for service in World War I and later rose high in the ranks of corporate America. John excelled in the law. He was Aunt May's special friend, while Seth, several years younger, was Mother's. He was also close to Uncle Vann. May could never bring herself to marry John, but they remained life-long friends.

Parker had expected to be nominated to the governorship by the Democrats in 1920, following the administration of Gov. Walter Bickett, a Monroe native and Mother's first cousin. His sister, Annie Bickett Ashcraft (Cuz Nannie), we considered part of our immediate family, almost like a grandmother.

Parker by 1920 was a prominent lawyer in both Monroe and Charlotte, and was considered a logical choice by Democratic kingmakers as Bickett's successor. I never learned why he was denied the nomination, but his response to political rejection was to switch parties. That hasty act may have cost Judge Parker a seat on the U.S. Supreme Court twelve years later. The political rift between Bickett and Parker did not, however, strain our friendship with Judge Parker, who continued to attend family functions, especially weddings and funerals, over the next two generations.

Parker, now a Republican, had been named by successive administrations in the 1920s (on the strength of his judicial talent) as a federal district judge for western North Carolina and later as a judge on the U.S. Fourth Circuit Court of Appeals. President Hoover in 1931 nominated Parker to the U.S. Supreme Court, having earlier obtained the support of the state's Democratic senior senator, Fernifold Simmons of Harnett County, cousin of Grandmother Mary S. Covington.

Opposition by Democrats and organized labor, however, doomed the nomination. Parker was accused of having an anti-union bias and an anti-labor judicial record, which later less impassioned analysis failed to justify. But 1932 was a presidential election year, the nation was in economic turmoil, the Democrats had gained seats in the mid-term elections, and there was no way any Hoover nomination to the U.S. Supreme Court would gain the Senate's approval.

So Parker's political shift in 1920, when Republicans ruled supreme, was paid for in 1932, a Democratic era. However, he remained Chief Judge of the U.S. Fourth Circuit Court of Appeals with his opinions seldom reversed. Fourteen years later he was named one of the Allied judges in the trials at Nuremberg.

The Simmons-Covington women, whose men had once occupied prominent places at both state and federal levels, held fast to their pride of place. They remembered all past achievements and family connections, however tenuous, and spoke of them often. As one in-law said of them, "These women recommend themselves highly."

As fortunes waned and fissures hitherto unknown appeared in the family foundation, the need grew to glorify and seek refuge in the past. The need intensified as the men in the family died early, leaving only female survivors and no one to carry on the family name. There was, however, substance to their claims: Both Aunt Eve and Aunt May became successful professionals before their time. Aunt Susie, widowed early with four children, rose in the ranks during the Depression, outstripping many men. Mother and Aunt Catherine married men who did well in the business and professional world.

Lessie and all her sisters kept up with relatives who were doing well, out of both affection and self-interest. They passed all this on to me. As a teenager I became family proud, more so even than they; I over-absorbed all the family stories. Mother was no snob. She probably didn't give a passing thought to "family connections" and "who was who" from one year to the next. Neither Mary C. nor Lil cared a rap, but I set out to learn and to know more.

Mother's stories were factually accurate. Judge Parker, a Coolidge appointee, was indeed a U.S. District Judge for western North Carolina; Mother's uncle-in-law Judge E. Yates Webb, married to her Aunt Willie Simmons, had held that same position under Woodrow Wilson. Looking ahead, her nephew James Braxton Craven, Jr would assume the same title by appointment from John F. Kennedy. Family friend Senator Sam Ervin, later of Watergate fame, was an influential Craven backer. Four years later Brack was promoted to the U.S. Fourth Circuit Court of Appeals by Lyndon Johnson and rose to become Chief Judge just like family friend John Parker.

Like Parker, Brack also came close to gaining a seat on the U.S. Supreme Court. In 1968 President Nixon, though he had been one of Aunt May's law school boys at Duke in the mid-'30s, wasn't about to nominate any Democrat to the highest court. Several Senators publicly suggested Brack as a highly qualified candidate of whom they would approve. Nixon instead made three disastrous nominations to the Court's first vacancy in 1970, all of them rejected by the Senate.

When the Democrats regained the White House with the election of Jimmy Carter in 1976, again Brack's star shone brightly. But the following May, before any vacancy occurred, he dropped dead on a tennis court in Richmond at age 59. He was playing with his third wife, Susan (an attorney herself and former law clerk to Watergate Special Prosecutor Leon Jaworsky), then only 29 years old. Brack, lucky in law, was never lucky in love.

There was another political event which involved a connection to the Covington family. In 1922 Luther Hartwell Hodges, a product of Leaksville-Spray, married Martha Houston Blakeney of Monroe, a cousin of the Covington girls and reared closely with them. In 1950 Hodges, a nationally known figure in commerce and industry, retired from the business world and returned home from New York to devote himself to public service. He was elected lieutenant governor in 1952 and two years later succeeded to the North Carolina governorship upon the death of Governor William Umstead. He was easily re-elected in 1956. Four years later President John F. Kennedy named Hodges to his Cabinet as U.S. Secretary of Commerce.

Brack's first professional break came when Hodges named him to the North Carolina Superior Court in 1957. During his twenty-one years as a judge at both state and federal levels, Brack's decisions were seldom overturned. He plowed important new ground in the areas of civil rights and personal privacy.

I learned of one case first hand that attracted national attention. Brack asked me to join him for lunch when he was visiting Washington in 1964, while I was drawing temporary duty with the Department of Commerce. He told me of the case of a man in Charlotte who had been sentenced to life in prison for committing oral sodomy in the privacy of his bedroom The case had been appealed on constitutional grounds—unequal protection of the law, inadequate legal counsel, and cruel and unusual punishment. North Carolina's antiquated law was not often enforced, yet the legal issues were not clearly defined.

Brack and I reminisced about the past. We recalled things said and done by adolescents as we were growing up. We agreed that human sexuality, as researched in the Kinsey Report (1948) and more recently by Masters and Johnson, was more fluid than society and the law acknowledged.

"Brack, the punishment obviously doesn't fit the crime. The law is seldom enforced. Of course you have to throw out the conviction and the law on which it was based," I argued. "Rely on ethical law and tell your clerks to research the matter and come up with some precedents and other legal justification. That's what the U.S. Supreme Court does all the time."

When Brack gave his decision, the man was released. Although the law remained on the books, it was further weakened. The ruling was widely praised in liberal judicial circles, Time devoted an article to it, and television covered it widely. The decision on appeal was not overturned.

Brack's language, considered progressive in 1965, would, however, be politically incorrect today and probably infuriate gay activists. Among other reasons for not confining the homosexual to prison, Brack argued that it would be "like throwing Br'er Rabbit into the briar patch." Why reward him? That sounds today about as insulting and regressive as President Clinton's "don't ask, don't tell" military policy. Forty years ago, it was avant-garde.

Mother could also lay claim—and often did—to a connection with the political leadership that had earlier emerged in Cleveland County known as "The Shelby Gang." This group included E. Yates Webb, who was married to Mother's Aunt Willie Simmons. Betty Webb's Aunt Faye Webb married O. Max Gardner, North Carolina governor from 1932-36 and later named Ambassador to the Court of St. James by President Truman. He never served, however, as he dropped dead from a heart attack the night before his ship set sail in 1948. Gardner's sister married R. Clyde Hoey of Shelby, one of the last of the old circuit riders to be elected governor of the state. He served from 1937-41. Governor Hodges in the 1950s named Hoey U.S. Senator when the incumbent died in office. Hoey had been an admirer of David Covington before the turn of the century and readily acknowledged the family claim on him.

In the mid-1930s Mother's second cousin on the Simmons side, Walter Lambeth, represented the Thomasville district in the U.S. Congress. Another cousin, John Kerr, after whom Kerr Lake near Durham was named, also served in the U.S. House of Representatives. Kerr's mother was a Foote from Warrenton, whose sister had married my great grandfather Gaston Simmons of Wake Forest.

By the time John F. Kennedy was elected in 1960, a new generation of political leaders had appeared in Monroe, some overlapping with older ones. Luther Hodges Jr. (whose first wife Dot Duncan, like his mother Martha, was from Monroe) was among the growing group. Luther Jr. ran for the U.S. Senate in the Democratic primary in 1978. A candidate of "the establishment," he was heavily favored to defeat his closest rival, Insurance Commissioner and populist John Ingram. Hodges was unexpectedly defeated, however, in a tightly contested second primary, having led handily in the first. A low voter turnout and over-confidence by his supporters are cited as causes. The conventional wisdom remains that had Luther won in June, he would probably have defeated Republican incumbent Jesse Helms in the general election, and North Carolina liberals would have been spared twenty-four more years of Jesse as North Carolina's senior senator.

# 15. Song of the Shirt

In 1934, five years after Aunt May had moved to Durham and Cousin Betty had gone to jail, Mary C. decided to transfer to Duke University, a co-ed school. Aunt May adored her niece as the child she'd never had, and the affection was intermittently returned, although sometimes in ambivalent and bizarre ways.

Aunt Eve had once been dean of women at Meredith College, and she and Aunt May thought it would be a grand finale to Mary C's two-year stay there to have a house party for her friends at Broadacre. They could easily persuade Lessie, who loved to put on the dog and identify herself with the younger generation.

Dowd might be a tougher nut to crack. In the depths of the Depression everybody felt dirt poor, whether they were or not. But while Aunt May had always been intimidated by Dowd, Aunt Eve was not. She was small and fragile, in contrast to Aunt May's raw-boned five feet eight; but, as Daddy once favorably observed, she thought like a man. Finding her immovable in one argument, he declared heatedly, "Miss Evabelle, you're the most butt-headed woman I've ever known." To which she replied, "No, Mr. Secrest, I just have a firmness of purpose," something, she added, that if Lessie had, both would be much better off.

So the house party was set. Four young men from UNC, Wake Forest, Davidson and Duke were invited to spend a long weekend with Mary Covington and three of her Meredith College classmates. It was a house party in the English style, of course, leavened by some of Daddy's country ways. It lasted from Friday until Tuesday, and included a fish fry, a hayride, an informal dance, a lot of music furnished by records on an old Victrola, movie attendance, horseback riding, card and parlor games, and on the Sabbath, Sunday school, church, and evening prayer services. There was an abundance of food but no alcoholic beverages. And no sex either. In those innocent days, such an idea, much less enterprise, would never have been thought of. Idealism? Yes. Romance? Yes. But sex? Before marriage? Nice girls would never consent to that, and nice boys wouldn't proposition them or, if they had, would want and expect a firm rejection.

Bill Finlater from Raleigh, whose sister Dot was one of Mary C's classmates at Meredith, was Mary C's beau for the weekend. Bill later was to make quite a name for himself as a liberal-minded Baptist preacher who managed to get his Pullen Memorial Baptist Church in Raleigh kicked out of the Southern Baptist Convention over civil rights. Thirty years after the house party I enlisted Bill's help on the North Carolina Volunteer Racial Committee attached to the Community Relations Service, which I was helping to organize in the Johnson Administration.

In 1934 he was already idealistic and interested in religious, political and philosophical questions. So was Lessie Covington Secrest. She and Bill hit it off from the start, each seeking to top the other with Shakespearean allusions and references to the Bible, to Goethe, and to other literary and religious figures. Daddy didn't think much of Bill. Mary C. didn't think much of Mother. Aunt May and Aunt Eve were enchanted chaperones. Lil and I drank it all in, free to participate as if we were part of the group. Mary C. was always good about that.

Mother observed, triumphantly I thought, that Bill came to Monroe in love with the daughter and left in love with the mother. My sister must have felt the same thing, for after that, her friendship with Dot cooled, as did that with Bill.


The year 1934 was also the second year of the Chicago World's Fair. Its theme was "Century of Progress," somewhat optimistic if not ironic, considering that the nation's economy and productivity had sunk below the level of 1912. But it was a great fair in a great city. Mother, Mary C. and Lil had gone in 1933 with Aunt Katherine and Brack and Aunt Susie, Earl and David. Daddy and I had stayed home.

Now, in the spring of 1934, Lil and I decided that Daddy should have his turn. We set out to earn the money to send him. We hitched Lady up to the buggy and drove all over Union County, mostly to small farm houses, to sell blackstrap molasses. Since the sugarcane was grown and harvested on some land on Parker Street and harvested by Heath and me, and since the molasses itself was homemade at Broadacre, I'm not sure we were really earning money independently. In any event, we poured the dark, rich homogenized black syrup into bottles, put the bottles into cartons, and trotted off.

Union County was large, with 639 square miles and a population of some 50,000, exclusive of Monroe and many unincorporated settlements. We stuck to the rural areas and country roads, some of them hardly more than paths. It was long, hot, dusty work and required some sales pitch, too. We worked from sunup till sundown. Neither Mother nor Daddy had the slightest idea where we'd gone. Anything could have happened to a girl 14 and a boy 10, but nothing untoward ever did. And we made a lot of money. We charged 25 cents a gallon, and by August we had accumulated enough, surely, to send Daddy to Chicago; maybe he would even take me along.

Daddy was pleased by our efforts. He thanked us but said the whole episode reminded him of something I'd done last year: bought four watermelons for the dollar he had given me and then turned around and sold them all for 50 cents. "Lil, you and Mac need to learn something about money," Daddy explained. "Times are hard, and I can't afford to go. And the money you collected was less than what it cost to make the stuff you sold. You didn't make any money, you lost it. Net profit is the bottom line. Income less expenses equals profit. Lil, you're a bright student. Use your head and figure it out."

Daddy gave other reasons for staying home. He had to work. We were poor. Mother wouldn't like it. And, finally, the real reason: he didn't want to go to the World's Fair. Daddy was a homebody who often said he'd never lost anything outside of Union County that he needed to go find. The year before, he'd been required to go to Detroit for a General Motors meeting and that had been more than enough for him.

Because of our father's volatile nature and contradictory personality, he did not command the kind of respect a parent is entitled to. We loved our unpredictable and ambivalent father, but he was often victimized by his children even if he was the initial cause of his predicament.

None of Dowd's children accepted his hard work ethic. I once reminded him of the Biblical passage in which we were told to "regard the lilies of the field; they toil not, neither do they spin." So why should we have to work all the time? Still later, after one of his lectures about the value of money and the need to live by the sweat of one's brow, we taunted him with lines from a poem Mary C. had brought home from Duke in her junior year. Filled with idealism and good intentions and a certain contempt for the fruits of capitalism, which is often learned on college campuses, Mary C. began to quote lines from Thomas Hood's "Song of the Shirt."

*"Stitch! Stitch! Stitch!"*

As Daddy's voice rose to denounce our collective laziness, Lil chimed in,

*"Work! Work! Work!"*

Soon I joined the chorus:

*"With fingers weary and worn*
*With eyelids heavy and red*
*A woman sat in unwomanly rags,*
*Plying her needle and thread."*

Then Mary Cov again:

*"Stitch! Stitch! Stitch!*
*In poverty, hunger and dirt,*
*And with the voice of dolorous pitch*
*She sang the 'Song of the Shirt!'"*

Now Lil:

*"Work-work-work*
*Till the brain begins to swim;*
*Work-work-work*
*Till the eyes are heavy and dim!"*

Finally, altogether:

*"Work! Work! Work!*
*My labor never flags*
*And what are its wages?*
*A bed of straw, a crust of bread*
*—and rags."*

The verse was a lament about the abuse of working women during the Industrial Revolution, especially in the sweat shops of the garment workers' district in metropolitan New York. This sentiment resonated with the feminism of the Covington women that was passed along to the Secrest children. It also appealed to their inclination to side with the underdog and have-nots, and to the notion of Christian charity. Mary Cov was already on her way to social work.

None of us realized the challenges Daddy faced every day to keep our heads above water during the depth of the Depression and the necessity for him to work and work, stitch and stitch from sunup till late at night. Surely no textile laborer worked harder or under greater pressure than he. So we jauntily disregarded his preaching of the Protestant work ethic and continued to taunt, flaunt, tease and badger him with strains from Hood's nineteenth-century poem. And to dodge nimbly out of reach as he occasionally struck out in exasperation.

That "The Song of the Shirt" accurately depicted the plight of working people, including women and children, was demonstrated by the Triangle Shirtwaist factory fire in New York on March 25, 1911, that claimed 146 lives. Government concern for industrial safety and zeal for reform of the abuses associated with the Industrial Revolution had declined since the Muck Raking Era associated with President Theodore Roosevelt ten years earlier. That tragedy deeply affected two women prominent in Franklin Roosevelt's first administration twenty years later, Eleanor Roosevelt and Frances Perkins, Secretary of Labor and the first woman to serve in a presidential cabinet. That fire and the conditions behind it strengthened a reform movement that eventually led to the Wagner Labor Relations Act of 1935 that regulated hours worked and wages paid, and set the stage for a resurgence of organized labor.

These facts were re-impressed upon me in 1958 when I won the Sidney Hillman Award for best editorial on civil rights and racial issues. The awards banquet was held in Atlantic City and the prize presented by David Dubinsky, president of the Ladies Needle Workers Union. Other winners in related categories included Eric Severeid for his television commentary and Wilma and James Stokely for their book on race relations, *"Neither Black Nor White."* Severeid, a hero of mine ever since he was the CBS radio voice during the fall of France in 1940 and whose memoir, *"Not So Wild A Dream"* years later I greatly admired, joined Ann and me for supper and a long talk. For years we kept up with the Stokelys too, once visiting them in their Newport, Tennessee home. James, a poet of note, has died, but Wilma Stokely is still writing good books from her home today in Asheville.

By the time Lil was fifteen and I eleven, we had grown weary of Daddy's sloppy bathroom habits and Mother's indifference to domestic law and order. There was never a clean bath or face towel to use, as Daddy would grab whichever one was available to wipe off dirt, sweat, grime and goodness knows what else.

Daddy had a lot of body hair, including thick bunches that grew along his shoulders and the top of his back as well as his lower belly and thighs. For some reason this bothered him, and he would periodically light some newspapers and burn the hair off, leaving behind a smell like that of a chicken plucked and deeply singed. Then he would dampen a towel and wipe away the lifeless hair, returning the dirty, smelly thing to the towel rack. Burning was a procedure often used in barbershops and not an unusual home remedy in the 1930s.

No one had a towel and face cloth of one's own, and we were all guilty at one time or another of sloppy bathroom habits. One day Lil and I decided to do something useful and forceful about the situation. We put up towel racks, laid out fresh towels, face cloths and wash rags (as !local folk called them), and labeled each one by name, printed on sheets of paper attached to the towels by straight pins.

Late that afternoon Daddy came home, made a beeline for the bathroom, took a shot of white lightnin', and brought out the lighted newspaper. Once the hair had been burned off, Daddy was quickly in and out of the bathtub, which he left uncleaned, grabbed the first towel he could reach, and started to rub himself vigorously.

Soon Lil and I heard cries of pain and expletives not deleted. Daddy took a quick look in the mirror to see bloody scratches covering his back, chest and legs, all from our pins. "Lil, Mac, come in here," he roared. "What's the matter with you—are you trying to kill me?"

Daddy had belatedly found our labels; he had taken Mother's towel and gotten scratched good and proper. Lil and I were genuinely sorry at first, but as Daddy refused to accept our explanations and apologies, and continued to rant and rave over our own lunatic behavior, we became defensive and defiant.

Lil was more sympathetic than I at Daddy's plight but less intimidated by his reaction. Always more self-possessed around him than Mother, Mary C. or I, she calmly explained that our towel plan had been designed to benefit the entire family. She pointed out that if he had only taken the time to notice that the towels were clearly marked, he would have avoided injury; in other words, it was his own fault. "Next time, look before you leap, Daddy," was his daughter's condescending advice.

"Next time?" Daddy growled ominously. "There's not going to be any next time," and he chased us around the house, wrapped only in his bath towel which kept falling off. We escaped, but Daddy was right; there was no next time.

Soon our bathroom was back into its usual state—wet, dank, dirty towels flung this way and that or lying in a sodden heap on the floor. And the irony lies in the fact that when Lil married and had her own family and her own bathroom to maintain, it wasn't a great improvement. John was like Dowd, Lil became more like Mother, and all the towels in the Buie household were up for grabs.

My wife Ann has fought a 55-year battle to keep the Secrest towels straight as well, sharply reminding me and our three children to "leave my things alone," and asking us sarcastically when we left sodden towels in a heap on the floor or pajamas not hung up, "Who was your maid last year?"

Ann, born and reared in an overly clean New England household, more prim and proper than the hectic southern Secrests, was a determined woman whose will prevailed. We were all remade in her image, although Ann herself was far from house-proud, being devoted to our cats and dogs. While she might have kept the closets and bathrooms clean, the towels separate, and the wash done, our house would never have made the cover of any magazine. Nephew John Vance once even called Ann's housekeeping at a beach cottage "slovenly." But then John was not one who should have talked. Years later, on the occasion of his son Ted's marriage to Michelle, we discovered that John, a forester and an environmentalist, allotted two sheets of one-ply toilet paper per bathroom visit. Maybe not slovenly, but how about wacko?

Bathroom casual became a generational thing. Lil's second daughter Ann found books and boys more interesting than laundry when she was a student at the University of North Carolina at Greensboro. When she finally got around to changing the sheets on her bed at mid-semester, the girls on her hall celebrated the occasion by announcing over the loudspeaker: "Attention, everyone, Ann Buie has just changed the sheets on her bed." That was big dorm news.

Today, down at the Secrest household in Atlanta, the scene is about the same. No one would ever accuse David and Mindy of becoming house-proud, although they entertain with a debonair insouciance, totally unashamed of that big hole in the ceiling or stacks of newspapers that David one day will take care of or the unemptied kitty litter box sitting by the front door to welcome unwary guests.

The towel episode was not the last time Daddy became the victim of his children. One evening Lil, Helen, Martha and I were home alone and decided to call the operator and play jokes on her. Busy, already harassed, she had no time for such tomfoolery. The next time we asked for "Central," she set off a loud, penetrating, piercing whistle into the receiver, leaving Lil momentarily deafened. In revenge I took our great-great-grandfather's hunting horn, designed originally to call the hounds to the chase, and after getting Central on the line, blew the horn as hard as I could into the telephone receiver, then quickly hung up.

A few minutes later, Daddy pulled up into the driveway, came into the house, and before he could even get to the lavatory, picked up the telephone on its first ring. BRRRINGGG! The loud, piercing blast was Central's answer to the latest retaliation. Daddy held the phone at arm's length, looked at it in disbelief, then shook his head to help rid his ears of the ringing.

"What in the devil was that?" Jiggling the receiver, he got the irate operator back on the line. He also got an earful about the treatment she had been receiving from his children. "Well, Mildred, I'm sorry," Daddy replied. "I'll speak to them about. But, listen, sister, don't do me that way."

Later on that year Daddy, given to imaginary heart attacks and genuine gastroenteritis, had been sent to bed on doctor's orders with a hot water bottle to relieve an aching left arm and shoulder and told to lie still. Lil and I were in attendance, sitting near his bed. Suddenly he gasped and started to sit straight up. Lil, ever vigilant, pushed him back onto the pillow. "No, Daddy! The doctor said you were to remain quiet." Up and down they went until Daddy finally managed to brush his daughter aside.

"Goddamn it, Lil, that hot water bottle is burning the hell out of me," Daddy bellowed. And sure enough, the boiling water had leaked out, scalding Daddy every time Lil forced him back down upon it. Life with Father never seemed to run smooth for anybody.

# 16. Broadacre and Monroe

Before one can grasp life at Broadacre, one should know something about the town of Monroe. Our family was not so different from others in the neighborhood and throughout the community.

Monroe in 1930 had a population of 6100, of whom 35 percent were black. Another group were known as "lint heads," people who worked in the local cotton mills. And there were transient railroad people and farm families whose children went to different schools. Some of these people lived across the tracks, removed from the mainstream of municipal society.

So the landowning, professional, and business classes were limited in size and scope. People largely knew everyone in their own circle. There were lots of not so well-kept secrets and a certain democratic tolerance and acceptance of individuals and their idiosyncrasies. As Julia Sugarbaker said in an episode of the sitcom *"Designing Women,"* "We Southerners don't hide our crazy relatives in our attics. We bring 'em out on the front porch and show 'em off! And," she added, "when we learn about someone's crazy kin, we aren't surprised. We just ask, 'On which side of the family?'"

Monroe was the place where records were kept and courts met to dispense justice. It was the site of the county jail, the "poorhouse," and the sheriff's office, as well as the municipal police department. Jesse Helms, Sr. served, at different times, as both police chief and fire chief. Prosperous upper middle-class ladies on Saturdays—the big Market Day—mingled shoulder to shoulder with black and white country folk as they held rummage sales on vacant town lots or on the sidewalks before storefronts. Streets and sidewalks were jammed both with people of varying hues and with beasts of burden. Stores stayed open till nine o'clock at night.

Mayor Sykes owned a livery stable a couple of blocks off the town square, equidistant between City Hall and the Ellen Fitzgerald Hospital. No one seemed concerned about the flies and horse pies and other unsanitary conditions near the hospital. Farmers brought their horses to be shod there and watered at a trough large enough for all the horses and mules that pulled the wagons from county farms into town, filled with cotton, grain, and other produce as well as people. While the townspeople knew each other and, if one were to look back far enough, were usually kin, some of their cousins also lived on the farms. In Union County and its county seat there weren't many degrees of separation among residents.

We had diversity and pluralism too. There was one Jewish family turned Methodist, the Icemans, who established the Icemorlee Cotton Mill in the late 19th century. There was one Chinese family, who ran the laundry, one Christian Lebanese family, consisting of the Saleebys and the Hobeikas, who owned The Candy Kitchen, one German family, the Hernigs, who operated the bakery, one Greek family, who owned a restaurant, and a young Italian fellow called Pedro, who had a fruit stand.

There were people of color, largely servants or small farmers, but one of them was a medical doctor who had some white female patients. Dr. Hubert Henry Creft had offices in a building owned by Dowd Secrest, and he sent most of his patients to Secrest Drug Store to have their prescriptions filled. A person called African-American or black today was called "nigra" (never capitalized), colored or darky, by the middle-class and educated, and nigger, jiggerboo, and other derogatory words by low-class white people who either didn't know any better or didn't care. Many were mulatto and often referred to as "high yellow." But the white women who frequented Dr. Creft's office insisted that he was Indian. Dr. Creft was an Indian to the extent that he was born in Grenada, British West Indies. He earned his degree from Leonard Medical School, Shaw University in Raleigh, in 1912 and practiced medicine in Monroe for over fifty years.

Everybody else considered themselves American and weren't aware of any ethnic differences among people who were largely Anglo-Saxon, Scotch-Irish, Celtic, Welsh or of an earlier German or Irish descent. They were just "white people." This ruling majority was unaware of what black folk—and some other people as well—called them.

There were no major European ethnic groups, certainly none from Central, Southern or Eastern Europe that I ever knew about. The Southeast, given its economy, history and heritage, never had a major port of entry for immigrants, never had the Ellis Island experience. The Latino influx, especially from Mexico, and the immigration of people from South Korea and Vietnam were yet to come. But we did have Puerto Ricans from Spanish Harlem with the Civilian Conservation Corps in the middle 1930s.

Blacks and whites co-mingled peacefully together in the stores and on the street, but you seldom if ever saw a black face behind the counter. Pretty young colored girls would come to town in elaborate evening dresses and formal gowns on Saturdays in mid-afternoon. Young white men, known as drugstore cowboys, could be found "standing on the corner, giving all the girls the eye," with long suggestive whistles directed at white and black alike. No one called it sexual harassment in those days. And no one ever shot and killed any of these white teenagers, either, as someone did the black 14-year-old Emmitt Till from Chicago one afternoon in a little town in Mississippi some twenty years later for whistling at a white woman.

Monroe was the only real town in Union County; outlying settlements were Wingate, Waxhaw, Marshville, Rock Rest. Most people in 1930 still lived out in the country—50,000 Union County residents vs. 6,100 for Monroe.

Charlotte, North Carolina's major metropolitan area twenty-five miles northwest of Monroe, was a world away, with lots of green space between. There wasn't much social mingling with people from Charlotte, and even had there been, Charlotte in those days wasn't all that different from Monroe in its cultural, ethnic, and racial makeup. A good many people emigrated from Union County and Monroe to help that city prosper and develop, especially the Belks and Sherrills of department store and cafeteria fame. But there wasn't much communication between the two county seats. Monroe certainly was not a bedroom commuting town for Charlotte as it partly is today.

Monroe with its political "Mafia," and Shelby, 40 miles northwest of the Queen City, with its political "Gang," furnished more politically prominent faces than Charlotte. The two smaller towns were historically more closely aligned. The Foote-Simmons-Covington-Secrest families were in both camps, through direct descent or by marriage.

A century and more earlier, Mecklenburg County and the area later to become Union County had produced national leaders. Andrew Jackson's family had migrated from Pennsylvania, along with the Secrest family— friends and neighbors—to Waxhaw before the American Revolution.

Jackson, our seventh president, and James Polk, our eleventh, were born and raised on the southern Piedmont frontier, only a few miles apart, Jackson in Waxhaw and Polk in nearby Pineville.

"Sweet Union" was to be carved out of West Anson and East Mecklenburg in 1840, and the little settlement of Monroe was to become the county seat. Andrew Jackson is Union County's most famous citizen, although he left the state before he was twenty years old, later making his political mark from Tennessee, as did James Polk. Both men were national Democrats and believers in America's "Manifest Destiny"—a nation indeed destined to rule "from sea to shining sea." Jackson believed in a strong presidency and an indivisible union, once threatening to hang John C. Calhoun, his vice-president from South Carolina, over the question of a state's right to nullify an act of Congress.

He was not interested, however, in freeing the slaves or in the welfare and tribal rights of Indians, ordering the wholesale removal of the Cherokee Indians from the Southeast to Oklahoma. When U.S. Supreme Court Justice George Marshall ruled against him, Jackson declined to enforce the court order, remarking, "Justice Marshall has made his decision. Now let him enforce it." A strong president, reflecting the national mood, Jackson got away with it.

Jane Jackson, a kinsman of Andrew whom she called "Cousin Andy," married a Gathings from western Anson County near Wadesboro. One of Jane's daughters married David Anderson Covington I, my great grandfather, thus giving Mother still another claim on a prominent Democrat.

James Polk, a generation after Jackson, was also a product of the frontier and a man whose personal and political background was reminiscent of Jackson's. Polk too dodged and danced around the domestic issue of slavery, preferring to dream of territorial conquest at the expense of Mexico. Under his regime, the U.S. claimed Texas (governed by Sam Houston, another national leader who had family connections in Union County) and that vast area of the Southwest, leading all the way to the Pacific Ocean.

So it was in this small, closely-knit society of like-minded people that I grew up. Monroe was never far from the country; many of its leading families came straight from the farm, and most were related to many who remained there. Nonetheless, if you came off the farm, the city cousins considered you a "country hick." Dowd Secrest, I suspect, always felt a sting from that.

In the 1920s and '30s Southern white children were taught that the Ku Klux Klan of the post Civil War era was originally a good thing, formed to rescue the people of the eleven Confederate states from black Republican rule. Men who rode by night during the Reconstruction Era, their faces covered, to burn fiery crosses and to bring vigilante justice were regarded as white knights, whose aim was to protect white women from black men and to redeem the honor and glory of the veterans of the Lost Cause from carpetbaggers and scalawags.

The revival of the Ku Klux Klan in the 1920s, with its nativism and xenophobia, was something different, a hybrid offshoot with roots more in the Midwest than in the Southeast. Its targets were Jews and Catholic immigrants from central and southern Europe even more than Negroes, although they were by no means excluded. There was also a different political agenda that reached into the legislatures and governors' mansions of states well outside those of the old Confederacy and into courtrooms and courthouses all across the land.

Coincident with the Klan's revival was the reissuance of the film *Birth of a Nation* in 1930, which I saw at age seven in Miss Rowena Shute's Pastime Theater. I still remember the excitement generated by the scenes of the white heroine played by Lillian Gish, threatened with rape by a black man, and the tragedy I felt when she and her mother jumped to their deaths rather than be dishonored.

I don't recall that D.W. Griffith's apologia *Intolerance*, made shortly after *Birth of a Nation*, first filmed in 1915, was ever shown in Monroe. It certainly was not reissued in 1930. A friend recalled seeing *Birth of a Nation* as a child. As she sat in the theater, frightened but mesmerized by the sight of costumed Klansmen galloping off on their white-sheeted horses, a man seated behind her shouted out, "Them's the Boys!" Her mother dispelled the illusion when she nudged her little pre-school daughter and whispered, "Bad grammar!"

Some racial feeling and sectionalism was also fueled ten years later with the release of *Gone with the Wind*, although that was an entirely different kind of film and times had radically changed. By then the Great Depression, the New Deal, and the start of the European war in 1939 had changed things forever.

The reception of token and stereotypical minorities who lived in Monroe prior to 1940 was typically benign and inclusive. Monroe had no modern Ku Klux Klan and few hostile feelings toward foreign newcomers. Racism, however, was deeply instilled and politically formalized. Black people were second-class citizens. Segregation was never questioned even as we condemned the rising tide of racism in Hitler's Germany and Mussolini's Italy.

The German Hernigs didn't really count as immigrants, as Jack Hernig had married a Union County woman with the substantial English name of Starnes. Their three children, Elsa, Margaret and Jackie (about the same ages as Mary C., Lil and me) were born and reared American citizens and lived across the street from Broadacre.

The Iceman family, whose patriarch was a Jew, didn't count either, as he married a genteel gentile from Alabama and joined the Methodist church. Their children (my mother's generation) all married people of English and Scotch ancestry. I was grown before I knew that Molly Bowie, one of the most popular girls in our class and a natural student leader way out of my league—and her equally revered younger sister Irene Carr ("Cutie") Bowie—were ethnically speaking one-quarter Jew and hence eligible for extermination had they lived in Nazi Germany. Molly and Cutie were indeed Little Miss Cutie Pies of Everything as teenagers. To land a date with one of them was a real feather in one's cap. Lou Wood and her gal pal Barbara Cheek were equally worthy. I had a secret crush on both of them, who would never turn their heads in my direction. Later, as adults, Lou and her husband Wilton Damon and I became good friends.

Margaret Hernig was a sweet, animated girl whom everyone liked. Margaret never dated much until she started going out with Bruce (June Bug) Snyder. His German ancestors had settled in Monroe many generations earlier and he, of course, was no immigrant at all.

June was Lil's age. A natural cut-up and a talented musician, he was the star of Monroe's high school band, later formed his own swing band, and entertained crowds at numerous civic and social events. His rendition of "Mama Don't 'Low No Banjo Playing in Here" always received a rousing reception by crowds at the annual Union County Fair, sponsored by the local chapter of the American Legion. They didn't come any cooler or more hip than Bruce Snyder.

Snyder joined the Tommy Dorsey Band in 1941, playing lead clarinet, and he swang with the best of them. His roommate on the road was Frank Sinatra. When Margaret and June were married in the early summer of 1942, the event was a local sensation. Sinatra had agreed to serve as a groomsman and to sing at the wedding. That he actually did so became an urban myth; the sad truth is that conflicting big band engagements made it impossible for Sinatra to show up.

Even so the wedding was equaled for excitement only by the nuptials a year earlier of Elizabeth Warren to Hamilton Long. There was nothing ethnic or foreign about that affair—English all the way. 'Lib Warren was in Lil's class and her chief academic rival through high school. Upon their graduation from Monroe High in May 1936, Lil was valedictorian, beating out Elizabeth by only a fraction of a point.

But socially Elizabeth Warren was light years ahead of Lillian Secrest, her life filled with dates with boys her age and older—all at her beck and call. Lib lived up to her high school achievements at the University of North Carolina at Chapel Hill, where she was named "sexiest coed on campus" in 1940. No mean achievement, though coed attendance at UNC was then capped at fewer than 200. Fifty-five years later I mentioned that to Elizabeth at a high school reunion. Lib laughed heartily at the memory.

"Do you know what Mama said to me when she heard about that?" Lib asked. "'Now, honey, don't you worry. I'll stand behind you.'"

Lib was really no different from other girls; she just knew how to turn the guys' heads around. At nearby Duke, Lil was no wallflower but remained shy, preferring her best friends, Catherine Johnson at Meredith College and Helen Saleeby and Amy Riser Harrington, Monroe neighbors and now Duke classmates.

Lil did manage to outshine her rival Lib in the academic arena once more, graduating from Duke "summa cum laude," with a straight 4.0 average. She also far outshone her sister Mary Cov, class of '36 and her brother, class of '44. Ditto friend Helen and cousin Brack, class of '39. As for her social life, Lil at twenty, a late bloomer compared to Elizabeth Warren, began to shine herself.

Lib's fiancé, Hamilton Long, was a native of Morganton, his father a psychiatrist at the State Hospital with some Monroe family connections. Hamilton was smart, good-looking, athletic, and, in 1940, a lieutenant in the Army Air Corps, the newest and most exciting branch of the growing U.S. military. German victories in Europe in 1939 and 1940, and the epic battles of Britain and the Blitz, all emphasizing air power, had focused attention on airmen, and Lieutenant Long cut a figure in his military uniform as glamorous as that of his bride to be. Everyone who was anyone (that is, from the proper social circles) attended that wedding held at the First Baptist Church on Main Street.

Morning glories fade fast in the light of day, however, and not long after that lovely wedding on a warm late summer night, the bright promise of a romantic young couple died with the fatal crash of Hamilton's plane, leaving Elizabeth Warren Long Monroe's first war widow on a soon to lengthen list.

# 17. Monroe: Tolerance and Bigotry

Before the United States entered the war in 1941, most of the immigrant families had departed. Pedro, the Italian fruit peddler, left shortly after Italy's conquest of Ethiopia. The Greek restaurateur soon followed. The Chinese laundry closed. Only the Saleebys remained—our Lebanese-American neighbors who arrived in Monroe prior to World War One.

Helen was five when she moved into her home on South Hayne Street in 1923, along with her mother, her father Najeeb David Saleeby, sister Eva, and brothers Alex, Edmond and David. A woman we called Aunt Halti, Helen's paternal great aunt, and uncles Willie and Joe Saleeby and John and Nick Hobeika completed the family circle, although not all under the same roof.

Helen remembers the Secrest family with affection, especially Mother and her sisters. "Those five Covington women were wonderful people, generations ahead of their time," Helen said to me some eighty years after we first became neighbors. "They were like surrogate mothers, welcoming me and my whole family with open arms.

Helen recalled how Miss Lessie had taught her uncle John Hobeika, then a teenager, to speak English, "even though your Daddy didn't want her to." And how Mother from Helen's earliest days encouraged her to read and gave her access to all the books in the extensive Broadacre library, "many with rich leather covers."

"Your mother not only welcomed us into her home, she encouraged her children to befriend us and introduced Mother and the rest of my family to her circle as well. She and Aunt May and Aunt Eve gave so much of their time opening doors for us and making us feel comfortable in our new home, thousands of miles from Beirut." Your Lockhart cousins just across the street did the same thing, as did Annie Bickett Ashcraft, the Belks, Heaths, and Bowleses."

Helen's mother was a religious woman of a philosophical bent. She soon had a good command of basic English, though spoken with a broken accent. She would listen by the hour to radio personality Tony Wons, who served up religious and philosophical homilies. "Are you listening?" Wons would ask his audience, mostly women, and Mrs. Saleeby would answer earnestly, "Yes, yes, Tony, I'm listening." Occasionally I'd go over to their house and find her arguing, agreeing, laughing, and crying as she talked back to Tony Wons.

She was a sympathetic soul, trying to say and do the comforting thing, even if it sometimes came out the opposite way. One day a friend of Mother's dropped by the Saleeby household for a little sympathy. Margaret Houston Payne, known by one and all as "Daughter," hadn't been feeling well. Her husband, a medical doctor, worked all the time and paid her little attention. Her two boys were nearing manhood and had little time for her these days. She felt lonely and nervous, nearing the change of life.

"I guess I'm just getting old," she complained, hinting for a compliment, searching for sympathy. Eager to comfort and reassure, Mrs. Saleeby replied in her broken English, "No, no, Mrs. Payne, you not old. You just look old!" Daughter didn't have any answer to that but did enjoy telling others the joke on herself.

Aunt Eve had a similar experience. She often recalled a visit she once made to Mrs. Saleeby who told her, "We talking last night, and I say it no matter Miss Eve have ugly face, she has a beautiful soul." My aunt said she cherished that compliment because, whatever truth lay therein, she owed it to "my parents and all the wonderful family and friends in Monroe who shaped my life."

Helen developed into a beautiful young woman, with olive skin, curly black hair, and deep, expressive brown eyes. She possessed a natural grace and a contagious energy and enthusiasm. She was loyal to a fault. Popular with her classmates and teachers and a member of the National Honor Society at Monroe High School, she continued her winning ways at Duke University, a member of Phi Beta Kappa.

Born into an Arab family with some Central European roots, she was of the Greek Orthodox faith. Her uncle became the head bishop of the church in Beirut. Even so, her Middle Eastern features and her religion precluded her from being asked to join several of the snootier sororities at Duke. She was rushed by a new sorority, soon to assume social status, Alpha Phi. Helen later regretted not joining the sorority. More outgoing then than Lil, she may have enjoyed the sisterly experience more. The Secrests, although members of fraternal organizations, really didn't think much of them.

Helen gave Aunt May credit for helping her adjust so easily her freshman year. Aunt May invited Helen over for tea with faculty friends and, with Mary Cov. and Brack, took her to meet President William Preston Few. She gave parties for her and her dormitory classmates. She took her and her friends on evenings out for ice cream and milkshakes at a popular dairy bar. In those innocent days such outings were a big deal for freshmen. She encouraged her to participate in student activities.

"Aunt May was like a little bit of a home for me," Helen recalled, "and kept me from missing Monroe too much. She kept on opening doors for me in Durham just as your mother had done for me in Monroe."

Helen helped Mary C., Lil, and Martha raise me, especially the year Mother wasn't home in 1927-28. When Helen was ten and I was four, I went over to her house one afternoon with the ring I'd found at the bottom of the crackerjack box, gave it to her and asked her to marry me. But Helen turned me down.

Lebanon, Helen recalled, historically had been caught among various religious factions. Several Saleeby families emigrated to North and South Carolina as early as the 1890s. When it became apparent prior to 1912 that the Moslems were gaining the upper hand and were intolerant of Christians, Najeeb David and his brothers Willie and Joe Saleeby, along with David's wife and two brothers, John and Nick Hobeika, decided it was time to get out. Mr. Saleeby came in 1912 and sent for his wife and their three children, Eva, Alex and Edmond, a year later.

Helen's Uncle Elia Saleeby remained in Lebanon, then part of the weakening Ottoman Empire, which became known as "the sick man of Europe." It fell apart in defeat in 1918. His home became a gathering place for the Greek Orthodox community. He became the Archbishop of Beirut in 1936, after Lebanon became a French protectorate under the League of Nations at the end of World War I. Elia later played a major role in resisting French power during Lebanon's political unrest, before it became an independent country in 1944.

Helen visited her uncle in the family home many years after the end of World War Two. "This lovely mountain spot looking down on the lights of Beirut, once known as the Paris of the Middle East, and the deep blue

Mediterranean Sea, is painted indelibly on my heart," Helen later recalled. "And my heart was shattered too when I learned that our ancestral home had been destroyed in the battering of Beirut during the war years."

But Helen's real home, as it was for all her siblings and for her mother and her maternal uncles John and Nick Hobeika, was Monroe, North Carolina, in the United States of America. The Saleebys owned the Monroe Candy Kitchen, a popular spot for teenagers to hang out. The Saleeby household became a favorite haunt for the young neighborhood crowd, rocking with energy and laughter as they sang, danced, played cards and various parlor games on weekends and throughout the summer months.

The Saleebys were big on food, providing us with dried sheets of apricots called Amerdeen and serving watermelon and homemade ice cream along with sweets from the Candy Kitchen. There was no home more American in Monroe then the Saleeby's.

We were especially close to "Uncle Johnny" Hobeika. He came to America knowing nothing of its language or its history but fell in love with both. In his senior year at Monroe High, he was chosen the best debater in North Carolina. Many people commented on his command of the English language and his fluency in both speaking and writing. Uncle John attributed his skill to Lessie Covington Secrest who had taught him to speak, read and write English. Miss Lura Heath, public school teacher, and her father Colonel Heath, son of a veteran of the Civil War, intrigued him with stories of that tragic era of American history. Robert E. Lee became his hero. So the Saleebys and the Hobeikas became not only Americans but Southerners as well.

The Saleeby household was nevertheless a troubled one. The oldest child Eva died a few years after their move to Monroe. Helen's mother blamed Mr. Saleeby for their daughter's death. She came to believe that Eva would not have died had they remained in Lebanon. Eva was born with a heart condition, incurable in those days and aggravated by the traumatic experience of a large dog jumping on her. She died three months later. No one was really to blame.

"The day Eva died was the day peace went out of that house," Uncle Johnny later observed. We seldom saw Mr. Saleeby, who stayed in the back room as the young crowd gathered up front. Occasionally I'd stray into the back and see Helen's uncle smoking the "hubble bubble" or Argeli, a long pipe out of the end of which extended some tubing that wound up in a bubbling glass bowl. It was a special blend of Turkish tobacco. But I assumed, as did many others, that the man was smoking hashish—just something that Arabs did and nobody paid much attention to. Helen later explained to me that it was just the way Turkish tobacco was used. She added that her grandmother Hobeika smoked also. It was acceptable for elderly women to smoke but not young ones. In any event, the "hubble bubble" was a far cry from American cigarettes and seemed exotic to me.

Bishop Saleeby recalled the family to Lebanon at the end of World War II. Helen's father returned in 1946 and Uncle Willie in 1948. Mrs. Saleeby and her four now adult children, along with her brothers Johnny and Nick, remained in Monroe. They later moved to Dillon SC. Helen returned to Duke to earn an advanced degree and taught English at Myers Park High School in Charlotte until her retirement. Her brothers did well in business.

They were a long-lived lot. Uncle Johnny died at 92. Uncle Elia lived in Lebanon until 97. Brother Edmund died at 91 in 2003 and was buried next to Mrs. Saleeby in Monroe. Helen is going strong at 86.

Who gets the credit for the tolerant, generous acceptance of a Middle Eastern family in a little Southern town, governed by an English tradition and dominated by a fundamental Protestant religion, predominantly Baptist? The people of Monroe or the Saleeby family?

I vote for Mrs. Saleeby. She was the one who told her family that they were Americans now and must make every effort to accommodate to the new culture in which they lived. She constantly reminded them of their obligation to be good citizens and to set a good example. Other people of Arab descent would be judged by the way the Saleebys lived.

The people of Monroe also get my vote, for reaching out to these foreign folk with their strange new ways and accepting them so readily. The Saleebys were a metaphor for the melting-pot experience. The question remains today: melting pot and assimilation, or diversity and multi-culturalism? The Monroe answer was to accept both. But if the Saleebys had resisted learning English, had isolated themselves into a tight little ethnic group or religious enclave, what would have been the majority response? Tolerance? Understanding? Acceptance? I don't think so.

Time brought Helen insight about her parents. "Daddy wasn't always wrong." Mr. Saleeby hadn't been responsible for little Eva's death. Nobody was. "Mama wasn't always right."

And over at Broadacre, Mary C., Lil and I also came to understand that "Daddy wasn't always wrong." He wasn't responsible for Mother's episodes of depression, even if he could have managed his reactions to them better. "And Mother wasn't always right."—a fact that Lil and I wouldn't admit until we were middle-aged but that Mary C. figured out much earlier. Such knowledge though, flawed as it was by her own rationalization and projection, didn't seem to help her any.

Helen's friendship with Lil and Mary C. which began one early autumn afternoon in 1923 continued uninterrupted for the next eighty-one years. She felt honored to serve as maid of honor at Lil's wedding to John Buie at Broadacre on August 28, 1942. Mrs. Saleeby joined the Methodist Church, but the other members of the family belonged to St. Paul's Episcopal Church, over which the Rev. Frederick Blount Drane presided for thirty years.

People in Monroe were not, however, always tolerant of minorities and could be harshly cruel. There was no Catholic Church, precious few Catholics, and those who lived there were sometimes mistreated. North Carolina, deeply entrenched in the Protestant religion, was also largely populated by Yellow Dog Democrats, especially down east, which dominated state politics. The first time the state voted Republican in a presidential election was 1928, against the Irish Catholic Al Smith. North Carolina went for Herbert Hoover.

That election year a Catholic second grader in Monroe's Primary School reaped the wrath of local Protestants. He was cursed on the playground, occasionally waylaid and beaten up on the way to or from school. He was mocked as a Roman, an agent of the Pope. He was ridiculed in his teacher's presence. No school official intervened, in the school yard or in the classroom.

The boy, made particularly nervous one day by such harassment, felt an urgent need to go to the bathroom. Up went his hand, one finger raised to indicate he needed to urinate.

"What do you want?" inquired his teacher, her voice rising with impatience.

"I need to go the bathroom, please," was the timid reply. His classmates burst into laughter, with taunts of "Sissy" and "Baby" ringing in his ears.

"No, Charles, you must wait. The bell will ring in a few minutes," his teacher replied. Actually it was nearer half an hour.

A few minutes later, Charles raised his hand again. The exasperated teacher asked, "What do you want now?"

The child raised one finger again, to be greeted by scornful laughter by his classmates. "I told you to wait, Charles. Don't interrupt the class again." Not long thereafter, a trickling sound could be heard and soon a thin yellow stream ran down the side of his seat and onto the aisle. The boy's pants turned dark where they were saturated with urine. Charles turned beet red and his face screwed up as he started to cry.

"Look at Charles," one boy shouted. "He's peeing on himself!"

"Baby! Do you wear diapers?" a little girl chimed in.

"Is that what you Catholics do at home?" inquired another.

The teacher, never one to tolerate disruption, reasserted her authority and soon had her charges under control. But did she reprimand them for their cruelty or bigotry or show any sympathy for the solitary Catholic child? No, indeed, she silenced her students only to take up where they left off, blessing Charles out for his failure to control himself and making him feel even more diminished in everyone's eyes, most particularly his own.

After recess, during the next classroom period, another child raised his hand, one digit to signify number one, and was promptly excused. Soon another raised her hand, one finger up and was also permitted to go. But then, little Ben was a Baptist and little Jean, a Methodist, so they didn't have to wait. No, Monroe wasn't always so patient with diversity and pluralism.

Yet how quickly things can change. Within fourteen years Monroe was filled with soldiers from all over the nation, stationed at newly established Camp Sutton, and there were many Catholics among them. These young men were welcomed into homes and churches and USO facilities without a hint of discrimination. Soon there was a Catholic Church and a parish priest. In 1942 young Monroe women—and some not so young—became betrothed to Catholic men—all Yankees, many sporting Greek, Polish, Italian and Irish names.

Eighteen years later, John F. Kennedy, Irish Catholic from Massachusetts, easily carried North Carolina in the presidential election of 1960. People had learned a lot since Herbert Hoover and 1928.

One friend of my mother, dissatisfied with her husband and with life in general, even left her Baptist Church and converted to Catholicism. Lessie was never sure how deeply theological the conversion was. "I think she fell in love with the man, but since she couldn't embrace the priest, she embraced the church instead." This judgment contrasted with Mother's usual sympathy with dissidents, but it didn't affect the friendship. They remained lifelong friends, growing closer as they grew older.

Sometimes a teacher's impatience with a pupil's needs has nothing to do with race or religion. In 1960, our son David, in the fifth grade in public school in Cambridge, Massachusetts, raised his hand for permission to go to the bathroom.

"What do you want, David?" Mrs. Buchanan asked.

"I need to go to the bathroom," our son replied.

"Well, it's nearly time for the bell to ring," his teacher replied inaccurately.

"But I really need to go right now," David insisted. And he started to leave the room.

"Get back in your seat," the teacher ordered.

David complained, "But I'm not comfortable. I tell you I need to go right now." Unlike Charles, David had his classmates with him, but to no avail.

"Suffer," was his teacher's final reply.

And suffer successfully he did, managing to hold on till the school bell rang—half an hour later. David came home and complained. But neither Ann nor I took it up with the teacher. Sometimes such lessons teach that life—and teachers—can be unfair. And Mrs. Buchanan, Boston Irish Catholic to the core, wasn't punishing a Protestant, she was just tired of kids always needing to go to the bathroom and interrupting the class. "Suffer" became a household word and family joke whenever the children wanted something and wanted it now. We even sometimes tell our dog and two cats today: "Suffer!"

# 18. Kissing, Kidnapping, and Regional Myths

Ethnic and religious prejudice were different, however, from a deeply ingrained faith in racial superiority and domination that became institutionalized by two centuries of slavery followed by another of segregation. These issues were aggravated by sectional rivalry that led to four years of civil war and ten years of reconstruction. Monroe in the 1930s had enjoyed "good" race relations in the sense that it remained free of civil strife and enjoyed a surface serenity between individual blacks and whites, largely due to acceptance of segregation as a normal way of life, enforced when necessary by "law and order."

North Carolina prided itself on its liberalism and progressivism, calling itself "a valley of humility between two mountains of conceit," that is, Virginia and South Carolina. Its neighbors returned the compliment, considering the Tar Heel state to be populated by a bunch of ill-bred, crude country bumpkins, many of whom, ironically, had emigrated there from the Palmetto State. When I moved to Cheraw in 1953, I soon learned that neither state's sense of superiority was justified.

South Carolina's political leadership, however, lagged far behind that of North Carolina, and its daily print media, unlike that of its neighbor, beat the drums of racial unrest and massive resistance to racial change between 1954 and 1964. Yet Cheraw escaped any major racial incidents during the Second Reconstruction while my home town of Monroe, just fifty miles away on the North Carolina side of the border, had two. The fact that Cheraw did have a liberal newspaper that supported racial reconciliation and integration may, however, partly explain the contradiction.

The "Kissing Case" was the first, the residue from which led to the second, "The Kidnapping Case," which catapulted Robert Williams, a young black firebrand and president of the local NAACP, into the international spotlight. The kissing case occurred in the late 1950s and involved four elementary school-aged children, two white girls and two black boys.

The kids were neighbors on Parker Street, a partially integrated neighborhood just behind Miss Ann Redwine's house on all-white, upscale Hayne Street. The four children were playing in a storm culvert near home when some affectionate physical display occurred. The two girls went home and confessed to Mama that they had been kissed by the two boys. Mama told Daddy when he got home.

Daddy allegedly reached for his shotgun and went looking for the boys. Word spread quickly around the neighborhood, then reached City Hall. The police were called, the boys arrested and placed in protective custody. Eventually they were tried in juvenile court and sentenced to an indeterminate term in a nearby youth correctional center, then called "reform school," and placed on probation.

The press had a field day. Reporters from leading national newspapers and some from overseas flocked to Monroe to report on Monroe's oppressive racial culture and its judicial mistreatment of minorities, even children yet. The reporters interviewed anyone willing to talk, the more flamboyant the opinions, the better the story. People took sides, many whites feeling misrepresented and defensive. The episode was a nine-day wonder, soon to disappear under the weight of matters of larger concern. But damage had been done. Judge J. Hampton Price, father of my best friend Bill, was pilloried. Governor Luther Hodges, whose wife Martha was a native of Monroe, came in for his share of criticism. Soon bumper stickers appeared: "No justice, no peace." The majority of people on both sides stayed neutral and quiet.

The incident preceded the lunch counter sit-ins that originated in Greensboro a year later, the Lumbee Indian shoot-out against the Klan in Maxton, and the Freedom Rides on buses by organized interracial groups all over the South in 1961. Most people in Monroe had never even heard of Malcolm X, the black separatist movement, or the Nation of Islam.

But Robert Williams, a black man my own age and a relative of Lindsay Williams, one of my black pals in the 1930s, had. Robert came from a family that took a deep historical interest in slavery and race relations. His father believed in self-defense, black pride and racial assertion. Martin Luther King, Jr.'s philosophy of non-violent and passive resistance leading to integration did not hold much appeal for Robert Williams. He believed in and wrote about "Negroes with Guns."

As black unrest in Monroe grew in response to that in other parts of the country in the early 1960s, demands were made and occasional rallies and marches occurred. On one day of confrontation, a white couple from Marshville, on the way home from Charlotte, got caught in the middle of a group of contesting whites and blacks. The man and his wife were seized and spirited away. The couple claimed they were kidnapped and held hostage. Robert Williams said they were taken into protective custody for their own safety.

Soon the incident turned into a national cause célèbre. Again the national and international media had a field day. Members of the protest group, represented by a coalition of black and white leaders, many of whom were from out of state, were arrested and charged with a number of offenses, including kidnapping. When trials were held, the national spotlight again shone down on the Union County Courthouse.

Several people received long prison sentences, later to be reduced, but Robert Williams was not one of them. He fled, one jump ahead of the law, first seeking sanctuary in Fidel Castro's Cuba, later in China, then in North Africa before returning to North Carolina from exile in Canada. Ultimately, Williams was granted amnesty and permitted to return to Monroe. He never was tried or convicted of anything. Later Robert lived in Charlotte, somewhat mellowed out and making no references to the communist or socialist utopias where he had once been granted safe haven. He died in 1996 and was buried in Monroe, eulogized by several civil rights leaders, including Rosa Parks.

During the trials a friend, John Herbers, a Nieman Fellow with me in 1961, wrote me a letter. He was covering the proceedings in Monroe for the New York Times. "Mac, I am surprised and disappointed in Monroe," he wrote. "Having known you, I expected better." Hmmm, I thought as I read on. This sounds like an Ersel compliment. "The courtroom scene is like something from a Faulkner novel, or Ernest Caldwell. There was the courtly male judge, the racist prosecutor, the all-white, all-male jury, all like some scene from a 1930s Hollywood movie about the benighted South."

Herbers went on to describe the crowd in the courtroom, many in overalls, held up by suspenders, chewing tobacco and filling the spittoons lying nearby. "There was even the village idiot, roaming around at will, making guttural sounds and laughing inappropriately as evidence was given."

I suggested in reply that Herbers, himself a native of Mississippi, had been around the New York Times too long. What he had observed was a bit of Americana, no doubt replicated in some degree or other in courtrooms all over the South and beyond. The courtroom gallery was hardly typical of Monroe. And as for the unrestrained village idiot, he was representative of the tolerance and respect for individuality that was to be found in the rural South. Good for him and for those who believed in his freedom. The trial showed the South in transition. Soon the area would show the same respect for its black citizens as it now showed for its village idiots.

Given a similar situation and faced with a similar challenge, would other cities and towns in other sections of the country look much better? Different, no doubt, but really better? A few years later, I had a chance to see for myself and found Northern urban areas, home to the ghetto and tolerant of de facto segregation, police brutality and a playing field far from level, different indeed but no, not much better.

### Regional Myths and Southern Belles

There are misconceptions and myths about the South that are hard to put to rest. Among the former is the idea that it is a monolithic region, all states possessing a state of mind that constitutes a Solid South.

In reality the eleven states of the Old Confederacy are as far-flung culturally as they are geographically. Charlotte, in Piedmont North Carolina, with its red clay soil, Anglo-Saxon and Scotch-Irish ancestry and Protestant religion is a far cry from New Orleans, with its Creole and Cajun folk, Catholic culture and delta soil, not to mention French cuisine. Virginia has more in common with Pennsylvania than with Florida. Even within the states themselves, there are variations. Southside Virginia is drawn more toward the Carolinas than toward Northern Virginia adjacent to Washington. South Florida, Mecca to northern snow birds and a large Jewish and Latino population, is different from Central Florida or the northwest Panhandle known as the "Red Neck Riviera." Northern Florida is indistinguishable from South Georgia, itself light years away from

Atlanta. The Low Country of South Carolina is self-consciously different from the Up Country and Charleston is a long way from Greenville, not only in miles but also in views and values.

North Carolina differs from all its neighbors: Virginia, South Carolina, Tennessee and Georgia. Within the old North State one finds, furthermore, decided variations stemming from geography and history among residents of the Coast, Tidewater, Piedmont and Mountains.

Despite these differences there are, however, other forces unifying the Southern states to create a Mind of the South. Most natives think of themselves as Southerners and look upon their neighbors, from Virginia to Florida, South Carolina to Texas, as relatives. People in Mississippi and Alabama often refer to the coastal Southern states as their ancestral home, much as some Virginians and Carolinians still regard England as theirs.

Southerners are also bound by a common history. Each state has had its frontier experience. All bear the guilt of slavery and segregation and the shame of military defeat and occupation. The South was politically solid for nearly 150 years, safely in the keep of the Democratic Party. Nearly every Southern senator as recently as 1956 signed a Southern Manifesto pledging resistance to Supreme Court decisions ordering an end to segregation in the South. For much of the twentieth century white Southerners from Texas to Virginia, Florida to Arkansas, stood up when "Dixie" was played at public functions. The area also shared generations of grinding poverty, ignorance, and a feudal economic system that led to a regional inferiority complex among those who were aware of the world beyond.

Southerners talk with similar accents. They think in common terms. A sense of place still draws Southerners home. The pace of life remains slower and more relaxed, surface manners more polite, people more unguarded and friendly, than in many other regions of the nation.

Southern states were late comers to an industrial and commercial revolution that others embraced a century earlier. The picture began to change in the twentieth century and accelerated enormously after World War II. Today the South is the growing, prosperous Sun Belt, while the Midwest is referred to as a Rust Bowl and the Northeast undergoes a population melt down. Although most of the eleven states of the Old Confederacy still lag behind others in the Federal Union in personal income and other indices of social progress, they are quickly catching up. They have the momentum.

The greatest myth is the romanticized pride of the Old South in its aristocratic traditions—which were short-lived at best and barely existed outside imagination. The ideal of the gallant knight and his fair lady, the first Southern Belle, is the stuff from which mythology is derived.

The South after 1865 became a matriarchal society. Both North and South suffered enormous casualties in the Civil War, but the Union, with a population five times that of the Confederacy, could more readily absorb the loss. Soon the tides of European immigration also reached the North.

Reliable figures on Southern casualties are difficult to come by, but it is probable that they averaged between twenty and thirty percent of the men in combat. That compares to about six percent in World War II. The white population of the South in 1860 was approximately six million; that of the Union 25 million. In 1940 the population of the United States was 132 million. The states of the Confederacy suffered the loss of a generation equal to that of France in the Great War of 1914-1918.

The law of supply and demand set in. Men became a precious commodity. Mothers spoiled and protected their male babies. The phenomenon of the "dutiful daughter and entitled son" emerged. Sons, idolized by mothers and sisters, became adults often unable or unwilling to work for a living. It was easy to romanticize the past and live in a more pleasant era. Why bother with ambition when loafing, hunting, fishing, drinking and fighting were a lot more fun?

Young men returned the love showered upon them by their women, but it often took the form of exaggerated respect for females in general. Women were placed on a pedestal, worshipped from afar but denied a sexuality of their own. Women accepted this role to please their men. While men may have idealized women, they expected proper ladies to remain pure and virginal, certainly until marriage, sometimes afterwards, except for obligatory motherhood. The inferior position of women was hardly confined to the Southern states. It was a national phenomenon for a large part of the twentieth century, and as anthropologists will attest, one that is even more pronounced worldwide.

Young gentlemen could get what they needed on the side, from prostitutes, lower-class girls of their own race, or, more often, from young black women who were still , despite emancipation, more like chattel. What proportion of African-Americans today have no white genes?

Before my wife, a true Yankee from New Hampshire, came south with me, she had been told, "Oh, you'll love the Southern men, but you won't like the women." She at first swallowed the myth of the Southern belle but discovered, to her surprise, just the opposite. "Where are all the southern belles I've heard so much about?" Ann finally asked. "Most of the women I've met are smart, funny, hard working, up front, and good sports. Why, they are a real sisterhood." She later wondered what had happened to the coquette, the man trap, the dumb, vapid, self-centered beauty who believed the chief goal in life was to get a man.

While Ann met Southern men to admire as well, she found others spoiled, chauvinistic, inattentive to women, anti-intellectual, often rude and inconsiderate. In the comparison with women they suffered: immature, irresponsible, emotionally dependent, especially on mama. "Good grief," she exclaimed, "why don't they grow up?" Since Ann had chosen to marry a Southerner, I didn't offer much defense.

Mary Cov and I, however, found Freudian explanations: the incest taboo, the phallic symbol, man's fear of female sexuality and its demands upon him, and an anger at maternal love that could be dominating and stifling. Much of this we believed came from the trauma of the Lost Generation of the Civil War. Men were not entirely to blame for their weakness. Women helped make them that way.

Whatever its merits, the Lost Generation and the female's indulgence of the male was the argument used to explain much of the South's backwardness between 1876 and 1940. But this Faulknerian scene was subject to change as the South began to catch up with the rest of the country after 1940. In some cases the Southern Belle became Rosie the Riveter. After the war many women remained in the work force, often to support husbands in school on the G.I. Bill of Rights.

Pity the young privileged woman, misnamed Southern Belle, of an earlier era. She was taught little and knew nothing except how to conduct herself socially according to prevailing custom. Little was demanded of her. But as soon as she married, things changed. She was expected to know how to please her husband, to care for infants, one after another, to run a household, often with very little money, and to train and direct servants. The home and the children were her responsibility, even if she lacked equal rights and legal authority. Hard work and submission, not social frivolity and independence, were her fate. No wonder so many Southern women had genteel nervous breakdowns.

She had, moreover, to learn all this before the days of household conveniences and supermarkets with delis and bakeries where prepared food is available, before anyone who didn't want to cook could send out for pizza or Chinese. Today, with men and women both in the workforce, things have changed. But not entirely. Surveys indicate it is still women who do most of the housework, all over the country.

Sociological analysis is partly speculation. Theories are hard to quantify. One risks oversimplification and meets so many exceptions that the rule itself becomes dubious. There were no doubt Northern Belles too. They just didn't become fictionalized. And a dominant personality will often control another despite lower domestic status. Stereotyping is a faux pas in our multicultural social and political environment. But all that would not cause Carl Jung much concern. He would consider the "Southern Belle" and the "Entitled Son" archetypes, a true expression of an earlier society and part of its present collective unconscious, which occasionally surfaces in movies, books and the popular culture. Some young women even today may imitate the myth, but the demise of the double standard for the sexes is gradually obliterating the Southern Belle.

# 19. By the Company One Keeps

If one is influenced by the company one keeps, an introduction to some of my childhood friends may shed further light on my formative years. By age twelve in September 1935, I had made lasting friendships despite my relative isolation at Broadacre, my preoccupation with my parents and sisters, and my basic partiality for Doll, Heath, and tenant farm kids like Murray and Lindsay, with whom I held top-dog status.

I had attended school with the same boys and girls since Miss Inez Flow's private kindergarten at age five. Miss Flow was an unmarried gentlewoman of indeterminate years, but I would guess about 45 when she had our class—the A section comprised of kids from the "good, old families" from the right side of the track.

Miss Flow was a warm-hearted, impulsive, loving woman who could discipline no one, let alone five-year-olds. I remember her kindergarten as glorified bedlam, dozens of children filled with restless energy running to and fro totally out of control. Little learning went on there, but there was a lot of music, storytelling and creative energy, and loads of loving, hugging and boosting of self-esteem, as well as plenty of sub-rosa bullying and a pecking order of which Miss Inez was blissfully oblivious.

Amid all that noise and confusion and disorganized chaos, no wonder Miss Flow would periodically take to her bed, immobilized, unable to do anything. Thus attendance was irregular, with our teacher often "indisposed." I didn't learn what that word meant until some years later. What it really meant was that Miss Flow was predisposed to periodic

134

"nervous breakdowns." Once her kindergarten was interrupted for seven years, when the lovable, loving, distracted teacher took to her bed unable to function, with a paid companion to look after her.

The world—let alone Monroe—didn't understand mental illness very well in the 1920s and early 1930s, and didn't use the word "depression" often, let alone "bi-polar" and "uni-polar disorder." Psychotherapy was almost equally unknown and psycho-pharmacology was non-existent. So Miss Flow was stuck in bed until one day she arose to announce, "I think I'll start my kindergarten again this fall," and so she did.

There were plenty of nervous breakdowns in Monroe, especially among middle-aged women, but the condition was accepted without stigma. Everybody was just glad to see Miss Inez up and around again, running her kindergarten the same old way and spending her days in contented harassment.

I became associated with many other children in kindergarten and during my first few years in public school. I was also bullied and at the end of the pecking order from first through third grade. By the beginning of the fourth grade though, at age nine, with my new farm-toughened self-assertiveness, I was no longer one to be taunted or trifled with. Cool, popular? Well, at least accepted at last.

### Moke and Bill

My earliest acquaintances—some of whom became friends later—were Bob Houston, Bill Price, Moke Williams, Philip Griffith, Emsley Armfield, twins Arnold and Donald McKenzie, Bill McLeod, Frank Howard, Sam Henderson, John Futch, Bobby Laney, Paul Triplett, and Caston Hunter, not to mention cousins Hill and Lee Wolfe and Vann Secrest.

I still preferred, however, the company of girls at this stage: Elinor Ellwanger, Eleanor Williams, Margaret Hamilton, Ruth Bankhead, Mary Jane and Irene Dillon, Mary Alice Vann, Rachel Hemby, Eleanor Howie, Ruth Hough, Sally Orr, Dodie Love. None of them were members of the self-appointed in-crowd and none made it their chief goal in life to be cute, cool or classroom cheerleaders; they were just likable, good students and fun to be around.

Even a year or two age difference is important in the early grades, and we didn't really know children a year or so behind or ahead of us. With only forty students in our A Section class the choice was limited, and even more so for me, as we lived out on the edge of town with few neighborhood children my own age to hang out with. Jackie Hernig and

Bobby Pfeiffer, two to three years younger and Bobby Cunningham and Johnny Sloop, a year or more older, didn't count. That of course changed once we reached high school.

My best friends from kindergarten days were Moke Williams, an only child; Bill Price, Ed Doster, Conrad Haney, another immature child overly attached to an older sister and his mother, a boy with a sad life and a tragic end to it, and Philip Griffith, the most unique, original character I've ever known and the one I perhaps remember the best and miss the most as we all grow older and apart and begin to fade away.

Friendship is a thing that resists analysis. Most early friendships flourish, then weaken with time. Similar experiences and shared memories, nourished by propinquity, are important ingredients. And friendships among women and those among men are different in substance, too. Women share emotional experiences and tell each other things. They are oral and co-dependent.

Men find common bonds through work, projects and shared interests that, when fulfilled, tend to dissipate. Once mature, they are usually more satisfied with their wives and significant others—partners is the preferred word today—as their friends and are more dependent upon them. Women, eager for affection, understanding and oral discussion, often find other women meet this need more easily than men. Women nourish friendships, men cultivate allies who may change as the project is completed. Women in general make and maintain the friendships established in a marriage, the men willing to follow their lead.

Some of this may be explained by basic differences between male and female, some in the way the social order developed, with men the historic breadwinners—earlier the hunters and warriors—and women the homemakers and caregivers. Testosterone and estrogen may play a part. Women console, understand and comfort. Most men aren't so good at that. As one astute social anthropologist has observed, "Testosterone blocks empathy."

But it is partly socialization as well, and as I was early on socialized on a feminine scale, I tended to make friendships based on emotional openness, memory and nostalgia. Even all that, however, can't survive lack of propinquity—separation by time and space.

Bill Price and I had similar temperaments. Our personalities seem to fit. We usually liked the same things. And we had a similar sense of humor—a recognition and appreciation of the absurdity of the human condition. We were completely unashamed of the fears and insecurities we both felt as we grew older, and openly discussed them. We arrived at puberty at the same time, which meant we had to deal with and discuss sex. That wasn't so rare.

The things teenagers did to themselves and others—sometimes in groups—to satisfy their curiosity probably rivals what their liberated grandchildren do today. My closest friends and I were less venturesome and experimental than many of the hip, cool kids who invented some really novel, creative things to try. At times we all bore the burdens of guilt and anxiety. At others we were shameless. Most of us got through it largely intact.

In this area boys and girls differ, their behavior not always in sync. They mature at different ages, leaving girls sometimes to become more aggressive, the teenage boys self-conscious and in retreat. While I believe in the fundamental difference between men and women—"Vive la différence!"—I also know that both sexes are bound by common humanity, far more closely united by the values they share than divided by differences.

There is usually a feminine side even among the most macho of men and a masculine side to the most feminine of women. If not, how would they ever manage to co-exist, let alone marry, establish families, and on occasion love, honor and cherish one another? Without such common bonds, no families could exist, no civilized societies flourish. They could only seasonally copulate and move on. Evolution does have some merit.

Lifelong friendships also change as people mature and personalities develop. Although Bill and I remain close friends at 80, the things that made us close at ten years of age were different from those which kept us close at fifteen, changing again by twenty, and yet again once we became older and more settled. We were inseparable in high school, even closer in college. My sophomore year at Duke I spent so much time visiting Bill and Moke at Wake Forest that their fraternity brothers considered levying Chapter dues on me.

What did we do together in our earlier years in Monroe? Play a lot outdoors, engage in sword play with long sticks and pared down tree limbs, pretending to be Robin Hood or Friar Tuck. Philip was usually Maid Marion.

We would play a made-up version of War, each representing a different nation. I was by turns Italy, France, Russia and finally Great Britain, as my political philosophy migrated from authoritative and imperial to democratic and parliamentarian. Jackie Hernig was forced to be Germany.

Individuals emerged as characters in these fantasies. We had to have heroes
and heroines. Philip had the most vivid imagination and would come up
with the best names.

At age ten, I identified with Benito Mussolini's youngest son Bruno,
a darkly handsome young aviator whose picture I'd seen in the Charlotte
Observer. Bruno was my role model, whose identity I'd assume in our
horseplay.

"Bruno needs a girlfriend," I announced one afternoon. "A beautiful,
dark-eyed, lithe young woman, with full lips, wasp waist, full bosom, and
double-jointed hips."

Philip immediately got the picture. "Yes, yes!" he squealed in
enthusiasm. "And her name must be Voluptuana!" And so it was, and guess
who played that role to perfection, even if he lacked the figure for it?

Moke was a lonely little boy. An only child, he was around his mother
Cleone and a much younger, pretty Aunt Cupie too much. Soon he began
to spend a lot of time at Broadacre, and if not there, he would be on the
telephone, to Lil's and Mary C's great displeasure.

"Mac," Mary C. would call out so he could hear, "It's Moke again,
for the fifth time in the last fifteen minutes." And she, or Lil, or one of
my parents would order us to get off the phone. Moke apparently found
my noisy, intrusive, opinionated household diverting, so different from his
isolation at home. I spent a lot of time at his house, too, finding in it a quiet,
peaceful sanctuary from the Sturm und Drang of Broadacre.

Opposites attract. Moke was neat, clean, quiet, and as he grew older, a
fashion plate, even natty. He got that from his mother's side of the family.
His maternal uncle Hazel Davis was nicknamed "Tweedy" because of his
preference for fashionable English attire. I was a slob, usually dirty, always
talkative—Mary C. didn't call me "Blab dirty nose" for nothing—with
animal hair all over dingy clothes and with filthy socks and smelly feet.

Moke's friends thought surely he would become a men's clothier,
owner of a haberdashery. He was no student in high school or college.
Who could ever have guessed that Moke would become a distinguished
psychiatrist, a guest lecturer at Princeton, the owner of a medical clinic in
Fort Lauderdale, Florida, that became a veritable cash cow? Moke, who
could never pass high school chemistry, was to become the disciple of
two-time Nobel Laureate Linus C. Pauling and to achieve considerable
recognition as a specialist in psychopharmacology.

Moke was full of surprises to a lot of people, but not to me. I knew
him well in high school and came to understand him better in college.
Moke was reined in. Few people knew of the heavy emotional baggage he
carried around all his adult life—something that set him further and further

apart from his Monroe roots. Moke was nevertheless in and out of my life and that of my family until his death in 1995, even as we drifted apart gradually over the years. Moke may have pretended to have many macho role models, but he really wanted to be Gertrude Niessen, a Hollywood song and dance performer who belted out hot jazz tunes.

Aside from playing basketball and tennis, we also re-enacted battles of the Civil War, fighting and always winning the great battles of Northern Virginia and Tennessee, and those along Sherman's march from Atlanta to the sea. We were unreconstructed rebels. This shouldn't be surprising. As history is taught, 1932 wasn't so far removed from 1862 and even less from 1876, the end of Reconstruction.

Mrs. Vernon Austin, my third-grade teacher whose own grandfather had participated in the Civil War, spent a good deal of classroom time talking about the "War Between the States" and states' rights. We even had to keep a scrapbook featuring heroes of that period: J.E.B. Stewart, Stonewall Jackson, and above all the sainted Robert E. Lee. Once I was sent home in disgrace because I brought to class my Civil War journal with a picture of Ulysses S. Grant on the cover. I was often a contrarian.

Mother was called, a parent-teacher conference held. I was supported at home, Daddy shouting so Mrs. Austin could hear, "Tell old lady Austin to get over it. My granddaddy was killed in that war and you don't hear me crying over spilled blood, do you?" He added that "she ought to be more concerned with what is happening in Europe and the U.S. today like her colleagues Miss Lura and Miss Annie."

While Mother agreed with Daddy on this occasion, she also was aware of the need for diplomacy and civility. "Hush, Mr. Secrest. And lower your voice. You don't want to offend Mrs. Austin or hurt her feelings. That's not nice."

But Daddy was not persuaded. "Nice?" he shouted. "Nice? I'm not trying to be nice." And with that he emitted a resounding fart, as he was prone to do, especially when excited, to relieve his chronic indigestion. As Mother reached hastily to close the door, I heard Daddy shout loudly, "Thank the Lord for that!"


*Ed Doster*

Broadacre's doors were open to anyone who happened by, and there were always some little boys underfoot to avoid. Ed Doster was another one, as was Conrad Haney. Ed had an older brother John Henry and an older sister Eleanor, both of whom were popular and cool and married well. Ed never was and never did, but in later life he migrated to Hollywood, became a celebrated couturier, and hung out with a pretty fast Hollywood crowd, including actor David Jansen. Years later I took Ann and our three children on a cross-country trip and stopped in California to visit my first cousin Sarah Secrest Handwork Sturm and her husband Kenny, and, while there, to look up Ed.

I had just turned 40, my hair thinning, revealing male pattern baldness. So I called Ed. "Hey Ed, Mac speaking," I announced. "We're in Whittaker and want to see you. I'm thinking about getting a hairpiece. Do you know anyone to recommend? I want one just like Fred McMurray's in "My Three Sons.""

After an enthusiastic response, Ed assured me that yes, indeed, he knew just the guy who operated a hair replacement center, a young Italian named Mario. We made an appointment for the next day. Ann, sons David, 13, and Phil, 12, and daughter Molly, 6, hesitantly entered the establishment with me near Hollywood and Vine that July 22, 1963. A husky young Italian-American came out to greet us.

"Come on around back," he suggested, and with the family waiting in the anteroom, I entered the hair salon apprehensive and self-conscious.

"So, what do you want to be?" Mario asked. "Blond or brunette? Short, long, curly, flat top? You name it. We've got it."

Anxious, mortified, wishing I were anywhere but there, I replied.

"I'm really just here to look around. I don't think I want to buy anything." That was fine with Mario. He assured me all his customers were initially nervous. I wasn't committed to anything at all. Just try one on.

When I continued to demur, Mario had a suggestion. "Here, take a little drink; it'll relax you," and he poured out a large jigger of Canadian Club.

"Bottoms up." And so I swallowed the burning liquid, chased quickly by a small glass of water, and let Mario place the hairpiece on my head.

"Ede—" (pronounced Ed-DAY) says you'd like a flat top—or something a little shorter like Fred's got. You know I make all of McMurray's hair," Mario assured me.

Good grief, I thought. Eday! Is that what they call Ed out here?

"Oh, really?" I replied, somewhat impressed. "Yes, I'd never know he wore a rug if I hadn't read it in TV Guide. But no, no, no. I just don't think I could ever bring myself to wear one. How does he keep it on?"

Mario assured me that a well-adhered hairpiece wouldn't come off in a hurricane. You could even swim with it. Seeing receding resistance, he poured out another two ounces of whiskey, handed it to me, and down the hatch it went.

"Well, okay, I'll try that brown one, curly in front and no part on either side." Feeling pretty confident now, I looked into the mirror. "Wow," I thought, "that's how I looked when I got married sixteen years ago." Not only did I have a headful of beautiful shiny real human hair, I seemed to have lost some wrinkles around the eyes, which looked much bluer, and my jaw line appeared firmer.

But again doubts assailed me. Don't be such a fool. Act your age. What will people say? Can I stand the ridicule?

I voiced all these objections and more to Mario, who assured me I looked fifteen years younger and fit as a fiddle. As he handed me another jigger of Canadian Club, which I didn't even bother to chase with anything this time, this young Italian stallion assured me no one would ever know. People would just ask if I had lost weight, or started pumping iron, or bought a new suit.

"OK," I decided, my stomach now full of whiskey, head dizzy, inhibitions gone. "Show me how to tape it on and the best way to comb and care for it." A few minutes later, out I walked with the hairpiece in place to unexpected, even enthusiastic, support from Ann, David, Phil and Molly.

They all assured me I looked great. But as I sobered up, off came the hairpiece. I let Molly play with it occasionally, but wear it I could not—not at least until November 22, 1963, when I decided to sport it at the Charlotte Country Club, where my cousin Hill Wolfe had invited me to luncheon. As we left around one o'clock I heard Walter Cronkite's familiar voice saying something about gunshots fired at the presidential motorcade in Dallas. Now I have two reasons to remember what I was doing the day President Kennedy was shot.

Stunned, I walked down Trade Street and over to the North Carolina National Bank to see Luther Hodges. Maybe he had not heard and would need to know; after all, his father was serving in the President's cabinet as Secretary of Commerce. He hadn't heard and was as shocked as I. Soon I drove back to Cheraw to be with Ann and the children, including Cousin Hill's two sons, Hudson and Johnny, and daughter Mary and their boxer dog, Duke. Hill's third wife Rosalie had left him earlier in the summer, with their son Wick and Hill's daughter Candy; the other kids were dividing time between Cheraw and Monroe until permanent plans could be made.

When I got home I discovered the house in an uproar. Not because of the assassination but from Duke's disappearance. I took Hudson and Johnny, now teenagers, to look for him, and we soon found his body on the Wadesboro highway, smashed by a car that had failed to stop…indifferent, uncaring, just so much road kill. Anxious and upset by the national tragedy,

I refused to let Hudson and Johnny cry over Duke: "Come on. Buck up. There are more important things going on now than this." I've always regretted those words.

Soon Ann had the boys and Mary, near Molly's age, packed up and ready to travel. We left Sunday morning. Monroe is about an hour's drive from Cheraw. We got to Mother's house just in time to see on television Jack Ruby shoot Lee Harvey Oswald. What on earth would happen next? I dropped Johnny, Hudson and Mary off at Aunt Mary Hinson's and headed back home, after promising Mary we would pick her up later to spend the year with us. That never happened, as Aunt Mary Hinson and Uncle Vann intervened. "Hill would drive you crazy," Vann warned. "Mary belongs in Monroe with her brothers," Aunt Mary added. It was just as well, for within eight months Ann and I had ourselves moved to McLean, Virginia.

### Philip

I became acquainted with Philip when Mother asked Mrs. Griffith if he could go to the movies with me for his sixth birthday. I had just turned five. This was the first time either of us had ever seen Mickey and Minnie Mouse and Donald Duck in action. I recall Philip's squealing in delight as the cartoon characters took pratfalls, pies in the face, and slid and slithered on and off chairs, ran up chimneys and popped in and out of unexpected places. Philip always squealed in excitement, even as a grown man.

Not long after that, he and I were cast as tiny telephone operators, equipped with toy telephones, in a local theater production titled "Oh, Doctor!" Philip was by ordinary standards an oddball, far more than I a boy set apart, and so he remained all his life. But everyone liked him for his sunny disposition, optimistic nature, and calm acceptance of people and circumstances, however he found them.

Philip was a great mimic and had an uncanny ability to spot some personal characteristic and imitate it to perfection. He liked people and loved to talk and gossip about them. If you knew something on somebody or had nothing especially nice to say about them, Philip, like Alice Roosevelt Longworth, would invite you to "come over here and sit by me." He had a keen sense of humor, often directed as much at himself as at others: sharp, witty, barbed, penetrating, incisive.

Philip had an older brother Paul, whose nickname was Ice, as cool and hip and in the mainstream as Philip was out of it, and a younger brother Hugh, a composite of the two. Their father had died by the time Philip was four years old, leaving him to be reared by a working mother and his grandmother, up to Monroe from her Georgia home to help her daughter. They were dirt poor, but the Griffiths were among the right people in Monroe and faithful Episcopalians, so that was okay.

They lived on Washington Street in a little cottage built around 1870, and there Philip lived and died from 1922 to 1998. Although he spent most of his adult working years as a professor of English literature at several universities, largely Tulane and Tulsa, he spent a large part of every summer in Monroe with his mother and maintained his hometown ties. So early retirement to Monroe when he was 60 years old was a smooth transition.

Philip was a member of St. Paul's Episcopal Church, formed in the late 1800s by a group of dismissed members from Monroe's Central Methodist Church. They were cast out because they had dared defy fundamental religious dogma by attending a circus in Charlotte on a Sunday afternoon. But I always thought Philip had progressed long past Episcopalian to Anglican. Later in life he spent several weeks each summer in London, holed up in the British Museum and University library by day and spending the nights with an Anglican order in the Westminster diocese—"all very strange," as he later confided.

After retirement he spent each May in Florence, Italy, staying at the celebrated and expensive Mona Lisa Hotel, owned by a Florentine contessa who had befriended him; then June and July in England. Philip had friends in high places all over—New Orleans, Charleston, Annapolis and Baltimore, Hendersonville and Camp Kanuga, Chapel Hill, Cheraw, South Carolina, as well as Florence, London, Cambridge and Oxford.

He had entrée into the society of old Charleston. Welcomed into antebellum homes, he became a friend of Alicia Rhett, a woman of impeccable lineage who played the role of India Wilkes in *Gone with the Wind*. Red-haired and five feet ten, Miss Rhett was a distinguished artist and portrait painter. She hated Hollywood and vowed never to return. *Gone with the Wind* was the only film she ever made, but in it she turned in a professional job.

Philip sponged off them all, never for less than two weeks at a time. He paid his way as an entertainer and conversationalist, sometimes court jester, often a parody of himself. Philip knew where all the bodies were buried—in Monroe and everywhere else—and always understood who was who and how they were related; he never forgot anything. Philip confided everything in me, and it was this shared memory and nostalgia and his sense of humor and ability as a raconteur that formed the basis of our life-long friendship. Philip also understood about propinquity; he made the effort to keep up and to stay in touch. In other respects we had little in common, but he seemed to love and respect me and my family. That was enough for me.

Philip's best neighborhood pals growing up were Kitty Jane Fairley and Mary Faith Douglas. On a rainy Saturday afternoon, he could be found more often making fudge with them than playing contact sports with little boys in muddy backyards. But he was a good sport, willing to take his turn on the playing field if he had to. One sunny, crisp autumn afternoon, as the pin and Spanish oaks and sugar maples were turning scarlet and gold, a group of boys and a few girls joined Philip and me after school to play pick-up.

"Let's make a pyramid," suggested one boy, "and see how high we can go!" The largest and strongest boys, which included me, stood on the ground as the next heaviest set climbed up on our shoulders. Then another set of lighter kids, including Kitty Jane, Mary Faith and Mary Alice, added themselves.

"Who'll volunteer to be the star?" Paul inquired. No one stepped forward. "Hey, Philip, how about you?"

Yes, we all agreed, Philip, slight and slender, would be perfect. So he was drafted—amiable, amenable, as well as quick and agile. With some pushing and pulling from bottom to top, Philip ascended, reached the pinnacle and held his pose for a second or so before the whole edifice collapsed. I could feel my arms weaken and knees buckle, along with those of my bottom-rung playmates, as Philip hurtled to the ground.

Aside from a few cuts and bruises, no one was injured except Philip, who writhed on the grass in pain. Lynn Griffith and Mrs. McMahon rushed out, along with John Vann. A doctor was called, an ambulance arrived, and Philip was taken to Ellen Fitzgerald Hospital. There Dr. Mahoney set his fractured left shoulder and bound up his dislocated right one.

There was no social security or aid to dependent children in 1934. Mrs. Griffith, a single mother, worked long hours at meager wages down at the Monroe ice plant keeping books for Mr. Dickerson. Dr. Mahoney waived his fee. The hospital charged a minimal rate. Daddy and friends and neighbors donated and collected money. And so the medical obligation was met.

After a week or so Philip, his upper body wrapped in bandages, was back in school. He remained his sunny self, cheerful, humorous, never complaining. His behavior in those circumstances, while typical, won him universal admiration, and he relished the approval and acceptance.

Philip always adored his mother, never apparently really wanting to cut the apron strings. As he grew older, he became what he loved but could not have. Naturally like his mother in temperament, he began to take on her mannerisms and her personality traits. He unconsciously imitated her, resembling her as some younger sister might.

Not long before his own death, but many years after hers, Philip said, "I miss my mother every day of my life. She was such good company and so much fun. Even after she became bedridden, she loved life and remained interested in everything and everybody." As I said, Philip really was a lot like Lynn.

Philip was to invent and reinvent himself. An outstanding student at the University of North Carolina at Chapel Hill, he became an adequate member of the military during World War II. He was an honor graduate student at Johns Hopkins University and became a distinguished professor of eighteenth-century English literature. Later he became a world traveler, a bon vivant, a problem drinker, a teetotaler, a man of Rabelaisian appetites, a wine connoisseur, a celibate, a southern gentleman, a continental sophisticate who could, and often did, successfully pass himself off as an authentic Englishman. But to me Philip remained just Philip, an original, and a lifelong friend.

Nothing said here diminishes Philip. He was a person of substance and consequence, of conviction, ideas and faith, all of which he was willing to express and defend. He had an admirable mind and character. Philip was not a man to be marginalized for his eccentricity.

In Florence, shortly after Philip's death in August 1998, I stopped by the Mona Lisa Hotel to notify the contessa and her staff. She wrote brother Hugh in Monroe a note of consolation, adding "We will always remember Dr. Griffith fondly, sitting quietly in our lounge in the evening enjoying a glass of wine." David and Molly joined Ann and me in signing the guest ledger "Requiescat in Pace" and proceeded to the Uffizzi Museum with Philip weighing heavily on my mind.

# 20. Family Friends and Unique Characters

Friends and relatives played important roles in life at Broadacre. They helped keep Lessie and Dowd on an even keel, and I was usually quite attached to them as stabilizing influences in my own life. Aside from the unusually close ones, there were others who were in and out of our lives and who may also shed some understanding of life in small towns all around North Carolina in the 1930s and '40s.

One such friend was Mrs. Calhoun Pruitt, who had a son Mary C.'s age. Mrs. Pruitt could be found almost any afternoon drinking Coca-Cola laced with ammonia in Secrest Drug Store and visiting with friends who happened to stop by. There was an ongoing debate among some of the men, and women too, as to who was the prettiest woman in town—Virginia Calhoun Pruitt or Lessie Covington Secrest.

There was never any doubt in the mind of Mrs. Pruitt, who was a coquette at heart and proud of her dark, stylish good looks. Mother willingly conceded the title, never thinking she was anything special to look at. Like many women of her time, she wore her long hair parted in the middle and done up in a bun on the nape of her neck. She had been grey-haired since thirty-five, soon to turn snow-white, and she dressed in a matronly style, a little overweight and tightly drawn in by heavy bra and tight girdle. Even so, she had her partisans.

One afternoon in the drugstore Mrs. Pruitt and Mother were comparing notes and forebears. To Mrs. Pruitt, a native of South Carolina, genealogical lines were important, whereas Mother always claimed she was more interested in where she was going than where her ancestors had been. But on that day there was heated argument. Finally Mrs. Pruitt, who had an overly dependent grown son and a husband who didn't amount to much, said, "Oh, Lessie, it just makes me so mad—to think that your cousin Andrew Jackson threatened to hang my uncle John C. Calhoun over a thing like nullification!"

That matter back in 1829 involved the question of South Carolina's right to nullify an act of Congress. President Jackson, the story goes, was moved to remind his Vice President Calhoun that "the federal union, it must be preserved," and to threaten to hang Calhoun from the nearest tree if he persisted in pursuing the argument.

*Rachel Howie*

Rachel Howie was another member of our extended family who was in and out of our lives ever since I can remember. Rachel was the younger sister of Betty, Dr. Marvin Smith's wife. She was so young in fact that she remained permanently twenty-nine years old.

Dr. Smith, whom we called "Big Doc," was my father's first cousin. He had a huge family practice for generations in Monroe and throughout Union County. He delivered me in 1923 and my first son 25 years later. Mother and Daddy lived on Windsor Street across from Marvin, Betty, and Rachel for several years before they returned to Broadacre after Grandmother Covington's death. The Secrests and the Smiths were close friends, with children all about the same ages: Mary C. and Peggy, Lil and Kelly Ann, Mac and George, who was called "Spud." Spud's own son, known as George the Third, was a student of mine at UNC-CH in 1971.

Betty was a warm-hearted, outgoing, good-natured woman with a strong sense of family obligation, as was her sister Blanche Howie Benton, who was still living at age 107 in Monroe in 2003. Rachel was cut from different cloth: spoiled, self-indulgent, not motivated to live on her own. Proud of her appearance, she lived vicariously through her two nieces Peggy and Kelly Ann and strove always to appear just as young as they.

Rachel was a frequent Broadacre luncheon guest and entertained us over the years with tales of Peggy's musical talents, her exciting social life at the University of Alabama, and later her married domestic bliss along with her radio and library careers in Monroe. Kelly Ann provided her aunt with as much or more interest: her popularity in high school, her successful academic career at Salem College, where she was one of Cousin Evabelle Covington's special girls, and particularly her selection to join the debutante ball in Raleigh. Rachel was ecstatic when Kelly Ann married Ed Carter during World War II, moved to Wilmington, Delaware, and enabled Rachel to claim a Du Pont connection.

Rachel's interests were movies and movie magazines, romantic novels, her nieces and nephew, and herself. As a young woman she had transient romantic attachments, but somehow they never came to anything. She was either too lazy or emotionally dependent to leave the sheltering arms of Betty and Marvin.

Having no money of her own, Rachel earned her keep and her lifestyle as Dr. Smith's receptionist in his offices above the Secrest Drug Store. She spent a lot of time during slack periods downstairs, drinking Cokes and visiting with whoever was at hand, usually Chatty Stack, Daughter Payne and Virginia Pruitt.

If I have pictured Rachel as vain and shallow, that is what she was. At age sixty-seven and in urgent need, she refused to apply for Social Security, for which she had been eligible for five years, lest her age become known. As she put it, "If you think I'm going to take Social Security now, and let Clara Laney (Union County's perpetual Register of Deeds) tell everybody in Monroe how old I am, you're crazy."

Betty Smith suffered from severe asthma and eventually had to be moved to the nursing home at the Ellen Fitzgerald Hospital, where she later died. Rachel remained in the home on Windsor Street with Big Doc and continued to serve as his receptionist.

Even before Betty's death, she tried to appropriate her sister's role, telling people how she had raised Peggy, Kelly Ann and Spud. Peggy and Kelly Ann came to resent Rachel's intrusion into the lives of their parents and particularly these claims. "She didn't raise us," Kelly Ann one day years later declared. "Our mother did. Rachel never changed a diaper in her life. And without a nickel of her own, she chose to depend on Daddy's support rather than admit to her true age. My Aunt Rachel was just a self-centered narcissist who never contributed anything to anybody."

Rachel, I think, was better than that. She never committed any indiscretion as Doctor Smith's medical confidante. She was genuinely devoted to her nieces and nephew. As the years passed, Rachel took to drinking heavily. One cold winter morning she was found lying outside in the Smiths' front yard, having fallen some hours earlier through a plate glass door. Her body badly broken and half frozen, Rachel spent a long time in the hospital and in rehabilitation, but she recovered from both the injuries and the addiction. That, at her advanced age, required strength of character.

After Betty's death, when Rachel continued to live under the same roof with her brother-in-law, some gossip circulated. One old farmer was overheard saying to his wife as they watched her at work in the office, "That's Rachel Howie—Big Doc's woman." The gossip was not true. Rachel just wanted to be provided for and live the life she had grown accustomed to. Until his death Dr. Smith took care of her, as Betty and Blanche would have wanted him to and as his conscience required. It took the death of Dr. Smith to move Rachel out of that Windsor Street house and into a room of her own.

Betty and her two daughters were all musically talented. They sang alto and soprano together. Betty was a faithful member of the First Methodist Church choir. I have an indelible childhood memory of middle-aged, matronly Betty Smith heaving a deep asthmatic wheeze, then belting out a good old John Wesley hymn, her heavy, velvety contralto in perfect harmony with the choir.

### Aunt Eve and Friends

When Aunt Eve accepted the position of professor of sociology and economics at Salem College in 1924, she quickly adapted to the social and economic climate of Winston-Salem. She joined the country club and became friends with various members of the extended Hanes family of tobacco and underwear fortune; the Gordon Grays, also of tobacco; Dr. Wingate Johnson, later one of the founders of Bowman-Gray Medical Center; Gordon Spaugh, Salem College Moravian minister, and his wife Catherine; Dr. Craig, an august internist and Hanes in-law.

Her closest friend and surrogate mother was Miss Mamie Dwyer whose brother Henry was owner of the Winston-Salem Journal and later a vice president of Duke University. Aunt Eve's personal physician was Dr. Phohl, an old and revered general practitioner to the rich and famous in both Old Salem and the new city of Winston. She became a close friend as well of Dr. Ronthaler, President of Salem College.

Some years later when one of her friends on the faculty, Dr. Ralph McDonald, regarded by some as a radical leftist, decided to run for governor against an old family friend, Clyde Hoey, she was torn as to whom to support. Hoey was commander-in-chief of the "Shelby Gang" and quintessential establishment Democrat, and his wife was a Gardner, aunt to cousin Betty Webb. Aunt Eve knew on which side her bread was buttered and finally backed Hoey, a sure-fire winner in any case. But Cuz

Nannie Ashcraft of Monroe, whose brother Walter Bickett was governor from 1916-20, supported and campaigned for McDonald, that radical New Dealer even accused of being a parlor pink.

### Miss Catherine Hanes

Of all Aunt Eve's trophy friends, the most memorable to me was Miss Catherine Hanes, a fabulously rich, extravagantly eccentric unmarried lady of the first Hanes generation that struck it rich with Reynolds tobacco and later with lingerie and hosiery. Miss Catherine rented the entire top floor of the Robert E. Lee Hotel, Winston-Salem's finest, as a part-time residence. A non-stop, compulsive talker, she loved Aunt Eve largely because the quiet college professor would listen and not interrupt her free-association soliloquies.

Early on Miss Catherine took a liking to me. I remember her escorting me from Winston-Salem to Greensboro in her chauffeur-driven limousine for dinner on the terrace at the top of Greensboro's leading hotel. Lessie, Eve, and Lil were tolerated, but not allowed to speak, as Miss Catherine and I chatted the fifty-two miles to and from Greensboro. Mary C. was usually not allowed to come because she would contend with Miss Catherine for the privilege of speaking.

It was not at all unusual for Miss Catherine to call, in the days when such calls were expensive, from Winston-Salem to Monroe, order Lessie to the phone, and talk for three to four hours. One hot mid-summer evening Daddy answered the phone and Miss Catherine's imperious voice ordered him to put Lessie on. "That cranky old maid from Winston wants you on the phone," Daddy called out to Mother, who was sitting on the veranda facing east, fanning herself to seek relief from the heat and the gnats. Daddy could see no advantage at all in having Miss Hanes as a friend.

"Lessie," Miss Catherine said, never bothering to identify herself, "Don't let that oaf of a husband back on the line to interrupt. Now, listen," and off she went. After an hour of standing up by the wall telephone, Mother summoned Mary C., Lil and me. "Take the receiver and just listen," she whispered. "You can take turns. No need to say anything but 'yes' and 'uh-huh' periodically. Miss Catherine will never know the difference. She'll just hang up when she runs down. But if you have to, you can come get me on the porch." Well past our bedtimes Miss Catherine did finally run out. She never caught on that Mother had left the phone. But Miss Catherine did retain her interest in me, always remembering me—never Mary C. or Lil—with expensive gifts at Christmas and birthdays.

Many years later, Miss Catherine finally dropped me. Ann and I had recently married, and we came by Winston-Salem. Aunt Eve called Miss Catherine, now quite ancient, to see if it were convenient for her to receive us. "Yes," she replied, adding rather severely, "But leave that Northern wife of his at home." We did so, and we had a pleasant visit, shorter than usual, our hostess relatively restrained.

I never saw Miss Catherine again. She died shortly thereafter in solitary splendor on the top floor of the hotel, attended only by an equally aging Dr. Phohl. When the will was read, my name was not among the beneficiaries, as I always thought Aunt Eve had secretly hoped. I think "that Northern woman" ruined my chances. But Aunt Eve ought to have known better. Money goes to money. Money marries money. It usually stays in the family.

But Aunt Eve remained close friends to three generations of Haneses: Big Nona, Little Nona, and the youngest Nona, and those friendships had nothing to do with high finance. Years later Ann and I and our three children attended young Nona's wedding in Winston-Salem. We had gotten to know her a few years earlier when she was a student at Wellesley College and I was a Neiman Fellow at nearby Harvard University.

We fixed her up with a Harvard student from Charlotte, Graham Allison, whose mother was from Cheraw. Graham later earned his doctorate and served some years thereafter as Assistant Secretary of Defense. Today he is a renowned academic at the nation's oldest and most prestigious university. In 1961 Graham, then a Harvard undergraduate, escorted Nona to the Big M, a black nightclub in Dorchester, with Ann and me and a friend, Jim Laue. The future academic spent most of the evening hoisting Nona on his shoulders to show what a big, strong man he was. But no, he and Nona were not soul mates, and each married someone else.

### Aunt Eve

Although much more than a friend, Aunt Eve herself was a memorable character, contradictory in many ways. She sometimes spoke to me of her love affairs, including one with Nicholas Murray Butler, President of Columbia University when she was a graduate student there. Butler, an internationally known educator and later Nobel peace laureate, twenty years older than she, enjoyed occasional picnics with Aunt Eve.

"He once said to me," Aunt Eve confided in her old age, "'You are the smartest student I've ever had. You sweet, pretty little thing—just a fragile bundle of brains and talent.' Wasn't that nice?" When Aunt Eve spoke of affairs, she meant symbolic romance, spiritual unity, occasional words of praise that were to her terms of endearment. Her mother Molly's earlier stern moral preachments precluded anything else.

I had heard from childhood of Aunt Eve's love affair with John Vann, Monroe lawyer, and how after she broke the engagement, he had impulsively runoff with a young woman from Wadesboro, who became Mrs. John Vann and the mother of their nine children. But every time Aunt Eve came to Broadacre, John Vann would come over alone to visit his former sweetheart. That continued until World War II, when Colonel Vann disappeared one night from the military transport ship which was carrying him to Europe and was never seen again.

When Aunt Eve was in her mid-eighties, she brought out from her desk a framed photograph of John Vann which had lain hidden there for decades and placed it among the other pictures of her loved ones on top of her bureau dresser.

Mary C. was unimpressed by Aunt Eve's lost loves. "Aw, bull!" she declared, and quoted her favorite line from Shakespeare: "Men have died and worms have eaten them but not for love." Aunt Eve never married because she never wanted to, my sister insisted. "And she would never have married John Vann, of all people, because she was second choice to her own sister. You knew, didn't you," she asked triumphantly, "that he only started dating Aunt Eve after Aunt Sue had thrown him over for Uncle Earle?" Besides, Mary Cov concluded, "Aunt Eve's true love wasn't John Vann or Nicholas Murray Butler, whom she really hardly knew. It was Miss Mamie Dwyer!"

Aunt Eve was a good Samaritan whose main goal in life was to be of service to others. She needed to be needed and to be appreciated. She did expect, however, to be rewarded on this earth, largely through reciprocal devotion. She was a loyal and loving aunt whom I always appreciated, even though I have often laughed with others over her and her foibles.

Once when I was well past middle age and was in Winston-Salem visiting her with Ann and our three children, she sent me up three flights of stairs with a dish she had prepared for a colleague whom she really didn't like much and with whom she had little in common. Miss Jess Byrd opened the door at my knock but ushered me out promptly with the message that she neither needed nor wanted the gift, but please to convey her appreciation for the thought. My aunt likewise refused to accept the rejection.

"No, Mac, she needs the food. She's just getting old and being difficult," declared the equally old Aunt Eve. "Take it right back up there and tell Jess how much we all hope she enjoys it, and that there's more if she needs anything else." Back up the rickety stairs I climbed, knocked on the door and was admitted, only to be told," No, Mac, I don't need a thing. Your aunt is just being overly appreciative of some little kindness I've recently shown her. Take that right back down again."

But Aunt Eve was adamant. Miss Byrd was to have that food. "Mac, honey, just run right back up there, but this time don't go in. Just set the food down on the placemat in front of the door, put this note on top, tap once lightly and leave." I did as I was told. I've never known what became of that dish or of the food it contained.

I was more appreciative than Miss Byrd of Aunt Eve's care and concern. When Ann and I learned in late April, 1966, of our teenage son Phil's serious illness, word soon reached North Carolina. Before the week was out, Aunt Eve appeared unannounced at our home in McLean, Virginia, to offer her support. She had sent herself "in passing," as she might some package, from Salem College to Georgetown, arranged to stay with Betty Webb and Roy Veatch, and had somehow gotten from there to McLean just to share her concern with us. A day later, after a quick visit to the clinical center at the National Institutes of Health to see Phil, she returned to Salem.

Two years later, when Phil, recovering from a secondary sickness caused by the effects of chemotherapy, was able to leave the hospital again, Aunt Eve gave him two hundred dollars, with instructions to take his girlfriend Jane Clayton out for dinner and an evening on the town and to spend every penny on having fun that night. That impulsive generosity and understanding of youth was typical of my "old maid" aunt.

Years earlier when our son David, then about ten years old, lost ten dollars in a restaurant where Aunt Eve had taken us for dinner, and I strongly reprimanded him for carelessness, Aunt Eve intervened. "It wasn't David's fault. It was yours, for letting a child carry that much money and expecting him to be responsible for it." I didn't mind being overruled and I didn't argue the matter. I had learned not to contend with Aunt Eve.

Lil was Aunt Eve's favorite until rather late in Eve's life, when nephew Brack Craven needed her more. She loved all of Lil's children, especially Kathy Buie who returned that affection and named her only daughter Eve. Lil and I used to laugh at Aunt Eve's managerial skills. We maintained she should have been United States Postmaster General, as she knew how to save on postage. She could write more on a postal card than most people could in a letter, filling both sides and placing the address in a clearly printed box in the middle. She seldom had to pay to mail packages, as she managed to send most of them "in passing," often at considerable inconvenience to the carrier.

Once she sent a Christmas gift to Beatrice Bulla, a Craven relative and supposedly, although I've never bothered to verify it, a kinsman of President Theodore Roosevelt on his maternal side, at her retirement home in suburban Baltimore. I was going to nearby Bethesda anyhow so, on my way, I came by Salem (considerably out of my way), picked up the package and left it at Miss Bulla's place in Baltimore (considerably out of my way). The value of the gift was small. There was no hurry, of course, Aunt Eve assured me, but she expected me to deliver it on time. However, Miss Bulla received her gift the following July; while I did not contend, I often did as I pleased, not as I was directed.

Aunt Eve was a smart businesswoman and put her knowledge of economics to the test in the stock market. When she died in August 1979, she left an estate, before taxes, of three-quarters of a million dollars, all of which she had earned from a meager initial investment. That is before the Dow had reached 1000, so one can see what her estate was worth based on values twenty-five years later. She could also be hard-headed about money. As she grew older, she sometimes lost track of assets. When the savings and loan association notified her of a $10,000 certificate of deposit long since mislaid and sent her a check for the full amount, she wrote a note of appreciation but inquired about the interest which had not been included. She got that, too.

In her mid-eighties, Aunt Eve came to the rescue of an acquaintance who lived in an apartment across the hall. The woman, many years Aunt Eve's junior, began to lose her memory, and something had to be done. Upon her friend's death, Aunt Eve, with family permission, went through all the accumulation of mail, unpaid bills, checks never cashed, income tax forms never filed, and cleared all matters up to everyone's satisfaction, including that of the Internal Revenue Service. She really was a bundle of brains.

Aunt Eve described herself as forehanded. I thought obsessive/compulsive might be more accurate. She bought Christmas cards in January and signed and sealed them for delivery the following December. She wrote thank-you notes for gifts she had yet to receive (but was sure were coming). Before her death, she prepared special dishes for guests at a luncheon to be held before the funeral and put them in the freezer for the guests to enjoy when the day arrived.

As Aunt Eve sensed the coming of the end, she planned her own funeral, asked me to write her obituary, edited it carefully to be sure she got a favorable review, and then asked me to deliver one of several eulogies at the Moravian Church on the campus of Salem College. She gave me letters and documentation, all highly laudable, and again edited what I was to say. Once the time had come, however, and she was past editing, I gave the eulogy as I saw fit. It was indeed worthy of Aunt Eve—so much so that Mary Cov termed it "fulsome," a word that made Mother indignant, as she felt everything I said was sincere and right on the money.

The church was packed, people of all ages coming from near and far to honor this remarkable little old lady, weeks shy of ninety, who had lived on the Salem College campus for fifty-five years. The Winston-Salem Journal had begun charging for obituaries before Aunt Eve died. When she learned about that, she decreed, "Don't pay one cent. If my death isn't front-page news, free of charge, omit it altogether." Not to worry. When the time came, she made the news, just below centerfold.

In the funeral procession, the Moravian Church bugle corps played a lively tune as Aunt Eve (cremated, ashes placed in an urn "not to exceed thirty dollars in cost") was carried to her final resting place in God's Acre at Salem. My aunt also planned the repast to precede the funeral, "a small but lovely luncheon" for relatives and dearest friends. "There are forty-three names on the guest list, but all things considered, I believe thirty-five will show up," Aunt Eve declared. At the luncheon, as her great-niece Kathy Buie recalled, "There were exactly thirty-five people; I counted them." Aunt Eve knew how to manage and to plan.

In her desire to serve and to be needed and wanted, Aunt Eve could intrude to an extent where she became neither. Brack began to feel put upon and to complain about our aunt's demands upon his time.

"On my way to court from Asheville to Richmond, I feel obligated to stop over at Aunt Eve's in Winston-Salem. She expects it. I feel now, after all she has done for me, I can't refuse. But I'd much rather go on to Durham and spend the night with Jim and Sarah. I hardly know my grandchildren."

"Oh, for goodness' sake, Brack. Skip Salem. Go on to Durham. Aunt Eve will understand. Even if she didn't, she's tougher than you give her credit for. She didn't want you to marry Susan. She really wanted to keep you more to herself. The night Ann and I spent with her before the wedding, she was in emotional distress. Her jaws locked and we had to call Dr. Huntley. He said she was 'just revealing a little human emotion.' But she couldn't bring herself to go to the wedding the next day with Mary C., Isabel Craven, Ann and me. Yet look how she quickly accepted Susan, even courted her for your sake. Do as I do. Say, 'Yes, Aunt Eve,' and then do as you please."

But we both instinctively knew what it must be like—to be old, in declining health, always second-choice to sisters who had children, sometimes lonely, anxious, "tired of living and scared of dying." So Brack kept on stopping over with Aunt Eve, until the day he died in 1977, ironically two years before she did.

# 21. Rosa, Skipper, and Jesse

Until the fall of 1935, times at Broadacre rolled by as usual, punctuated by exploits of our pets and neighbors, outbursts from our unpredictable father, and the uncovering of a family secret that had waited for nearly 60 years. The question "Who is Mrs. Thompson?" was finally answered, and the matter of "Rosa's Odor" fully aired.

Rosa Parker was a family friend as well as relative. Her mother Margaret Houston Blakeney, known as Maggie, was Mother's first cousin. Rosa's grandmother was Susan Gathings Covington who had married Hugh W. Houston, known as "Black Hugh," not because of any blemishes of character, although he had plenty, but due to his dark, swarthy complexion. Maggie died young at age 38 but had been confined to a wheelchair years before that. Rosa was one of those "plantation-reared" Covington-Houston-Blakeney girls with connections to people in high places. But Hugh's family had lost a lot in the Civil War and Reconstruction, and Black Hugh lived the good life, well beyond his means to pay for it. Rochel Edward Blakeney, Rosa's father, was a man cut from the same cloth.

The Houston name was a prominent one, however, both in North Carolina and Virginia and finally in Texas. David Franklin Houston, a cousin, was born and reared in Monroe. An academic and a businessman, he was appointed by his close friend President Woodrow Wilson to be Secretary of Agriculture (1913-20) and later Secretary of the Treasury. Prior to public service he had served as president of both the University of Texas and Texas A & M. Later he became Chancellor of Washington University in St. Louis. At the time of his death, he was serving on the Board of Trustees of many of the Fortune 500 Companies.

157

Connected families, whatever the degree of separation, looked after their own in small Southern towns in the post Civil War era. The Covingtons, especially twins Martha Wall Lockhart and Susan Gathings Houston, David and Mary Simmons Covington and Mary and Thomas Bickett (my grandparents and great aunts and uncles) answered the call for help whenever and from wherever it came.

Rosa was a freshman in high school when her mother died, leaving six children to be cared for. Rosa spent a good many of her teenage years with the family of Annie Bickett Ashcraft, her mother Maggie's first cousin. Rosa was a family-minded woman, always close to her great aunt Martha, as well as to her grandmother Susan. In fact Rosa closely identified with her Covington kin, naming her firstborn daughter Annie Bickett after Cousin Annie.

Rosa and Mother, first cousins once removed, were about the same age. Rosa always liked me and my sisters, but she and Dowd could never get along. Rosa thought Dowd Secrest was a crude, vulgar man. She could "never understand why Lessie married him." Rosa, married to Carl Parker, was a capable woman, a schoolteacher and administrator, and a yellow dog Democrat who enjoyed dabbling in politics and public service.

Her sister Martha, Mrs. Luther Hodges, was First Lady of North Carolina 1954-61. Among the six sisters Rosa and Martha were the closest. When Rosa lost her husband and soon thereafter had to place her younger daughter in a nursing home with a paralytic condition, she had a nervous breakdown. Martha and Luther were a great help to her during this troubled period despite their official obligations in the Governor's Mansion in Raleigh, encouraging her to stay with them while she received psychiatric treatment on an ambulatory basis from South wing at UNC Memorial Hospital.

Daddy thought Rosa was bossy and abrasive. On one occasion he asked her: "Rosa, how do you do it? How can you keep Carl's tail measured and kept under your doorstep?" To which Rosa, bristling and rising to the bait, replied, "Mr. Secrest, that is a very offensive remark and entirely untrue."

Daddy continued, "Parker waits on you hand and foot and gives you whatever you want and he can't afford." Then rising beyond the occasion, he added, "allowing all of you in these hard times to ride on rubber and fart through silk."

"Dowd," Rosa replied, red-faced and dropping the courtesy title, "you're a crude, unrefined man. You're no gentleman." Reduced to repeating her familiar opinion, "What on earth Lessie ever saw in you, and why she ever consented to marry you, I'll never understand," she drove off in a huff with Daddy's laughter ringing in her ears. But Rosa was a forgiving soul and Daddy, who always liked women who stood up to him, had a sneaking admiration for Rosa.

Not many months had passed before Rosa, according to Daddy, dropped by Broadacre again. She and Carl and their three children had lived for many years in Albemarle, some forty miles from Monroe. Carl and the children seldom accompanied Rosa on her visits to see Lessie and "Cuz Nannie," as we all called Annie.

If we weren't home, Rosa felt free to use the facilities. Hardly anyone in the early 1930s locked their doors when they were away. On our return home from Lake Junaluska, after one of Daddy's hurried and harried weekend "vacations," we found a note in the front door from Rosa. She was sorry to have missed us, sent her love, and hoped to come back soon. It was late in the day and, ready for a quick jigger or two of bootleg whiskey, Daddy hurried for the bathroom—the only place Mother allowed strong drink to be consumed.

He soon charged out, denouncing "Rosa's odor." "She always uses our bathroom, and she never raises the window afterwards," he complained, loudly and bitterly. "And the next time she comes, I'm going to tell her," he vowed.

Mother replied, "Mr. Secrest, do lower your voice, and don't you dare ever mention such a thing to Rosa, or to Cuz Nannie, either. Why do you go out of your way to misbehave for them?"

He denied that he did, adding ungraciously that "Cuz Nannie," whose "illustrious brother" was North Carolina's wartime governor, always managed to visit Lessie just at suppertime. Good as his word, Daddy told Rosa the next time she visited Broadacre please to remember to raise the window, received as many insults in return as he clearly deserved, and watched Rosa drive off in high dudgeon after telling Lessie again what a fool she'd been to marry Dowd Secrest.

Whether Lessie had been a fool to marry Dowd or vice-versa was a matter of opinion. Despite Rosa's view, life at Broadacre contained as much love, laughter and general gaiety as mood swings and conflicts. Mother's life was filled and largely fulfilled with community projects, church work, women's club activities, family, bridge, travel and entertaining. Daddy's was largely filled and fulfilled with work, at several simultaneous enterprises but always, and above all else, by supervision of his beloved farms. Before I was 11, Daddy had long ceased to be a working farmer. I never saw him with hammer or saw in his hands. I never saw him hitch up a wagon, or plow a furrow, milk a cow, or operate a tractor. A handyman around the house, he definitely never was.

But I guess he knew how to do all these things and to supervise others. His farms were mechanized early on, his cows vaccinated against tuberculosis, and his feed and seed the best to be had, but the back-breaking reality of picking cotton and bone-wearing job of grain production and the general soul-searing life of a tenant farmer, cropping on shares, were things Daddy either did not know or had long forgotten.

Instead of doing manual labor together, he and I would get into one of his new Buick demonstrator cars and ride along bumpy country roads, dirt paths, and through rutted fields on inspection tours. He'd stop and converse with some farmer called up from the fields by an imperious honk of the horn. As I grew older and more averse to hard work with Heath around the barn and crib at Broadacre, I said to Mother and my visiting aunts one day, "When I grow up, I want to become a ride-around farmer like Daddy."

For some reason they thought this was a very funny remark, revealing a trenchant observation of which I was unaware. But the remark was relayed to Dowd by his wife and sisters-in-law, who teased him unrelentingly.

Brack Craven and I agreed on that aspect of country life. Brack's father, Uncle Jim, was a land-owner in Union and Anson Counties as well as a Methodist preacher. In 1935 he was pastor of the Myers Park Methodist Church, as well as a presiding elder. He and his brother-in-law Dowd Secrest were good friends.

Dowd was a reluctant but faithful churchgoer. At one time he served as chairman of the Board of Stewards of Monroe's Central Methodist Church, an architectural jewel and twin of the Union County Courthouse just across the street from the Secrest Drug and Feed and Seed Store. Dowd was also a generous contributor to the church. Unlike Lessie and Jim, he was not interested in theology or church history, but he and Uncle Jim loved to ride around their farms and Jim, whose holdings were far less extensive, listened to Dowd's advice about agriculture. Brack and I would occasionally go with them, both uninterested in and ignorant of the economics involved.

Kenneth Goodson, a protégé of Uncle Jim and young Methodist minister himself, often came along. Goodson later made a name for himself in the church hierarchy, becoming a bishop in Alabama and later in North Carolina. Thirty years later I had occasion to call on Goodson for help when negotiating a civil-rights dispute in Alabama, involving Gov. George Wallace. Goodson had been a regular in the bathroom drinking routine with Daddy, Uncle Jim, Cyclone Mac and me during Prohibition days. At age seven I was served only ginger ale, but would imitate the men, tossing back my shot and going, "Ahhh!" like they did.

160

Brack, imitating his father, one day got out of the car, put his hands above his eyes to shield them from the July sun and peered all around, finally calling out, "Sam, where's the cotton!" Then he shook with laughter. As he climbed back into the big town car Uncle Jim was driving, Brack declared, "That's all Daddy knows or really cares about farming. And me too." We both thought it was okay to have other people do your work for you as long as we could remain just "ride-around-farmers;" the proper term of course was "gentleman farmer." But my increased resistance to farm work as I became a teenager did not result in release from such duties.

Mother and Daddy, despite their differences, seemed to enjoy a social life together, sharing friends and whatever else a small county seat town had to offer. Their best friends were Fred and Kathryn McDowell Huntley, major stockholders in the Henderson Rolling Mill, the only flour mill in town.

Hargrove and Kelly Bess Bowles were other good friends. They had four children. Hargrove's father had been a Methodist minister. Hargrove himself was a banker. Their four children were John, Hargrove Jr. nicknamed "Skipper," James, and Richard.

The Bowles family lived across from the Huntleys on Maurice Street, having moved from their first house on Hayne Street next door to Aunt Eve and Aunt May. Mother, Kelly Bess and Kathryn were all close friends. For reasons never revealed to me, Kathryn and Kelly Bess fell out, and each would pour into Mother's ear the latest dreadful things about the other. Mother, a peacemaker at heart, remained close to both of them.

"Lessie, listen to me. Your friend Kathryn is a cheat and a liar," Kelly Bess declared. "And she's as tight as the bark on a tree. She underpays her help in order to inflate her unearned bonuses." She wasn't through but Mother simply said, "No, Kelly Bess, I really don't think Kathryn is dishonest."

And Kathryn confronted Lessie with her suspicions: "Your friend Kelly Bess is on drugs, Lessie."

"Why on earth do you say that?" Lessie asked. "I've never seen any such sign."

"Oh, Lessie, do wake up and look around you. You always think the best of everybody, but everybody isn't either sweet or sick and deprived. Some people are just plain mean. And self-indulgent. Look how Kelly Bess is always rubbing her nose, practically wipes it off her face. Look how she's always sniffing up. I tell you, that woman is on cocaine."

"No, Kathryn. I'm quite sure Kelly Bess is not a drug addict," Mother replied and tried to change the subject.

Kelly Bess's husband Hargrove was a gentle man of fine character and strong principles, never much interested in money. But one day in 1933 he came into the Secrest Drug Store and begged Daddy for a job. His bank had gone bankrupt, and he had lost most of what little he had.

"I'll be glad to do anything, Dowd," Hargrove pleaded. "Help Mr. Starnes in the seed store, sweep out the place, work behind the drugstore fountain." Daddy, his own head barely above water, had to tell Hargrove he really didn't have anything for his friend to do.

Hargrove had a cousin who continued to work at the flour mill for Kathryn Huntley after her husband Fred died unexpectedly in the summer of 1935. Aunt Kathryn, a firm, decisive woman when holding the business reins, was always complaining about her chief assistant Bowles, so maybe that was the cause of her feud with Kelly Bess.

Kelly Bess didn't share her husband's indifference to money. She had a rich, unmarried uncle in Greensboro to whom she paid close attention, and she often told her sons, according to Mother, that they should marry well.

" It's just as easy to love a rich girl as a poor one," Kelly Bess was quoted. Brack used to say that to me, too. It doesn't always work out that way, but, again, sometimes it does.

The Bowles children were smart. Skipper, a classmate and friend of Lil's, was not especially talented academically, but he had common sense, business acumen and a way with people that spelled future success.

After college and World War II, Skipper married a wealthy young woman from Gastonia, whose father's wholesale grocery business was subsequently merged into the Winn-Dixie supermarket chain. Skipper helped to manage the family business and rose high among the ranks of corporate leaders and civic-minded citizens who helped build and develop Greensboro and eventually North Carolina and its institutions after World War II. Chapel Hill has a Skipper Bowles building in the medical complex of the University and a Skipper Bowles Road leading down to the Dean Dome, where Skipper's beloved Tar Heels play ACC world-class basketball. Skipper led the campaign to finance the sports complex.

Skipper and his wife had several children, including Erskine Bowles, who served as President Bill Clinton's White House Chief of Staff and in 2002 sought office as U.S. Senator from North Carolina. He was beaten by Elizabeth Dole, former Secretary of Labor and Transportation under

Presidents Reagan and Bush and later head of the American Red Cross. She graduated from Duke University fifteen years after her brother John Hanford and I graduated in the early 1940s.

Erskine married an heir to the Springs' textile fortune, his grandfather-in-law being the fabled Elliot White Springs of Lancaster, South Carolina. So Kelly Bess's ambitions for her sons were realized. They all became rich, richer, richest. In 2000, Erskine Bowles' family fortune was estimated at between $900 million and $2 billion. Erskine's defeat by Elizabeth did not end his political ambitions. He is running for Senator John Edwards' (D. NC) seat in 2004.

Hargrove and Kelly Bess's older son John was one year younger than Mary Covington. They were good friends. Mother was at heart a matchmaker, but like Bill Finlater before him, John started off liking Mary Cov and wound up liking Mother even more. That may have irritated my sister considerably, but not for any love lost over John. Mary C. really regarded him as another brother or cousin, like me, Brack, Claude, or Earle. Her interests lay elsewhere.

John, after naval service in World War II, rapidly rose to the top of the pharmaceutical corporate world, becoming chairman of both national and international boards of Rexall Drug Stores. He too married a rich girl, heiress to the Holland Furnace Company in Michigan.

In 1955 Mother stopped off in Los Angeles to catch a slow boat to Tokyo to visit an old college friend whose husband now served in the Japanese Diet. John Bowles met her at the airport with a huge bouquet of flowers and a bottle of champagne. Nothing was ever too good for Miss Lessie in John Bowles' eyes. And Mother, the teetotaler, thought the champagne was delicious.

The other two Bowles boys made Greensboro home. James, born with a mild mental disability, later married, worked in the family business, and died without issue in 1986. Richard, a year younger than I, married a girl from Sanford with the substantial name of Horner. He has enjoyed a successful personal and professional life and been one of Greensboro's municipal movers and shakers, as well as an active supporter of the greater University of North Carolina.

But Skipper is the one people still remember when they hear the Bowles name. And Monroe, not Greensboro, is where the family originated. Hargrove senior and Kelly Bess started their married life there, all four of their boys were born and raised there, and John and Skipper graduated from Monroe High School. John had completed college before Hargrove Sr. and Kelly Bess moved to Greensboro in 1937, and Skipper was by then a student at UNC-Chapel Hill.

So when Skipper ran for governor of North Carolina on the Democratic ticket in 1972, we felt a native of Monroe was the candidate, not anybody from Greensboro. And Skipper would have been a shoo-in too that fall if it hadn't been a Republican year, with Governor Martin sliding in on Richard Nixon's coattails.

Skipper attended a Monroe High School reunion in June 1971 to honor Monroe's principal and founder of its first high school band, R. W. House. Jesse Helms called me about the reunion plans and sought my help in its organization.

Present with Jesse, future Republican candidate for U.S. Senate, were Skipper Bowles, soon a Democratic gubernatorial candidate; Henry Hall Wilson, former assistant to presidents Kennedy and Johnson, now head of the Chicago Board of Trade, and later an unsuccessful candidate himself for the U.S. Senate; and James (Bud) Nance, U.S. fleet admiral, who in the Reagan administration served as interim chief of the Joint Chiefs of Staff for one day and later emerged from retirement to become administrative assistant to Senator Helms.

Trailing considerably behind was Andrew McDowd Secrest, once a White House luncheon guest of JFK, a former Neiman fellow at Harvard, a former staffer of the Community Relations Service in the LBJ administration, and currently a candidate at age 46 for a doctorate in history from Duke University.

All of us were born, raised and educated in Monroe, North Carolina, and all were members of the "Monroe Mafia," now on a par with the "Shelby Gang" which generations earlier had dominated N.C. politics and been connected with Monroe through D. A. Covington, Walter Bickett and Mary Foote Simmons Covington.

But no matter how rich and famous a family may become, tragedy and irony often lie in wait. So it was with the Bowles clan. Kelly Bess developed a neurological disease and died fairly early in Greensboro. Skipper and one of his daughters later developed Lou Gehrig's disease and died, he in his sixties and she in her forties. Erskine and his family have to live in this fearful shadow.

Former President Jimmy Carter and First Lady Roselyn share a similar concern. Carter's father and several of his siblings died of pancreatic cancer. The Carter family are part of an NIH study to find causes and a cure for this dread disease. But the parents must feel concern for daughter

Amy and her brothers. And the Reagan family must live under the cloud of Alzheimer's Disease which claimed both President Ronald Reagan and his mother.

Of the hundred people at the reunion, only Jesse Helms achieved a long-lasting political career. And what a career! Jesse, elected in the fall of 1972 to the U.S. Senate, was the first Republican senator from North Carolina at least since Reconstruction. And when Jesse retired in January 2003, he had served longer than any other senator from the state, including my distant collateral kinsman Fernifold Simmons, who served from the turn of the century till the early 1930s.

Jesse has a closer connection to the Secrest family than he probably would care to acknowledge, since we were Yellow Dog Democrats and he, formerly one himself, had switched parties to become one of those new Southern Republicans. His marriage to Dorothy Coble has been a successful one, but his political success has not been due to her money. Jesse combined determination, ability, character, good luck and some negative campaigning to become and remain a winner.

To paraphrase the Great Emancipator, no elected official can be loved by all of the people all of the time. Helms, like FDR, whom he had at one time professed to admire, attracts the lightning. You either love him or hate him. I'm one of the few who, while often disagreeing with him, both on principle and in practice, neither love nor hate Jesse, but I do have a certain admiration for him. His greatest legacy may not be found so much in his service on the Senate Foreign Relations Committee as at Wingate University, once a little two-year Baptist junior college six miles from Monroe that he attended and which my grandfather Covington helped establish in the 1890s. Jesse established the Helms Center there which houses his state papers, and he has drawn national attention to the school.

Jesse is connected to the Secrests through his older brother Wriston's marriage to my first cousin Martha Hamilton, whose mother was my father's oldest and favorite sister, Bertha. In other words, my first cousin is Jesse's sister-in-law, and in the South that is kissing kin.

When Jesse's mother died some years after he had been elected to the U.S. Senate, his father married Ethel Blackwell. Ethel's first husband George had worked as a clerk in the Secrest Drug Store for what seems to me generations. I can still hear the harsh rasping in his chest when he laughed, an aftermath of his having been gassed in the battle of the Argonne in France in 1918.

165

Mr. Blackwell was a loyal, faithful servant of the Secrest family. His wife was a respected, pretty, good-natured woman who ran a beauty parlor in the basement of the store, washing, setting, and styling hair, polishing nails, and helping customers coordinate their makeup. Mr. and Mrs. Blackwell were what Mother would call "good, plain people" in an unconsciously condescending way. Lil and I, while very fond of them, would call them petit bourgeois. Mary C., less judgmental, would just call Ethel "a good egg" whom she liked.

There are Helmses and there are Helmses. Most of them were from German-English extraction. Some lived on original royal land-grants out in Union County. They were very prolific, and today's Monroe telephone book lists page after page of Helmses. Most used to be Democrats; I don't know about today. Aunt Matt (Martha) Secrest married a Helms—"Tip" Helms—who was once considered to be a good catch but turned out pretty much no-account. We blame him for G.W.

Jesse's father, "Mr. Jesse," was an agreeable, affable man about whom few people ever said a bad word. He served at one time or another as Monroe's fire chief and police chief. In a town the size of Monroe in the '20s and '30s, one might imagine what salary Helms commanded. He and Mrs. Helms raised two boys, Wriston and Jesse, and one girl. Again, the Covingtons would describe that Helms family as "good, plain people."

The elder Helms was a segregationist (what white people weren't in Piedmont North Carolina in the '20's and '30's?), but he wasn't a racist. Reports of his police brutality have been wildly exaggerated by Robert Williams, a black racist in Union County who later became a fugitive from justice and whose stories about white men prancing around naked before black women near Monroe's railroad depot were simply products of Williams' imagination. Responsible journalists and historians who reported such yarns in national publications and history books should have known better.

His son Jesse, the senator, has displayed, however, racist tendencies, judging by changing times and standards. He was slow to change his racial ideas and often used racist tactics to win elections. His spoken record up through 1968 reveals racist ideas and attitudes, much like those of his colleague, Sen. Strom Thurmond.

Aunt Eve might feel less charitable, as she never forgave Jesse for calling her nephew Brack "Ravin' Craven, that red judge from Asheville" for Brack's opposition to the Vietnam War. Lessie didn't appreciate it when Jesse also criticized me as a red-leaning editor from Cheraw, South Carolina. Earlier still, Aunt Isabel Wolfe—and all the rest of us—resented it when Helms played a key, and we thought underhanded, role in the defeat of Frank Porter Graham by Willis Smith in the 1950 United States Senatorial primary election. Aunt Isabel, Daddy's youngest sister, was a close friend of Mrs. Graham, a sister of Monroe's long-time Episcopal minister, Dr. Frederick Blount Drain, the pastor and across-the-street neighbor of the Wolfe family. His daughter Rebecca was a childhood friend in Monroe and remained a friend once we both moved to Chapel Hill.

That was when Jesse was a member of the Fourth Estate and later the conservative voice of WRAL-TV in Raleigh. But Jesse was a Monroe, not a Raleigh, product, and Monroe and Union County properly and proudly claim him as their own.

It's funny, though, the things you most clearly remember about celebrated people—things when they were still children themselves. The last time I saw Hargrove "Skipper" Bowles until after the war was mid-summer 1942, shortly before most of the young men of our generation were to ship out for service in World War Two. Skipper had come home from Greensboro to see old friends, including Lil, a public school classmate since first grade. He and Lil had been paired off as sweethearts in the third grade and had remained good friends, but not in a romantic way, ever since.

Hargrove had an enthusiastic, optimistic personality and the more he talked, the more animated he became. Though never feminine, he demonstrated a dramatic, almost girlish quality when he started to tell a story, playing all the roles as the characters came forward. On this particular hot summer day, as he and Lil sat on the front porch swing and I on a nearby chair, Skipper grew increasingly excited as he told some long, convoluted, no doubt embellished yarn about some crazy character that had done some outlandish thing.

"You know, Lil," Skipper declared, "I didn't know what to say or do. The guy was so funny! I declare, I think he must have been disarranged!"

Skipper was not a scholar nor a star English student. Lil's and my eyes met in an amused but indulgent acknowledgment of the malapropism. And that's the indelible image I retain of Skipper, despite many later memories and a full understanding of the man he became and of his important achievements.

I remember Jesse Helms in an equally unfair way. People do change and grow up, so why remember them in earlier, more impressionable years? I suspect most people remember others when they knew them best and retain these images regardless of later accomplishments.

Jesse as a mature adult cut a large and imposing figure and showed a remarkable amount of self-confidence and self-possession in the U.S. Senate. As a prepubescent kid and teenager, he didn't cut an imposing figure at all. I remember Jesse as a nice, decent, well-behaved youth, two years older than I. Far from being cool, he probably was considered by his peers square, something not prized then but which today I count to his credit. He was skinny, with large eyes sunk deep into their sockets, an unmuscular frame, and flat biceps. In the gym, guys in those days would be divided into burly and chicken legs; Jesse was definitely in the second category.

A member of Monroe's prize-winning marching band, Jesse played, of all instruments, the tuba, which wrapped itself around him, making him almost disappear as he staggered along under its weight; but he handled the instrument and the music to the satisfaction of the demanding band director, Principal W. H. House, whom Jesse revered.

At age 13, Jesse resembled E.T. (as in the movie) more than any other image that comes to mind. My cousin Martha Hamilton, three years older than Jesse, had a crush on a boy named John McDonald when Jesse was about fourteen. Jesse's older brother Wriston had a crush on Martha. Jesse at this stage in his life was something of a loner and perhaps lonely as well. He spent a lot of his time in Rowena Shute's Pastime Theater. When Martha and Lil happened to attend the same movie at the same time, they'd purposely sit behind Jesse and pick on him.

First, they'd put their knees against the back of Jesse's seat and bump him intermittently. Martha would occasionally lean over and yank his hair. Eventually Jesse would go out and report them to Miss Rowena, who'd send Pickett around to reprimand them. But as soon as Pickett disappeared, the torment would resume, depending on whether the movie entertained Martha and Lil, until Jesse, reduced to tears, would start to cry and place his tormentors on report again.

Then Lil and Martha would taunt him as a crybaby or tit-tat-teller. And that is the image I retain of Jesse when I knew him best—a crybaby and a tattletale. Today I think that Jesse was fully entitled to his rage and impotent tears and that the older female bullies should have been dismissed from the theater. I never pushed my knees against the back of Jesse's chair or yanked his hair, but I thought it was funny when Lil and Martha did and felt no sympathy for their victim.

But life is full of ironies. McDonald, Martha's fanciful flame, never gave her any encouragement, whereas Wriston, Jesse's older brother, persisted in wooing and pursuing her until her interest was piqued. They were married several years later and named a daughter Jesse.

# 22. Miz Thompson and Cyclone Mack

The front hall at Broadacre was a huge room, extending across the entire width of the house. On its walls hung a large number of pictures, which Mother and her four sisters had brought back from the obligatory Grand Tours of Europe that refined young ladies of their day took before settling down to the grimmer aspects of reality, usually marriage and child rearing, or, if one were to remain unmarried, wearing the label of spinster and competing with the privileged sex in the business and professional world to earn a living.

There were pictures of London and the royal palaces during the celebration of Edward VII's accession to the throne, thus ending the Imperial era of Victoria's reign. Other drawings and sketches depicted the Grand Canal in Venice, the Roman Colosseum, the ruins of Pompeii and Herculaneum, scenes from the Holy Land, and a particularly memorable one of Mother and Aunt May astride camels before the Great Pyramid.

Mother described to me her feelings upon first sighting the Bay of Naples and understanding the saying, "See Naples and die." She also regaled her children with stories about her adventures in Italy and France in August of 1914. She caught one of the last available taxicabs in Paris to see the Louvre Museum, just as all drivers were being called upon to rush troops up to the front for the First Battle of the Marne. Mother was a good storyteller, and she breathed life into all these pictures.

But the great hall at Broadacre was dominated by two large oil paintings enclosed in gilt-edged frames. One was the portrait of a man who resembled Grover Cleveland; the other was of a handsome, younger man with clear dark eyes and a quizzical expression. From my earliest days, I had been told that they were paintings of my grandfather David Anderson Covington II and his son David III—"Brother" to his devoted sisters.

The Covington men were short-lived. Grandfather David had died in 1898 at 45 when Mother was six years old. Uncle David was only 24 when the Grim Reaper called for him in 1908, Mother being then sixteen.

Great Uncle James Covington, David II's younger brother and at one time mayor of Monroe, died at age 42, leaving no children. His wife was the former Elizabeth Andrews, my beloved Aunt Lizzie. She lived to a ripe old age and was at one time high school librarian, though she was no better at maintaining discipline there than Miss Inez Flow had been in kindergarten. My great-grandfather, David Anderson Covington I, who was born in Rockingham, N. C., and lived his early adult years in Cheraw, S.C., survived to the ripe old age of 59.

All of these short-lived Covington men were, however, apparently early bloomers, who achieved quite a lot in the little time allotted to them. They represented an unrealized promise to their abandoned and bereft women, who sought to perpetuate their legacies to subsequent generations through carefully selected and edited memories.

Great-grandfather David Anderson Covington was one of the original founders of Union County and its county seat, Monroe. Union County was carved out of western Anson and eastern Mecklenburg counties in 1839-40. David owned much of the land incorporated within the original city limits of Monroe.

The Covingtons were landed gentry, controlling all the territory from where the Ellen Fitzgerald Hospital later stood in downtown Monroe on Hayne Street to the point where Hayne and Church Streets merged, several miles south of the courthouse square, to form Wolf Pond Road leading to the South Carolina line.

They were also professional folk in the fields of law, education, and politics. They, their descendents and relatives served over the years as mayor, county commissioner, judge of the original Union County Courts, and as members of boards that founded, first, Wake Forest College in 1834, Old Trinity College in Randolph County in 1838, later to become Duke University, and Wingate Junior College in 1896.

David Anderson Covington II, attorney, landowner, and businessman, also served as federal prosecutor for the Western District of North Carolina, where it is said that he never lost a case, and as a Superior Court Judge. He was named nearly sixty years after his death by the State magazine as one of the top ten attorneys in North Carolina. His nephew, Governor

Walter Bickett of Monroe, later of Louisburg, and Democratic governor from 1916-20, was often referred to as "a poor man's David Anderson Covington II."

He was nominated for the United States Senate and led in the first election by a large margin, only to be defeated by one vote in the runoff when one of his opponents threw his vote to another candidate. In the late 19th century, before senators were elected by popular vote, candidates were selected instead by the N.C. General Assembly.

A Covington was "somebody in particular." They all, like their Simmons in-laws, "recommended themselves highly." The women were expected to marry well, which some did, and some, conspicuously, did not. It probably irritated my father that my sisters and I were raised with such reverence for our male Covington ancestors, men who, perhaps because we had never known them personally, gradually attained mythical status for us. My grandfather and his son had six women—my grandmother, mother, and four aunts—devoted to keeping their bright flame burning in the minds of their descendants.

In this endeavor, they were successful. Aunt Sue named one of her sons David and tried to persuade him to change his last name from Fowler to Covington so that the family name could be carried on. Her son refused but did become, like his uncle David, a renowned scholar of the classics, having devoted his professional life to finding the missing literary key between Beowulf and Piers Plowman. To this day, international medieval scholars beat their way to his retired doorstep in Seattle to learn more about the literature and history of that period, as well as folklore and religion. Aunt Sue's love of "Brother" and her reverence for the Covington family perhaps played a role in her son David's career choice, as did his own father, Earle Fowler, himself a professor of English at Chicago and Louisville and a personal friend of David III.

My deceased twin brother was christened David, and I have never been sure that the Covington women, Mother included, were not disappointed that it was I, named Andrew McDowd Secrest after my father, who lived instead of David Covington Secrest, named after all those prior Davids in the direct family tree. When my wife and I had a son, we too named him David, partly from family fealty but, who knows, perhaps by this time, partly out of habit, too.

So it was with great surprise that my sisters and I discovered one Sunday in late January 1933, while the country was locked deep in the Great Depression and waiting in hope for the inauguration of FDR, that at least one of these exalted men had had feet of clay.

That Sunday was not different from any other except that James Braxton Craven, pastor of Myers Park Methodist Church in Charlotte, presiding elder of our district, was to be guest speaker at Central Methodist Church in Monroe.

I didn't like Uncle Jim very much. He was an in-law, married to my mother's much older sister Katherine. If truth be known, I wasn't any too crazy about her either. Aunt Katherine failed to make much over me, give me lots of presents on my birthdays and Christmas, and in general spoil me extravagantly, as did my two maiden aunts, and, to a lesser extent, Mother and my older sisters. No, neither Aunt Katherine nor Uncle Jim believed in over-praising children. My father apparently agreed with the Cravens, for he would often say, "Leave the boy alone. He's here, and we just have to put up with him."

Aunt Katherine was not demonstrative and seemed sort of sad, despite the fact that she was a compulsive talker who darted from one subject to another, pausing just long enough to catch her breath and to hold up her hand—just as Great Uncle Henry Simmons used to do—to prevent any interruption. Being the oldest of five sisters, she had talking rights, I guess, based on seniority. I had to become considerably older before I understood and could empathize with that sadness I saw in her and come to know the fine, strong character she really was, and admit, as well, that I had also misjudged Uncle Jim.

"Spiritual" in those days was the last word that I would have used to describe Uncle Jim. I avoided him because he seemed brusque and impatient and made me feel inadequate and immature. I had never really been taught how to tie my necktie or use my knife and fork properly.

"C'mon, Mac," Uncle Jim would say, "don't be such a baby. Now here's how you do it." And he would make me hold the dinner utensils just so and cut my own meat. He would also, roughly and impatiently, place my tie beneath my shirt collar and demonstrate how to loop one end over the other, move it up, through and down until a proper knot appeared, always much too tight around my neck.

On that particular Sunday, the only good thing I could say about Uncle Jim was that he wouldn't preach long. "Fifteen to twenty minutes is about the attention span of a congregation," he told my father. "If you haven't made your point by then, you've lost your audience."

Uncle Jim and Daddy had little in common beyond a few points: they had married sisters and shared a love of the land; neither believed in spoiling or over-praising his children or his wife, and both enjoyed a good stiff drink after the Sunday sermon.

After church and just before Sunday dinner, Uncle Jim, Daddy, and I would go to the bathroom lavatory, where my father would bring out three glasses and a mason jar of moonshine whiskey known as "white lightning." He would pour out about four ounces into each of two glasses. Then he and Uncle Jim would toss it down quickly, chasing it with tap water, and go, "ahhhhh," as the burning liquid found its way into their expansive bay windows. Then Daddy would pour some ginger ale into the other glass which, imitating them, I would toss neatly down and go, "ahhhhh," and wait for their approving laughter. Maybe I was a baby about neckties and dinnerware, but I felt I had earned Big Boy status here.

Prohibition was soon to be repealed with the election of Roosevelt, but alcohol would remain prohibited in "dry" North Carolina. Bootleg, or moonshine, whiskey was still the only kind you could get. In addition to being illegal, it was socially unseemly, Mother thought, to serve strong drink. Women of her time, age, and station in Monroe did not approve. The fact that strong drink and over-indulgence may have shortened the lives of her idealized ancestors had also set her dead against it.

So if her husband and her Methodist preacher brother-in-law were to drink, they would have to go to the bathroom to do so, as hurriedly and uncomfortably as possible. She did not like my being in on the action, even with ginger ale, but there were some things she just couldn't help.

The Methodist Church in the 1930s in the South was still fairly fundamentalist, if not primitive, and Monroe's Central Methodist Church, while more sedate and refined than its country cousins, had its own "Amen Corner" up front, consisting largely of elderly white men, some even veterans of the Civil War and all of them highly vocal.

The church frequently held revival services, with special guest speakers, in which members were urged, when the spirit moved them, to come forward, kneel at the altar rail and confess their sins (as silently or as loudly as they pleased). As the congregation surged forward, the organ boomed out such old standbys as "Washed in the Blood of the Lamb,"

"Love Lifted Me," and "Power! Power! Wonder Working Power!" Young to aging spinsters were prominent among these repentant sinners. One young woman in her mid-30s was so swept away by the tidal waves of emotion that she made eight pilgrimages toward salvation in one evening. Lil and I counted them and laughed out loud, though we tried to stifle the sounds and pretended to be crying.

The church also participated in week-long Camp Meetings, during which entire families would live in tents and permanent lean-to's and enjoy fellowship, singing, prayers and preaching, liberally intertwined with gossip, neighborly visitations and, sometimes, assignations. One time a town official was found in a compromising position with his neighbor's wife, whom he was supposed not to covet, and on another, a visiting Baptist minister was caught consorting with a madam of a Charlotte bordello, a good-hearted farm woman with Union County roots who had become a highly successful businesswoman in the world's oldest profession in the Queen City.

Camp meetings had a lengthy local history, extending to a time long before my day or that of my parents. The Covingtons and the Secrests usually disdained such carrying-on. But Mother, when she was about 90 years old, confided in me that one of the more prominent social arbiters in an earlier Monroe had as a young girl attended such events enthusiastically. She eventually acquired the nickname of "Picnic Drawers" because of the frequency and rapidity with which she dropped them, always in the company of some boyfriend, when they both apparently became sufficiently infused with the holy spirit.

As respectable and conservative as Monroe's Central Methodist Church had become by the 1930s, it would still sponsor visiting evangelists, one such being "Cyclone Mack," regionally known for his dynamic, blustering, theological theatrics. He reminded me, in retrospect, of Sinclair Lewis's Elmer Gantry or the real-life Billy Sunday. My father, although serving as Chairman of the Board of Stewards, regarded such religious excess as Chatauqua or theater, if not burlesque. He never hit the sawdust trail to confess his sins, nor did Mother, not because they didn't have any but because they both felt their sins were their own business and that of the Lord but certainly no one else's.

Both Daddy and Uncle Jim thought people like Cyclone Mack were good entertainment as well as interesting Southern sociological specimens. Whenever the evangelist swept into town, Daddy would invite him over for Sunday dinner and for the pre-dinner drink of bootleg booze with Uncle

Jim and me. With Cyclone Mack, one drink led to another, and often he would rant and rave against the evils of demon rum from the pulpit to a rapt Sunday evening audience, fully tanked himself.

Mother and her more theologically restrained kin disapproved of these "overly emotional Methodist ministers" and their moral double standards, if not downright hypocrisy, but to Daddy and Uncle Jim it was all fun and games, and in this area Mother could exert no control over her husband, her son, or her Methodist preacher brother-in-law.

As I lay under the covers, dreading to get up, on that last Sunday in January 1933, Heath came into the room with an armload of kindling and stove wood to start a fire in the grate. "Pretty cold out there this morning," announced the voice that only a handful of people on the planet could translate. Heath was then about twenty-one years old and tongue-tied. Because he could not speak clearly, most people assumed he was mentally deficient, but he wasn't—far from it.

As I grew older, I discovered that Heath had quite an active social life and was very popular with girls of his own age and class, who didn't seem to mind his speech impediment at all. I later learned more about some aspects of life—and some facts of life—from Heath, his friend Murray and my two closest black friends, Lindsay and Doll, Jr. than I did from my parents, siblings, or classmates, or from what I observed of the social behavior of Broadacre's abundant animal population.

Having heard Heath announce that it was cold outside, I asked my usual question, "Reckon it's going to snow today?" And Heath, knowing what I wanted to hear, replied, "I wouldn't be surprised. It's getting cloudy and smells like snow."

"Yeah, I bet," I thought to myself. "It looks like snow and it always rains." Rainy days and Sundays got me down, but today there was something else to dread. What was it? Oh, yes, Uncle Jim and Aunt Katherine, with son Brack, six years older than I, were coming to Sunday dinner, and I had to go to church to hear Uncle Jim preach, and, worst of all, this was the last Sunday in the month, which meant that Miz Thompson would be with us too.

To get from my bedroom to the bathroom, I had to go across that unheated, wide front hall, seeing my frosted breath at every step. And I had to pass beneath Grandfather David's and Uncle David's portraits, sometimes feeling that they knew my every wicked thought and bad deed.

Over-sensitized to their premature deaths and convinced of their perfection, often at night I felt as if I were praying to them rather than to God. They certainly seemed more real to me, as God has always been a nebulous figure I had trouble much believing in.

When I was even younger, I often confused Jesus with Santa Claus, as both were celebrated on the same day. I preferred Santa to Jesus, as he was obviously more generous. When I learned that Santa Claus was a mythical character about the same time I learned the facts of life, I began also to doubt all those Biblical tales of divine miracles, leaving me something of a "Doubting Thomas." To Mother it seemed only three perfect men had ever trod the earth: Jesus, Papa, and Brother, and not necessarily in that order. As I went past their pictures, I wondered if they would approve of my negative attitude towards Sundays in general and toward the approaching Sunday dinner in particular.

Mary Covington, seventeen, home for the weekend from Meredith College, and Lil, thirteen, and I shared a curiosity and an embarrassment about Miz Thompson. I'd known her, I suppose, since I was born, but what did I know about her? Where did she live? Where did she come from? Did she have a family of her own? Why did she speak, dress, and act so differently from my mother and aunts? And why did Daddy, usually so casual around visitors, accord her so much deference?

Mother was painfully polite to her, yet formal, somewhat distant, not at all her usual spontaneous self. The same seemed true of Aunt Eve, Aunt May, Aunt Sue, and Aunt Katherine. There had to be some history about this plain country woman, a sort with whom we ordinarily would not associate.

On this particular Sunday, the family had attended church as usual. Uncle Jim had delivered his brief sermon; he, Daddy, and I had completed our lavatory ritual; and now we gathered in the dining room for Sunday dinner, with Miz Thompson the guest of honor. Aunt Eve and Aunt May, home from Salem College and Duke University, joined Mother, Daddy, Uncle Jim, Aunt Katherine and Brack, Mary Covington, Lil, and me as we sat down at the dinner table. Only Aunt Susie and her family from Louisville were missing from the family reunion.

The dining room at Broadacre was itself a long way from the kitchen, originally separated from the main house as a safety precaution. There was a dinner bell placed under the table beneath the carpet, within leg reach of the person occupying the host chair, to notify the servants when it was time to serve dinner.

As we seated ourselves, in walked Miz Thompson, escorted by Gene Watts. Dressed in a dark blue silk dress, Miz Thompson, in her customary, self-possessed manner, took her place beside Mother, who presided at the head of the table. "Good afternoon, Lessie," Miz Thompson said to Mother, whom most other people called "Miss Lessie."

"How do you do, Dowd?" she asked of my father, whom nearly everyone, including his own wife, called Mr. Secrest. She greeted my aunts in the same familiar way—Kate, May, Eve—and then spoke in turn to each of the children; she always called me "Mackie." We dutifully returned her greetings, and the group turned to small talk until Mother placed her foot on the bell and dinner was served.

Miz Thompson had always seemed old to me. She was then perhaps sixty, older by twenty years than Mother, the youngest Covington girl, and by seven years than Aunt Katherine, the oldest. Her speech placed her as a country woman. Her rough hands indicated a life of hard farm work. She flattened her vowels, especially the letter "I," much as some people still do out in the county or in some areas of Tennessee and Kentucky. Her pronunciation of words like white, ice, nice, and light, is easy to imitate but almost impossible to spell phonetically.

Being ill-mannered children at times, we mocked her speech. Lil, speaking to Mary Covington, asked, "Would you please pass the why-ut bread?" And Mary Covington, in reply, passed it on to me, "Mac, would you like some ny-us, ly-ut bread?"

And I replied, catching on to the game, "Why yes, please, I'd like some ny-us, ly-ut, why-ut bread." Soon, Brack joined in, asking me to please pass the ny-us, why-ut ry-us. Then the four children, three of them teenagers, including one in college, exploded into gales of laughter.

Miz Thompson, with a show of innate dignity, ignored the by-play, busying herself with eating the dinner in her own unique way, quickly and greedily. A tall, raw-boned woman, not thin but stringy, she had limp, greasy, pure white hair, cut short in a scraggly style across her brows, and rheumy light blue eyes.

As she started to speak, she coughed and wheezed, then sneezed loudly, spewing forth food particles and phlegm onto the linen table cloth. She casually ran the back of her hand across her nose and gave her wrist a quick flick. She then wiped her nose on the sleeve of her silk dress.

"You all will just have to excuse me," she said calmly with that same unyielding self-possession, "but I done forgot my snot rag." After a moment's stony silence, the room was filled with frantic adult conversation. But as Brack's, Lil's, Mary Covington's, and my eyes met, first in surprise, then in amusement, we once again burst into uncontrollable laughter.

Mother quickly excused herself, summoning her unrepentant children and bewildered nephew into the kitchen, far removed from Miz Thompson. "I've never been so mortified in my life," she hissed at us. "Don't you have any manners at all? The idea of mimicking Mrs. Thompson like that. Don't you have any consideration for other people's feelings? She noticed all right—she's no fool, you know." The more Mother talked, the madder she got.

"She can't help the way she talks, and the poor old thing can't change the way she was reared." Finally, resorting to the Bible and to Job's wife to express her feelings toward the children who were now very much in retreat, she cried. "Oh, I'm so angry I could curse God and die!" After a moment's hesitation, she ordered, "Now go back and get your plates and finish your dinner in the kitchen where you belong—that is, if the servants will have you."

After Mother returned to the dining room to salvage what she could of the Sunday dinner, Hattie, an elderly black woman who had been Mother's nursemaid, said, "You children ought not to treat your mother like that. Nor Miz Thompson, either. You ought to show some respect to your elders, if not your betters, seeing as how she's related and all...."

At first, I didn't understand what Hattie was saying, but later that afternoon, Mary Covington said to Lil, Brack, and me, "Have you really looked at Miz Thompson? Think about her. If she rearranged her hair and dressed better and didn't murder the King's English—and wipe her nose on her sleeve—who would she look like?"

Over several days the image grew. Lil noted that Miz Thompson had "the same Jimmy jaw as Aunt May. Her bottom teeth do sort of overlap her upper ones, don't they?" I offered that Miz Thompson was "about the same height as Mother, with the same blue eyes and white hair." All the Covington sisters had prematurely white hair. And we all agreed that now we could see in Miz Thompson that same sad expression that we observed in Aunt Katherine's eyes, and, sometimes, in Aunt May's and Mother's as well.

We looked at each other in dawning recognition of a truth as undeniable as it was unbelievable. We had heard, of course, of how Grandfather David had married twice, once when he was only eighteen years old. His wife Ellen Howie, herself only seventeen, had died eleven months after their marriage, leaving no children.

After Grandfather David was widowed, he went to Wake Forest College and read law up there. When he was 27 years old, he married Molly Foote Simmons and moved back to Monroe with his bride to re-establish himself in his community and to rear his family. So what, we wondered, had happened in the time between Ellen Howie and Molly Simmons?

Eventually, we confronted our mother and aunts with our circumstantial evidence, and they confirmed the story we had already pretty well surmised. Grandfather David, that most sainted of men, he of the gilt-framed portrait, had at age 22, while overseeing the Totten Place, taken up with an older, married tenant farm woman from one of Great Grandfather's farms. So that is where Miz Thompson came from! Later Mother defended her father on the grounds that men in that time and age did such things, adding that if Lord Randolph Churchill did it, contracting syphilis in the process, without harming Winston's career, she saw no need to apologize for her father.

In the repressive, hypercritical Victorian Age, with its sharply defined social classes and racial distinctions, such affairs were covered over, hushed up, denied; but a gentleman's code of honor also compelled the father to assume at least some financial responsibility for the mother and illegitimate baby. Miz Thompson already had a mother, a foster father, and half siblings with whom to make her home.

The child, with Covington blood in her veins, could never be legally recognized or socially accepted, but neither could she be completely disregarded. So Grandfather David gave Miz Thompson's mother and legal father money until his premature death, and his widow continued to meet the obligation, however shocked or wounded her puritanical nature may have been. When Grandmother Molly died in 1917, the Covington sisters assumed the role from a sense of justice and Christian charity as well as of "noblesse oblige." As Grandmother Molly may well have reminded Mother and her sisters, "Old sins cast long shadows."

My father, perhaps feeling that his father-in-law's indiscretions enhanced his own position, appeared glad to have Miz Thompson in the family Bible, so to speak, and willingly helped finance the continuing expense. Miz Thompson married early and had her own family, sharecroppers like her own mother and foster father, but she knew she was a Covington and let it be known that she considered herself Somebody in Particular.

Whatever became of Miz Thompson and her descendants—my half aunt and my half first cousins? Her visits became fewer and farther between. I do not remember ever seeing her again after 1935. Her own children were a generation older than Lessie's and Dowd's. We never saw or heard from any of them, and if Mother or Daddy did, they weren't talking.

And today, who knows? With the New Deal, World War II, and the economic and social changes that come with new technological revolutions, my Thompson kin may well be my economic and social superiors. There is a tide in the lives of families—here today, gone tomorrow. Up one or two generations, down the next. From shirt sleeves to shirt sleeves in three generations.

Even before the first David Covington, there were men and women known as "Silk Glove" Covingtons and others called "Hoe-Hand" Covingtons. This curious split in families is well described as a common Southern phenomenon in W.J. Cash's *Mind of the South,* which explodes the myths of Southern aristocracies that arose largely after the Confederate defeat in the Civil War. Without the right of inherited wealth, who can predict who will rise to the top, sink to the bottom, or just stay where they are?

There is often some family feeling of superiority—usually ill-founded—over one's in-laws. And in my own family I discovered, just as the Covingtons felt superior to the Secrests, to my father's continuing chagrin, so the Simmons of old Wake Forest felt superior to the Covingtons "in that little frontier town of Monroe, N.C." And the Footes of Warrenton, from whom my grandmother Molly partly sprang, felt superior to everybody, claiming a close association with George Washington.

Mary Covington, Lil, and I were, however, impressed by Miz Thompson and her story, and we would often call her up as an antidote to hearing too much about the deceased male Covingtons and their perfections. We lacked compassion for everybody involved, and found the whole episode and the distress it caused more funny than sad.

As Earle Fowler, Aunt Susie's oldest son, said to me years later, when he first heard of Miz Thompson, as Aunt Susie apparently never shared the story with him, "Well, what do you know? I'd always heard Grandfather David was like Caesar's wife, above suspicion. Even on his tombstone, the inscription proclaims, 'Behold! The Perfect Man.' Now, I feel better about my late and overly lamented Covington kin."

# 23. Family Secrets

Content with my friends and satisfied at school, the year 1934-35 passed by happily enough. I completed the sixth grade successfully, despite unintentionally insulting my teacher "Flossie" Redwine.

At last I had overcome a prolonged resistance to learn to recite the alphabet. I also abandoned my resentment at having to prove that I understood my native tongue and could write and read well without having to learn English grammar and diagram sentences. Even my understanding of math, always a challenge, improved.

Lil, barely 15 years old, remained an honor student in her junior year, making all A's and the National Honor Society. Mary C. had transferred to Duke University and was, as usual, ambivalent, loving it one day, hating it the next and keeping Aunt May upset. Things rocked along between Mother and Daddy as usual, at least I didn't notice much difference.

Things began to go downhill in the early summer of 1935 when Uncle Fred Huntley died of a sudden heart attack at age fifty-two. Fred and Kathryn were my parents' best friends, and Mother appeared to take his death unusually hard. Then in July word reached Broadacre that Uncle Earle Fowler had died unexpectedly at fifty-eight in Louisville.

Mother, Aunt May, Aunt Eve and Aunt Katherine Craven drove out for the funeral and brought the younger Fowler children back to North Carolina because Aunt Sue, their mother, was burdened with other obligations. David, near Lil's age, came to Monroe. Earle, a year older than Mary C., remained in summer school at Antioch College.

Daddy had never liked Uncle Earle, often ridiculing his professorial airs, although he did like and respect Aunt Sue. Mother noticed that Daddy treated David poorly, and she deeply resented it. Earle Fowler and her brother David, dead for nearly thirty years, had been good friends, and Mother interpreted Daddy's attitude as evidence of his dislike for her Covington kin in general.

"Boy," Daddy said to David one day at lunch, "You don't like our southern cooking, do you?" To Daddy anyone from Kentucky was a Yankee, especially from a city as far north as Louisville. "All you ever want to eat is peanut butter and jelly." He pronounced the word "jelly" to give it a decided Yankee accent and proceeded to mock David's speech. He also complained about our going to the movies all the time. Nothing we did—or didn't do—seemed to suit him, but that seemed normal behavior for Daddy those days and I thought little about it. Certainly he never expressed any sympathy to David for the loss of his father, paid much attention to him, or took him anywhere.

Mother became incensed when Daddy decided to take me and Doll Jr., but not David, to Myrtle Beach to see Locke Everette. David had never seen the Atlantic Ocean, and she felt that Dowd was slapping him in the face. Mother spoke openly of this to me but never said what she thought to her husband, turning her anger inward.

I didn't sense the slight. After all, David was nearer Lil's age than mine, and I detected no disappointment in my cousin when he wasn't included. Given Daddy's erratic behavior—irritable, unreasonable, and getting worse—I imagined everyone at home would be delighted to see us go.

We didn't stay long, as Daddy never liked to be away from Monroe for more than a couple of days. Doll and I had a great time. Doll had never seen the Atlantic Ocean, either, as the white tenant farmers didn't tolerate a little black boy as part of their annual entourage. Poor whites and black people competed both economically and socially and didn't seem to get along very well in the mid-1930s, especially in the presence of upper-class whites.

Locke had a place on the ocean front. It was all right for Doll to appear on the beach once it was clear he was there as the playmate of an approved white child. And anything Locke decreed was undisputed in Myrtle Beach. Locke favored Gothic decor and kept a human skull on the lamp table. At night he lit a candle inside it and read aloud his original poems that sounded much like Edgar Allan Poe's. I even learned a new word to add to my growing vocabulary—tintinnabulation—which I sprang on my classmates on our return, to their growing exasperation.

Doll was awed by the roar of the ocean, the pull of the tide, the crashing of the breakers as the waves rolled toward shore. He'd run out up to his knees as the water receded, and then flee toward shore as it returned farther up the beach. Doll couldn't swim, but he finally worked up the courage to go out to the breaking waves and eventually to trust Daddy and Locke to carry him out far beyond them, resting high on their shoulders.

Doll and I retired early after a fried fish dinner following a recitation by Locke. The lighted skull appeared to be listening and wore an evil grin. We started out in separate beds, but I later awoke with Doll clutching me around the waist. The growing sound of the sea at high tide and dreams of that human skull had awakened and frightened him; he felt safer by my side.

We went home the next day. In August Mother took David home. She remained in tight emotional control around us children, but not around her recently widowed sister, Aunt Susie later told me.

Pacing up and down restlessly in the Fowlers' living room in Louisville, Mother repeatedly asked, "What is the matter with him? Why does he act like that? What on earth am I going to do?" The questions were largely rhetorical, as she paid little attention to anything Aunt Susie had to say.

"How could he have treated David like that?" she cried. "Imagine leaving him home and taking Doll Jr. instead. You just don't know how cold and unfeeling he was about Earle and how mean and sarcastic he could be. Just hateful, hateful, hateful." And again she would pace restlessly, hands agitated, eyes darting here and there.

As she continued to pour out her frustration at her husband's unpredictable behavior, her growing fear of him, her disillusion with love, marriage, life itself, she talked incessantly and repetitively until the sky began to lighten. Her face was distorted, her voice shrill and hoarse by turns, her eyes as dry as stone. In her self-absorption Lessie had forgotten it was her sister who had recently been widowed, who had four children to raise, now as a single mother, with very little money.

Finally Aunt Sue raised her voice. "Lessie, get control of yourself. Surely you exaggerate. David had a wonderful three weeks in Monroe. Whatever Dowd's attitude, I can assure you it all went over my son's head. Dowd may have a strenuous personality, and can behave impossibly at times, but I'm sure he meant David no harm. And even if all you say is true, you have no reason to be so obsessed." She went on to say that as much as she loved her late husband and missed him, "no man who's ever lived could so negatively affect or rule my life the way you let Dowd rule yours."

But Aunt Susie, who was the most like Lessie in personality and often called her "my twin sister" although she was five years older, knew that Lessie was right now beyond help. Nothing anyone could say or do could shake her out of her growing obsession with her husband, her marriage, her family, her future, and her fears about her own failing health.

One day in mid-September 1935, a loving mother was there providing all the care and support a boy on the edge of puberty needs; the next day she was gone. No goodbyes, no explanations; no reassurances. I had just turned twelve; my mind flashed back to the time when I was four. Second verse, just like the first, but with no Miss Julia or Miss Olive. Only Glennie in the kitchen and Nina Mae cleaning upstairs and Heath and Murray out in the crib and over at the barn.

Mary C. told me that our mother had gone to a sanatorium in upstate New York for rest and recuperation. It was a psychiatric hospital in Clifton Springs, New York, near the Finger Lakes. "What's the matter with her?" I asked. "She seemed OK to me."

"Remember when Mother was away for about a year eight years ago?" Mary C. asked. "She was just down in the dumps and felt she couldn't cope. You were only four then so you can't really recall that, I guess."

Well, yes, I could. I remembered Miss Julia. And Miss Olive. And Vancy and Mary Garrison, and missing my lively, beautiful mother who brought light, laughter, and love into our lives. It seemed then as if she had been gone forever. "When will she come back? She'll be home for Christmas, won't she?"

"I sure hope so," my sister replied. "But no one really knows right now."

Mary C. and Aunt May returned to Duke that weekend, leaving Lil, now a senior in high school, me, and Daddy at home. Aunt Eve had already returned to Salem College. Surprisingly, I did not miss Mother much. God, Hitler, Mussolini, and Franco intervened to distract me from preoccupation with her depression and absence from hearth and home.

The winter of 1935-36 was unusually harsh. For me, still obsessed with snow, it was like a dream come true. The Piedmont of North Carolina had one snowstorm after another, starting on Mary C.'s twentieth birthday, December 23rd, 1935, and ending on Daddy's fifty-second, March 18th, 1936.

That same year Mussolini, with my approval, directed his Roman legions in the conquest of Ethiopia, and Hitler, to my dismay, remilitarized the Rhineland. For the past several years, it seemed to me, Broadacre itself had been a war zone. Children are ill-equipped to make objective evaluations about such matters, but Mary C., Lil and I blamed Daddy, whom we viewed as a bully seeking to control and dominate a free-spirited, often willful wife, who may also have been a "co-dependent enabler" as today's psychiatric jargon would have it. During those years Mother was viewed as the positive force, Daddy the negative one. So when the marriage fell apart and Lessie was shipped off to Clifton Springs, Dowd was blamed.

One night shortly before Thanksgiving, Lil and I were in the living room doing our homework. Arithmetic was proving problematic. If a train headed north at 66 miles an hour toward a destination 300 miles away, and another train headed south at 40 miles an hour toward its destination 430 miles distant, which train would reach its station first and how long would it take each train?

"This problem doesn't make any sense," I complained. "What has one train to do with the other?" The more often I read the problem, the more opaque it became. "Who cares about the trains?" I re-read it. Stubbornness took hold. Read it again. Anger flared. "I hate this stuff," I cried. "I hate Miss Strawhorn."

Lil came over to me. She read the problem. "It's simple. All you have to do—" Lil always found homework easy. Everything was simple to her. I slammed the math book shut and hurled it across the room. "I hate you! I hate you! I wish you were dead!" I shrieked, now out of control and crying bitterly.

Lil started to retort but thought better of it. Instead she put her arms around me and murmured, "There, there, you poor little boy. You just miss your mama, don't you?" And with that we both sobbed softly but long and bitterly, until we heard Daddy call out, "Lil, Mac, time to go to bed." So we dried our tears, washed up and went to bed. That is the last time a harsh word passed between Lil and me.

Children whose families become dysfunctional (a word never used in 1935) form close bonds. We became inseparable allies. Mary C. later borrowed the title of a movie, *These Three,* script by Lillian Hellman and starring Miriam Hopkins and Merle Oberon, to describe us. We had recently seen it at Rowena Shute's Pastime Theater. The Hayes Office, an organization formed in 1932 to censor film content, required that all hints of lesbianism be removed from the script, and the public's innocence was saved. The censorship was strict—no nudity, no profanity, no explicit sex, nothing that would violate traditional community values was allowed. Married couples occupied twin beds, exchanged only a chaste peck on the cheek goodnight.

All traces of sibling rivalry disappeared. It was all for one, one for all as we volunteered—or were we drafted?—into a three-and-a-half-year struggle between our parents and against clinical depression. We were faithfully assisted by Aunt May, Aunt Eve, Aunt Sue, Aunt Katherine, Aunt Bertha and Uncle Charlie, Aunt Kathryn Huntley, Mrs. R.B. Redwine, Aunt Mary, Aunt Isabel, Uncle Vann, Aunt Matt, Miss Ann Redwine, Cuz Nannie Ashcraft, Kelly Bess Bowles, and many others. Views and loyalties varied, but all were dedicated to helping out.

Daddy, widely respected in the community, felt and often in fact was misunderstood at home. Temperamentally ill-suited to deal with such a domestic situation, he handled it poorly. He was defensive, but needed to be understood, even if he had to burden his children with unsettling information. One evening after Christmas he sought to explain things to Mary C., Lil and me.

"Your mother is not entirely to blame for her illness," Daddy said.

"Tell me something I don't already know," was my inward reply.

"You see, your grandmother suffered from the same condition," Daddy continued. "It was diagnosed as involutional melancholia." Daddy now told us that Grandmother Molly fell ill in the spring of 1916 at the age of fifty-six. She had become obsessed with unnamed but unforgivable sins she believed she had committed: she had failed her family; she was an unworthy soul, condemned forever to be separated from her faith and her Lord and Savior.

So she was sent off eventually to a psychiatric hospital in Richmond, Virginia, where late one evening after rounds, her doctors found "Mrs. Covington considerably better." Before dawn, however, she had hanged herself with a belt affixed to some timber overhead. Unfathomably, she had done the deed on Mother's twenty-fifth birthday, September 16, 1917.

But Grandmother Molly's vulnerability to emotional instability had been foreshadowed. At 31, shortly after giving birth to Aunt Eve, she had been "indisposed" for months, a condition that today would be called a clinical post-partum depression. "Recidivism," given such tendencies, is not unusual but is unpredictable. Episodes can occur many years apart.

Although the death notice had appeared in the Richmond newspapers and the facts were generally known in Monroe, the local newspaper carried the cause of death as Bright's Disease, as reported by her family. Surely no one was fooled by such pretense, as that condition, the one from which both her husband David and his brother James had died years earlier, is both rare and never contagious.

Grandmother Molly had been a pillar of the Monroe community, a founder of the first women's book club, a faithful member of her church, a doer of good deeds to the rich and poor, and she was a Democrat. A graduate of Peace College, Raleigh, she was respected as a highly educated, cultivated Christian woman.

Widowed at thirty-eight, this woman managed to rear and educate six children and see them all through college. She oversaw her husband's estate, including the land and all the tenant farmers who lived thereon. She even assumed his obligation toward Miz Thompson. She took her daughters on tours abroad. Although connected to the Covingtons only by marriage, she maintained close ties with her sisters-in-law (many years older), and took in as part of her own family nieces, cousins, and others as circumstances required. A strong, accomplished, loving and giving woman, she accepted with steely determination the death of her only son at age twenty-four ten years after she lost her husband. She traveled to Chicago and nursed him for weeks until he succumbed to scarlet fever, aggravated by heart disease related to a defective valve.

Daddy also mentioned something about Mother's great-uncles on the Simmons side and their peculiarities. Molly was not the first to be affected by what Mary C., Lil and I later termed "the Simmons Curse," a tendency toward emotional and mental instability.

These revelations left a deep impression on Mary C., Lil and me. What were we to make of all this—that Mother would hang herself too and that we must all live under a shadow of inherited insanity? Good grief! What a time to share such family history. And was the danger limited to the Simmons line? Did the Covingtons—not to mention the Prices and Secrests—also have secrets to share?

It all sounded too much like those novels by the Bronte sisters. I shrugged and dismissed it from my mind, but like many other accumulating things, this new information lay submerged to be reviewed another day.

*Lessie seated in bay window at Broadacre, Monroe NC 1928.*

*Dowd, businessman and civic leader, Monroe 1930.*

*Mac with Lil, 1923.*

*Most happy fella, Mac at nine months.*

*Back: Lil & Cousin Martha; front: Doll, Jr. & Mac with pal Joe, behind Broadacre root cellar & storage building 1929.*

*The Saleeby-Hobeika family, our neighbors, 1926: Helen center front, her mother middle row right, her father back row left.*

*Mary Cov at Mars Hill College, summer 1930.*

*Hilda Outen and Mary Cov on front porch at Broadacre, 1931.*

*Dowd flanked by two tenant farmers in Houston Crossroads cotton field, Union County 1934.*

*Mac at 12 on eve of second separation from Mother, September 1935.*

*Portraits in front hall at Broadacre: my grandfather David A. Covington II and*

*David A. Covington III (Brother).*

*Lessie (left) and Aunt May in Egypt 1914. A large print hung also in the Broadacre front hall.*

*Moke Williams at Broadacre, 1949.*

*Philip Griffith (left) reinvented, with Mac,1979.*

*Bill Price (right) at the Copacabana with Mac, Tave, and Teensie, NYC 1944.*

*Mary Cov, a senior at Duke, 1936.*

*Dowd Secrest, 1936.*

197

# Part II

# Adolescence to Maturity

# 1936-1948

# 24. *Franco and the Flu*

Aunt May, instead of coming home for Christmas that year, elected to go to New York to check on her youngest sister. But Aunt Eve was on hand to keep our spirits bright, as was Mary C. Our aunts gave us multiple presents, gloriously wrapped, and the gifts were piled high beneath our Lebanon Cedar Christmas tree standing tall in its accustomed place in front of the big bay window.

Aunt Katherine and Uncle Jim invited the Secrest family and Aunt Eve to dinner at their home in Charlotte on Sunday, December 23. It was Mary Cov's twentieth birthday. Brack, in his freshman year at Duke, was on hand for the reunion. It was a cold and cloudy day. Daddy for some petulant reason declined to go, so Eve, an uneasy rider at best, directed him to turn over one of his newest Chevrolets for her to drive.

We got to Charlotte safely enough to hear Uncle Jim preach the sermon at Myers Park Methodist Church. Dinner followed at one o'clock. I kept peering hopefully out the window as the sky grew darker, the air damper, the breeze more brisk. Soon I saw something falling heavily into the nandina bushes, then heard a dry, sharp pinging—sleet! Soon it was falling in sheets, followed by large thick snowflakes.

"Oh, my goodness!" Aunt Eve exclaimed. "Look at that! We must leave at once." So immediately after an abbreviated meal, we all got into the car and she slowly made her way out of the driveway and onto the open road. In 1935, U.S.74 was a narrow, curvy, two-lane highway between Charlotte and Monroe 25 miles away. Since we were driving southeast, Aunt Eve reasoned hopefully, "Perhaps the snow will soon stop." Snowfalls didn't usually amount to much in the southern Piedmont.

Twelve miles later, just past Matthews, things became worse. As Aunt Eve approached the hill leading to the bridge, she failed to accelerate and the car slid backward. Unaccustomed to driving much and almost never in snow, Aunt Eve now pressed down too heavily on the accelerator. The wheels spun rapidly without traction. Down more firmly went the accelerator. Forward leapt the Chevrolet, as the back wheels began to skid. Having reached the apex of the hill and picking up speed as she drove down the other side, Aunt Eve slammed on the brakes. The car fish-tailed. The dizzy and frantic driver dropped the wheel and grabbed her stomach, gasping, "Ooh, ooh, ooh!" Soon we were in the ditch, shaken up but uninjured.

Some good Samaritans came along to push us out of the ditch and send us slip-sliding our way home. Aunt Eve crept along at a snail's pace, occasionally losing control as she forgot to turn in the direction of the skid, but we finally made it. "Why didn't Aunt Eve let me drive?" Mary C. later complained. "She's a lousy driver herself and practically killed us all. I could have made it with no trouble. I've been driving for four years. She's so bossy and thinks she knows it all."

The only casualty was Aunt Eve's well-being; she developed a weak pulse and erratic heartbeat, and Dr. Smith promptly put her to bed, where she remained until time to return to Salem College in early January.

Late Saturday afternoon, December 29, a much larger storm arrived. Daddy and I were at the motor company, ready to come home for supper when I, ever eagle-eyed for snow, spied the first flake. Soon you didn't have to look for it. The snow fell silent, fast, furious but to me beautiful, all through the night and well into the next afternoon. Daddy and I bonded on such occasions; his patience held out as I woke him every hour to peer out the window to be sure the snow was still falling.

What excitement! The next day we made snow ice cream. Heath and I took the wheels off the buggy, hitched up Lady, attached some bells to our sleigh, and rode all over town. Later Lil and Mary C. helped me build an enormous snowman. Later still, as the thermometer continued to drop, Heath made an igloo, pouring water over the snow to encase the structure in ice and provide insulation. Who could possibly miss his mother in the midst of such divine intervention?

Lessie, isolated in the sanitarium in the snow belt of the Empire State, was probably less enthusiastic about wintry weather. Things were wintry enough inside her soul. Aunt May had left Durham for Utica, New York,

December 19. We waited anxiously for a first-hand report. Mother had not written since she left in September, not even at Christmas. We looked for a letter from Aunt May or a phone call, but neither came. Now here it was the first week of January, and still no news.

At last the letter arrived, a full ten days after Aunt Eve had landed in bed from her trauma at the wheel. Daddy, feigning indifference, placed the letter on the mantelpiece and said, "We'll read that later on tonight after supper." No one complained, but after Dowd had left for the motor company, Aunt Eve spoke up. "Mary C., get May's letter and open it. It's addressed to Mr. Secrest and the family. He can read it later if that's his choice."

So Mary C. opened the letter and handed it to Aunt Eve, who proceeded to read it aloud. Lessie seemed somewhat better. She had regained most of her weight loss and was sleeping well. She showed interest in all of us, although she still declined to mention Dowd. She showed no inclination to come home right away, nor did the doctors recommend it. She did not like Clifton Springs and thought even less of the medical staff. Aunt May found the place comfortable and well equipped. The patients were well cared for in a protected environment. It was certainly no nineteenth century Bedlam, but neither was it on the cutting edge of psychological knowledge or investigation. It was essentially a rest home for the wealthy. The doctor would be in touch with Mr. Secrest soon. Aunt May recommended leaving Lessie where she was until spring, then seeking re-evaluation.

Soon Lil and I were left alone again with Daddy once more having to be "Mother and Daddy both." Mary C. had returned to Duke and Aunt Eve, having recovered from her hysterical heart attack, was back teaching at Salem College.

The first few months of the new year passed rapidly. Lil and I became latch-key kids, except that no one ever locked any doors. On Friday nights Daddy took us to dinner at the Gloucester Hotel, later renamed the Joffre Hotel, a late Victorian structure near the Seaboard Railroad Station, which catered to both passengers and workers. Even now I recall the food served there as the best I have ever tasted, although it was no doubt home-style Southern country cooking laced with fat.

One evening in early February Lil and I ate there without Daddy, since he had to attend a civic meeting elsewhere. A gentle snow started to fall as we ate. We finished in time to go to the Center Theater, operated by Margaret Hamilton's parents, to catch the seven o'clock feature. *Kind Lady* was a creepy little yarn about an elderly woman living alone in her London house, not unlike Broadacre, and threatened by pathological crooks—led by Basil Rathbone—seeking to keep her captive as they took over her life and her home.

Deliciously frightened, Lil and I raced in swirling snow after the movie to our dark and shuttered house about a mile away. But we had not been left alone. To be sure we were safe and sound, Daddy had arranged for Heath and his buddy Murray to "babysit" for us. How two single men, now in their early twenties, semi-literate and unimpeded by high moral standards, would guarantee our safety is not clear.

But not to worry. Lil, just turned Sweet Sixteen (and still romantically unkissed), was very much in charge. It was a Friday night and we could stay up as long as we pleased. What to do? Simple. Lil arranged Heath, Murray and me around the card table and proceeded to teach us how to play contract bridge. Since she had been trying to teach me since I was four, I could help her a little.

Daddy got home around midnight. Never patient with Mother and her bridge clubs, he hardly expected to find Heath, his favorite field hand, and Murray playing cards under Lil's strict direction. The men were pretty quick studies, too, and probably the only tenant farmers in Union County in the mid-1930s to learn all about Ely Culbertson.

I would have missed Mother more if General Franco had not started an insurrection in 1936 from northern Morocco and the Canary Islands against the Spanish Republican government, weakly clinging to power in Madrid since 1931. The Spanish conflict became a metaphor for all the political unrest in the western world. The military, backed by the Catholic hierarchy and the remnants of royalty, sought to overthrow the loyalists, representing the duly elected government. But soon it was conservative against liberal, reactionary against radical, orthodox against reform, church against state, with Fascists and Communists playing both ends against the middle. Domestic and state terrorism played their parts. Soon Mussolini and Hitler intervened, eager to promote Fascism in the Iberian Peninsula and to test their new fighters and bombers.

The Western democracies clung devoutly to neutrality and isolationism, which tilted the balance toward Franco. The battle raged for three years, with the bombing of Guernica—made famous by Pablo Picasso's mural—and bombardment of Barcelona the most infamous events. The war, later immortalized by Ernest Hemingway's *For Whom the Bell Tolls,* commanded my attention. Torn between my enthusiasm for Mussolini's empire-building in Africa and my sympathy for the Spanish loyalists as well as my dislike of the Nazis and growing enthusiasm for the Russian experiment in establishing "communism in one country," I spent little time missing my mama.

In 1936 and 1937, Hitler also was pursuing his program of anti-Semitism and rooting out Jews and their influence from German culture. Hitler enforced the Nuremburg laws, reoccupied the Ruhr, and remilitarized the Rhineland. In 1936 Hitler had not only left the League of Nations but also flouted the Versailles Treaty and was fast building the most powerful army and largest air force in Europe. These he tested daily in Spain.

The news flashes and daily reports from the world's diplomatic and military fronts were of far greater interest and excitement to me than any Southern Conference football or basketball game, although I liked those, too. But the little Friday afternoon football games at Monroe High School and the basketball games in the gymnasium seemed insignificant.

"Two-four-six-eight! Who do we appreciate?"

The cheers seemed absurd. The band formed recently by Principal House, which I had dutifully joined, paraded around the field as the crowd sang:

Monroe will shine tonight.
Monroe will shine!
Monroe will shine tonight.
Right down that line.
When the sun goes down
And the moon comes up
Monroe will shine!

As the song continued and I tootled on my clarinet, faking it half the time, and Jesse Helms tottered under the weight of his tuba, I thought, "How silly. How trivial, while mean men in Europe are threatening the world with war and aggression and killing hapless minorities who don't look or act as a tyrannical majority demands." But the cheering never stopped.

"One-two-three-four-five-six-seven;
All good children go to heaven.
When they get there they will say,
Monroe, Monroe any old day!"

I was definitely set apart. No one else my age knew or cared anything at all about Europe, wars or rumors of wars that, once unleashed, would surely reach our shores. I was not worried or frightened, just fascinated by unfolding events and thrilled by accounts of human conflict.

Daddy and I shared some of these interests, as did Uncle Charlie Hamilton. We also continued our trips to Charlotte for boxing, wrestling and rodeo exhibitions. Johnny Yow, Arbor Miller, and Oza Leach were three older Monroe youths on whom I developed crushes as they competed for the Golden Glove title.

When Joe Louis was unexpectedly knocked out by the German Max Schmelling in late 1935, I was crestfallen. How could such a thing have happened? But then Jesse Owens won the big race in Berlin at the summer Olympics. The nations of the world, having disgraced themselves by awarding the Games to Nazi Germany, now could enjoy the spectacle of an American black man beating a member of the master race. Hurray for Jesse! Hurray for the USA! And to hell with Hitler. My father and I were again briefly on common ground.

Eight years later I met my boxing hero in person. I had just arrived in New York's Pennsylvania Station in 1944 and had several hours to spend before returning to my ship in the Brooklyn Navy Yard. On my way through the waiting room I saw a familiar figure in an army uniform. Joe Louis, I thought, and moved closer to make sure. Yes, it was!

Never one to hold back, yet careful not to intrude upon the privacy of a celebrity who might be temperamental, I introduced myself. Joe wasn't touchy at all. An army corporal, he asked me, a navy ensign, to sit down on the bench with him.

Talk turned to his unexpected defeat by Schmelling, his third-round knock-out of Schmelling two years later, and speculation about his adversary today, serving somewhere in Europe with a German airborne unit. Joe too had a long wait until his train was due to take him down to Alabama.

"Want a beer?" I asked.

"Sure."

"Let's go over to the Café Rouge," I suggested. We talked for a couple of hours over several glasses of beer. The navy patrol twice came over to see why a commissioned officer was drinking with an army enlisted man, and a black one at that, but when they recognized Joe Louis, they left us alone. All except one army M.P. who was such a fan that he sat down and had a beer too. Joe, who lacked a formal education, was plenty smart, talked easily and shared stories of his beginnings in Alabama, his upbringing in Detroit, and his life as world boxing champion.

Twenty years later I met another world boxing champion. In September 1964 I had been sent on a racial conciliation mission to Fort Lauderdale. An outdoor theatre located in a black residential area was showing *Mondo Cane,* a sociological study of human behavior around the world. The strictly segregated theatre had a fence that separated the white and black entrances. The movie screen was high, and it tilted in such a way that some black residents could see the action from their homes. At the scene of a black woman in Africa holding a little pig to her breast to suckle, a great protest had arisen. The purpose of showing the extreme poverty and hardship in an African village, and the importance of preserving a baby pig so it could later provide food for many people, was lost on some who did not want their children to see black people so depicted.

Local civil rights leaders used this unrest to protest the segregated arrangements at the outdoor theatre. My mission: to talk the white manager into taking down the fence and integrating the viewing area, as well as helping civil rights leaders persuade black parents that the film itself had educational and social value, was not a racial slur, and could not be censored.

When I boarded the plane at National Airport in Washington for the flight to Florida, my seatmate was Cassius Clay, who seven months earlier had knocked out Sonny Liston to claim the world title. Unlike his later public persona as Mohammed Ali, Clay was then reserved and not inclined to talk much about himself. But during the flight he warmed up, and when we landed at Fort Lauderdale in the middle of a storm that soon turned into a hurricane, he became much more animated.

Rain fell in sheets, the wind blew at one hundred miles an hour, our umbrellas turned inside out, and taxis were at a premium. We finally found a driver who would take us to our respective destinations, miles apart. Before the evening was out, I felt that Clay was indeed one of "the greatest."

The solution to the racial dispute was simple. Providence again intervened. The hurricane blew down the fence dividing the white and black parking areas; the manager, who didn't really want to go to the expense of replacing it, agreed to let it lie, and the film in dispute was in its last showing. I returned to Washington amid considerable acclaim for having done absolutely nothing.

The father-son bonding at Jesse Owens' victory in 1936 did not last long. Daddy was easily irritated, and I was no doubt an irritating and baffling child...lazy, impudent, and argumentative. One day when Lil and I had come home from school for lunch, Daddy was there to supervise a surprise feast prepared by Glennie Williams, our cook.

"Look what we have today!" Daddy exclaimed. "Fresh, home-grown squab." Lil and I looked at each other.

"What's that!" I asked, thinking the baked delicacy looked a lot like a pigeon.

"It's like a dove," Daddy answered. "They are wild game. Be careful. There may be some buckshot still in them." I did not believe him. Neither did Lil. We declined to eat it. We would not even taste it.

"You can't fool me!" I shouted. "That's one of my pigeons. It might even be Pidgy-Widgy." Daddy denied it. He cajoled, pleaded, scolded, and threatened to no avail. Lil and I both stubbornly refused to eat a bite.

"I'd feel like a cannibal," Lil declared.

"Me, too," I echoed.

After a while Daddy had had enough. He denounced us as "sorry, ungrateful, spoiled, good-for-nothing" children and ordered us to bring in a load of wood for the heater and get back to school. We retreated to the back porch where Heath had stacked the wood. It was Lil's idea to break off two little twigs. Each holding one between forefinger and thumb, extended out in front of us as far as we could reach, we marched back into the house past Daddy, placed the twigs on the hearth and fled out the front door.

We ran as fast as we could, but soon I heard the sound of a familiar engine. Nemesis in his Chevrolet was in hot pursuit. Lil, three and a half years older and longer-legged, ran ahead, tore through the cemetery and achieved sanctuary. Retribution caught me at the edge of the graveyard and gave me a pretty good licking. I cried at first but regained my dignity before Daddy let go and ordered me to school. Being a fair-minded child, able to see both sides of an argument, I decided later that I really had deserved that whipping. But I never did eat that squab, which I remained convinced was kin to Pidgy-Widgy. In any event, that was the last time my father laid his hand on me.

Lil was never in danger; at sixteen and a girl, she was well past corporal punishment. In fact, when Daddy sought to restrict her to the house for the day and disallow the outing she had planned with friends, she taunted him with this verse she had earlier communicated to them:

"If I'm not there,
You'll know the reason why.
I'll be at home,
Eating pigeon pie!'"

Stress can affect the immune system. Lil and I were under a lot while Mother was away, and we fell victim to a virus. In the 1930s, influenza posed a serious public health threat. The respiratory disease then is not to be confused with the 48-hour virus people call the flu today. Each year someone at Broadacre came down with it. One day in January 1936, Lil came home from school with cough, nausea and upset stomach; two days later, so did I. It was the real thing. We burned with fever. After it subsided about two weeks later, we lay abed for days, weak, wan, listless, without appetite or energy.

As we began a slow recovery, we needed entertainment and diversion. Darling Baker, Senior, was summoned to provide it. With an imperious clap of hands from Lil and me, Doll would appear on stage, as it were, before our beds for a command performance. A lay preacher, this usually dignified, reserved black man, father to Doll Jr. and sister Virginia (practically our siblings) would divert us with recitations, minstrel song and dance, and a sermon full of old-time religion associated with the African Methodist Episcopal Zion Church.

Moved by all that creative energy from Doll, whom we never called Mr. Baker, Lil and I would sing and clap and egg him on. And we began to feel better. It was an unconscious show of racism, revealing, as I realize now but did not then, arrogance and a sense of entitlement. It was also a show of disrespect for a man old enough to be our own father, who had standing and respect in the black community.

We were not raised to consider colored people, or "Nigras," as we pronounced the word, inferior. We were never mean-spirited. We liked our numerous black friends and did not consciously intend to insult them. We would have been shocked had we ever been accused of such a thing and would have denied it vehemently. Didn't Doll Jr. practically live with us? Didn't he often receive favors at Lil's and Mary C.'s expense? Yet we were all guilty of institutional racism. We accepted both de jure and de facto segregation as a perfectly normal arrangement, really just a fact of life. We regarded black folk in general as a servant class, whose obligation it was to wait on us, to work for us, and, when times called for it, to entertain us.

What do you suppose the Reverend Mr. Darling Baker, Senior really thought and felt as he played the court clown for Mac, twelve and Lil, sixteen? Dowd was never called upon for a return engagement if and when Doll Jr. and Virginia got sick. Maybe they weren't supposed ever to come under the weather.

Sometimes influenza got so bad it was beyond the reach of entertainers. Often it turned into pneumonia. People died. Cousin Hill Wolfe became sick a year later. His fever rose. His lungs filled with fluid. Soon he had double pneumonia. Uncle Vann called Aunt Isabel.

"No, Vann, Dr. Smith just left. Hill's not one bit better."

Vann called his brother. "Dowd, you've got to get over to the Wolfes. Isabel is frantic. And you know Hilliard isn't much help. That boy's temperature is 104 degrees."

Dowd went. Soon Aunt Mary Hinson stood watch. Then Vann. Day after day Hill lay in bed as his fever rose. He was delirious, the fever climbing to 106 degrees and holding. A few days later Dowd was on the phone again with his sister Isabel. Her voice quivering, she told her brother that Dr. Smith had said the crisis would be reached soon. "The fever has got to break. It just has to—or," and my aunt's voice broke again as she hung up the receiver.

But it didn't break right away. It seems now that Hill's life lay in the balance for another week, the fever raging at 105-106 degrees. How high could it go? How long could it last? A couple of nights later, the phone rang. It was Uncle Hill. Dr. Smith had just left. Hill, Jr. was wringing wet and deadly quiet, but the fever had broken. It was down to 102 degrees and Hill, in a semi-coma, was at least no longer delirious. Dr. Smith said he had passed the crisis and barring complications, should recover.

I suppose he did. At least he gradually regained his strength. His lungs were clear, as was his memory. But my cousin seemed changed. Always bright, he remained an honor student. He played in a neighborhood dance band. He regained his status as a popular kid, far more so than Vann or I. He went on to UNC, joined the DKEs, did well in college. Hill was not, however, the same. His judgment seemed impaired. He became erratic, unpredictable, his attention span abbreviated. Soon he developed diabetes insipitus and became subject to headaches and occasional blackouts. Otherwise, he was physically as strong as ever.

Hill was in and out of our lives, especially Mary C.'s, Vann's and mine, for many years to come, all through his serial marriages, career changes and unpredictable behavior. As an adult he had one crisis after another, most of his own making. My sister and I later concluded that the part of Hill's brain that regulates judgment and emotion had been damaged—partly burned out—by the prolonged high fever when he was so sick so long at fourteen years of age.

It was either that or some peculiarity inherited from his grandfather Wolfe, who had, after all, run out on his wife, Miss Minnie, and just disappeared, only to be found years later, living in Baltimore with another woman. Yes, it had to have been the influenza or to have sprung from the loins of grandfather Wolfe. Such behavior couldn't possibly have originated from some recessive Secrest gene. Could it?

# 25. Blessed Be Thy Name

While Mother was at Clifton Springs, from September 1935 to March 1936, Lil and I didn't do much to keep the house neat. Christmas decorations put up in December remained there until the great day of anticipation, March 15. One of our favorite decorations was a pair of large Santa Claus lamps, screwed into sockets on the dining room wall on either side of the hutch. For the last two months we had agreed daily that "we really ought to take those down," but it was a chore that we never got around to.

On the Ides of March, the air thick with excitement, Lil and I hurriedly removed the Santa lamps and picked up half a year's accumulation of junk, trash and dirty clothes. We washed, scrubbed, folded and tucked away, working alongside Alice Bowell, drafted for the occasion.

Broadacre looked pretty good when Mother got home. She looked wonderfully good to us. Things didn't go so badly at first. Mother tried to take up where she had left off, going to church, playing hostess to her church circle, the book club, her bridge foursome. She was not, however, her old self, and Daddy offered her little support; he still resented her getting sick in the first place. Lacking introspection, he didn't have any patience with depression. He called it a "sit-down strike," a new concept applied by labor leaders up north to organizing industry. Soon the Congress of Industrial Organizations emerged, later to be joined with the older American Federation of Labor. Daddy felt Mother's condition was spitefully aimed at him, and in some ways it may have been.

Daddy's disposition did not improve when Mother, on occasion immobilized, failed to carry her weight or do her share around the house. Mother admittedly was no bundle of joy. She would occasionally play the piano and sing religious hymns. One line I learned to dislike in particular was, "For his eye is on the sparrow, so I know he watches me." Following these words, she would rest her head on the piano keys and heave a deep sigh. "Some eye," I thought to myself.

Another hymn was "In the garden." The words: "And he walks with me and he talks with me and he tells me I am his own. And the joy we share as we tarry there, no other can ever know," all seemed so sad, joyless, false. If that is the comfort provided by faith, I decided, it's best to remain a heathen. What good is faith if you lose it when you need it the most? Why re-embrace it later? Sickness and health, happiness and faith. What has one to do with the other?

So the parental war, which had been going on, it seemed to me, ever since I could remember, was still being waged. Mother's depression was to Daddy like a red flag to a bull. She lived in the past. She talked about all the things she used to do. "I wish I were able," was the reply to any suggestion that she throw herself back into life. She made picky comments but skillfully deflected any critical reaction by heaping all blame on herself. She would ask obvious questions, seemingly unsure but actually knowing the answers. I soon became somewhat impatient myself, labeling such inquiries F.Q.'s, for Fool Questions.

Mother felt guilty because she could not plan menus, let alone prepare meals. She walked with an unsteady gait, stiff and unnatural, as if she were literally unbalanced. She had no appetite. At meals her nose drew up as if everything smelled bad. She picked at her food. Out of frustration, Daddy would start to bully and berate her, and she would revert to a self-punishing passive aggression that was equally withering.

She didn't spare Lil or me any description of her symptoms, and we heard daily that her head felt stuffed with cotton or like a block of wood. She was self-absorbed, yet obsessed with her husband. When we walked downtown, she would turn and look toward some man and ask anxiously, "Is that your father?" My answers became increasingly unsympathetic: "At this time of day? In this place? Of course not. And why do you care?" She couldn't eat. She couldn't sleep. She was always tired. She couldn't see. Her eyes bothered her. Her walk wasn't right. Nothing was.

Yet there were times of brief remission and astonishing revival. Mother was never as sick as she thought she was, was far more functional than she realized. Her hearing, her memory, her ability to think clearly, even to perform creatively at times were unimpaired.

When Lil was named valedictorian of her class and needed some help in researching the topic of her address, Mother was an asset. In 1936, North Carolina schools had only eleven grades. The school year was eight months, not the national norm of nine. A campaign was launched to extend the school year and to add a twelfth grade. That was Lil's topic. Her address won great praise. The editor of the Monroe Journal published it in its entirety, calling the speech an astonishing achievement for a girl of sixteen and a credit to Monroe's education system.

Not so surprising, I thought, seeing as how Lessie, forty-three, and depressed, had written most of it. No, Mother wasn't so sick as she thought and at times behaved. Her condition really did not bother me much except when Daddy was around; to me he was the fly in the family ointment. And when Mother was not around, Daddy was all right. I just couldn't abide the combination.

Lil, barely sixteen when she graduated from Monroe High School, had been accepted at Duke. With a straight-A average, Lil had been actively recruited by Duke, received a scholarship, and won exemption from the required English grammar class taught by the dreaded Professor A.C. Jordan.

Anna Bernard Benson, dark, diminutive English teacher at Monroe High School, had drilled Lil and later me in grammar so thoroughly that there was no part of speech we didn't understand and no sentence too complex to be diagrammed. Known for her acid tongue, Miss Benson brooked no nonsense from her students. Even the most difficult behavior problem submitted to her tyranny.

Anna Bernard, attractive and youthful, was in her late thirties to early forties when she rammed and crammed the English language down our throats. Some, like Lil and me, thrived. Others barely survived, but few failed and no one ever forgot Miss Benson. At the 1971 high school reunion more than thirty years later, arranged to honor Principal House, she outshone him by being voted the meanest and most memorable teacher of all.

A woman of many parts, Anna Bernard loved drama and the arts. She was director of the dramatic club at school and often took students to Charlotte to see little theater productions or Broadway shows on tour. Whether students loved or hated her, all feared and respected her. She was an animal lover and organized a kennel club in Monroe. Lil and I were avid grammar students, but we stayed on her good side also by giving her an Eskimo Spitz puppy.

In 1943, at age forty-five, Miss Benson surprised Monroe by running off with a twenty-nine year old lieutenant stationed at Camp Sutton. Before he went overseas, Lt. Bamberger and his wife performed as exhibition ballroom dancers in U.S.O. shows. After the war the couple lived in his home town of Baltimore, where they operated an antique business.

When he was 62 and she 78, they retired to Monroe. Mr. Bamberger died of a heart attack at 65, leaving Anna Bernard to live in solitary splendor among her antiques in the old Blakeney home. A few years later, Mrs. Bamberger moved to the Penick Episcopal Retirement Home in Southern Pines, where she lived to be nearly 100, happily dominating all those other old folks around her.

But in 1936, Anna Bernard was still teaching English at Monroe High School and putting the fear of God in her students. When Daddy heard Lil exclaim over her exemption from the grammar class at Duke, his reaction was a shock.

"Lil, you're to take that class. It will do you some good."

"I will not," she replied defiantly. "Why should I? Miss Benson taught me everything there is to know about English. The other day I even caught her in an error."

Lil enlisted her teacher's help. Anna Bernard came by to see Lessie and Dowd. "Mr. Secrest, I do hope you'll reconsider. Lil does not need any corrective grammar class. She can spend her time and energy much better in other study."

Daddy listened but said very little.

"And how is Mrs. Secrest?" the teacher inquired.

"She seems to be some better," Daddy replied guardedly.

"You mean, don't you, somewhat better," Miss Benson corrected. She went on to explain the precise difference between some and somewhat within the context of his usage. Then she added, "Well, I'm glad that Lessie is somewhat better, and remember, Lil is not to be forced to take a course at Duke she does not need from which the University has exempted her."

Miss Benson's father had been a Seaboard Railroad man, but her mother had been a McCauley-Tallyrand-Redfearn, a lineage to be reckoned with. Daddy waited until Lil's former teacher had left before exploding to Lil, "You can tell Anna Bernard Benson to go to hell. You're going to take any course that is required of any other student. You don't know it all!"

Soon Daddy had someone from Duke on the telephone. No, he didn't want to speak to any admissions director. No, he didn't care to speak to the chairman of the English department. Put Dean Herring, Vice President for Academic Affairs, on the line.

"Now look here, Dr. Herring," Dowd Secrest started. After some courteous give-and-take, Daddy declared "Well, if Duke University doesn't have any professor in the English Department who knows more than my 16-year-old daughter, then I guess she's enrolled in the wrong school." Before it was all over, Dowd had even gotten President William Preston Few involved. For once Miss Benson appeared bested, and for a change Lil didn't get her way. Duke knuckled under. If her father wanted his daughter to take grammar, she would be so required.

Everyone seemed to benefit. Lil took A.C. Jordan's English in stride. At the end of her first semester, still sixteen years old, a product of the eight-month school year and eleven grades, she received a card on which A.C. Jordan had underlined the letter "A". Many students two years older and from New England prep schools had flunked, and only one "A" was given.

Six months later at a family gathering one summer evening, after a feast of watermelon, roasted corn on the cob, cider and homemade peach ice cream, all the adults in our extended family discussed the question of divorce while Mary C., Lil, and I listened from an upstairs bedroom window. Daddy appeared to be the one forcing the issue, Mother distressed and in retreat. Once again I agreed with Daddy but not for the reasons he advanced. Brack, also on hand and accustomed to a peaceful household, murmured, "Oh, you poor kids," as raised voices wafted through the billowing curtains.

It turned out that there would be no divorce. It wasn't done in decent circles in Monroe in 1936. Daddy, when reminded of that point by Aunt Eve, and of the criticism he would receive if he were to desert a clinically ill wife, especially a member of the Covington family, quickly relented. Dowd coveted community respect, and a final family rift would not be good for business, either. Again he paid attention to Miss Evabelle, who had good judgment and "thought like a man."

That memorable evening, with all the usual suspects present, was soon followed by a terrible ordeal which led to a setback in Mother's condition.

Once the marriage was back on track, Mary C. asked if some friends of hers could come over from Charlotte for a party. She had graduated from Duke and received a convertible Chevrolet as a graduation gift, which her friends could use to come. "Sky" Kline, former captain of the Davidson basketball team nicknamed for his height, and his three friends had basically constituted the team, which in those days ranked high in the Southern Conference; other members were Duke, UNC, NC State, and Wake Forest.

Sky was a particularly close friend of Mary C. He was the only child of a widowed mother, who doted on him but not to his detriment. Sky was a natural-born winner: athletic, smart, handsome, good-natured, popular. He and my sister were just buddies. At five feet, eight inches herself, she preferred tall men but they were hard to find. Although a graceful athlete and a good dancer, Mary C. felt awkward at being the tallest girl around. Later her height became an obsession, and I came to hate the issue. Who, besides her, gave a damn? Certainly neither of her two husbands, both of whom were shorter than she.

Mother and Daddy held the usual backyard fish fry, complete with hush puppies and coleslaw, augmented by pork barbecue and cold drinks supplied by the Drug Store fountain. The usual early bales of cotton and straw were supplied for seating, and "Fiddlin' Bob" from one of the farms came over to perform. This fiddling virtuoso and yodeler was a model for later country singers such as Randy Travis, also born and raised in Union County. Bob was probably the more talented, but he was born fifty years too soon; the Nashville sound was yet to be invented.

"Why hello, Miss Lessie!" boomed Sky, as he and his buddies entered the house.

"How do you do, sir?" he asked respectfully of Mr. Secrest. Sky then introduced his friends.

New York Cal, ever the self-confident extrovert, slapped the reserved Dowd on the back and inquired, "How you doin', Skipper?" Daddy winced.

Texan Hoxie McMillan, as shy as Daddy was reserved, said, "How do you do, ma'am," and "Pleased to meet you, sir."

Dave from Charlotte had been to Broadacre with Sky before. He greeted my parents with a "Hey, folks, good to see you again" and walked across the front hall out to speak to Lil and me sitting with Helen and Doll Jr. on the porch swing. Mother was gracious and charming, in her element with the younger generation.

Sky gave Lil a brotherly hug, asked how "my girl" was doing, then gave me and Doll Jr. a playful punch on the arm. Before long the Victrola was playing swing tunes from the latest hit parade, and the rug was rolled up for dancing. Dave and Cal were arm wrestling, and when Cal unexpectedly pushed Dave's arm down and held it, Doll Jr. and I cheered. Soon Cal and Hoxie, sleeves rolled up, were competing to show off their biceps and offering rides to the impressed twelve-year-olds. They swung us around and around till one or the other became too tired or dizzy to continue.

The eating, singing, dancing and horseplay continued throughout the early evening, punctuated by Fiddlin' Bob's plaintive wailing. Youthful exuberance eventually gave way to casual conversation and some minor romancing among the boys and girls who had joined us for supper.

Servants prepared the food and did all the work. Mother and Daddy never did any of that stuff, but they planned the affair, supervised it, closely chaperoned everyone and saw to it that no one consumed anything alcoholic. Daddy told everyone at ten o'clock it was time to go home. They had a twenty-five-mile ride back to Charlotte, and another twenty to Concord once Dave and Cal had been dropped off. Best to get an early start and to bed. Tomorrow everyone—at Broadacre at least—had to be up early for Sunday school and church.

We all hated to see them go. So much good-natured energy had brightened our cheerless household. Sky and his friends, acclaimed athletes and scholars both at Davidson, left in high but sober spirits, still filled with a sense of adventure, optimism and immortality.

The next morning, as the family was about to leave for church, the telephone rang. Mary C. answered.

"Hello, Mary Cov. This is Peggy. Did you hear the news on the radio?" Peggy was Dr. Marvin and Betty Smith's older daughter, who had been part of the party at Broadacre the night before.

"No, what news?" But Peggy couldn't speak as she began to cry. Soon Peggy's Aunt Rachel Howie and her niece Elizabeth ("Lick") were vying to tell about some terrible wreck in Matthews.

"Oh, it's too horrible to talk about," Lick declared. Peggy, now composed, got back on the line.

"Mary Cov, you aren't going to believe this, but Sky had a terrible accident. His car struck that big oak tree, you know the one standing right in the middle of that sharp curve as you come into Matthews. The car was demolished. The report said there was only one survivor. But they didn't say who or what shape he's in."

Mother was soon on the phone, talking first to Rachel, then to Betty. Then Daddy, talking to Big Doc.

"Killed? Three of them? Good God, how did it happen?" Daddy asked. " Damn young fools. Probably speeding. But at two o'clock this morning? Why, they left here at ten last night."

As told later, Sky and his friends had encountered a woman and her daughter at a drive-in all-night restaurant. The women were on their way to the Monroe Country Club for a party. Would the boys like to join them? Sure, why not? So the group went to the party, accepted a drink of bourbon brought up from an ABC store in nearby Chesterfield County, South Carolina, and started to dance the night away. The boys were unaccustomed to alcohol. One drink led to another.

Sometime after midnight, with one more for the road, the four young men weaved their way out of the clubhouse, got into Mary C.'s car, Sky behind the wheel, and lit out for Charlotte. The social set—considered smart by some standards—had done nothing to restrain the youths from overdrinking; in fact, they had supplied the whiskey. The concept of a designated driver was then unknown.

Although none of the Secrest family was in any way responsible, everyone—with their over-developed super-egos and sense of personal responsibility—felt guilty. "If only I hadn't planned a party," Mary C. lamented. "If only I hadn't offered them my car. If only you hadn't given me a car," she said to Daddy. "I'm to blame. I feel so guilty." My sister would level that charge against herself in different arenas for the rest of her life. She never learned the lesson of self-forgiveness.

Mother was so sunk in shame and sorrow that she was of little help to her daughter. She relapsed into deeper depression. We all attended the funerals. "The Lord giveth; the Lord taketh away. Blessed be the name of the Lord." I stirred restlessly in my seat. To hell with that, I thought. I always disliked the book of Job. And I didn't think too well of God, either. I didn't understand "why bad things happen to good people." Sixty-seven years later, I still don't.

Mrs. Kline was a rock of Gibraltar and a pillar of faith. We met Hoxie's and Cal's parents, up from Texas and down from New York, and Dave's in Charlotte. We later went to the Presbyterian Hospital to visit the only survivor of that awful carnage on U.S. 74. There was no sign of anybody from the Country Club.

When we entered the hospital room and Daddy approached the bed occupied by a body wrapped in bandages from head to toe, we heard a cheerful, cocky voice, "Hi, ya, Skipper? What's up?" Irrepressible, irresponsible, happy-go-lucky Cal. On that late summer's night, he'd had angels riding on his shoulders. Cal recovered completely—not even any scars, unless psychological ones. What life still held for him I'll never know, as his path and Mary C.'s later diverged.

# 26. The Great Sperm Race

After that August tragedy, and with Lil's departure for Durham, things went from bad to worse. I now label 1936, 1937 and 1938 as "The Nightmare Years." But even so, happy, nostalgic memories of my early and mid-teen age years crowd out the more unpleasant ones.

Aunt Eve and Aunt May spent a lot of time those days at Broadacre with Mother, Daddy, Mary C., Lil and me. Our aunts, equally concerned, had different approaches in helping their nieces and nephew cope with parental problems. Aunt May preferred diversion and indulgence. She proposed movies, card games, visits with relatives and neighbors, eating out and changing the subject.

Aunt Eve opted for discussion. She preferred explanation, understanding, solutions and, lacking that, coping skills. Lil and I still remember vividly sixty-seven years later Aunt Eve's lying on the bed with us, repetitively drawing patterns with her fingers on the bedspread, as she sought to help us understand and see everyone's point of view.

They both cared so much, in their own different ways. They seemed like lifesavers to me during those years. They were partly responsible for my subsequent happy memories of a harrowing time and for a normal teen-age adjustment. In what may have become selective, revisionist memory, I recall many more good times than bad, indeed, an average, happy adolescent life.

With so much time and attention devoted to domestic problems, I was, however, often bothered, preoccupied, inwardly harassed. During the school year there was no Aunt May, Lil, Aunt Eve or Mary C. to serve as barriers and buffers. On occasion I was drawn away from friends and school activities, distracted from academic interests. I could not concentrate. My grades plummeted. I hated algebra even more than Latin.

Eight years earlier Mr. Hall, the math teacher, had endured a year with Mary C., who also hated algebra. She just did not get it and did not care. She also hated Mr. Hall who disliked her with equal intensity. Mr. Hall simply could not believe it when Mary C's little sister entered his class. Oh, no, he must have groaned. Not another Secrest. He also could hardly believe it when Lil liked algebra and aced every problem. Final term grade:100. Mr. Hall loved Lil and Lil loved him.

When I came along four years later, Mr. Hall looked forward to having me for a student. Alas, I took after my older sister. I hated algebra. I just did not get it. Soon I too hated Mr. Hall. The feeling was reciprocated. Mother, naturally good at math, did not feel able to offer any help. Daddy lacked the time. It looked as if I would flunk both algebra and Latin, even have to attend summer school.

One evening, frustrated by everything, I became infuriated and, just like that night a year earlier when I had slung the math book across the room and told Lil I hated her and wished she were dead, I now threw both algebra and Latin texts across the room and shouted at Mother and Daddy that I hated them and wished they were both dead.

That was when they arranged a tutor for me. Miss Connie Horne, a funny little bird-like woman who lived with her older unmarried sister, Miss Allie, on Hayne Street, agreed to take me on. Miss Connie was known to be peculiar but a good teacher and self-possessed. She did things for herself. When her roof sprang a leak, she got a ladder, roofing, hammer and nails and fixed it. She ought to be able to handle me. I gave her a hard time. More than once she was ready to throw in the sponge.

"Mr. Secrest," she told Daddy one early spring night in the second semester of the eighth grade, "I don't think Mac is ready to learn much right now. He has too many other things on his plate. Why don't you give him a cow and let him stake it out the rest of the year? Give him some time to sort things out." Mother and Daddy decided I should continue with Miss Horne if she were willing. I was confronted with a choice—buckle down and do better or face the prospect of repeating the grade.

I buckled down. I learned the nominative ablative and how to conjugate enough verbs to squeak by, always wondering whatever happened to the pronouns, somehow concealed within the verb itself. I reluctantly accepted the fact that Caesar, "after having whipped up his horses" had indeed "conquered all Gaul," which he proceeded to divide into three parts. But I never could understand Mother's insistence that the study of

Latin made an understanding of English easier. What a circuitous route. Why not put the time spent on Latin into the direct study of English? But Mother, like Lil, was a whiz in both Latin and mathematics, indeed, in all foreign languages. She had an ear I didn't. But thanks to a dedicated English teacher I did learn English to a faretheewell.

Whether I would pass algebra was not certain until the final exam. I squeezed past with a D, relieved to be rid of Mr. Hall forever.

I had managed to get through my first year of high school, still faking it in the band, living at home without the help of Lil and Mary C. except on an occasional weekend or holiday. Miss Connie Horne's older sister, by the way, nearly sixty years old in 1942 also got married like Miss Benson did, thanks to the arrival of Camp Sutton and all of those men in uniform. She enjoyed thirty-five years of marital bliss before dying at the age of ninety-five.

When school ended in early May, 1937, I continued to work part time at the motor company. I hated it. There no one told me what to do, or when they did, how to do it. So I mainly sat down, feeling useless, bored and resentful. My main distraction was to take rubber bands and shoot them at flies. At least I learned to be a good shot, knocking out flies on the wing with great accuracy. It was almost as exciting as the Battle of Britain three years later.

As Lil and I were close, we inherited each other's friends. Catherine Johnson, later to marry Ed Jackson, son of a professor at Davidson College, was one of Lil's friends who left me two legacies: the first a love of music, the second a devotion to dogs.

Catherine was the person largely responsible for Lil's meeting her husband, John McNair Buie of Wagram, not that Catherine approved of John much. Catherine was a many-faceted personality, a combination of good and bad, conventional and peculiar but a devoted, loyal, life-long friend.

She was a talented musician, an accomplished pianist with a rich contralto voice. As a teenager she instilled in me an appreciation of composer Jerome Kern, especially his tunes "Old Man River" and "Without a Song."

Catherine was smart, too. As an adult she was not only a wife and mother but also a skilled writer, editor of a medical journal, and later author of a successful paraphrase of Biblical scripture. As occasion required, she and Ed opened their hearts and home in Durham to me in 1969 when I needed a place to stay when I first returned to Duke at age 46 and three years later to Lil's daughter Celeste when she needed some special tender loving care.

Peculiar she was, too, in her middle years embracing a fundamentalist, charismatic religion although she came from traditional, conservative Baptist and Presbyterian faiths. She took to speaking in tongues on occasion and once had her Riverton home exorcised of demons. Yet her religion served her well, making her a kinder, gentler person and fortifying her with courage when she had to confront death in the form of terminal cancer.

Catherine's second legacy was a passion for Albert Payson Terhune's Sunnybank collies in Pompton Lakes, New Jersey. Catherine had a beautiful rough-coated tawny collie named Lad, whom I greatly admired.

One Saturday afternoon in December, 1936, Mother and Daddy drove me to Southern Pines, seventy-five miles from Monroe, to visit Terhune's uncle who raised and bred Sunnybank collies. The breeder had no puppies available but recommended a kennel in Ohio.

I later saved $50 from work at the motor company to order a registered collie from a breeder in Galion, Ohio. The puppy arrived at Broadacre on June 7, 1937, a date easily remembered as that was also the day I heard on the radio that movie star Jean Harlow had died. She was only twenty-six years old. An abusive husband and a stupid mother—a Christian Scientist who refused her daughter medical treatment—were responsible.

Already scared to death of dying, the "Blond Bombshell's" untimely demise haunted me for days. The tragedy was enhanced when Bruce, my collie puppy also named after one of Terhune's fictional heroes, died a week later. Dr. Alexander said Bruce, only ten weeks old, already had distemper when he arrived. Daddy said I could not have a replacement, but of course I got one, an all-white collie shipped free. Christened Bruce, the Second, he arrived at ten weeks of age, hale and hearty and full of wonderful puppy mischief.

Thirteen is a sorry age. I was a miserable master: neglectful, inconsistent, lazy and resentful when I was expected to train Bruce properly and clean up after him. I quickly lost interest in him, who represented more of an ideal, or obsession, than a reality. Bruce was neither fed nor watered well, seldom de-fleed, never washed or brushed, inconsistently vaccinated—free to wander outside and to play in traffic. Yet Bruce was loyal and loving, always thrilled to see me. He lived, inexplicably, until he was ten years old, left for Mother to care for, until a year before I got married.

Many years later, when son David was thirteen, one of his jobs was to clean up and shovel after Atlas, our 180-pound black Great Dane. How David hated that job and Atlas for producing such enormous loads.

"Why do I have to do this?" David asked. "Let Phil do it."

"Because you're older and bigger and it's the job you've been given," was the parental response. "Just go ahead and do it, dump it in the lot next door." Mumble, mutter, bitch and grumble, David was required to do what I should have done twenty-five years earlier.

Did it make any difference? Ten years later, after David and wife Leslie (Mindy) Fuller married, they bought a black Great Dane named Baron, after football star Eddie Lebaron. They soon acquired a cat, and the competition began: whose job was it to feed, water and walk the dog and whose to clean out the kitty litter box? Some things never change.

Mary C. and Lil had seen a movie titled "Three Smart Girls" and decided it was up to "These Three" (Lil, Mary C. and me) to emulate these film heroines in patching up our parents' unraveling marriage. The film starred Deanna Durban and featured Nan Grey and Barbara Read as the three sisters. I could see the parallel between my sisters and Deanna and her screen siblings, but where was I to fit in? Apparently I was to be cast in yet another female role.

The three Secrest children had by force of circumstance been thrust into the center of their parents' personal lives for a long time, but the fantasy of Mary C., now twenty-one, that she, Lil and I could serve as marriage counselors for Mother and Daddy was fated to failure. They would have to work out their own arrangement. By the time the movie's sequel, "Three Smart Girls Grow Up" was released in 1939, Mother and Daddy had worked things out on their own, and no one even considered that I, at sixteen, should be cast as any sort of girl, smart or not.

The powers that be (which probably meant Aunt May, Aunt Sue, and Aunt Eve) decided that I was to spend the summer of 1937 in Louisville with Aunt Susie and her children—three of whom were near enough my own age to be compatible. It wouldn't do to have me carry the burden at home alone any longer, simmering angrily and in frustration down at the motor company. Mary C. had a job as a social worker with the WPA. So it fell to Lil, home from her freshman year at Duke, to stay in Monroe with Mother and Daddy and serve as referee, buffer and negotiator.

One June afternoon, three months before my fourteenth birthday, I went over to the barn to help Heath, working on birthing a calf. The cow was having a breech baby; that is, the calf was coming out all four feet first. The calf would have to be turned. The whole process is time-consuming, involving all kinds of implements, and potentially dangerous to the life of both mother and baby.

Once the ordeal was over, with a great sense of relief for everybody, Heath and I were left alone. Discussion of the birth led to discussion of pregnancy. The talk turned from animals to humans, from pregnancy to sex. Earlier in the year my friends and I had seen some of the little pornographic comic books that Heath and Murray were laughing over.

We asked to see them. What we saw was a series of drawings, depicting Flash Gordon, Superman, Tarzan, Popeye, Jack Armstrong, All-American Boy, and many other fictional heroes, in the nude, engaged in explicit sex acts with Lois Lane, Olive Oyl, Tess and other girlfriends. All the images pictured the heroes and heroines in highly exaggerated form.

I asked Heath to see the comic books again. He pulled a few out of his pocket and tossed them over. Distant memories returned. Some of this I seemed to sense. Other stuff puzzled me. What really happened? What did that picture mean? What were they doing? Why? Heath, being tongue-tied, was not accustomed to teaching orally or verbally. His strength lay not in description. Heath was visual. In school he would be better at show than tell. He taught best by hands-on experience.

Oh, so that was what happened. But what did girls get out of it? Did the same thing happen to them? How can you tell? The more answers I got, the more questions I had. I was really disappointed. If that was sex, it sure seemed to be overrated. What was the big deal? But that was enough for today. I didn't really feel guilty but kind of ashamed. I would have to tuck all this away, not repressed or forgotten, but set aside—postponed for another day. Gosh, I'm hungry. I wonder what's for supper.

Soon thereafter I left for Louisville. I didn't see Heath until September and hadn't really wanted to. Once back home, the episode was dismissed from my mind. Things were changing. Now fourteen, I saw less of Doll Jr., also reaching puberty. I worked less on the farms; I seldom hung around the barn anymore. I was growing up. I did not blame Heath. Why should I? After all, he had more to do with rearing and educating me in some ways than anyone else and had for years. I had been the initiator in June's little episode. Heath was no pedophile like Dr. G. was reputed to be. And he certainly wasn't homosexual. In his own ignorant, primitive way, he had sought to educate and to inform.

The barn episode was far less intimate and potentially harmful than all that earlier feminine seductivity when I was too young to know much or to be able to do anything about it, accompanied as it was with all that moral nay-saying. Within a year Heath was to introduce me and my friends to Rachel, a pretty young tenant farm girl who came to live-in with us. Within another year Heath had married. Before my first year in college was completed at age seventeen, Heath had left Broadacre, and I seldom saw him again. But in a way I remember him fondly as a foster parent.

The same summer I spent in Louisville, Aunt Eve and Aunt May attended school at the University of Nova Scotia. There they met another pair of unmarried women many years their junior. But the four hit it off from the start.

Laura Phillips and Eleanor Varney, public-school teachers in Laconia, New Hampshire, were natives of Concord. As the four women visited one evening, talk turned to their families. Laura spoke fondly of her eldest niece, Ann Louise Eastman, daughter of Laura's sister Louise, seventeen years her senior. Ann had recently graduated from Kalamazoo, Michigan, high school and planned to attend the local branch of the University of Michigan that fall, later to transfer to the University of New Hampshire in Durham..

Aunt Eve and Aunt May replied that they had a niece, Lil Secrest, the same age at Duke University. Her brother Mac, nearly fourteen, was to be a sophomore in high school that fall. Lil was an all-A student, but they were concerned about their nephew. He was an underachiever, did not really know how to study and stubbornly refused to learn anything he didn't already know.

"Really, I believe he can't concentrate," Aunt Eve explained. "You see," and she lowered her voice to a confidential whisper, "his mother—our youngest sister—has been emotionally disturbed, and there's been a lot of tension in the home."

Aunt May added that Mac had to assume entirely too many adult responsibilities now that his sisters were away. "I'm really quite concerned about him."

Soon conversation turned to more impressive topics—family achievements and important connections. Here May and Eve met their match. Laura spoke proudly of her English heritage. Her grandfather once owned the granite quarry in Cornwall, the stone from which was used to build the famed lighthouse at Land's End. Her father Harry Phillips, who had settled in Concord shortly after the American Civil War, had pursued the trade in New Hampshire and successfully built upon the family fortune.

Furthermore, niece Ann's father Harold Moses Eastman was from an old New England family that had settled there in the mid-1600s. He was related to U.S. Senator Moses from New Hampshire and was a second cousin of George Eastman of Eastman Kodak Company. Eve and May were hard pressed to equal that. But they tried. At the end of the summer term, the two Carolina ladies were invited to visit Laura's ancestral home and have lunch with sister Mildred Hanna, whose husband was president of United Life and Accident Insurance Company. Then there was a visit with sister Winifred Johnson, whose husband was New Hampshire's Highway Commissioner. The visit was climaxed with a tea at the home of the governor, Dr. Blood, senior partner in the medical partnership Blood, Graves and Coffin. Dr. Blood had delivered their niece seventeen years earlier. Clearly, the Phillips and Eastman families were "somebody in particular" in New Hampshire's capital city of Concord.

The next summer, not to be outdone, Eve and May returned the compliment. Laura and Eleanor came to North Carolina to be wined and dined by Aunt Eve's intellectual, moneyed and social set in Old Salem and Winston. Aunt May demonstrated equally impressive connections at Duke and Wake Forest, all capped off by a tea at the Governor's mansion in Raleigh where R. Clyde Hoey, whose wife was a Gardner and hence provided a family link, however tenuous, presided as governor.

How all this came together in the fall of 1946, ten years later, and once again united these New Hampshire and North Carolina families is a coincidence worthy of Ripley's "Believe It Or Not." As I came to know the Phillips and Eastman families and learned some of their secrets too, I concluded that when our families met, it was: "Tennessee Williams, meet Eugene O'Neill."

During the 1936-37 school year, I had continued to play buffer between Mother and Daddy, absorbing much of the depression from one side, anger from the other. And my obsessive fear of the dark returned. Broadacre loomed large and lonely—sitting there isolated and remote among its growth of huge old shade trees. The headlines carried stories of a serial killer on the loose, a headhunter leaving torsos scattered here and there around the countryside.

Although none of his victims were anywhere near North Carolina, let alone Broadacre, I carried my fear of him and the dark to bed every night. I took that fear with me to Louisville where the headhunter really did lurk nearby. My anxiety became so intense that Aunt Susie said I would have to go home if I couldn't control myself better than that. My fear did not affect cousins David, Bill and Caroline. I began to learn from Aunt Sue to control what I could and accept what I could not. Where a situation arose not of my own doing, I would have to learn to get used to it or get over it. In final analysis, no matter how much others wanted to help, nobody could do it for you. It was a lesson I took to heart and have remembered all my life: help others but remember, the good Lord helps those who help themselves.

When I got home in late August nothing much had changed. But I had. When I saw "Night Must Fall" with Rosalind Russell and Dame Mae Whitty scared witless by Robert Montgomery's carrying around heads in hat boxes, I shrugged it off as just another movie and went to bed alone in the dark and sound to sleep.

In my ninth and tenth grades, I further distanced myself from parental conflict. The years 1937 and 1938 passed by slowly, sometimes painfully, but I stayed on an even keel. I may never have gotten Latin or algebra, but there was nothing much in English, history, and social studies that I didn't know.

I did a courageous but unpopular thing by dropping out of the band, along with my friend Moke, because I was no good on the clarinet and did not enjoy it. We had to endure the slings and arrows of an outraged majority—our peers calling us "quitters and sissies" for having the courage of our convictions. It was cool to be a band member and one of "Mr. House's boys," and here we were, flaunting our independence. I did discover sports, both participatory and spectator, and girls. But even as a sports fan, I was different—a passionate Duke Blue Devils fan while most of my friends were Tar Heels, born and bred. I later became one also.

Fifteen is in a different way as difficult an age as thirteen. Hormones rage. Independence flares. Control by adults is swapped for control by the peer group: the pack instinct is dominant. Subservience to age is replaced by subservience to flaming youth. Most teens manage to eat, dress, act, look, and think alike despite the need to become nonconformists.

Teenagers, defying authority and striving for individuality, identify with each other. They are often led—and misled—by aggressive, self-appointed leaders. These kids seem to grasp control instinctively and know how to circumnavigate the dictates of parents, teachers, and other mature role models without overstepping the bounds of conformity and authority. That is a rare gift. Few succeed all the time. Most get into a little trouble now and again, which elevates them even more in the eyes of their followers. They always manage, it seems, to land on their feet.

Due to family preoccupation and a natural inclination toward perversity, I was neither a leader nor a follower to become. Then, as now, whenever I felt myself too comfortable with the majority, I began to back away. Too much individuality can lead to opposition or to ostracism. I sometimes experienced both, seeming to court it, often to welcome it.

Sex in a boy of fifteen is big. It was with me, although I pretended otherwise. Despite my encounter with Heath, and frequent self-indulgence, I was also something of a prude, a Puritan, a religious zealot. Mother's earlier frequent preachments, Biblical prohibitions and morality plays were not entirely forgotten.

So I was not so much trouble in the classroom as were some of the cooler kids, most of whom were a year older. Eugene and Kirk were two of the ringleaders. Eugene was a shark, whether at billiards in the pool room or at pocket pool in school.

I sat across the aisle from Eugene on my right and Kirk on my left. Mary Charles was a seat ahead of me, Myrtle one behind. Eugene could not carry any change in his left pants pocket. He had cut a hole so as to make himself more accessible. Kirk had done the same. Soon evidence of physical arousal became evident.

"Pssst!" Eugene called over to Kirk, now in concert with his ally.

Kirk, taking his cue, whispered to the girl across from him, "Mary Charles, look!"

Mary Charles, a right and proper girl in the eyes of her elders, looked. She turned her head, saw the rough outline beneath Eugene's pocket, turned red, and looked back toward the teacher.

Seeing that Miss Smart was facing the blackboard, saying something about verbal conjugation, the teenage girl looked back at Kirk, then across at Eugene. Eugene's grey trousers now revealed a spreading stain. On his face he wore what we called "a shit-eating grin."

Soon Myrtle, responding to a poke from Mary Charles, turned around and looked first at Eugene, then at Kirk, now at me. Feeling protective of both girls, I indicated they should turn around and ignore the pool players. It was wasted effort. The girls not only looked, they laughed, they whispered and passed notes to other students, many now distracted from Caesar's exploits in Gaul. Kirk and Eugene's activities were more immediate and to the point. For my Goodie Two Shoes intervention, I was considered a square, the word "nerd" not yet having been invented. I wasn't the only one not to learn much Latin from Miss Smart, who remained unaware—or pretended to be—of what was going on behind her back.

A young teacher's assistant also played a part in such high jinks. Newby resembled an "idiot savant," brilliant in science, erratic, immature and deficient in social skills. He was handicapped by his appearance and personality. He looked like some Dr. Jeckel who had swallowed only part of his potion and had turned about half-way into Mr. Hyde. His hair was thick and wiry—growing every which way. It grew everywhere, out of his ears and nose and sprouting along his shoulder blades. His face was deeply scarred, perhaps by an earlier round with acne. One might have thought smallpox, but Monroe had not had any cases of that in generations. We had all been vaccinated.

Newby was physically ugly. He had no close friends, girl or boy, only an elderly single mother and a younger brother and an older sister, neither of whom suffered from his handicaps. The young man had been hired to help Mr. Watson in the chemistry lab. But after hours the teacher was not privy to some of Newby's experiments, egged on by some of his more precocious students. Newby would do anything to gain the approval and companionship of the older, hip guys, and they did not hesitate to use him for their own personal pleasure.

Someone got the great notion that it would be fun to hold a sperm race and bet on the competitors. What was a sperm race?

Newby explained. The contenders would master their own domain, place the semen on glass slides, adding dye to differentiate them. The sperm then would swim upward upon the slides. The slide which contained the sperm that reached the top first was proclaimed "Winner!"

Each donor put down a dollar before the race began. Bystanders were free to bet as well—winner-take-all. The Sporting Life was alive and well at Monroe High School under Newby's supervision in chemistry lab, safely after Mr. Watson had left for the afternoon. The alleged betting ring was never discovered, but Newby's contract was not renewed in 1938. At least that is the story that went around. It may not have been the real low down. I wasn't there and can't vouch for it. The mere fact that it was generally believed says a lot about the mindset of teenagers in the South of the 1930s.

# 27. Richard Nixon and Me

In the fall of 1936 and the winter and spring of 1937, I spent several weekends with Aunt May at Duke. Lil was a freshman in Brown House. Since Aunt May did not have an extra bedroom in the faculty apartments on East campus, she had me bunk in at night with one or another of her law school boys in their cabins in Duke Forest.

One young fellow was a dark-haired, reserved, sober-sided student from Whittier, California. Richard Milhaus Nixon spent most of his time in the library, so I didn't see him much. On an occasional evening he would, however, come home early and engage me in casual conversation. He was impressed by my knowledge of European history and interest in the international situation: the Civil War in Spain, communism in Russia, Nazism in Germany, militarism in Japan, the growing impotence of the League of Nations, a defeatist peace-at-any-price appeasement in western European democracies and isolationism in America. A loyal Republican, he would also test my polemical skills as an equally loyal Democrat in defending Roosevelt and the New Deal.

In 1937 Nixon was a Fortress America isolationist along the lines of Senator Robert Taft of Ohio. He deplored FDR's New Deal as economic "class warfare" and his political methods of "tax and tax, spend and spend, elect and elect," as once voiced by presidential advisor Harry Hopkins, whom Nixon dismissed derisively as that "little half-assed social worker."

Sporting a deep five o'clock shadow even then, Nixon was a serious student. Aunt May, a confirmed FDR Democrat, called him "brilliant," arranged a National Youth Administration (NYA) job for him in the law library, and sometimes had him and his cabin-mate over to the apartment for dinner.

The law school cabins in Duke Forest were primitive. There was no insulation, central heating, or hot water. The students were often cold and hungry. I never heard Nixon complain. I do remember him being idealistic and believing both in doing good in the private sector and in observing honesty, justice, and devotion to law in executing public service.

On one occasion he challenged me to defend racial segregation, a challenge I failed miserably and knew it. While he too deplored the Nuremburg Laws dictated by Hitler in 1935, he asked me to explain why legal separation and discrimination based on race was not only legal but defended as moral in the American South yet condemned as legally and morally wrong in Nazi Germany.

I slept over with a lot of law school boys. As there was no reason to anticipate Nixon as a major force in the nation's political life fifteen to forty years later, I did not pay a lot of attention to him. But as one of "Aunt May's boys" and one of the few who would engage me in conversation about something other than Wallace Wade's Blue Devils, he stands out, retrospectively, from the rest.

In 1937 I saw nothing in Nixon of what set my teeth on edge many years later. Nothing to indicate his campaign tactics against Jerry Voorhies and Helen Gahagan Douglas to gain a seat in the U.S. House and later the Senate. Nothing to suggest the Checkers Speech in 1952. Certainly nothing to suggest the Watergate tapes in 1974.

I subsequently agreed with Nixon on some of his anti-communism stands, including his condemnation of Alger Hiss who was convicted of lying to Congress about his former membership in the Communist party.

Even here, however, my attitude was, "So what?" Many Americans had been Communist in an abstract, idealistic kind of way in the 1920's, 30's and 40's. Many had been "parlor pinks" and "fellow travelers." Others were moved by the Soviet Union's massive military contributions as allies against the Axis powers in World War Two.

So when Nixon became an early Cold War warrior, I often agreed with him, while deploring what appeared to me to be tactics somewhat reminiscent of Senator Joe McCarthy. I voted against Nixon in 1952, 1956, 1960 and 1968. In 1972, however, with the Chicago Democratic

Convention of 1968 still in mind along with President Johnson's Vietnam disaster, I finally capitulated and voted for Nixon's re-election (along with nearly everyone else), only to have Watergate explode in my face.

After Nixon's defeat in his campaign for governor of California in 1962, followed by a momentary withdrawal from political life along with a sarcastic comment to the press that "you won't have Nixon to kick around anymore," he launched one of his several comebacks.

Soon he was back on the rubber chicken and green peas circuit, giving speeches and raising funds for Republican candidates. On reading that Nixon was to appear in nearby Salisbury, N.C., I wrote a column in my weekly newspaper, The Cheraw (S.C.) Chronicle, recalling my teen-age acquaintance with him at Duke.

Cousin Hill, who had become a Republican, sent a copy to Nixon. Soon I received a note from the former vice president, saying he did indeed recall those days in Duke Forest and that despite our continuing political differences, any nephew of Miss Covington's would always be a friend of his. He invited me to sit on a platform with him (since I wouldn't stand on his political one).

I declined, observing that "I couldn't afford" to be identified with North Carolina Republicans, so "thanks but no thanks." Today I view that reply not only as rude, but also supercilious and arrogant. I can only plead youth, but I really wasn't all that young----having already turned thirty-nine.

The months from September to May, 1937-38, passed slowly, with "war within, war without." War within myself and the family, with Mother home part of the time, sometimes visiting Aunt Eve or Aunt May, with an occasional stay-over at Duke Hospital for evaluations. One Saturday afternoon in Wallace Wade Stadium, a good, underrated Duke football team outplayed the No. 1 nationally ranked Pittsburgh Panthers, only to lose 10-0 when Elmer (Honey Boy) Hackney, quarterback from Pittsboro, fumbled both opening half kick-offs to set up the only Pitt scores. The next year it was a different and much bigger story.

Football was a huge sport in the '30s, the rivalry between Duke and UNC far greater than today. At half-time the cheerleaders put on grand displays comparable to those in the Big Ten. The Duke Blue Devil, complete with horns, tail and a real pitchfork, pranced up and down the sidelines, occasionally hurling his spear, much, I thought, as Zeus would hurl his thunderbolts.

At one game, attended by Mother, Lil and me, the Blue Devil at halftime limbered up as the band played Duke's anthem "Dear Old Duke" followed by the rousing "Fight Song." Caught up in a collegiate chauvinism, I was no longer contemptuous of such ovations and demonstrations, as I had once been about Monroe High.

After equal time had been granted to the Tar Heel band and Ramses, the UNC mascot, had trotted around the field, out sprang the Blue Devil. Back went his arm. Thrusting forward, he flung the sharp, metal pitchfork into the air. It sailed up high, briefly gleaming silver, before it plunged earthward and lodged its blades into the back of a Duke cheerleader.

The youth fell to the ground. The stunned crowd of 45,000 released a roar of disbelief. Medics ran over. Distant figures stood over the boy for what seemed like hours, as a bewildered Blue Devil circled around and around in dismay. Finally an ambulance arrived and the cheerleader was whisked away. After that the Duke pitchfork was made of stiff cardboard with soft rubber blades.

What happened to the victim? I was led to believe that he recovered without lasting paralysis. The Blue Devil and the institution and team he represented escaped without legal penalty. For him the careless mistake itself was punishment enough.

Mother took that awfully hard. As her best lifelong friend, Miss Ann Redwine, later observed under different circumstances, "Your mother always seemed to believe her feelings went deeper than anyone else's." Maybe they did. She learned a lot later on. As for me, the memory did not linger. I certainly was not traumatized. I had other things on my mind.

In March, 1938, Hitler marched into his native Austria and declared the Anschluss. Neville Chamberlain unfurled his umbrella and declared the annexation a natural unification of a people of the same race and language. Besides, the Fuhrer had declared this was his last territorial demand. Mr. Finlay and Mr. Huffman, my high school social science and history teachers, knew better. So did my parents. So did I.

Aunt May had arranged through the Perkins Library for me to receive some educational materials from the recently opened Soviet Embassy in Washington. The Simmons and Covington kin, largely academics, believed in information, education, the free flow of ideas and opinions, in truth triumphant, once free to combat ignorance and censorship. What they did not fully appreciate was that education and propaganda meant the same thing in totalitarian societies. Truth and error were never left free to contest their merits.

Soon I was thrilled over Soviet accomplishments such as the dam at Dnieprpetrovsk in the Ukraine, the success of the second Five Year Plan, and the collectivized farms, even if it did mean the ruin of those rich landowning Kulaks. I had to figure out on my own that Stalin's forced industrialization was an ecological disaster; that collective farming resulted in the starvation of millions of peasants and that the Kulaks were, by American standards, impoverished serfs, now servants of the state rather than the Boyars.

Neither did I understand the implications of the Third International, the Byzantine, tyrannical nature of the Kremlin, or of the enormous oppression of people by any totalitarian society. I knew nothing of class warfare or of Marxist-Leninist theory, as modified by Josef Stalin.

I was a teen-age idealist, temporarily hooked on the principles of a theoretical communism that was never fully practiced except possibly during those "ten days that shook the world" and a few months thereafter when individuality, free love, anarchy and a hatred for all things personally oppressive held sway.

The massive purges and show trials were still in the not-so-distant future. The Gulag was largely unknown. The novel *1984* was yet to be written. All I knew was that the ugly, repressive, reactionary regime of Imperial Russia had been overthrown. Change and reform were in the air. The Soviet Union was a mortal enemy of Fascism and Nazi Germany, eager to erect a barrier of collective security against Axis aggression.

By late 1939 I had learned better. But in 1941 I was happy to welcome Russia into the last European war. When that war became a world war, the Allies were eager to welcome the Soviet Union as an ally. Even Winston Churchill, long a foremost enemy of communism who had twenty years earlier attempted to strangle the infant in its crib, held out a hand of friendship. Even he acknowledged that it was the Soviet Union, its Great Patriotic War thrust upon it, that had "torn the guts out of the German military machine" and in the process had suffered injuries no other nation could have endured. I've always felt a certain appreciation for that. Stalin, by stopping the German blitzkrieg for the first time in December 1941, and Truman, by dropping "the bomb" on Japan in August 1945, inadvertently may have saved my life.

So it was with such recognition in mind that I viewed Russia as a wartime ally but with few illusions left. The onset of the Cold War soon to follow victory in 1945 came as no real surprise.

The year 1938 did not start out much different from the year before. Mary C. was teaching at Mount Olive. She disliked her principal, Kenneth Stabler. He was a stickler for rules and regulations. My sister always had a problem with those and with male authority figures, a difficulty that stemmed, I believe, from conflicts with her father and which was reflected later in both her marriages.

Mary C. was a good, creative teacher but impatient and tactless with her rule-bound boss. She invited me and friend Bill Price to visit for a weekend. Hamp and Amelia Price were perfectly willing for Lessie to drive us all the way from Monroe to Mount Olive, even if Lessie remained depressed and expressed her willingness to do so "if only I were able." She was able enough to do it without mishap, although Bill and I tried to make the task more difficult by humming loudly, denying all knowledge of the origin of the sound when Mother asked if we heard it too and wondered where it came from. We also ridiculed her obsessive habit of repeatedly taking her hand on and off the manual gear shift while we were riding along at sixty miles an hour with no need to shift gears.

Mary C. was a good hostess. She encouraged her favorite student Charlie Kraft to introduce me to his friend Jean Barbour at a party Saturday night. Jean was a dirty blonde who looked just like Priscilla Lane, a Warner Brothers contract player. I fell in love for the first time, experienced my first heart-driving kiss, an affair that lasted the entire weekend---and as quickly forgotten.

Mother, Mary C., Lil and I spent that summer at Lake Junaluska, where Duke University held an annual summer school. Mother, Mary C. and Lil all took classes in Shakespearean drama. I was alone a lot, hung around my sisters too much, and made friends with the local folk, many living unbelievably isolated lives.

We made friends with a young fellow named Joe, who worked around the place and enjoyed visiting with summer people. Joe hung around the evening pavilion, playing ping-pong, strumming his guitar, and singing mountain songs. One Saturday night he failed to appear. We asked about him, only to be told that he had been killed the night before on the road to Waynesville.

It seemed as if many people were getting killed in wrecks back then. Statistically, highway deaths were much higher then than now. By 1938, perhaps 50,000 Americans died on the nation's highways annually out of a population of 130 million, compared to about 40,000 in 2000, when the population was over twice that of 1938. Sometimes things do get better.

There was an occasional hint of summer romance. A boy next door up from Greenville, N.C. whose mother was a friend of Miss Ann Redwine developed a crush on Lil. She typically avoided and dismissed him but Mary C. and I teased her mercilessly. "Lil is ripe for romance," Mary C. declared. When Moke and Bill came up for a week to visit me, Lil's name changed to Ripe.

When Daddy came up for a weekend and took all of us over to Grove Park Inn in Asheville, twenty-five miles away, for dinner, cupid hit Mary C. A business friend of Dowd's joined the group. Mary C. found Mr. Geough to be "tall, dark, and handsome." The strong, silent type, he was about forty, "far too old for Mary Cov," then twenty-two, Mother declared.

We were all impressed by the glamorous setting---a beautiful five-diamond dining room, with a lavish display of food, served in many courses in great style. The room provided a panoramic view of the Blue Ridge Mountains to the northeast and of the Great Smokies to the west. Nearly fifteen, I no longer was a spoilsport when the family dined out, nor did I object when Daddy began to flirt with the waitress. I even did a little myself.

Mary C's flirtation with Mr. Geough did not last long. In fact, she never saw him after that night, but she talked plenty about him. Later that fall, however, she forgot all about him when she met Nick Clodfelter, the first real romance of her life.


Despite Mother's successful coping with family, friends, visitors, housekeeping and Duke summer school classes at Lake Junaluska, appearances were deceiving. She was no better. In fact she got worse as soon as we returned to Broadacre.

Back home in a hideously hot August, I spent a lot of time with Vann, Moke, Bill, and Philip. Hitler pressed his demand for the return of the Sudetenland, now part of Czechoslovakia, to the Third Reich. Chamberlain dispensed Lord Runciman to the various capitals of Europe to seek a peaceful solution which in those days of appeasement meant a Prague surrender to Berlin. But President Edward Benes proved stubborn. Great Britain and France warned Germany they wouldn't force their Czech ally to surrender. The Soviet Union urged "collective security." The world moved closer to Munich.

Of all this, most of my friends were blissfully unaware. If some did hear of it, they did not seem to care or understand. The national mood was one of isolation. Even President Roosevelt issued calls for world peace, declaring that "All of us are pacifists." When school began in September, crowds gathered at the Friday afternoon football games. "Monroe will shine!"

I had not noticed any difference in Mother since our return, but one day in September there was a hushed conference among my father, Aunt May, Aunt Eve, Aunt Catherine and Aunt Sue. Aunt Eve had received a call from Frances Adams, a former student at Salem. Could she and Mr. Secrest come by the Adams house that night?

Our whole entourage went. Old man Bruce Adams had begun to act strangely earlier in the summer. Now he was accusing his wife of infidelity. His accusation was not only unbelievable, his behavior was also bizarre. He developed an *idée fixe* about poor old Mrs. Adams who had never even looked at another man, as, in all probability, no other man had ever looked at her. Elderly, plain, decent, "a good Christian woman," the whole notion was just plain crazy.

Exactly. That's what daughter Frances thought and son Henry feared. Father Bruce was losing it, possibly becoming dangerous. Knowing that Mother had been coping with depression for three years and had been hither, thither and yon for help, the adult children of Mr. and Mrs. Adams thought the Dowd Secrest family could offer some help.

Medical knowledge did not then understand the differences among the various kinds of mental and emotional disorders. No distinction was made between neuroses and psychoses. No one mentioned character disorders or borderline personalities. There was of course a world of difference between the simple, unipolar disorder from which Mother suffered and the madness into which Mr. Adams had descended. His proved to be a form of systematic delusional paranoia for which no medication was then available. So Bruce Adams was sent off to the North Carolina State Hospital for the Insane in Morganton, where years earlier John Redwine had gone.

The memory of that evening in the Adams household is seared in my memory. What a fight. What a scene. What a fright. What a sight!

Mother went home, took an overdose of aspirin, and later fell down the front porch steps. Soon, at her decision and with the bills to be paid from her own money, Mother left for Phipps Psychiatric Clinic at Johns Hopkins Hospital in Baltimore. She went alone, committed herself. "It's always darkest before dawn," so the saying goes. "The tide is at its highest just before it ebbs." Often in depression, a patient is at his worst just before the darkness lifts. That is the way it worked with Lessie when she left us for the third time on my fifteenth birthday, September 15, 1938, one day before her forty-sixth.

Life is full of ironies. Fast forward forty years, from 1938 to 1978. Substitute the name Henry Adams for Bruce Adams and you would find a repeat performance at the same brick house on Houston Street now occupied by Henry and his wife, Caroline. Bruce's son Henry had early on shown signs of a fragile nervous system. Childless, his wife was careful not to allow too much pressure to be placed upon him. She and Henry took care of nearly all of our family's insurance business. Mother and Henry had remained friends. As recently as 1957 Lessie had unexpectedly encountered Henry and Caroline walking along the Champs-Elysées while on separate travels to France.

Twenty years later Henry began to have strange ideas and behave in bizarre ways. He suspected his wife of having an affair. How? When? With whom? He did not know, but he was determined to find out. The accusations against Mrs. Henry Adams were as unfounded as those against Mrs. Bruce Adams had been forty years earlier. Eventually Henry had to be sent to Broughton State Hospital in Morganton, just like John Redwine and Bruce Adams before him. As Caroline said to me at a reception we had given Mother in 1981, "It's just the most frustrating thing one can ever imagine." Perhaps an understatement.

Frances Adams married late in life, but in time to have a daughter. Aunt Eve kept up with her Salem girls and was pleased to report in 1979, shortly before her own death, that Frances enjoyed a happy, normal family life, somewhere out west. Idaho, I believe---far removed from the family sadness that had haunted their home on Houston Street in Monroe.

# 28. Rachel, Recovery and the Rose Bowl

Mother's departure for Baltimore was overshadowed for me by European developments: Chamberlain's trips to Berchtesgarten to seek some solution with Hitler, the digging of ditches in London streets to provide air raid shelters, the sand-bagging of Buckingham Palace, Westminster Abbey, and Parliament buildings, riots and strikes in Paris, saber-rattling in Rome, ranting and raving by radio and press in Berlin.

As the crisis neared, Chamberlain broadcast from London: what a pity, how incredible, that the world stood at the steps of another war over a quarrel so far away among peoples about whom the British people knew nothing. "What inspiring leadership," Philip and I declared, sarcastically. "Say what?" and "Huh?" was the reaction of most of our peers. Again, I lived a life separate from most of my friends.

As London's air raid sirens sounded in practice drills and Chamberlain wrung his hands, a reprieve was granted. Mussolini, with FDR's encouragement, called for a four-power conference. Hitler agreed, the meeting to be held in Munich, with Germany, Great Britain, Italy and France. Czechoslovakia, whose fate was to be determined, and the Soviet Union, were excluded. Within days, Chamberlain and Daladier, the French premier, had returned to their respective capitals, the French leader at least looking embarrassed and ashamed. The British Prime Minister was triumphant, waving a piece of paper Hitler had signed. The agreement meant "peace with honor in our time."

Winston Churchill, still a back bencher in his "Wilderness Years," arose from his seat in Parliament to declare that his country had suffered an "unmitigated defeat." He later declared that Chamberlain, "given a choice between war and dishonor... chose dishonor (but) he will have war..."

That prophetic view was realized less than one year later. But back home exciting things were happening. Two events of about equal importance to my adolescent mind occurred. Duke's Blue Devils, boasting a defensive line of the Seven Iron Dukes and quarterback, Eric "The Red" Tipton with his magic kick, were going into their final game undefeated, untied and unscored upon. If they could defeat the nationally ranked No. 1 Pittsburgh Panthers in the final game of the season, Wallace Wade's Blue Devils would surely be invited to play in the Rose Bowl for the mythical national football championship.

The other news came from Johns Hopkins. Mother was much better. In fact, she was well, but not quite ready to acknowledge it. She slept well, had a hearty appetite, interacted well with other patients and staff, and spoke lovingly of her husband and children. She expressed a desire to be back home with them.

On the phone with Daddy, with Lil and me on the extension line, the doctor said, "Your wife isn't clinically depressed. She is well. This kind of quick, spontaneous recovery is not uncommon. It's largely a matter of time, which, frankly, we do not fully understand ourselves. I suspect Mrs. Secrest was getting well in September when she made her own decision to come here. She arrived only a couple of months ago. She seldom talks about herself now, far more interested in other patients and helping them."

The doctor said that Mother's expression was pleasant, her sense of humor keen, her walk balanced and graceful. Most importantly, Mrs. Secrest had a deep and penetrating insight into her condition and the roles her personality and family environment had played in her illness.

In reply to Dowd's question about coming home, the doctor replied, "She's probably ready now. But we want to be sure her progress holds. Sometimes mood swings occur and apparent recovery doesn't last. If she continues as she is now through January, come take her home." Then the doctor, a woman yet, said, "And when you do, Mr. Secrest, you and I need to talk."

"Fat chance," I heard Daddy mutter as he hung up the phone.

Soon calls and letters were flying among family members and friends elated at the good news from Baltimore. Lil, Mary C., and Aunts May, Eve, Katherine and Sue, plus Monroe relatives and friends and, of course, Rosa Parker and Betty Webb were ready to welcome Mother —back into the daylight of life.

Aunt May told Brack that he was to have me up for the big game against Pittsburgh. No, it was too cold out there in Duke Forest. I was to stay with him and his fraternity brothers at Kappa Sigma. He could find an extra bed.

The night before the big game I even got Eric Tipton's autograph. The fabled kicker was Brack's fraternity brother. Brack himself had become a Big Man On Campus: president of the Panhellenic Council, soon to be initiated into Phi Beta Kappa. In those days, the Craven-Covington names were still an advantage.

That late November Saturday is still a day to be remembered. Daddy, Lil, Aunt May and I crowded into Duke stadium. Shortly before kick-off, snow began to fall. By half-time the field was lightly covered. Pittsburgh's dream backfield swept up and down the field, but the Seven Iron Dukes always held on downs within the shadow of their own goal posts.

Tipton gave the performance of his career. Despite the slippery ball, often having to be wiped off due to the heavy wet snow, the quarterback time and again got off long, booming kicks to place the ball within Pitt's 10-yard line. On what was to be one of the final plays of the day, Eric the Red took the ball on fourth down, put his toe into it and sent it sailing up, up and away, a high spiraling kick that landed 50 yards down field and rolled out of bounds on the Pitt three-yard line. With the clock running out, the Duke line rushed the Panther quarterback on fourth down, and blocked the kick. One of the Duke linemen recovered the ball for a Duke touchdown. The extra point was good. The final score: Duke 7-Pitt 0.

So Duke had ended its first undefeated season: untied and unscored upon. Before we had left Durham for Monroe, the snow still falling, the Durham Sun had published an extra. "Duke Wins! Accepts Bid to Rose Bowl!" It didn't get any better than this. No way could Mother's recovery compare with that in the mind of a fifteen-year-old boy, no matter how over-attached he may once have been.

After Mother had sent herself to Johns Hopkins in the early fall of 1938, Daddy hired Rachel as a live-in housekeeper. That may have been all well and good, except Rachel did not know much about keeping house and had little interest in it. Her tastes turned to other things—such as movies, beauty pageants, parties and pictures of herself in bathing suits which she had taken downtown in Monroe's professional photography shop.

Rachel, daughter of Fiddlin' Bob and niece of a Charlotte woman of considerable note, was star-struck. A first cousin was a starlet in Hollywood. Within four years Virginia Dale was playing Fred Astaire's girlfriend in the film "Holiday Inn," in which Irving Berlin's tune "White Christmas" was introduced. It's probable that the nationwide motel chain borrowed its name from that Tinsel Town production. Miss Dale remained in show business, in movies and television, until her death in 1995.

Virginia Dale's older sister, Rachel insisted to me, had really won the Miss America contest in Atlantic City in 1936. She never received the crown, however, after it was discovered that she had previously been briefly married, a violation of pageant rules. Since then, Rachel's cousin had pursued a lucrative modeling career in New York City and had been pursued by nearly every eligible man in the Big Apple. Soon Rachel was modeling bathing suits for me, Vann, Bill Price, Bill Hemby, Moke and Philip. Wow! Forget about Heath's and Murray's earlier little funny cartoon books.

One afternoon Vann and a couple of other friends were over playing. Rachel was out, perhaps at the photographer for more pictures. Daddy was working. Despite my experience with Heath the year before, despite Rachel's innocent provocations, despite my frequent self-indulgences, I retained a puritanical, goody-goody, judgmental attitude—ambivalent, erratic, contradictory leftovers from earlier maternal warnings and moral teaching. Sometimes I didn't approve of drinking or cursing at any age under any circumstances. It was immoral. Vann and friends were less inhibited. Vann, who knew about Daddy's lavatory drinking habits, decided that afternoon to sample the bootleg whiskey.

"You can't do that!" I exclaimed, in moral outrage.

"Oh, come on. Uncle Dowd won't miss it," Vann countered.

"It's not that. I don't want you to. It isn't right. You shouldn't drink whiskey," I insisted.

"Where does he keep it?" Vann asked, dismissing my disapproval. And he ran into the bathroom, wrestling me to one side as he looked among the bottles of bay rum and other skin lotions.

"Aha! Here it is!" he proclaimed, bringing out a Mason jar nearly full of a clear liquid. "I bet that's white lightnin'."

So Vann and Bill each took a belt, then gagged, belched, groaned and opened their mouths to gulp down cold breaths of fresh air as they ran for ice water in the refrigerator. Well, if you can't beat 'em—so I took a swig, too, and joined them in hot pursuit to the kitchen.

I never told Daddy, I don't think Vann confessed to Uncle Vann, but a few nights later, Uncle Vann did come by the house. I heard him talking to Daddy.

"Dowd, what's the matter with you?" the brother, nearly nine years younger, asked in a stern voice. "Have you lost your senses? What do you mean by having a young woman like Rachel living here with you and Mac?"

Daddy said something in self-defense, but Uncle Vann wouldn't hear of it. "No, Dowd, I'm not saying anything against Rachel. She's probably a nice, sweet girl. And I'm not accusing you of anything improper, either. But consider how things may look to other people. Appearances do matter."

Vann mentioned me and Vann Jr. He said Rachel could prove a temptation to us—at least an unhealthy preoccupation.

"It just isn't right, Dowd," Vann repeated. "The boys are unchaperoned. You don't know if one thing may lead to another. Think about it. You don't want another Mrs. Thompson in the family, do you?"

Daddy pooh-poohed any such idea, adding that any such suggestion was an undue reflection on Rachel. Vann replied that aside from Vann and me, there was the possible perception of impropriety.

"People will talk, Dowd," Vann warned darkly. "About you and Rachel. Some like to think the worst, even if you are innocent. They'll say you are being unfaithful to Lessie while she's sick and away, you'll see. And," he added, "Vann, Jr. can't come over here any more as long as this arrangement continues. Vann will be spending his time after school working at the drug store. Maybe you ought to think about some similar arrangement for Mac."

Daddy ignored his brother's warning, but none of my uncle's fears came to pass. Soon Vann was temporarily side-tracked by a belated circumcision. Again, Uncle Vann showed more common sense and understanding than Dowd (fifteen a far more psychologically appropriate age for such a procedure than four).

When Mother returned home well, in charge, a different woman, a few months later, Rachel disappeared within a week. I remember Rachel, as I do all the women in my life, with fondness and affection, appreciative of her star-struck innocence, enthusiasm, warm-hearted indulgence and good-natured sense of fun.

Mary C. was not asked to return to Mount Olive for the fall term of 1938. In view of her open show of contempt for Principal Stabler, that came as no surprise. Nor was it any disappointment to her. She had no intention of accepting reappointment, having already gotten a better position in an experimental school in Ellerbee.

This little community in Richmond County, about fifty miles from Monroe, was proud of its model progressive school, in which "hands-on" teaching was emphasized. Teachers were encouraged to be innovative and creative. The students, the theory assumed, were so motivated and kept so busy, there were practically no disciplinary problems.

That was fortunate for Mary Cov, as she was not a good disciplinarian, usually siding with the student against the authority figure, often laughing with her charges at their antics. The classroom was not a quiet place of repose. Her students were not expected to keep quiet or stand still. The day I visited her in action in Mount Olive the room was rocking.

That approach was just fine in Ellerbee. Mary C. was in her element. She coached the girls' basketball team to victory in the divisional championship. The faculty was comprised of idealistic young men and women, all devoted to intellectual ferment and having a good time. As an added bonus, my sister met a man whom she felt was the man of her dreams. Her parents feared he might become her worst nightmare.

One problem was Nick Clodfelter was a railroad man. He'd never been to college. He liked to party. He liked to drink. He liked to carouse. Around Daddy Nick was the perfect gentleman. Around Dowd's daughter, he was also a gentleman but not, thank goodness, my sister said, perfect. In Daddy's eyes, the railroad man from Hamlet was not good enough for his daughter. "Would any man ever be?" Mary C. wondered.

That fall, Mary C. and several of her friends, sometimes including Nick, spent an occasional weekend in Monroe. Rachel took those weekends off. I looked forward to these house parties, as Mary C. and her friends brought with them good humor and high spirits. They played swing and hit parade tunes, danced, played cards and parlor games, especially Murder and Charades. Daddy kept his bootleg whiskey securely locked up. None of Mary C's friends were interested in drinking except Nick, and when he was around her, he wasn't, either.

On a Saturday night in late October, while the Ellerbee guests were in residence, someone said he smelled smoke. Seated in the kitchen facing south, I saw a faint glow near the barn.

"Hey, Daddy, look over there. Is that light coming from the barn?" Even as I spoke the light grew brighter, orange tongues of flame licking around the sides of the wooden building.

"Call the fire department!" Daddy shouted, as he ran for the car. "Go get Heath," he added, indicating to Nick that he should take me. The whole house emptied as everyone started toward the barn only a block from Broadacre.

As we approached the building, we could feel the heat. A large crowd had gathered. Ropes blocked traffic in both directions on the unpaved road. I could hear a great commotion from within, horses whinnying and neighing and kicking against their stalls; cows, calves, sheep, goats, all in growing panic. No sound came from the chickens and turkeys.

Heath, Murray and Doll Jr., soon to be joined by me and Nick, and then dozens of rural neighbors, ran rapidly in and out, opening doors and lowering ramps as the livestock seemed somehow to flow out of the burning building.

We were lucky. The fire had been discovered early. The flames had not spread to the animal compounds before rescue workers had gotten there although some of the thick black smoke had. Contrary to Hollywood versions of such fires, where horses freeze with fear and have to be led out, blinders over their eyes, nearly all the animals bolted on their own as soon as the gates were opened. But the fire raged out of control. The barn burned to the ground. Luckily, only the chickens and turkeys had burned with it.

On a subsequent Saturday night, in April, 1939, the same thing happened, only this time it was at Dr. Sam Alexander's barn on Franklin Street. Dr. Alexander was not so lucky. Many of his animals, including 31 horses and mules, were killed. On several other Saturday nights that winter other, larger fires occurred. The police soon concluded that a fire bug was responsible. Casualties grew, but none was human. The pyromaniac was never caught.

These incidents occurred just as the Nancy Drew films—grade B Warner Brothers programmers—were released. The first, *Nancy Drew, Detective,* followed by *Nancy Drew, Reporter,* caught my imagination. I wanted to become a policeman and find that fire bug. Then I decided it would be better to be an investigative reporter, not only covering exciting events but also helping solve crimes. Later I did become a reporter. I would like to credit more masculine elevated role models, but the truth is that at age fifteen I was motivated by Nancy Drew, played to the hilt by Bonita Granville, with whom I simultaneously identified and wanted to hit on.

Over the next several years I did elevate my journalistic sights, now becoming inspired by real-life radio reporters, foremost being Edward R. Morrow ("This—is London"); Eric Severeid ("Reporting from Paris"); William L. Shirer ("Coming to You From Berlin"); Larry LaSueur—all great voices from CBS and reporting on the first years of the Second World War: 1939-1941.

The new year opened with great excitement. Duke's Blue Devils were to face Southern California's Trojans in the Rose Bowl at Pasadena at 5:00 o'clock Eastern Standard Time. A largely defensive team with little offensive punch, Duke was still a slight favorite over USC, which had lost two games earlier in the season. But the Trojans had a mighty aerial offense, sure to challenge the Seven Iron Dukes.

Lil, Daddy and I listened to descriptions of the Rose Bowl parade, the pre-game hype, the sportscasters' knowledgeable analysis. Then, the kick-off. Although the Trojans put on an aerial circus, completing pass after pass, and unleashed a ground offensive that carried them deep into Duke territory time and again, the Duke line held on fourth downs. The half-time score remained: Duke 0-USC 0.

The same story was told in the third quarter. But early in the fourth Duke managed to take the ball down to the Southern California sixteen yard-line, where on fourth down, the Blue Devil place kicker sent the ball through the uprights, placing Duke ahead, three to nothing. So it remained until the final minute of play. With the Trojans in possession within the shadow of their own goal posts, Lil and I felt sure our team had won.

With the clock ticking off the seconds, the California quarterback began to connect with his receiver. The combination Nave to Doyle ran off one first down after another. As the announcer told us that sixteen seconds remained on the clock, the USC quarterback on the Duke 32-yard line threw a Hail Mary pass. As related later, the sidelined Duke captain put his head down on his knees, daring not to look up.

"Did he make it?" the boy asked Coach Wallace Wade, as the roaring crowd furnished him the answer.

"Yep, 'fraid he did, son," was the coach's reply. The California team lined up quickly for the extra point, kicked perfectly. The final score USC 7-Duke 3. The previously unbeaten, untied, unscored upon Blue Devils saw the national title slip from their grasp.

Almost immediately the phone rang. A collect call from Baltimore. Would we accept the charges? Yes, yes, of course.

It was Mother, calling to commiserate with her children. At the sound of her voice, Lil cried. When I got on the line, I cried, not so much because I was hearing Mother's voice for the first time in four months as because my favorite team had lost.

When Daddy was finally allowed to speak to his wife, he did not cry. He was brief, businesslike, unemotional. Mother was well. She was coming home soon. Discussion concerned hospital logistics and transportation.

"Tell the doctor to send me the bill," Daddy said abruptly, "And come home on the bus."

Dowd was being difficult again. This later led to an argument with Lil.

"What do you mean, telling Mother to take the bus home?" my 18-year-old sister asked. "Of course you're driving up to get her. What's the date?"

"She is being discharged by the end of the month." Daddy said. "No, we're not going up to Baltimore. She went up there alone. She can come home alone—good connections by bus or train."

"Well, if you're not going, Mac and I will," the defiant daughter declared.

"And what will you use for money?"

"Don't be concerned about that. I can type term papers and tutor friends for their final exams. And borrow. Mac can clerk at Belk's after school. We'll take the train from Hamlet to Washington. Stay with Betty and Roy. They'll drive us over to Baltimore. Don't worry about it." With that, Lil pressed her lips together into a tight line, looking just like Aunt Eve, once she had made up her mind.

Later that evening we called Aunt Kathryn Huntley. She drove over, spoke to Dowd, came out a few minutes later to announce that we were all going to Baltimore to get Lessie. Yes, of course Dowd was coming, and Lil and me too. She preferred to do most of the driving in her new Buick, as it was roomier than Dowd's car and she was a better driver. She trusted us to make suitable arrangements in Baltimore. Direct, decisive, accustomed to dealing with men in a man's world, Aunt Kathryn knew how to deal with Dowd. She had been a buffer, absorbing much of the tension between our parents since Uncle Fred's death four years earlier.

Aunt Kathryn regarded Mary Cov, Lil and me as children she and Fred never had. She was equally devoted to Lessie and Dowd. She was so closely aligned with us so often when Mother was away that Lil and I occasionally wondered if Mother were ever jealous.

"I don't see how she could have helped it," Lil said years later. But Mother never was, and in her faith, she was fully justified.

The trip to Baltimore and back was uneventful. We stayed at the Double Door Inn next to Johns Hopkins. The doctor had her interview with Dowd, whether he wanted it or not, and at her insistence, with Lil and me, too. Given Daddy's attitude, I did not view a prospective reunion between Lessie and Dowd at Broadacre with any great optimism. Caution in the form of separation seemed to me to be the better part of valor.

The afternoon at the hospital as I waited my turn with the doctor, I learned about anorexia nervosa. I saw a young woman lying on a bed and asked if she would like to play Chinese checkers. She agreed. She was so thin you could see right through her. She couldn't have weighed sixty pounds. I asked her why she was so skinny. "I'm not!" she declared, "I'm too fat! I hate the way I look." At age fifteen I had learned a lot. No one else in Monroe knew about such things. Not many medical people did. Eating disorders weren't discussed much until fairly recently and became women's issues.

No one else seemed to agree with me about parental separation, so back we drove to Monroe with a night's stop-over in Betty Webb and Roy Veatch's home in Georgetown. The only memorable thing occurred when Lil and I, both of us too keyed up to sleep, met at midnight in Betty's kitchen to discuss our parents' situation; then, remembering that delicious chocolate cake we had been served at dinner, opened the refrigerator, found the half cake remaining, divided it evenly and ate the whole thing. Anxiety can give one a mighty appetite.

# 29. An Anniversary and the Blitz

Lil went back to Duke to complete her junior year. Mary C. finished her year at Ellerbee's progressive school and applied for admission to the School of Social work in Richmond. She spent the summer out west and in Hollywood, coming back with all kinds of exciting tales. I continued to dance in nervous attendance as a parental go-between, but gradually reduced my vigilance as Mother appeared able to cope all right on her own. Daddy remained unpredictable, ambivalent and contradictory, sometimes unreasonable, argumentative, emotionally and physically self-indulgent; at others, unexpectedly patient, jovial, cheerful and good-natured.

I became a better student again, making A's on almost everything but still largely removed from campus life and much too late to make the National Honor Society or to top any list of classroom superlatives. Moke was named Best Looking Boy, but the honor didn't seem to make much difference in his popularity or self-esteem.

Rachel Hemby agreed to go to the Junior-Senior banquet with me. Daddy provided Gene Watts as our chauffeur, as I had just turned fifteen, much too young to drive. After dinner—suffocatingly chaperoned, with teen-age exuberance appropriately stifled—Bill and his date, Moke and his and Rachel and I headed out for Charlotte with Gene at the wheel. We went to WBT radio station, the CBS affiliate, to watch local celebrities perform and to request our favorite tunes to air.

My request, "I Get Along Without You Very Well" dedicated to my parents, Mr. and Mrs. Andrew M. Secrest of Monroe, N.C., was indeed broadcast shortly after midnight to the tolerant approval of Lessie and

Dowd. What they failed to appreciate was that even at the Junior-Senior banquet, my parents still weighed heavily on my mind. It was a hollow declaration of independence.

Mary Cov had had a more liberating experience at her Junior-Senior banquet eight years earlier. Her date, William (Shug) Huntley, was already seventeen years old and had his driver's license. Mary Cov told him he could drive her to the party in one of Daddy's demonstrator automobiles. Daddy said he couldn't. After the customary head-banging, Daddy won.

But Mary C. had the last laugh. She got Heath and me to hitch Tom to the wagon, filled with hay, and with Mary C. at the reins, off she and Shug went, on a hayride.

" Cool!" was the reaction of her classmates. She and her date clearly had achieved peer approval, something Shug had rarely attained before.

Lil, enjoying more establishment status than her older sister or younger brother, had been both planner and participant at her Junior-Senior Banquet in 1936. She played the role of Harriet Hilliard to Skipper Bowles' Ozzie Nelson in a take-off on Ozzie's network radio musical program. Lil's only problem: she couldn't sing, so rival Elizabeth Warren had to render the musical numbers.

In July 1939, Aunt Eve decided that Mother and Daddy should spend the rest of the summer alone to readjust. With Mary C. and Earle in California, she arranged to have Lil and me, along with David, Bill and Caroline Fowler from Louisville spend several weeks in July and August with her at Salem College. Brack had a job at Myrtle Beach. The three boys were put up at Miss Teague's boardinghouse in the heart of what today is Old Salem, just across from the Moravian Church on the Salem College campus. Lil and Caroline stayed in Aunt Eve's apartment next door.

Aunt Eve was an unrivaled organizer and planner. She called all her connections into play. The result: swimming and games at the Country Club; daily movies, parties at Catherine Johnson's and her friends, dinners at Salem College's cafeteria or at Miss Teague's. Miss Catherine Hanes came across, as did the Spaughs and various faculty members.

Best of all, however, was the camaraderie among the Secrest and Fowler cousins. Although part of each day was reserved for reading, instruction and quiet time, we played cards constantly. With international tensions rising and actual war only weeks away, the card game "War!" was by far our favorite. I insisted upon being either Great Britain or Russia—until August 24 when Hitler and Stalin signed their friendship pact. Then we made Caroline and Bill, the youngest, represent Germany and Russia.

David, although nearer Lil's age than mine, and I bonded closely that summer. We both were sprouting hair on our chests. We experimented with cigarettes. We shared a mutual sense of forbidden pleasure when we accidentally walked in on Nancy Teague, then a stacked and sophisticated eighteen, as she was taking a bath. Standing tall and totally nude in the bathtub, slathered with soap, she looked up in surprise as we bumbled in without knocking. Then, seeing who we were, she smiled broadly and asked, a mocking tone in her low, sultry voice, "Why, hello, boys, what do you want? Anything I can do for you?"

David and I fled in confusion. Nancy no doubt got a big laugh out of that. Reduced in circumstances by the death of her husband, Nancy's mother had been forced to take in roomers. She and her daughter lived from hand to mouth but maintained their position in Old Salem. Nancy graduated from college and later married the head man of Piedmont Airlines and became a prosperous corporate wife, as Piedmont morphed its way through mergers into British Airways. But fortune is a fickle mistress and suddenly frowns as quickly as she smiles upon her favorites. Before Nancy reached middle age, cancer claimed her as it had her mother a few years earlier.

The movie highlight of that last peacetime summer was "The Wizard of Oz." I came home barely a week before Hitler first demonstrated the blitzkrieg. I wandered around beneath the grape arbor at Broadacre, groaning under its heavy load, plucking occasional muscadine and scuppernong grapes, thinking about the pending war and humming, "Somewhere, Over the Rainbow."

Could Poland successfully resist Nazi Germany, threatened as she now was by Russia from the East? Would France and Great Britain honor their pledge to come to her assistance if Germany attacked? Had the appeasers stopped asking: "Why die for Danzig?" Wouldn't they find some belated reason to back out of war one more time? With memories still fresh of the killing fields in Flanders drenched in blood only twenty-five years earlier, why wouldn't they be tempted? If they did declare war, how could they help Poland? Only partly re-armed, could they defeat Nazi Germany, now protected from a two-front war?

Daddy and I occupied the same bedroom Thursday night, August 31, leaving the radio on to catch the latest news. At dawn, we heard the familiar voice of Robert Trout, CBS reporter, announcing that German troops had crossed the Polish frontier and were rapidly driving east, as German aircraft bombed Warsaw. My questions were soon answered. Poland was finished within thirty days, invaded from the east by Soviet Russia on September 17. Warsaw surrendered on September 28. A so-called "Phony War" then set in as Germany prepared the conquest of Britain and France.

Now sixteen and in my senior year, I substituted my preoccupation with family matters with one concerning the European conflict. Russia invaded Finland in December. Despite initial defeats, by March 1940 Stalin had imposed his will upon his little neighbor. Soon the Soviet Union had occupied the Baltic states of Lithuania, Estonia, and Latvia and regained land lost to Romania and Poland at the end of the last war. Clearly the stage was set for something big to happen.

Now the battle to repeal neutrality laws began at home. The move to aid the allies, led by a wily, cautious commander-in-chief, Franklin D. Roosevelt, backed to the hilt by most Southern Democrats, was opposed by some of his Midwest progressive former supporters, such as Burton K. Wheeler of Montana, as well as isolationist Republicans personified by Senator Robert A. Taft of Ohio, Senator Nye of North Dakota, and the unholy trio—quoting FDR—of "Martin, Barton and Fish." President Roosevelt even presented journalist Frank O'Donnell of the New York Daily News an Iron Cross at a news conference for "aiding and abetting the enemy"—a gesture unimaginable by a president in peacetime toward the Fourth Estate half a century later.

At home things settled down. My parents and I shared the same views on local and foreign policy issues, so domestic harmony reigned on that front. Mother had at last learned to lead her own life, with Dowd when he wished, without him when he did not. Lessie planned a big party at Broadacre to celebrate her and her husband's silver wedding anniversary. An elaborate, catered affair, nearly everyone we knew was invited. It was also a party for those who had loyally rallied around Mother during her four-year hiatus and whom she had never repaid.

Everybody apparently was to come—except one. Daddy decided he would not attend. Mother had redecorated the house for the occasion. She had a silver gown designed. She arranged for Lessie and Dowd gifts to be presented. Engraved invitations were sent to family members, nuclear and extended, on both sides as well as to long-time friends. Welcoming RSVPs came from all over—inside Monroe and well beyond it. Everybody it seems except from her husband. He would not come. He would spend the evening, December 9, 1939, down at the motor company with Gene Watts, Bright Beaton and Wilma Joyner.

Concerned about propriety and appearances, as well as for Mother's sake, I was upset. "What on earth are you going to do?" I asked Mother in considerable agitation. "Daddy won't come. It will be just terrible."

"Why, give the party and have a good time," was my mother's confident reply. "I can't be responsible for your father's behavior. If he wants to stay down at the motor company, that's up to him. But he'll be there alone. Gene, Wilma and Bright will be here. They've already accepted." After voicing further doubts, I tried to follow Mother's advice not to worry about it. "We're having our twenty-fifth wedding anniversary, and I'm going to have a wonderful time," she declared.

With everyone in place, Mother made her entrance, looking radiant and, I thought, breathtakingly beautiful in her silver dress. As the servants opened the sliding French doors from the living room to the dining room, there stood Daddy—even dressed in a tuxedo—standing over the punch bowl, flanked by Uncle Vann, Aunt Isabel Wolfe and Aunt Mary Hinson. Mother—along with Neville Chamberlain—had learned at last that appeasement did not pay.

The rest of my senior year was largely uneventful. I shook the dust of my parents' marital discord from my feet and moved on. One evening in early spring, 1940, Moke and I came back to Broadacre after seeing the film *Rebecca*. Still immersed in the scene where Lawrence Olivier is reunited safely outside with Joan Fontaine as Manderly goes up in flames, we were well inside before we smelled the smoke, then saw the fire licking around the grate. The space heater had already fallen through the floor.

We ran outside, grabbed the garden hose, pulled it through the bay window and poured water on the flames. My shirt pulled over my head to guard against the heat and smoke, I reached the phone to call the fire department. Once sure they were on the way, I called my parents who were at a dinner party at the J.C. Willis home. That fire was not the work of the arsonist. The furnace itself was defective. The damage was so extensive that Mother, Daddy and I had to move to an apartment in the Monroe Hotel and stay until the end of my senior year while Broadacre was repaired, refurbished and redecorated to Mother's taste.

Aside from the war now beginning to rage in Scandinavia and Western Europe, one other memorable event stands out. One late spring night Moke and I on impulse stopped by Molly Bowie's and asked her if she would like to go for a ride. Molly, still way out of our league, condescended to go, suggesting we pick up Lillian Younce to complete the foursome. Both Molly and Lillian were accustomed to dating older boys more socially mature than Moke and I. Before long we were parked in a little spot off the Wadesboro highway known as a local lovers' lane. Once there Moke and I didn't have a clue as to what to do next. Molly and Lillian were no help.

We didn't have long to wonder. A car drove up. Several boys got out... all older, bigger. Molly and Lillian looked guilty, embarrassed to be caught socially slumming with the likes of Moke and me, just sixteen and rarely been kissed. We rolled up the windows and locked the doors. I heard threats and shouts of derision as our tormentors demanded we get out of the car and give up the girls.

"No, don't get out," Molly warned.

"Just ignore them," advised Lillian. Not an easy thing to do as Daddy's new car was being damaged by flying debris, then rocked left and right until it nearly flipped over. Snarls, threats, epithets continued to spew from the mouths of our older tormentors, as Moke and I suffered the humiliation of impotent anger and fear. What an impression to make on such popular girls. What a thing to have to endure now, not to mention certain harassment in school on Monday. We would never live this down.

Somehow we did. Such injury to the male ego is slow to heal, however, and the event is still a painful memory sixty-five years later. Now, when I look through the university alumni directories and see that I have outlived all my tormentors that night in 1940, I feel vindicated, even glad. Dead? Serves them right!

In my seventeenth year, I grew emotionally more independent. I got a job on weekends clerking at Belk's and spent my own money for the cigarettes I had begun to smoke. I didn't date individually but several of my friends and I spent many a Friday and Saturday night at the home of Mr. and Mrs. Thomas Percy Dillon who had five girls, three of whom were more or less our contemporaries. Irene became my main squeeze; Mary Jane, Moke's. We called the senior Dillons Mr. and Mrs. Bennett, after the family in *Pride and Prejudice*.

At sixteen one is often in love with love. I was no exception. Romance became far more important than sex. Popular music, a stolen kiss that "sent my heart a-dancing," and eating—always eating—set the routine. Swing was the music to dance by. The main dance was the jitterbug, a variation of an earlier one called the Big Apple.

As the European conflict widened, jazz and swing began to be replaced by romantic tunes with a slower, more romantic sound. Vocalists— male and female—began to overshadow the hard-driving sound of the instrumentalists. Tommy Dorsey with his new male singer Frank Sinatra remained the favorite, but the sweeter sound of Glenn Miller's band was soon alongside Dorsey's in the charts. These tunes were laments of unrequited love, full of longing, desire, nostalgia—all appropriate for that age and time. When Paris fell in June 1940 I felt that I too, along with Frank Sinatra, would "Never Smile Again."

After the British army escaped from the continent through the English Channel port of Dunkirk in May, Britain itself was threatened by invasion. When Churchill's "Few" won the Battle of Britain, the Luftwaffe launched "The Blitz." The American public loved the romantic ballad, "A Nightingale Sang in Berkeley Square." The lyrics were so right to describe the times in which we lived... "the whole darned world seemed upside down." The popular culture of 1940—music, drama, the press, radio and the movies played a significant role in mobilizing public opinion behind FDR's program of avoiding war by aiding the Allies. For fifty-seven nights London was hit by explosive and incendiary bombs. The aerial attacks then extended into the countryside—Bristol, Birmingham, Coventry. Every week for eight months Great Britain suffered the equivalent of the terrorist attacks on the United States on September 11, 2001.

From August through October, every day then was like Super Bowl Sunday now. Who won? Who lost? What was the score? How many planes shot down? The entire world was composed of fans, awaiting results in breathless anticipation. British Prime Minister Winston Churchill inspired the democratic world with his fearless rhetoric. Franklin Roosevelt mesmerized us as he accepted an unprecedented nomination for a third term and went on to win the election in November. This was no football game. Far more than a mythical title was at stake. Western civilization, democratic values, individual freedom, even personal survival depended on the battles fought—some won, some lost—in 1940. At least that is how we saw it at Broadacre.

# 30. New York, New York!

I graduated from Walter Bickett High School in May, 1940, at sixteen. I ranked eighth scholastically in my class of forty. The twelfth grade was added that year but was optional for seniors. Most of us headed for college decided to graduate, as the future appeared so uncertain. Moke, Vann and I were accepted at Duke, Bill elected to go to Wake Forest, Philip to Carolina and Conrad to Clemson. Ed decided to complete the twelfth year. I had not been a distinguished student in high school. I did not make the National Honor Society, was not a student leader, did not participate much either in sports or extra-curricular activities. The reasons for this lackluster performance having been clearly set forth, I offer no apology or further explanation. I was relieved to discover later that research found no correlation between membership in such organizations and subsequent success in life. I always suspected as much.

Despite my fascination with European history and considerable knowledge of international politics from an early age, I was essentially untutored about American social history. Having been educated in schools where history was taught from a Southern perspective, by teachers for whom the Civil War and Reconstruction were still part of their collective subconscious, I developed a distorted view of how Americans in places outside the South lived. The year ahead at Duke University was to be an eye-opener. While it may be true that the South of the first half of the 20th century remained as much a state of mind as a geographical expression, I didn't even understand the enormous differences among the Southern states themselves, or the different kinds of people who lived there.

The nation was judged by the prevailing standards of Piedmont North Carolina, as filtered through the minds of teachers, preachers and other adult mentors outside my family and who taught and interpreted life well beyond the prescribed state-approved textbooks and public-school curriculum. Nothing Mother and her more sophisticated sisters said could completely offset that influence. Many people in Monroe were still infatuated with the myth and romance of the Lost Cause. The public schools observed Confederate Memorial Day on May 10, ignoring the national commemoration on May 30. Thirty years later they were still doing that in Cheraw, South Carolina where I then lived and served that community as editor-publisher of the Cheraw Chronicle.

Consequently, I remained a provincial child, limited in social scope and vision, until my first trip to New York, followed by my freshman year at college. Until then, I viewed anyone reared outside the eleven Confederate States as "Yankees," as foreign as people from a nation overseas. I understood that there were some English-speaking people in some of the New England states who reached our shores early on. There were blue-blooded Boston Brahmin discriminating against and exploiting some immigrants, largely Catholic Irish who were rapidly outbreeding and replacing them. As for all the other Northerners, they lived mainly in the Northeast corridor of the Atlantic Seaboard, mostly in Pennsylvania, New Jersey and New York. These people, I assumed, were largely oppressed wage slaves, victims of robber barons and Republican industrialists, who, when they were not holding down their own workers, were hatching schemes further to oppress and discriminate against the South by unfair tariffs, taxes, and railway freight rates.

Northerners lived in big city slums, never in houses of their own with yards and gardens but always in little crowded apartments above the businesses they ran. Every neighborhood was a "Dead End," as depicted in a MGM film. Rich Northerners were *nouveau riches*, their fortunes recently acquired in trade or manufacturing and on the backs of their underpaid employees. Those in the Social Register of big cities, such as New York's Four Hundred, were not in the same class as old monied Southern families, where money did not count so much as status and tenure. Southerners did not need social registers to tell them who they were. They already knew.

As for yeoman farmers in the Midwest and prairie states who actually worked the land themselves and sent their children to college, I knew nothing. Even less about merchants, small businessmen and middle class professional families in small towns like my own. To me there were only two classes outside the South: the capitalists and the workers, mostly immigrants since 1865, who, when they weren't being exploited by their masters, were misled and betrayed by big city bosses and crooked labor union leaders.

I was surprised to learn through travel and at the university that I not only had a thorough misconception of American life in nearly all its aspects, but also that I had to correct equally egregious misconceptions about the South held by fellow students from the North. Fortunately young people are quick studies and before long we were all fellow Americans, fully united by the time Japanese bombs fell on Pearl Harbor December 7 and Hitler and Mussolini declared war four days later.

Lil graduated summa cum laude at Duke in June 1940. Her name, listed alphabetically in the program, bore an asterisk which simply stated at the bottom: "Top-ranked student academically with a 4.0 average." There was no other recognition, no doubt to her great relief, but the members of the Duke football team were introduced individually to the audience with great acclaim. Aunt May thought that was scandalous. I did not then, but I do now. Soon after graduation, Mother and Daddy drove Lil from Monroe to Kannapolis to interview for a job as a high school English teacher. On the radio we heard the voice of President Roosevelt in a graduation address at the University of Virginia declare: "Today, Monday, June 10, the hand that held the dagger has plunged it into the back of its neighbor." Italy had declared war on France, now in its national death rattle, and Great Britain. Mussolini had feared an Allied collapse before he could join. He need not have worried, Churchill dryly noted. He was soon to get all the war he wanted. Great Britain, its army safely home from Dunkirk and rapidly rearming, had decided to fight on alone.

Soon home again with job in hand, Lil was notified by Mayor John Sikes that he had named her Miss Monroe and that she was to compete for the state beauty title at the annual tobacco festival in Wilson.

"Heavens, no!" was Lil's response.

"Yes, indeed!" was Daddy's reply.

"I certainly will not," Lil reiterated.

"Lil, honey, it might be really nice," Mother suggested gently. "You're so pretty. You'll meet some interesting people. Why not give yourself a chance?"

Mary C., home from Smithfield for the weekend, itching and irritable from all those gnats and mosquito bites, teased Lil. Her sister was again "ripe for romance." She was bursting out of her bra. Her little sister had become a glamour girl, besieged by at least three men, soon to become four. "Lil—North Carolina beauty queen. She will win in a walk," was her final word.

"Well, I'm not going," was Lil's semi-final reply.

But Daddy insisted, saying that Lil was entirely too clannish and shy. "You have just graduated from college. You will soon start a teaching career. You'll be living alone in a new town. It is time to become more congenial with people your own age." Lessie backed Dowd. "Yes, honey. It'll be fun. And don't worry. You can select any wardrobe you want."

Lil still protested. She did not care about fashion. Or makeup. Or playing any phony "Lady Graciosity" role and pretending to be a recent graduate of any charm school. She accused her parents of wanting her to go for their sakes, not hers. "My hair is horrible. I have nothing to wear. I don't know anyone to ask as my escort. I don't really like to dance. I'll feel like a fool walking down some plank 'oozing charm' before a bunch of judges. And I'm not a fool. I didn't go to Duke to become "Miss Monroe, Beauty Queen." Good grief. Tell Mr. Sikes 'thanks, but no thanks.' Get Lib Warren. She would be perfect."

Mother was persistent. As for an escort, how about Hargrove? No. Lansing? Absolutely not. "Besides, he's your boyfriend, Mother. Not mine." Lil had not forgotten how Lansing, halfway between herself and her mother in age, had cottoned to Lessie, another suitor of a Secrest girl who enjoyed making literary allusions and quoting poetry with the mother. Nor had Lil liked it any more than Mary C. had earlier, when Lessie was overheard telling a friend that Lansing had come to Broadacre in love with the daughter only to leave in love with her mother.

Well, how about John? No!

Harold? Absolutely not.

Arnold? Oh, Mother, please.

Archie? Nope.

A brother is not one to ask if his sister is attractive. The incest taboo is too strong. But others were commenting on what a beautiful young woman Lil had become. By the time the argument was over and Lil had succumbed, largely as a result of Aunt Eve's pronouncement that the pageant "would be a good growth experience," and Aunt May's enthusiastic endorsement, "You sweet darling, adorable, precious girl, you'll just be the belle of the ball," she was, I guess, a knock-out.

People said she looked every day more like Lessie when she was twenty. She possessed finely-chiseled features, a classical face—intelligent, expressive—framed by a thick, luxuriant head of chestnut brown hair—

her crowning glory. Ethel Blackwell, in her beauty salon in the back of the drugstore, fashioned it into a glamorous page-boy style, just like Ginger Rogers in "Kitty Foyle." The Lady Eve was ready to be launched.

Almost, but not quite. Lil refused to ask any of the men she had dated. She asked me instead—nearly four years younger. I had gotten my driver's license at sixteen only five months earlier, hardly an experienced man behind the wheel. But off we drove the two hundred miles to Wilson with parental approval in spite of all those earlier warnings and actual examples of the dangers of highway accidents.

Lil's Lady Eve persona soon evaporated. At her suggestion we skipped most of the festival's activities. She preferred to stay in our boarding house and play two-handed draw bridge or go to a movie. We did go to the formal dance. In 1940 couples danced together. A stag line formed, and men were free to cut in and dance with any girl who caught their fancy. Before long I was cut in and Lil was waltzed away. Relegated to the sidelines, I watched as Lil was tagged time and time again. Aunt May was right. Lil was at least one of the belles of the ball.

Never particularly shy, I joined the stag line and cut in on a few girls who had caught my attention. They must have wondered what this callow kid was doing at the dance but no one said so. I was having a great time until shortly before midnight Lil appeared with the order, "Come on, Mac, time to go home. Let's get out of here."

We got home safely, despite the odds. Lil's verdict: "Well, thank goodness that's over. I'll never do that again. But, we had a pretty good time, didn't we?" That was the last time I ever had to escort Lil anywhere. From then on, she had more bona fide boyfriends than she knew what to do with, and I was not lacking in girlfriends, either. Our next joint venture was just down the road. Our first trip to New York.

Upon my graduation from high school and Lil's from college, our parents gave us a two-week tour of New York City as a gift. What a magical place: the Wrigley building, Times Square, the Empire State Building, Broadway shows, movie palaces where you could actually smoke in the balconies, Rockefeller Center, and Carnegie Hall, Madison Square Garden, French restaurants and, above all, the 1939-40 World's Fair.

In early July while we were at the fair, news came of the British attack on the French fleet, followed by a bomb explosion at the French exhibit as we stood nearby. There was a great deal of excitement, some property damage but no injuries. I recall visiting the Palestinian exhibition staffed entirely by Jews and largely reflecting the Jewish culture and tradition, especially in Jerusalem. There was little evidence then of a dominant Arabic presence in what today is the area claimed by the Palestinian Authority, the "occupied territories."

One could walk the streets of Manhattan at two o'clock in the morning and be among a sea of people. After midnight, Lil and I attended the film, "All This and Heaven Too," starring Bette Davis and Charles Boyer, the start of my life-long love affair with the actress later famed as the "Magnificent Popeye" and the "Fourth Warner Brother." It didn't get any better than this, at least I didn't expect it to—until we went to dinner on the sky-light roof of the Hotel Astor and heard Frank Sinatra sing to the music of Tommy Dorsey and his orchestra. The main attraction to me, however, was the city itself—as O. Henry had once dubbed it, this "Baghdad on the Hudson:" its ethnic neighborhoods, its architecture, rivers, cathedrals, historic monuments, museums, national treasures. What a fabled place! New York was my home port for a while during my Navy years. I have never gotten over my love for the Big Apple. Nor, I suspect, will I ever get over the terrorist attacks on New York September 11, 2001. Like my Confederate ancestors: Forget? Hell!

Mary C., down from Smith College, joined us for a couple days at the Taft Hotel. One day as she and Lil were visiting elsewhere, Martha and Luther Hodges, recently moved to New York from North Carolina, took me to Jones Beach with their daughters, Nancy and Betsy, then thirteen and fifteen years old, and son Luther Jr., three. After a swim, Martha and Luther, family friends and kinsmen, treated me to lunch at a Howard Johnson restaurant which offered a variety of ice cream flavors that boggled the mind. The Secrest Drugstore fountain never saw anything like that. What an indulgence! We could have as many ice cream cones as we desired. Before we returned home, Lil and I took a trip up the Hudson to West Point.

Back home we spent time at Riverton, near Wagram, where John Buie began to pay attention to Lil as Lil turned hers to Archie McMillan. I stayed glued to the radio with Mother to listen to the Democratic political convention where FDR was nominated for a third term. Mary C. had decided earlier to break up with Nick Clodfelter, largely due to pressure from Daddy although she always blamed Mother. That was unfair as Mother, who agreed with Daddy that Nick would be a poor choice, argued that her older daughter should make her own decision.

"Otherwise, she won't get it out of her system. I know my daughter. She'll romanticize about her first love forever and hold any interference against you. It's better to let her learn the hard way." I agreed with Mother.

Besides, I liked Nick. Mother was proved right. But it did her no good. She got blamed anyhow. Mary C. herself could hardly claim to have been emotionally damaged by the end of the relationship. One of her favorite quotes was, "Men have died and worms have eaten them but not for love." She frequently said that about some man or woman who claimed a lost love as the reason to stay single. "All rationalization to escape sexual intimacy" was her explanation.

Mary Cov was offered a job as social worker at Smithfield. She really wanted to go Smith College to earn a master's. Daddy balked. She would get no money from him. Mother refused to intervene. Mary Cov could not make up her mind. Lil and I labeled her indecision her "Smith-Smithfield neurosis." Mary C. laughingly agreed with the diagnosis. Aunt May and I urged Mary Cov to dump the Smithfield job and go for Smith. "You say you never go anywhere or do anything and don't know anybody," I reminded her. "All you've done for two weeks is sit on the swing on the landlady's front porch each evening, bothered by gnats and bitten by mosquitoes. Why stay on? And if you really want to become a social worker, why not go to the best school? And Smith is the best."

Mary Cov was still uncertain. Daddy would not like it. Mother would not advise her one way or the other. "It's your decision," was her inevitable reply.

"Where would I get the money?" my sister asked.

"I'll lend it to you," Aunt May, who had precious little to give, declared. And so she did, and my older sister chose the road less traveled, a turn that took her into a new direction that fundamentally altered her life. But she had wanted to become a social worker ever since she and I had seen the movie "Dead End" at Rowena Shutes's Pastime Theater in 1937. The film starred Sylvia Sidney, Joel McRae and Humphrey Bogart and featured the Dead End Kids. The movie adaptation of the Broadway play was done by Lillian Hellman. Mary C. was Sylvia Sidney, I, Billy Halop, the younger brother whom she protected. The movie was typical Hollywood fare. Society was to blame for individuals gone wrong. But it was a brilliant film.

The brightest thing to happen that summer of 1940 was to meet cousins Betsy and Nancy, nieces of Rosa Parker and daughters of Rosa's younger sister Martha. Betsy's and Nancy's father was Luther H. Hodges, a vice president of Marshall Field's. He had recently been transferred from Leakesville-Spray, N.C., to New York City. They now lived in Grammercy Park, soon to move to Bronxville, where they lived in the home formerly occupied by composer Jerome Kern.

Luther was already a nationally known figure. He was soon to become one of FDR's "Dollar-A-Year" men to help convert the economy to wartime production and make the U.S. "the arsenal of Democracy." Later he served President Truman in the Marshall Plan to rebuild western Europe, again largely without pay. In 1950 he and Martha moved back to N.C. In 1952 Hodges ran for Lt. Gov. and won on a ticket headed by William Umstead. He became governor upon Umstead's death in late 1954.

Martha Blakeney Hodges was only nine when her mother died in 1906. She and her five sisters and one brother now had to find other homes in which to live. While Rosa found a place with Cuz Nannie Ashcraft, Martha stayed first with her Covington cousins at Broadacre, and later divided time among them, her grandmother Susan Covington Houston and Great Aunt Martha Covington Lockhart (twin sisters of my grandfather D. A. Covington). Her aunt and uncle Virginia and Whiteford Blakeney also opened their home to her as did Cousin Lillian Brewer of Wake Forest, another Covington daughter who had married into the Brewer family who had helped found Wake Forest College in 1834. Martha's childhood experience was not unusual in the post-Reconstruction South. Repeatedly, extended family members, collateral kin and in-laws took in children whose families had fallen on hard times and treated them as their own.

Martha attended Monroe and Wake Forest public schools, graduated from the Women's College of the University of North Carolina at Greensboro, and later studied at Columbia University and the University of Chicago. She met her future husband when she moved to his hometown of Leakesville-Spray to teach history at the local high school. She taught for three years, also serving as principal the last year.

"I loved my job. When I married Luther, they lost the best history teacher in North Carolina," Martha once said, only half joking. Martha went on to contribute to North Carolina history herself, serving with dignity as First Lady when Luther was Governor from 1954-1961. She later served with equal distinction as wife of the U.S. Secretary of Commerce when Luther was appointed to that office and became a member of the cabinets of President John F. Kennedy and Lyndon B. Johnson from 1961-1965.

When Martha and Luther were married in the Blakeney home in Monroe on June 24, 1922, Lessie and Dowd had given the bridal luncheon the day before and Mary Cov was flower girl in the wedding. Cousin Vann's mother, Mary Gordon Secrest, and friend Bill Price's mother, Amelia Houston Hawfield, Monroe college classmates of Martha, were part of the wedding party. When Mary Cov was doing her internship in New York for Smith College in 1940-41, she sometimes babysat for Martha and Luther. She fell for the whole family. Betsy and Nancy were smart, talented, sweet, artistic, creative, imaginative, polite, mannerly. On and on the superlatives flowed. And there was only one word to describe Luther Jr., just turned four: "adorable." I was programmed to like them.

When the Hodges family returned to their home in North Carolina in June, 1940, to check out Salem Academy as a school for Betsy that fall, they came by Monroe to see the Secrests. That started a friendship that has lasted ever since and which led to unexpected ramifications in subsequent years. Betsy and I were Duke classmates for a year, in 1942-43, I a junior, she a freshman. When she later transferred to Sarah Lawrence College, I saw her on occasion in Bronxville while on leave from the USS Hammann, a destroyer escort upon which I served in the North Atlantic during World War Two. At Salem Academy in 1940-42, Betsy became one of Aunt Eve's girls. A generation later, Betsy's daughter Martha at Salem College inherited the mantle. Betsy's other daughter Carol and Nancy's daughter Vary were at Duke in 1968-72 along with Ann's and my sons, David and Phil.

# 31. Duke Freshman

As a freshman at Duke in 1940 I did better than I had in high school, occasionally making the Dean's List. Not bad for a student two years on average younger than most of his classmates. I had a lot of catching up to do socially, too. Here I began to shine. I joined Pi Kappa Alpha fraternity, despite my disapproval of such organizations as elitist and snobbish. I remembered Mary Cov's feeling of rejection when, as a transfer from Meredith College to Duke University, she was not asked to join Alpha Delta Pi, to which her mother had belonged at Brenau College.

To my credit, I made a lousy frat boy, finding the whole thing silly and trivial. Mary C. never quit talking about A.D. Pi, however, holding it against not only the sorority and Duke, but also Mother for her not having been rushed. She never mentioned, however, that she had expressly forbidden Mother to write to the sorority on her behalf. So how were they to know? When Lil went to Duke four years later and did ask Mother to write, Mother did so, Lil joined and she, also to her credit, made a mighty poor Greek, finding most of her friends among those whom the frats dubbed GDI's (Goddamned Independents).

Many years after I had graduated from Duke, Luther Hodges told me that he believed the only things I had learned at Duke were to speak pig Latin, smoke, drink, swear, and chase skirts. I disagreed, pointing out that I had already started smoking before I had ever enrolled. I loved Duke long before I was a student there. Thanks to Uncle Vann, Aunt May, Mary C., Brack, Helen, Lil, and Amy, it was already a familiar place. Some people chose Duke because it ranked well academically, an Ivy League school down South. My reasons were less elevated: I liked the Duke football team and the sweet rolls served in the student cafeteria.

Professor Alan K. Manchester, dean of freshman at Trinity College (the Gothic West Campus where only male students were permitted to reside) took a special interest in Vann and me. He never seemed to learn that we were not brothers. The Dean was impressed by my fascination with and considerable knowledge of history. But although I thought I knew it all, he did not. Like A.C. Jordan four years earlier with Lil in English, Dean Manchester really did have something to teach me. He really did know more than I. I have never forgotten the fundamental principles of historical understanding and interpretation that he imparted.

Next to Manchester came Dr. William "Wild Bill" Hamilton, an intimidating professor of Political Science who was to that subject what A.C. Jordan had been to English. Seldom if ever known to award an A, Professor Hamilton was a stimulating lecturer, so intense that by the end of each class his forehead was beaded with perspiration, his shirt underarms soaked in sweat. Maybe that is why he dropped dead one day before he was fifty years old.

By year's end there was little about political theory I did not know. In those days we were spared the computer models in vogue today that have emphasized the science and killed the art in the study of politics. In 1940-41 political science was dynamic, full of fire, passion and humanity. In 2003, the few courses I have audited have been as dry as dust, robbed of their essential humanity.

I had often spoken to Aunt May of my admiration—and fear—of Dr. Hamilton, unlike Dean Manchester hardly an approachable person. But how I admired the working of his brain, the knowledge and understanding of the political process it contained, and his ability to communicate all that to his students —that is, the few who had the wit and will to receive it. A couple of weeks before the final exam, wily Aunt May had lunch with Dr. Hamilton in the faculty dining room. "You have my nephew, Mac Secrest, in your freshman class," she informed him. "He admires you so much. He told me just yesterday that if he were grading his professors, you and Dean Manchester would get A plus."

You never know who may be susceptible to blandishment. Dr. Hamilton did not appear to be one who was. But when my grade card was returned to me several weeks later, there was the grade, an A. When the class sheet was later posted, I had received the only A in the class. How much credit belongs to me and how much to Aunt May, I will never know, but I am claiming it all.

Professors Wilson and Hoover in Economics were other rarefied academics internationally known for their mastery of "the dismal science." Early on Wilson was called by the government for special wartime work in South America but not before my freshman and sophomore years when I garnered another A, difficult to come by in Dr. Wilson's classes. Aunt May was also close to him, but I don't think she ever tried to butter him up. Again, that A was my own.

I remember Dr. Hoover for a lesson he taught me outside the field of economics. One day I handed in my assignment late. "I'm sorry to be so tardy, Dr. Hoover," I explained, "but I haven't been feeling very well." The professor looked askance, then replied, "Mr. Secrest, most people often don't 'feel very well.' Indeed, the work of the world is done by people who probably aren't 'feeling very well.' I wonder how the boys on Corrigador are feeling this morning. Probably "not very well." You understand my rule. No paper, no matter how good, gets more than a C if turned in late, unless you have an excuse from the student infirmary. And I do hope you're feeling better tomorrow." What a lesson! Don't go through life making feeble excuses. Go ahead and do your work, even if you aren't "feeling very well."

Professor Petrie was Vann's and my professor in Religion, a full year requirement at Duke in 1940. Thank God for Dr. Petrie who made the Old Testament come alive as no preacher ever had. And who resurrected Jesus and all his parables. Dr. Petrie, who may have understood my Doubting Thomas stand in regard to a personal God or any New Testament promises of personal immortality, was no rant-and-rave fundamentalist. He did not get bogged down in fruitless arguments about faith versus science, dogma versus evolution. He just taught the Good Book, explained the Gospels and did so in a way that made sense.

He was also inspirational, leaving me at year's end no more a Christian than I had been before, but somehow a person with a deeper understanding and appreciation of all religions and the vital roles they play in our everyday lives. I learned to appreciate the Bible as great literature. I still enjoy leafing through it not for any personal salvation but for an appreciation of its literary beauty and for its wisdom and its compassionate humanity. But I did not make an A in Religion. I had to settle for a B. I still believed faith without good works was dead. I've always been a devotee of the social gospel.

I placed out of A.C. Jordan's English class and Daddy did not force me to take it. Had he done so, of course I would have, like Lil, made an A. We both had Anna Bernard Benson in high school. In my other English courses I excelled. In French, with the aid of a pony, I scraped by. I avoided math and science courses like the plague, only to have to face the reckoning later when my future depended on it in the Navy, first in the V-12 program at Duke and a little later in Officers' Candidate School at Harvard.

At seventeen I was a tall, well-proportioned young man, on the slim side but in pretty good shape, thanks to all that earlier farm work. What I lacked in bulk, I made up for in definition. I blame my being left-handed for my inability to play tennis, softball and golf well. Anything that required much of a swing got past me. I excelled in physical education generally, getting A's in basketball, handball and swimming. I was poor at gymnastics, requiring assistance from classmates—pulling from the top, pushing from the bottom—to get me to the top of that damned rope, limply dangling from the Card gym ceiling.

Duke's campus character who captured the affectionate if condescending attention of Duke students for over three decades was a former professor named Nurmi Shields. Nurmi had been a brilliant young student of physics. But something happened along the way. He lost his grip, then his job, then his mind. And Duke University, playing its proper role of sanctuary for all (and looking after its own), allowed Nurmi to stay on, well beyond his ability to perform in classroom or laboratory.

Nurmi decided that he was the world's greatest long-distance runner. All day long, as the campus bus made the two-mile trip between East and West Campus, Nurmi would line up alongside it parked in front of Duke Chapel. When the bus left, Nurmi would take off as fast as he could, hoping to beat it to East Campus. Sometimes he would run out of breath too soon, but that did not matter. Crowds of students, usually led by campus athletes, would lift Nurmi to their shoulders, proclaim him winner of the race, and bring him back amid popular acclaim to the chapel steps.

In his earlier days in the 1930s, Nurmi usually made his run all the way. When I returned to Duke in 1969 to pursue a graduate degree in history, one of the first people I saw was Nurmi, still lining up against big new campus buses, ready for the race. A new generation of healthy, corpuscular young athletes were there to cheer him on. He never got beyond the first circle past Duke Chapel, but Duke students still hailed Nurmi as a conquering hero, and Nurmi seemed happy and content.

Nurmi in 1940 seemed funny, but when I saw him still at it in 1969, I thought his situation tragic. The student response was well-intentioned and kind; the university's attitude humane and tolerant. But what had happened to Nurmi? Why could not something have been done at Duke

Medical Center to help this troubled, talented, gifted man? Why was he allowed to remain a delusional buffoon, an object of ridicule, however benign?

The mystery of human behavior, the contradictions in the human character, the ambivalence of the human spirit—as personified by Nurmi and his fans—bothered me a little, but not much, in 1940. It both baffles and bothers me a lot more today.

Thirty-five years ago, I moved to Chapel Hill. Nearly every day since, when I am in town, I have walked my boxer dogs, one after another, on campus. Perhaps some former student sees me three-plus decades later and thinks, "My God! That can't be Dr. Secrest! Why, he must be a hundred." Maybe they regard me now as I did Nurmi sixty-five years ago, although I don't think I ever seemed delusional.

The first professor I met in 1969 welcomed me back after a twenty-five year absence with this enthusiastic declaration, "There's a dandy new book out on Teapot Dome. You'll love it!" I bet, I thought. The same old academic irrelevance. I felt as if I were in a time warp. Some things never change. Fifty years from now, long after other scandals, I bet some professor will be enthusiastically trumpeting still another "dandy new book" this time on Watergate.

I had a wonderful time my freshman year at Duke, 1940-41. I remember blanket and beer parties at a nearby lake in the spring. My dates were either "townies," that is, girls from Durham all older than I, or coeds, most of whom dressed, talked, acted and looked alike in their pastel brushed wool pull-over sweaters, pleated skirts, bobby socks and saddle shoes. I thought they were the most beautiful creatures on earth. And so exciting. They came from all over, too—quite different from the small town sisterly girls I was accustomed to. Bill Price, over from Wake Forest, and I were smitten with Durham beauties Norma York, green-eyed Jean Garrett, Carolyn Strong, and many other coeds.

By far the most glamorous were Eunice Patten, whose father was president of Louisburg College and a Methodist minister, and Julia Booker, daughter of renowned Professor Booker of the UNC English department. Eunice was stacked—as the saying went—"every brick in place." She had dark hair and eyes, a brunette complexion.

Steamy, smoldering, sophisticated Eunice had a close friend, Julia, who dated a Duke medical student. Julia too had dark hair and eyes and, as I recall, a dry, droll wit. Both she and Eunice smoked, even drank a beer (against the rules), occasionally would utter a mild expletive. Julia had style, like those women who could "never be too rich or too thin."

How did J. Kempton Jones, a sophomore and PKA brother, do it? Kemp was no glamour boy. Kind of roly-poly, no athlete, with a fair complexion that sunburned easily, he couldn't even boast of much hair on his chest. He seemed open and innocent. I felt comfortable around him. He was almost as socially immature as I. What did Eunice see in him? What did Kemp have that I didn't? How did he fit in with Julia and that Howard guy?

But fit in he did, as Eunice married Kemp, Julia married Howard, and 62 years after those PKA blanket parties each couple was still sharing blankets—one in Chapel Hill, the other in Savannah. Kemp settled down to practice medicine and became one of the leading doctors in the Southern Part of Heaven. Julia's husband also became a doctor. One day I called Kemp and Eunice, whom I hadn't seen in years, to share these memories and ask if my recollections bore any resemblance to reality.

"You got me about right," Kemp said. "Here, I'll let Eunice tell you what she thinks."

"Why, hello, Mac," the same low, soft, sultry voice, sounding not a day older. "How're ya doin'?" A perfect take-off on Mae West. Then a big, hearty laugh. "I don't think you got it quite right, but I sure hope so," Eunice said with a laugh. "I can't wait to call Julia and tell her what a glamour girl she was. Yes, we thought we were sophisticated. But really, we were so innocent. By today's standards, we were downright prudes."

When I wasn't "smoking, drinking and chasing skirts," I was either deeply immersed in study or preoccupied with the German-British war, personified by Adolf Hitler and Winston Churchill. The first part of the year went well. Our potential ally won the Battle of Britain, survived the Blitz, redeemed Ethiopia and practically destroyed the Italian navy. A small British army nearly chased Mussolini's army out of North Africa. The British also removed pro-Axis governments in Iraq, Syria and, ultimately Iran, securing the Middle East from a potential German occupation.

Even Greece defeated the Italian invaders. The Serbs overthrew a pro-German government and made common cause with the British and Greeks. Was a united Balkan front in Eastern Europe possible? Could Britain re-enter Europe through the back door? What affect would all that have on the Soviet Union, now described by Winston Churchill as "a riddle wrapped in a mystery inside an enigma?" Soon the answer came. No, they could not. The small British expeditionary force sent to help the Greeks was hurled out of Greece, then Crete. Rommel landed in Libya and drove the British out of Cyrenaica and threatened Egypt. Yugoslavia was crushed by the German army within five days.

Why should I include a thumb-nail sketch of the European war in a memoir? Because the struggle was to me as real as —and far more important than— any Rose Bowl game, or beach blanket bingo party could ever be. I spent many hours with Dean Manchester and other Duke professors talking about the war, our first peacetime draft in history, and the struggle between the interventionists and the isolationists who were dividing the nation into two hostile camps.

Most of my fellow students either did not know or did not care about any of this. The big fall and spring dances at Duke and Chapel Hill, and the football and basketball games, were far more interesting and important. So where did that leave me? Out in left field again—somewhat set apart—but not so much so as in earlier days. I had learned also to go with the flow.

In late May and early June the only light from abroad were Rudolf Hess's flight from Berlin to Scotland to seek an unauthorized negotiated peace with Great Britain, the British navy's sinking of the Bismarck, and President Roosevelt's slow but sure victory over the isolationists and American Firsters, resulting in repeal of the Neutrality Acts. Roosevelt provided real leadership and showed a sure hand in guiding the nation, even if he had to resort to misdirection, manipulation, and occasionally outright lying. He waged a naval war against Germany in 1941 before Pearl Harbor. As he confided to Winston Churchill at their first personal meeting in mid-summer, "I will wage war but I may never ask for a declaration of war. Were I to ask Congress, they would debate it for months," by which time, he added, it might be too late.

Moke had not been happy at Duke and decided to transfer to Wake Forest the next year. He had had a miserable experience one spring night when he joined a group of fraternity brothers on a visit to "Katy Mae's" in Raleigh. "Katy Mae's," to put it bluntly, was a whorehouse. Moke, unsure of his own sexuality and expecting too much of himself at only seventeen years of age, had not been able to go through with it. He didn't even get his clothes all the way off. How he agonized over that.

Thirty years later Moke made out okay. He met Oscar-winning actress Susan Hayward in Ft. Lauderdale and had a brief but passionate love affair. It burned too hot not to cool down. Besides, Moke never could fully free himself from his attachment to Mom and Aunt Cupie, even though they wished he could.

But in 1940 Moke was still trying. "Good grief, Moke," I asked him, "What did you expect? You're not that kind of boy. All you could probably think about was your mother and Aunt Cupie, were they to know. What's the hurry?" In those days Moke trailed after me. I was his father confessor.

"Do you really believe all that stuff some of these older guys from New Jersey tell you? Hey man, they're making most of that up. They boast and brag and lie so much that eventually they just have to do it. But you're not like that. Do you really want to be?"

Well, maybe he did. I sure didn't, although the next year I joined a group of DKE's from Carolina and went with Cousin Hill to some such similar establishment. But Hill and I never had any intention of having a sexual experience. We went to observe. We viewed this outing as a sociological experiment.

When we got to the place and met the girls, we engaged them in conversation. Where are you from? How old are you? Do you have parents or a family? Do you go to church? Do you do this for fun or profit?

"Hell, Mac, given the way we were raised," Hill recalled years later, "do you think we could have behaved any other way? Good gosh, we thought if you kissed a girl you were practically obligated to marry her." Maybe that explains some of Hill's five marriages. A lot of Hill's youthful respect and idealism evaporated. Maybe it has to, at least to some degree, as one grows older.

In late June Moke's Aunt Cupie was planning a weekend at Carolina Beach with her friend Helen Craven (no kin to Brack). They had older boyfriends to accompany them. Jesse Lockhart, who dated Helen that weekend and whom he later married, was my second cousin. He lived on Hayne Street across the street from Broadacre. They agreed to let Moke and me tag along.

On Saturday afternoon, June 21, Moke and I bumped into Sally and Dodie of Monroe on the beach. What do you want to do? Let's go for a ride. OK! Moke had Helen's car keys. She and Cupie were out with others—we'll take her car.

So we did. We went to a bar, pretending to be eighteen, drank a beer. Got away with it. Went to another bar, had another beer. Got away with it. And so it went, until Moke and I were thoroughly dizzy. I got the girls safely home around nine o'clock. Upon backing up from the curb my foot slipped off the brake, onto the accelerator and Helen's car flew across the street and into a steel utility pole. What a mess. Luckily, no one was around. The pole wasn't damaged. The car drove all right. Maybe Helen wouldn't notice.

"Won't notice? Mac, how can she help it? The whole trunk is caved in. Of course she'll notice it," Moke exclaimed.

"Maybe we can get the car back into the same parking spot she had," I suggested hopefully. "You put the key back where you got it. She'll think somebody else did it." So much for honesty and youthful idealism when you've got your ass in a sling.

The next morning all my angst about Helen's car disappeared. The morning headlines: Germany invades Russia. At last, a reprieve for hard-pressed Britain. Maybe the Soviet Union would surprise the world and successfully resist. At the very least Britain would escape a second invasion threat from an apparently invincible Germany. I hoped, and feverishly prayed, that Hitler had now repeated Napoleon's mistake of 130 years earlier. Most military experts didn't think so. Many expected the Soviet Union to collapse like France, within six weeks. The muse of history, to whom I turned so often, assured me that it would not. Surely Hitler had made his first fatal decision. What did a little auto accident in Carolina Beach matter now? It even made an honest man of me. Moke and I showed Helen and Cupie what had happened to her new car. I promised Helen that Daddy's body shop would repair it. Maybe Daddy would even give her a new one.

Helen and Cupie were unbelievably forgiving. "It was an accident. Just inexperienced driving. At least drinking wasn't involved." Uh-huh. "But don't you ever use my car again without my permission," Helen warned. "That is close to stealing."

Back in Monroe Daddy too was understanding. The boys meant no harm. No one was hurt. Thank the Lord for that. And he did satisfy Helen about the car. Whether he repaired it or gave her another, I never knew and didn't ask. I really didn't care. Germany was driving ever deeper into Russia. Smolensk, key railroad site on the road to Moscow, was surrounded. Could the Soviet Union hold out until General Winter came to her side? With the world holding its breath, why should I care about Helen Craven's car? I held my breath the next five months.

# 32. A Summer Southern Wedding

In August the family gathered in Morganton for Brack's marriage to Mary Kistler. The couple had met the summer before at the Patricia Inn at Myrtle Beach, where Mary was vacationing and Brack was on a working vacation as night desk clerk. The summer romance ripened during the following year when Brack was a law student at Harvard University. Mary completed her education at St. Mary's in Raleigh, and spent some time in Boston with an uncle and financial guardian.

The wedding was a lavish affair, typical of many such events in pre-World War II small Southern towns, featuring beautiful young brides of wealthy leading families. Mary Stoney, mother of the bride, was, in Mother's words, "originally a poor woman who married a rich man." When Mr. Kistler died, he left Mary with two young children, Mary and Andy. Some years later Mrs. Kistler remarried and became—Mother's words again—"a rich woman who now married a poor man." Stoney, who had served a term or two in the North Carolina legislature, was not wealthy but Mary could afford him. Mary Kistler, Brack's bride, claimed direct descent from Gov. Craig, a claim which irritated Mother who preferred to make such claims on prominent people for herself and her own children. I sensed a touch of malice in Mother's comments.

Lil and I were in the wedding, which took place in Mary's ancestral home in the high rent district of Morganton, a Tara-like mansion supported by stone columns, faithful to the Greek architectural style so prevalent in the early 20th century South. Uncle Jim was permitted to assist in the Episcopal ceremony, despite his being a Methodist. Mary looked lovely to me—a little blond doll, radiant, mischievous, cool, in charge—while Brack matched her with an assured, masculine charm. Lil was a dutiful bridesmaid, but her heart was not in it. She was diffident and preoccupied. As an usher, I was way out of my league—younger by six years than most of the other male attendants. Mary herself was only a year older than I but light years ahead in social sophistication, as were her bridesmaids, all, that is, except Lil, who stayed largely to herself. Aunt Katherine appeared elderly compared to Big Mary but was her usual calm, composed self. Aunt May was unusually quiet and withdrawn—a shadowy figure on the sidelines. Mother was at her Lady Graciosity best, charming, witty, socially competitive. Aunt Eve also managed to hold her own, working the crowd, eager to help manage things if the opportunity arose.

Mary C. was on hand as a Greek chorus, recording impressions, largely negative, to recite later. When Mary tossed the floral bouquet after vows were exchanged and as the reception drew to a close, Lil quickly stepped aside to let other grasping hands win the prize. Both Mary C. and Lil had long claimed Brack as their own, as they had me. Brack's Covington aunts May and Eve had considered him almost as their own son, as they had me. It was not easy for these loving but possessive women to give him up. His own mother Katherine was quite willing to do so. Time to move on. The marriage had her blessing. Brack's cousin Isabel Craven, however, felt more like my sisters. She too had gone to Duke with Brack and staked a claim to him.

Brack was two years younger than Mary C. and nearly two years older than Lil. He was five years old when his older sister little Katherine had died. She had been buried in the Monroe cemetery next to her Covington grandparents. Brack spent a lot of his childhood and teen-age years at Broadacre. Mary C. had taught him to dance. Lil had taught him to play cards. Mary C. fixed him up with dates and introduced him to movies and a world of play and make-believe. Most of these worldly if innocent pleasures were not encouraged in the home of a Methodist minister in the 1920s and '30s.

When Mary C. finished college and moved out into the world, Brack and Lil gravitated more closely together. She should have gotten him to take her to the Wilson Miss Tobacco festival rather than me. So none of Brack's female relatives were really ready to let him go. They were not particularly inclined to like Mary or cut her any slack. Nor was Mary inclined to want any special attention. She had no intention of becoming one of Aunt Eve's girls or an out-of-town member of the "I declare Miss Lessie!" fan club of Mother's youthful but old maid admirers.

Female intuition may have warned her off Mary C., Lil and Isabel. In any event, she did not much cotton to them or them to her. But I liked her and I think she liked me. After Ann and I were married in 1948 she was invariably friendly and cordial on the few occasions our paths crossed.

Mary C. found Mary Kistler much too short for her cousin Brack. "She can't possibly be five feet tall," she declared to me during the reception. "She looks like a child dressed up in adult clothes, compared to Brack's six-foot, four-inch frame. Why, when they dance, her head must bob up and down against his stomach just like yours used to on mine, when we both took ballroom dancing classes. You were four, I was twelve, and when we danced, that's exactly what happened. We looked ridiculous."

"I think she's pretty—thin but well-proportioned, with every brick in place," as I liked to say.

"Just wait. By the time she's forty, she'll have a middle-age spread," Mary Cov decreed. " A little frame like that cannot handle extra weight."

I disagreed, insisting that small women often kept their shapes better than large ones. "Look at Vivian Leigh," I said. "She's tiny and must be getting pretty old, but she's still pretty as a picture." I had recently seen the actress in "Waterloo Bridge" and "That Hamilton Woman" and was still entranced. "I bet you Mary will be just like her." Mary C., still uncomfortable with her five-foot, eight-inch frame, remained unconvinced.

"Oh, Mac, for goodness' sakes. You think you like short girls because Lil and I are tall. That's just your defense mechanism against being overly attached to us. It's the old incest taboo at work," Mary C. reminded me. "You know that." Well, I'd heard it often enough. Damn Sigmund Freud. Lil was largely noncommittal but did make the catty observation that Mary elected to get married in August, just a month before her birthday, so she could tell people later that she was "only eighteen when I got married."

Aunt Eve had only nice things to say about the new in-laws. Little Mary made a "lovely bride." Big Mary was a "lovely" hostess and made a "lovely" mother of the bride. They were welcome to her home at Salem College any time. That remained her attitude. Mary did later visit her there frequently, finding Aunt Eve's apartment a convenient place when she came to Winston-Salem.

Mother spared little Mary but was less charitable to her mother. In the spring of the following year, Mother stopped by Mary Stoney's house, with its big Greek columns and circular drive, on her way to Ridgecrest to visit the Cravens. Mrs. Stoney looked out her window, recognized Lessie and called out, "Oh, it's you. I wondered who that was driving on my lawn."

"Well, it certainly wasn't I," was Lessie's quick rejoinder before she entered the house to drop off some gift and pay her respects. She did not stay long but the remark lingered. More than once I heard about the tactless greeting and unjust accusation she had received from Mary Stoney. I suspect it was Mother who had left tire ruts on Mary's nice new grassy lawn. Mother was unobservant about mundane things such as grassy lawns and flower plots. She had given up on that at Broadacre a generation earlier when husband Dowd had turned her one-time showplace into an in-town barnyard. By nature Mother was more at home with ideas, philosophy, religion and literature than with gardening gloves or with directing maids and yard men. She and Mary Stoney would never have had much in common.

She probably did not negotiate that winding driveway well, running off and on it in a preoccupied hurry to get the duty visit over with and go on her way, leaving in her wake a muddy mess. I never succeeded in persuading Mother that she may well have been in the wrong. "Even if I had," she would argue, "that is no way to greet a guest." Even an unannounced, unwanted, obtrusive one?

Sixteen months after Brack and Mary were married, Jim arrived. During Christmas when Aunt Eve was spending the holidays with us at Broadacre and with the Cravens in Charlotte, Lil and Mary C. joined us for a few days, leaving recently acquired husbands at home. Mother decided we should drive to Morganton to see this first-born baby of a new Simmons-Covington generation. Forget about the Cravens and Kistlers, apparently. Brack was at Guadalcanal with the Seabees. Both Big and Little Mary were happy and proud to show Jim off.

Daddy, who had declined to go to the wedding the year before, decided he would not go to Morganton to see Jim, either, and neither would anyone else from Monroe. We'll see about that, Mother replied. She called Gene Watts at the motor company, directed him to deliver one of Daddy's used cars, along with required gasoline ration cards. Before we go, Eve cautioned Lessie, be sure to unlock one of the bay windows. No one ever could find any door keys as we never locked any doors.

"Why do that?" I wondered. Morganton is about 80 miles from Monroe. The weather was bad. Gas supply short. It was a long day but well worth seeing the heir apparent. Jim was acclaimed "adorable" and "precious" by

Mother, Eve, Lil, and Mary C. We did not overstay our welcome, getting home just before dark. Broadacre, however, was blacked out and locked up. Shades were drawn, shutters closed.

"What in the world——," Mother's voice trailed off. "Why is everything so dark?"

"Lessie, Honey, just slide open the bay window and climb through," Aunt Eve directed. "You can unlock the doors from inside." Once in the house, we found the pantry cleaned out, the refrigerator empty. With the rest of us standing around speechless, Aunt Eve called the Star Market, ordered a long list of supplies to be delivered, and then proceeded to restore everything as it was before.

Lessie was told to fix supper, including a place for Mr. Secrest, and when he gets home—and he will come soon, Aunt Eve assured us—do not say one word about the reception we received. Do not mention Morganton. Act as if nothing has occurred. If your father asks questions, you may discuss anything except our activities—or his—today. Daddy soon came home, was treated with affection by some, respect by all, and told nothing. Soon he was laughing, calling Lessie a "cat bird," and Miss Evabelle "something else." Aunt Eve handled and managed Dowd till the day he died, always saying how devoted she was to him.

The Craven-Kistler marriage came to a close in the summer of 1950, when the couple's sons, James Braxton III and Steven, were seven and two years old respectively. Aunt Eve was called upon to help out. And she did so for years, working in harmony and mutual respect with Mary Stoney, about whom she never uttered a critical remark. She managed to keep close ties with them all, too close to suit some of them subsequently.

Brack and Mary later married other people. Brack married Jean Bible from Asheville in 1952. They had a daughter Betty. The offspring of these multiple marriages turned out well—accomplished, well-adjusted, attractive adults. No harm done. Who knows what the results may have been had two people remained united in unholy bonds of matrimony "for the sake of the children?"

Brack had come to Lake Placid in 1948 to ski not too long before Steve was due. I was living in nearby Saranac Lake. He called Ann and me up. We arranged to go skiing one afternoon followed by dinner at the Mirror Lake Inn. We visited until late in the evening, eating hugely, drinking heavily, having fun. Even so, it struck me as odd that Brack would leave his pregnant wife to go skiing alone. Had Aunt Eve sent Brack up there to check on Ann and me? Not likely. In any event, two years later the news that Mother termed "a bombshell" came out. Brack and Mary had called it quits. Had Brack been afflicted by "The Seven Year Itch?" Or had Mary? Probably not. They had married too young. Their interests diverged. One did not outgrow the other; they just grew apart. It happens.

Isabel Craven, thirty-two years later, was riding in the car to Richmond with Mary C. and me to attend Brack's third marriage to a young woman named Susan, twenty-six years his junior. Talk turned to Brack's marriages to Mary and then to Jean. "Oh my goodness," Cousin Isabel declared. "I could never get close to Mary. Whenever she came around any of us Cravens, she acted as if she'd gone slumming." I cannot vouch for the accuracy of Isabel's complaint. I never saw any such sign of snobbishness in Mary.

Aunt Eve was hard-headed about business and inclined to appreciate success. She admired people who accumulated money and could manage it well. She advertised the Kistler wealth widely. I never heard Mary Stoney or her daughter brag about it. Nor was I particularly surprised to learn later that Mary was not much richer than Isabel Craven or Dowd Secrest.

When I was growing up I surely never felt rich and we never lived as if we were. Others, however, saw us in a different light. Cousin Martha Hamilton, writing about the family in a brief memoir for her children, referred to "Uncle Dowd's estate" and his "immense wealth." If so, why did we live so frugally? True, we did as we pleased. We got what we wanted. We could afford to go where we wished. Money, like sex, is important only if you don't have it. In 1946 when Daddy died, the Internal Revenue Service and inheritance taxes managed to relieve us of most of it.

Over lunch one day in Durham, a generation after Brack and Mary had split, Jim asked me why his parents had parted. Divorce involving young children is difficult, even in 2003 when it is as much a rule as an exception. In 1950 divorce, especially involving a Methodist minister's son, was viewed as a scandal. I had not seen it that way in 1945, when Mary C. and husband Albert Odmark divorced. Mother and Daddy did, but I thought Mary C. made the right decision, not only for herself but also for Albert. When Mother told me about Mary and Brack's separation, I was neither shocked nor judgmental, thinking once again that the two people most intimately involved knew what they were doing.

Mother was excited; I believe she felt Brack's pending divorce somehow justified Mary C's earlier one and freed her, as a mother, of any culpability. She certainly did not seem especially concerned. She just did not care for Mary and her mother much. The feeling probably was mutual, if and when either Mary thought about Lessie at all, which most likely was seldom if ever. I was unable to answer Jim's question. I didn't know. But the two adult individuals most involved had their reasons. They knew what was best for them and I always have respected their decision.

# 33. Stalin, Sex and Virtual Unreality

The German offensive stalled for several weeks on the central front. Hitler now turned south to capture the Ukraine, Russia's breadbasket. The situation appeared increasingly desperate. If Stalin made a separate peace, or the Soviet Union collapsed, where would that leave the United States? We were already deeply committed to aiding Great Britain and waging a shooting war in the Atlantic against German U boats.

The nation remained torn between isolationists and interventionists in the late summer and early fall of 1941, although the President appeared to be gaining the upper hand. It was obvious to me that Brack and Earle would soon be swallowed up in the military and that if the Soviet Union didn't remain a viable ally, the war would ultimately swallow me up, too. And all my Fowler, Secrest and Wolfe cousins and close friends as well. Yes, Smolensk mattered a lot more than Morganton or anyone's wedding.

Those five months between the German invasion of the Soviet Union on June 22 and the Japanese attack on Pearl Harbor December 7 held as much angst for me individually as it did for the world collectively. Mary Covington was home from a year of psychiatric education at Smith College which included two summer terms at Smith followed by a two-semester internship at a mental hospital in New Jersey. She had at last realized her academic potential, fully Lil's equal, achieving honors in all course work and excelling in the practicum and field work. Now back at Broadacre before taking her first job as a psychiatric social worker in Miami, she exuded Freudian theory from every pore. Soon Philip, Bill, Moke and I were reading *Introductory Lectures on Psychoanalysis, Interpretation of Dreams,* and *Totem and Taboo.*

Aunt Sue, back from Louisville for a visit, had been promoted Chief of the Venereal Disease and Control Center in Kentucky's Department of Public Health. Mother, immersed in all things psychiatric since regaining her health two years earlier, was in the center of all this intellectual ferment and conversation.

Sex, symbolism, dreams; sex, repression, projection, the Id, Ego, and Superego; sex, resistance, denial, substitution, defense mechanisms, sublimation, rationalization, disassociation; sex, childhood traumas, borderline personality and character disorders, transference and counter-transference; more sex—you name it, you got it at Broadacre the summer of 1941.

"I never heard or saw anything like it!" Philip exclaimed many years later. "Oedipus and Electra complexes, castration fear, climax anxiety, penis envy, masturbation, oral and anal-retentive personality development? Good heavens! In Monroe? A Freudian salon at Broadacre at the same time Miss Lessie was teaching the Methodist Women's Sunday School class and conducting the Women's Missionary Circle? It was all very stimulating, I must say. But Mac," and Philip's voice jumped several octaves, "it was simply astonishing!"

Did anyone in Monroe object, even when Freudian interpretation began to creep into the Sunday school class and infiltrate into the consciousness of those early middle-aged maiden ladies who comprised Mother's cheering section? No, indeed. Delightfully shocked, deliciously titillated, they just shook their heads in awe and declared in unison, "I declare, Miss Lessie!" They reacted the same way whenever Mother put on her adolescent hat and sang songs of the popular culture of that day, demonstrating her ability to stay young and in sync with the younger generation.

Not everyone approved. Aunt May retreated. Daddy scoffed. Aunt Eve, faced with the latest evidence of psychological symbolism, replied, "I don't think so" and closed her mouth into a firm thin line. Mary Cov had just informed her that the gift box containing candy which Aunt Eve had given her for completing her education was shaped in the form of a casket. "You aren't really congratulating me. You're saying 'Drop dead!'" Mary C. exclaimed triumphantly.

Aunt Eve, reluctant to sound retreat in the face of an argument in which she knew she was right—which was most of the time—continued to disagree. "No, Mary Covington, you have misapplied the symbolism. One of my Salem girls once gave me a box of candy exactly like that. The container resembles a violin case much more than a casket, dear."

Before her niece could respond, Aunt Eve, sounding more like Agatha Christie's lay detective Miss Marple with every word, added, "You remind me so much of that girl. She was so sweet and thoughtful and just devoted to me." Seeing parallels between her niece and her student, as Miss Marple always saw between her nieces, nephews and neighbors in the village of St. Mary Mead, Aunt Eve concluded, "Just as I am to you. Why, I would never give you anything that even suggested a negative thought."

My sister started to reply, "No, of course you wouldn't consciously, but sub-consciously, you may well ..." but was cut off with her aunt's firm but final comment, "No, dear, I don't think so," once again compressing her lips into one thin, determined line.

Mary Cov may have swallowed the Smith line then but much later denounced it, calling the dean of the School of Social Work "a crackpot and a lesbian. Some role model," she snorted, "for impressionable young women like me."

Lil listened selectively, often engaged, sometimes skeptical. But it all proved too much for me. By nature suggestible, I could never have become a doctor, as I would have developed symptoms of every disease I studied. Now I had to wrestle with all this new information—or speculation—about prevention, cause and cure for mental and emotional disorders cloaked in mysterious terms such as neurosis and psychosis. I felt more at home with the good old-fashioned term "nervous breakdown."

When Aunt Susie told tales of her work in rural Kentucky, dealing with syphilis and gonorrhea, I was ready to collapse. Could you get it from this? Or that? How about the other? Philip and I walked around with cold hands and feverish minds half the time. At least no hair had started growing in the palms of our hands — yet. Movies were no longer a joy, as each was subject to a Freudian interpretation. Nothing could be as it appeared or was intended. Everything was a reversal or mirror image of what it projected. I lived increasingly in a world of virtual unreality.

Adjustment after one's freshman year in college is tough enough: all those new people from everywhere, advocating this or that idea which was often in conflict with your own accustomed ones, was culture shock enough. I came down with a severe case of summer flu, followed by a listless recovery: no energy, no appetite, no real zest for living. Once out of bed, Mary C. and I went to a movie, "Rage in Heaven," featuring Robert Montgomery and George Sanders. The plot seemed simple enough: the character played by Montgomery committed suicide and arranged to have it appear as if his best friend had murdered him. Why? Because they were both in love with Ingrid Bergman, and if Montgomery couldn't have her, Sanders certainly couldn't.

"No, Mac, you just don't get it," Mary C. assured me. "Montgomery wasn't really in love with Ingrid, he was subconsciously in love with Sanders and had repressed his true feelings, projected them on to his friend, his love having turned to hate and so...." On and on the lesson went. Apparently the plot was more convoluted than I had first thought.

I returned to Rowena Shute's Pastime Theater to see the movie again. Well, yes, the script did suggest something was awry. It did indicate some Freudian theory, not quite daring to spell it all out, perhaps due to the Hayes Office's influence that still pervaded Hollywood. The Freudian theory? Repressed homosexuality apparently led to paranoid schizophrenia. So now I had to worry about what my Id and my subconscious were up to, let alone all those conflicting conscious thoughts that my first year away from home had prompted.

I shrugged the worries off. I didn't have any subconscious. I remembered everything, even if I did set them aside. I never repressed anything, unable to get at the source. I didn't have much of a censor or mental inhibitor to interfere with my internal communication system. Besides, all this new psychological stuff had an old ring to it. Looking back, it did not sound so unfamiliar. Freud may be interesting but he wasn't always right. There was also behaviorism and biology. Time to shake the dust from my feet again and move on back to Duke for my sophomore year.

One September afternoon in 1941 while Betsy Hodges was visiting me at Duke from Salem Academy, I got a phone call from Aunt Eve. Could I somehow manage to get Aunt May over from Durham to Winston-Salem? Why couldn't Aunt May drive herself, I wondered. No, she couldn't, Aunt Eve assured me. I could not use her car, either. My friend Charles Smith from Tenille, Georgia, whose mother Erin had been a sorority sister of Mother's at Brenau College, had a car. He, Vann, and I had plans for Betsy and some Duke coeds for that evening. Maybe Charlie could take us.

At sixteen and eighteen, Betsy and I were not the epitome of sophistication. We conversed in pig Latin. Our idea of humor was to ring doorbells of downtown Durham funeral homes and inquire of the proprietor if "Dearly Beloved," the name of a popular tune of that day, had passed away. When Aunt May came stumbling out of her apartment, wan and weary, nervously twisting her hands and squinting her eyes, we laughed. Lacking a clue as to what was wrong, Charlie, Betsy and I mocked Aunt May's squint, repeating everything she said exactly as she said it.

"I can't see a thing... My eyes feel so funny... It's so stuffy and hot... I'm so dizzy." The litany of complaints was long. Much of it familiar. But the three teenagers still did not understand. We told jokes, laughed and mocked everything, until Aunt May said, "I declare, you young people are so much fun—just a breath of fresh air. I feel better already."

The seventy-mile drive was not comfortable. Charlie's car was a sport convertible, not really big enough for four people, plus all that baggage. But we got to Salem safely, deposited Betsy at the Academy, and delivered Aunt May to Aunt Eve. I was not to learn until a few weeks later that the "Simmons Curse" had struck Aunt May. Her address, like Lessie's three years earlier, was now Phipps Clinic, Johns Hopkins Hospital, Baltimore, Maryland.

Of all those people at the Kistler-Craven nuptials in mid-August, 1941, I was perhaps the only one more interested in Smolensk than Morganton. A huge battle centered around this vital railroad link in the Soviet Union fewer than two hundred miles from Moscow. By September the Nazi blitzkrieg appeared momentarily stalled on the central front as Hitler directed his army to turn south. Soon the Ukraine, breadbasket of the Soviet Union, was occupied. The drive toward the oilfields near the Caucasus Mountains accelerated. More millions of Russian troops were trapped by encirclement and either killed or captured.

Could the Russians hold out until the winter? Most military experts in Great Britain and the United States continued to doubt it. Churchill thought they could and pledged what little aid Britain could spare. Roosevelt believed they would and made similar pledges to Josef Stalin. But the truth was that the United States was practically disarmed itself, and while industrial mobilization was underway and our military potential unlimited, there was really nothing much anyone else could do now to help our communist ally. If Russia were to hold out until General Frost came to her aid, she would have to do so on her own.

# 34. Pearl Harbor!

When I returned to Duke in September, the Battle of the Atlantic and the fighting on the steppes of Russia occupied my mind far more than did classroom lectures. Just like the Battle of Britain a year earlier, every day was like an NCAA basketball game. Who won? Who lost? How close were the Germans from the Kremlin? At last a heavy snowfall in November! But the Germans could see the domes of the Kremlin from a Moscow suburb only fifteen miles away. The Russian government moved to Kuibyshev, four hundred miles distant, but Stalin elected to stay in Moscow. One could literally feel the earth sway under one's feet—at least I could.

There was also talk about an oil embargo against Japan. Isolationist sentiment still lingered. The Senate had recently approved extension of selective service by only one vote. Good God, Almighty! Didn't the American people understand anything? Few of my Duke classmates seemed to. And most of the professors in my history classes droned on about the Teapot Dome scandal of 1924 under President Harding. We never even got up to the Great Depression.

Despite such preoccupations, I remained a teenager at heart, deeply committed to getting to know every beauty queen or wannabe on East campus. I first met Anne McClenagan of Raleigh through fraternity brother Bill Cozart. She was interested in a DKE at Carolina, a friend of Cousin Hill. I was in love with love, fantasizing, romanticizing, idealizing every girl I dated—largely girls from Kappa Kappa Gamma come to mind followed closely by Pi Beta Phi, Alpha Delta Pi and Alpha Theta Pi.

Anne, with her long thick ash-blond hair worn shoulder length in a peek-a-boo style popularized by movie star Veronica Lake, was the object of my first affection. Anne, a Daddy's girl, was a flirt. She soon had me and several other boys wound around her little finger. She was tall, willowy, graceful, with an unconscious but provocative swing to her walk. She was also good-natured, a good sport, with a pleasant disposition and spirited sense of humor. Anne was also a pretty good athlete and could run faster than I.

Yes, Mary Cov, I know she was nearly as tall as you, and therefore, I could not possibly—but I did, anyhow.

Anne had an acceptable pedigree. Her mother, a member of an old Raleigh family, was a sister of Mrs. Edwin Pate of Laurinburg. The McNair-Pate dynasty dominated Laurinburg and owned a good part of Scotland County in the 1940s and '50s. Fiquet Pate was Anne's first cousin, and Fiquet, another tall ash-blonde and Duke classmate, was a social force herself. She married Pou Bailey, later a well known jurist who died in early 2004. Fiquet herself suffered an early stroke and died a generation or more earlier.

The McClenagan name was a good one in Florence, South Carolina. The town's high school was named in its honor. The McClenagan house on Peace Street in Raleigh was an historic property. It was there, one source claimed, that the governor of North Carolina had said to the governor of South Carolina, "It's been a long time between drinks."

I have never known what that remark meant or why it was so often repeated as part of state history. Does anyone know, or care if they do? I may have houses mixed up. The comment could have originated in Anne's grandparents' ancestral home in eastern North Carolina. Why would I have cared about a girlfriend's family tree anyhow? Because I had unintentionally been reared a snob and remained one, a condition typified by an observation I made one day at Lake Junaluska in 1938.

Lil, Catherine Johnson and I were hitchhiking to nearby Waynesville. Car after car passed us by without even slowing down. Finally, hot and tired, I turned to the two girls and said, "Just think how embarrassed these drivers would be if they knew they were ignoring children from one of the most prominent families in North Carolina!" Lil and Catherine could not believe I said that, much less meant it. It was a remark they never let me forget.

With Anne's pedigree defined, I thought I was in love with her but never really was. We were just good friends. She certainly was not infatuated with me, although one night she did accept my fraternity pin. It meant as little to her as it did to me. Soon she was two-timing me for a student one year ahead and nearly three years older. She and Lauch Lanahan married before war's end, had three children and enjoyed fifty years of life together before he died shortly after his 50th class reunion in 1993. Anne died suddenly ten years later. One always suffers a pang when a love of one's youth, however shallow, passes on. I felt bereft when I learned of Anne's death, even though I hadn't seen her in eight years.

Mary Cov had been a classmate of Anne's sister Marian at Duke in 1936. She cared little for either girl, insisting that Anne had no interest in me, only using me until someone better came along. She also reminded me that I would unconsciously make a sister of any girl who showed too much interest in me. It was a defense mechanism against an over-attachment to Lil, her, Mother and all those other dominating, possessive women in my early life, she condescendingly explained—again. She assumed full blame and felt "so guilty," except for the part that belonged to Lil and Mother.

Oh, yeah, the old incest taboo again. Now I had learned to laugh about such interpretations. "That's right, Mary C. But, what the heck? You know what they say about incest: 'It's a game the whole family can play! '" But where psychological insight was concerned, my sister was sometimes right.

The annual Panhellenic Dance was the big social event of the first semester at Duke. What excitement! Pi Kappa Alpha had a big party in the chapter house, featuring a lethal alcohol punch called "Purple Jesus." Most of the brothers, me included, would drink too much, get overly steamed and super-charged—young males behaving badly, but not to rival "Animal House."

I invited Julia Scott, a freshman at Agnes Scott College in Decatur, Georgia. I had met Julia in August when Moke and I visited Charlie Smith, Moke's roommate from Tenille. What a knock-out! Julia, like Jeannie, had light brown hair, thick, rich and luxuriant, hanging down far below her shoulders. She had seafoam green eyes, which I thought must have been an inspiration for the song "Green Eyes" which Jimmy Dorsey and his vocalist Helen O'Connell had just made famous. Forget about Anne—at least for the moment.

The dance was set for Saturday night, December 6. Julia came the day before. Charlie, Vann, Moke and Bill (over from Wake Forest for the event) and their dates and Julia and I attended a fraternity dinner-dance Friday night. At Charlie's nudging, I even bought Julia a corsage. Charlie Spivak and his orchestra provided music for the Saturday night dance. The Spivak band was apparently at the top of the charts, approaching popular culture status then that some rock star like Bruce Springsteen might enjoy today. I had become a pretty good dancer. Only Art Vann, later a well-known Durham trial lawyer, could do the jitterbug better than I.

Julia was a sensation at the Saturday dance. The stag line rushed her all night. The cooler guys at ATO, SAE and Phi Delta Theta monopolized her. Those Yankee kids could not get enough of this sweet Georgia peach and her Southern drawl. I seldom saw Julia that night. Carlisle Groom, fraternity brother from Greensboro, had the family car for the weekend. He and his date Jane, whom he soon was to marry, drove Julia and me back to Greensboro in time to put Julia on the two o'clock morning train to Atlanta. I spent the rest of that night with Carlisle. Happily my room had a radio. I turned it on, hoping to hear late news from the Moscow front. Were the Russians still holding?

Soon the bulletins started coming. The battle for Moscow had turned. Siberian reinforcements, about whom the Nazis had known nothing, had not only repulsed the German assault, they had actually taken the offensive. The German army all along the central front was in retreat. For the first time, the German blitzkrieg had been stopped—just barely and just in time. The news from North Africa was equally good. The British had defeated German General Erwin Rommel, relieved Tobruk. The Italian and German forces were in full retreat toward Libya.

I slept the sleep of the saved, assured now of a long war which we surely soon would enter. Maybe we would even win it before I had to go. That night any thought of Japan never entered my head. I never saw Julia Scott again. She wrote a short thank-you note. But she was no longer interested. I could not compete with those older, more sophisticated SAE youths from New Jersey who did not have to wrestle with any sister or mother complexes and could devote full attention to Julia. I was dumped. In retrospect I did pretty well, however, on the female front. Thereafter I was chased more often that I had to chase. When I did get into the race and actually caught my quarry, I often didn't know what to do with her. "Chased" might better have been spelled "chaste."

On late Sunday morning, December 7, Mr. and Mrs. Groom pulled an unwilling son and his equally unwilling friend out of bed, gave us a hasty brunch and shortly after noon we were driving back to Durham. Around Burlington Mr. Groom switched on the radio. Soon we heard the bulletins—this time from Honolulu and Washington. The news had nothing to do with the Russians and Moscow or the British and Egypt. It was all about the Rising Sun and the Japanese attack on Pearl Harbor.

Stunned, excited, thrilled but anxious, I now knew we had won the war but at what cost? Who could say? Winston Churchill in his memoirs recorded similar sentiments: "So we had won after all."

I went to prayer services with friend Alex Radford, Big Brother Henry Hall Wilson and Cousin Vann in Duke Chapel. Later that night we ran in a blackout from West to East campus—goodness knows why—gulped down two chocolate floats each at the Toddle House, then proceeded to the Centre Theater to see Gary Cooper in "Sergeant York." What a movie to absorb the night of the Pearl Harbor attack.

Duke's winning football team was the big news on campus that fall, second only to the coming of the war. For the second time in three years the Blue Devils had been invited to the Rose Bowl, now to face Oregon State for the national championship. With the West Coast still in partial panic, California officials expecting further Japanese attacks, would the game be canceled? No indeed. In the 1940s football was still a popular obsession, in close competition with baseball as the national sport. For the good of morale, the game was to go on—only it was to be transferred to Duke's Wallace Wade stadium. This was the first and last time the game was played anywhere else but in Pasadena. That event remains a favorite sports trivia question more than sixty years later.

Daddy, Mother, Uncle Vann, Cousin Vann, Lil and I were present in Durham that January 1, 1942, to see Duke, heavily favored, take and maintain an early lead, only to fall to defeat 20-16 in the final quarter. Duke's Rose Bowl record has remained 0-2. With the university's changing attitude toward de-emphasizing football—following a much earlier Ivy League trend—it is likely to remain that way.

At the homecoming game that 1941 season I met a girl about whom I had heard but had never met. My freshman roommate John Coffee Brooks from Miami, Florida, (he pronounced it "Miama") had a date with Octavia McRae and introduced us. Tave, as everyone called her, was a pretty, stylish girl, with a model's figure. She was somewhat self-conscious of her six-foot frame but carried herself straight and tall and did not eschew high heels. A generation later she would have viewed her height as an asset. Thin, willowy, small-boned, Tave made people turn around and look. She closely resembled Loretta Young.

I had heard about Tave because she had Monroe roots. Her mother was from Monroe and had been a close childhood friend of Lessie. Tave had a slightly younger sister Virginia, nicknamed Teensie, who was a legendary glamour girl at St. Mary's school in Raleigh. Virginia Lee, Tave's and Teensie's mother, had married Will McRae of Rockingham. Mr. McRae had grown rich in textile stock and land speculation in Richmond County. He was a doting husband and father, letting the women in his life spend his money as they wished and lead the lives they wanted.

Virginia's ancestors included the Monroe Lees, Laneys, and Ayscues, among whom numbered that social arbiter of an earlier era who carried the sobriquet "Picnic Drawers" as a consequence of her activities at Union County camp meetings in the 19th century. Whenever we drove from Monroe to Durham, we passed right past the big brick house in Rockingham, and every time Mother would say, as if for the first time, "That's where my friend Virginia Lee lives now, with husband Will McRae and their two little girls."

We never stopped to see them, however, and I never realized that Tave and Teensie were frequent visitors to their aunts in Monroe, Mrs. Dorothy Redwine and her only daughter Dolly B., and Dorothy's two maiden sisters, Marion and Margaret Lee. Dorothy was the widow of Worth Redwine, brother of Florence (Flossie), my seventh grade English teacher, and John, Flossie's ill-fated brother. As I have repeatedly shown, individuals from old Monroe families were seldom distanced by many degrees of separation.

Dorothy and her sisters were proud Episcopalians and friends and neighbors of Aunt Isabel and Uncle Hill. Cousin Hill had long known Tave and Teensie, but somehow Vann and I had not. Now all that changed. Tave did not take to her date John much that Duke homecoming day and I did not cotton much to mine, so little in fact I cannot remember her name or what she looked like. But Tave and I did take to each other, struck by the coincidence of our meeting as well as the mutuality of our interests.

That Christmas the girls visited Monroe and Bill Price and I took them out. Tave and Teensie pretended to be sophisticated. They seemed so cool when they drank beer from bottles in the backseat of the car, smoked cigarettes, and occasionally bellowed out profanity when they spilled beer on their elaborate evening dresses. Teensie was interested in the theater and was the more dramatic of the two girls. She considered herself more glamorous and assumed a sense of entitlement. Both were good-looking, intelligent, high-spirited, independent young women, not atypical of other girls of their time, place and privilege.

For the next several years, Tave was the girl I saw the most and liked the best. Gradually an informal understanding developed. Someday we would probably get married. Before that feeling was firmly set, however, I still had Anne McClenagan in mind, a dilemma she soon resolved by dumping me. Soon after returning my fraternity pin, Anne accepted Lauch's. One spring evening soon thereafter, the men of Beta Theta Pi gathered outside the Pegram House on East campus to serenade Anne and to perform the brotherly rituals that formalized the pinning.

On the floor above Anne's room, a group of Pi Beta Phi girls decided to have fun at Anne's and Lauch's expense. They pulled down their window shades, focused bright lights upon them, and then one Pi Phi girl after another, to the beat of "Strip Polka" by the Andrews Sisters, walked slowly and seductively past the shades and began to strip. First the gloves, then the hat, now the stockings, next the skirt, the blouse, and so it went. The silhouettes appeared in perfect focus on the screen as the crowd gathered below. Soon cheers and laughter drowned out the singing brothers of Beta Theta Pi. This was to me a fitting climax to my Duke University experience, now drawing to a close.

When Vann and I joined the United States Naval Reserve in 1942 and were subsequently called to active duty, we were stationed for a few months at Willow Grove Naval Air Station outside Philadelphia before going on to Harvard for officers' training. During the fall we spent frequent weekends with Mary Cov and her husband Albert Odmark, in New York, and we would invariably call Tave and Teensie to spend a night out on the town. That winter we repeated the process, traveling down to New York City from Boston. By the time we received our commissions, Vann and Teensie, Tave and I must have hit every trendy nightclub in Manhattan. We swam at Long Beach, bicycled in Central Park, lunched at the Tavern on the Green. We had come a long way from Monroe.

Tave and Teensie were handily available as they were doing their "My Sister Eileen" thing, Teensie studying drama at the Neighborhood Playhouse and Tave taking a course at Katherine Gibbs business school. Father Will willingly paid their expenses, although Tave took an occasional job and finally did get a position as personal secretary and assistant to actress Helen Hayes, known then as the First Lady of the Broadway stage.

The McRae sisters lived in a little Greenwich Village apartment on Christopher Street, just across from the Women's Detention and Correctional Center. On a quiet night one could hear the inmates screaming and yelling obscenities at people passing by. On May 31,

Vann and I received our commissions as ensigns, USNR, just twenty years old, and finally went our separate ways. He wound up on Okinawa and in China, and I on a destroyer escort.

# 35. Navy Blues

The U.S.S. Hammann (DE-131) plowed the North Atlantic on anti-submarine patrol and convoy escort duty for weeks on end, going from Boredom to Tedium and back, with an occasional excursion to Ennui, to paraphrase Henry Fonda in the post-war play "Mr. Roberts," later to be made into a Warner Brothers movie and shown perhaps in Miss Rowena Shute's Pastime Theater. I saw it, however, at the theater in Cheraw, South Carolina, my future home.

For a while the Hammann's home port was New York. In the evenings I usually took Tave out although sometimes she and Teensie would join me and my new buddies in the ship's wardroom for dinner. Soon David Alcorn, a red-haired Scotch Irishman from Philadelphia, was Teensie's escort and Frank Shubeck, of Austrian descent from Detroit, was squiring Kate, a southern belle up from Georgia who was fast becoming a top model.

There were 212 enlisted men on board the destroyer escort, the smallest major warship in the U.S. Navy, and 14 officers. I was the youngest officer aboard with the lowest rank when I first came aboard. Soon other shave tails reported for duty and I rose in seniority. The Hammann was staffed entirely by reserve officers. There were few career sailors and no Annapolis graduates aboard. Thanks to our captain, Charles L. Gould, and the executive officer, Charles A. Rueger, the atmosphere was highly informal and civilian.

I tried to adapt to naval lingo, but to me the deck remained the floor; starboard and port still right and left; topside, upstairs. Navigation remained largely a mystery and when I gave the command, "left rudder, full speed ahead," I did not have much idea of what I was doing. Fortunately the older enlisted regular Navy hands did know what they were doing, as did the senior reserve officers. At least I think they must have, as we always got where we intended to go and usually ranked number one in rescue mission and gunnery practice. The Hammann had more than its share of cross marks on its bow to indicate submarine kills.

We once rescued more than 200 merchant mariners from a sinking cargo ship in a hurricane in the Caribbean, not far from Bermuda. We rigged a chair lift, pulled by ropes anchored from our destroyer escort to their merchant vessel, and brought them over to safety aboard the Hammann. The wind raged so furiously that both ships swayed port and starboard forty degrees and more. Men on the chair lift often were submerged in the foaming sea, waves breaking high over the bow and washing away everything on deck not anchored down. But we didn't lose a man and later won a Navy commendation for that feat.

The duty suited me. It was long distance killing, seldom seeing the enemy. It did not become personal. It was nothing like the kind of trench warfare I had envisioned in my pre-teen years that scared me to death and made me wonder whether it would have been better to have been born a girl. Nor was it anything like what soldiers had to face in Normandy, Marines in Pacific island hopping, sailors in kamikaze attacks, air crews in combat or on bombing missions in every part of the globe. I felt lucky.

New York was the place to be for a young naval officer. Bulletin boards in leading hotels carried information about where to go and what to do. Want a weekend at an estate of the rich and famous in Westchester County or the Hamptons? Just sign up. How about free tickets to the hottest Broadway show in town? Or an evening, compliments of the house, at El Morocco, the Stork Club, the Copacabana? Give us a call. If that did not suit, you could always go to the Stage Door Canteen to meet and dance with stage celebrities. Sometimes, although it was against the rules, you could even escort one home. I met Marilyn Maxwell, a hot ticket in 1942, that way.

The most famous and ubiquitous character to emerge in World War II was Kilroy. He was everywhere, at home and overseas. Kilroy was a drawing, just a pair of eyes and a long nose peering over a line. He looked a little bit like my friend Frank Shubeck. Beneath the drawing, which appeared in every men's room I frequented, was the line: "Kilroy was here."

Soon some aspiring poet wrote this little verse beneath the identifying line:

Here I sit
Broken-hearted
Tried to shit
But only farted.

That too became ubiquitous. One evening I attended a soiree at a debutante's home in the Hamptons. The girl's mother, a fashionable, sophisticated woman in her early forties, made a charming, gracious hostess. She was entertaining her guests with a long story about a difficult but amusing social situation, the solution to which she was uncertain. By turns brittle, ironic, humorous, delightfully self-deprecating, she neared the climax of her anecdote: "So there I sit..."

And I blurted out: "Broken hearted!"

The woman stopped in mid-sentence. An audible gasp was followed by a prolonged silence. I turned beet red. Thankfully some senior officer with braid all over his cap and several stripes on his sleeves laughed loudly. Soon everyone else joined in. The older man slapped me on the back and brought me a drink which I obviously did not need. Apparently everyone knew of Kilroy's poem, which must have appeared in women's restrooms as well.

Captain Gould was fourteen years older than I. At thirty-four he still possessed movie-star looks. Women chased him. Men liked and envied him. A native of Ohio, he had come out of a Hearst newspaper background. He knew the Joseph Kennedy family. He and John F. Kennedy had double-dated. He was at home at the Stork Club. His current girlfriend was Robin Chandler, who later married actor Jeffrey Lynn and later still, Andrew Biddle Duke, who became chief of protocol in the Kennedy administration.

Gould himself rose in the ranks of the Hearst organization after the war. He became publisher of the San Francisco Chronicle after leaving the New York Journal American. By 1970 he was head of the Hearst Foundation and was frequently seen on television as Hearst family spokesman in 1974 when Patty Hearst was kidnapped by the Symbionese Liberation Army. The captain adopted an avuncular attitude toward me, and we remained lifelong friends. For some reason he found me worth keeping up with. He married late, an attractive and talented girl named Peggy. They had two sons.

Ann and I visited them once at their place in Westchester County, taking our two boys, ages one and three, and our boxer Misty, still a puppy but housebroken. Peggy looked askance. I could see why. She had decorated everything in pure white—walls, sofas, chairs, carpet. Just married, neither was used to children or indoor pets. Charles was unfazed. "Come on in. What will you have?" They served cocktails and hors d'oeuvres. Charles and I were soon deep in political discussion. He was delighted that Ike had won and Adlai had lost in the recent presidential election.

The captain and I had differed during the war on politics. Most of the officers aboard the Hammann were mid-western Taft Republicans with a few Southern Democrats, all opposed to the New Deal, and "that man in the White House," even if he were their Commander-in-Chief. Some were apolitical. Levy and Schwartz, two Jewish officers, quietly agreed with me but did not say much. David and Frank, who along with me were dismissed as "the three young fops," also were Democrats.

Acosta Nichols, of Oyster Bay, New York, was a neighbor of the Theodore Roosevelts. He was first cousin of Arthur Bliss Lane, ambassador to Poland in 1939 and author of the book *I Saw Poland Betrayed*. Corky, as we called him, was a friend of the Pratt family, co-founders of the Standard Oil Company. Best described as an internationalist Republican, his views corresponded to the liberal editorial policies of the New York Herald-Tribune.

Corky was a New York bluestocking, something my pre-college Southern prejudices did not allow me to recognize. Even now, aboard the Hammann, I was occasionally surprised. N. Philip Frye was a bluestocking from Chicago, something Acosta Nichols would call an oxymoron. Frye, four years older than I, was a graduate of Princeton. There was an antebellum tradition of young Southern gentlemen attending that New Jersey Ivy League school. Woodrow Wilson, a Virginian by birth and a North Carolinian by education and vocation, was a president of Princeton. But how could an heir to the Princeton tradition be a troglodyte Robert Taft Republican, especially one from Illinois?

That was a question over which Frye and I constantly wrangled in the wardroom when there was nothing better to do. Ed Pepper, a proper Bostonian, was the same age as Phil Frye but a graduate of MIT. Ed had the usual arrogance and unconscious air of superiority of the New Englander, casting a doubtful eye upon anyone from New York and especially upon people south of the Mason-Dixon line. He also was disdainful of any liberal arts college. Princeton was hardly MIT and Duke did not even register on his radar screen. What an experience, to be treated as Nobody in Particular.

Ed was somewhere between Phil and Corky in political opinion, but all were to the right of David Alcorn and me, the two radical leftists on board. Charles Rueger, a Virginia gentleman and a graduate of Mr. Jefferson's university, stayed above the fray. Totally sure of his own elevated identity, he did not need to worry about who was who. Kind, gentle, considerate, he was concerned only about the safety and well-being of the crew and with the military efficiency of his ship. He and Gould were a perfect match.

Whenever we were not standing watch on the bridge, often soaked to the skin by waves breaking over the bow, four hours on, four hours off, or engaged in drill or actual combat, we spent time playing Hearts.

"Watch out for Frye," Ed warned. " He's a shark. He's trying to sweep."

"Hell, don't let him do that," Stillwell shouted. "Smoke out the bitch!" He was referring to the queen of spades who counted 13 points against the player who got caught with her in his hand. Phil usually won. Phil was married to a pretty young woman named Pam. Ed went with a blonde girl named Pat. Pam and Pat. Pat and Pam. It seemed as if that was all we ever heard. How about a girlfriend with seven or eight letters in her name, like Octavia or Virginia?

Soon, however, I had a Pat of my own. Captain Gould had gone to a party on Park Avenue, met a captain who had a daughter twenty years old. Fresh, star-struck, ripe and ready, Pat Cullen thought Charles Gould was wonderful. Charles thought she was too young for him but just right for me. Pat, another natural blonde with thick hair down to her waist, looked like a super-stacked Alice in Wonderland. She was not beautiful in the traditional sense, but she had the kind of sex appeal that personified Clara Bow as the "It" girl in the Roaring Twenties.

Pat had a wild imagination. On our first date I picked her up at her Park Avenue apartment. Neither parent was home. She asked me in, gave me a drink of Daddy's prized Scotch whiskey. Soon she hatched her latest scheme.

"Come on, Mac, try on Daddy's dress whites." I didn't think so. I was now a twenty-one-year-old ensign, with one stripe on my sleeve. Her dad was a captain, just below an admiral, with four stripes on his. His hat was emblazoned with insignia, disrespectfully termed scrambled eggs. Mine had none.

"You must be crazy. I would never get away with that," I protested.

"Oh, don't be such a stick in the mud," the captain's daughter replied. "It will be fun. Just try the coat on for size."

It was a good fit. So was the hat. After another slug of Scotch, I put on the captain's clothes and off we went. First stop : Mama Leonie's for dinner. No one paid the slightest attention. Next, the Persian Room. Again, no head turned. The Russian Tea Room. No reaction. With growing self-confidence, we went from one place to another, descending the scale of social acceptability. Before midnight we were in bars in Union Square, frequented exclusively by enlisted men. There our luck ran out. Military police and Navy patrolmen stopped to question us.

"You are kinda young to be a captain, ain't you, sir?" inquired one.

"Let me see your identification, sailor," ordered another.

Pat started to explain but was politely told to be quiet. It was nearly dawn by the time Captain Cullen and Commander Gould came down to the bar to straighten things out. The captain heeded his daughter's plea to let things go. It was all her idea. Gould told the patrol he would see to it that I received proper discipline once back on the Hammann where he had jurisdiction.

The next day Gould called me into his stateroom, listened to my explanation, then declared, "Well, Secrest, I always knew you were a young fool, but I had no idea you were this young and this big a fool." He acknowledged some responsibility, however, as he had introduced me to Pat. Captain Cullen felt some responsibility too as his daughter had played the role of Eve. Or was it the snake? Captain Gould's verdict: go and sin no more. The captain was less patient later with Lieutenant Corky Nichols.

Corky Nichols entered the Captain's stateroom in a state of high anxiety. Usually beet red, his face was ashen. "You have to do something about this," Corky declared. "Really, this is terrible! If this got out, what would our fellow officers think? And the enlisted men? Charles, what are you going to do?" Captain Gould had no idea what his chief communications officer was talking about but soon pieced it together. Terry, old time Navy chief boatswain mate, apparently had put his hand on Corky's knee and said, in effect, "How about it?"

The Hammann had been at sea a long time. Terry had misinterpreted Nichols's manner. One misunderstanding led to another and now to this. The situation seemed almost comically ironic to Gould, involving as it did the ship's chief communications officer. Corky could see nothing funny about it. The Captain thought Nichols "doth protest too much," that this Oyster Bay, New York, bluestocking who didn't approve of women guests in the wardroom and seemed uncomfortable in their presence unconsciously may have given off vibes to Terry subject to different interpretations. Besides, the Chief was an invaluable asset, more important to the ship's operations than Lieutenant Nichols. The Captain didn't want to lose him.

Corky was determined, however, to be vindicated. A formal hearing must be held, disciplinary action taken. The discussion was lengthy. All officers were called in for consultation. After listening to Corky's lengthy complaints, Captain Gould finally snapped, "Corky, if you haven't tried it, don't knock it!" That was hardly regulation manual response. Corky was not amused.

Finally Gould agreed to do something. He asked me, as personnel officer and paymaster, to arrange transfer papers for Terry and to give him leave for two weeks upon our arrival in New York. I was to date Terry's return orders one day after the Hammann was scheduled to leave on her next North Atlantic run. The orders were carried out. Terry missed the ship and was declared Absent Without Leave. On the Hammann's return to home port some weeks later, Terry was retrieved from the brig where he had been detained.

The wrong date on the boatswain mate's orders was blamed on a clerical mistake. Terry was cleared of the AWOL charge. Corky calmed down. No mention was made of the original indiscretion. No one's reputation was ruined, no careers damaged, the ship's efficient operations insured. By no means regular Navy procedure but highly effective.

In the early war years, there were no Naval regulations dealing with homosexuality. Individuals were left to deal with it the best way they could. Sometimes they were caught and punished. Usually, the situation was ignored and nothing made of it. But homosexuals, usually referred to as "queers," were also sometimes victimized, beaten up and "rolled," that is robbed, and blackmailed. Ultimately the Navy recognized the problem and assumed its responsibility.

Homosexuals, if caught, were given Section Eight discharges, for the good of the Service, and returned to civilian life. There was no dishonorable discharge and no further stigma attached. Section Eight releases covered more than sexual misconduct. The change was viewed as a progressive step forward, removing misfits from harm's way and protecting them from mental and physical abuse or, in extreme cases, death. Today Section Eight discharges are viewed as regressive and benighted. But they did not differ greatly from "Don't ask, Don't Tell" that is today's regressive policy.

Corky was a good friend. Secure in his lordly social status, he was above snobbery. Aboard ship, he often sided with me in defense of the Democrats and FDR. And he defended me when I pronounced the Kentucky whiskey "BourBON" after the French royal dynasty, not "BURbun" as everyone else called it. "Mac's exactly right," old schoolmarm Nichols would say. "He's given the proper French pronunciation, which most of you ignoramuses don't even comprehend." Yes, Corky was okay.

Ed did not marry Pat. He chose Ruth instead. When my wife Ann and I years later visited Ann's relatives in New England, we occasionally met Ed and Ruth for lunch. We once spent a weekend at Ed's parents' home to attend a regatta. The elder Pepper spoke condescendingly of his childhood acquaintance with Rose Fitzgerald and her Irish clan. It was obvious that this WASP Back Bay Brahmin considered himself superior to those "Pig Parlour Irishmen," no matter how long the Kennedys and the Fitzgeralds had been over here and no matter how rich and politically powerful they had become.

Terry's appetite, satiated by shore leave, was apparently permanently appeased. But he continued his old Navy ways, blowing the wake-up whistle at five o'clock each morning, shouting through the ship's loudspeaker system: "Now hear this! Now hear this! Sailor, drop your cock and grab a sock. All hands on deck! Sweepers, man your brooms. Clean sweep down, 'fore and 'aft." As Shakespeare said, cribbing from Proverbs, "All's well that ends well."

The 1941 regular Navy was an elitist organization: class conscious, racist, sexist, conservative, resistant to change. The influx of reservists altered much of that, but the reserve officers themselves were in turn influenced by the old guard. The officers aboard the Hammann reflected the contradiction despite mavericks such as Charles Gould. There was a wide gulf between an "officer and a gentleman" and the enlisted man. I never met a black officer or any female ones, either, except in the Waves. Women were not allowed to serve aboard ships.

The wardroom was a haven for the privileged—all officers with college degrees. Blacks were relegated to service in the laundry, galley and as servants in the wardroom. Officers on our destroyer escort were waited on by Hatten, a semi-literate, "Step 'n Fetch It" young black from Virginia. Most of the officers ignored him, speaking in his presence as if he were the original invisible man. Captain Gould, always kind-hearted, was good to Hatten but found him to be a laughing-stock figure. Only Lieutenant Rueger and I, both Southerners, treated Hatten as a human being, but even we dealt with him from a vantage point of noblesse oblige and condescension.

On board there was camaraderie among officers and white enlisted men, but our social lives were tightly drawn. On leave or at liberty, the policy of no fraternization was strictly observed. Most of the men I was supposed to direct were older and knew more than I did. Whenever I made a suggestion or had a complaint, my subordinates would usually reply, "Don't worry about it, Mr. Secrest." I learned to let well enough alone... in everything except where money was concerned. As paymaster, I had custody of lots of cash, sometimes millions of dollars, and I was determined to keep tight control of that and account for every penny.

Once a recently arrived young ensign came across a group of enlisted men playing poker in midship. The officer placed his foot upon the cards, hands upon the pile of money, and told the group he would place them all on report. Amid great protest, Chief Boatswain Mate Terry declared, "Oh, c'mon, sir. Cap'n Gould don't care if we gamble a little. In fact, if you'd been here a minute earlier, you'd have caught him, too." Indeed, Gould was at that minute hiding in a nearby locker, hoping the young officer would not discover him.

I kept up with several of these men after the war. David Alcorn and I see each other every year or so. Frank Shubeck, also, but more rarely. Ann and I saw Corky Nichols and Ed Pepper frequently the year I was at Harvard as a Nieman Fellow in 1960-1961. Corky had returned to his position as schoolmaster at Groton, that quintessential Ivy League prep school whose headmaster was once old Mr. Peabody when FDR was a student there. Corky never married. He wasn't a lovable Mr. Chips, being overly concerned lest our visiting children raise their voices too loudly in the library or scratch the furniture.

Ann and I visited Charles Rueger and wife Harriet in Roanoke. Later in Richmond and Williamsburg we saw him and his second wife Ellen. We were guests of Charles and Peggy Gould in New York and later in San Francisco, when our daughter Molly and her husband lived in nearby San Jose. I last saw Charles there in 1985, three years before his death.

Phil Frye's wife Pam died in 1964. Prior to that time, I occasionally drove up from Cheraw to see them when they were down from Chicago to spend time in the spring at the family's horse farm in Tryon, North Carolina. Phil was loaded, by 1960 a leading corporate attorney in Chicago. His father earlier had largely owned the White Sox baseball team. Once Ann and I stopped by their home in suburban Chicago. I called Phil "the big noise that blew in from Winetka." Mostly, Phil and I stayed in touch by mail and telephone, especially during election years, when we would renew our earlier political arguments, still trading insults over our party preferences.

There were other friends, as the fortunes of war removed some, who were then replaced. Ted (Tex) Eubanks and I, fellow iconoclasts, read the entire Bible to seek answers and wound up with still more questions. On the same page politically, we liked to read the comic strips, especially "Little Orphan Annie" and scoff at Daddy Warbucks, that rich Republican plutocrat.

Bob Bourne was a young officer from Bronxville, whose family was also up to their armpits in money. He had an aunt so socially exclusive that, according to one society reporter, "She has never even been seen." Largely on my initiative, we kept up, as I sought to teach these men the virtue of "propinquity," either by pen, phone calls, or, when possible, by personal visits.

We saw Bourne often in Cambridge in 1960-61, helped nurse him through his failing marriage. He even came to see us in Cheraw, shared his bed with our boxer Misty, and celebrated his second marriage with us. As the years pass, it becomes more difficult. Numbers dwindle. Father Time claims his own. Frank, David, Bob... but not many left. Charles Rueger, at ninety-four, is, however, still clear-headed and caring.

En route home from the Pacific after the atomic bombs had fallen on Hiroshima and Nagasaki, the Hammann spent two weeks at Pearl Harbor, where I paid my respects to cousin Lee Wolfe, a twenty-year-old military policeman who had committed suicide a few months earlier. Lee, Hill's younger brother, had apparently had a brief affair with a Hawaiian girl, felt guilty over his unfaithfulness to fiancée Virginia Hamilton and in remorse had shot himself. His buddies told me that Lee had become obsessed, terrified that he had contracted a venereal disease. Ironically, an autopsy revealed he had not.

Even if he had, in those days of recently discovered penicillin, what if he had? No, Lee's guilt had deeper psychological roots. He had been favored by his grandmother Miss Minnie Wolfe; indeed had slept in the bed with her far too long. Mary C. and I, soon to compare notes, decided Miss Minnie had laid the groundwork for his excessive sensitivity and vulnerability. It was her fault, not Aunt Isabel's. But there's always some reason. Poor Miss Minnie was compensating for the desertion of her husband, who had turned up years later in Baltimore, living with another woman.

Again underway, we soon passed through the Panama Canal, losing one sailor who drowned when he became tangled up in the anchor as he and several others jumped overboard to swim. I had become hardened. Such tragedies never cost me a night's sleep. Ten days later we dropped anchor in the Charleston, South Carolina, harbor. Locke Everette's sister, her husband and their five daughters, ranging in age from fifteen to twenty-three, welcomed me and my naval friends into their home at Three Atlantic Street. They opened doors to an old Charleston society many of my friends would otherwise never have known. There is an ingrown, old-world charm about Charleston and its social structure that can be described but never fully understood unless you were reared there.

By October the Hammann set sail for the last time. The destroyer escort was put to rest at Green Cove Springs, Florida, where it was moth-balled for several years. Ann and I stopped by to pay it a visit in 1954. Later the entire fleet there was dismantled.

The six months I served in Florida were happy and carefree. I spent a lot of time with Aunt Ruth, one of Daddy's younger sisters, and Uncle Ad Benton. Aunt Ruth introduced me to Josephine McRae, whose father was a major Ford dealer and self-made millionaire.

Mr. and Mrs. McRae opened their lavish home on the St. Johns River to the officers of the Hammann. Dave and Tex were more enamored of Josephine and her friends than I. Another McRae girl—Tave—still held first place in my heart. But Josephine's parents intrigued me. Typical of many *nouveau riches* in the mid-century South, they were impressed by style, pomp and circumstance. They appeared overwhelmed by Gould's glamour, Corky's elegance, Pepper's unconscious arrogance.

Every night was party night at the McRaes. They were super-patriotic; nothing was too good for Uncle Sam's boys in blue. They were also good, down-to-earth people without pretension. They had money and they flaunted it. They also shared it. It was as simple as that. While they were climbing the social ladder, it was mostly for Josephine's sake, who had, however, already made it: serene, confident, with entree into any social set in town.

They also seemed devoted to each other. So it was a real shock to read in the headlines of the Saranac Lake, New York, Daily Enterprise a year later of a double murder in a mansion in an exclusive section of Jacksonville. Mr. McRae had shot and killed his wife and a family friend whom he had found in bed with her. Months later McRae was acquitted of all charges, the jury finding him innocent because of the nature of the act: a crime of passion. Such verdicts were not unusual in the South sixty years ago. I was soon to learn another legal concept in South Carolina—"friendly murder"—and how one could get away with that.

In the mid-20th century, men who avenged their honor by violence were usually acquitted of any crime. Women had far fewer rights and less protection than today. The idea that a wife could be raped by her husband and he could be tried and convicted of such a crime was practically unheard of, particularly south of the Mason-Dixon line. The idea that a woman's body was entirely her own was not a widely-accepted concept.

# 36. Saranac Lake and Psychoanalysis

On May 15, 1946 I returned to Monroe, once again a civilian. Mary C., married to Albert Odmark in 1942, whom she had met a year earlier on a New York subway train, was divorced and back home from a two-year stint in India with the Red Cross.

Weird coincidences occurred during World War II. Walking down a street in Delhi one day in 1944, she bumped into Joe Presson, an earlier member of her entourage at Broadacre. Joe in the 1930s had worked behind the soda fountain in the Secrest Drug Store. Now both in India, neither of them had any idea that the other was in the Orient. As Mary Cov later told the story, accompanied by her usual refrain, "I feel so guilty," they made the most of their brief encounter, enjoying a nostalgic and romantic reunion.

A decade earlier, Joe had continued to work at the drug store as many of his friends went off to college. One day Uncle Vann discovered that he had over several months been tapping the till and taken a considerable amount of money. Daddy, angry and disappointed in his teenage neighbor, was initially inclined not only to fire Joe but also to prosecute.

Upon further reflection, after consulting with Mother and Uncle Vann, he decided upon a different course. Joe was a good worker. Why not teach him a lesson but give him a second chance? Daddy told Joe he could keep his job provided he repaid the money by deduction from his weekly wage. The matter would be treated as an interest-free loan, not a theft, on condition Joe acknowledged his mistake and promised never to repeat it.

"Joe, you're not a bad boy," Daddy said. "But remember the old hymn, 'Yield not to Temptation.'" A deal was reached. Satisfy the loan. Attend Central Methodist Church regularly. And Daddy would not refer the matter to the police or tell Joe's parents or anyone else. Joe's father had been unable to work for several years since suffering a serious injury in a local bank robbery. Of course Mary Cov, Lil and I knew, as we knew all the family secrets. But we never let this one get outside the inner circle.

Joe would have the same chance of promotion and salary increase as before. He kept the faith, and even managed eventually to attend nearby Wingate Junior College. He and his sister Hannah Lee and Mary Cov remained friends. After Pearl Harbor Joe joined the army and followed the path destiny had set that led to his reunion with Mary Cov in India.

This incident was one of several in which Mother and Daddy showed generosity and understanding of young people, especially those who got into trouble. Just like when Bat-Eye Bailey, another kid with no money, had taken Mary Cov and Cousin Claude on that unauthorized joy ride years earlier which landed them in the middle of J.C. Penney's plate-glass window.

Mary C. liked but never really loved Albert. In her first show of sibling rivalry, she had married in haste when she heard of Lil's plan to marry John Buie of Wagram in August 1942. "If you think I'm going to let my little sister beat me to the altar, you're crazy!" Mary Cov exclaimed. So she quickly arranged for a nice big wedding in Monroe's Central Methodist Church on July 9, six weeks ahead of Lil.

Lil in 1946 now had two daughters, Kathy, two and a half, and Ann, ready to celebrate her first birthday. Mother, well now for over seven years, had retained her good health. Aunt May had recovered hers in 1943 in Lexington, Kentucky, after two years, and was back home in time to lend a hand in caring for Aunt Katherine Craven, who died of liver cancer in November.

Lil had taken a belated interest in a young lieutenant at Camp Sutton in June of 1942. Daddy had arranged with army authorities for Paul, a pharmacist, to work at the Secrest Drug Store on his off hours. Civilian pharmacists were nearly impossible to find in war time, and it was a good deal for all concerned. Especially for Lil, who was taken with Paul, who in turn was obviously smitten with her. Lil dated Paul up to a week before her marriage to John. Paul, a native of California, was soon, however, to ship out. Plans had been made. It was too late for anything to change. But I often wonder what might have happened if Lil had had a little more leeway.

Lil, Vann, Uncle Vann, Mother, Daddy and I all worked at the drug store that summer. With Monroe full of soldiers now that Camp Sutton had been established there—thanks largely to Mayor J. Ray Shute—all Blue Laws were repealed. Movies were open on Sundays. People started playing cards on the Sabbath. Mother, that staunch member of the Women's Christian Temperance Union, sloshed beer to customers in the store (but "Never on Sunday") when she wasn't working at the USO canteen across the street.

Camp Sutton was named in honor of Frank Sutton, Union County's first war casualty. Frank had enlisted in the Canadian Air Force in 1940 to help the British, then alone. Ironically, he was killed in Libya on December 7, 1941, never to learn about Pearl Harbor or America's entry into the war, insuring the Allied victory Sutton had so early recognized as essential to his own country's security.

Lil, Vann and I worked from 8 am till closing time at 11 pm. One evening a soldier spied Lil, found her fetching, and sidled up to her.

"Where do you keep your rubbers?" he asked suggestively.

"Our what?" Lil asked. Puzzled, that was one product she didn't know anything about.

"Oh, you know," the corporal persisted. "Your Trojans." Lil was still at a loss. She didn't have a clue.

"Hey, Vann," she shouted across the store to her younger cousin. "Where do we keep the Trojans?" Vann turned red. The usual hubbub in the store stilled. Everyone looked toward Lil, who just stood there, repeating the question. "You know, our rubbers."

Paul, the Camp Sutton pharmacist, thought that was hilarious, but he came to Lil's rescue. "C'mon back here, soldier," the lieutenant directed. And the behind-the-scene transaction took place, with Lil still in the dark over the commotion she had caused.

Six weeks before her marriage to John Buie and Lil still knew nothing about contraceptives. After her marriage she didn't care about them. Lil was sure she would be a good wife. But she wanted even more to be a mother. She could hardly wait to get pregnant. She had always adored babies. But how could she be sure she was fertile?

Six months after Lil's marriage she still had not conceived, but she did not give up easily. Later John remarked to me, "You know, Mac, your sister kept me plumb wore out!" I soon relayed that message to Lil and others in the family who now had fun at Lil's expense at family gatherings over at Ma's house on Saturday nights, only Ma was no longer there to join in the fun. She had died in December 1939. Aunt Mary and Uncle Henry Hinson now lived there.

Lil took the ribbing with her usual self-possessed good humor. "I don't remember John complaining at the time over all that work I put him through," she remarked drily. "And man, was it ever worth it. With the investment, look at the priceless dividend we received—Kathy, born December 5, 1943, 'the perfect child.'"

Although I stayed busy at the drug store, too, I kept one ear out for war news from CBS radio. The second summer of a German offensive in Russia had begun. Again the German army sliced through Soviet defenses with apparent ease, first the Crimean peninsula, then the rest of the Ukraine, followed by a drive all the way to Stalingrad and the Volga River. The oil fields just beyond the Caucasus mountains were by summer's end within reach. It looked as if nothing could stop the Germans and the Japanese—now pushing west through Burma, Java, and Singapore to threaten India and Madagascar—from joining forces in the Middle East and isolating the beleaguered Russians from Allied assistance through Iran.

Again the question arose: Could Russia hold out until General Winter set in? Rumors were rife that the Soviet Union, always suspect under a perfidious Joseph Stalin, was on the verge of arranging for a separate peace.

The British fared no better in North Africa. Six months after the Singapore fortress fell—once believed impregnable—Tobruk in Libya surrendered with the loss of the entire British garrison. Soon the British Eighth Army was in full flight back into Egypt, stopping to regroup at El Alemein only forty miles from Alexandria. The British position, never strongly held in her pro-Axis colonies of Syria, Iraq, Arabia, and Jordan, was in jeopardy throughout the Middle East.

Japan swept everything before her in the Pacific. Only the naval battle of Midway in June 1942 provided any hope for Allied prospects. Every day the earth seemed to tilt, just as it had a year earlier, first one way, then another, but usually in favor of the Axis powers.

Like us in the Secrest Drug Store that summer, Americans never doubted that they would eventually win. But now the length and the cost of the war seemed certain to be far longer and greater than we had originally envisioned.

But shortly after I had returned to Duke in September 1942, the tide turned. A new British general in North Africa, Bernard Montgomery, took the measure of General Rommel, defeating him in the decisive battle of El Alemein in October. Soon thereafter an American-British expeditionary force landed and freed French North Africa of Vichy and German control. Churchill and Roosevelt met in Casablanca to plan future operations, just as Warner Brothers released Casablanca, starring the unforgettable quartet: Humphrey Bogart, Ingrid Bergman, Paul Henreid and Claude Raines.

In August the American army landed in Guadalcanal to stop the Japanese Pacific campaign and remove the threat to Australia. The British secured India, even if Churchill had to jail Ghandi and Nehru in the process.

Above all, the Russians held at Stalingrad. By November they had trapped an entire German army which surrendered the following February.

The British and Americans had also captured an entire German army by May 1943 in Tunisia, clearing all of Africa of the Axis presence. Soon Sicily was also captured, Italy invaded, Mussolini deposed. Italy switched sides and the Allies had re-entered Europe through the back door. Germany was being laid waste by the British and American airforces. Neither side concerned itself with "collateral damage." The people were viewed as the enemy and the more civilians died, the more welcome the news.

Germany's huge seaport city of Hamburg was the first victim. British and American planes, using both high explosives and incendiary bombs, produced the first "firestorm" in military history, wild fires burning out of control, creating hurricane-force winds that sucked men, women and children out of their homes and incinerated them. Over a three-day aerial offensive, an estimated 60,000 people died. An unrepentant Winston Churchill declared: "They have sowed the wind. Now let them reap the whirlwind." He also said, almost in truth, that "before the battle of El Alemein we never had a victory. After it, we never had a defeat." He also declared that the 1942-43 victories "are not the end. They are not even the beginning of the end. But they may be the end of the beginning."

Two more years of hard fighting were to remain after Hamburg's destruction. Hitler speeded up the Holocaust. Churchill also pointed out that Hitler, had he not been obsessed with exterminating the Jews and banishing "Jewish science" from Germany, may well have won the war.

With June 5 and 6, 1944 came the surrender of Rome and the Normandy invasion. By May 1945 the war in Europe was over and Hitler was dead. Japan, now the target of our aerial and naval war, every bit as destructive for the Japanese as Hamburg and Dresden had been for the Germans, was ready to surrender. After the dropping of the atomic bombs on Hiroshima and Nagasaki in early August 1945, Japan too surrendered. The bloodiest war in the history of the world came to an end, an estimated 50 million dead, millions of others permanently displaced, most never accounted for. I had been in the service on active duty for three years.

Daddy was the casualty now, slowly and painfully dying of cardiovascular disease. He was a difficult patient and help was nearly impossible to find. Mother needed help, but she was reluctant to ask her children to stay home to provide it. I would have refused had she asked. I did my share of nursing that summer, but I felt I had done my bit of parent-sitting in earlier years. Now it was time to make decisions about my own life.

Mary C. did not look well herself—too thin, tired, wired, strung out. The years in India had proved physically and emotionally stressful. She was offered two jobs, one as case worker with a mental health agency in St. Petersburg, Florida; the other, in Rochester, New York. She could not decide. Lil and I termed it the Smith-Smithfield neurosis in redux. "Why would anyone want to go to an old folks home like St. Petersburg, Florida?" I asked. "New York is much better." Little did I anticipate the Sun Belt boom or the Snow Belt meltdown. In any event, I think I influenced my sister in her choice of Rochester, where she was to meet her second husband and where he and she were to raise their future family of three girls and one boy.

Mary C. had lived and worked in New York City from 1942 to 1945. While there she decided she would benefit personally and professionally if she were to undergo psychoanalysis. She had met Dr. Carl Herold, a former professor at a Viennese university with a doctorate in philosophy. He had later entered medical school, developed an interest in psychiatry and still later studied under Dr. Freud himself at the Psychiatric Institute in Berlin.

Of Austrian nationality, Dr. Herold had left Germany in 1935 and later established a properly certified practice in psychoanalysis in New York City. Mary C. believed that self-knowledge would unlock all the secrets of one's psyche and thus inoculate one against the virus of mental or emotional disturbance. Anyone with a history of psychosis in the family should certainly seek such protection. She convinced me. She also persuaded me that Dr. Herold—a Renaissance man learned not only in the science of medicine but also in the art of philosophy and healing—was the one to see.

Service overseas in the Red Cross and her doctor's bout with tuberculosis interrupted Mary Cov's experiment. By 1946 Dr. Herold was recuperating in Saranac Lake, New York. Although she did not tell me at the time, the phenomenon of transference and counter-transference had also interfered with her analysis.

It was a truism, but a false one, in the 1920s and '30s that a patient always fell in love with her analyst. I don't know what happened, if anything, between my sister and Dr. Herold in 1943. But if anything did, it would have been the fault of the analyst, a person of authority and in a position of power and a man twenty-three years my sister's senior. At the least it would have been highly unethical and today a cause for a medical malpractice suit or loss of one's medical license. But I heard nothing of this for ten years. It is a story for my sister to have told, if she had so chosen, not me. It was not a part of my life, and I never let it become so.

In any event, as I talked my sister into taking the job in Rochester, so she talked me into going to Saranac Lake for my mental health vaccination. To some extent, then, each of us was responsible for the decisions taken that summer that determined the paths we were later to walk. I'm glad we did. I believe Mary Cov was, too, even if at times she felt as if she could not live with, or without, her future husband, Dr. W. H. English, soon known to us all in the family as Bill.

She later turned against Dr. Herold and psychoanalysis, denouncing it all as "nothing but a cult." The union between Bill and Mary C. produced four great dividends, however, as did my subsequent one with a young woman in Saranac Lake. Nature has a wonderful way of balancing things out. Life is like the weather. When you encounter stormy weather, just wait awhile. Things clear up. They do get better . . . even good . . . sometimes great.

In August I made my first trip to Saranac Lake, New York, a beautiful little town nestled amid the Adirondack Mountains and the multiple lakes that inhabit the region. It is only ten miles from Lake Placid, site of the 1932 Winter Olympics, scenes from which I'd seen in Mrs. Rowena Shute's Pastime Theater in Monroe when I was eight years old. Ever since then I had wanted to ski and bobsled. Here was my chance. Saranac Lake had its own reasons for national recognition. Its altitude and climate had made it a medical mecca in the treatment of tuberculosis since the 1880s.

By 1946 there were many sanatoriums, the best known being Trudeau Sanatorium. The medical director was the grandfather of Gary Trudeau, later of "Doonesbury" fame. Will Rogers Sanatorium was established to treat and care for patients from the entertainment world. The Veterans Administration maintained an enormous center in nearby Tupper Lake. And there were others. During the two years I lived in Saranac Lake, I met the heir to a Bolivian tin fortune; Ralph Ingersoll, journalist and publisher of P.M., a new and controversial newspaper; Lila Lee, silent film star; Lady Cunliffe, a British aristocrat if not a royal one; and many other people, young and old, rich and poor, interesting and dull, from all around the globe.

I also met Ann Eastman Convel, fresh out of graduate school at the University of Wisconsin who had just accepted the job of head librarian at the Saranac Lake Free Library. Her aunt Laura Phillips and Laura's friend, Eleanor Varney, were the women from Concord, N.H., with whom Aunt May and Aunt Eve had made friends in Nova Scotia nine years earlier. Saranac Lake was a vacation destination as well as a medical center. Home to summer camps of the rich and famous, its part-time residents included the Rockefellers, the Haneses, the Walgreens, and many other names among the Fortune 500. Albert Einstein and Marc Chagall were two visitors I recall in the summers of 1947 and 1948.

Death was a frequent but silent and largely unseen visitor in Saranac Lake. The town had dozens of cure cottages where patients on bed rest lay out in glassed-in porches in dry sub-freezing temperatures to help rid their lungs of the tubercule bacillus or at least seal up and contain those lethal germs. Late at night hearses drove down the narrow service alleys to pick up the corpses of patients who had died earlier that day. The only evidence left were the empty beds on porches to be remade and soon occupied by other patients, of whom there was an endless supply.

Saranac Lake had a permanent population of eight thousand residents, most of whom were descendants of families who had come generations earlier for the cure. Doctors there were pioneers in new surgical techniques to treat tuberculosis and local laboratories were engaged in research and development that soon led to a chemical "magic bullet" for this disease—long known as "the white plague"—that had indeed plagued mankind since the dawn of civilization.

One quickly became blasé, however, about tuberculosis in Saranac Lake. Patients were taught techniques of personal hygiene. Only patients who registered "sputum negative" were allowed in town. Everyone, sick or well, learned never to spit in public places on peril of arrest. People did not need to be reminded to wash their hands. Rarely did anyone catch TB from anyone else in Saranac Lake. Yet the prevalent mood among the residents was fatalistic, even reckless. "Eat, drink, and be merry..." was then an animating philosophy. I was reminded of Thomas Mann's The Magic Mountain.

Dr. Herold and I got along fine from our first encounter. He proved flexible, willing to meet my agenda. No, I did not want the conventional psychoanalytic technique. There would be no lying down submissively on a couch with a revered doctor sitting behind me taking notes and (who could tell) perhaps dozing off between occasional "uh-huhs." There would be no free association or uninterrupted flow of ideas.

I insisted on cognitive therapy, with well-defined problems properly identified relevant to my own personality development. Of course that may require delving into one's early childhood, with distant memories recalled and perhaps emotionally re-experienced, but forget about any rigid conformity to Freudian dogma. Don't get hung up on dreams or symbolism. Remember Freud's wisecrack that "sometimes a cigar really is a cigar."

I required a therapist with imagination, insight, and a mind of his own, blended with a sense of humor and human understanding gleaned from personal experience as well as theoretical knowledge. Freud had a lot to offer, but so did Pavlov, Watson and Jung. So did the new school of behavior modification. There was stimulus and response, conditioning, deconditioning and reconditioning. There were new studies redefining normality. And there were heredity and environment as well as looming discoveries involving genetics. Even Freud, later referred to as a "biologist of the mind," had conceded that the future of psychology lay with physiologists and chemistry.

"You appear to be a normal, happy young man," Dr. Herold observed. "Why do you want to see me, anyhow?"

"Looks can be deceiving. You can't judge a book by its cover." I took refuge in clichés. "You don't know me. How can you tell? I want to grow, develop and mature gracefully." I explained that I felt that due to family circumstances, I had become too dependent upon the women in my family. "Who would want to marry a Mama's Boy or a Baby Brother? I want to be worthy of the woman I marry."

Besides, I had another agenda. What did I want to do with my life? That decision is one of the most difficult and important a young person can make. Later on when I was a teacher myself, I empathized with seniors who still did not have a clue. I had long believed I wanted to be a history professor.

Mother and my maternal aunts, with their beloved "Brother" David still in mind, had implanted the seed early on. My cousin David Fowler, with his literary bent, and I, with my historical inclination, could fulfill Uncle David's unrealized promise. David, also recently out of the Navy, was already on his way, now enrolled at the University of Chicago where "Brother" had studied forty years earlier and where he had died at age twenty-four, his life and career cut short. I explained all that to Dr. Herold. "I want to earn my doctorate in world history."

"In that case why don't you apply to a university and start the process?"

"Because I want to be sure," I replied. "My college education was interrupted by the war. It was incomplete. I was too young. Besides, I need to make peace with my past and to know myself." I asked Dr. Herold if he did not agree with Socrates—that 'an unexamined life was not worth living.'"

I was sixteen when I graduated from high school, nineteen when I left Duke University. With nearly four years in the U.S. Naval Reserve, largely spent at sea on active duty, now I was back home still only twenty-two years old. No wonder I was unsure. Of course I needed further formal education.

My plan was to examine significant changes in the world—political, intellectual, scientific, cultural, economic, religious, social, philosophical—and learn how the historical process worked. One way to proceed was to examine the lives of great men and women who were catalysts for change and, one hoped, for a positive progression of mankind through the ages.

A simple accumulation of facts was not adequate. History was more than just "one damn thing after another." It could be understood, and if so, perhaps not repeated. Generalized history was not a promising field, nor an interesting one. A scholar needed a special area of investigation, leading to original interpretations that would command academic attention and lead to success and recognition. I had personal ambition and a practical approach. Why not specialize in biography? To do so, would I not have an advantage if I could gain psychological insights into historic personalities? Psychoanalysis was still a hot intellectual property. Why not kill two birds with one stone?

I proposed a study of biography through the eyes of a trained psychologist. And since human behavior is often best revealed in literature, why not study the one hundred greatest books, as proposed by the University of Chicago? Dr. Herold's job would be to lend a Freudian interpretation not only to world leaders, past and present, but also to great literary characters. With his knowledge of philosophy, he should also be able to help me understand the ideas of the classical Greek philosophers, as well as those of the Great Enlightenment and the 19th century romantics and skeptics.

In the process, perhaps we could find parallels to my own life. I agreed with Dr. Herold. There was not much the matter with me. My personality might be compared to underground wires or pipes. If something were amiss here or there, we could dig up that particular connection, unplug or rewire it, and set things right, without having to replace the entire system.

As for finances, well, Dr. Herold was at a disadvantage. Tuberculosis, not psychological disorders, was the medical preoccupation in Saranac Lake. He needed to work, financially and emotionally, himself. I was a veteran; he was a refugee. I was entitled to some consideration. I could afford five dollars an hour (a full 60-minute hour, please) the first year. If we persisted, and went into a second year, then I might be able to manage ten dollars an hour. The schedule would have to be flexible: an hour a day, five days a week, arranged around whatever work I could find in a little town like Saranac Lake. In 1946, these fees were not greatly out of line with prevailing ones elsewhere. A college graduate could expect an initial annual salary of perhaps $3,000.00 a year.

So it was arranged. I got a job as manager of a restaurant, the Blue Gentian, owned by two women, one German, the other Swiss, who also ran a second restaurant by the same name in winter in Sarasota, Florida. They had decided to keep the Saranac Lake restaurant open for the first time year-round that winter of 1946-47. The Blue Gentian was located next door to the Saranac Lake Free Library, which I frequented in my search for books. I was soon to be immersed in Dostoevsky, Thomas Mann, and Theodore Dreiser.

But I was not so submerged as to be unaware of the pretty young woman behind the desk. Her red hair framed her freckled face. I imagined her as a model posing for a Titian painting. Who could help but notice her? She was five feet, two inches tall, and weighed perhaps 98 pounds wringing wet, yet was well-proportioned. She had deep dimples when she smiled and big brown eyes, soft or snapping in turn.

My first impression was of a girl who wore her skirts just right, had good but expensive taste in clothes and radiated good taste, good breeding, good looks and money. "Probably one of those rich girls who got and beat tuberculosis and work in the library to have something to do," was my conclusion before I left in late August to return home, pack and return on September 15, my twenty-third birthday.

I went home by way of Rochester to see Mary Cov. She still wasn't herself, overly anxious, full of regrets and unwarranted guilt, lacking her usual energy, nerve, and animation. Always professionally conscientious, she lacked interest in her job. But as usual around me, she perked up, her sense of humor, now ironic and sardonic, returning. Soon we were hip deep in psychological interpretations of various family members, including ourselves.

That evening she introduced me to a doctor she had met on the job and was seeing socially, Dr. William H. English. Bill, as I was soon to call him, was a psychiatrist and head pathologist at the State Hospital. A native of England, he had lived in South Africa and Canada before migrating to the United States. He spoke with an English accent and had a cultivated manner. He was about Mary C.'s height. He took us out to dinner at an expensive restaurant. I was impressed. He must have been also, but why favorably, I now wonder, as my sister and I talked a mile a minute about personal matters and people he did not know, paying him little attention.

Back at Mary Cov's apartment, she said accusingly, "You think he's too old for me, don't you?" Mary C. was thirty to Bill's forty-three.

"No, I don't. And I think he seems to be a good guy and is very nice looking." I did wonder about his having two teen-age boys, but my sister had not known him very long and she wasn't looking for a husband right away, was she?

I left the next day for Bronxville, New York, to attend Betsy Hodges's wedding to Duke classmate Donald Bernard. It was a lavish affair with many former Duke students on hand. Donald's parents were from Texas, his father now advertising manager of the Washington Post, so Donald should be good enough for Betsy. But I was unsure. Few people in my opinion would have been. Fifty-seven years, three children, and ten grandchildren later, they are still together, so they must have been good enough for each other. The New York Times headline above the wedding account read, "Bride has ten attendants." Well, so what? Betsy had a lot of friends. She was worth it.

# 37. Love and Marriage

Back home I got my stuff together, said goodbye to my parents, friends and all those other people who had played such important roles in my life and headed for upstate New York on the Seaboard and New York Central railroads to chart a new course. When I stepped off the train two days later, Mary C. was on the platform to meet me. The date: September 15, my twenty-third birthday. For the next two years each of us traveled the road from Saranac Lake to Rochester and back many times. These visits drew us closer together even as we grew somewhat further apart.

My job at the Blue Gentian ended before Saranac Lake's long winter did. The owners decided to close late in the season due to a lack of business. Thereafter I had a succession of jobs: assistant auctioneer, furniture store employee, proctor at the exclusive Lake Placid School for Boys, liquor store salesman, day laborer, digging ditches in earth frozen solid in several inches of frost. Between jobs I joined the "Fifty-Two, Twenty Club," a government program that paid veterans $20 a week up to fifty-two weeks while unemployed. But usually I found work.

In November 1946 Mother called to say that Daddy had taken a turn for the worse. The doctors suggested that members of the family gather around. I took the first train home. Mary Cov and Bill, married in October, had already returned from an abbreviated honeymoon. Lil was one floor above Daddy in the Ellen Fitzgerald Hospital sick with flu. Uncle Vann, Aunt Mary and Aunt Isabel joined us in a round-the-clock vigil. Mother, Mary C. and Bill, and I were softly speaking with Daddy when he suddenly turned to the left and asked, "Why, Bird, what are you doing here?" and breathed his last. "Bird" was Daddy's affectionate diminutive for his oldest and favorite sister, Aunt Bertha Hamilton, who had died eight years earlier of a stroke at age fifty-eight.

I stayed in Monroe just long enough for the funeral and then headed back to Saranac Lake, my heart heavy, not so much from Daddy's death as from a feeling of regret that he and I had never really managed to bridge the gulf that so often separated us. I suspected that I had been a disappointment to him, as he had been so often to me. In some ways, his death came as a relief. Daddy was sixty-two when he died. He had been in declining health for two years. Age is a relative thing. In the eyes of a twenty-three year-old man, sixty-two is old. My attitude: well, he had lived to a ripe old age, a long if not an especially happy life. In 1946 people did not live as long as they do in 2003, so perhaps I was not so callous as I sounded.

Aboard the Seaboard passenger car in Hamlet, white and black passengers were segregated until the train reached Washington, and no alcohol was served. But once past Virginia, things changed. Then I went to the lounge for a beer. A young white woman came in shortly thereafter and took the chair next to mine. She had finely-chiseled features, a face so fragile I felt she might break at the touch. She looked as if she had been sculptured from porcelain—delicate and vulnerable. Her eyes were gray, hair pale, almost like a halo. I offered to buy her a beer. She accepted. I had a second. So did she. After a third, she began to tell me about herself. A native of Atlanta, she was on her way to New York to visit a college roommate.

Why did she seem so unhappy? She soon told me. Married less than a year, her husband, back from the war, had recently walked out. No reason given, he just didn't love her anymore. She could not understand it. She could not accept it. What was the matter with him? With her? She blamed herself. Could anybody ever love her? We talked a long time—words uselessly spent. She was afraid. She was lonely. Would I come back to her Pullman compartment for a little while? Sure, why not?

Once inside, she quickly changed into a gown and negligee and asked me to lie down beside her. She wanted me to put my arms around her, hold her close until she fell asleep. She needed to know someone could still care for her. I lay close beside her, clothes still on and securely buttoned, aroused but in control, careful to behave as a caring, responsible human being should. As soon as I heard her breathing evenly, deeply and felt her body relax, I slipped my shoes back on and quietly closed the door behind me. I never saw her again. We were ships that had passed in the night, leaving in our wake a deeper awareness of the mystery that lies beneath so much of human behavior.

Saranac Lake had its first snowstorm September 30. Jane Tomlinson, a girl up from the Main Line, Philadelphia, and I were on our first date. We were drinking beer at the Dew Drop Inn overlooking the Saranac River when I saw the first flake fall. Had I died and gone to heaven? Soon I would buy skis and pursue a fifteen-year-old dream . . . to become a ski bum.

Jane was the girl I dated that autumn. Father, vice-president of Temple University, mother and daughter had all contracted tuberculosis down in Philadelphia, all had recovered, now "sputum free," but had remained in Saranac Lake to make sure the cure was to last. The fatalism that tuberculosis promoted among residents led to a quick ripening in relationships. Nice girls did not question whether it was proper to kiss on first date, and their parents did not care. Jane and I were left alone a lot in her little stone cottage off Old Military Estates.

We became good friends, enjoying swapping stories and telling lies. Jane was no beauty. She couldn't begin to compare with Ann, the librarian, whose eye I had caught but whose reserve I couldn't break. My first encounters with Ann were usually good-natured arguments over library fines. I sometimes returned books late. Ann expected me to pay the few pennies owed. I declined to do so. We argued and bantered about it, but she ended up paying the fines for me. Aha! An indication Ann had blinked first. I did not see Jane upon my return to Saranac Lake after going to Monroe for a few days at Christmas. She had left town for several weeks to visit a friend at a dude ranch in El Paso, Texas. By the time she returned, I only had eyes for Ann.

David Alcorn and Frank Shubeck came up to visit me in late December and early January. Both were soon to be married. Frank asked me to be his best man when he married Gennie in Detroit in February. Frank arrived with little notice. I gave him my date for the evening—a hot-to-trot girl of eighteen from Columbus, Ohio, recently cured of tuberculosis and now full of energy and zest for life. She was cute and funny, loved to dance, exhausting and inexhaustible. She and Frank would be a good match.

That freed me to do what I had wanted to do since the previous summer. I asked Ann, the librarian, for a date. To my surprise, she looked up, smiled and said sure. Later she told me she regretted acting on impulse and would have called to cancel but didn't even know where I lived, much less my telephone number.

That first date was a memorable one. Frank, one of nine children, was more than a match for his date. When she decided to go home early, Frank accompanied Ann and me to Ann's apartment, where he commenced to wrestle and generally roughhouse with her. After an especially hard tackle, Ann had had enough and gave him a sharp, stinging kick in the shins. Having two older brothers and eight male first cousins, she knew how to take care of herself. Frank fell to the floor in feigned agony, asking pleadingly, "What did you do that for?"

"Serves you right, Frank," was my reply, and pulling Ann down on my lap, I proclaimed Ann was sure to become my "Woman of the Year," like a cover on *Time*. Thereafter I spent all the time Ann would consent to with her. We skied on moonlit nights on nearby slopes, with only rope tows to reach the top. She was always better than I. I developed speed and displayed panache but little finesse or control. Even after I had lessons and practice, Ann remained a better skier. She also beat me in golf, tennis and ping-pong. It's a wonder we ever got married.

I fell "in love" three times in rapid succession in Saranac Lake, each time in different ways and at different levels. The first time was with a German boxer dog, "Cuno of Bavaria," that my roommate, Bob Allen, had brought home from Germany a few months earlier. For the next two years Cuno played a big part in the lives of Bob, Ann and me.

Bob had come to Saranac Lake in September to attend the newly established college of Paul Smith nearby. A native of Baldwinsville, New York, he had spent a weekend in late September across the hall from me at my rooming house operated by Mrs. Van Brackle at Two Church Street. He couldn't move in with me, however, as I already had a roommate, a former Marine from Georgia, up to take the cure but now well and soon to return home.

In early December Bob came back by the house, and finding Pete prepared to leave, asked if he could move in. Sure, it was okay with me. Bob never said anything about a dog. When I unlocked the door to my room upon my return from Monroe shortly after Christmas, I sensed a presence, then heard heavy breathing, next felt something pounce upon my chest. Soon the thing had its front paws hugging me around the neck, tongue washing my face, rear end wagging furiously. That really was love at first sight. It was an affair that has lasted a lifetime, including eight other boxers.

The feeling was contagious. Ann got it and she gave it to her Aunt Mildred Hanna's family in Concord, New Hampshire. Later we transferred it to sister Lil and the Buie family in Wagram. When Bob returned to the room shortly after Cuno's welcome, he wondered about the dog and asked if it were still all right to move in. I replied: only if Cuno comes as part of the package. Bob, Cuno and I became like the Three Musketeers, soon to be expanded to four as Ann joined the ranks.

My second love was with Bob himself. We quickly formed a close affiliation. Like Doll Jr. many years earlier, Bob became an alter ego . . . my doppelganger. Different in personality and temperament, we complemented each other and soon were close friends. Four months later Bob joined me in North Carolina for spring break. I met his train in Hamlet and we drove over to Wagram to spend the night with Lil, John and their two little girls, Kathy and Ann. The next day we drove over to Pine Bluff, twenty miles away, where we met Mother and Bill English.

Mary Cov had become upset after our father's death. In November the anxiety and frustration she had experienced the previous summer had deepened. She again felt guilty and depressed. In early December she left Rochester and husband for Monroe and mother, a move that did not please anyone, herself included. Mary C. wanted to live at Broadacre with Mother and clerk at the drug store. Out of the question, everyone agreed. Soon my sister descended into a much deeper, darker depression, accompanied by increasing mental and emotional confusion. She talked in circles around the clock and needed to go somewhere for professional help. Mother made the decision to enroll Mary C. at Pine Bluff Sanitarium after the New Year, another move that pleased no one, but what were the alternatives?

Over the ensuing months, Mary Cov seemed no better. Bill decided in April, in consultation with Mother, that it was time to intervene. He and the doctors agreed to administer a few shock treatments on an ambulatory basis. Soon the whole family ensemble was commuting between the Buie household in Wagram and the hospital. Bob and I had arrived just in time to participate. He took it all in stride, as if the situation were a perfectly normal one to experience during spring break. Maybe for the Secrest and Allen families in those days it was. Both were a little over the top. By week's end the whole entourage was en route to Monroe. Mary Cov felt much better, seeing light at the end of the tunnel. Before week's end, she and Bill returned to Rochester.

Bob and I spent several more days at Broadacre with Mother. A large number of high school friends back from war, many now married, gathered for a party at the farm home of cousins Wade and Betty Secrest. (Wade, a distant cousin but close friend, and I, along with most of my navy buddies, had quite by accident celebrated V-E day May 8, 1945, in Portland, Maine, together.) Booze flowed freely, stories and old memories shared. Friends Moke, Philip, Ed, Paul, Caston, and Bill, and cousins Vann and Hill were on hand to pledge anew eternal friendship.

As quickly as it began, as quickly it was forgotten. The next morning, hung over and disgruntled, Bob and I packed, kissed Mother good-bye and drove off in Daddy's Chevrolet, a gift the day before from Mother, as part of Daddy's estate. Daddy had left us all well off, even after the IRS had taken about four-fifths—the prevailing 1946 estate tax rate. I had no real money troubles while I was in Saranac Lake. In one sense, Daddy was now paying for my analysis. Well, why not? He and Mother were in large part responsible for my feeling the need for it, weren't they?

In 1947 there was no interstate highway system and few dual lanes on federal roads. We even had to take a ferry across Chesapeake Bay to reach Pennsylvania from Delaware. The 650 miles from Monroe to New York City took seventeen hours. The 310 miles from New York to Saranac Lake across narrow, curvy mountain roads took another eight. We were glad to get back to Saranac Lake in a spring snowstorm. Within a day or so, we were as good as new. No sign of emotional or physical exhaustion remained. Youthful energy when put to good use is a wonderful thing.

Ann Eastman Convel was the third object of my affection. She may have placed third chronologically but of course was "win, place and show" from our first encounter that evening with Frank Shubeck. Looking back, I now know my interest really started that day the preceding August when I first saw her in the Saranac Lake Free Library. As Johnny Mercer once wrote, "When first we met, I felt my life begin . . ." Ann did eventually open up her heart and let me rush in. I've always been glad that she did.

In June Bob and I got jobs at Saranac Inn, a popular summer resort twelve miles from town. Dozens of students, from colleges all over the country but mainly from the Northeast, also worked there through Labor Day. Ann frequently visited me for dinner and to swim and sail in Upper Saranac Lake. Again, she was more at home aboard a boat propelled by air-filled sails than I, but in this sport, I was a quick study.

I was assistant paymaster at the Inn, working under Mr. Curtin, a former TB refugee from New Jersey who lived with his wife and children next to Carl and Mercedes Herold on Riverside Drive. Most of the college kids served as maids, cooks, dishwashers, waiters and waitresses or worked on the grounds, in the golf shop or in the stables. Due to my white collar status, Bob and I got good rooms in the main hotel and three free gourmet meals a day.

It was party time every night. Students gathered after work at a nearby tavern to drink beer, sing, dance and generally engage in mating rituals that one can see repeated today at any college watering hole. Only the sounds and sights of the popular culture then and now are different. *Plus ça change, plus c'est la même chose.* Girls were in great abundance, and they chased Bob, Bill Leitheiser and Don Hinman, both former Duke classmates up for the summer, and me with ruthless abandon. Like son David a generation later, I was often and easily caught.

One girl from New Jersey was my nemesis. She would not leave me alone. Never having mastered the rudiments of English grammar, she didn't know the difference between the subjective and objective cases, let alone proper tense. She wouldn't have recognized an intransitive verb if one had landed in her ear. She said 'git' for 'get.' I tried to teach her the difference between 'who' and 'whom' to no avail. When I avoided her ardent advances, she took to her bed for hours. She refused to accept my evaluation of her conduct as neurotic and her headaches as efforts to win attention and sympathy. Whenever Ann came out to see me, my pursuer made catty and insinuating remarks. What a difference from Joan from Worcester, Mass., and Peggy from medical school in Cincinnati. Now they were worth the chase.

While I had a good time that summer of 1947, my heart had already been claimed by Ann and my mind by Dr. Herold. To paraphrase Cole Porter in Kiss Me, Kate," I remained "true to them both in my fashion, always true to them in my way."

In July Ann and I joined Mother, Aunt Eve and Aunt May in Nona Hanes Porter's New York apartment on Park Avenue for a long weekend. Nona's husband was a recognized sculptor who now had peer juried exhibits in some of New York's leading galleries. Aunt May, who had spent every weekend throughout the winter driving to Pine Bluff from Durham—seventy miles each way—to see Mary C., was herself again the cause for concern. She had just returned from a two-week stay in Rochester to see how her beloved niece was doing and was not reassured.

Mary C. had recently had a miscarriage and now, pregnant again, was on bed rest threatened with another. She was still too thin, restless, edgy, difficult. Seeing Aunt May, and remembering Durham and 1941, I was more concerned about her. Her eyes bothered her, as did her legs. She was unusually quiet and withdrawn and when she did speak, it was to obsess about my sister. It was "déjà vu all over again."

I called my sister and could detect nothing wrong. As usual the telephone conversation lasted forever with Mary Cov dominating the flow. I reported to Mother and her sisters that everything seemed SNAFU in Rochester—a World War Two acronym for "Situation Normal: All Fucked Up."

Ann, Mother and I met Captain Gould and Robin Chandler for lunch at the Tavern on the Green. I dismissed any further thoughts of dismay, opting instead to have a good time. In times of stress, I recommend that. As it turned out, Mary C. and Bill did have a difficult year of adjustment, aggravated by a series of miscarriages extending into 1948. I drove over to Rochester several times, once with Ann, once with Bob, always with Cuno or Liberty Belle, whom I had acquired to become Cuno's mate, and each time I opted to have a good time.

In return Mary Cov came over to Saranac Lake several times, once near Christmas time. Ann had been invited to a cocktail party given by a member of her library board. She had asked if I could come. Now she called back to see if my sister could as well. Ann and I have never agreed on how long one should stay at parties. She wants to come late, stay a few minutes and leave. I want to arrive on time and stay till the end. That Christmas Mary C. agreed with me. She was having a great time. So was everyone else. In hedonistic Saranac Lake, everyone always did. Ann nudged me when board members began to sit on each other's laps and whispered, "Time to go."

I didn't think so, but having been in similar situations before, I knew when to agree. Mary Cov did not. She saw no reason to leave. She opted to continue having a good time. Ann reminded me that one of her bosses on the library board had already extended her invitation by two to accommodate my sister and me. She did not feel comfortable over-staying our welcome or remaining as the party possibly careened further out of control, something board members might recall with embarrassment in the cold light of the morning after. "I'm leaving," she declared. "And you're coming with me. Your sister can find her own way home." Faced with the ultimatum, Mary Cov agreed to come with us. We adjourned to Downing's, a popular restaurant, and had a pleasant dinner, all three opting to have a good time.

In April, 1948, Ann, Libby, a Boxer I had recently bought as a mate for Cuno, and I drove to Rochester to see Theta Hansen, one of Ann's former classmates at the University of New Hampshire. Libby and I stayed with Mary Cov and Bill and teenage sons Billy and Keith. Leaving Libby locked in the guest bathroom, I headed after dinner into town alone to check out Rochester. It was already getting late and time for Mary C. and Bill to retire, as she was recuperating from still another miscarriage.

I met a guy at one of the taverns in town. He was waiting to meet a friend to take back home for the continuing celebration of the marriage of his sister. "Ever been to a Polish wedding?" my new best friend asked. Nope, I never had, but always interested in social history, as evidenced by different ethnic practices, I sure wanted to. "You got wheels?" Joe with-the-unpronounceable-last-name wondered. "Good. I'll take you to one—or what's left of it."

So I spent that night and most of the early morning hours at some stranger's house in a Polish neighborhood where guests drank, sang, toasted, danced and carried on presumably until the sun rose. Like Mary C. I liked to stay till the party is over, but I did leave before dawn. Once back in the English apartment, I remembered Libby. I had left that poor, pregnant dog shut up in the bathroom for hours. In her desperate need to go, she had dug out several tiles from the bathroom wall. What a careless, stupid, thoughtless thing to have done. I had behaved as badly to Libby as I had to Bruce ten years earlier.

Forty years later, whenever Mary Cov and I had an argument, she would remind me of that night in Rochester when I left my dog shut up for hours and she had dug out tile from the English guest bathroom. Clearly I had not yet finished "Climbing Fool's Hill."

The expression "Fool's Hill" originated with Mrs. Myrt Harrell, proprietor of the Pageland, S.C. Hotel. Daddy would stop at Myrt's for dinner on the way home from Myrtle Beach during the mid-1930s. One night Lil and I began to laugh at something Mrs. Harrell had said and couldn't stop. After awhile Daddy upbraided us for such uncontrolled misbehavior. "Oh that's all right, Dowd," Mrs. Harrell said indulgently. "They're just climbing 'Fool's Hill.'" Getting the "silly giggles" is something Lil and I, soon to be joined by Ann, were prone to, usually at inappropriate times and places, such as funerals and church services. Maybe I never will reach the top of Fool's Hill.

A few months later Mary Cov was pregnant again. This time there were no problems. Indeed, whenever hormonal changes occurred during her normal pregnancies, my sister thrived. She was like a different person. On June 6, 1949, Mary Ann arrived, "a perfect baby." This was a pattern that defined all three of my sister's successful pregnancies.

Libby had an equally easy time when she delivered a litter of five puppies in mid-May, 1948. Ann and I had acquired Liberty Belle of Mazelaine in March from a breeder on Long Island. We stayed with Ann's Aunt Ruth and Uncle Wes Andrews and their sons Wes Jr. and David. Libby was a litter mate of Warlord of Mazelaine, winner of best in show at New York's Westminster dog show earlier that year. I spent $300 for her, which was a lot of money then. My original plan was to breed Libby to Cuno, keep the male pick of the litter, then sell the mother and her other puppies to the highest bidders. But love has a way of changing one's best laid plans, and Ann had fallen in love with Libby. She had rescued Libby shortly after I had bought her.

Without consulting my landlady, I had brought Libby into my upstairs bedroom, where I left her during the day without supervision. She quickly took to the best chair, opting to leave it only at night to crawl into bed with me. Soon Libby was doing to my bedroom what she was yet to do to Mary Cov's bathroom. In my absence during the day, she barked constantly, relieved herself on the carpet and clawed the furniture. Within two days I received an ultimatum: get rid of the dog or find other accommodations.

Now living next door to Ann at 10 Helen Street, having moved from Saranac Inn at the end of the season in September 1947, I walked over as soon as she got home from work. What was I going to do? "Oh, I'll take her!" Ann exclaimed. "She'll be no trouble. I'll walk her at lunch and you can when you get off work. It will be okay."

Ann did not tell Mrs. McKee, her landlord, of her decision. She assumed the arrangement would meet with her approval. Mrs. McKee did not live far away, just across Church Street and down a block. There is no way she wouldn't find out. But even if she did, people in Saranac Lake adopted an indulgent view of just about anything, so why would Mrs. McKee care about a dog, especially a well-behaved one like Libby?

And so it worked out that way. Ann and I had been seeing each other every day and night since September after my summer at Saranac Inn had ended. We made trips on weekends and holidays to Rochester, to Montreal, to Ithaca for Cornell football games, to Concord to see her favorite aunt and her family, Mildred and John Hanna, over to Fort Ticonderoga and down to Glen Falls.

Ann had ordered a car. Automobiles were still difficult to come by as the domestic economy shifted from wartime to peacetime consumption. When the car finally came in January, 1948, a neat little gray two-door coupe, she only needed $300 to close the nine hundred dollar deal. I lent her the money as a short bridge loan till her next paycheck. When Ann's mother, Louise Eastman, heard about that all the way from Cleveland, Ohio, she was loud in her disapproval.

"Ann, what are you thinking? You know he'll have to be repaid, and in what way, do you think? I doubt he'll accept any coin of the realm. He will expect to be repaid in other ways," Louise warned darkly. Ann was in danger of becoming a fallen woman. Tess of the D'Urbervilles had faced no crueler fate. "Oh, I'm so grateful I was born a woman," Louise declared. "Those poor, weak, vulnerable men—just a prey to their passions!"

Louise need not have worried. Ann was now twenty-eight years old. She had been married briefly five years before to a young bombardier who had been killed shortly thereafter in an air raid over Germany. She knew her own mind. If she had wished to preserve her virtue, she could hardly have been bought for three hundred dollars.

Ann had not learned to drive before her car arrived. I taught her, and she was a quick study, learning in rough winter weather in the mountainous terrain of Saranac Lake. On our first trip out, she put the gear in reverse, stepped on the accelerator and promptly slammed into a fire hydrant.

Before that was repaired, friend Bob Allen came by to ask if he could borrow Ann's car. His old pre-war Hudson had broken down. "Sure," was Ann's good-natured reply. "Just don't run into any snowplows." A couple of hours later Bob returned, embarrassed, ashamed, hesitant to confess that a snowplow had indeed run into him. Ann's new car had not been totaled, but it had sustained two hits before she had even obtained her driver's license. But there was a good body shop in Saranac Lake and soon her car looked as good as new.

There is a technique to driving in snow. In 1948 snow tires were still unavailable. We occasionally had to put on chains, a nuisance at best, so we usually just drove around on regular tires. The only wreck I ever had was on the way home from Lake Placid after that evening out with Brack Craven in late winter of 1948. During the evening a cold front had moved in, rain on the roads had frozen, on top of which a few inches of snow had fallen. Accelerating to get up a long hill, my pre-war Chevrolet with its thin tire treads suddenly spun out of control and careened over an embankment and dropped a considerable distance, rolling over twice before coming to rest on its roof, all four wheels up in the air. Luckily we landed in deep snow. Ann and I quickly discovered neither of us was hurt, but Ann announced, seeing that her door wouldn't open, "We can't get out of here."

"I don't know about you," I replied gallantly, "but I sure can," and rolled down her window, crawled over her and climbed out. The only injury that night was the bruise Ann sustained when my ski boot hit her leg on my way out. I then helped her out, and we climbed up the steep embankment to hitchhike a ride home. A New York state patrolman soon stopped, took us to the nearest barracks but showed us little consideration as he peppered us with questions. Had I been drinking? No, I lied. Did I have a driver's license? Of course.

The only charge to come out of that was my failure to have a New York driver's license. We finally got home in the patrol car at three o'clock in the morning. Now my car was in the body shop. With cars at a premium, the dealer offered me $1,100 for the automobile, "as is, where is." I accepted the offer and now was dependent on Ann for transportation. I soon got a New York driver's license in nearby Malone, county seat of Franklin County.

Time passed quickly. In May Libby had her litter of puppies, delivered without a problem by Dr. Bouton, our dour veterinarian who much preferred animals to people. But he had been a huge help in breeding Libby and Cuno the previous March. They had had difficulty coupling. Libby was too frisky, Cuno overly eager. He tired easily and Libby just would not stand still. I think she wanted to be boss. She was experienced, Cuno was not. I didn't know dogs could have such problems. Our hounds at Broadacre never did.

Bouton was patient, and he showed Bob and me how to hold Libby while reassuring and calming Cuno. Two months later Libby whelped. Her puppies were all beautiful—championship stock for sure. As we watched this sweet picture of Libby nursing her puppies a few days later, I turned and asked, hardly realizing I was doing so, "Want to get married?" Without so much as looking up, Ann replied "Sure, why not?"

Earlier that year Aunts Eve and May had written to me that their dear friend Laura had a niece in Saranac Lake. Would I want to look her up? Aunt Laura had written a similar letter to Ann. But by then, a lot had already gone over the bridge. Shortly after my romantic proposal and Ann's passionate response, the phone rang. It was Mrs. McKee. "I understand you have a dog with puppies there," she declared. Ann confirmed her suspicion. "Well, you can't have them."

Ann, whose red hair suggested a quick temper, replied, "I'll be glad to move. You have my notice." Places were hard to find. Where would Ann—and, more importantly, Libby and her brood—live? We later said that we had to get married because our dog was pregnant.

A day later we rode out into the countryside. Ann wondered if we shouldn't talk, make plans, think about the future. Did I want children? Sure, if that should happen. What if we couldn't have any? "Ann, I'm not marrying you for children," I replied. How many? Who knows? Que sera, sera.

As things turned out, we had five pregnancies, four children, none planned, all wanted. Bob Allen was best man at our wedding May 31, 1948. Ann's Aunt Mildred was matron of honor. The Presbyterian minister, Mr. Hurley, conducted the service at the chapel in Trudeau Sanitarium. He gave us a good start by turning to the wrong page and beginning to read the funeral service. Louise and Mildred fulminated, Ann and I laughed.

I liked Ann's parents from the first time I met them a couple of days before the wedding. They didn't interfere. Harold was a gentleman, Louise a far cry from the earlier Victorian voice who had warned about taking loans from men who hadn't made commitments. She proved to be flexible and able to move with changing times. We got along well, even if she and Harold remained ideological, if not pathological, Roosevelt haters. Two weeks later Ann and I drove over to Concord, New Hampshire, for the wedding of Jack Hanna to Evelyn Manchester. The "greatest generation" was getting ready to give rise to the Boomer Generation. Everybody it seemed was getting married and quickly establishing families. It became the thing to do.

Soon a young disabled soldier from Kansas claimed a classmate of Jack Hanna's as his bride. Bob Dole spent the nights with the Hannas during his stay in Concord. But after the wedding he never wrote Mildred and John a thank-you note. "No manners," Aunt Mildred complained years later. "And what a thing to do! Just up and leave your wife one day without explanation." By 1996, however, Jack and Dole's first wife both voted for Dole in his race against Bill Clinton. I don't know what Mildred and John would have done. I voted for Clinton, a vote I came to regret.

Ann worked the rest of the summer at the library, giving notice that she would leave September 1. I worked at Tousley's Liquor Store and Fur Storage Company, to Mother's reserved disapproval when she came up to see us for a couple of days en route to a trip to Quebec. We agreed then that Ann and I would move to Monroe. I would work for the various family enterprises to decide what I wanted to do with the rest of my life.

I notified Dr. Herold of my decision. Two years of self-absorption was enough. I had stuck to my study and had derived what seemed to me to be the equivalent of several years of course work toward a doctorate in history, even if I were to gain no academic credit for it. And I believed I had benefited from revelations of self-knowledge and had a beneficial growth experience. Now it was time once again to move on. He agreed. Bob Allen, having completed his two-year education at Paul Smith's, was accepted at Duke University—at my urging and with family recommendations—and moved south with us.

Ann and I took a circuitous route home, driving west to see Bill and Mary C., now living in relative peace and harmony in Rochester near to our belated honeymoon destination, Niagara Falls, and then on to Cleveland to spend a week with Ann's parents. Ann tired easily and cried intermittently. Her mother took her to see a doctor. His diagnosis: Ann was a little anemic—and a whole lot pregnant.

I became overly solicitous, taking a week to drive through the Shenandoah Valley, squeezed in among Ann, Libby, and Libby's son Onuc, now four months old. We arrived in Monroe on my twenty-fifth birthday—exactly two years after I had moved to Saranac Lake. Mother, Aunt Mary Hinson, Aunt Isabel Wolfe and Norma Smith were playing bridge when we pulled into the driveway, emptied out the car and opened the front door to Broadacre. Libby and Onuc rushed up, and ran under, around and about the bridge table to greet Mother and guests, a greeting that was to replicate itself to many different people over the next fifty-five years through a procession of eight boxers.

*Broadacre 1940.*

*Lil Secrest before her marriage to John Buie, 1942.*

333

*Anne McClenaghan, Duke heart throb, 1942.*

*Tave McRae, girlfriend 1943-46.*

*Uncle Hill and Aunt Isabel Wolfe at home, Monroe 1943.*

# Part III

# Family Life

# 1949-2004

# 38. Death in the Afternoon

There had been almost no housing construction during the war. Places to live in Monroe were nearly impossible to find, but this was a national problem. Leavittown, Pennsylvania and New Jersey, had yet to be completed. Ann and I moved into the little apartment in the back of Broadacre, consisting of the old sun parlor, where several years earlier Betty Boop and Wimpy had eaten Daddy's dinner; the old kitchen, unchanged since Doll Jr. had discovered the roach in the fudge, still lit by the bare bulb overhead, hot water still supplied by the tin boiler, rumbling ominously and turning bright red whenever heated by the attached wood stove.

There was of course no central heat. Just a space heater in the big, bare back bedroom, formerly used by the live-in help. Welcome to a new life, Ann, Southern style. So this was the fine old estate Ann had heard about. Well, at least it had in-door plumbing, even if it were nearly sixty years old.

We looked for places to rent. Few existed. Those that did would not accept a couple with two boxer dogs. Even if they had, they were little improvement over where we already were. Mother remembered that the old Carpenter house on Tallyrand Avenue had been damaged by fire shortly before it was to go on the market. Perhaps she could buy it at a bargain basement price and have it repaired. Nick Didow from Connecticut, a young officer at Camp Sutton during the war, had married Jean Presson, Lil's close high school friend. Jean had brought Nick back to Monroe to live. He had started a construction business. Maybe he would give Miss Lessie's request top priority.

Nick agreed. He was a skilled builder and fast worker. Soon the old Carpenter place looked as good as new, now divided into apartments, one to be occupied by Ann and me, the other rented to Leo Bragg, Monroe's new sanitation officer, and his wife Catherine, and their two young daughters, Barbara and Julia.

Nick's son, Nick, Jr., a generation later became a professor of economics at UNC-Chapel Hill. He served as chairman of the Chapel Hill Board of Education for several years and remains a member of the Board today as it faces the controversial question of merger with the Orange County School Board.

Shortly after Thanksgiving, Ann and I, Libby and Onuc moved. We settled down to sweet contentment. Domestic life suited us. Ann had an easy pregnancy. She liked my family and they liked her. Ann adjusted quickly to small-town southern life. On Sunday we attended Central Methodist Church. Monday was Jaycee day for me. Friday, the Rotary Club. Ann joined various women's clubs to please Mother. Saturday nights were spent at the country club. Lil and Ann became good friends as well as sisters-in-law. Within two years they had bought a beach house together at Garden City, S.C., a self-indulgent, impulsive, irresponsible move that proved to be a bonanza for everybody. The ocean-front cottage, consisting of three bedrooms, two baths, living room, kitchen with a large separate dining room, and a screened front porch overlooking the sea, cost—fully furnished—$10,000. There was even a full roughed-in basement waiting to be completed.

I was less satisfied at work. I clerked at the drug store, and after hours and on weekends tried to manage the farms. I felt and was inadequate. Uncle Vann was patient and helpful. But he was really the manager and was grooming Vann Jr., now in his last year in pharmacy school at the University of North Carolina, Chapel Hill, to run things the next year. He would be qualified to do so. That was important to the family-held enterprise. Registered pharmacists were as hard to come by as new houses. I was really marking time, uncertain as to what to do or how to do it. I had led a structured yet carefree existence for eight years: three in college, three in the Navy, two in Saranac Lake. Now I had a wife, and a baby on the way. It was a time for decision.

I recall few events of interest during those months in Monroe. Harry Truman's upset victory over Thomas E. Dewey in November ranks first. Mother and I sat up all night listening to the election returns on the radio. The final result was not known until several Midwestern states finally tumbled into the Democratic column the next morning. Truman, the underdog, had defeated not only the Republican candidate but also Strom Thurmond, the Dixiecrat candidate from the right and Henry Wallace, the Progressive Party candidate from the left. The Secrest Yellow Dawg Democrats were ecstatic.

The second memorable event was less cosmic. The Tar Heels had a good football team. Their quarterback Charlie "Choo-Choo" Justice was a sensation, as much of a star on the football field then as Michael Jordan was on the basketball court forty years later. I let the customers wait that Saturday afternoon as I stayed close to the store radio. Carolina defeated the heavily favored Texas Longhorns 34-7 to launch the Charlie Justice era.

A third memory of married life in Monroe had to do with Christmas. Friends Bill, Moke and Philip came by our house on Christmas Eve to help decorate the big cedar tree that Ann and I had gone out to the farm to cut down ourselves. I even managed to build a stand to support it. Ann, on the wagon, did not drink the wassail she had prepared. But my friends and I did.

We drank, smoked (everybody did in those days), swapped stories of the past and shared plans for the future until well past midnight. Philip was in graduate school at Johns Hopkins University. Moke, who had switched schools six times between 1940-1947, finally had settled down. Now back at UNC, he was prepared to enter medical school the next year. Bill was already in his second year of dental school at Temple University in Philadelphia. Already our paths were diverging: only I, with all my earlier schemes to get to "Know Thyself," seemed restless and unsure.

In October Ann and I had gone to New York City where I attended Navy reserve training for two weeks, grasping at any straw to avoid working at the drug store. In November I had gone to Duke University to look into Duke's program in clinical psychology. I had stayed with Bob Allen and Cuno and linked up with John McMillan, brother of Lil's Riverton friend Archie.

But nothing really appealed to me. Looking back, I think I was still in recovery from all that intellectual immersion and self-examination in Saranac Lake. There is a condition some people develop from analysis that I now term "psychoanalosis." Like a lot of things that end in "osis" (such as halitosis, silicosis, tuberculosis and cirrhosis) it can be very disagreeable. Mary C. developed it, too. It takes about two years to get over. Some people never do.

Ann was eight months along when she broke water and went to the Ellen Fitzgerald Hospital for an unexpected early delivery on January 31, 1949. Dr. Smith delivered the four-pound, eleven-ounce baby boy. Everything appeared to be all right. We named him Andrew McDowd Secrest, III. He had a lot of red hair, the color of Ann's brother Harold's.

A few hours after his birth, the baby began to have trouble breathing. He turned from ruddy red to pale white. He was returned to the hospital nursery. Soon Dr. Smith came by to explain that the infant appeared to have developed Halbran's membrane disease, a sticking together of the air sacs in the lungs. It was associated with prematurity. Andrew McDowd was not much below weight. The extent of the disorder was not yet known, but he had not sufficiently dried out.

In 1948 there were no incubators or respirators in Monroe or Charlotte, probably not anywhere. I held our baby and watched him change from a deadly quiet, ghostly white wraith into a loudly yelling, red-faced infant as I gently thumped the bottoms of his feet with my forefingers. This unpredictable condition continued on and off the rest of that day and night. The next morning Dr. Smith suggested Andrew McDowd and I go by ambulance to Charlotte's new Memorial Hospital to see a specialist. Uncle Vann followed in his car. By the time we got to Charlotte, the baby was no longer responding to my finger tapping. His eyes remained open, but his breathing became more irregular, his color again translucent.

The woman doctor took him in at once. Soon she appeared to say she was sorry, but there was really nothing anyone could have done. Sometimes these things happen. When the same thing happened fourteen years later to President Kennedy and Jackie's baby Patrick, the first baby to have been born in the White House since Grover Cleveland's day, it made international headlines.

But had Andrew McDowd or Patrick been born thirty years later, treatment and survival would have been routine. As Hegel observed, the human race does go forward. We do progress. Things get better. Only it is a slow process, two steps forward, one step back, as we move ahead.

Mother had left Monroe for a trip to Mexico before the baby was born, so it was left to Aunt Isabel Wolfe and Aunt Mary Hinson to offer Ann and me the tender loving care Mother would have otherwise supplied. Just before she was expected home, I sent her a telegram at the residence of Betsy and Don Bernard in New Orleans where she was to stop.

Ann's mother Louise came from Ohio to give her daughter support. Lessie followed close behind. She and Louise hit it off well. Ann was soon up and around, quick to dismiss the whole episode as much as she could. She was better at that than I. By April I had given up on the family business.

Ann and I took a short trip to Hollywood, Florida. Thereafter I applied to law schools at Columbia, Yale and Harvard, to the Wharton School of Business in Philadelphia, and to the graduate school at the University of North Carolina, was accepted by them all and now had to decide.

I chose UNC, the easiest way out. My emotions were raw and on edge. I had no appetite and slept poorly. I lost weight. I had mood swings—up one day, down the next. My physical balance was impaired. Sometimes when I drove the car, I felt as if I were riding backwards. Mother was concerned about me, as I was about myself. Was the Simmons Curse to strike for the seventh time?

I thought back: grandmother Molly Simmons Covington in 1917; Mother in 1927, again in 1935; Aunt May in 1941, again in 1948; Mary C. in 1946. And now me? Not if I could help it. Theoretical knowledge about one's self was one thing. Doing something practical about it was something entirely different. I kept my own counsel, but stayed in touch with myself. I compartmentalized my life, dealing with one item at a time, changing what I could, accepting what I couldn't, resolved to handle things in my own way without burdening others.

Ann was helpful but matter-of-fact. She was, like the biblical Ruth, willing to go when and where her husband chose but not prepared to become an enabling, controlling or co-dependent wife. I had sought outside help before. Now the solution lay within me.

Ever thinner, I, like Cassius, had a lean and hungry look. And I came to believe, like Cassius, that "men at some time (must become) masters of their own fates, (that) the fault... is not in the stars, but in ourselves..." I learned to bear the burden alone and gain strength from it. I learned to dissemble. Perhaps it was time to act as I wished to feel and thereby bring about a self-fulfilling prophecy. I had made the effort to know myself. Now it was time to forget myself, to lose an intense awareness of the self in concern for other people and out of an interest in other things.

Hard physical labor is another recommended recourse. I later got a job roofing a service station on West Franklin Street in Chapel Hill. Pounding nails with a heavy hammer and working with roofing in our unrelenting August sun crowds out negative thinking and absorbs a lot of nervous energy. I lost weight, built muscle, regained my appetite and came home too tired to worry much about anything.

By June we were in Chapel Hill with Libby, but with no place to live. Housing was as tight there as it had been in Monroe. Victory Village was full. We finally found a place off Airport Road. Marion Boggs, former wife of a Spanish professor, agreed to rent us a room, with kitchen privileges. The house survives more than a half-century later, serving today as the Rape Crisis Center on Estes Drive, a street then non-existent.

Around the corner and down Airport Road lived Charlie and Sarah Justice. They had a boxer and a baby boy. Across the road near what was to become Colonial Heights lived John Swainson, a law student, and his wife Alice, who owned a bulldog. They were also expecting a baby. I could not have known, or John have expected, that he, a double amputee from World War II, would within ten years have become governor of the state of Michigan, successor to Governor "Soapy" Williams.

Ann had earlier thought that she might be pregnant again. Just before we left Monroe she had gone to see Dr. Smith. He dismissed the idea. "It is much too soon," he declared. "The wish, my dear, is father to the thought." So we had blithely gone to the beach with Lil and John and friends Mary and Dusty Odom, rode the ocean breakers and then the bumper cars, the Tiltawhirl, and rollercoaster with the Buie and Odom youngsters near the pavilion without further thought.

But Dr. Smith was wrong. Back from the beach in early July, Ann went to see doctors Easely, Podger and Pearse in Durham. Dr. Easely found her to be three months along. Podger and Pearse agreed. Libby had come into heat soon after we learned of Ann's great expectation. We decided she too should have another chance. We had earlier given her son Onuc to Ann's brother Phil in Windsor, Connecticut. A retired Army colonel had a boxer kennel in Hope Valley, Durham. His stud Duke of Durham had a pedigree that Libby could accept. By early October Ann, Libby, and Alice Swainson were all expectant mothers.

On October 9 Libby, now a week overdue, was panting and restless. I called Dr. Louis Vine, the only local vet with offices way out on East Franklin Street, a narrow two-lane road that seemed to be half-way to Durham. Mrs. Vine was herself pregnant and late, too. Lou Vine had a great idea. "Let's take my jeep, Mac: load up my wife, you and Libby and ride over some bumpy country roads. That might shake something loose. I'd rather not give any medication to Libby or resort to a Caesarean if we can induce labor the natural way."

The experiment worked on Mrs. Vine, who gave birth to a baby boy later that night, but not with Libby, now really sick—restless, panting, in pain, refusing food and water. So a Caesarean was performed. Five beautiful puppies were soon happily nursing, and Libby was content, despite being all stitched up, now resting comfortably in her box beside our bed.

Throughout the early hours of December 11, I walked the halls and climbed the walls of Duke's delivery room as Ann delivered David over a period of several hours. Again, the baby was coming a month early. Surely the same thing wasn't to happen. But despite his early arrival, there was nothing premature about this baby. He weighed nearly seven pounds; he bawled loudly whenever he was removed from his mother's breast, nursing hungrily. A replica of Andrew McDowd III, David Kilton Secrest also had a full head of red hair, only his was Titian like his mother's.

What a beautiful boy. So he was, so he became, so he remained, at least in the eyes of his parents. It seemed ironic to me, however, that whereas twenty-six years earlier, it had been Andrew Jr. who had survived and David who had died, this time it was reversed. Of our "Irish twins" in 1949, Andrew died and David lived.

Again nature had balanced the scales. Ann and Alice Swainson occupied beds next to each other in Duke's lying-in nursery. In 1949 women stayed in the hospital several days after giving birth, no drive-through delivery in those days. I was at home looking after Libby and her five. Moke, now in medical school, and Bill Leitheiser, known as "Shoulders" by the girls at Saranac Inn two years earlier and who was now up from Florida to visit his father, a patient at Duke, were frequent visitors to see Ann and David. They also came over to admire Libby's puppies, two males and three females, now two months old—playful and adorable—who provided David stiff competition.

Soon Mother and Lil were up to see the newest members of the family. Louise came down from Cleveland to lend a hand. Friends Philip and Bill did not lag far behind. There was plenty of company in Marion Boggs' house that Christmas and New Year's. Marion was interested in the baby, but she was becoming uneasy about the Secrest take-over of her house. She had rented a room the previous summer to a young couple with a dog. Now she had a wailing baby and five noisy puppies in her guest bedroom, not to mention this invasion of visitors every day, often late into the night. She became increasingly cranky.

One day she appeared with a loaded shotgun and threatened to shoot some dog that had appeared at the front door. She grew verbally abusive of her former husband who had dumped her several years earlier for some woman from the Dominican Republic to whom Marion now referred to as "that nigger." She found fault with our housekeeping. She felt that Ann was reflecting upon her intellectual tastes when Ann expressed a preference for the Sunday *New York Herald Tribune* to Marion's *Durham Morning Herald*. Ann and Libby, new mothers, did not need this kind of nervous tension. I became increasingly uneasy.

In mid-January, 1950, I went over to Durham to see Mr. Alex Muirhead, developer of the Glen Lenox apartments. Only a few units had been completed. Few roads were yet paved. The place was a sea of mud. There were hundreds of applicants, eagerly awaiting entrance. I laid out my case before Mr. Muirhead. I was at my most persuasive, embellishing and exaggerating as necessary. I took the prettiest puppy with me, along with a long list of personal references. I told him about the shotgun incident... our disappointment a year earlier... our "Irish twins."

Before I finished, the move had become a matter of life and death. Mr. Muirhead agreed to let us occupy the next apartment to become available if we did not object to living in one where some additional work must be completed and the yard was still a sea of mud. No objection at all. We moved in on February 1, the second family to live in Glen Lenox. The first? Our Hamilton Street neighbors, Charlie "Choo-choo" Justice, wife Sarah and son, and their boxer. We lived there six months. The Justices were modest, unpretentious people, despite Charlie's fame as an athlete. We became casual friends. It was with a sense of sadness and nostalgia that I read of his death in late 2003, and of Sarah's in February, 2004.

Soon another student family moved in next door, Marie and Tom Sawyer and their young son. Marie, like every other woman we knew, was expecting another child. Tom, a native of Swan Quarter, later became manager of urban redevelopment in Charlotte. Wife Marie was a native of Norfolk, Virginia. For years we remained friends, just as we had with Alice and John Swainson, but at some point, they disappeared from our radar screen. That happens as people grow older, especially if they are widely separated by time and space. At least that is a partial explanation, but I never fully understand why.

In early 2004 I found Tom in Virginia Beach and called him. He and his two sons were fine, as well as a grandson, now a pre-med major at UNC. But Marie had suffered a stroke three years earlier, leaving her paralyzed and cognitively impaired. Tom is her caregiver. Love and heroism take many forms and can be found in many places.

Bob Allen's father died the year Bob entered Duke in September, 1948. A year later Bob's mother moved to Durham and rented Hollow Rock Farm, a beautiful, historic old house that came fully furnished, even with a live-in cook. An heir to the Chicago Tribune had owned it but due to some personal misfortune, he had agreed to rent it at a nominal sum to someone who would keep it up. We attended many memorable parties at the Allens' temporary home in 1949-50. This house still presides in solitary dignity over that area in Orange County, just across from the Hollow Rock Tennis Club.

Carolina was still on the academic quarter system. I stuck with the graduate history program through the summer and early fall, but grew increasingly restive. Journalism appealed to me more. I needed to work and support the family. Spending another four to seven years in academic study, followed by years of travel on the road to tenure, from teaching assistant, to assistant professor, to associate professor, maybe to full professor with tenure, depending upon one's record in research and publication, appeared increasingly burdensome. There is a close correlation between history and journalism and an immediacy and activism to the latter that now appealed to my restless nature. So far, I had not heard anything in my history courses that I didn't already know.

So I switched to journalism. I'd become interested in the *Chapel Hill Weekly*. I came to know Louis Graves, its publisher. Community journalism appealed to me. That is what I wanted to become... editor/publisher of my own newspaper in a nice little town where I could become a big fish in a little pond. My other role model, who had already earned a national reputation as a small-town journalist, was Hodding Carter, Jr., of Greenville, Miss.

I was in one of the last classes of students to benefit from the wisdom of Oscar Coffin, Phillips Russell, and Tom Lassiter, lecturer-on-leave from his newspaper, the *Smithfield Herald*. I quickly became a friend as well as student of Walter Spearman and Stuart Sechriest. I found my fellow students in journalism somehow more stimulating than those in history. My career goal remained consistent and clear. I left Chapel Hill in August 1950, to begin my apprenticeship in journalism; first a year at the *Laurinburg Exchange*, then a year at the *Charlotte News*, and finally a third job at the *Westwood News*, in Westwood, New Jersey.

# 39. The Snake Pit

Just before we moved to Laurinburg, Ann and Lil bought an ocean front cottage in Garden City Beach, South Carolina, ten miles south of Myrtle Beach. Neither Ann nor I cared for the heat and gnats of Scotland County or the dinky little frame house on Williams Street, the only place in Laurinburg we could find to live. We liked the people, however, and the location, only 75 miles from Monroe and 100 miles from the beach cottage, named the Seabuoy. And we loved the icy cold water of the Lumbee at Riverton, less than a mile from Lil and John's home in Wagram. And who wouldn't love the yet largely undeveloped beaches along South Carolina's Golden Strand? In 1950 no one even imagined what a hurricane named Hazel could do just four years later.

Bill Price asked me to be his best man when he and Nancy Cutchin from Whittakers, a village near Rocky Mount, were to be married in October. Soon Bob Allen asked me to serve in the same capacity when he and Phyllis Moore, whom he had met shortly after arriving at Duke in the fall of 1948, decided to get married in Duke chapel in January, 1951.

In late November Ann found out she was expecting a third child. The baby boom had really hit home. Mary Cov and Bill had their first, Mary Anita, in June, 1949; Lil her third, John, Jr. in August. David arrived in December. In February, 1951, Mary C. had another girl, Susan Vanessa, followed quickly by Lil's third daughter Celeste in July and by our third son Andrew Phillips August 5. Two years later Mary C. had twins, Andy and Bella. In another year, Lil had Jim. Our fourth, Mary Ann, trailed along in December 1956, the last of Lessie's and Dowd's grandchildren. We dubbed her "Molly Finale."

Mother, who loved babies, welcomed all these grandchildren with generosity and enthusiasm. The christening of Mary Ann English at Broadacre in late August, 1949, was an affair to remember. Mary Cov was at her most loquacious and provocative. Kith and kin from all over turned up, including most of the women from Mother's Missionary Circle, as well as ardent members of her "I declare, Miss Lessie!" fan club. In all the hubbub, Mary Cov had lost her milk but that, she assured one and all, including the minister, Mr. Sprinkle, back on special invitation, did not matter. Satisfaction of the oral instinct, the natural bonding of mother with child, was what counted.

"See?" she asked, as she plopped out one breast and offered the nipple to her infant daughter, who willingly accepted it. "Now she's perfectly content. Nourishment for the body may come out of a Similac can, but the love that nourishes and develops the soul must come from the mother's body." Mary C. had become an expert on breast feeding and was prepared to share her knowledge with all who would listen. Further nuggets of Freudian wisdom spilled out. Everyone present seemed to find this S.O.P. (naval lingo for Standard Operating Procedure). The capacity of people from small Southern towns to accept with tolerance and understanding those of their own was demonstrated once more.

Optimism at home and abroad was the dominant theme when the war ended in late 1945. It didn't last long as the Cold War began in 1946 and managed to heat up to a Soviet blockade of Berlin in 1948 and a shooting war in Korea in the summer of 1950. In Europe, Asia, everywhere, hope contended with despair in the aftermath of a worldwide conflagration that had claimed 50 million lives, exposed unbelievable atrocities including the Holocaust and opened up the possibilities of a nuclear abyss. In China Mao Zedong's Communist party overwhelmed Chiang Kai-shek, driving him and his dynasty to Formosa, later to become Taiwan, in 1949.

This bipolar global situation was reflected in the personal lives of many of those who lived or used to live at Broadacre. It is generally true that when things go badly, if one waits awhile, there will be a change for the better. But one can also look at life the other way around. When it's nothing but blue skies all the day long, just wait awhile. Before long, often without warning, thunder rumbles, lightning strikes. And one gets stormy weather. Mother Nature is an unpredictable, ambivalent, often cruel mistress. So is Providence. So is Human Nature.

Lil's and John's son, soon known to all as Jon-Jon, proved to be a Down Syndrome baby, severely afflicted, never able to care for himself. Before disbelief and denial were overcome, Lil was expecting a fourth baby. John was also a problem. The youngest of four children, he had been spoiled and over-indulged. When Lil later told people she had five children, I thought to myself, "No, six. Husband John is the biggest and most difficult child she has."

John did not know himself and had no intention of becoming intimately acquainted. He was Mr. Denial personified. He had a pleasant disposition, loved Lil both as a husband and as a child, possessive, dependent, insecure. They had moved back to Wagram from Wilmington after the war. John had been a worker at the Naval shipyard in the port city. Away from sheltering arms, good at his work, making a good living, supporting his wife and daughter, John was happy and apparently self-confident.

Back in Wagram, it was a different picture. Basically shy, John appeared to be an extrovert. He projected a "hail fellow, well met" image. He had the personality of a salesman and was good in that line of work. There was nothing wrong in that. As Governor Luther Hodges, known by some as the "Businessmen's Governor," later remarked, "Nothing ever happens in the economy until somebody sells something."

John had an obsessive-compulsive personality. He got the idea that he could become wealthy in automatic coin machines, especially scales of all kinds. He wanted to be his own boss and a traveling man. The idea itself was not flawed, although Dowd warned one would never get rich collecting pennies, nickels and dimes, but the manner of execution was. John was not a good businessman. An eternal optimist, he never allowed a realistic audit to stand in the way of a great expectation.

Nor was experience a good teacher. He did not learn from his mistakes. John never let a legitimate self-doubt rise to the level of consciousness. I never saw any evidence of an introspective thought. Business was always great. The only problem was there never seemed to be any profit at the end of the year. He never had any money. When income flowed into the pipeline, expenses flowed out. John, figuring over his accounts, was elated at the amount of money he was making.

John liked to live well. He stayed at the best places, ate at the most expensive restaurants. When promises of checks to come from his boss Mr. Maddox were "in the mail" but somehow never materialized, they were entered as accounts received. When March 15 came around and federal and state income taxes were due, somehow John never had the money with which to pay them. John is the only person I've ever known who lied to the Internal Revenue Service in reverse. He reported large net profits which he had never made in order not to have to admit that he was not supporting himself, let alone his growing family.

His reaction to reality was to deny it, to take refuge in emotional withdrawal. Each March 15, later changed to April 15, John would wind up in bed, sleep deeply, refuse to shave, dress or talk. Dr. Edwin Womble, family physician, would come, put John on intravenous glucose, then send him to Presbyterian Hospital in Charlotte where John would stay for a couple of weeks until Lil paid his fantasy income taxes. That done, John quickly recovered. Lil found it cheaper to pay off the IRS than to continue to pay rising hospital bills. John was no con artist. It was no intentional scam. He was not dishonest except where it came to dealing with himself. Ever the optimist, next year would always be better. To prove it, he mortgaged his house three times.

There is irony in this story. John, self-employed, always paid the top in Social Security tax. When he took early retirement at sixty-two, he received top dollar in Social Security checks. He never had another depressed day. And he loved doing his own taxes, now accurate and honest. Coincident with his retirement was the settlement of the Buie family trust. Like many Southern families, the Buies, while comfortable enough, were "land poor." Over the years land grew in value, as did the heavy growth of timber. There were other assets. When these were distributed, John now had a large income and, as the stock market surged, a considerable estate. When he died in 1988, John, if not a millionaire, wasn't far from one.

But Lil could not foresee the silver lining in 1950. She felt trapped in her marriage, much as her mother must have felt in 1935. She grew to hate the scales, now accumulating in large numbers in the yard, over-crowding the garage. To accommodate the overflow, John built two more. She also grew to hate John's boss, Mr. Maddox from Chicago. When he visited Wagram, Lil, like her mother Lessie earlier, made it difficult for her husband and boss. If they wanted a beer, they could go out into the garage with the scales, heat and gnats and drink out there—as uncomfortably as possible.

Kathy was seven, Ann five, Jon-Jon only a year old, his disability ever more apparent. Now Lil had discovered she was expecting again, and the house was mortgaged... for the third time. Then the thunderbolt struck. Mother, recently home from Memorial Hospital in Charlotte for a minor operation, awoke the day before Thanksgiving to find herself locked in a deep depression. The great black hole that had sucked her up in 1935 and from which she had emerged three years later stronger, healthier, better than ever, had dragged her down again. The Simmons Curse had returned, this time without warning.

Mary C. and Bill were expected to stop by Broadacre for Thanksgiving Day dinner and spend the weekend before returning to Rochester from their trip to Hollywood, Florida. Mary C., with Mary Ann only 18 months old and now in her sixth month of another pregnancy, had her own hands full. "We were expecting Mother's usual happy welcome, only to find her depressed, anxious and nervous, demanding to be taken somewhere. Somehow she had broken suddenly like a cracked egg," Mary C. later told me.

Mother, recently turned fifty-eight, had become the mainstay of the family since her recovery in 1938. She had helped with Aunt May twice, coped with Mary Cov's problem in 1946-47, adapted well to living alone after Dowd's death, worked hard and successfully at his remaining enterprises, had agonized with me over Ann's and my loss of our first born, and provided strong moral and financial support for Lil over Jon-Jon.

By nature extroverted and altruistic, she lived in the present, optimistic and upbeat. Mother, who had hoped to prove to the whole extended family that depression could not only be overcome but also permanently conquered through psychological insight and understanding, was thought to have become invulnerable. Earlier times were dimly remembered or disregarded altogether.

Aunt Eve came down from Salem for Thanksgiving with the Buies. The following Saturday she came to see Ann and me. She obviously dreaded telling me the news, fearing what my reaction might be. She needn't have worried. I was of course surprised, even shocked, initially inclined angrily to deny it. But within fifteen minutes I had absorbed and accepted it. Now I was more concerned about what to do about it.

Mother had insisted Mary C. and Bill take her immediately to Pine Bluff, the place from which she, Bill, Lil, Bob Allen and I had extricated Mary Cov herself less than four years earlier. Given their situation and the need to return to Rochester, they had little alternative. Before long Ann, Lil, and I were at the hospital, taking turns. Mother, perhaps out of a sense of guilt for having placed her older daughter there, had insisted upon returning to the "scene of the crime" and demanded shock therapy. Since that was the treatment du jour in 1950, the doctors were only too happy to comply.

After the first four treatments, spaced two days apart, the phone rang. It was Mother, her voice alive, vibrant, confident. She was just fine, in fact, she felt great. The episode she had experienced had just been a little flashback to some frightening childhood experience that was of no consequence now that she had remembered it. "Yes, of course, come see me anytime," she said. "I'll be going home soon. I'll call back."

What a relief! Shock therapy when it worked was a miracle. It had achieved the same trick with Aunt May in 1943. But why had it not worked so well when she got sick again in 1948? The call back never came. Three days later I called the hospital. May I speak to Mrs. Secrest? No. Why not? She doesn't have phone privileges. When should I come see her? We don't know. She isn't allowed visitors at this time.

What on earth had happened? I jumped into the car, drove the twenty miles over to Pine Bluff, demanded to see my mother. Denied that, I asked to see the doctor. Denied that, I walked into his office and asked for an explanation. Mother had had an unexpected setback. The shock had interfered with her memory. She had become resistant, hostile, suspicious, fearful. She was in a locked ward. The shock treatments, far from being discontinued, were now being given daily.

This situation continued for a week. First I, then Lil, next Ann, often all three together, would go over to Pine Bluff daily. One afternoon while the three of us were there, Lil discovered she was bleeding. Now in the first two months of her pregnancy, she was threatened with a miscarriage. Ann drove her home, and Lil was promptly put on bed rest by Dr. Vita McLeod, her obstetrician from Southern Pines. Ann, about as far along in her own pregnancy, remained so far unthreatened.

Within the week, I met with Mother's doctor, asked to be taken to see Mother in the locked ward and was aghast at what I beheld. There was Lessie, strapped to a bare examining table, long white hair loose to her waist, a front tooth missing, looking wild-eyed and disoriented. But she recognized me immediately. What she said was illogical, inconsistent, incoherent but I got the drift. This place was a house of ill repute, run by a den of drug traffickers. No one here was as they represented themselves to be.

Further conversation with Mother was useless, but I had plenty to say to the doctors and aides. How many shock treatments had Mother been given? How far apart? With what result? How long do you plan to continue them? Has this confusion been going on uninterrupted since last week? When—and how—do you expect this situation to clear up? What caused the loss of her front teeth? Her bruises? The injury to her arm and hip? Do you see any cause and effect between Mother's present psychosis and shock therapy? How often does this happen and what is the prognosis?

It soon became apparent that the doctors and nurses did not have a clue. They had no plan except to give more of the same. "Have my mother dressed, her things packed, and ready for discharge in thirty minutes. I'll wait in the lobby," I ordered. When the head psychiatrist protested, I cited habeas corpus, patients' rights, threatened legal action, agreed to sign discharge papers assuming all responsibility for subsequent consequences. We were out of there well within my deadline and on our way back to our little frame house on Williams Street in Laurinburg.

Mother stayed with us for a month, her fear, dependency and confusion gradually subsiding, her memory and lucidity returning. As the mania disappeared, the deep depression resurfaced. It was clear to me Mother was depressed, but she was not suffering from manic depression. The mania had been induced by adverse reaction to the shock treatments, a condition not uncommon. The proper medical protocol is simply to stop the treatments. Even I, at twenty- seven and a layman, although with many years of on-the-job training, understood that.

During that December, 1950, Ann, now three months pregnant, and I slept on the fold-out couch in the living room, giving Mother our bedroom. David, barely one year old, stayed in his little room with Libby, our boxer, claiming her space beneath his crib. On New Year's Day, 1951, Mother and I climbed aboard the Seaboard Silver Meteor in Hamlet for Baltimore, where after a twelve-year hiatus, she once again entered Phipps Clinic in the Johns Hopkins Hospital. Once again I spent the night at the Double Door Inn although the occasion was a mirror image of the one Lil, Daddy, Aunt Kathryn Huntley and I had spent there in January, 1939.

Mother's illness once again had to run its course. She spent a year in Baltimore, a year in Louisville, first with Aunt Susan Fowler, then at Norton's Infirmary there, and finally a year back home at Broadacre, with Mary Simmons, black nursemaid who lived and later died in service to our family, as her caregiver. Ann and I, married less than three years, and having had two children, lost one and with another on the way, had to get on with our own lives. I needed to concentrate on my apprenticeship training. Mother, presumably well cared for, would have to take a back seat. And that is the way she would have wanted it.

Even so, I still had to assume some responsibility: correspond with her doctors, see that bills were paid and insurance coverage provided, pay attention to property, farms and businesses in Monroe—seventy-five miles away—although Uncle Vann was a mainstay. The situation was further complicated by conditions in Wagram and later in Rochester. The years

1951-55 were not easy on any of us, made even more complicated by three more job changes, first to Charlotte, then to New Jersey and finally to Cheraw, South Carolina.

In retrospect, the energy and resiliency of youth strike me as little short of miraculous. Surprisingly, those years were filled with achievements, unexpected recoveries, learning experiences and memorable opportunities. I often discovered, while looking for one thing, something else of greater value. Serendipity indeed. Today I still remember those years with pride and satisfaction, associated with personal growth and a lot of fun. Even the grim episodes were interesting and informative. I've always found life to be like that—a fascinating mix that is totally unpredictable.

# 40. Baby Boom and Custody Fight

"These Three" siblings from the 1930s and early 1940s were now contributors to the post-war baby boom. As earlier foretold, Mary Cov's second child Sue arrived in February 1951, followed by Lil's third daughter Celeste in July. Ann's and my third red-haired son Phil came along soon after on August 5. On August 27, 1953, Mary C. delivered twins, Bella and Andy. Four children in four years.

Cousin Hill beat me to the altar by a year, Vann behind by only one. Hill's first wife was Lillian Cannon from Charlotte, related to the Kannapolis-Concord Cannons, but a lesser one. Even a lesser Cannon from that branch was, however, well heeled. Before that marriage fell apart, Hill and Lillian had two boys and two girls in rapid succession. Despite latter day upheaval in Hill's personal life, characterized by multiple marriages and unpredictable behavior, all five of Hill's children matured into successful, well-adjusted adults. That was not just by happenstance. Whatever his faults, he never turned his back on his children. The Secrests, especially Vann Jr. and Sr., and Aunt Mary Secrest Hinson, never failed to lend a helping hand. Mary Cov did the best she could.

Vann married Jane Hunter of East Orange, New Jersey. Bright, attractive and talented, Jane was a musician by education and training. Her parents had roots in South Carolina. Hill, then working for Col. Elliot White Springs, founder and owner of Springs Textile Mills in Lancaster, S.C., with whom Mr. Hunter was also associated, brought Vann and Jane together. Learning that Hunter's daughter was to attend UNC-CH in the fall of 1948, where Vann was already enrolled, Hill had suggested to Vann that he look her up. He did, and the rest, as they say, is history. Soon Vann and Jane joined the baby boom, ultimately adding four more Secrests to the growing family chain.

Friends Bill Price from Monroe and Bob Allen, from Saranac Lake and Duke days, both got married about the same time. Bill's Nancy was a beautiful, talented young woman—a glamour girl who never thought of herself as one. She had a lovely, trained voice and was a radio-TV entertainer in Richmond when Bill wooed her away from career and into multiple motherhood. Bob's Phyllis, a pretty, brainy, somewhat introverted young woman, proved to be a perfect match for Bob's pomp and circumstance. They too soon contributed to the country's burgeoning population.

Hill and Lillian lived in New York during Hill's turbulent and short-lived association with Colonel Springs. Hill's job was to create raunchy advertisements for Springs textiles and to persuade respectable mass-circulation magazines to accept them. A memorable, politically incorrect one in *Esquire* was a drawing of a muscular young Indian brave, clad only with a feather protruding from his headdress, looking happily dazed and exhausted in bed alongside a curvaceous Indian maiden clad only in a smile. The caption: "A buck well spent on a Springmade sheet!" The reluctance of major magazines to carry these ads stemmed not from any sensitivity to the feelings of Native Americans but from a concern over sexual content and double entendres that might offend morally uptight readers in mid-century America.

Fifteen years before Hill involved Ann and me in one of his wilder shenanigans, he and first wife Lillian and their children visited Mary C. and Bill in Rochester on several occasions. Ann and I visited him and Lillian several times in New York, once in the summer of 1948 when we came down from Saranac Lake. The four of us, joined by Teensie McRae and her husband, Tommy Guthrie of Charlotte, now a resident at Columbia University Medical School, attended a new Broadway play, "A Streetcar Named Desire," starring Jessica Tandy and her unknown leading man, Marlon Brando. Having read the play, I was disappointed in Brando's performance. He played the part largely for laughs and mumbled his way through the Tennessee Williams script so that it was almost impossible to understand him. Ann's and my verdict, "That guy will never go far in show business."

Another highlight was the walk to the theater next to Joan Bennett and her new husband Walter Wanger, who was almost as tall as his diminutive wife. This was a little before Wanger had shot, though not killed, a romantic rival in some Hollywood love triangle. Teensie, a recent mother herself, ran alongside Miss Bennett and Mr. Wanger for blocks, still the starry-eyed, stage-struck kid from her Neighborhood Playhouse days during World War II. Guthrie had earlier achieved his fifteen minutes of fame when, as a member of the 82nd Airborne Division, he had captured top Nazi figure Franz Von Papen in 1945 somewhere in Eastern Europe.

Hill understood about propinquity and made an effort to stay in touch. Ann and I saw a lot of him and family in 1952 and '53 when we moved to New Jersey and even more when he and third wife Rosalie moved to Cheraw, South Carolina, ten years later. Hill's family was star-crossed, though, seldom one step away from tragedy.

Only five years after her son Lee's death in Hawaii, Aunt Isabel was killed one rainy spring night in 1950 as she crossed Franklin Street on her way to a meeting of Gold Star Mothers at the Monroe Hotel. Perhaps thinking of her son Lee, and partly blindsided by her umbrella, she was struck and killed by a woman also on her way to the same meeting held to honor the men who had died in the war so recently concluded. Aunt Isabel was only forty-nine years old. Uncle Hill died not long thereafter. Cousin Hill himself was not long-lived, but the ultimate tragedy came many years later when Hill's oldest son Hudson, still in his thirties—and never a smoker— died of lung cancer.

Ann's and my turn to suffer from Hill's poor judgment came some years later—in December 1963. Hill stopped by our house in Cheraw, South Carolina, unannounced, to drop off his son Wick, then four years old. "Mac," Hill asked, "Can you and Ann keep Wick a few days while I help get the other kids settled in Monroe?

Sure, why not? Hill's got enough to handle right now. Ann agreed. It never occurred to us to ask any questions about custody. All I knew was that Rosalie Wickersham, Wick's mother and Hill's third wife, had left Hill without warning the preceding August and taken Wick and Candy, Hill's older daughter by his first marriage to Lillian Cannon, back to New York.

Wick was a handsome, good-natured, happy little boy. Our daughter Molly, now nearly seven, enjoyed playing the role of older sister. David and Phil were equally good with him. I took him and Molly to Cheraw's annual Christmas parade, where everyone scrambled for the candy tossed out to the crowd by Santa Claus. We attended a party at the Indian Head Finishing Company where Wick got to sit on Santa's lap and share his wish list. We took him to Miss Ruth Funderburk's Ding-Dong pre-kindergarten school to play with boys and girls his own age. Every evening Ann read him stories and told some tales before he was put to bed in the same room with Phil.

On Christmas Eve his stocking was hung on the mantel along with those of everyone else. Wick was crazy about Misty, our boxer, then experiencing a false pregnancy. She was constantly stealing Molly's dolls and furry toy animals, which Misty took to a nest she'd made in Molly's closet and arrayed around her feeding station, her nipples now filled with milk for her imaginary litter. Wick was kept busy in a tug-of-war with Misty, seeking to retrieve Molly's dolls for her. Wick had been raised with a male boxer, Duke, whom he obviously had missed since August.

I became aware that something was wrong when Rosalie's father, Colonel Wickersham, called me at my office a few days before Christmas. Wickersham was a man to be reckoned with. Partner in a large, prestigious old law firm in Manhattan, his own father, George W. Wickersham, had been U.S. Attorney General in President William Howard Taft's administration 1909-1913, and had been known for his trust-busting prosecutions. Wealthy, privileged, powerful, a member of New York's Republican establishment, young Wick's grandfather was not accustomed to challenge.

"Mr. Secrest, I understand you have my grandson at your house, is that correct?" I acknowledged that that was so. "Well, return him immediately. Wick belongs with his mother." I agreed but explained that I couldn't bring him up there myself right now. His father had entrusted him to our care, and I couldn't act without prior consultation or parental consent. Couldn't Rosalie come down to get him? I would arrange for Hill to be present.

"No, indeed!" thundered Wickersham. He then proceeded to accuse Ann and me of being accessories after the fact of kidnapping across state lines (a federal offense), of aiding and abetting a criminal (Hill), harboring a fugitive (Wick) and a whole litany of other high crimes and misdemeanors. Rosalie's father was an elderly gentleman, well over eighty, older then than I am now. He certainly had provocation. Hill had acted impulsively and probably vindictively. But that would be par for the course. How in hell did I get in the middle of this?

I apologized, explained, reassured, sympathized and agreed, but nothing apparently could assuage Wickersham's indignation. All I got in return were more threats and vituperation. Finally, I had had it.

I had just turned forty years old. I had lived in Cheraw for ten years. I felt just as secure as a Southerner and a Democrat as Hill's father-in-law did as a Northerner and a Republican. I outlined the situation as I saw it.

359

Hill and Rosalie were not divorced or even legally separated. She had left him, without notice, taking not only his son Wick but also Candy, Hill's eleven-year-old daughter by Hill's first wife. No custody agreement had been reached. Was Hill any more guilty of kidnapping Wick in December from New York than Rosalie had been in taking Wick and Candy from Cheraw in August?

"I don't believe any crime has been committed by anybody, Colonel," I said. "If any has, it was without my approval or prior knowledge. My wife and I simply saw a need and sought to meet it." I assured the anxious grandfather that Wick was in a safe and secure setting. He was not in his father's custody. "Wick is having a good time with his second cousins. Yes, he should be with his mother, and I'll send him back to her on a direct flight from Charlotte to New York shortly after Christmas. I'll send you his flight schedule as soon as I know it."

Until then, I added, "Don't get so bent out of shape about it." As for the legal threats, they fell on deaf ears. As a respected member of my community in South Carolina, I doubted that he would succeed in any extradition proceedings, certainly not before Wick was back in New York. If any charges were brought against me, the case would be tried at some point way down the road, by which time the whole thing would have become moot.

"And you wouldn't win. No jury would convict me down here in a lawsuit brought by you from New York, if for no other reason than sectional and political bias. I would win. My attorney L.C. Wannamaker would see to that.

"Instead of being angry, hostile and insulting, just say 'thank you for taking such good care of my grandson.' And don't worry about expense. I'll assume responsibility for Wick while he is under my roof and for his safe return to New York."

And that is the way it ended. After Christmas I drove Wick to Charlotte seventy-five miles away, put him on a plane under the watchful eye of two stewardesses and notified Colonel Wickersham's secretary of the flight schedule. A few days later I received a phone call from Wick's grandfather, full of apology and of appreciation for all Ann and I had done for his grandson. The colonel was a nice old man. He had deserved better than Hill.

I have seen Wick a few times since then. Now a grown man nearing middle age, Wick is a tribute to both sides of his family. And he is the spittin' image of his late older half-brother. Again, Providence, by any name one wants to call it, had sought to balance the scales.

After Wick's safe arrival in New York, Ann and I settled down, waiting for Hill to drop the other shoe. He did so many times. The phone would ring at eleven o'clock at night. It would be Hill. "Mac, I've got to see you. Can you come over to the hotel at Southern Pines?" It was a distance of fifty miles, but I would go and calm my hectic cousin down as best I could over some minor matter. Another evening the call might come from Monroe, fifty miles in the other direction.

Things eased off when Ann and I moved to McLean, Va., and Hill married Mary, his fourth wife, and settled down for a while. But even after his fourth marriage, Hill would be in and out of Chapel Hill and Durham with some major problem that had to be solved that night. There was no explaining him. Hill was just Hill, and I felt that I had to put up with him.

Hill was a great gambler and spent his wives' money freely. One night he bet his gambling buddies $500 that the Silver Meteor, express train from Miami to New York, would stop and pick him up in Southern Pines, although that town was not on the train's schedule. Prior to the bet, he had pulled some connection with the Seaboard Railroad and persuaded them to make the unscheduled stop, having let them in on the bet. Sure enough, to everyone's disbelief, the big train slowed to a stop, and Hill, after collecting his bet, climbed aboard and headed for New York City.

# 41. The Sixth Commandment

Shortly after Celeste Buie's birth in midsummer, 1951, Lil began to show signs of stress. On bed rest during much of the pregnancy, the arrival of a healthy, normal baby, especially in view of Jon-Jon's Down's syndrome less than two years earlier, came as a great release. But the pent-up anxiety, aggravated by worry over Mother's health and her husband John's dependency and occasional bouts of instability, demanded an outlet. Lil held it in from Ann and me. Others didn't understand or couldn't offer the help she needed. Instead of ventilating, Lil repressed her feelings, bottled up her emotions and tried to ride things out.

I could see what was coming. There must be some way to prevent the Simmons Curse from striking for the ninth time. Jon-Jon was a problem. Lil, slow to accept a definitive diagnosis, had taken him from one medical clinic to another, from Charlotte to Wilmington. Now nearly two years old, he hadn't developed at all, weighing nearly the same as he had at birth.

Trying to get food into his mouth, much less swallow, was an exhausting enterprise. He cried most of the waking hours of the day and nearly all night. When he was quiet it was worse. Then one was more aware of his broad nose, slanted eyes, and overall deformity. Lil was a demonstrative mother. She held him close to her breast, rocking and swaying, singing songs, telling stories, cooing and whispering sweet nothings in his ears. If nurturing could do it, Jon-Jon should thrive.

But he didn't, and there was nothing anyone could do about that. Down's Syndrome comes in different degrees. Some children are only mildly retarded. Others, while more so, can learn to care for themselves and later even hold down jobs at a menial level. Others never develop, or if they do, only enough to sit up and perhaps to walk. Jon-Jon was so severely disabled he would never be able to care for even his most basic needs, let alone talk, learn or survive independently. Yet like all such afflicted children, in moments of repose he showed a sweet and loving disposition.

His condition was breaking my sister's heart, ruining her physical and emotional health, which she needed for her six-week-old baby daughter. John, in predictable denial, was doing the best he could but it wasn't good enough. Lil's two older girls, Ann and Kathy, six and eight, needed their mother now and would need her even more down the road.

This was the situation Lil faced in August 1951, as we gathered at the Seabuoy, the cottage at Garden City Beach. Lil and I had just returned from a hideously hot visit to Dr. Sidberry's pediatric clinic in Wilmington where Lil was told yet again of Jon-Jon's condition and given the useless advice to place him somewhere, when there was no such place to be found.

Weary from the trip, oppressed by the heavy ocean air stirred by a hot land breeze, everyone decided to go swimming. The surf was rough and roiling, so Ann took David, now twenty months old, and Phil, not yet one month, out, well covered, to splash at the water's edge. Lil, John and Fanny Mae, the colored teenager on hand to help out, watched Kathy and Ann, up to their knees in the foaming water and eager to venture farther out.

I picked up Jon-Jon, and holding him close to my chest, swam out toward the breakers. The little boy liked the water. Unable to cling to me tightly around neck, he nestled down in my arms, content to have the warm salt water wash over him, head and all. Soon I was beyond the breakers, up to my armpits, then neck, as the large swells moved up, around and over us.

That's when the idea occurred to me. Why not loosen Jon-Jon's light, tenuous hold and let him drop to the ocean floor? It wouldn't take a minute. No one could prove that one of the breaking waves had not torn him away. It would be so easy. So right. What was one useless, hopeless, miserable life compared to so many others: my sister, with whom I had gone through so much for so many others over so many years; my brother-in-law, whose own sometimes tenuous hold on reality required help; and, above all, my three nieces who had a right to a safe, strong, happy environment in which to grow up?

My little nephew would not suffer. I would be doing him a favor, along with everybody else. He might otherwise live for years. With penicillin now available, disabled infants whose life expectancy once was measured in a few years, if not months, now could live to middle age or longer. What would become of him? I dropped my right arm from his waist, then looked down for one last time before loosening my left hand.

I saw this tiny little piece of humanity at my mercy, felt his deep, loving trust, and realized that I did not have murder in me, not even what I then would have considered a mercy killing. I, who had always been puzzled by Providence's plan, certainly couldn't play God now, even if I didn't believe in Him. Steeped in God's Law, I could not violate his commandment. Unable to create life, I could not voluntarily take one, unsanctioned by state law or a federal military.

Now holding Jon-Jon closely against my face, I made back toward shore, relieved of a great burden, confident somehow that a solution could be found, even if the family might have to endure another round with the Simmons Curse. And sure enough, nine months later when I knocked, a door did open and a path more frequently taken appeared. Milton was right: "They also serve who only stand and wait." But the waiting is less long if you also seek and find. Later Lil and John found their own—and better—solution for Jon-Jon. Fifty years later, the entire Buie family felt strengthened, even enriched, for having had their Down's syndrome son and brother in and out of their lives for so many years.

In 1971 I told Aunt Sue about my near brush with a mercy killing twenty years earlier. Now eighty-four years old, she nodded her head. "I know exactly how you felt," she said. "It must have been a great temptation. I'm just thankful for your sake you stopped in time. It would have haunted you the rest of your life. Oh, you would have gotten away with it as far as the law and society are concerned. But knowing you, it would have been the proverbial albatross."

She nodded her head again. "But it was certainly an understandable, human reaction. And even had you done such a thing, you still would have been my lovable, admirable, strong and compassionate nephew. We humans are a strange and contradictory lot. A person is never as bad as his worst moment," she added emphatically. "That's one reason I oppose the death penalty." But, she added ruefully, "Neither is a person as good as his best moment."

She recalled what an elderly caregiver hired to help with her first born Earle had said to her in 1914 when she and Uncle Earle lived in Chicago. In her enthusiastic, effervescent way, the young mother had been boasting about her firstborn: beautiful, sweet-natured, good as gold, brilliant, adorable—no adjective could do justice to this most wonderful of babies. "Yes, Mrs. Fowler," the old lady replied, "He certainly seem to be all that but you can't never tell. He may one day hang."

Recalling that day Aunt Sue began to laugh until her shoulders shook. Lessie and May laughed like that, too. Aunt Katherine and Aunt Eve never did, satisfied with a self-indulgent smile. Fortunately Earle, despite an occasional emotional problem, never did hang or get into serious trouble. In fact, he became a prominent lawyer in Louisville and a man of accomplishment and renown. But the Simmons Curse did leave its mark on him and his family.

My concern about Jon-Jon's presence in the family that summer of 1951, however, was justified. The Simmons Curse now was to strike for the ninth time, taking the form of post-partum depression. This can be a devastating physical illness. Lil's case was aggravated by reality problems in her own life. Like Lessie in 1935, she was forced to face questions about her marriage, complicated as it was by four children, including a two-year-old Mongoloid son and a newborn baby girl.

Unlike Mother, who would cave in without warning, Lil put up a courageous battle. She got help at home. John stepped up and assumed his responsibility. Aunt Eve and friend Catherine Johnson Jackson did what they could from Winston-Salem. Ann and I, preoccupied with our own growing family and one hundred miles away, also did what we could from a distance.

Aunt Eve enlisted medical help from Dr. Wingate Johnson at Bowman Gray Medical Center where insulin shock was one course of therapy. Nothing seemed to work. Wagram, a small village near Laurinburg, was like an extended family. John's elderly, ailing parents couldn't offer much assistance, but John's sister Mary Pence and sisters-in-law Jean and Lottie Mae Buie were towers of strength.

Lil stuck it out at home for six months. Then she agreed to seek additional professional help, capably arranged for by husband John. Once again, time played a key role. After six months, it was time for Lil to get well. Within six weeks and after a few electroshock treatments at a South Carolina Hospital, she was back home with her family. A strong, well-adjusted woman, she never again required clinical treatment, even after a fifth child arrived in July, 1954, this time a big, healthy boy named James Archibald Buie after a deceased young uncle.

Yet there remained one problem to be resolved: what to do about Jon-Jon, who was destined to remain an infant forever, impossible for Lil to keep at home and do justice to herself and her other children. I was a reporter with the *Charlotte News* when I found a solution. It is difficult in 2004 to understand the lack of facilities—public or private—in 1952 for the severely retarded. There appeared to be no way out. Using my connections as a reporter, I contacted the city's Department of Social Services and got the name and address of a well-recommended home in the mountains of West Virginia. The home was owned and operated by "Miss Ruth." I called her, made a hasty inspection tour, and impressed by what I saw, inquired about admission policy, available space, waiting list and cost. Miss Ruth's met every test except the vital one of availability. There was no room.

I had heard that before. I remembered when Mr. Muirhead had said the same thing about housing in Glen Lenox in 1950 in Chapel Hill. Never give up. Never give in. Never surrender, Winston Churchill had said. But Daddy, also believing in persistence and determination, when hearing the aphorism "If at first you don't succeed, try, try again," had replied, "Well, yes, but don't be a damned fool about it, either." One does have to learn about rejection, reality and acceptance.

The situation, however, had to be resolved. Miss Ruth's was the answer, and after a weekend of discussion and persuasion with Miss Ruth at her West Virginia home, she agreed to make room for one more. Soon Lil, John, Jon-Jon and I were on our way back to West Virginia where my little nephew found tender loving care. My mountain solution was better than my unfulfilled beach one.

A few years later Lil and John placed their son in the recently opened Caswell Home for Children near Goldsboro. This proved to be a fine state institution that provided Jon-Jon with the kind of professional care and support he required. When this perpetual baby died at age 53, personnel from the institution attended his memorial service and interment in Wagram, beside all the members of a grateful family.

The rest of the Buie family story is for them to tell. Lil and John and their four other children remained closely aligned with me, Ann and our three children. Lil and John worked their way through their problems as married people committed to each other must. He loved her unreservedly, if selfishly and possessively, and allowed her to make family decisions and to rule the roost. And, like Dowd and David N. Saleeby, John "wasn't always wrong." I regret now that I didn't understand him better and the social phobias from which he suffered, probably from some errant gene in the Purcell strain of his family. People liked John. He accepted his several disabilities without complaint and faced amputation and death bravely when it came at age seventy-eight in 1988.

Lil returned to teaching in 1957 and reigned in the English classroom for twenty-five years, every bit as effectively and much more beloved than her mentor, Anna Bernard Benson. In her last year of teaching in 1983, she was honored as North Carolina's English Teacher of the Year. During her tenure she also earned her master's degree in English from New York University, traveled extensively, took students on educational trips abroad and raised three daughters and a son who as adults have been a credit to her. She and Mother were instrumental in establishing a network of support groups for the mentally disabled through the North Carolina Association for Retarded Children.

Lil and I, assisted as much as time and space permitted by sister Mary C., also provided the support Mother needed when she was sidelined again in 1959. Mother, a strong woman, managed to survive all that, but without her children's support, it would have been a dicey proposition. When Mother had a mild stroke at age 88, she lived the last two years of her life with Lil and John, who showed as much deference to Miss Lessie as he would to his own mother, even though Mother never liked John much and did little to conceal her feelings. Mother spent every holiday from 1959 with Lil. She was in Wagram so much that her Buie great-grandchildren were surprised to discover later that she didn't live there year-round.

When Phil, our third son, developed a serious illness at age fourteen in 1966, Lil was never far away. And when Lil's youngest daughter Celeste developed emotional problems her sophomore year in college, Ann and I remained close at hand. Celeste spent the academic year 1971-72 with our family in Chapel Hill on her road to recovery, working part-time for retarded children at the Rev. Robert Seymour's Binkley Memorial Baptist Church.

Sister Mary C. and her four children were equally involved with Phil's and Celeste's well-being, just as Lil, Ann and I had been with her family's, when Mary C. had fled Rochester years earlier and descended upon Mother in Monroe four months after the twins were born. Mother's recovery from a debilitating illness between 1950 and 1954 didn't just happen. It required family solidarity and hard work. It sometimes resulted in hand-to-hand combat with seasoned professionals. It cost all of us a lot in time, pain and money.

# 42. Lobotomy, Anyone?

Mother's experience at Johns Hopkins Hospital in 1951 was no better than Aunt May's had been in 1941 and was certainly not the triumphant one Mother had enjoyed in 1938. Aunt May had to return to North Carolina first and then go to Lexington, Kentucky, to recover in 1943. The problem both times lay with the medical staff's failure to recognize the importance of time in treating depression.

Fifty years ago shock therapy was still the preferred treatment. Psychotropic drugs and anti-depressants were yet to be developed, although thorazine, an industrial strength chemical soon to be in wide use to keep patients dull and docile, was in its early stages of development. Later its overuse and abuse led to patient cleansing of state hospitals, with disastrous individual and social consequences, unforeseen and unintended.

Really effective biological treatment of mental illness was still several years down the pike. Even with the successful use of such drugs today, one has to guard against side-effects, drug interaction, overdosage and dependency. Research indicates that cognitive therapy continues to play a significant role, along with drugs, in an effective treatment and control of mental disorders.

Unipolar disorder, once known simply as depression or nervous breakdown, usually disappears—and possibly reappears—spontaneously. Even without professional help, most patients eventually get well. Many, perhaps most, stay well. A time cycle, both as to onset and recovery, is involved. In the interim, good care can do much to speed up and fine-tune the process, mitigate suffering and offer maximum protection during periods of greatest danger. Counseling, communication, self-understanding and a support system all help in a complicated therapeutic process until Mother Nature calls, "Time!" That is when shock therapy can play a key role in jump-starting recovery.

Having observed this time factor in Mother's prior bouts with depression, and later with Aunt May and Mary Cov, I alerted the medical staff at Johns Hopkins. With the memory of Mother's adverse reaction at Pine Bluff still reverberating, I warned doctors against leaping to conclusions and stipulated that no shock treatment or experimental drugs were to be used without my written approval. I then dismissed the matter and except for a rare trip to Baltimore placed most of my attention where it belonged: with my wife, my sons, my dog and my work, first in Laurinburg and then in Charlotte.

After a year in Laurinburg in 1950-51 with O.L. Moore and son John Henry as my bosses, I resigned to become police and crime reporter for the *Charlotte News*. At the *Laurinburg Exchange* I learned about city and town governments and made friends with a Scotland County native, then a rising young attorney in Fayetteville, Terry Sanford, with whom I maintained a life-long acquaintance.

In Charlotte my principal colleagues and friends were Vic Reinemer, editorial writer who later became chief aide to U.S. Senator Mike Mansfield of Montana; Pete McKnight, editorial page editor who resigned to become the first director of the *Southern School News Service* (a clearing house for information on compliance with U.S. Court decisions and publisher of a periodical founded to keep tabs on public school integration); Cecil Prince, later a Nieman Fellow at Harvard and soon to suffer an untimely death; Holly Mac Bell who later carved out a career with the U.S. Information Agency; and Tom Fesperman, widely-read columnist. Overseeing us all was Broady Griffith, managing editor and benign father figure who encouraged young reporters to follow their own lead, until he on occasion felt forced to reign us in. And his boss, equally benign Bill Dowd, owner and publisher.

Another reporter with whom I felt a strong rapport was a pretty, dark-haired, brown-eyed girl from Rock Hill, SC. I was struck by her resemblance to my sister Lil. When I learned her name was Claire Simmons, I began to wonder, and we discovered that her grandfather Henry Simmons was my grandmother Molly Covington's brother. Claire and I were second cousins.

Claire was a talented writer but a gifted musician. She was a coloratura soprano soon to become the diva of the Charlotte Opera Company. In 1958 Ann and I drove from Cheraw, picking Mother up in Monroe, to attend opening night of Puccini's *Madama Butterfly*, in which Claire sang the title role. This was her final appearance in the Queen City before she left for Europe to study voice.

She pursued a professional career abroad, appearing on the concert stage of several opera houses in Italy, Austria and Germany before returning to Charlotte. Here she married (again), divorced, and kept herself and the community stirred up from time to time. Later she gave voice lessons, specializing in the Bel Canto technique and preparing her most promising students for try-outs with the New York Met.

Later I met many of Uncle Henry's other descendants and attended Simmons family reunions in Gainesville GA, where Uncle Henry and Uncle Tom had run Brenau College years earlier. Henry's grandsons David Lide and Hayne Palmour III excelled in science and technology while David's brother Miller became an actor. Another grandson, Bill Simmons, was a professional singer. Bill had another claim to fame. His first wife was the daughter of Col. Harlan Sanders of Kentucky Fried Chicken.

Uncle Henry, teacher, scholar and non-stop talker, produced four girls, three sons and innumerable grandchildren. None of those I have known in Columbia SC, Gainesville GA, Raleigh, Washington, New York or Pittsburgh seems ever to have heard of the Simmons Curse. Although Uncle Henry's son Henry Jr., took his own life shortly after World War II.

*The Charlotte News*, an afternoon daily, played second fiddle to the larger, older morning paper, the *Charlotte Observer*. *The News* was looser, more permissive, liberal and Democratic. Both the *Observer*, conservative and respectable, and the *News* were family-owned enterprises. That changed when the Knight-Ridder chain bought the *Observer* in the late 1950s and later acquired the *News*.

For the next fifteen years I maintained personal and professional ties with the Charlotte press from my place as editor and owner of the *Chronicle* in Cheraw, seventy-five miles southeast of the Queen City. In the mid-fifties, I became acquainted with Charles Kuralt, later a CBS television journalist but then a *Charlotte News* reporter, a casual friendship maintained until his death in 1999. The same was true of Julian Scheer, also a *News* reporter, later to become a big-wig with the U.S. space agency.

My colleagues and I in 1951-2 formed a liberal cell at the apartment of Harry Golden, editor of the *Carolina Israelite* and social progressive who asked provocative questions about Southern racial practices and poked good-natured fun at conservatives. Harry achieved a measure of fame and fortune with his various "plans" to achieve racial integration, using humor to disarm his critics, and with his colorful phrases, especially "Only in America," the title of one of his books and a short-lived Broadway show.

Golden had an enormous ego, always full of himself and was, subconsciously, a male chauvinist. He did not enjoy the intellectual company of women, although he did come to like Mother with whom he engaged in spirited discussions of religion and politics. He gloried in his Jewishness, often engaging in self-parody, and enjoyed shocking and jolting Southern Christian fundamentalists in a tolerant, affectionate way. I found his ideas and manner of expressing them stimulating. After I left Charlotte we remained in touch. Over the next couple of decades we drew closer—if not intimate friends, certainly solid allies.

In 1962 Harry was asked to be guest speaker at the annual dinner of the Low Country Jewish Community in Charleston, South Carolina. When Tom Waring, fire-eating editor of the Charleston *News and Courier*, learned of the invitation, he raised such editorial hell that the Community was intimidated into disinviting Golden. Several such invitations, including one from Winthrop College, were rescinded as racial tensions mounted in the Palmetto State between 1954 and 1964 and academic freedom and First Amendment rights were trampled.

The Jewish community then turned to me, now in Cheraw, only to discover that editor Waring found me to be even more of a bête noir than Golden. Soon a note came in the mail, suggesting that I too may want to reconsider their invitation. I declined to be uninvited, telling the chairman that I would attend the dinner as scheduled and give my talk—fee waived—unless I found myself locked out. The Jewish group gracefully agreed to let me in.

I delivered my address in which the editorial irresponsibility of the Charleston press was my topic. The newspaper's reporter was on hand to cover the event, and I was Waring's editorial target the next day. No harm done. The David and Goliath editorial battle between the *Cheraw Chronicle* and the Charleston *News and Courier* lasted for about fifteen years with the *Chronicle* landing on the right side of history.

The argument was heated but civil, and eventually became friendly, with Peter Manigault, publisher, inviting me and my family and friend David Alcorn and his family into the patrician's antebellum home for tea and later a tour of the family's 17th century Mulberry Plantation. We were all properly impressed by an original Gilbert Stuart portrait of George Washington hanging above the drawing room mantel.

I did an adequate but perfunctory job at the *Charlotte News*, 1951-52, spending a good deal of time on the road looking for a newspaper property of my own to buy. *The Cheraw Chronicle* was possibly available but at a price then beyond my ability to afford. I looked elsewhere—Clifton Forge, Virginia; Owego, New York; Berlin Beach, Maryland; and finally Westwood, New Jersey.

I had only one headline story at the *News* bearing my byline. Assigned as my photographer was a young man who became an artist with the camera. "Jeep" Hunter was not only "Johnny on the spot," always ready to go and always on time, he was an intuitive genius in capturing the essence of a story on film. His photos probably were worth a thousand of my words.

I was on a routine trip to the Lawyers' Building to interview an attorney when a man holding a smoking gun stepped into the elevator with me on the third floor. He looked wild and disheveled. There was no problem getting the story. He was babbling almost incoherently, eager to tell it.

Anxious to score an exclusive, I kept pushing elevator buttons as we rode up and down to keep *Observer* competitor Kays Gary, who had the same beat, from gaining access. The middle-aged man from Myrtle Beach, South Carolina, had just shot and killed a leading Charlotte attorney, claiming the man had ruined him personally and financially. He handed me his gun, rambling on and on as we rode up and down, up and down until he had finally run out of words. When we got out of the elevator on the ground floor, the police were waiting for us.

The man was obviously out of control and temporarily out of his mind. But I got a great interview. Ironically the man's father a generation earlier had shot and killed his daughter-in-law—this man's wife. Maybe violence was something that ran in his family. Or perhaps he suffered from post-traumatic stress disorder. Again I was reminded that "the child is father to the man," that "as the twig is bent, so the tree inclines." The fellow was convicted of some murder charge, but not in the first degree. I have long since forgotten what his sentence was but do recall testifying at his trial. No, I was not charged with hindering or delaying a criminal investigation even if I were technically guilty.

Before I left Charlotte, I arranged for Mother's transfer from Johns Hopkins to Louisville to stay with Aunt Sue. The medical staff had earlier notified me of their decision to give Mother a series of shock treatments. The therapy had progressed, before I intervened, to the point where the doctors had managed to induce the predictable mental disorientation and confusion, followed by the customary psychotic episode. The condition, termed "catastrophic" by the psychiatrists, soon cleared up. But the treatment was unauthorized, unnecessary, unwise and, above all, untimely.

It was also frightening and unpleasant for Mother and upsetting for her family. At least Hopkins, unlike Pine Bluff, had the good sense to stop as soon as the predictable reaction set in and to notify me promptly.

The episode again demonstrated that doctors, even specialists, are not always right. They should listen more closely to their patients and their families, who may not know as much about medicine but more about the patients. Again the time factor had not been appropriately gauged. In 1951 the technique of shock therapy, while useful, was not the refined procedure it is today. Curare, a drug to relax muscles, was not always effective and could be toxic. Patients could, sometimes did, suffer broken bones. Sometimes they died. The young wife of one of the Reynolds tobacco heirs had succumbed from such a procedure in Winston-Salem only a year or so before. A useful tool, it was not to be used lightly and indiscriminately.

By the end of the century the procedure has become much more benign. New drugs to keep limbs limber are safer and more effective. The shocks are milder, cause only mild tremor with no convulsions, and little, if any, memory loss. They may be administered routinely on an outpatient basis. Even fifty years ago problems could be modified and positive results magnified if proper care and consideration were provided. Today layman concern over occasional medical arrogance and lack of experimental restraint remains justified.

If Johns Hopkins lacked restraint in 1951, Norton's Infirmary in Louisville was unrestrained to the point of malpractice in 1953. After a few weeks, Lessie's depression proved too much for Aunt Sue to cope with at home. My aunt held chief of staff Dr. Ackerley not only in affection but also in awe. A long-time family friend, he had become acquainted with Uncle Earle and Aunt Sue when Earle, Jr. was a teenager. Thereafter, Aunt Sue thought he could do no wrong.

It was agreed that Lessie should enter the Louisville hospital. She was there from the summer of 1952 until early spring, 1953. Hospital costs in mid-century had not yet careened out of control. There was some rational connection between prices charged and services rendered. One could make some sense out of itemized bills. Mother was covered by health insurance provided by the Secrest Drug Store. The premiums were relatively low, the coverage adequate. Damage suit lawyers had not yet made medical liability premiums prohibitive nor had American society become the litigious one it is today.

As incredible as it may seem, it was less expensive to keep Mother in a hospital such as Johns Hopkins or Norton's Infirmary than it was for her to live at home with a caregiver. And even that remained comparatively cheap through the first three quarters of the 20th century. The real inflationary cycle, especially in the medical field, did not begin until the Vietnam War era and the Johnson-Nixon-Carter years, aggravated by Middle East conflicts from 1966-1973 and a domestic war against poverty. The nation learned that you cannot have guns and butter without inflation.

While it may have been cheaper to live in a hospital bed than at home, it is not necessarily the preferred medical treatment. There is the danger of the patient's becoming institutionalized, too isolated from the stimulus of real life. There's a greater danger of over-treatment and lack of medical restraint. At Norton's it seemed as if the decision were either to kill or cure. Mother hadn't been there long before the old tried and true method of shock therapy was again recommended. Preoccupied with my own family and profession, I had delegated responsibility to Louisville authorities. My only role was to see to it that the bills were paid.

So I received a shock of my own to learn that the doctors had yet again resorted to shock therapy. By this time Mother's system had become so inured to the procedure that she had been given more than sixty treatments before the experts had managed for a third time to induce mental confusion and still another psychotic reaction. Again the medical teams had failed to take into consideration the time factor and the proper environment before such methods were used. Again they were shocked themselves at the "catastrophic" results.

Didn't anybody ever pay attention to a patient's history and look at her chart? Aunt Sue, who had been such a mainstay—and would be again— had never seen Mother in a disoriented state. Now she was as alarmed as I was disenchanted. We were both aghast when we were informed of Norton's next recommendation. What about a brain operation? A pre-frontal lobotomy!

Don't people ever learn? Don't they remember? I did. I remembered Aunt Isabel's friend, Mrs. James from Laurinburg, who had undergone a lobotomy a few years earlier. Left alone, Mrs. James would have recovered eventually on her own. As it was, her pre-frontal lobes were cut, leaving her cognitively impaired, a woman without personality or control, someone who needed permanent custodial care. The depression may have disappeared, perhaps permanently, but at what price?

I also remembered the wife of Archie McMillan, Lil's teen-age flame down at Riverton. Mrs. McMillan suffered from a more severe form of mental illness. Shock therapy would not have helped. Perhaps nothing would have, except possibly the passage of time and that was by no means certain. Today drugs that reintegrate personality would control her condition. But that was then. The option: the new, improved, wonderful surgical breakthrough, a lobotomy!

The new Mrs. McMillan was not an improvement. Her mania disappeared, but in its place came cognitive dysfunction, uncontrolled emotional outbursts, unexpected four-letter expletives expelled in the middle of church services. She became an indifferent mother, a careless dresser, a sloppy eater. She was no longer the pretty, graceful, intelligent young woman conversant with the world of literature, politics and religion and must remain without hope of ever becoming so again.

Years later, her son Frank began in his early teens to display signs of instability. His despairing father, unable to face the music a second time, one night gave his son an overdose of some drug sending him into a peaceful, permanent slumber and then fired a bullet into his own brain.

Today I read of wonderful new advances in brain surgery, of how tiny incisions and little implants at just the right location, found by MRIs and CAT scans and guided by laser beams, can eliminate symptoms of derangement without damage to personality or intelligence. I hope so. But I've heard that song before.

With the memories of Mrs. James and Mrs. McMillan in mind, I was not inclined to accept the doctors' recommendation concerning Lessie. Neither was Aunt Sue, who understood Mother's intellectual gifts and the pride she'd always taken in them. I wrote Mother a letter, saying it was time to move back to Broadacre and resume the life of the living among family and friends who cared about her and about whom she cared as well.

Mary Simmons, who had helped raise Lil and was like a family member herself, was prepared to serve as Mother's live-in caregiver. I also remembered Miss Inez Flow, a kindergarten teacher who had spontaneously picked up her bed and walked after so many years of self-imposed confinement. Many similar episodes could be found in Monroe and lots of other places, too. Best to face the shadows of the past, to return to the scene of the crime, as it were, and slay old dragons, to mix a few metaphors. Given a change from hospitals where she had now spent the better part of three years and nearing the climax of her cycle when Mother Nature would surely soon shout, "Time!", she would get well again.

Mother returned home March 1, 1953. Later that same month, I decided to buy the *Cheraw Chronicle*, with the help of Uncle Vann, who arranged financial loans and secured the assistance of Secrest Drug Company auditor James Bevis of Charlotte to verify the business figures offered by *Chronicle* owner James Law. Cheraw is only forty-eight miles from Monroe, less than thirty miles from Laurinburg. A Southern sense of place, asserting its traditional centripetal force, was drawing us all back home. Soon Mary C. was to succumb to its gravitational pull as well.

A few months after I had settled down in Cheraw as a community editor-publisher, I read an Associated Press story about two prominent Democrats buying the Saranac Lake *Enterprise*. Cheraw and Saranac Lake were about the same size. Their job would be similar to mine. The partners were Roger Tubby, a native of Vermont who had served as President Truman's press secretary, and James Loeb, a party activist and co-founder of the left-leaning liberal organization, Americans for Democratic Action (ADA). I wrote them a tongue-in-cheek letter of congratulations and commiseration, along with a few tips on how to deal with community conflict.

Soon Tubby and Loeb answered in kind. That correspondence led to a personal friendship that lasted in Tubby's case for forty years, including visits to each other's homes. In 1956, when Tubby was on leave of absence as media director of Adlai Stevenson's 1956 presidential campaign, he and his wife Ann came to Cheraw. He arranged admission for my wife Ann and me to a political rally in nearby Southern Pines where Stevenson was to appear with Governor Luther Hodges. We even got a ticket for die-hard Democrat L.C. Wannamaker, my Cheraw attorney. Wannamaker, a gifted gardener who grew prize-winning camellias, garnered a large pile to present to the candidate. One of my fondest memories of that year was meeting my idol Adlai, who may have lost the election but had won lasting honors for the quality of his campaigning, and hearing Governor Hodges introduce me as his nephew when in actuality I was only second cousin by marriage.

Tubby took another leave of absence in 1960 to help with John F. Kennedy's campaign. It was through my friendship with Tubby that I came to write some campaign literature for Kennedy from my position that fall as a Nieman Fellow at Harvard. Tubby was then named Assistant Secretary of State and later still served as a U.S. representative to the United Nations in Geneva, Switzerland, in the area of human rights and humanitarian affairs.

Tubby served through the Johnson, Nixon, Ford and Carter administrations, returning to Saranac Lake with the election of Ronald Reagan in 1980. Ann and I visited Ann and Roger Tubby several times thereafter in their house on Trudeau Road, overlooking White Face Mountain in Lake Placid, not far from the Trudeau Sanitarium Chapel where Ann and I were married in 1948.

James Loeb stayed in Saranac Lake and ran the *Daily Enterprise*, until he was later tapped to be ambassador to the Republic of Ghana in Africa and later still as ambassador to Peru. Ann and I were equally good friends with Jim and wife Ellen, visiting them in their Riverside Avenue house in Saranac Lake in the late 1950s. But Jim was touchier and more on edge than laid-back Roger. Neither did he welcome differences of opinion. In 1970 when I wrote an op-ed piece on Richard Nixon's efforts to end the Vietnam war with his "secret plan" and sought to explain his and Kissinger's rationale for ending the Viet Cong's sanctuary in Cambodia, Loeb was outraged. He wrote me a brief note, dismissing me with the line, "Sorry we lost you, goodbye." And that was the last I heard from him.

Ann and I also kept up with friends we had made the two years we were in Saranac Lake, especially Bill and Peggy McLaughlin and their children who were about the same age as ours. Bill's father had never moved to Saranac Lake, remaining in New York City, an Irish-American political boss in the Manhattan Democratic Party that had emerged from the days of Boss Tweed and a reformed Tammany Hall. Bill was a wild and crazy guy who never grew up, but he had a winning personality and was a good friend of Bob Allen and me. Even so, we both knew Peggy had her work cut out for her.

Mrs. Ruth Worthington, Ann's predecessor at the Saranac Lake Free Library, was another person with whom we maintained ties, although she was old enough to be Ann's mother. Coincidentally, Mrs. Worthington had been reared with Ann's father in a little New Hampshire town. She was also a friend of Bob Allen's father later in New York state where the Worthingtons and the Allens had raised Morgan horses. Mr. and Mrs. Worthington had planned to retire in Saranac Lake until "that damned leukemia claimed my husband in mid-life, leaving me alone," forcing her to return to library work.

We kept up with Carl and Mercedes Herold too, until Carl's death in 1954 from complications from his earlier bout with tuberculosis, and hers a few years later. In 1949 the Herolds were a great help when our boxers, Libby and son Onuc, chased porcupines up nearby Baker Mountain and failed to return. As we sat in the Herold living room late at night, we heard the dogs howling from the summit but neither answered our repeated calls. Finally we got the New York State Forest Rangers out to search the mountain. Libby finally returned, face full of porcupine quills. We later found Onuc wedged between two boulders, unable to move but with a dead porcupine between his paws. His face too was a mass of quills. With the help of the Rangers, we got him loose.

After midnight we roused a disgruntled Dr. Bouton, and took the dogs down for sedation to remove all those quills. It was a painful ordeal for everybody, but we all survived.

We also visited Nona Hanes Porter at her summer camp on Upper Saranac Lake, one of many vacation homes in that area for the rich and famous. Big Nona had gotten to Saranac Lake generations earlier when her husband had developed tuberculosis. Aunt Eve's friend, "Little Nona" Hanes Porter, had attended high school there. The family, once recovered, returned to Winston-Salem, but they kept their "camp" for seasonal vacations.

# 43. Flying High and Diving Down

In 1953 the baby boom was in full swing. Lil announced in November that she was expecting another baby. Mary C., always competitive, had already topped that with twins in August. Ann and I, thank goodness, were on a sabbatical. Mother, still locked in her emotional deep freeze, got interested in spite of herself. There was a constant flow of friends in and out of Broadacre to welcome her home from Baltimore and Louisville. She was comforted at the prospect of her son and his family living nearby and relieved that I finally appeared to have decided at twenty-nine what I wanted to do with my life. Always crazy about babies, Mother couldn't help showing some animation over the upcoming births.

Everything was not, however, consistently coming up roses. Mother had her setbacks. We ran risks. Mary Simmons was not a health provider and Mother saw no doctors. Broadacre could still exude a dark, depressing emotional odor. On Mother's sixty-first birthday, one day after my thirtieth, the telephone rang by my bedside at our home on Christian Street in Cheraw. It was Dr. Smith.

"Mac, you'd better come up here right away and see about Lessie."

"Why? What's the matter?"

"Your mother swallowed a bottle of aspirin—I don't know how many, but Mary Simmons couldn't wake her up and called me. She's still pretty groggy. You need to come right now." And Dr. Smith hurriedly rang off.

I was at Broadacre in less than an hour. I did as Dr. Smith directed. Filled Mother with steaming black coffee and started walking her around the house, assisted by Mary Simmons. Mother regurgitated, drank more coffee, walked some more, the process repeating itself until her head was clear.

I was more honest and blunt than loving and tactful. "Mother, I wish you'd stop sending out these cries for help. You aren't suicidal. You knew you wouldn't die from the aspirin you took. You're a smart, capable woman. If you had wanted to kill yourself, you'd have found a way. Your mother did. What do you want … to go back to a hospital like she did?"

What was it that made her birthday so special? "I know your mother took her life on your twenty-fifth birthday. So what? Do you think she did it to spite you? But have you noticed how nearly every time in the past when you've wanted change or some special attention, you have chosen your birthday to dramatize it?"

Warming to my task, I added, "So recognize what you're doing, do not do it again and quit trying to ruin my birthdays. Mine was yesterday, you should remember, and I had a great time. Now I've got to go back to work, and I don't want to be called on any such fool's errand as this again." Relenting enough to give Mother a quick hug and kiss, I thanked Mary and walked out the door.

Mary C., usually competitive with Mother, was at peace with herself and everybody else during her final pregnancy. She was positively elated when she gave birth to full-term babies, a boy Andy and a girl Bella on August 27. Unlike Lessie's, both of her twins survived. Unlike Lil and Ann, she had lost no babies nor given birth to an anomaly. Having overcome the miscarriage problem, she now reigned supreme as Supermom!

But elation and emotional high flying can lead to a bumpy landing. Mary C. came to earth quickly. Within weeks she was feeling rocky and unglued. Defensive and into denial, the change was all husband Bill's fault. What was he up to with that Croatian woman assistant of his? He didn't want the children. He didn't want her. And she wanted out.

By late November she was calling long distance every day, usually from some pay phone "in the ice and snow where Bill can't hear me." She had to call collect. She eventually ran up hundreds of dollars in "emergency" long-distance calls. I paid the bills and kept track.

Eventually I presented the bill and got my money. I usually do. And Mary C. was never stingy. When back on track, she was quite willing to repay. In early December she called for the last time, now from the Rochester airport. She and her children, Mary Ann, four, Sue, nearing three, and Andy and Bella, now a little over three months, were landing in Charlotte on Eastern Airlines the following evening and I was to meet them and put them up in Monroe.

We were playing bridge at our house on Christian Street in Cheraw when the call came. I didn't mention anything about it to Ann or Lil, over from Wagram for the evening. I would meet the plane as instructed. Luckily the *Chronicle* had already been published. We would work something out. I left for Monroe early the next day after calling Mother's cousin, Ann Brooks, now teaching in Rockingham.

Ann was Cuz Nannie Ashcraft's only daughter and had lived most of her younger years in her mother's shadow. When she was in her late thirties, she enrolled at Columbia University, bobbed her hair, met Everette Brooks, a Canadian, and married him. Despite the Depression, Ann (she had dropped the name Annie Mae), found a job at Macy's department store and rose to the level of buyer in the jewelry department.

Married too late to start a family, she and Everette lived the good life in New York City until the mid-'40s when Everette dumped her for another woman. At first stunned and humiliated, Ann picked herself up, dusted herself off and went back to school, earned her teacher's certificate and returned to North Carolina.

Rockingham, only fifty miles from Monroe and twenty miles from Cheraw, was a convenient location. "Ann, could Mother stay at the teacherage with you for a few weeks after Christmas?" I asked. Yes, Ann replied, she thought she could arrange that, a private room with meals supplied and if needed a temporary live-in maid. The next call was to Lil. Could Mother come down to Wagram and spend a few weeks until school reopened after Christmas? I explained the situation. Mother would be well out of the house before John had his annual income tax crisis.

"Of course," was Lil's immediate reply. "We will all love to have her. It will be great to have a fourth on hand for bridge." Mary C. had been on the phone to Uncle Vann as well as to Dr. Smith. Since they were already alerted to her arrival, it should be easy to implement my plan. Move Mother out of Broadacre and transfer her to Wagram until the public schools reopened in early January. Then she could stay with Ann Brooks in Rockingham until the situation in Monroe was clarified.

Mary C. and her four children were to live at Broadacre with Mary Simmons to help out. And so it came to pass, with a little fine-tuning here and there. Mother was informed, accepted the fact that her daughter and her four English grandchildren must now be given priority. She was packed and ready to leave by the time I got to Monroe. She was in Wagram with the Buie family, including three granddaughters, now nine, eight, and two, (with another grandchild on the way) by mid-afternoon, and I was back at Douglas Airport in Charlotte by eight o'clock, awaiting Mary C's touch down.

At this point I was past conjecture. How can anything good come of this? Shakespeare reminds us that "sweet are the uses of adversity." At the moment I couldn't see its advantages. What else was looming down the road? The Bible warns us that "sufficient unto the day is the evil thereof," which to me means, "Don't borrow trouble." It would find you soon enough. Just deal with life's problems as they arise and hope for the best. *Que sera, sera.* The surprising thing is that my sister's post-partum flight to Monroe set in motion all the right moves that soon restored all branches of the family to an even keel. Providence does indeed move in mysterious ways, her wonders to perform, egged on by those who have the wit and will to help themselves.

Mother benefited from her month's stay with her daughter and three grandchildren in Wagram, although she showed few outward signs of it. Lil handled the situation well, assisted by Hattie and Olivia, kitchen help and housemaid. Kathy, Ann and Celeste proved irresistible even to Mother's emotionally anesthetized state.

Wagram, the village, now became an extended family. John was kin to half the people there and Catherine Johnson Jackson to most of the others. Among the Presbyterian and Baptist churches, neighbors Mary and Dusty Odom, Sunny and Anna Covington, Rush and Mrs. Lena Wooley across the street; John's sister and his brothers' wives, Mary Pence, Jean and Lottie Mae Buie and their extended families—with all these, Lessie had plenty of diversion and Lil plenty of help. Even Florence Redwine, my former seventh-grade teacher in Monroe, now teaching school in nearby Maxton and living with her older sister, Sara McKinnon, dropped by for visits.

In Rockingham, the environment was less intimate but perhaps more restful. Ann Brooks, a brisk woman of considerable self-possession, was the perfect foil for Mother, immune to symptoms of her depression. At the teacherage, there were plenty of women to provide companionship and social diversion but no one emotionally vulnerable to Mother's condition. Many of them probably had had experience with someone in a similar state in their own families. Ann and I, only twenty-two miles away in Cheraw, also kept tabs on Mother, having her over for an occasional weekend as well as driving over to Rockingham once a week.

I even unearthed second and third cousins, some once or twice removed, with whom to renew or establish friendship. During the three months Mother lived in Rockingham, people I shook out of the family tree—all descended from our common ancestors from the latter part of the 18th century and all who came to know and like Miss Lessie—included the Coles, the Walls, the Dockerys, the Gathingses, the Covingtons, the Monroes, the Coppedges, the Usserys, the Ledbetters, and the McRaes, among others.

Mother was at the teacherage from January to April. Over Easter weekend, Ann Brooks said it was time for Mother to return to Monroe. Mary Cov had notified her of a vacancy at the Ellen Fitzgerald Hospital. That facility had been converted into a nursing home when the new Union County Memorial Hospital was completed. It was designed for both short-term and long-term care. Near the center of town and now home to many of Mother's older friends, the Ellen Fitzgerald Hospital became the epicenter of elderly social activities.

I moved Mother from the Rockingham teacherage to the Monroe nursing home on Easter Monday. Her roommate was her friend Betty Smith, Big Doc's wife, who was hospitalized with chronic asthma. In an adjoining room was Mother's "Aunt Lizzie," wife of Uncle Jim Covington, widowed for the past fifty years. Elizabeth Andrews Covington, a maternal woman who had never had children, was our former high school librarian. There she mothered all the students, even the most unruly, unable to discipline anybody. The library soon became the place where teachers sent their worst disciplinary problems. There they were hugged and kissed and loved into submission. But the library was the noisiest, most rocking room in school. Aunt Lizzie's library reminded me of Miss Inez Flow's kindergarten many years earlier, totally out of control and hence a favorite student haunt. But unlike Miss Flow, Aunt Lizzie did not have a delicate nervous system. She thrived on the bedlam.

Anna Bernard Benson's mother was another resident, along with other old friends, some temporary, some permanent residents. Someone was usually in the room visiting Lessie practically all day. Not the least of whom was daughter Mary C., often accompanied by one or all of her children. Soon Mother's room was a center of social enterprise.

At Broadacre with Mary Simmons, Mary C. herself was quickly overcoming her earlier panic. She made new friends, renewed old ones. Soon she had Mary Ann and Sue enrolled in kindergarten and a preschool center for half a day. In time away from her infant twins, now both thriving, she stayed busy at a variety of activities, including work at the Methodist Church.

By May Mary C. was feeling fine and ready to move on. She took Mary Simmons with her to Hollywood, Florida, where she bought a house and, before the year was out, had flown back to Rochester for an amicable reunion with her husband, who gladly welcomed her and their four children home. Before that reunion, however, Mary Simmons had been injured in a gas explosion at Mary Cov's Florida home. Badly burned, she died some weeks later during a skin graft. Mary C. was heartbroken and of course felt guilty, although the explosion was beyond her control and she had assumed responsibility for every cent of medical cost.

Mary Simmons' loss was deeply felt by everybody. She was highly respected in Monroe. She had quit moving to the back of the bus from Charlotte to Monroe in the 1930s, a good twenty years before Rosa Parks refused to do so in Birmingham, Alabama, because she was tired and her feet hurt. Mary was a woman of deep and abiding faith leavened by a keen sense of humor. Before the operation following her injury she declared, "I know I have a heavenly home awaitin', but I ain't one bit homesick!"

The English family now established a pattern that enabled two incompatible people to co-exist despite irreconcilable differences. Bill was chief pathologist at the state mental hospital in Rochester. Now fifty-three years old, having two difficult teen-age boys from a previous marriage and four young children, including twins, with Mary Cov, he needed some time and space to himself. The solution? My sister would spend several months each winter in Hollywood, Florida, in the home on McKinley Street that she had bought a year earlier. The rest of the year she and the children joined Bill in one of the large houses provided for the hospital staff on the grounds of the State Hospital at 1600 South Avenue. Their housekeeping needs there were largely met by the state.

In Florida Mary C. enrolled the children in the private Palm Manor School, paying tuition by serving as the school's publicist. She also wrote a column for the *Hollywood Tatler* and later the *Miami Herald*. She managed to create a daytime radio/television show entitled "Aunt Mary's Stories" occasionally featuring her photogenic, precocious kids. When the children weren't in school, their mother had them involved in some other organized activities. She kept herself and them on the go.

She located my friend Moke, now a psychiatrist, in Fort Lauderdale and kept him uncomfortable, trying to match him up with every pretty girl she met, which was the last thing Moke now had in mind. Moke, who never could decide which gender he preferred, was unable to establish long-term relationships with women. Fortunately, he realized this and wisely chose not to marry.

In Rochester Mary Cov became friends with several of the wives of psychiatrists on the state hospital staff, especially Rosemary Grofero, Blanche Steckle, and Eleanor Reynolds, second (but not the last) wife of the chief of staff, whose older daughter Nancy later married her childhood sweetheart, Pete Pagano. Pete's parents, first-generation Italo-Americans, owned a produce market and lived above their store across the street from the state hospital. I remember Pete and Nancy from my visits to the English family in 1947 and 1948 but, barely teenagers themselves, they wouldn't remember me. The family represented to me a typical and inspiring American success story.

Nancy as a teenager sometimes babysat for Mary C.'s and Bill's growing family. Pagano earned his medical degree in Rochester and later became Director of the Swing Cancer Research Center at the University's Medical Center in Chapel Hill. Nancy became the first ordained female Episcopalian priest at Chapel Hill's Chapel of the Cross and served as assistant pastor there for several years.

My sister, the mercurial extrovert, set the social agenda for husband Bill, the introvert. Among the many other friends she made were Mr. and Mrs. Ernest H. Schopler. Schopler was a Rochester attorney who had been chief administrator in the denazification program of Germany under Gen. Lucius Clay at the end of World War II. The couple's two sons, Eric and John, both earned doctorates in psychology and became tenured professors at the University of North Carolina in Chapel Hill. Eric's son, Dr. Bobby Schopler, is now a Chapel Hill veterinarian once associated with the Orange County Animal Protection Society and more recently involved in establishing a wildlife and raptor center in the Triangle area.

Mary C. even had a fling in Rochester politics, nominated as a candidate for alderman on the Democratic ticket. She proved too flamboyant even for those liberal Democrats, but then in that Republican stronghold, she never had a chance to win. When I asked Eric Schopler half a century later if he remembered my sister, he replied with a laugh, "Mary English? How could anyone ever forget her!" adding that she did have a "wonderful vocabulary."

Throughout the 1950s and early '60s Mary C. visited Mother, Lil and me en route to and from Florida, riding the train and stopping off in nearby Hamlet. That way her children, Lil's and ours grew close, more like siblings than cousins. Mary Ann, David, Sue, Celeste and Phil became the self-proclaimed "Big Five," condescendingly terming the younger Jim, Bella, Andy and Molly the "Little Four" and the two older Buie girls, Kathy and Ann, the "Over the Hill Two."

Lessie's grandchildren, too young to remember the turbulent early post-war years—indeed some then not yet born—enjoyed a care-free youth, happily recalling family gatherings at the beach, at the Lumbee River in Wagram, at the lake at Cheraw State Park and at their homes in New York and Florida.

After John Kennedy was elected President in 1960, he began a large military build-up. While the alleged missile gap that he campaigned against failed to materialize, the conventional army was enlarged and re-equipped. It was then put to the test in huge maneuvers in the summers of 1961 and 1962 called Swift Strike I and II. The epicenter was the sandhills of South Carolina, with headquarters at Cheraw. These events also provided excitement and diversion away from home for my nieces and nephews.

Army public relations personnel came by the *Chronicle*, arranged for me and any staff or guests I chose, to cover the maneuvers from mobile ringside seats. On several occasions Ann and I took David, Phil and Molly to see the huge tanks and new jet fighters in action. One morning, joined by nieces Mary Ann and Sue English, we all sat on top of an army truck as the jets thundered overhead, so close we could feel the heat from the engines. We would involuntarily duck each time a plane took off, narrowly clearing the army trucks as it zoomed past leaving long vapor trails. The noise was deafening, creating vibration on the roof of the vehicle.

Cheraw was the chief military objective, and it exchanged hands several times as the thousands of men from the 82$^{nd}$ and 101$^{st}$ Airborne Divisions, representing the white and red armies, fought for the prize. Yes, there was lots of excitement for the Secrest, Buie and English cousins in those summers. The military exercises were a prelude to the Cuban missile crisis during the thirteen days of October, 1962.

My sister moved back to North Carolina in 1964 to be near Lil and me. I missed the initial adjustment, as Ann and I had just moved to Washington, D.C., where I was to work for the Johnson Administration for over two years. Mary C. settled in Laurinburg and taught at several schools in the area. At the Laurinburg Institute, where Dizzy Gillespie once attended, she claimed to have recruited Charlie Scott, UNC's first black basketball player. She also taught at St. Andrew's College and at North Carolina's predominantly Native American school, Pembroke College. She and her children continued to spend summers in Rochester, and Bill spent as much time in North Carolina as his work allowed.

Mary Cov was better with young children than with teenagers. As hers grew older, she was reluctant to let go. The more independence they demanded, the more she intervened. She talked more and listened less. When Andy and Bella enrolled at the University, Mary C. persuaded Bill, now of retirement age, to move to Chapel Hill. They came to the university town in 1971, the same year I joined the faculty at the School of Journalism. Mary C.'s presence, despite my affection for her, proved to be one of several family liabilities that made a professional life at UNC impossible.

Four years later, Bill left permanently for their home in Hollywood. Thereafter, Mary C. divided her time between North Carolina and Florida, a model of perpetual motion, darting in and out of Monroe and the lives of her mother, sister, brother, children, nieces, nephews, and cousins, but always on hand for any major family event. Whenever Lil and I were not available to be monopolized, she turned her attention to Cousins Hill and Vann, with an occasional excursion to my friends Bill and Moke.

Mary C., like Cousin Hill, was a mercurial and unpredictable personality, sometimes over the top and beyond the realm. But she never neglected her children. Nor did they ever neglect her when she grew old and sick.

My older sister played a major role in my life. A caregiver and advocate, she never targeted me for criticism until after we were both married with children. Later she changed her sights, and we engaged in numerous spirited fights.

The first time Mary Cov saw me occasioned a fight. When she and her chum Virginia Redfearn peered into my bassinette shortly after my arrival, Virginia declared, "My, what an ugly, red-faced baby!"

"He is not. He's beautiful!" Mary Cov shouted and delivered a ringing slap to her belittling friend. From then on she was my champion, guardian, loyal friend, devoted sibling and, sometimes, merciless tyrant.

When I was nine years old, some kids ridiculed me as a "sissy" because I was so often in the company of Mary C. and Lil. They bullied me, among others, mercilessly. When I complained to Mother, her advice was to ignore the mistreatment, rise above it, turn the other cheek.

That didn't appeal to my combative sister, who understood that one cannot afford to be cowed by schoolyard bullies. "I know Fred," she declared. "He's really a coward. Call his bluff. Knock the devil out of him." With a little training from Heath and Lindsay, I was soon ready for the ordeal. I picked a fight and won it, to the delight of many of my classmates. Mary C. was a good child psychologist. Self-respect and peer approval are especially important to a pre-teenager.

I had my "mid-life crises" early. Each time I turned to Mary C. for help and advice. And it was always forthcoming: helpful, caring, reassuring, comforting and sensible. I like to think that, whenever she had hers, I did as well by her.

In our adult years we remained close, even as we engaged in occasional knock-down, drag-out arguments over matters both large and trivial. But we didn't hold a grudge; we fought, forgave, and forgot. And then we'd go at it again.

In 1962, at a family reunion in Hollywood, Florida, she and I had a furious argument over this cosmic issue: Who was the greater movie star— Bette Davis or Joan Crawford? She was in Joan's corner, I in Bette's. Later, after two searing books came out about those Mommy Dearest moms by two angry daughters, each of us yielded to the other. In my mid-teens I had stubbornly refused to give up crushes on female celebrities. Mary C. and Lil were equally determined to set the standards by which I was to judge women. So the 1962 row had its origins in earlier years.

Mary C. was family-minded. She naturally enjoyed people, but her first love and loyalty lay with the family—nuclear and extended. She might raise Cain on occasion with cousins Vann and Jane, and Sarah or Hill, Jr., but let anyone else do so, and look out! The same principle applied to Lil and me, to Mother and Daddy; and later to husband Bill and children Mary Ann, Sue, Bella and Andy, and on up and down the line.

My sister was a hard worker and a tough fighter, both traits I grew to admire, even if occasionally she mistook her target and found herself, in the words of a popular tune many years back, "shadow boxing in the dark." In my youth, she was the chief cheerleader and ringleader, but always leader, in good deeds and bad. She was a rebel at heart, but it must be said, as she grew older, "a rebel without a cause."

When the new Methodist minister came to call at Broadacre in 1934, Mary C. gathered Lil, Helen Saleeby and me into an adjacent room and instructed us to start singing as loudly as possible as soon as the preacher began to say his farewell prayer. We were to go truckin' on down through the living room singing, "The lady in red, the boys are all crazy for the lady in red. She's a bit naughty and gaudy, but Lawdy, what a personality!" We did as we were told, before a mortified Mother. Mary C. like to shock people, especially her parents. Why did she do it? Why did we follow? As Lil has recalled, because we were her willing and devoted slaves.

In her first year of teaching, in Mt. Olive NC in the fall of 1937, she invited me and my best friend to visit her. She prompted us to act up in the classroom and mock her principal, who, she said loudly so he could hear, was "snooping" on her just outside the doorway. She disliked authority figures. A contrarian, she would argue with a circular saw and usually win, as its engine would fail before her voice did.

But she really had the heart of a social worker. She championed the underdog, which included the have-nots, the "challenged" of any variety, black people, or anyone else in a minority or in momentary need. If you were down, you could count on a helping hand up. But if you were up, she would also try to smack you down.

Phil loved his Aunt Mary. Sick on and off for seven years, he was to her a perpetual underdog, off-limits to any criticism, even deserved. And to the best of her ability, Mary C. helped him all that she could. That help, largely through her children, was a huge benefit to him and the rest of us throughout his life. Later, when our daughter Molly fell temporarily into parental disfavor and hence became an underdog, her Aunt Mary Cov predictably championed her cause and persuaded others in the family to do the same, often to her parents' chagrin.

As she grew older, she took to calling me on the telephone at all hours, usually to catalog my faults. One night she rang at 11 o'clock and talked until 1:40 A.M., listing all my shortcomings without once repeating herself. The next day I wrote her a twenty-page letter detailing a few of her own. Soon both of us had dismissed the incident, and neither could remember a single fault we were supposed to have. That was a good lesson in the futility of name-calling. One can better spend the time considering the beam in one's own eye than dwelling on the mote in another's.

Mary C. was a study in contradiction and contrast, a complex personality of many colors and shadings, as little understood by herself as by others. She certainly had industrial-strength vocal cords, kept in shape by constant use, a feature shared by relatives of two earlier generations, especially Great Uncle Henry Simmons and Aunt Katherine Craven.

When my sister lost her health and became unable to make telephone calls and excoriate me, I came to miss them and her, as I have every day since her death on February 2, 2001.

# 44. Recovery!

In mid-July 1954, Lil's friend Mary Odom called Mother. Lil had given birth to a son, James A. Buie, both mother and son well and healthy. I was up from Cheraw to visit Mother when she received the news. The expression on Mother's face was a revelation. I hadn't seen that once familiar benign look for nearly four years. I then whispered to Ann, "I think Mother Nature is about ready to say, "'It's time!'""

Once back in Cheraw I asked my office manager, Mrs. Mabel Clark, if she would be willing to move in with Mother at Broadacre and be her paid live-in companion. I had come to know Mrs. Clark as a dependable employee. I liked and trusted her. Nearly seventy years old, she was about eight years older than Mother, but strong, healthy, a woman of good judgment. She had often expressed a wish to leave Cheraw for a while and live elsewhere. Yes, she would. That settled, I called Dr. George Mundorf, a former classmate at Duke who had recently opened a psychiatric practice in Charlotte. I dialed George's number.

"George, Mac Secrest speaking. Can you handle a new patient?"

"Good to hear from you, Mac, after—gosh, how many years? Twelve? Well, I've just opened my practice. You have a mortgage-lifter for me? Tell me about it." We arranged an appointment in Charlotte.

"George, are you willing to accept my mother as a patient and follow my instructions? You know medicine, I know the patient and her history. Can't we collaborate—work together on this?"

"Tell me more." So I related to George the family history, the mixed results achieved from shock therapy, Mother's repeated adverse reactions to it at Pine Bluff, Johns Hopkins, and Norton's Infirmary.

"My belief is that shock therapy is the method to be used to jolt Mother out of her depression once certain conditions are met. It must be the right time. It must be given on an ambulatory basis from her own home, in a familiar setting and accompanied by people she loves and trusts. She can receive no more than six. They should be given on alternate days. If she shows improvement by the fourth, wait a week, then if her condition remains stable, give two more, spaced one week apart. After she has received six treatments and says she feels better, stop. If she does not improve or begins to show signs of confusion and hostility, do not continue."

We talked and planned most of the afternoon. I explained why I believed timing was important. Mother's previous illnesses had come and gone in cycles. The environment was right. After years of legitimate concern about her children, things had settled down, everyone was looking up. All Mother needed was an extra boost to get her over the hump.

George agreed. I went back to Monroe, lined up friends who would go with Mrs. Clark and Mother from Monroe to Mercy Hospital where Dr. Mundorf practiced. I would go the first time. Two days later, Aunt Kathryn Huntley. Next, Miss Ann Redwine. Then, Miss Lura Heath, my first grade teacher whose younger sister had once experienced a similar condition. I would come back up for the last two treatments if they proved warranted.

It worked out as planned. I kept in touch with George and Mrs. Clark by telephone. After the first treatment, Mother returned home and slept away the afternoon. After the second, she did the same. After the third, she made an appointment to have her hair washed and set and again, slept the sleep of the saved. After the fourth, she said she felt different. Better? asked Mrs. Clark.

"Yes," Mother replied.

"Well?" her companion pressed on.

"I believe so."

On Friday, October 16, Ann and I received news that Hurricane Hazel had struck the South Carolina Grand Strand and destroyed Lil's and Ann's cottage, the "Seabuoy." The hurricane cut inland, crossing Cheraw, Monroe, and Charlotte as it made its way toward Canada. Travel was impossible. So was communication. Power and telephone lines were down.

It had been a week since Mother's fourth treatment. I could not get up for the fifth. How had it gone? Had the improvement held? Or was Mother to repeat the Pine Bluff experience of 1950—apparent recovery, euphoria, elation, followed by confusion, suspicion, and psychosis?

On Saturday morning, still unable to get through by telephone, I drove to Monroe, up and around the winding driveway at Broadacre and parked in front. There Mother and Mrs. Clark were in the dining room preparing to have lunch. After an affectionate greeting, Mother inquired about Ann, David and Phil, then expressed concern about the beach destruction. She didn't mention her health or appear in any way depressed.

When I asked her about it, she replied in an off-hand way that she was just fine. She acted surprised that I had inquired, as if there had been no cause for any anxiety. Mrs. Clark said Mother had been just fine for the last week. Dr. Mundorf had said there was no need to continue treatment but had made an appointment for a checkup next month.

A serious mental illness of four years leaves one physically depleted. Mother still had backaches but the local chiropractor was to give her weekly massages. She remained for awhile in a somewhat weakened, fragile state. We enlisted aging Alice Bowell to help pound and rub Mother fully back to normal. Mrs. Clark in an aside said that Mother showed no signs of mental confusion, was not depressed, had no complaints, and slept and ate well. She showed an interest in contemporary events and in other people, expressed no anxiety and no longer lived in the past.

By Christmas Lessie looked younger than her sixty-two years. She was again attending church, teaching Sunday school, playing bridge, hosting the book club and holding forth for the benefit of her rejuvenated fans of the "I declare, Miss Lessie!" club.

In February, 1955, Mother bought a house nearer town and moved out of Broadacre forever. In April she left on a cruise to Hawaii and Japan, where she was guest of a classmate of hers at Brenau College in 1912, whose husband was now a member of the Japanese Diet. From pictures she later showed me, it appeared she was the life of the party aboard the cruise liner.

In her absence, I asked Aunt Sue to come to Monroe and help out with Aunt May. The family she had lived with for five years in Roanoke, Virginia, needed her room. Aunt May's teeth needed attention as did her general health. She had never fully recovered from her breakdown in 1948. She had gone to live near her cousin Nan Trantham Poe, herself an occasional victim of the Simmons Curse, in Roanoke. Over the years we had seen her less and less. Increasingly she had become dependent on the kindness of strangers. Perhaps Mother Nature would call "Time!" for Aunt May, now sixty-nine. In any event, let's give it a try.

Aunt Sue, herself sixty-seven, was as usual game. Again George Mundorf was enlisted. Aunt May did have severely infected gums. Her teeth would have to come out, dentures fitted. It was arranged to have all this attended to at Mercy Hospital in Charlotte. Her physical problems required a hospital stay of a month. To cheer her up and lend encouragement Judge John J. Parker, her old high-school sweetheart and life-long friend, was enlisted. He came by several times to see her. So did nephew Brack.

When it came time to try shock therapy, I drove up from Cheraw each time to take Aunt Sue and Aunt May, now back in Mother's new house in Monroe, to see Dr. Mundorf in Charlotte. Due to her age and condition, the treatment took longer. The results were somewhat mixed, but on balance, positive. Aunt May had no loss of mental capacity. She survived the ten treatments without physical injury. Her depression lifted, her appetite restored, sleep patterns normal.

She didn't, however, regain her old contagious enthusiasm and spontaneous expression. She still seemed to me restrained, somewhat remote and inaccessible. But she was not unhappy or agitated. Those who had not known her before would not consider her in any way disabled. I considered the effort a mixed bag, with something gained and nothing lost.

Later on, the original Aunt May did return a year before her death and who's to say that what we did in 1955 didn't have something to do with that? In August 1959 Aunt May emerged from her twelve-year emotional deep freeze. She began to talk and talk. She wrote effusive and affectionate letters to nieces and nephews. Mary Gene, first cousin David Fowler's wife, declared from their home in Seattle, "Why, it's the same old Aunt May!" The recovery didn't last long, however, as she was felled by a series of strokes a few months later. Aunt Eve arranged for her to stay at a Wake Forest nursing home, where Aunt May in lucid moments introduced herself as Mrs. John Parker, and later at Broughton Hospital in Morganton, where Judge Brack Craven saw to it that she was provided the best of care. Aunt May, now semi-comatose and bedridden with a broken hip, died in August 1961 at seventy-five.

A strange postscript to this story. Dr. Mundorf was the only figure in the saga to get sick. He later came down with cancer of the breast, rare indeed for a man. I lost track of George after 1960 but I learned that he got over his problem. I have since learned that breast cancer is growing among men, affecting 1,500 each year and claiming nearly 500 lives. The diagnosis and treatment are the same as for women: mammograms, MRI's, and, if trouble is detected, surgery and chemotherapy. Former Senator Edward W. Brooke of Massachusetts, one of the first black men to serve in the U.S. Senate since Reconstruction, is one victim of this disease who is doing something to heighten public awareness of its dangers.

Mother's mental health problems did not end, however, with her recovery in October, 1954, at sixty-two. One afternoon five years later the telephone rang in my office as I prepared a story for the next day's edition of the *Cheraw Chronicle*. The voice on the other end was that of a woman with a foreign accent. At first I thought someone was playing a practical joke or making a threatening anonymous call. That happened fairly frequently.

But I soon discovered this was no laughing matter. A nurse from a psychiatric clinic in Lausanne, Switzerland was calling. Mother, on a European holiday, had come down with the flu. A few days later she complained of feeling depressed, unable to make decisions or to do anything. Would I please come get her right away?

Initially surprised and alarmed, I quickly became angry as well. Now sounding more like Dowd than the dutiful son, I snapped, "No, indeed, I certainly will not." I had responsibilities at home and a life of my own to lead. "Did Mother ask that I come?"

"No, but we can not assume responsibility for her."

"I didn't think she did," I replied. "And you and the clinic needn't assume any legal obligation for Mrs. Secrest. I'll send a wire, relieving you of all that. Just put her on the flight to New York City tomorrow night and call me back within three hours with the travel information. She has plenty of traveler's checks to pay her bill and buy the ticket."

I assured the nurse that Mother was not suicidal. "What do you expect her to do?" I asked with exasperation. "Pull open the airplane's pressurized doors and jump out? Just pump her full of tranquilizers and get her on that plane. I'll meet her at Newark Airport early Friday morning."

I called my high school chum Elinor Ellwanger, now head nurse at Charlotte's Presbyterian Hospital, and asked her to make arrangements for Mother's admission late Friday afternoon. She agreed to contact Dr. Mundorf for me. Ann drove me over to Hamlet after supper, where I caught the Silver Meteor for New York, arriving there Thursday morning in mid-October, 1959.

I now had the rest of the day and all night to kill before meeting Mother's six o'clock plane Friday morning. I spent a pleasant, warm, sunny afternoon in Washington Square, talking to an assortment of Greenwich Village characters, street people, and several shadowy young men I assumed to be drug dealers. Autumn in New York is a lovely time of the year. Then on impulse I called Judge J. Waities Waring, formerly of Charleston, South Carolina, now a refugee from the eternal city and living on Long Island. Luckily he had a listed number.

I had never met the judge but knew a lot about him. He was the man who had ruled South Carolina's lily-white Democratic primary elections unconstitutional in 1948. He had become a pariah in his home town, not only because of his decision but also because he had divorced his first wife, a member of an aristocratic Charleston family, and married a Northern woman. Judge Waring was a cousin of my editorial nemesis Tom Waring, editor of the Charleston *News and Courier*.

The judge answered the phone. I identified myself, explained my situation and the time on my hands and said I would like to interview him and to hear more about his famous case and his experiences in Charleston. "Why certainly," the judge responded with typical Low Country hospitality. "Come on out here and meet the family. Stay for supper." And that is what I did. I have found it useful not to waste time mulling over misfortune if one can avoid it. It was an evening well spent and made for an interesting column in the *Chronicle*.

I did not bother to go to bed that night. By the time I had returned to Manhattan from Long Island, reached the New York Port Authority and the Newark Airport, I had only a couple of hours before Mother's plane was due. When Mother came down the ramp shortly after six o'clock unassisted, I recognized the signs: unsteady gait, sad expression, nervous mannerisms—all totally foreign to her natural self. She grasped my hand, expressed concern for me and everyone else. "I know dear that you are broken-hearted and your life is ruined," she murmured.

The Dowd in me stirred again. "Not likely, Mother. This is hardly new. We've been through this before... three times. You know the saying, 'three strikes and you're out.'" I bit my tongue, "Come on, you can do better than that," I said inwardly. Then I grew more sympathetic and reassuring. I told her of the arrangements I had made. I was sorry she felt bad but wasn't overly concerned. "Mother, you always get well. And when you do, you are better than ever. A lot of progress has been made in five years. You'll be over this in short order."

I was off the mark by a mile. Mother remained depressed for eleven more years, from 1959 when she was sixty-seven to 1970 when she was seventy-eight. But I was also partly right. This time was different. After a two-week stay at the hospital with George Mundorf in attendance, Mother remained home with a series of housekeepers and care providers. She required no real nursing. Anti-depressants may not have provided a cure but they did put a floor under the black moods. Mother was never so bleakly depressed or so uncomfortable this time. Over the years she was periodically checked by a hospital physician but no treatment other than medication was recommended, nor did Lil, Mary C. or I press for any.

Mother again withdrew from life. She didn't go to church or to club meetings. Once more she had lost insight into her condition and her faith. Her verve and vitality were drained but she remained the mistress of her own home. She saw close friends, played occasional games of bridge, could even read books. She was included in family events, visited in Wagram, Cheraw and Laurinburg, had grandchildren thrust upon her. My sisters and I pursued our lives as if she were well, the main difference being that she now had live-in help, whose shelf life was about three years each.

Mother's first caregiver was recommended by Dr. Vita McLeod. "She's smart and reliable," Dr. McLeod said, "But hard-favored. She can be sensitive and pout. On such occasions she resembles a venomous old toad." When Mother heard that, she cracked, "Vetoed!" No, Mother wasn't as deeply depressed this time. Occasionally she would show wit and humor.

Then one day in October, 1970, while Aunt Sue was visiting from Louisville, Mother got up from her habitual rocker before the television set to which she had been glued for eleven years and announced, "I'm not depressed anymore. And I don't believe I have been for months." Aunt Susie smiled, nodded and replied, "Oh, I know that, Lessie. I've just been waiting for you to knowledge it." Just like Miss Inez Flow, I thought, back when I was in kindergarten.

Mother recovered completely, insight regained, faith restored, energy returned. Soon she was entertaining the Methodist Women's Circle, her book club, once more an active member of Monroe's Business and Professional Women's club. I called her General Bull Moose, after the character in L'il Abner who would periodically jump into the deep freeze only to emerge years later no older than before. When Mother emerged from her emotional deep freeze, she neither looked nor seemed any older than she had eleven years earlier. Providentially, she even recovered those lost years, now in retrospect seeing life then through new lenses, the proverbial rose-colored glasses.

She got to know her younger grandchildren, some now in college, and they her. She was a help and comfort to Ann and me during Phil's illness just as she was to Lil and her daughter Celeste when Celeste was having troubles of her own only a year after Mother's recovery. She dismissed her help, preferring to live alone and do her own work. She became an ardent Democrat, delighting in Nixon's Watergate discomfort and an ardent supporter of McGovern in 1972. She later became a Jimmy Carter fan.

Even after a brief reactive depression following a broken hip at eighty-two, followed by extensive dental work, Mother bounced back. She demanded lithium at Duke where the doctors said it probably would not be effective in older, unipolar depressive patients. She insisted, she got it, and was back to normal within six weeks. They wrote that one up in the medical journals. Even a mild stroke at age eighty-eight did not keep her down for long. Mother lived twelve good years after her recovery 1970. She was physically, mentally and emotionally younger and healthier at eighty-eight than she'd been at sixty-eight.

Rosa Parker declared at a family party in 1972: "That Lessie is amazing—here she is like the phoenix, once again risen from the ashes." Mother was not a neurotic woman. She was just prone to cyclical depressions due, perhaps, to some bio-chemical imbalance in the brain, some occasional short-circuitry of the electrical system, caused by a kind of malfunctioning internal computer. Electrical signals may have misfired along the neural pathways and failed to make contact with the brain's receptors and synapses. Perhaps a lack of lithium or serotonin or an incomplete absorption accounted for part of the problem.

Then the electrical circuitry would clear up. The computer virus would disappear. The time clock would start ticking, the cause and cure never fully understood.

But psychological factors and personality formation at an early age cannot be totally overlooked. How one reacts to stress is determined early. As to cure, one cannot neglect environment: family infrastructure, adequate finances, insight and understanding, all of these play important roles in recovery. Left alone, neglected, without monetary support and medical attention, a patient's fate would indeed have been uncertain. All things considered, Mother proved to be a strong, durable woman who made her way through life very well indeed, given the heavy burden Mother Nature had hung around her neck.

# 45. Psychiatric Quarrels

The disagreements I had with psychiatrists at Pinebluff in 1950, at Johns Hopkins in 1952, and Norton Infirmary in 1953 were replicated at South Wing in UNC Memorial Hospital in 1971, the National Institutes of Mental Health in 1973, and at Duke in 1974, 1980 and 1989. The arguments, which could become heated, were not due to my bad disposition or from any systemic institutional defect. Overall, I admired these hospitals and their medical and nursing staffs.

But nothing is perfect and too many mistakes were made to let pass without notice. A patient must assume some responsibility for his own care, but when that becomes impossible, another person often must act as his advocate. Otherwise, one can be neglected in a large bureaucratic organization such as a modern hospital or get lost in the cracks.

The young woman psychiatrist at South Wing, at UNC-CH, assigned to look after my teen-aged niece in 1971 meant well, but she was careless about keeping appointments, making records, checking patient charts and keeping medications straight. She was inconsistent in treatment, contradictory in advice, careless about security.

Admittedly I was under some stress myself and hence sometimes hyper-vigilant, cross and cranky. But I kept track, documented my observations and presented them to the doctor and her supervisors. As a result we all benefited and learned. At South Wing they couldn't even keep the clocks set properly. Every clock told a different time, none of them correct. Resetting the clocks for daylight-saving time was totally beyond their reach. For patients who are already uncertain about their sanity, it can be unsettling to read ten different times on the same hall.

Later at NIH I encountered a social worker who was tactless, secretive, defensive and I thought temperamentally unsuited for her job, which she appeared to dislike. She did not like my niece or her mother, so they came not to like or trust her. Soon the social worker came to dislike me as well. After a trial period, changes should be made if a patient and therapist aren't a good match. I was at NIH a lot so it was easy to keep watch. At last I confronted the woman with our dissatisfaction and recommended my niece be assigned to someone else. The therapist instead of cooperating became combative.

"You're interfering," she informed me. "You're a troublemaker. You're ungrateful." She warmed to her subject: "Do you realize we're providing your niece with treatment—much unavailable elsewhere—and at a cost of thousands and thousands of dollars —free of charge? Why, it's priceless! And you don't even appreciate it."

"My niece is here partly as an experiment. She is really your guinea pig," I replied. "You're glad to get her or you wouldn't have accepted her. And you don't know yet how valuable the drugs are. No matter what their cost, if they don't work, they're worthless. So far, I can see no improvement." I added that she and my niece weren't a good therapeutic match, an observation that should be viewed as constructive criticism, not a personal attack.

We took it up with the medical staff, and a change was made. My niece's doctor was a wise and confident man who encouraged family input and welcomed suggestions. I had no quarrel with him. But some of the psychiatrists on the staff seemed to need treatment themselves. They over-identified with their patients. I would find them huddled over and cuddled up with their charges so closely one couldn't tell who was doing what and to whom, much less why. Physician, heal thyself! But since those situations did not apply to my niece, I stayed out of that. Even so, the National Institutes of Mental Health seemed a far cry from the National Cancer Institute only a few floors below.

I preferred the psychiatric clinic at Duke Medical Center to South Wing at Chapel Hill or to NIMH, not to mention the now-defunct Pinebluff Sanatorium or the Johns Hopkins Hospital or Norton Infirmary of an earlier day. But on occasion you might not have guessed it, as on several occasions Duke too was found wanting and got told about it in no uncertain terms. I like to think we all benefited from such exchanges.

In 1974 Mother at eighty-two had fallen at her home in Monroe and broken her hip. Alone at the time, she was severely injured and could easily have died. Fortunately she was able to pull the telephone down and over to the floor beside her and call Uncle Vann. Soon she was in Memorial Hospital in Charlotte for the operation and then in rehabilitation. After several weeks she was on a walker and recuperating with Ann, Molly and me (and our two boxers Duchess and Daffy Down Dilly of Dilbury). Before long, probably out of habit, she lapsed into a depression.

This was no deep, endogenous depression. It was a superficial, reactive one. Even so, Mother when depressed was no day at the beach. After staying with us for three months, during which time she had extensive dental surgery, she was sent home with a highly-recommended practical nurse to live in with her and serve as her care provider. What I did not know until some weeks later was that the care provider was a spree drinker who was neglectful and when in her cups could act abusively. When Mary C., then in Monroe, discovered that, she dismissed the woman on the spot and literally drove her off that night. But what were we to do with Mother?

I called Duke and got her prompt admission. So there was Mother, in a clinic occupied by mostly young, physically fit patients, herself nearly eighty-three years old, able to move about only on a walker. Good help was expensive and hard to find. The prevailing philosophy was for the patients to do things for themselves—wash their own personal laundry, comb and set their own hair, go through the cafeteria line and serve themselves. All perfectly good practice for physically unimpaired patients. But for Mother? On a walker? Depressed, unmotivated, without appetite and elderly?

Mother liked Dr. Pfeiffer and so did I. He was a geriatric specialist who actually seemed to like and to understand old people. A rare bird. He took a special interest in Mother. He admired her intellect. He found her extraordinary. Mother had read that lithium helped depressed patients. He said the evidence did not support the belief that it was effective in unipolar or reactively depressed patients—only those in the manic phase of bipolar disorder, which she did not have. Nor had it ever been tried on people her age.

Mother was stubborn and persistent. "Come on, Doc, what's the problem? Why not try it?" I asked. He finally agreed. Mother stayed one month at Duke, showed little improvement. I took her back to Monroe with another caregiver and a bottle of lithium tablets. Before she left, Dr. Pfeiffer had accepted a position in Colorado. I went over one day to discover Mother with no food. The nursing staff apparently expected her to go through the cafeteria line, carrying her own tray as she gripped the walker with both hands, fearful as she was of another fall. That had been going on for days—ever since the doctor had gone. She hadn't even been seen by a replacement. Mother was undernourished, dehydrated, over-medicated and losing weight. That was when the nurses' station got instructions on how to treat physically disabled patients in Marine drill instructor language.

Rude, crude, impolite, not nice? "Hell, I'm not trying to be nice!" The thought occurred: I sound just like my father used to. But it was effective. The next evening I went over at mealtime to find a nurse helping Mother eat as a doctor stood by, talking to her. "Dr. Secrest, Duke is a great medical center. But sometimes we stink" the doctor said. "Thanks for your input."

Discharged and back home in Monroe again, Mother had still another caregiver. Mary Cov had found this one, who was another disappointment: cold-blooded, rough, uncaring, and none too bright. Just what Mother needed. One morning when this woman was sharply pulling back Mother's hair to put it up in a bun on the back of her neck, Mother winced, then depression turned outward into anger, and she snapped, "You're fired. Leave now and don't come back."

She asked Mary C. to take her for the weekend to Seabuoy II, the beach cottage Ann, Lil and I had bought a year before in North Myrtle Beach. They arrived in humid ninety-five degree heat, wilted but in good humor. "Man, am I hot!" Mother declared. "Get me a Gatorade." The lithium apparently had kicked in. That was on Lessie's eighty-third birthday, September 16, 1975.

Mother maintained her emotional equilibrium, getting younger and stronger every day. She maintained, however, her association with Duke and with Dr. Pfeiffer's successor. They quickly established a rapport. When Mother died seven years later, the doctor wrote a note to the family, expressing sympathy and declaring, confidentially, that "Mrs. Secrest was my favorite patient." The feeling was mutual. Mother admired him without reservation. That professional association later was extended on occasion to Lil and her daughter. They all agreed that the Duke doctor was the greatest.

But he and I did not always agree, although our differences lay with his support personnel, the nursing staff, over whom he had little control, or his resident associates. In April 1977, now eighty-four, while visiting Lil, Mother had a brief recurrence of depression, followed by an adverse reaction to lithium. She did not require hospitalization, however, and soon was back home, raking leaves and running her own household with far more energy and ability than her paid companion.

In July 1980, now 88, Mother had a mild stroke. Over several days she had become confused and disoriented. Her speech was affected, as was her eyesight. She lost her appetite. Given her history, Lil and I assumed she was also depressed.

Back I took her to Duke. There she became worse. When I went over to see her, she was lying on a narrow single hospital bed, no rail up, in a private room. No one was around. The bell at the head of the bed was out of her reach. When I rang it, it apparently was out of order, as no one answered, even after repeated attempts. Mother would get out of her bed onto her walker and go to the bathroom herself. The pitfalls were obvious. I went to the nurses' station. The nurses were busying themselves with charts, records, clerical work, the glass soundproof partition securely closed. No one looked up.

I found a pen and sheet of paper and made a list of things that needed to be done and a list of things that would probably happen if they weren't. First among them would be a fall from the bed if rails weren't erected and, at bed time, a strap placed across her legs to prevent her from getting up alone but not in such a way as to entangle her. I also wanted to be given names of recommended caregivers whom I could hire to be on duty at night to see that no accident would happen. My requests were ignored. But I had copies made and sent to the nurses' station, night duty nurse, supervisor of nurses, and other appropriate personnel.

The next afternoon I went over to see Mother again. She wasn't in her room. Where was she? I went to the nurses' station—door and window closed, heads down, eyes averted. I rapped on the glass so long and so loudly that someone was finally forced to answer. Where was the patient in Room 123? We don't know. Well, find out. They did. She was down in the basement getting X-rays to check for possible fractures from having fallen from the bed during the night.

I found my way ultimately to the X-ray room, discovered Mother alone, lying on an elevated, narrow metal examining table a good four feet off the floor and without benefit of any strap or restraining device. She was in the usual flimsy hospital garment, shivering in a room that could hardly have been 60 degrees Fahrenheit. Her mind was clearer, speech better, memory returning. We talked as we waited for forty-five more minutes until the technician reappeared. Mother had been left there stranded in the air for more than an hour. What might have happened had I not come to see her?

When I received a bill from Duke, unitemized, totaling thousands of dollars, I returned it with a request for a line-by-line explanation for each charge. Whenever I came across any charge that had to do with examination or treatment for injury caused by the fall from the hospital bed the night before, I crossed through it with a red pen. The new total—$750—I paid. It was accepted without question.

Later the doctor told Mother, "You have a caring and attentive son, but he does think he knows it all." My reply to her (but not to him): "That is because I do. And I am so tired of always being right." Jim Craven, mother's great nephew, was faithful in his visits to her at that time, just as he and his wife Sara had been when I was laid up in Duke Hospital the year before with a prostate cancer operation.

My last run-in with doctors at Duke occurred in 1988 when my niece had a brief recurrence of an old illness. She had been subjected to a lot of stress in her job teaching in the elementary grades of public school. Forty students to a classroom, no teaching assistant, required to give nursing services, even catheterization, to students for which she felt unqualified. So when a guest speaker from an administrative office in Raleigh addressed a teacher workshop and assembly, promising corrections to all these problems, she gave him the raspberry from the back of the room and declared she had heard that song before and walked out.

Soon she found herself a voluntary patient in Duke's psychiatric ward. That was all right with her. She probably did need help and was among friends, especially her old doctor. My niece had not been at Duke a week when I went over to see her. As a new patient she was in a closed ward, not allowed to see anyone but family members. Even I had to wait. As I did so, in walked a delegation from her school: the superintendent, the principal, the chairman of the school board, the board's attorney, and, in addition to all those, a lawyer from the North Carolina Department of Education.

How nice, I thought, for all these people to come see their colleague and to wish her well. How kind. How thoughtful. How considerate. I went over to speak to them. But they were there for another purpose. They wanted my niece's signature on a resignation form. The state attorney wanted it on another form. What for? Let me see it. I assumed they were there to fire my niece and to get her agreement not to contest it, despite her tenure protection, and to agree further not to seek a disability pension neither the state nor the school district wanted to pay.

"Well, you can't see her now," I assured them. "She has only recently been admitted. The doctor wouldn't hear of it." But her regular doctor wasn't on duty. Only the resident assistant was. It wasn't long before I saw her, alone, insecure, uncertain and non-assertive, walk into the room. Pretty soon the educational professionals and the two lawyers were all over her, handing her papers and pens to sign away whatever it was they wanted.

The resident appeared. "What do you mean allowing visitors in here in violation of hospital policy?" I asked. "Do you consider my niece on a level playing field with these people? Where's your obligation to protect your patient? Who's paying you, them or her? Whose side are you on, anyway? Do you think my niece will have any reason to trust you after this? Does your supervisor know you've given permission for this invasion of the patient's privacy? Do you know anything at all about patients' rights and confidentiality? Or about medical ethics?"

The doctor stared at me and at the educational delegation. "Well, what have you to say about all this?" I demanded.

"I'd say you would make a damned good patient advocate," the young man replied, and turning to my niece, said, "Let's go on back to the ward." It worked out okay for everyone concerned. But what if I hadn't been there?

A few weeks later my niece felt better. She wanted to go home. The doctors felt she wasn't ready. Neither did I. But she was determined and exercised her rights under recently passed patients-rights legislation, sponsored by Senator Ervin, to demand a court hearing. Her doctor was a female Iranian who spoke broken English, a poor choice for therapist, I thought, in view of the hostage-taking in Teheran in 1979-81 with the name of the Ayatollah Khomeini still clearly remembered. It was confusing enough for anyone, not to mention an emotionally agitated patient.

The young foreign doctor was little help in the courtroom. It fell upon me to testify before the judge that I felt my niece should remain somewhat longer under the care of the hospital for her own good. Five years later Cousin Vann and I had to perform the same favor for Mary Cov, now seventy-seven years old, frail and infirm, who had insisted upon leaving a Charlotte facility before she was ready and with no place else to go. In both Durham and Charlotte I found the medical and judicial systems woefully inadequate, the law poorly constructed, and the judges rude and unsympathetic to both patients and family, even if we did prevail.

But things, as usual, worked themselves out. My niece upon discharge rapidly improved. Within a few years she was married and has enjoyed since then good health and a useful, happy life. Now she and her husband have been able to provide her aging mother, a victim of Parkinsonism, the kind of tender loving care her mother had before given her.

*Family gathering at Dowd's funeral, Monroe 1946: Mac, Mary Cov, Aunt May, Mother, Aunt Sue, John Buie, Lil, Aunt Eve holding Kathy Buie's hand.*

*Gennie and Frank Shubeck, seated bride and groom, with Gennie's sister as maid of honor and Mac as best man, Detroit 1947.*

*Ann and Mac Secrest on their wedding day, 1948.*

*Liberty Belle of Mazelaine, first in our long line of boxers, 1948.*

*Ann and Kathy Buie, flower girls at family wedding, Wagram 1948.*

*The Carpenter house, our first home in Monroe, 1948.*

*Nancy and Bill Price, just married in Rocky Mount NC, 1950, with Mac as best man and Nancy's sisters as flower girls.*

*Ann, Phil, Mac, David, and Misty at the Seabuoy I, Garden City SC, 1953.*

*Mary Cov, Mary Ann, Sue and Bill English, 1951.*

*Sue English, 1953.*

*Mary Ann English, 1953*

*"Mammy Mary" Simmons with twins Andy and Bella English, 1954.*

*Cousins Ann and Kathy Buie standing behind Phil and David, Cheraw 1954.*

*Lessie's passport picture after her recovery in 1954.*

*Home from Harvard, Cheraw SC 1961.*

*Celeste and Jim Buie with David, Phil and Molly, Cheraw 1961.*

*Molly, Little Red School House (kindergarten) graduate, 1963.*

*Mac at 40, as racial conciliator with Community Relations Service in Washington D.C. 1963.*

*David, valedictorian of the Cheraw H.S. class of 1968.*

*Molly "Finale" in middle school, Chapel Hill NC, 1969.*

*Jane Clayton and Phil, Junior-Senior Banquet, Cheraw 1969.*

*Phil with John Bartley, Cheraw 1969.*

*Our cabin on Mt. Mitchell, Burnsville NC 1971.*

*Mindy and David cut the cake, 1973.*

*Mac, Ann, Molly, Mindy & David at a family wedding, 1976.*

*Lessie the phoenix at 88, 1980.*

# Part IV

# Professional Life

# 1950-1985

# 46. Cheraw: A Country Journalist

What I have told so far of my adult life is not the whole story. A large part has been spent in other pursuits of my own choosing. I have enjoyed two careers, one as editor-publisher of a weekly newspaper during a bitter racial and sectional divide when the deep South was saying "Never." The other was a long-delayed arrival into Academia, an ambition from early childhood that I thought would never be realized. I have largely liked whatever I did and seldom failed. But in retrospect I find that I practiced better than I preached.

My experience as a Southern newspaper editor began in Cheraw, S.C. in March, 1953, the year before the United States Supreme Court in Brown I ruled segregation in the public schools unconstitutional, and ended fifteen years later in 1968 after passage of the Civil Rights Act of 1964 and the Voting Rights Acts of 1965 and 1966.

In between I spent one year at Harvard University as a Nieman Fellow (1960-61) and two years as a racial mediator with the Community Relations Service housed first in the Department of Commerce and then in the Civil Rights Division of the Justice Department (1964-66). These were years of social change and political turbulence, recognized today as a Second Reconstruction. The post-Depression, post-World War II South was already moving—from agrarian to industrial, rural to urban, poverty toward prosperity. Now it had to move "with all deliberate speed" from racial separation toward integration.

Cheraw, South Carolina, was in many ways similar to my home town of Monroe, forty-eight miles up the road in Union County, North Carolina. One hundred years older, it had even more curious characters about whom one could spin yarns for years. But these will have to be told by someone else. Cheraw was a growing, prosperous community, deserving of its self-designated title: "Cheraw—the Tip Top Town: Prettiest Town in Dixie." I thought it would be a comfortable place in which to live, work, and raise a growing family. So I bought the *Cheraw Chronicle*, a weekly newspaper with a tradition dating to 1819. It had been operated for years by printers who had little understanding of what a community newspaper might achieve.

Cheraw is located in the sand hills of north central South Carolina on the banks of the Pee Dee River, one hundred and ten miles from Chapel Hill, seventy-five miles southeast of Charlotte, ninety-eight miles from Myrtle Beach and one hundred miles northeast of Columbia. Cheraw is the largest town in Chesterfield County but not the county seat, that distinction belonging to the town of Chesterfield, twelve miles northwest.

A black belt town in a red clay county, it was settled early by planters and tradesmen who enjoyed a prosperous commerce on the Pee Dee River with earlier settlers from Georgetown and Charleston. It was an active trading village by 1730 and a thriving town by 1776. In the churchyard of Old St. David's Anglican Church (1767) lie buried British Redcoats and Hessians from General Cornwallis's army which occupied the town in 1781, later to be joined by Union and Confederate soldiers who fell in battle on Market Street when Sherman marched through in 1865. Sherman briefly made Cheraw his headquarters, and the town was spared the torch, it is said, because of his friendship with a Confederate general from Cheraw who had been his classmate at West Point.

Still standing on the town green is the old law office where, it is alleged, the South Carolina Ordinances of Secession were first drafted. Nearby stand the Old Slave Market (1836) and Town Hall (1838). Farther along Market and Third Streets you'll find a Catholic church built in 1828 as well as many other dwellings and structures dating from the Colonial Era, the Federal Period, and Antebellum times. Washington slept there; Lafayette danced there; and Sherman ruled there, and all the houses where these momentous events occurred still stand there.

In the *Chronicle's* files is a notice from an issue dated 1831 that refers to a group of cotton merchants returning home from a business trip "to the little village of Charlotte." By 1852, Cheraw may have been larger than either Charlotte or Atlanta. But the town languished after the Civil War and the First Reconstruction, apparently asleep, perchance to dream of past glories. In 1953, the population was listed as 5000, of whom 35 percent or so were African-Americans. But the city limits hadn't been changed in many years, and there were at least 15,000 people living in the Cheraw school attendance area and another 50,000 in Chesterfield County, as well as many others just across the river in Marlboro County.

While the *Chronicle* ultimately garnered its fifteen minutes of fame— or infamy—from its stance on race relations, it was equally noted at home for its local news coverage and community service, irrespective of race. The challenge was how to cover the news fairly and accurately and still survive. Supposedly nothing ever happens in a small town. As it turned out, everything happened in this small town, and people, often already clued in, would read the local newspaper to see how much the editor dared to print.

There was seldom a lack of sources for news or of subscribers eager to read about the activities, good and bad, of their neighbors. And while everyone seemed to be all for a free press, when their particular ox was gored, they then, of course, wanted to shoot the messenger. In the course of my tenure, I was, literally and figuratively, shot at. But as people came to appreciate the proper role of an editor, acceptance replaced suspicion, and many even grew protective of their eccentric editor, replying in effect to outside critics, "Well, he may be a son of a bitch, but at least he's our son of a bitch."

It is said that names make news, and nothing succeeds like success. In telling this tale of people, great and small, and of battles, won and lost, I drop a few names and claim credit where credit is due, without false modesty. I operated the *Chronicle* as a throw-back to the 19th century penny press: personal, partisan, combative, sometimes subjective, a harbinger of the old "New Journalism" yet to come. I was big on civic journalism. But I was guided by these journalistic commandments:

An editor should tell people what they need to know, not just what they want to hear.

In setting the news agenda, an editor should not tell people what to think, but what to think about.

In preparing his editorial menu, an editor should provide food for thought in a palatable way that helps his readers digest it.

A community newspaper editor should avoid "Afghanistanism," the practice of "viewing with alarm" and "pointing with pride" to those things far from home and ignoring problems close at hand.

An editor must do for his subscribers what they cannot do for themselves—gather, report, edit, and interpret news, including meetings held and business conducted behind closed doors or in executive session.

An editor automatically becomes part of the power structure. But he must occasionally step aside from it, free to report, comment, and criticize without succumbing to pressures to conform. There is an inherent conflict of interest that can never be completely resolved. One must also understand what a community is. A town is far more than its Chamber of Commerce, its business, civic, and religious leaders, and its professional organizations and cheerleaders. It is a combination of all kinds of people, races, classes, and cultures, often divided by clashing interests but all united by a common bond, their sense of place. Each group is entitled to representation in its newspaper.

An individual plays many roles as editor: doctor, lawyer, teacher, judge, preacher, and politician, with a mission to "comfort the afflicted and to afflict the comfortable." An editor must also be aware of the cult of personality. It is essential that his readers support him, often by unconsciously adopting his ideas as their own.

I was sitting at the typewriter on a Monday afternoon in 1958 when the phone rang—a long-distance call for A.M. Secrest. "Who do I know from Chicago. Oh, it must be Phil Frye, hoping to get a rise out of me about Ike and his latest efforts to lift the country out of its recession."

"Hey, is this the editor of the *Cheraw Chronicle*?" inquired a 'colored' voice, as people said back then.

"Yes. Who's this?"

"Man, what kind of guy is writing that stuff about white and colored folks living together equally? Is you crazy?" Then a hearty laugh, followed by an introduction, "This is Dizzy Gillespie talking. I wuz born and raised in Cheraw. My aunt sends me my hometown newspaper. I've been wondering 'bout you." He pronounced the name of the town like all natives do—"Chee'raw."

Gillespie, who had developed a transitional sound in pop music— somewhere between rhythm and blues and soul, known as Bebop—had become famous for his new technique on the trumpet. Unlike trained musicians who compress their lips and hold in their cheeks while blowing the horn, Gillespie's cheeks expanded until he resembled a bullfrog. It was a wonder he didn't blow his eardrums out or damage his mastoid bones.

"Secrest, I'm gonna come down to Chee´raw one of these days soon and meet 'the man,'" Dizzy declared. "And tell Mr. Jim Powe hello for me. The Powes and Gillespies (the white ones) owned my family way back yonder. Tell 'im Ah'm gonna ride up in a big limousine and come in the front do'," he added, and rang off.

Gillespie, a sophisticated, educated man, was a natural story teller and put on "black speech" whenever he elected to play the role of a "darkie" for mocking effect. He did this in a humorous, good-natured way, never with malice or self-deprecation.

Our paths crossed several times, not only in Cheraw but also years later in a classroom at UNC and later still at our home in Chapel Hill at a time of personal loss. A member of the Ba'hai faith, which is ruthlessly persecuted in Islamic lands, particularly Iran, Gillespie neither drank nor smoked nor swore, viewed all people equally and treated everyone with compassion. I never saw him in ill-humor.

In January 1959 I had the idea of a Dizzy Gillespie Day and got the Cheraw mayor, council, and chamber of commerce behind it. They then organized the whole affair. The idea was to demonstrate that whereas in 1958 a crowd drove Nat King Cole, a native son, from the concert stage in Birmingham, Cheraw honored its native son with pride, white and black together.

So the town did proclaim a Dizzy Gillespie Day in February 1959, complete with a downtown parade, civic banquet and key to the city. It made good sense—politically, economically, racially, and morally—and reflected well upon Cheraw in the national news.

The editor's job is a demanding one, in which his reach always exceeds his grasp. But you've still got to try to get it right, for if you ever become a mouthpiece for any particular group instead of the entire diverse community, you either go broke or become a prostitute who accepts the dictum, "Whose bread I eat, his song I sing."

I understood this. P.D. East, publisher of the *Pedal Paper* in Magnolia, Mississippi, was less fortunate. East struck an early courageous note against racial injustice, but in such a careless and misguided manner that he alienated everybody and ultimately was reduced to bragging that his was the only newspaper in the country without a single paid subscriber in his home town.

Predictably he went broke, exerted no influence on public opinion and could, therefore, make no contribution to social change. Instead, he became dependent on hand-outs from groups in faraway places such as Oregon and Wisconsin and remained largely irrelevant to problems close to home. In contrast, the *Chronicle* managed to deal honestly with race relations at home and abroad over a 15-year period, combining information and civil discourse in the newspaper with participation on human relations boards, civil rights committees and interracial councils, and did so while increasing paid circulation, advertising lineage and net profit every year.

Fellow white liberals whom I remember most clearly working with in those times were James McBride Dabbs, a genuine South Carolina aristocrat who lived on his plantation in Mayesville; Leslie Dunbar, director of the Southern Regional Council in Atlanta; Marion Wright, an attorney from Conway, S.C. and later president of North Carolinians against Capital Punishment; Alice Spearman, a real Southern belle, if an aging one, who was director of the South Carolina Council on Human Relations in Columbia; and Courtney Siceloff, director of Penn Community Services in Frogmore, St. Helena's Island, S.C. Alice combined beauty and brains with a magnanimous spirit. Later she and Marion Wright married. Ann and I often visited them at their home in Linville Falls, N.C., not far from our mountain cabin near Burnsville some years after we had moved to Chapel Hill.

The job of community editor was never easy. In 1954 and 1955, after the Brown I and II decisions, I pointed out that Supreme Court opinions that exercised judicial oversight of laws passed by the legislative branch had been accepted as part our constitutional system since *Marbury vs. Madison* in 1803. I advised calm compliance with the decisions, as their full implication was revealed over the next few years.

Over the ensuing years, the Chronicle stood for law and order and cooperation and discussion among whites and blacks and against demagogic political leaders and state massive resistance laws, which could (and did) lead to years of racial strife, domestic discord, regional antagonism, personal injustices, and a weakening of the moral fabric of the country. I believed that the court decisions were right, morally and legally. It was clear, furthermore, where the power lay and who would ultimately prevail, and having, as a white child of the Old South, lost one cause, I saw nothing romantic about losing another.

I have never taken to role models or to hero worship. I am too aware of the clay in the feet of my idols, thanks to my early relationship with my father. By now, what would you expect me to say, raised as I was on the teat of Freud and psychoanalysis?

I have had a few heroes: Roosevelt, Churchill, the stable of CBS radio foreign correspondents in World War II, Roy Wilkins (Executive Director of the NAACP 1955-77), and, fleetingly, Adlai Stevenson and JFK. That's about it, except for two small-town editors, William Allen White of Emporia Kansas, who provided important assistance to Great Britain during the contest between isolationists and interventionists in 1940 and 1941, and Hodding Carter, Jr., of Greenville MS, whose example above all else influenced me to become a journalist.

I met Carter at last in the fall of 1955 when he delivered a lecture at Coker College in Hartsville, S.C., 25 miles from Cheraw. President Robert, who had taught history at Duke fifteen years earlier, invited me, and I asked Walter and Dale Spearman at UNC to join us.

Carter was nationally known as a voice of reason on race relations in a Mississippi otherwise gone mad. He was not a disappointment. I placed him on the Chronicle's mailing list and we later exchanged letters and phone calls. He even expressed a hope that his son "young Hodding" and I could some day edit a newspaper together.

Hodding Carter III is thirteen years younger than I, and I didn't meet him until May 1989, well after his term as press secretary to President Jimmy Carter. Ann and I were in Upton, Mass., awaiting the birth of grandson Abraham Alexander, when a dinner was scheduled at Harvard to honor retiring Nieman Curator Howard Simons, who was terminally ill with cancer. It was a poignant evening.

Since Ann elected to stay home with Molly, I asked niece Bella English, a columnist with the *Boston Globe*. At our table were three members of my Nieman class of 1960-61, Ellen Goodman, syndicated *Globe* columnist and her husband Peter, Belle, and I. Seated at the next table were Hodding Carter III and his wife. He was easy to recognize, and I introduced myself. Gifted with Mississippi charm as well as professional ability, he instantly recalled who I was. His father had died, but his mother was still alive and well at her Greenville home.

Hodding and I hit it off right from the start. His father was right, we would have been a good team, but Hodding III had long since moved far ahead of me. I saw him on other occasions when he came to Chapel Hill, the last time in the mid-'90s. The Greenville newspaper remained a family-owned enterprise but Hodding never returned to Mississippi to run it. Today he is president of the John S. and James L. Knight Foundation in Miami, active in promoting ethics in journalism and devoted to improving the quality of the mass media.

In 1955 the *Cheraw Chronicle* and briefly the *Florence Morning News* were alone among South Carolina newspapers in refusing to trumpet abuse of Negroes, their organizations and leaders, and any white moderates who diverged from the official party line of the state political establishment. Surprisingly, we developed a considerable amount of support in town. Governor George Bell Timmerman and House Speaker Sol Blatt, leader of the "Barnwell Ring" that spawned Strom Thurmond, led the public to accept the results of the infamous "Thou Shall Not" sessions of the S. C. General Assembly in 1956-57. The new laws, among other things, outlawed the NAACP, infringed upon academic freedom, and arranged to shut down the schools, universities, parks and all public accommodations and facilities (if they might ever come under court order to integrate). Indeed so much was forbidden and curtailed, and everyone's constitutional rights so trammeled, that visitors often remarked that South Carolina by 1958 resembled South Africa more than any other Southern state. Timmerman and his successor Fritz Hollings seemed to vie with Faubus of Arkansas, Wallace of Alabama, and Maddox of Georgia for the title, Most Racist Governor in the South.

As the crisis deepened through the years 1956-1964, I occasionally received unsigned hate mail and anonymous telephone calls. Signs reading "For Sale" and "Moving Out" appeared in the front yard. Occasional pellets peppered our living room picture window. These threats, plus ample evidence of violence against people and property elsewhere, prompted me to take certain precautions. I'd place a penny on the window of my car or tie a thread from hood to bumper. If the penny had dropped or the thread was broken, I'd check to make sure I hadn't been booby-trapped.

In 1957 I was one of several people statewide to contribute to a publication of essays entitled: *South Carolinians Speak: a Moderate Approach to Race Relations*. It was the brain child of Episcopalian minister John Morris, a red-haired native of Georgia who had married Patsy Pratt of New York and Massachusetts, whose grandfather had been co-founder with John D. Rockefeller of the Standard Oil Co. John at the time was minister in Dillon, thirty miles from Cheraw. He was a genuine liberal in race relations. He could afford to be, but that shouldn't lessen appreciation of his devotion to the cause. Our friendship has continued even into his and Patsy's retirement in Atlanta.

Public reaction was mixed. One contributor's house was fire-bombed. Another was intimidated into recantation. Some withdrew into silence. Others, including me, just hung in there. So my concern about car bombs and booby traps was not entirely misplaced.

# 47. "Wild Bill," Thurmond, and the KKK

I never really knew, however, whether threats I received over these years emanated from racial tension or simply came from people whose ox I may have gored through routine reporting and commentary on the news. Here are a few examples of such journalistic enterprise, which had nothing to do with race.

*The Chronicle* exposed the use by Marlboro County's Senator Paul Wallace of state Highway Department labor and materials to build a dam on his farm. He was forced to repay the state and the chief highway commissioner apologized for his role in the scheme. We researched the record of Wallace's son Tom, who had been made a highway patrolman without proper qualifications or training. His record revealed several drunk driving convictions and vehicular homicide. These revelations resulted in the patrolman's resignation and brought a pledge from the commander of the South Carolina Highway Patrol that greater care would be taken in future appointments.

Another story resulted in the defeat of the county coroner "Son" Redfearn in the upcoming election after he had ruled accidental death in the case of an elderly woman whose body, clad only in her thin nightgown, was found in 18-degree weather, stuffed in the backseat of her car, while a transient lodger was missing with her car keys and pocketbook.

The coroner's brother, probate judge William Redfearn, soon followed suit after a kidnapping and shooting gone wrong. The judge had been campaigning for re-election in an auto tour of Chesterfield County. Propped up beside him was a 45-year-old mummy called "Spaghetti," an embalmed body the candidate had snatched earlier in the day from a funeral parlor in Laurinburg.

Judge Redfearn, a "good ole' boy" who proudly went by "Wild Bill" or "Sweet William," was performing to the applause of his largely rural, red-neck and rough-neck constituents. But on this occasion one of "Wild Bill's" former buddies, who had recently found the Lord, stepped out from the crowd assembled in front of the Court House in Chesterfield and called to him: "Bill, Bill! Stop! Don't act like this. Give up your sinful and godless ways and follow me. You need the church, Bill! And the church needs you!" Whereupon "Sweet William"—or should I say "Wild Bill"— spouted a few choice S— and F— words, drew his pistol from his pocket and shot his erstwhile friend dead on the spot. Just another day in the life of a candidate on the political hustings in Chesterfield County.

Redfearn was tried and convicted on a manslaughter charge and given six years in prison. While awaiting trial he campaigned for re-election behind bars, using surrogate speakers on the stump and broadcasting on the radio by audiotape recordings. When the votes were tallied, the election ended in a tie. The County Election Board, unable to reach a decision, sent the case to the State Election Board, which ultimately referred it to the state Supreme Court. The Court ruled a man in prison could not effectively perform his official duties and handed the office to reform candidate Margie Pusser of Pageland. Within a few years Redfearn was out of jail and back home in Chesterfield with his South American lover and boasting that he had never lacked for cigarettes, booze, drugs, or sex either, while he did his time.

It was not too long after that incident that Senator Wallace met his fate. He was shot dead on election night by his disappointed opponent, Marlboro County Clerk of Court Rogers, who had led in the balloting all evening only to lose in the final minutes as late-arriving ballot boxes, bearing possible evidence of tampering, robbed him of his victory. Voters took their politics seriously in the sand hills of South Carolina.

Did the *Chronicle* ever endorse candidates in local elections? Sometimes. An official in the South Carolina General Assembly, believing one good term deserved another, was running for re-election. But despite his many qualifications and assets—scion of an old and distinguished family, lots of money and a fine education (UNC undergraduate, Columbia University Law School, Rhodes scholar)—his public performance was deeply flawed. He had placed private interest above public gain. And although he must have known better, he supported both in and out of office all the racially hateful legislation during the "Thou Shalt Not" session of the legislature.

Nor did we find his domestic agenda progressive. A public library? Not needed. A county bookmobile can meet community needs. A school lunch program? Too expensive. The kids can take an orange to school. No, he didn't quite say, "Let them eat cake." A county hospital? A waste of money. "Mac, we'd never use it. We'd go to Duke or Charleston, wouldn't we?" And never mind, apparently, all those who couldn't afford out-of-town medical care. Old Commodore Vanderbilt couldn't have said it better: "The public be damned."

Yet this man, like Caesar's wife, remained "above suspicion," even after it was learned that he was both the attorney and the only beneficiary named in the will of his recently deceased maid and long-time family retainer. She had many relatives who could have benefited from her meager estate. Talk about paternalism. Talk about *noblesse oblige*. No one, it seemed, was willing to observe: "But the emperor wears no clothes."

Fed up with his unearned pristine reputation, I decided to oppose his re-election, which he was heavily favored to win. In the first of a series of editorials, I proclaimed, to get readers' attention, "We've got news for you folks. Your senatorial candidate is not God. He's not even Jesus Christ. And it is sacrilegious to worship graven images, dead or alive."

Later I observed in quieter tones that "this political emperor is not only unclothed but stands naked of any political principle except to win this election" and proceeded to document the case against him. After the campaign smoke had cleared and votes were counted, the legislator was down by sixty-seven votes. Shortly thereafter I received in the mail a picture of a Bengal tiger. Beneath the picture, the candidate had written, "Why bother to be merely unpleasant when, with a little more effort, you could be a real son of a bitch?"

When the Hospital Board selected Cheraw as the site for the Chesterfield County Memorial Hospital in 1957, using Hill-Burton federal money to fund the project, a great hue and cry arose. People in the town of Chesterfield and those living farther west protested that Cheraw was not in a central location and was unfairly favored. When argument failed, a suit was brought against the Board. The case on appeal wound up in the South Carolina Supreme Court.

The *Cheraw Chronicle* had been in the thick of the fight, first to secure a hospital and second to locate the facility in Cheraw. It became both a hot political and legal issue. L.C. Wannamaker, a trial lawyer and political maverick, was the *Chronicle's* attorney. Mr. Wannamaker was a member of the Wannamaker-Duvall family dynasty, an old, large and extended family that exercised considerable influence and control over local affairs. Its members were social arbiters and largely in the conservative camp. But L.C. (Caston) Wannamaker was not. He was a yellow dawg Democrat to the bone. He also represented the have-nots in Cheraw and sided with the Court House gang more often than with his kith and kin.

An elderly, courtly figure, Caston was old enough to be my father. He adopted an avuncular attitude toward me, approving of my Democratic editorial policies and even defending what my more conservative vocal critics called my "nigger-loving" ways. Caston had in his day been a political figure in his own right, running and nearly winning the position of lieutenant governor in 1912. His great nephew was Paul Hardin, who seriously considered going into practice with his uncle in 1946. Hardin decided, however, to return to his home town of Charlotte, although he remained a frequent visitor to his Cheraw relatives. He later became chancellor of the University of North Carolina at Chapel Hill and remains today a well-known figure in the Research Triangle Park cities of Durham, Raleigh and Chapel Hill.

Hardin's Uncle Caston was like a figure out of some Dickens novel. His smooth, suave, diplomatic manner concealed a certain devious streak. In some ways Wannamaker was a lovable, ruthless rogue. He was a portly man, and when amused he would giggle until his false teeth clacked. Were he to audition for a Warner Brothers movie starring Humphrey Bogart, he would be cast as British actor Sidney Greenstreet. He was exactly the kind of lawyer I wanted to help keep me out of trouble.

One day Caston came by my office. "Mac, what say you and I take a little trip down to Columbia tomorrow?"

"What for, Caston? What's up?"

"Well, you know the hospital case is coming up soon. My Wofford College classmate is Chief Justice of the State Supreme Court, you know, and I thought perhaps you would like to meet him." Well, yes, I acknowledged, that would be interesting.

"Now, you understand, of course, we cannot discuss any aspect of the case before the court," Caston cautioned me.

"No, no, of course not. That would be the epitome of impropriety," I agreed, in all naive sincerity.

But there would be no harm in letting the jurist know of our interest in the case and his meeting Caston's young journalist friend who had been so instrumental in arousing public interest in a humanitarian situation so important to everyone in Chesterfield County. No, no, no harm at all.

So Caston and I drove to Columbia, had lunch with the Chief Justice, with the smooth old attorney hosting the affair and in the most subtle manner imaginable, laying out hypotheticals about reasonable hospital locations, without once mentioning Cheraw or Chesterfield County. As we were about to leave after the two-martini lunch, I saw the judge wink at Caston and say, *sotto voce*, "I've got the picture, friend. You and your little editor don't have a thing to worry about."

A few weeks later a decision in the hospital case was handed down. The hospital was to be located in Cheraw. The legal opinion dealt with statistics, census tables, industrial employees, hospital insurance policies, Hill-Burton federal funds and state finances, and various legal terms and precedents. But I believe the real deal had gone down in that Columbia restaurant many weeks earlier.

Another political lesson learned. Judges do decide cases on considerations other than the law. Sometimes influence, friendship and old school ties play a part in public controversies that are part legal, part political—at least they did in South Carolina in the late 1950s. Many Democrats believe this lesson was demonstrated again on the national scene in December, 2000, when, they claim, George W. Bush was "selected," "appointed" and "anointed" President of the United States.

Did I make enemies as a country editor? Probably, though that was never my intention. And not very many friends but plenty of opponents and allies. Alliances are made, break up, and reform, as the occasion requires. Friends are forever. The editor's chair is a poor place to make new ones. My opponents were usually bigger than I and always in the public eye and hence, fair game.

Did I ever report rumor and gossip? Sometimes. If I believed there were substance behind the talk and had made every effort to determine the facts, but had been stymied, stumped, and stonewalled by the persons involved and if the reports involved public figures and the public interest, I would usually go with the story. It was sometimes the only way to smoke people out and arrive at the truth. Under such circumstances, the public interest outweighed the private right.

I tangled with U.S. Senator Strom Thurmond in 1967 when he came to Cheraw and urged local civic and political leaders to form "safety committees" to censor what school children could read and to purge the shelves of the public and school libraries of any books that even implied acceptance of integration and thus posed a threat to "our Southern way of life." Senator Thurmond was keynote speaker at the annual joint meeting of the Greater Pee Dee Area Medical Association and the South Carolina Bar Association held in Cheraw that year.

As publisher of the town's only newspaper, I was invited to sit on the dais with officials and featured speaker. I listened, took notes, wrote an objective story, quoting the Senator carefully. Then I put on my editor's hat and wrote an opinion piece titled "A Profile in Extremism." To add insult to injury, that article won first place for editorial writing in the annual South Carolina Press Association contest. Outgoing governor Donald Russell made the presentation at the banquet in Columbia which the Senator attended.

The following year the Senator and I were on the same flight to National Airport in Washington. Seeing a familiar face but clearly unable to place me, Senator Thurmond asked if I would like a lift into town. "Why, thank you, sir," I replied. "That is very kind of you." To satisfy his curiosity, I identified myself. The Senator stopped abruptly, peered into my face, shook his head and snapped, "Forget it," leaving me to get to Bethesda the best way I could.

Thurmond had a remarkable career. The people wrote in his name for U.S. Senator in 1954, as a protest to the U.S. Supreme Court's Brown decision. No candidate had ever been elected by a spontaneous write-in vote in the history of the state. They re-elected him time and again. He served longer than any other senator in history, until his death at nearly 101 in 2003. His defenders say he mellowed and changed with the times. Why, he even eventually appointed black people to his staff.

But the record will show he was well past fifty when he first went to Washington, nearing sixty when he conducted a one-man filibuster against a pallid civil rights bill in 1958, and nearing seventy when he launched his tirade against the First Amendment in Cheraw and sought to intimidate not only his black constituents but also white progressives with whom he disagreed. It was a conversion too late in the coming ever favorably to impress me.

When widely known rumors about Senator Thurmond's having sired a black child out of wedlock were confirmed in December 2003, I wasn't surprised. It was common knowledge in Cheraw in the mid-1950s. I don't think any better or worse of Sen. Thurmond for his "youthful indiscretion," although he was 22 years old and had taken advantage of a sixteen-year-old servant in his parents' home. Some people might consider that statutory rape. But it was hardly an unusual event in the early twentieth century South.

Indeed, it reminded me of my grandfather David Covington's indiscretions with Miz Thompson two generations earlier. But at least Ms. Thompson's mother was an older, married woman and there was no racial implication. I'm willing to give credit to the senator for acknowledging his relationship to his daughter when she was sixteen years old and lending her affection and emotional support and some rather meager financial help as well. But on balance, my opinion of Sen. Thurmond hasn't changed. He was a hypocrite, and he placed his political ambitions above the good of his progeny and of his country.

I had occasion to brush against the Ku Klux Klan three times. Once was in Alabama when co-worker Abe Venable, black, and I, white, occupied a motel room in the mid-1960s when we were on a racial conciliation mission with the Community Relations Service. When we turned off the television and were ready to sleep, we heard voices from the next room. They belonged to members of the local Klan, talking about plans to frustrate the Feds who were coming to Lownes County to force race mixing and miscegenation upon the God-fearing white people there. We kept quiet the rest of that night, slept in late the next morning and reported the incident to the F.B.I., and that was the last anyone ever heard about that.

The next time was when the Grand Wizard of South Carolina held a meeting in a barren, wind-swept cotton field one winter night two miles across the Pee Dee River in Marlboro County. They had invited Eddie Sweatt and Kevin Mackey, *Chronicle* associate editor and photographer, and me to sit on the platform. To their surprise, we showed up and listened as they harangued Cheraw's "nigger-loving newspaper" and all those "wishy-washy civic leaders" we had "brainwashed" over the past dozen years.

Eddie calmly recorded the proceedings which we dutifully reported in the next issue of the paper. We weren't foolhardy. In anticipation we had notified the sheriffs of Chesterfield and Marlboro Counties who were also on hand. And these sheriffs were nothing like Sheriff Price in Philadelphia, Mississippi, who had presided over the deaths of several young men with the Student Non-Violent Coordinating Committee (SNCC) in July, 1964. Burke Marshall, chief of the Civil Rights Division of the Justice Department, and I were monitoring events in Washington when news of the bodies endammed in Philadelphia reached us.

The last time I had any truck with the Ku Klux Klan was when I was still working in Washington. Eddie called to say the F.B.I. had infiltrated the Cheraw Hunt and Rifle Association and had discovered it was a front for the Klan. Names I would never have associated with it appeared on its membership rolls. Later, hearings were held in the capital and charges were brought. But I never felt that this group constituted any personal danger. The members were young, dumb, largely uneducated. Their activities seemed to provide them a social outlet. The Cheraw black population didn't appear any more intimidated than Eddie or I.

# 48. Chutzpah

The job of a community newspaper editor can be demanding. I had to work hard, first with Mayor Russell Bennett, then with Mayor Miller Ingram, to help establish a county hospital, a tech school and a community college, and to keep open the Cheraw State Park and town library, despite efforts by state leaders to close both or to convert them to private use to prevent even token integration.

The job is not for a shrinking violet. I learned to become self-assertive. I relied on lessons learned early from my Methodist upbringing. "Seek and ye shall find. Knock and the door shall be opened. Don't hide your light under a bushel."

I brought this advice into play in March, 1963. President Kennedy had initiated a "seduce-the-press" program, in which he invited editors and publishers to White House luncheons for an exchange of views and an inside look into his administration. Yet, when South Carolina's turn came, I was ignored. There were few daily newspapers in the Palmetto State. The luncheon was to be small, up close and personal.

Among the several men and women invited, few were supporters of the President. They were Republicans in Democratic clothing. I had supported JFK for the nomination, had written speeches for his campaign in the fall of 1960 when I was at Harvard. I had stuck up for him in 1962 when he had to send U.S. Marshals, soon reinforced by an airborne division, to Ole Miss to enforce a federal court decree—over the armed opposition of Governor Ross Barnett—requiring the admittance of James Meredith, the first African-American to be accepted there. Now I was to be overlooked?

438

Impulsively I reached for the typewriter, banged out a letter to Press Secretary Pierre Salinger, giving him all the reasons I should be invited. I sent copies to Luther H. Hodges, Kennedy's Secretary of Commerce, to my congressman, to North Carolina Senators Sam Ervin and Everett Jordan, and to Senator Hart of Michigan, at whose behest I had earlier gone to Washington to speak on behalf of pending civil rights legislation.

Back came a letter from Salinger, expressing appreciation for past favors rendered. He acknowledged my political support, but rules were rules. And the rules specified that only publishers of daily newspapers were to be invited, plus the officers of the state press association. That left me out.

I answered immediately, asking who made the rules, if not the President's press secretary? "Who said rules couldn't be changed? And since when did the Kennedys themselves always play by the rules? Unless I hear to the contrary, I will appear at the West Gate on April 11 for the luncheon. Thanks in advance for the invitation." Again, copies were mailed out to people in high places in Washington.

The following week I received a telegram. "You are invited to have lunch with the President on April 11." It included detailed instructions.

Martha Hodges invited me to stay with them. Lacking an extra guest room, she asked Senator and Mrs. Sam Ervin to put me up for the night. The President seemed impressed when I told him the next day that Chesterfield County, with an overwhelmingly Protestant population, had voted more heavily for him proportionately than any other county in the country, a fact for which I gave the *Chronicle* considerable credit. Later I told Mr. Kennedy that while many people in South Carolina were now divided in their political support, they were united in their pleasure at the prospect of the birth of the first baby in the White House since the administration of Grover Cleveland. The President looked surprised, even stammered, as he replied "Oh, uh, no, Mr. Secrest, you're, uh, confusing Jackie with Ethel. She and Bobby are the ones always having children." Martha Hodges and Mrs. Ervin had been my sources. They weren't likely to have made it up or have been misled. They had said nothing about the pregnancy being a secret or the story regarded as confidential.

The luncheon lasted until mid-afternoon. Some of my colleagues later said that I had talked too much and was inclined to monopolize the conversation. I replied that was because most of them were too witless to ask questions, let alone have opinions. When we met reporters outside, headed by Merriman Smith, dean of the White House Press Corps, they bombarded us with questions. I had earlier gone by the office of James O. (Scotty) Reston, Bureau chief and syndicated columnist of the *New York*

*Times*, and his assistant Tom Wicker, and promised to give them a report of any part of the conversation not considered off the record. Now I did have the denial by the President of any White House pregnancy.

The next day the *Times* printed the denial. The following day Pierre Salinger confirmed the report that Mrs. Kennedy was expecting the couple's third child in September. Unwittingly, I had smoked them out. The *Times*, struck by the contradictions, joshed in its capital column the next day that Jack and Jackie should establish a hotline, similar to the one recently set up between Kennedy and Khrushchev, so they could know what was going on between them.

I had been equally self assertive a few weeks earlier when Senator Hart of Michigan asked me to testify before his committee on the 1963 Civil Rights bill. The committee's counsel, a Mr. Creech from Wilmington and an Ervin appointee, sought to minimize everything I had to say. Finally in cross examination, he asked if I had not come to Washington for publicity and personal exploitation. That suggestion was so silly, I replied, that if that were the best he could do, Senator Ervin should send him home to Wilmington. My testimony would not help me or my business in Cheraw. And I had come up at my own expense. No one had even met me at the train station. The total cost—coach, not Pullman, plus other related expenses—exceeded one hundred dollars. The senatorial committee was so cheap, I added, that they hadn't offered to pay for anything. At the end of the testimony, with the usual show of bi-partisan courtesy and good nature, the committee chairman handed me a check for the cost of the trip.

Several months earlier, in October 1962, Reston had called me. He was planning a trip to South Carolina, now the last holdout to school integration. The test case was soon to come with Harvey Gantt at Clemson College. What was the mood of the people? Would Governor Hollings follow in the footsteps of Governor Faubus at Little Rock in 1957? Would he emulate Governor Barnett at Ole Miss in 1962? Was South Carolina's governor to behave more like North Carolina Governors Luther Hodges and Terry Sanford or attempt a stand in the schoolhouse door like Alabama Governor George Wallace did later and proclaim, "Segregation now, segregation forever?"

Reston, accompanied by his wife, arrived in Cheraw on a Friday in early October. I gave them the usual tour of the town and arranged for him to talk to civic leaders, town officials, political bigwigs, officers of the local NAACP and members of the black ministerial association. On hand was Levy Byrd, secretary-treasurer of the South Carolina NAACP, who some years earlier had been featured in a New Yorker personality profile along with Thurgood Marshall. Byrd was a plumber who walked all over town pulling a little wagon with his toilet plunger and other equipment to provide service to the big houses on Market and Third Streets occupied by white people. Byrd had many years earlier served fifteen years in prison for the passion-killing of his wife. Or so I was told. Reston also met John McCall, black attorney who five years earlier had successfully defended his African-American client before an all-white, all-male jury in Chesterfield against the charge of rape of a white woman. That feat, ignored nationally but highlighted in the *Chronicle*, excelled anything the fictional Atticus Finch achieved in *To Kill a Mockingbird*.

Before Reston left Cheraw on Sunday, I had assured him that South Carolina would not react as Arkansas and Mississippi had, and as Alabama still threatened to do. Models for the Palmetto State, whose people believed in law and order, were North Carolina and Virginia. In the Old Dominion, massive resistance had collapsed in 1958 under court orders from both the Virginia and U.S. Supreme Courts, despite the Byrd machine.

Reston went on to Columbia and Charleston, where he absorbed a lot of nostalgia for the romantic days of the Old South from the editors of *The State* and a lot of fire-eating rhetoric from Tom Waring of the *News and Courier*. In a series of articles, Reston concluded that Cheraw reflected more accurately the changing mood of South Carolina than its capital city or that Eternal City standing proudly at the confluence of the Ashley and Cooper Rivers "which meet to form the Atlantic Ocean."

The first of Reston's three-part series appeared in the *Times* on Sunday, October 21. The next day Kennedy addressed the nation about the Cuban missile crisis. No one paid much attention to anything else after that for nearly two weeks, by which time any national interest in Cheraw had long since evaporated.

But when Gantt was admitted to Clemson in January 1963 without fanfare, the Secrest-Reston view was vindicated. Later that year the first integration of a public school in Charleston occurred under a federal court order without incident. A lone, unarmed guard watched as the black students entered school unmolested. The worst that Tom Waring and the *News and Courier* could do over the past ten years had not proven effective enough.

Five years later when integration was voluntarily attempted by the Cheraw school board, with the full support of the *Chronicle*, an irate crowd overturned the school bus and ran the black students off. So much for the power of the press in either town. The next year, however, Debra Crawford, daughter of the *Chronicle's* black linotype operator James

Crawford, volunteered to integrate the Cheraw grammar school. This time all went off without a hitch. And the integration process proceeded peacefully apace.

Zalin Grant worked part-time and in the summers in high school and college at the *Chronicle*. As editor of the *Tiger* at Clemson, Zalin championed the cause of civil rights when Harvey Gantt enrolled there under court order. At my suggestion, Zalin welcomed Gantt to the campus and was the first student to break bread with the beleaguered youth, refusing to follow former Governor Byrnes' advice to Clemson students to "shun" the young, lonely black student and make him feel unwelcome. I editorialized briefly: "Welcome to Clemson, Harvey. I hope you make A's on everything !"

Later Gantt, a Charlotte architect, ran for the U.S. Senate against incumbent Senator Jesse Helms twice. Both times he lost, but in close elections. Zalin Grant served with the Green Berets in Vietnam. After the war he worked for *Time* and the *New Republic*, before settling down with a French wife in Paris to write books.

There was one other time when I found it necessary to assert my position in order to cover a local story from which I was initially excluded. President Eisenhower's secretary of the army, Robert Stevens, was coming to Cheraw to inspect Delta Finishing Co. Stevens was a top executive at the JP Stevens Company and Delta, one of their plants, had been charged with pollution of the Pee Dee River and other environmental violations. Stevens' guest was Henry Luce, publisher of *Time* and *Life* magazines. This was a big deal.

A public relations person came by the *Chronicle* office with a prepared story for release. There was to be a luncheon at the plant, with a tour of the facilities followed by a reception for local bigwigs. I wasn't among them.

"Thank you for the information," I said. "I always find public relations people so helpful for information and background briefings. But I never reprint canned stories. We cover the event and write our own. Ask Secretary Stevens or Mr. Luce to call me.

The call, of course, never came. Two days before the event I called Mr. Luce, got past his secretary, and said, "Mr. Luce, as a courtesy to another member of the Fourth Estate, you should invite me to the Delta luncheon."

"Mr. Secrest," Luce replied, "I'm just a guest myself. I'm not in charge of the event."

This I acknowledged but reminded him that he had the clout to include me if he wished. The least he could do would be to grant an interview, but there was no justification for my exclusion as I was the publisher of the local newspaper. "It isn't collegial; it isn't professional. *Time* and *Life* are international media giants. Compared to you, worldwide, I'm unknown."

But, I added, he and Stevens were not visiting worldwide, they were guests in Chesterfield County, where the circulation of the *Chronicle* was many times that of his publications. "Furthermore, I represent the people of Cheraw, and it is for them that I should be included."

I made similar calls to Dick Thomas, Delta's public relations man, and to the plant's manager Mr. Harrell, both of whom I knew personally. In fact, the *Chronicle* did much of the job printing for Delta.

Later that afternoon I received a call from Luce. He laughed out loud at my chutzpah, but he acknowledged my point of view. "Come on to the dinner, Secrest," Luce said. "Stevens and I want you at the head table."

The question remains, why was it that the *Chronicle* and I, as its editor, not only survived but thrived over a fifteen-year period of mounting racial tension? I had opposed the state's policy of massive resistance with mounting conviction and by participation in such organizations as the South Carolina Council on Human Relations in Columbia; the Southern Regional Council, in Atlanta; Penn Community Services, near Beaufort, which provided the only interracial conference and training center in the state. I had accepted appointment by President Eisenhower in 1959 to the South Carolina Committee to the U.S. Commission on Civil Rights.

The committee subsequently held hearings all over the state and aired grievances by anyone who felt they had been denied justice or equal protection under the law. I'd even taken a year off to attend Harvard University, not a popular move in South Carolina in 1960. The current joke: how does one get to Washington? Go to Harvard and turn left.

It would have been easy for outraged readers to drive me out of Cheraw at any time between 1954 and 1968. I could well have become the target of political extremists, citizens' councils, individual vigilantes or organizations advocating the use of economic pressure against "a liberal press dedicated to subverting Southern life and tradition."

But that never happened. Why, eventually, did the views of the *Chronicle* prevail over the much larger, more powerful voices of the *State*, the *Greenville News*, and the *News and Courier*? Could it have been that South Carolina was far more reconstructed than its political leadership would admit? Had the average citizen moved more into the mainstream of American life, especially since the Great Depression and World War II, than the old regime, which owned the large daily newspapers, realized?

There must also have been deep affirmative bonds among many individuals of the two races that went deeper than the surface fear and resentment the court decisions aroused and politicians exploited. There was also the presence of strong, well-organized Negro organizations. Black people weren't afraid, or, if they were, they overcame their personal fears out of a devotion to a larger cause. Black people voted, usually in a bloc. They counted with politicians. And while their skin was black, their money was green, and merchants did not want to lose their patronage and good will. The economy of the state was already thoroughly integrated into the national economy, and community leaders wanted it to become even more so. World War II had made South Carolinians more aware of the opinions of other people and the importance of other cultures.

Furthermore, the folk in South Carolina had a long collective memory—something Carl Jung would call the "collective subconscious." This memory extended to an historical era preceding the Civil War, back to the ideals of the American Revolution and the Founding Fathers and their ideas of equality, justice and democracy as enunciated in the Declaration of Independence, the Preamble to the Constitution, the Bill of Rights, and the Federalist Papers. There was also the undergirding, unifying bond of a shared religious faith.

At some level, people remembered—and still revered—that 18th century concept of liberalism, anchored in the Age of Reason and the European Enlightenment, perhaps best expressed in the Declaration of the Rights of Man and The Citizen and earlier by Voltaire: "I may hate what you say, but I defend to the death your right to say it." And because they remembered, they tolerated and on occasion responded to editorial arguments in the Chronicle.

Finally, our readers accepted the Chronicle because it remained a community newspaper, neither obsessed by nor avoiding discussion about race relations and related political, legal and constitutional issues. Cheraw was a microcosm of small towns all over the post World War II South, and there was plenty to write about besides racial matters. Any honest reading of the *Chronicle* or understanding of my personal activism would reveal my pragmatism and moderation. To call me a radical, a communist, fellow traveler, outside agitator, carpetbagger, scalawag and so on was just too laughable to be believed. A carpetbagger? Well, yes, some South Carolina extremists considered a liberal editor from North Carolina close enough to be called one.

By 1963 I was well established in Cheraw and generally accepted. Predictably, when things settled down, it was time for change. Everything seemed different somehow after the November 22 tragedy.

In April following Kennedy's assassination, Ann and I took David, Phil and Molly out of school, as usual, and went to Cambridge, Mass., for a reunion of Nieman Fellows at Harvard. Pierre Salinger, Kennedy's press secretary, was there, now seeking the Democratic nomination for the U.S. Senate from California. He recognized me from the White House luncheon a year earlier.

Salinger was described as "ebullient" by the press during his campaign, and that day he was indeed excited, as he was favored to win in the upcoming primary. He was less ebullient a couple of months later after he had lost. In those days Salinger was funny, sensible and likable. I found him less so in later years when he lent himself to all kinds of conspiracy theories, mostly derived from unsubstantiated reports on the Internet.

He claimed, for example, that the TWA Boeing 747 crash that killed 230 people on July 17, 1996, had been the work either of terrorists or of U.S. missiles fired upon the aircraft off Long Island. Increasingly Salinger lost his credibility, his humor, and his charm.

On the way home from the reunion, we stopped in Briarcliff N.Y. to spend a couple of days with Ann's parents. Across the street lived a young woman from Cheraw, Sue Kirkley, whose nephew Miller "Pokey" Ingram was a friend of David. Sue had married a young man from White Plains, N. Y., whose brother was with the ABC television network. It is a southern custom to look up people from home who are living in a "foreign land" if one finds himself nearby. This custom suited my intrusive personality and insatiable curiosity, and my choice "to live in a house by the side of a road and be a friend to man."

Sue's brother-in-law Miller Ingram, mayor of Cheraw, had given me her number and she was pleased to hear a voice from home. David and I went over to visit while Ann, Phil and Molly decided to stay with Ann's parents.

Sue and Jerry, her husband, made a handsome couple, and they were enthusiastic Democrats. She introduced us to her redhaired look-alike brother-in-law, over for a visit. In referring to the recent assassination and Johnson's sure hand on the tiller, he remarked, "It just shows what a powerful ticket we elected in 1960. Johnson is sure to persuade the Congress to approve the civil rights bill, something Kennedy himself could never do," a view Jerry heartily endorsed.

445

That was how I met Roone Arledge, soon to make a name for himself as a TV producer associated with such shows as ABC's Wide World of Sports. When Arledge died in 2003, he was recognized as a leading figure in network television. It really is a small world. Close neighbors of the Arledges the year before had been Cousin Hill Wolfe and his family.

Before we left the Arledge home, we had talked about the proposed civil rights bill and especially Title Ten that included the creation of a Community Relations Service to negotiate racial disputes. "That's something I could do," I exclaimed. It was there that the idea to seek a job with the Service was conceived. I acted upon it as soon as we got back to Cheraw.

# 49. Selma and Martin Luther King

I soon got to Washington, accepting a request from Secretary of Commerce Hodges in June 1964 to co-chair a task force to prepare for the formation of the Community Relations Service. This agency had been provided for at the insistence of Senator Lyndon Baines Johnson. After passage of the law, I joined the agency and for more than two years was involved in attempts to settle racial disputes and disagreements all over the country. The idea was to offer mediation and seek compliance with civil rights laws and thus avoid lengthy and aggravating litigation and to get the problem off the streets and out of the courts. Anticipation of problems and prevention when possible, conciliation when not was the goal.

I first met Dr. Martin Luther King, Jr. in the late 1950s at Penn Community Services in Frogmore, South Carolina. He was there to attend a seminar on passive resistance and civil disobedience. Dr. King then was known largely as a supporter of Rosa Parks who had declined to move to the back of the bus in Birmingham, Alabama, and as founder of the Southern Christian Leadership Conference (SCLC). I met him again seven years later in Selma, Alabama. That is when I had an opportunity to play a small role in an event that led to the passage of the Voting Rights Acts of 1965 and 1966.

John Griffin, manager of the Conciliation Division in the Community Relations Service, and Calvin Kytle, acting director, decided to send me to Selma, Alabama, in early January, 1965, in anticipation of racial conflicts soon to surface. My job: to try to ameliorate the rising tensions at the local level, revolving around disputes between the Selma branch of the NAACP and the Civic Improvement Association on the one hand and the white

447

power structure on the other. At issue were questions of voting restrictions on the minority population, police brutality at the hands of Sheriff Jim Clark's posse, unequal protection of the law, denial of black representation on municipal ruling bodies, and a steadfast refusal by the all-white local government to obey provisions in the recently passed Civil Rights Act, especially in the area of public accommodations. There were also issues of separate but unequal schools and lack of economic opportunity.

At the same time the Southern Christian Leadership Conference, under the leadership of Dr. King, had earmarked Selma as a test case over voting registration rights to be played out on the national stage. Utilizing the already existing racial unrest among black citizens of Selma, and reinforced by every other civil rights group, plus a nationwide religious movement, the SCLC was well prepared to make its case. It wisely chose to focus on the voting restrictions placed upon black people in clear violation of the U.S. Constitution. Here was clear-cut evidence of racial discrimination that no one could deny and around which most people all over the United States could rally.

The Reverend F.D. Reese, pastor of the Tabernacle Baptist Church, and Mrs. Amelia Boynton were the major local black leaders. Reese lacked the necessary fire in the belly to prove a strong leader. Mrs. Boynton was made of sterner stuff. Knowledgeable, convinced, dedicated and a formidable personality, Mrs. Boynton was also physically impressive. A large woman, perhaps tipping the scales at two hundred pounds, she was an effective debater and an intimidating presence. Her deceased husband had been a civil rights activist in the 1940s and '50s; she was his worthy successor.

Selma's mayor was Joe Smitherman, a young man of modest means whose natural political constituency came from a white lower middle class, members of which had common interests with many of their black neighbors. But these groups had also historically been rivals for the relatively few menial jobs available to them in commerce and industry. They were often skillfully manipulated by upper class white people in control of the political, economic and social power structure.

These men—and some women—were backed to the hilt by the establishment churches and the press. Mayor Smitherman was their Charlie McCarthy, mouthing the words of his ventriloquists. The Selma *Times-Journal*, masquerading as a voice of moderation, revealed its true nature when an article about black people carrying the identifying slug, Nigger News, was published with the mortifying slug inadvertently still attached.

Smitherman, in contrast to Mrs. Boynton, was not an impressive physical specimen. Of medium height, he had a slight body, thin neck and chicken legs, weighing, ringing wet, perhaps one hundred and thirty pounds. But he had weighty political support which he exercised with the help of Sheriff Jim Clark, Public Safety Commissioner Wilson Baker, and the ascendant local political authority.

When the SCLC, along with college youths, white and black, from the Student Non-violent Coordinating Committee (SNICK) headed by John Lewis (now a Georgia congressman); the national NAACP and the Congress of Racial Equality (CORE), arrived in late January, action on the national stage heated up. There were spontaneous marches throughout town, with or without a permit. There were mass rallies every night at Brown's Chapel Baptist Church. Boycott of local merchants followed. Soon the SCLC was joined by religious leaders—Protestant, Catholic, and Jewish, white and black—from across the country. Later political leaders at state and national levels reinforced the throng. Malcolm X, in transition from the Nation of Islam but still at odds with Dr. King's non-violent philosophy, was in and out of town.

Dr. King voiced a demand for a march on Montgomery to demonstrate the need for a national law to end the systematic disenfranchisement of black citizens. He argued from solid ground. The Dallas County and Selma Election Boards used complicated civic and legal examinations, graded selectively, to disqualify practically all black people who tried to register to vote. By February 1965 only fifty-seven black applicants, which included professors with Ph.D. degrees, had been reviewed and all had been rejected by the Board of Registrars. Soon adversarial groups were facing each other across roped-off lines, manned by local police, shouting arguments and hurling epithets at each other. James Bevel, the Reverend C.T. Vivian, and Silas Norman, brother of future opera diva Jessie Norman, are the protest leaders I remember most clearly.

Gov. George Wallace refused to issue a permit for the march on Montgomery on the grounds of public safety. The Alabama State Highway Patrol, led by Commander Al Lingo, blocked passage across the Edmund Pettus Bridge spanning the Alabama River. On the Selma side of the bridge, Baker's and Clark's men occasionally manhandled the crowd. Soon the attention of the White House and the Department of Justice was focused on Selma. There was excess on both sides. Black secondary school children were used. Many in SNICK openly flouted local law and custom, sometimes engaging in public displays of interracial sexual co-mingling to enrage the local white population, who predictably over-reacted to any provocation.

The national, then the international, press flocked to Selma. The mass media focused its spotlight on the scene. As chief conciliator with the Community Relations Service, I was given some help from other staff members, chief among whom was Jim Laue, my young friend from Harvard four years earlier and who had written his dissertation on the SCLC and the use of non-violent civil disobedience to achieve social change.

He knew King and his chief assistant, Andy Young, far better than I. I also called upon members of the Mississippi Citizens Advisory Committee to help out, as well as the few moderate politicians, professors, and businessmen I could find. I even called upon federal judges on occasion for advice. But I possessed no carrots, in the way of federal funds, to bribe and no sticks, in the form of legal authority, to coerce anybody to do anything.

The battle came to a head one Friday in early March when the protesters, now thousands strong, white as well as black with a strong contingent of religious leaders, moved to break through the barricade and flow across the Edmund Pettus Bridge and begin their unauthorized march on Montgomery.

Sheriff Clark's men moved forward. The posse, riding their horses and cracking their whips like Russian Cossacks on some pogrom, attacked the marchers. Blackjacks came out. So did police dogs. Some cattle prods came into use. The marchers—once a primarily middle-class crowd, with a sprinkling of intellectual, religious, media and political elitists among them—became a disorganized and demoralized crowd, running helter-skelter for their lives. Hundreds were injured, some seriously. John Lewis had his head laid open. Nuns, other women, and children were among the casualties.

This scene, broadcast on television Friday night, was flashed around the world. The nation found itself in the grip of a racial crisis. I flew home that night. I had been away for two months, with only an occasional weekend back in McLean with the family. I was exhausted. I hadn't been home long before the phone rang. It was Leroy Collins, former Governor of Florida and now head of the Community Relations Service, telling me that President Johnson had asked that Collins and I return the next day to Selma in an Air Force jet, leaving from Andrews Air Force base. We landed at Clark Air Force Base at Selma, were greeted by a military honor guard and put up in bachelor officers quarters. The message: "The Feds are here and we mean business."

The protesters were remobilizing. A crowd, far greater than the one on Friday, converged on Selma. Volunteer workers rode around the clock between the Montgomery Airport and Selma, ferrying civil rights advocates. Dr. King vowed that the march to Montgomery would resume on Tuesday.

Alabama authorities responded in kind. Al Lingo, long-time nemesis of the civil rights movement, lined up hundreds of highway patrol cars to block passage across the bridge and was authorized to use whatever force necessary to prevent its crossing. The struggle intensified in Selma itself and in surrounding rural counties where an occasional body was found dead in associated conflict. Clark's posse was ready. So were Baker's police. I can't recall if the National Guard had been placed on alert.

On Tuesday the two groups once again faced each other on the same spot where Friday's melee had occurred. The marchers awaited a signal from Dr. King to move ahead. Gov. Collins and I met the SCLC leader at the home of Dr. Sullivan Jackson, a local black dentist. There we had a pleasant conversation, mainly concerned with the superiority of Southern soul food, enjoyed by both blacks and whites, over Northern cuisine.

You can sense when someone likes you. King, a few years younger than I, liked me and I returned the feeling. He and Gov. Collins got along equally well but became side-tracked on religious and philosophical questions while the main and immediate issue remained unresolved. Andy Young, King's man, and I, representing Collins and the Johnson administration, became restive. Time was running out. With tensions rising, anything could happen at any time.

The day before I had called Kenneth Goodson, now a Methodist bishop in Birmingham, to meet me in Selma and to talk with Governor Wallace, a fellow Methodist, in his command car across the river. He agreed to come. Goodson was the young protégé of Uncle Jim Craven back in the mid-1930s. He had been a frequent visitor to Broadacre when Uncle Jim, Brack, Dowd and I—not yet a teenager—would, as "gentleman farmers," ride over the cotton fields in Union and Anson Counties and confer with the tenant farmers who did the actual work. Goodson had even been in on some of the hasty bootleg whisky drinking around the Secrest lavatory when Cyclone Mac had been in town in the early 1930s. So I cashed the Bishop card.

While Bishop Goodson was talking to Wallace and Lingo, urging them at least to pull back their troopers and get control of the Selma Posse, Young and I met with march leaders and urged them to agree to halt voluntarily, once they had made the symbolic move across the bridge. If that were achieved, an agreement about a march on Montgomery later would be easier to get.

The civil rights leaders agreed. They were worn out. The governor agreed. He and his troopers were, too. No one really wanted a repeat on Tuesday of the hateful thing that had occurred the preceding Friday. Now all Andy and I had to do was to get Gov. Collins and Dr. King's approval. We presented our plan. The governor and Clark and their men would move back several hundred yards and allow the marchers to cross the bridge. The protesters would in turn stop voluntarily once they had made their symbolic march, proclaim victory, and then return to Selma to lay further plans. We got each side to initial the agreement I had scribbled off on the back of an old envelope.

King conferred with Young. Collins conferred with me. Then we swapped conferees. "Do you really think I ought to do this, Secrest?" Dr. King asked me. Yes. I did. Collins asked the same thing of Young. Yes, he did. Together Young and I, given a police escort through the crowd, rode back to Governor Wallace. A temporary solution had been found. Before the end of that month, a permanent one was reached and the march on Montgomery was held, with Peter, Paul, and Mary leading the crowd and a host of celebrities in singing "We Shall Overcome" from the Alabama Capitol steps.

Collins and I flew back to Washington that night. The President asked us to come to the White House to thank us for what we had done to "save the nation from another day of shame." With astonishing speed the Congress passed and the President signed a new Voting Rights Act which occasioned an eventual political revolution in the South and a realignment of the Democratic and Republican parties.

My role in Selma did not end there, however. The national civil rights groups moved on out, with SNICK leaders promising to show up three years later in Chicago. But the civil rights struggle at the local stage between Mrs. Boynton and Mayor Smitherman continued. Nor had the violence dissipated. Upon my return to Selma, a white Unitarian minister, the Reverend Mr. Leeb, was set upon by a group of young white toughs and beaten so severely he died the next day. It was my unhappy duty to meet his family at the Montgomery Airport and take them to Selma and to express the government's regrets.

A little later a young white woman from New Jersey—Viola Luizza—was shot to death in her car by a group of white men as she ferried still more civil rights protesters into Selma. In that car was an F.B.I. informant who led to the arrest of the killers. I attended the trial of the young gunman, named Collie, some weeks later.

Most of the negotiations between local factions in Selma occurred in the street, up front and personal. One could never tell when they might begin or end or what the immediate issue would be. The news media from all over the world were on hand to watch, eavesdrop and record what they could. Most of the reporters, many now dead or retired, I can't even recall. But one young, jug-eared fellow who looked just like Alfred E. Newman on the cover of *Mad* magazine I still see every weeknight on the ABC television network show *Night Line* with Ted Koppel. Others were Nelson Benton, Jack Nelson of the *L.A. Times*, Robert Novak and Nicholas von Hoffman, all nationally known journalists. These reporters never got any news out of me, however, conscious as I was of the penalties of violating the confidentiality requirement of the Service: a year in jail and a $10,000 fine.

The conciliation process went from the sublime to the absurd. One hour I might be on the phone, asking a district or appellate federal judge how to interpret his latest order. The next I may have been measuring the distance from a store window to the protesters on the sidewalk and chalking it off, as contesting and protesting antagonists squared off and shouted at each other.

One morning I had awakened late. I tossed on my clothes without bothering to wash my face or brush my teeth. I tossed on my hair piece which I had invariably worn since the day President Kennedy had been assassinated sixteen months earlier, and hurried to the Albert Hotel, scene of that day's action. I need not have hurried, as the marchers had not yet arrived. The movement operated by what reporters came to call CPT: Colored People's Time.

But when they did arrive, the demonstration and the shifting demands became particularly noisy and confused. Jim Laue had returned the day before to give me a hand. It was hot and humid that day in Selma. As the Reverend Mr. Vivian of the SCLC, Police Commissioner Baker, Jim and I argued over some minor point, I began to sweat. As perspiration accumulated under my hair piece, which needed fresh tape, beaded up on my forehead, and began to roll down my face, I kneeled down to the sidewalk to illustrate a point with some chalk. As I did so, off slid the hair piece.

I reached over to grab it just as Jim, ever the clown, snatched it away, shouting, "Oh, oh, what is that? A coon skin? A squirrel tail? Anybody lose something?" And he paraded up and down the battle line, twirling my hair piece as the crowd began to laugh and make catcalls. An unusual but effective way to break tension and get the negotiation process started again.

Life in Selma led to irregular hours. After a day on the street, there would be an evening at a religious rally in Brown's Chapel, informal headquarters for the local movement. Singing, clapping and preaching could last for hours. One ate when and where one could. Such a lifestyle caused irregularity and that, added to standing on my feet all day long, led to hemorrhoids. That called for relief which I found in a tube of Preparation H.

One day I carried a used tube in my pocket to the usual street meeting. Finally growing physically weary, I bent over to give my aching back a rest when out plopped the tube of Preparation H. Again Laue was too quick for me. He grabbed the container, danced around before the crowd, and shouted, "Oh, look what I've found! Did somebody lose this ointment? Anybody in pain and need relief?" Again tension gave way to laughter. I had long since passed embarrassment. Life every day was informal and personal. I got my Preparation H back from Jim, stuck it in my pocket and went back to work. Soon we had reached an agreement on the issue of the day, whatever that was.

I liked the people of Selma, black and white, and I believe they liked and trusted me. Mediators from the Community Relations Service, then housed in the Department of Commerce, were different from representatives of the Justice Department or from the agents of the F.B.I.. The people from Justice were too formal, remote, legalistic, armed as they were with their walkie-talkies and seeming to view the white locals as yokels and the black civil-rights activists as some kind of illegal aliens from another planet.

The men from the F.B.I. were worse—arrogant, secretive, watchful and intimidating, if not downright hostile, armed as they were not only with sophisticated communication equipment but also with guns. To their credit, they learned, and later, when CRS was transferred to the Department of Justice, we learned from them, too, and benefited from the carrots of persuasion and the sticks of enforcement they provided. But I believe the people of Selma preferred to work with CRS, wherever we were housed, at least until Mayor Smitherman came to Washington.

In late spring, when I was finally back in the Washington office, the CRS staff decided it would be a good idea to invite Mrs. Boynton, Mayor Smitherman, the Reverend Mr. Reese, Hosea Williams and a couple of others to the capital for discussions on how best to resolve their differences. It fell to me to meet the group at National Airport in my own nine-passenger Chevrolet station wagon, as their plane was to arrive after regular office hours.

The two Selma groups, one white, the other black, left the plane separately, neither side looking at or speaking to the other. How was I to get all six people into my car? The back jump seat was occupied by Duchess, the family's new young boxer. The car itself, left in its usual state of disarray, was dirty, the floor filled with bird seed, some of which had sprouted a few days earlier when I had forgotten to close the car window and it had rained in. It seemed as if I would have to mow rather than sweep out the interior.

I welcomed the group, now standing a few feet apart, backs turned to each other. "Welcome to Washington, Mr. Mayor," I said to Smitherman, and extended my hand. Then I went over to Mrs. Boynton, took her by the arm, and led her over to Smitherman's side. "Did you have a nice flight? No turbulence, I hope. Come on, let's go to my car and I'll take you all to the hotel. I've made your reservations."

The mayor was accompanied by Wilson Baker and another man, representing the Selma Chamber of Commerce. Hosea Williams, Atlanta SCLC representative, and the Reverend Mr. Reese were Mrs. Boynton's companions.

"Let's see now, how are we all going to fit in here?" I asked as we reached my Chevrolet. Mrs. Boynton tried the front passenger seat, with Mr. Williams but found it too small and crowded. Smitherman had already taken a seat alongside Mr. Reese. Duchess reached forward and started to wash their ears. Both men began to laugh. After several trial seating combinations, it was obvious that people would have to be mixed up pretty thoroughly. It ended with Mrs. Boynton—all two hundred-plus pounds— sitting on Mayor Smitherman's skinny lap, while Hosea Williams, a large man himself, held up Safety Commissioner Baker. The other passengers squeezed in as best they could, all submitting good-naturedly to Duchess's enthusiastic welcome.

Before we had left National's parking lot, people who had traveled all the way from Alabama without speaking, were laughing together and soon cracking jokes. I purposely took the scenic route through Washington, hoping to extend this new "era of good feeling" as long as possible. When we unloaded in front of the Mayflower Hotel, I asked Mayor Smitherman and Mrs. Boynton to have dinner together, reservations already arranged, to work on an agenda for the early afternoon meeting the next day at the CRS conference room in the Department of Commerce. Bidding each representative good night, Duchess and I then drove back to McLean some ten miles away for a rare late dinner date at home with Ann.

When I got to work the next morning, the office was alive with conversation. "Hey, Mac, how about that Mayor Smitherman? Did you set that up?" What were they talking about? No, I had not heard any early morning news on the radio. No, I had not seen the *Washington Post*.

"Well, look at this," and a co-worker handed me the paper. The headline read: "Selma Mayor Levels Flim-Flam Charge." The story suggested Smitherman himself was being questioned about solicitation. What had happened?

Apparently Smitherman, away from the racial restraints of Selma and euphoric with his new-found friendship with Mrs. Boynton and Hosea Williams, had ventured out on the streets of Washington late in the evening after the other visitors had gone to bed. A young black woman had approached him, propositions were made, plans exchanged. The woman's manager had insisted on an advance down payment for any services later to be rendered. The girl in question would show up at a later hour at which time the balance would be due.

She never showed. The mayor waited and waited. When he finally realized there was to be no action, he felt cheated and angry. He reported the incident to the police. A report was filed and dropped into the hopper, which was available to the area press. *The Washington Post* police reporter made his routine check shortly before deadline, started to turn away when the name Smitherman caught his eye. It rang a bell. Could that possibly be the same Smitherman who had been so much in the national news all spring? The next day, the Selma mayor dominated the headlines of the Capital city's press.

I did not go by the Mayflower as planned later that day. I have no recollection of any meeting at our offices that afternoon. I don't know what happened to the Selma delegation or how they got home. The episode was certainly not of my doing but somehow I got blamed for it—at least by the white leadership in Selma.

The Washington incident did not, however, spell the end of Mayor Smitherman's political career. He returned to Selma as mayor and won reelection time and again, finally relinquishing office toward the end of the twentieth century. Even as blacks came to serve on the town council and Board of County Commissioners and other municipal boards and law enforcement agencies, Smitherman remained as mayor, a continuing reminder of the complexity of Southern racial politics.

I did not return to that town again, but within two months I was back in Alabama on a conciliation mission to Tuskegee, home of the famed institute founded by Booker T. Washington. Racial tensions had flared in Tuskegee when a group of black citizens, angered by the killing of a black man by a white man with the name of Segrist, of all things, attempted to integrate the white Methodist church. For several Sundays, black men, women and children had marched on the church and asked to attend the eleven o'clock morning worship service.

The congregation closed the door upon them. Now the whites in the church, feeling besieged and threatened, armed themselves with shotguns and threatened to fire into the black crowd. I was sent down to try to cool passions on both sides. My surname—Secrest—may not have helped much. I felt the need of back-up. Once again I called upon the head of the Alabama Methodist church—Bishop Kenneth Goodson. He again answered the summons.

Goodson and I met with the black Tuskegee group. Then we met with the Methodist Board of Stewards. On Sunday morning the preacher allowed me to address the congregation from the pulpit. Up from my subconscious and out of my mouth flowed Biblical references, allusions, and lessons I didn't even know I knew. When I had finished, Bishop Goodson took up where I left off.

But the front door of the church remained closed. Our mission did not succeed, but there was a victory of sorts within defeat. The good Methodists promised not to fire into the group seeking entrance into the sanctuary the next Sunday. They would lock, bolt, bar, if necessary nail shut, the front door to the church, turn their backs and worship the Lord the way He would have wanted, praying all the time for the forgiveness of the sins of their tormentors.

That was my last trip to Alabama, as future missions tended to take me farther north and west. It was also about the last of Goodson's term as Alabama bishop. He soon was to return to his native state of North Carolina and become a Methodist bishop there, with a home in Winston-Salem.

But before I left the region, I had made trips to Bogalusa, Louisiana, and McComb and Natchez, Mississippi. In Natchez, I discovered a tradition of a tough, river-boat gambling society blended with an early 19th-century Southern aristocracy derived from the cotton trade. In 1965, Natchez had a mayor of Arab descent, a strictly segregated society, and many social and racial problems, some of which were associated with the mayor's own close relatives. Needless to say, I didn't accomplish much in Mississippi and Louisiana. Progress there depended upon the Justice Department, lawsuits and slow political liberation made possible by the Voting Rights Acts of 1965 and 1966.

Over the last thirty-five years, Martin Luther King, Jr., the man, has been transformed into Dr. King, martyred saint. It is difficult to arrive at a true assessment. I suspect if he were alive today, he would not be a favorite of the conservative right who selectively use quotes from his Washington speech in 1963 to advance their own agenda. I believe King would have been pulled to the left, not only out of political necessity but also out of inner conviction.

He would have more aggressively opposed the Vietnam War, become more closely allied with the black underclass, and may have beat the drum of racial reparations. He certainly would oppose school vouchers, favor affirmative action, argue against a greater military budget in favor of a renewed war on poverty and universal health care. I can't imagine his favoring foreign wars that I believe he would call military adventurism.

As his friend Ralph Abernathy said in 1968, "Martin wasn't perfect." He had his flaws. Although he fought racism and was martyred for it, I sensed in King a distrust of many whites, particularly politicians. How could a man his age, raised in segregation and subject to all the humiliation such a system caused, have helped feeling some resentment? His treatment at the hands of J. Edgar Hoover and the F.B.I. didn't help matters. I am uncertain that the notion, so dear to all these white conservatives today who hated it in 1963, that people should be judged by the content of their character and not by the color of their skin, would be paramount in King's thinking were he alive today. He would understand that race problems in America would not yield with integration and that the whole question is far more complex than skin color and character content.

# 50. Family Life and Something Stupid

We enjoyed a good family life in Cheraw. David, Phil and Molly liked school, made many friends, and successfully picked up where we left off once we returned from periodic sabbaticals. But I could never have enjoyed the freedom to roam as I did while publishing a community newspaper without Eddie Sweatt, George Law and Jim Crawford on my staff. Eddie and Jim called me a benevolent boss, but I was perhaps more dependent on them than they on me.

George, son of the man from whom I bought the paper, could have resented his father's decision. But he was always a reliable, loyal production manager, even during tough times when association with the *Chronicle* was not a popular thing. He was particularly helpful the three years Eddie was away in military service.

Eddie was a Renaissance Man at printing and publishing. He had a lot of apprenticeship training, having been a "printer's devil" since his mid-teens. I relied upon him to price the job printing, to perform all aspects of the mechanical work, and upon his return from military duty to become general manager. He learned to fill every slot, from selling and designing advertising copy to hot type composition. When I left for a year in Cambridge, Mass. in 1960, he ran the paper, gradually learning the editorial as well as the production, advertising and managerial aspects of the business. He was honest, capable, and reliable.

Three years later we left again, away this time for more than two years. Once again Eddie assumed command, with never a word of complaint. More remarkably, he expanded his vision as well, embracing a generous, tolerant philosophy that enabled him to accept the *Chronicle's* editorial policy and eventually to push me further to the left than I sometimes thought I should go. I continued, however, to set the editorial agenda, writing editorials from afar and using Cheraw residents sympathetic to *Chronicle* policy to submit opinion pieces as well. Like Mark Twain and his *Letters from Abroad*, I was never mentally fully removed.

Jim Crawford, a Charleston native, married a Cheraw girl from a prominent black family. His niece, Margaret Ann Reid, became a colleague and close friend of Ann's. Margaret Ann later earned her Ph.D. in English literature and is a recently retired professor from a university in Baltimore. Another niece graduated from Duke and became a judge in Washington, D.C. Jim had contracted tuberculosis and cured in a South Carolina facility before moving to Cheraw looking for work. He couldn't find any.

Jim had, however, before his illness worked as a linotype operator. I was in great need of one. Most of those I could find were transients, given to booze and drugs, seldom competent or reliable. One of Jim's friends once remarked, "Crawford had to face a double stigma in the workplace. He was a recovered tubercular patient, which scared a lot of people, and he was a black man. In the 1950s newspaper publishers in South Carolina didn't hire black linotype operators. But Secrest didn't pay any attention to stigmas. Jim had a health certificate. He was proficient in his trade. Race didn't matter. He hired Jim, paid him the prevailing wage and just saved his life."

Jim's friend gave me more credit than I was due. He didn't understand that Jim was just as important to me as I was to him. Eddie, Jim and I became friends as well as colleagues in a relationship that lasted for over forty years, well beyond the time Eddie and I had both left Cheraw.

Without a dedicated staff, it would have been more difficult to do what on occasion I had to do for Mother and others in the family. It would have been impossible to travel so often and widely. After the first five years in Cheraw, Ann and I would often leave impulsively on trips, yanking the children out of school when necessary. We hoped that travel would broaden their horizons and knew they could make up the school work.

In 1959 we went to Saranac Lake. In 1960 to Cambridge, Mass. In 1963 we took off on a six weeks trip out West. A year later we were in McLean, Va. We traveled to Florida, New York and New England. In 1967 and 1968 I spent both summers in graduate school at Duke. Whenever the wandering spirit called, we answered. The *Chronicle* never missed an issue nor lost a dime.

Life in Cheraw revolved around family, church, school, men's and women's civic organizations, and the country club and golf course. Ann and I attended the First Methodist Church. I was a member of the Kiwanis Club. We also belonged to a dinner dance group, several couples bridge clubs, and a progressive dinner and gourmet group.

Ann was a housewife and mother, kept busy at home with David, Phil and Molly, a late arrival in December, 1956. Once Molly was old enough to enter Miss Ruth Funderburk's "Ding-Dong" school, however, Ann re-entered the work force as a school librarian. Before then she was a cub scout leader. But we were never accepted as bona fide Cheravians. To achieve that status, one had to be born and raised there. Our three children were accepted, therefore, as natives, but not their parents.

We were well liked and respected as residents of the community but always a little on the outside, not only because I came from North Carolina and Ann from New Hampshire but also because I was something of a hair shirt as editor of the town's only newspaper. In social gatherings it was understood: never talk about politics or race relations.

We did our civic duty and met our social obligations. There was hardly a wedding or a funeral of consequence we didn't attend. In the mid-20th century South in small towns it was considered commercial, tacky, if not downright common, to hold a wedding reception anywhere except in one's own home or church hall. A restaurant or hotel was out of the question. So were alcoholic beverages.

One of Aunt Eve's Salem girls from one of the town's best families had landed a good catch. The wedding was a command performance. Mr. Micklejohn, a native of Wisconsin who had married into a "right" family generations earlier, was standing next to Ann and me that early June night in a lengthening line two blocks away from the stately home where the reception was held. As we inched along the candle-lit path through an aromatic garden, awaiting our turn to go through the receiving line to meet the radiant couple, proud parents, extended family and close friends, and to see the lavish display of wedding gifts spread out all over the room, and, finally, to gain a seat and receive a cup of tepid Russian tea, some homemade roasted nuts and a few butter mints, the elderly gentleman muttered to me, "Mighty poor entertainment." But at least it beat the funerals.

On an occasional Saturday afternoon I would drive David and Phil to UNC or Duke to see a football game. As we drove into Chapel Hill one day in 1957 up Columbia Street, we noticed a commotion around Fraternity Row. Carolina was then a male-dominated campus, coeds in relatively short supply. Youthful voices were raised in a familiar tune.

David, then eight years old, recognized the gospel song recently popularized by Mahalia Jackson, but somehow the words weren't right. The students were singing the song, "He's got the whole world in His hands," but the lyrics now rang out:

We've got old man House by the balls,
We've got old man House by the balls,
We've got old man House by the balls,
Yes, we've got the whole man in our hands."

At the end of each stanza they would shout, "Squeeze!" The frat boys, protesting some restriction handed down by Chancellor Robert B. House, were whooping it up in traditional collegiate style.

House was Manager of General Administration (the title that evolved into Chancellor) from 1934 until 1957. He then returned to teaching English literature and the classics until his retirement in 1962. House played the harmonica and would give impromptu recitals on official occasions. He loved playing the clown and won the hearts of his students and his colleagues by his informal manner. The fraternal serenade that Saturday in 1957 didn't faze him in the least. House had family connections in Chesterfield County, and the *Chronicle's* "Society Column" often recorded his Sunday dinner visits with them.

Some things never change. UNC fraternity behavior in the late 1950s was of a piece with Duke's in 1941—with our potent "Purple Jesus" parties after football games—and with Carolina's in 1942 down in the PKA "Passion Pit," which I visited frequently that year after friend Moke had transferred yet again. Hard to please, Moke spent his freshman year at Duke, his sophomore year at Wake Forest, his junior year at UNC, and in 1943 went where the army put him, the University of Connecticut at Storrs. The Wake Forest students, kept under a stricter Baptist code, were forbidden to drink or hold dances on campus. They had to drive all the way to Raleigh to raise hell, but they managed some mischief in their own frat houses as well.

Harvard in 1960, Duke in 1969, when I was a graduate student there, UNC and NCCU between 1971 and 1985 were much the same. Judging from what I observe at UNC today and read about Duke, the lowest common denominators remain: alcohol, sex, and protest against authority—all apparently part of the process of growing up and establishing one's sense of identity. In some ways things were looser then than now. Most students smoked and the drinking age was 18.

Regardless of the hi-jinks, students in each generation have managed to get a good education, remain well-mannered, polite and friendly, somehow ready after four years of "hanging loose and laying out."—soaking up suds and sun—to play their part as responsible citizens in a democratic society.

As David and Phil got older, we'd drive up to the Reynolds Coliseum in Raleigh to catch some basketball games, usually played at night. David and Phil learned about the Everette Case basketball tradition at N.C. State. Our tickets invariably were high up in the bleachers, above the smoke ring that hung like a miasma below. In the early 1960s everybody, it seemed, smoked like a furnace at the games. Later we went more often to Carmichael Gym and Cameron Indoor Stadium. Cheraw, located so close to the North Carolina line, was pulled in two directions: South and west toward USC in Columbia, Clemson College and the Citadel, and north toward UNC, Duke, Davidson and Wake Forest. We went to games in Columbia and Clemson too. Although David, Phil and Molly, raised in Cheraw, were accepted as natives and so considered themselves, their educational and sports loyalties lay to the north.

They were programmed early to favor the Duke Blue Devils, followed closely by the Tar Heels and Wake's Demon Deacs. Molly was too young to go to these weekend or late evening events. However, being a light sleeper like her father, her feet would hit the floor when she heard us come in at one or two in the morning, and she'd run to greet us. After the boys went to bed, Molly (between the ages of two and six) and I would sit up in the big recliner and watch the late, late show together.

Often I wouldn't get home until early morning after putting the paper to bed. Molly and boxer Misty would hear the car and both would be waiting to greet me at the sliding glass door. Then we would settle down to watch the late show, usually an old Bette Davis movie. Molly never wanted to acknowledge that anything had ever happened before she was born.

Anxiety and stress were constant companions after Phil developed a potentially deadly systemic disorder in 1966. These emotions affect the weakest links in one's psyche. Although I had recovered quickly from the onset of obsessive-compulsive behavior in McLean where he first became sick, the problem would reassert itself occasionally back in Cheraw and later in Durham. I learned coping skills that overcame the symptoms, even as the impulse remained.

When I found myself setting down the salt shaker five times, I would say out loud, whether alone or in the company of family or friends, "Look at the fool thing I'm doing! Now why do you suppose a sensible fellow like me would act like this?" And the impulse would disappear. If that failed to work, I'd intentionally knock over the shaker, spilling some salt, which is supposed to bring bad luck, and say, "to hell with it." That always worked.

This disability, which had first surfaced when I was four and Mother disappeared, was not habitual. I was unaffected by it entirely between the ages of nine and forty-two. It seldom surfaced beyond the family circle. Few friends and no professional colleagues ever glimpsed this personal peculiarity. I was never anything like the character played by Jack Nicholson in the film *As Good As It Gets*, or the television character Adrian Monk.

But during Phil's illness, even after the sale of the *Chronicle* and I was in graduate school working on my dissertation, I would sometimes succumb to my own expression of the "Simmons Curse." I would check the doors late at night, shaking the knobs over and over again just to be sure they were locked. I would inspect the electric range to make certain all four burners were turned off, twisting each one a dozen or so times till I broke one clean off. I would turn the light switches on and off five times (never four or six). And I would count to one hundred and then down from one hundred to zero, skipping six numbers at a time.

I learned to control this again by calling attention aloud (usually to myself, as everyone else had long since gone to bed). "What an idiotic thing to do!" I would shout. "C'mon, you know better than this. How is this helping Phil—or anybody else?" And the impulse would dissipate. Another trick—do just the opposite of the impulse. If you start fiddling with the lock, unlock the door entirely and leave it that way. What were the odds of any intruder, anyway, compared to the chances you could tear yourself to pieces by such uncontrolled behavior?

I got over this on my own and learned that in some limited ways one can exercise free will and decide not to become or remain a victim. Largely on my own, but one night in Cheraw I got some help from David and Phil.

They slept downstairs. Late at night, I would creep down to be sure Phil was all right. While I was there I might as well check on David too. David, now a senior in high school, was 18 years old. Strong and muscular, he was a starter on Cheraw's football team and the picture of health. Phil was at the moment doing well. They were not exactly candidates for Sudden Infant Death Syndrome. Yet I would stand over them to see if they were warmly covered, then stoop down to see if I could hear them breathing.

After several nights of this, David and Phil caught on, but they never said a word. Not until one night when, as I assumed my listening position over David, I felt something hit me behind the knees, causing me to fall to the floor. As I fell, a sheet was flung over my head. Then I received a strong shove to my chest from the opposite direction, followed by another sheet.

Then David and Phil, laughing with glee, dragged me over to the front door, rolled me out and locked the door. Unexpected physical intervention proved to be an effective behavior modification technique. That was the last time I checked on my two practically grown sons for SIDS.

The situation was so ridiculous I couldn't help but laugh as I knocked on the door to be re-admitted. Once inside, we all had a good time at my expense. It was a good-natured protest with a warning behind it. I got the message to leave them alone.

I gradually got over O/C/D, but remnants remain. There's one hurdle I have never been able to clear. I cannot abide a label on any towel, sheet, or washcloth. For some reason Ann always hangs them up label out. I come along and turn them over, label in, edges exactly even. I've tried all the old tricks, even cutting the labels off. But nothing works. I can still see where they have been. So I spend more time than I want to turning towels, washcloths, face towels, and sheets over or inside out. When I explain to Ann I'd prefer she leave these things as she finds them, she refuses. "Why?" she asks. "I have no intention of becoming an enabler to crackpot behavior."

David himself got locked out in Cheraw not long after he and Phil locked me out. I was at Duke in summer school and Ann was working at the school library. David came upstairs just before bedtime to announce that he was going over to see his girlfriend.

"I don't think so, David," Ann said. "It's nearly midnight. You have to be at work early and I have to get my sleep. Besides, this is no time to go calling on a girlfriend."

"Well, I'm going anyhow," David replied.

"Oh no, you're not," his mother declared. Down the stairs David bounded and out the front door. Phil and Molly were already asleep. Ann locked up and went to bed and sound asleep. She was awakened early the next morning by a knock at the door. It was David, wanting in.

He was admitted, with this ultimatum. "David, I am a working mother. I'm also responsible for you three children while your father is away. I need your help. Now you must decide whether you want to remain a member of the family or become a paying guest." Ann explained briskly, "If you choose the latter, you'll get a room, fresh towels and sheets once a week, no meals, no laundry, and pay a rent of ten dollars a week. I'd much rather you remained in the family, but it's up to you. You're eighteen and of legal age."

David was a good boy. He'd never been any trouble. His chin trembled as he replied, "I'd rather remain a part of the family." That's one family dust up I missed, but everyone agreed that Mama had handled it just right.

It wasn't the last one. Phil's turn came as did Molly's, as they all reached those difficult adolescent years. We had decided after Phil's diagnosis that it would benefit no one to exempt him from rules that applied to his brother and sister. There weren't many. The children didn't require them.

I wasn't away a lot in summer school, commuting often, spending long weekends at home. We managed to make a festive event out of Phil's nightly chemo pop in his gluteus maximus. One memorable evening it was my turn to inject the syringe. Everyone was on hand—Ann, David, Molly, Duchess the boxer and Sheba and Delilah the cats.

Originally chicken about giving shots, I'd been tutored by the doctors at NIH and practiced repeatedly on an orange, and so had become accustomed. Phil and I were clowning around. David brought in the record player and put on the flip side of Sinatra's recent hit, "Strangers in the Night." It was the Frank & Nancy duet, "Something Stupid."

"O.K., now, ready, Phil, here goes!" And I plunged the needle into my thumb instead of Phil. Everyone thought that was a hoot, something stupid for sure. It didn't hurt much. I later asked the doctor at NIH if one could contract Phil's disease from a contaminated needle. What effect would chemotherapy have on someone not in need of it? "No, none, and don't worry about it," was the reply. "If such a mistake could harm you, the medical staff up here would have long since been decimated. We've all done that."

During David's and Phil's teenage years in Cheraw, I was sometimes an overprotective and "buttinsky" parent. Using my journalistic shield, I would inquire into matters that the boys and Molly would just as soon I left alone. When I heard about "spearing" at football practice, I intervened with the coach. I disagreed with the coach's selection of helmets. In 1968 it was felt one shouldn't drink much water in hot weather during August practice. I was concerned about dehydration and heat stroke. So David and his friends had to have access to plenty of water, start practice early, or late, out of the noonday sun.

I was equally vigilant about drinking and driving. The legal age for drinking was 18, for driving 16. Every time David and Phil left the house, Ann and I made sure who was driving, who was going where, and when they were to get home. They learned early about designated drivers. Other parents, relieved that someone else did the dirty work, would say, "Well, if David and Phil are going, I guess it's all right."

The Coachman was a favorite night spot among teenagers. Located twenty miles away in Bennettsville, the cinderblock building had no fire code. It was often overcrowded. I went over for an inspection, insisted upon additional well-lit exits and adherence to a capacity code. I relied upon the threat of unfavorable reports in the press to get desired results.

Family reunions at the beach with cousins were always placed ahead of weekend football practices, especially on Labor Day. David was benched more than once because of his enforced absenteeism. He was always a good sport about it. Ann, the librarian, and "Stormin' Norman" Wilde, the football coach, were usually at odds, as Ann let it be known that while she was a football fan, the sport, compared to player safety and family activities, was way down on her list of priorities.

Molly was seven years younger than David. She was only twelve when we moved to Chapel Hill. Her turn came later as Ann and I had to keep track of her, chasing her down well after midnight from a swim party and keeping tabs on her whereabouts in the afternoons as one boy after another came calling after school. Compared to her brothers, Molly had it pretty easy. She had a trip to Europe with a school group when she was only fifteen, followed by another to Newfoundland. She was active in Chapel Hill High's drama department and sang in the school choir. In many ways we were more permissive with her than with David and Phil, probably because she was more difficult to handle.

Phil got no special dispensation because of his illness. Once I woke up at three o'clock in the morning to discover he still wasn't home. I tracked him down at Jane's. I was determined to keep them all alive till they reached twenty-one if it killed me.

The last time David gave me any grief was when he was playing club football at Duke. There was a big game with Coastal Carolina down at Myrtle Beach. I got a call late at night from an irate motel manager full of complaints and threats over the behavior of a bunch of boys there. They had gotten into pillow fights, spilled beer all over the beds and rugs and generally trashed the place.

"Why call me?"

"The rooms were registered in your son's name."

I wasn't any too sympathetic with the manager, who seemed overwrought, but promised I would bring his complaints to David's attention. With David I was a little more severe. "You'll have to pay for the damage, David. Get your teammates to do their share. You're all equally responsible. But don't expect me to pay for your mistake. And, by the way, let somebody else sign the room registration cards next time."

David was a popular boy and easy to identify because of his red hair. Everybody liked him. One day in his senior year in Cheraw, a friend of his called out to me, "Hey, Mr. Secrest, I saw David in Charlotte last night." What would David be doing in the Queen City seventy-five miles away? I thought he had spent the evening with Brenda Brown or Nubbin Brown, whom we called "Breathless" because she was inclined to hyperventilate when something upset her.

I told David that Skipper had said they'd been in Charlotte the night before. David denied it. And he has never admitted it to this day. Now when I ask, he just grins and says, "I wasn't in Charlotte." Anyone care to bet?

# 51. NIH and Leukemia

The editorial policy of the Chronicle, both before and after the move to McLean, was not dominated by race, although that topic attracted the greatest attention. I was an early voice against American military involvement in Southeast Asia. When President Kennedy raised the question of Laos in 1961, in his first televised news conference, I called an implied intervention there "a lousy idea."

As early as 1963 the *Chronicle* warned against U.S. involvement in Vietnam, recognizing that conflict for what it was—a civil war in which we had no national interest. I later also argued against the manner in which it was waged, by draftees, too young, poor or ignorant to be able to avoid the draft by going to college or joining the National Guard, and least able to afford the sacrifice. I got into a rhubarb with Adjutant General Pinckney, Commander of the South Carolina National Guard, when the *Chronicle* called his organization a refuge for privileged draft dodgers.

That editorial dogfight still pleases me as much as anything I ever wrote. It was closely allied to civil rights and race as the South Carolina National Guard was then largely closed to young black men who were, as a class, unable to avoid the draft due to their relatively low economic status. For most of them the college option was out of the question. But, once we were deeply enmeshed in the war, I could see no easy way out. I had nothing in common with "Hanoi" Jane Fonda who once posed in a tank in the North Vietnam capital, or other war protesters who sometimes victimized those very soldiers who had been drafted to serve. As usual, I found myself somewhere in the middle, catching heat from both sides.

Many other questions arose during my Cheraw tenure. Sometimes I may have skated on thin ice. But I understood the laws of libel in South Carolina. I made sure of my facts, relying on truth as an absolute defense. We never published with what the courts call "malice." Had I abused my constitutional protection under the First Amendment, I believe I would have been successfully sued for libel, but I never was, even though the *Chronicle*:

1.   Reported the rumor that a prominent planter had kept migrant farm workers locked up in pens, feeding them slop from troughs and hauling them to and from the fields for substandard wages or no pay at all. He was later convicted on the unusual state charge of peonage.

2.   Printed gossip about sub-standard conditions at a county prison farm, including reports of oral sodomy among other abuses, which prompted a civil rights investigation and a subsequent conviction of some of the personnel in command of the facility on federal charges.

3.   Published reports that a county commissioner was using public equipment for private use, including home improvements, a report which he denied but said, in effect, he wouldn't do any more.

4.   Revealed a conflict of interest involving a corporate executive (a school board member himself) who successfully persuaded the school board to sell his company property—in some kind of convoluted financial deal—that had been used by the Negro high school as its athletic field, leaving the school "bare-backed and empty-handed." After this revelation, the county school board overruled the action of the local district board and returned the property to the black school.

5.   Called upon the county solicitor—and he agreed—to bring additional charges, other than "simple affray" (which was the original complaint) against a father and his bevy of grown sons who, in a family feud, had exchanged gunshots across busy U.S. Highway 1, endangering the lives not only of people in the neighborhood but also tourists on a heavily traveled highway from Maine to Florida. The boys later came to see me at the office. I almost got my clock cleaned that time, but *Chronicle* employees came to my rescue, just before I left Cheraw in June 1964 for a two-year tour of duty in Washington.

Phil, 13 years old when the family joined me in McLean, Virginia in August, had one cold after another that fall. He ran low-grade fevers which came and went. His color was often ashen. He began to lose weight. But then he would pick up again, seldom missing school, never complaining.

In early January, just before I left for Selma, Ann took him to a doctor. Ushered into the inner sanctum by the office nurse who was overly solicitous of her boss, Ann took her seat alongside Phil and waited and . .

. waited . . . and waited. The doctor looked up from his desk, then without a word, resumed his reading. Ann took out her knitting. After about half an hour, the doctor said, "Mrs. Secrest, put aside your handwork. I'll be with you shortly."

"Whenever you are ready, sir, we will be right here," she replied, as she brought out another ball of yarn and resumed her work. As the minutes ticked slowly by, the doctor occasionally looked up reprovingly. Ann's needles clicked more rapidly and loudly. Finally, the doctor got up, walked over to her. "Madam, I'm afraid I cannot help you."

"You don't need to, I'm not your patient. Phil is. You need to examine him."

"What's the matter with him?"

"That's what I'm here to find out," Ann replied, "but he's not been well for several weeks. He's losing weight."

"He's not too thin," the doctor replied.

"Well, take another look at him. Any fool can see he's thin as a rail. This weight loss, intermittent fever, sallow complexion and …"

Before she could continue, the doctor—still apparently miffed by her knitting in his presence—interrupted. "I do not consider you or your son my patient," he said sharply, and called his nurse to show them the door.

When we received a bill for $75, I took my time answering it. Finally, home briefly from Selma in April, I wrote on the third bill, "No examination, no prescription, no advice, no diagnosis, no prognosis, no payment." By early April Phil had picked up, gained weight, felt fine. I reported the doctor to the Better Business Bureau and local and state medical associations. No action was ever taken.

That summer I began to receive calls from a bill collector, threatening legal action and damage to my credit if prompt payment of the doctor's bill wasn't made. Harassing phone calls were made, many late at night. I managed to get the name and telephone number of the bill collector. Ann and I then enlisted David, Phil and Molly in a counter-harassment campaign—right down a teenager's alley.

Whenever the collection agent called, the kids were instructed to blow whistles and horns into the receiver. If we left town for a weekend, I'd call his home, give him my vacation address and telephone number, and urge him to call as we had grown accustomed to his voice. It was a replay of the way Lil and I had harassed telephone operators in Monroe 35 years earlier. I ridiculed any threats to my credit rating. We were beyond his reach. By the following January, he had given up.

In March, a year after seeing the first doctor, Phil got sick again. He couldn't throw off the effects of one virus after another. The low-grade fever returned. It was bizarre, as his condition would fluctuate from listless and wan to robust and energetic.

In late April, just before I had to go to Memphis on a racial conciliation mission, Phil came down with a high fever. By Sunday night it had broken, but he was weak and wrung out. Phil's flaming red hair and freckles stood out in sharp contrast to his alabaster skin, now so white he looked as if he didn't have one red corpuscle in his body.

Ann took me to the airport and Phil to the doctor—not the same one she had consulted the year before. This doctor was as good as the other had been bad. Phil got a thorough physical, including a blood panel study, results to be back Friday. I returned to McLean Thursday night. Phil still was home in bed, white as the sheets he lay on. The report the next day told us that Phil, at nearly 15 years of age, had developed acute lymphocytic leukemia, the kind that usually affects much younger children.

Phil was immediately accepted into the first on-going group of patients being treated at the National Institutes of Health with chemotherapy. At the time life expectancy of most patients with this disease was eighteen months. Many children enrolled in the NIH program were alive and in remission after three years and still going strong.

He entered the clinic in Bethesda, Maryland, that same night, April 22, and was back in McLean in full remission in less than a month. He tolerated well the side effects of the four toxic experimental drugs—Vincristin, L-mercaptupurine, Methotrexate, and Prednisone— given in combination called the pomp cycle.

Emotional stress is often manifested by physical distress—insomnia, loss of appetite, a sinking feeling in the pit of one's stomach. While Phil accepted the diagnosis with his customary aplomb, I did not. At first I had all these psychosomatic complaints. They were soon displaced, however, by a return of symptoms of an earlier problem: obsessive/compulsive disorder, which hadn't bothered me since early childhood.

I began to bargain with God again. If Phil were to be saved from leukemia, I would change my Doubting Thomas ways and become a true believer. When I took long walks during lunch at the Dept. of Justice, I would be careful not to step on any cracks in the sidewalk. I would always start off on my left foot and count up to 100. If I got out of step, so that my right foot came down on an uneven number, I would do a little hop to rectify the count and hold my breath for 30 seconds.

Bizarre? Nuts? Well, anything to save my son. A good dissembler, I disguised my OCD from others until I soon got it under control. But I discarded one peculiarity only to substitute another.

One evening while Phil was still in the NIH clinic, I drove down to McLean's Dart Drug Store to pick up a paperback book that contained material on a subject Phil needed for a school paper. He should keep up with his school work. The distraction would be good for him.

I leafed through the book that retailed for $1.98, found 45 pages that related to his topic, and ripped them out. Carefully concealing them in my raincoat, I sauntered out of the store. "Look what I found at the drug store for Phil," I announced to Ann at home, and pulled out the rumpled sheets.

Ann looked, first out of interest, then in disbelief. "Mac, you're nuts! What do you think you're doing? Don't you know that's stealing?" She reminded me that I could not only be prosecuted for shoplifting, but also lose my job.

I then remembered that Stewart Udall, a member of President Johnson's Cabinet as Secretary of the Interior, had been arrested only a few days earlier at that same drugstore for putting a cigar in his coat pocket and forgetting to pay for it. Udall clearly was not a kleptomaniac. He'd paid for his other purchases, but an overzealous manager had refused to accept his explanation and called the cops. The incident made headlines in the *Washington Post* even though Udall was exonerated.

"Think of the risk you ran," Ann said. "You don't think we can afford $1.98 for a paperback book? Besides, it is dishonest. Go right back over there, stick those pages back into the book and then buy it—and hope the clerk doesn't notice anything."

I did as I was told, now fully aware of what I had done and the risk I had run. I learned a lesson I never forgot as well as insight into another facet of human nature. People will do strange things sometimes under stress. Everybody needs to understand that. The Dart Drug Store incident was the first and last time I ever shoplifted anything.

Before Phil got sick we enjoyed life in McLean, especially after I got a desk job and was promoted to my level of incompetence. We even briefly entertained the idea of staying there permanently.

As we had in Cheraw, we joined a Methodist church and took, rather than sent, David, Phil and Molly with us. Ed Wright, a Baptist turned Methodist, was our activist minister, a strong believer that faith without good works was dead.

He called one day in early 1966 to ask if Ann and I could put up a couple of students from Wofford College touring the Northeast with the college choir scheduled to present a concert at the church Saturday afternoon and on Sunday morning. Sure, we could do that.

Will Williman from Spartanburg, S.C. and his roommate James Rivers from Chesterfield were our guests for two nights. After the Saturday concert and dinner at our house we took them for a tour of the nation's capital by moonlight—the tidal basin, the Jefferson Memorial, Lincoln's monument, the White House, the U.S Capitol, the eternal flame at Arlington National Cemetery.

Ten years later we met Williman again, this time as pastor of the North Myrtle Beach Methodist Church. We had bought a house at the beach and attended Sunday morning services on the frequent weekends we spent there.

Some years after that our paths crossed yet again, as Williman came to Duke to be associated with Duke Chapel. Today Will is chaplain of Duke Chapel and an activist pastor, concerning himself with student activities, including problems of binge drinking, auto safety, and inattentive academic enterprise.

I don't see Williman much. I don't go to Duke Chapel often. But over the years we've exchanged notes. I last saw him, his wife and a couple of youngsters walking down Franklin Street in Chapel Hill, licking ice cream cones. Williman's name in 2003 got on a short list for bishop of North Carolina. I hoped he would stay at Duke. But in July, 2004, William was named a methodist bishop, sponsored by the S.C. Diocese and left the campus.

We decided to leave McLean when Phil was discharged from the Bethesda clinic in early June. He could live anywhere and still be under the care of NIH and their specialists. I had wearied of the tension and travel associated with my work at the Community Relations Service. David, Phil and Molly were anxious to return to Cheraw. Ann was willing. Her job as librarian at school awaited her. Duchess, our boxer, and Sheba, our orange tabby cat expecting her second litter of kittens in three months, and her husband Purr didn't seem to care. I had been away from the *Chronicle* long enough and Eddie Sweat, my right-hand man, had borne the responsibility entirely too long. We came home August 1, 1966.

Long High School had a long, proud and segregated history in Cheraw. As a reluctant concession to integration, moves were now being made to place some Caucasians among the faculty. Ann agreed to work at Long High as librarian, one of two white faces there. David and Phil returned to all-white Cheraw High School, merger of the two schools and integration of students being still three years away. David's closest friends since age four at the Little Red School House, George Walters, Skipper Nock, and Pokey Ingram, welcomed him back. So did Phil's and Molly's buddies.

Years before Ann joined the Long High School faculty, an incident occurred there that enables me to claim a momentary association with a man later to become a musical icon. Entertainers are overpaid, overly admired, and usually irritate me. I don't like *People* magazine, the epitome of a kitch culture obsessed with celebrity. I don't claim to understand or to appreciate popular music that emerged in the 1960s and became louder and more invasive with each passing decade and gained international acclaim. Maybe "fifty million Frenchmen can't be wrong," but I don't have to pretend to like it.

Yet I do like two musical celebrities whose artistic gifts I have never understood. Dizzy Gilllespie I came to know and admire personally. James Brown I never met beyond the following brief, indirect encounter. He was an energetic, slim, handsome young man when he came up with The Flames from N. Augusta, S.C. to Long High School in Cheraw one day in the late 1950s or early '60s. I was invited to attend the concert. Police Chief McLaurin and a deputy were also on hand.

In the middle of the event, which had the all-black audience rocking, something went awry. Lights went out, the cash box fell to the floor, money sliding all over the floor as fists began flying in the air. Brown and his band tried to scoop up their money as others contended for it. The police sought to intervene, and Principal Otis Ford tried to restore order, but to no avail. Brown and The Flames ran out the door, jumped into their cars and took off, as gunfire was heard from some unidentified quarter.

A few years after that Brown made his big breakthrough in California and earned his title, "Godfather of Soul." Since then he has fallen and risen, re-inventing himself as the times demand. Out of all that has emerged an admirable, likable man, honest and direct, revered by black and white fans.

"The black man will never gain justice in America," Brown was recently quoted, but he has remained a patriotic citizen who loves his country, seeking to become part of a solution, not the problem. And because I was at Long High School one day early in his career, I can say, with some exaggeration, that "I knew him when."

Phil had to go to NIH monthly for treatment and tests. Home only six weeks, he relapsed in mid-September. For the next three months, he received massive amounts of chemotherapy intravenously. The protocol was five days at NIH, five days back home in Cheraw. Ann and I took turns driving or flying to Bethesda, staying with him at a nearby motel, then returning to Cheraw. By late December, he was back in remission, though weak and emaciated from the ravages of chemotherapy.

The Cancer Institute at NIH was a wonderful place. It combined the best of two institutions that often disappoint: the medical profession and the federal government. NIH provided the treatment and the funding, the patients provided the bodies. It was all new and highly experimental. Drugs were administered in unprecedented high dosages. No one could be sure of the consequences. It was largely a matter of faith and hope, wait and see.

After December Phil began to pick up. Again in remission, his treatment changed. Now NIH provided us the medication complete with injection kits. We were to give him shots twice a week at home. Once a month we would take Phil to Bethesda for five days of more intensive therapy given by the NIH medical staff. Phil regained his hair, weight and strength.

When Phil re-entered NIH in late June 1968 with high fever and pale as a ghost, the doctors thought he had relapsed. But he had not. Then they said he had tuberculosis. I disagreed. I remembered Aunt Sue telling me about her grandson Mark Martin's having contracted histoplasmosis several years earlier, and I remembered the symptoms of tuberculosis from my two years in Saranac Lake. Phil's symptoms were compatible with the Ohio River fungus, not with TB. I urged the doctors to test him for and to give him antibiotics for histoplasmosis. They agreed. In this case, Daddy really did know best.

For three months he remained in intensive care at NIH without any chemotherapy. The drug to combat the fungus infection could not be given with the anti-leukemia medications. Yet he never relapsed. Once again he had dodged death and come home, soon as good as new, to start his senior year.

While Ann and I took turns at NIH that summer, with Lil and Molly often by our side, I again took advantage of an opportunity. Ralph Abernathy had led a poor people's march on Washington that July. His civil rights group, largely SCLC and SNCC volunteers, camped on the outskirts of the city much as the homeless veterans had done in the early 1930s. I took time off to go see them and to speak with Abernathy. That was when he shared his view that "Martin wasn't perfect."

Phil did not suffer a bone marrow relapse for nearly seven years although he did have problems with occasional errant malignant cells in his blood that infiltrated his central nervous system, requiring chemical injections by way of spinal taps. In his spring term as a Sophomore at Duke in 1971, Phil had to go to NIH every day for treatment for five days straight for six weeks. Ann and I took turns driving to Bethesda and back to Chapel Hill the same day. Phil usually did much of the driving himself. Again the treatment worked.

Despite his illness, with all its ups and downs, Phil never complained, indulged in self-pity or feared death. As he lived with this dreadful disease, he was in fact pretty well. But his weight recycled, up to a husky, robust 160 pounds, then down to 120 when some subsidiary illness or new medication weighed him down.

After he became sixteen, Phil could go back and forth to Bethesda by himself. He usually stayed with the parents of his best friend in McLean, John Bartley. John's parents, Whit and Betty, became our close friends as well. Phil came to regard them as his other set of parents. Ironically Phil's friend John, never sick a day, was killed in an auto accident in July, 1972, while on an archaeology dig in Wyoming. We all attended John's funeral in McLean, staying with Jane Clayton and her parents.

David and Phil were both good students in high school and college. Unlike their father, neither son was set apart. Both were popular with their peers. Phil's classmates admired his courage and supported him. They cheered the debonair manner he wore his red hairpiece at basketball games after his hair fell out. Not to worry. It would grow back. The people of Cheraw will always have my affection for the manner in which they accepted Phil and held him close for the three years before we moved to Chapel Hill in September, 1969. Unlike dear old dad, both sons and later daughter Molly were members of the National Honor Society. David in 1968 was valedictorian of his class. Phil, despite all the time he had to miss from school, was valedictorian of his class in 1969.

# 52. Back to Duke and Chapel Hill

I sold the Chronicle in 1968. Pressure from constantly living on the center stage of community life and from parental responsibilities was beginning to take its toll. David enrolled at Duke in the fall. Phil followed in 1969. So did I, entering graduate school the same year. I had already attended summer school at Duke in 1967 and 1968, gathering hours and credits with the possible purpose of earning a MAT degree in history.

Ann and I felt the need to be near Phil but didn't wish to hover. We decided to live in Chapel Hill. Molly enrolled in the seventh grade of Guy B. Phillips Junior High School. She was to prove as good a student as her brothers. I was fortunate in having Robert Durden as my advisor. He was a firm but kind mentor, turning himself inside out to help me get every scholarship available. Durden, later to become the Duke family biographer, knew how to rein in my undisciplined temperament. He and I. B. Holley, Harold Parker and Theodore Ropp were faculty advisors I remember best. They encouraged me to move along rapidly. They wanted me up and out into the work place before I qualified for social security. Within two years of entering graduate school, I had completed my course work, written my dissertation and successfully defended it.

David and Phil loved Duke. They joined Sigma Chi fraternity. I taught Phil's roommate, a pre-med student, how to give Phil the shots Ann and I had given him for three years. I remember smelling the whiffs of marijuana that hung in the air as I walked down the dormitory hall. It was the era of campus revolution. The age of Aquarius and the Woodstock Nation had arrived. *Hair, Jesus Christ Superstar*, and a little later *Miss Saigon* were the popular road show attractions reflecting the generation gap and the

Vietnam agony. Phil's girlfriend from McLean, Jane Clayton, also attended Duke. Jane had been in our lives since 1964. David met his "Sweetheart of Sigma Chi," Leslie (Mindy) Fuller, during his sophomore year.

The student revolution had begun as early as 1963 with the free speech movement at Berkeley. Bob Dylan was already warning parents that times were a'changin'. Jack Kerouac's *On the Road* had appeared, as the bible of the Beat Generation. *Easy Rider*, an early film about "alienated youth," was to appear only a year after Ann and I moved back to Chapel Hill. The Beatles had appeared on the Ed Sullivan Show as early as 1964.

The Vietnam War, the civil rights movement, drug use, and other events reaching back even earlier partly explain the generation gap and cultural revolution that followed. The three P's were cited: penicillin (thought to be a cure-all for sexually transmitted diseases), the pill (freeing women from fears of unwanted pregnancy), and permissivity (Dr. Spock's child-rearing advice to the "Greatest Generation"). By 1968 Gay Rights had joined Women's Rights in the over-all movement toward liberation of youth.

The stage was set for a campus revolution that burned most brightly in California, the Northeast, and Midwest. The academic citadel with its old-fashioned notions of in *loco parentis* was overrun as easily and quickly as the Maginot Line had been in 1940. The revolution spread more slowly in the South, traditionally more socially conservative. But at both Duke and Carolina the impact was felt.

Student newspapers soon joined the fray. The *Daily Tar Heel* even carried a sex information column written by a Dr. Takey Crist, a member, as I recall, of the N.C. Memorial Hospital staff. This column was similar in content to *Loveline* (and Dr. Drew) on MTV a generation later. The column had a question and answer format. One question that appeared shortly after I'd returned to college and admittedly shocked me, was: "What is the nutritional value of semen?"

The answer, clinical and non-evaluative: none, except for the female egg. "Good grief," I complained to Ann, "is this what kids come to college to learn these days? Surely they must already know that." But that was thirty years before a survey on college campuses (in 2000) revealed that oral sex was the preferred sexual practice. Why? Because it relieved the male of anxiety about exposure to HIV and females from concerns about pregnancy and the abortion alternative. Although oral sex can work both ways (check the *Vagina Monologues*), it is usually the male who gets the quick, impersonal service, often in anonymous "hook-ups," and the coed who gets short-changed and runs the greatest risks.

Still in my liberal mode, I was glad to be back in school, despite such culture shock. Chapel Hill was a bastion of free thought but a town which had faced the challenge of racial integration only six years earlier and had been found wanting. In 1963 Chapel Hill was challenged to practice what it preached and to integrate its churches, schools and places of public accommodation. Protests arose, riots broke out, violence occurred. Chapel Hill was little better than Oxford, Mississippi, had been in 1962.

In those days I would drive up from Cheraw to see what was happening. I met with Gary Blanchard, a native of Maine, editor of the *Daily Tar Heel*, and encouraged him to lead the campus newspaper in the right direction. He occasionally reprinted pro-integration editorials from the *Cheraw Chronicle* in the *Daily Tar Heel*.

Gary became critical of Raymond Mallard, presiding judge in Hillsborough who was hearing cases arising out of the racial protests. Mallard, a native of Tabor City, North Carolina, who was an uncle of cousin Brack Craven's law clerk, entrapped Blanchard. He ordered the campus editor to repeat in the courtroom what he had written about the judge in one of his editorials. If he refused to do so, he would be held in contempt of court. If he did repeat the criticism in the judge's presence, he would also be found in contempt of court.

There were some voices raised in protest, especially those of Charlie Jones, University Presbyterian minister and his followers, whose church was split by the controversy. But the silent majority was little better in Chapel Hill than in Selma two years later, or in Cheraw before and after that.

One voice that had a Monroe connection was not silent. Dr. Critz George, no native Southerner he, was professor of anatomy and biology in the medical school. He had married a gentle Southern lady from Monroe, a sister of Miss Wilma Green, close friend of Lessie Secrest. Dr. and Mrs. George had kept up their ties with Union County. When my friend Moke Williams had been about to flunk out of medical school twelve years earlier, Dr. George helped keep him in.

Dr. George, with claim to knowledge of genetics, was a racist. He believed the Negro race was inherently inferior to the Caucasian race, lagging behind it by some twenty thousand years due to a glitch in the evolutionary process. He belched up his theories with a lot of so-called scientific data. Tom Waring, editor of the *News and Courier* in Charleston, and a leading "bitter-ender" in the struggle against integration, often cited George's work.

The UNC faculty polarized around Dr. George who found considerable support for his notions in a "liberal" UNC in the 1950s and early 1960s. The *Chapel Hill Weekly*, then edited by Jim Shumaker, steered clear of the fray. With friends on both sides and a lot of advertising at stake, the liberal editor, whose personal sympathies lay with the black protesters, decided there was little his newspaper could do to help restore reason and civility to the fury swirling all about him. He decided for the most part to stay on the sidelines. It was not Shumaker's finest hour—a fact he acknowledged to me at the time and later openly admitted. It was an uncharacteristic lapse on the part of a fine newspaperman—a man usually of forthright views and extraordinary courage.

Gary Blanchard thought I was not entirely fair to Shumaker. "Remember, Mac, Jim had a job and a family to support. Feelings, as you know, were running high. Orville Campbell, publisher, wouldn't print editorials supporting integration and criticizing the bitter-enders that Shumaker wrote," Gary recalled.

The former editor of the student newspaper, recalling in 2003 events forty years earlier, added, "Jim Shumaker, frustrated by Campbell's timidity, wrote some of the editorials that appeared in the *Daily Tar Heel* under my name. " Gary then told me something which he said had never been revealed before. "Jim wrote the editorial that so infuriated Judge Mallard and almost landed me in jail!"

Now sixty-four years old and living in retirement in New Jersey, Gary declared, "Mac, it's so great to hear from you again. What a blast from the past! I remember how you worked with and counseled me and my co-editor in those days. Every time you left I'd pray to God I'd see you again. I feared you might come to a sad end at the hands of people who really were worked up. I never believed you realized the risks you ran down there in South Carolina."

Gary also recalled working with Bill Friday, university president, and Bill Aycock, chancellor. "I remember Friday, Aycock, Shumaker and you as the four men, each in your own different way, who helped me and the *Daily Tar Heel* the most and taught me the value of ethics in leading a worthy, principled life."

Welcome words of praise from a man I only knew when he was a youngster of twenty-three and twenty-four and I an "old man" of thirty-nine and forty. Welcome, but somewhat overstated. I may have encouraged and supported Blanchard, but he was his own man who knew what he had to do. "Don't forget Walter Spearman, your journalism professor, and his enduring support and words of wisdom," I reminded Gary as we concluded our long-distance cell phone conversation.

In 1969 the University's reputation was still recovering from the speaker ban law earlier imposed on it by the N.C. General Assembly. The law had disallowed any speaker on campus who espoused communist doctrine. But by now the whole climate of negative social protest had changed. The integration process, while not smooth, was progressing. Ann and I found the political climate less oppressive than that in South Carolina at least. There the last places I would have expected support from were the places of higher education or the church. In Cheraw only two ministers over the fifteen years I spent there lent me any support from the pulpit—Fred Harris of the First Methodist Church and Father Walter Melfi of St. Peter's Catholic Church. Fred Harris wasn't there too long and Father Melfi soon kicked his habit, left the church and got married.

So when Ann and I came back to Chapel Hill that September of 1969, one of the first things we did was look around for a church we thought we might feel comfortable in. I had heard about the Rev. Dr. Robert Seymour, a Baptist preacher of all things, at the Binkley Memorial Baptist Church. I called Dr. Seymour and asked if I could come see him. He said he would come call on us instead. When he came I proceeded to cross-examine him, as if he were a hostile witness in court. I wanted to be sure Bob Seymour was liberal enough for Mac Secrest. What a laugh. Seymour and I remain friends, but now I view him to the left of me and he probably sees me as a member of the moderate right. People and times change, but Seymour, in retirement, remains a living legend and local treasure. The same can be said of our mutual friend, the Rev. W.W. Finlator of Raleigh, now pushing ninety and still going strong.

I enjoyed meeting students on campus, too, at Duke and at Carolina, and engaging them in conversation, sometimes controversial, often in agreement, always stimulating. One of the first students I met was a youngster I understood was a Junior transfer from Northwestern University—bright, opinionated, full of intellectual curiosity. Michael Barefoot was a native of Johnston County, son of the county agricultural agent there. Mike was a handsome kid, with bright hazel eyes and thick chestnut hair that curled in ringlets all over his head and which obviously hadn't been cut in years. He wore cut-off jeans above the knee and a dirty old tee-shirt bearing some liberal slogan of the day. It was standard student attire.

Mike was interested in history and social philosophy and, of course, the student movement. I was interested in student mentality. Initially attracted by Duchess, who always went with me on campus walks, Mike soon became interested in my experiences as an editor and my decision to return to school at the ancient age of forty-six.

We discussed capitalism, communism, socialism, Marxism, the New Deal, Richard Nixon, war and revolution, and, especially, the Vietnam War and campus reaction. Kent State was only a few months away. I lent him my favorite study of the Soviet experiment, *Three Who Made a Revolution*, by Bertrand Wolfe, biographies of Lenin, Trotsky and Stalin. Always skeptical of the communist experiment in Russia, of all places, I was already slowly turning to the right. I'd written extensive comments in the margins on every page. I gave the book to Mike.

Like many students of that era, Mike also seemed to be suspicious of anyone over thirty. He didn't really trust me, suspecting that I may have been an F.B.I. agent or a narc. That seemed to be an impression many students of that era had of me. I didn't see much of Barefoot after 1970, as he was soon to graduate and move on.

A few years later I met him again at the Wildflower Kitchen, a vegetarian restaurant on West Franklin Street, when Professor Walter Spearman and I went there for lunch. Mike was a waiter there, preparing to go to school at UNC-G to study food and merchandising. Walter, a friend of mine since 1949, had also been Mike's faculty mentor years later.

Before long Barefoot had returned to Chapel Hill to become associated with another restaurant. Soon he started his own enterprise, A Southern Season, which has become a nationally-known food and specialty shop including a popular restaurant, the Weather Vane. Today A Southern Season is a major Chapel Hill landmark and employer, recently to become a major "anchor store" at the University Mall. Mike is a major wholesaler and retailer, shipping goods all over the country.

He is also a buttoned-down, well-dressed model of what a bright, educated, motivated, ambitious young man or woman can achieve in a free-enterprise economy. How the boomer generation has changed. I seldom see Mike anymore. He is busy. I'm retired. Our paths wouldn't cross. But every time I go into A Southern Season, I'm proud of him and of the society which produced him.

Phil had a bone marrow relapse in September, 1972, his senior year. He divided his fall semester between Duke and NIH, spending his outpatient time with his second parents, Whit and Betty Bartley, who showered him with the attention and love they could no longer give to their son John.

Despite Phil's frequent absence from class and the gradual decline of his health, Phil continued to make the Dean's List. He was able to spend Christmas with Ann and me, David and Molly at our mountain cabin near Burnsville, North Carolina. He felt good, again in remission, full of Christmas spirit.

But in late February, his white blood count spiked. We flew with him to Bethesda where NIH found him in relapse, his system overwhelmed by the rapidly multiplying malignant white cells. They had grown resistant to all forms of chemotherapy. His injured bone marrow was unable to make platelets. Newer drugs proved no more effective than the old ones. His depleted physical condition was too weak to risk a new bone marrow transplant procedure, even if one could have found a match. Ann, David, Molly and I had been tested the preceding September. None of us was a match.

Three months earlier Phil's first cousin Celeste Buie had entered the clinic at Bethesda for treatment at the National Institute for Mental Health. More like a sister than a cousin, Celeste temporarily set her own troubles aside. She came down from the sixth floor to visit with Phil by the hour. As he became weaker, more comatose, she continued to sit quietly by his bedside.

Phil was allowed no such peace and quiet on weekends. David, now in the U.S. Coast Guard and stationed in Washington, and practically all of Phil's brothers from Sigma Chi, came up and filled his room, standing, sitting, squatting on the floor to lend their support. Julya Rose Hodge and Ed Robeson, Phil's best friends from Cheraw, were on hand as well. It was ACC Tournament time and March Madness was in full sway. Phil's room rocked with cheers as all eyes, Phil's included, were locked on the television screen.

Ann and I took turns, going up on long weekends, sometimes with Molly and Lil. I was now teaching at the School of Journalism at the University of North Carolina. It was my turn to go on Friday, March 23. I stayed with Phil and Celeste during the day, spent the nights with Whit and Betty. I had a miserable cold. I was pissed off at Richard Nixon over the unraveling Watergate scandal, the Christmas bombing in Vietnam, frightened at the disintegrating situation in the Middle East. My concern over Phil sank so deep I couldn't even feel it anymore.

As I lay awake in the downstairs bedroom of the Bartley home at three o'clock Sunday morning, I heard the phone ring. Brnng! Brnng! Brnng! The urgency of the sound carried its own message. Let it ring. I already knew. The phone did keep on ringing. It would stop briefly, then resume. Not wishing to disturb Whit and Betty, I finally got up and took the message. Phil had died, quietly and peacefully, alone at last.

Phil had become a believer a few years earlier by the influence of a woman whose son was also a patient at NIH. A stylish, painted woman who looked more like a model than a born-again Christian, she was a comfort to Phil, often relieving him of constant physical pain by a simple laying on of hands. Her name of all things was Mrs. Ghost. Whether she was really filled with the spirit of the Holy Ghost I never knew. I always left the room when she and Phil had a session as I did not want my negative vibes to interrupt any spiritual transaction. Maybe Phil wasn't alone when he died March 25, 1973.

The J-School faculty, led by Dean Jack Adams, came by the house the night after the memorial service for Phil in Cheraw and the funeral and burial in Monroe. They had prepared a dinner and served it themselves to Ann and me, David and Mindy, Lil and Celeste, and Jane, Phil's girlfriend, and Jane's mother Martha. They returned after dinner, cleared the table, put away the leftovers, and did the dishes.

Someone notified Gillespie in New Jersey. Soon the phone rang. "Hey, man, this is Dizzy. Comin' down to see you tomorrow." And so he did, to pay his respects, to listen more than to talk, but sharing some of his Bahai faith. Knowing my reservations and discomfort with personal prayer, he simply talked about living and dying and his acceptance of all religions and belief in a unifying, universal spirit beyond human comprehension that uplifts all mankind. He didn't stay long but his message and his presence were a comfort.

I didn't see much of Gillespie after that, occasionally receiving telephone calls to see how "my man" was doing. Dizzy died twenty years later, in 1993. He left a personal legacy far more important to Ann and me than his musical legacy to the world.

Duke University was sympathetic and generous to us as well. When Ann and I went over to the Bursar's Office to pay off the balance on Phil's considerable student loan, the officer replied, "Oh, no, Phil was a fine young man, an excellent student, an uplifting example to others. We were lucky to have him. I just want to express the sympathy of the University to you and your family." I always found Duke to be responsive to human need, in this case in sharp contrast to Wake Forest University, which rejected Phil's application in 1968 presumably because of his illness. They knew the odds—as did Duke. Apparently, in their view, why run the risk or waste the money?

How do you get over the loss of a child? In a sense, you don't. You never forget. You wouldn't even want to. Give yourself some space. Gradually angry resignation is replaced by peaceful acceptance. Father Time and Mother Nature eventually take care of everything. I don't question any more. And happy memories have crowded out the sad ones.

# 53. A New Career: UNC and NCCU

In 1969 I had returned to Duke as a graduate student in the History Department. By 1971 I had completed my course work and dissertation. The School of Journalism at the University of North Carolina at Chapel Hill then offered me a five-year contract as associate professor to begin in the fall semester. I wasn't to receive my degree, however, until graduation in May, 1972. David and I received our degrees on the same day. Walter Cronkite, CBS news anchorman, was the commencement speaker.

That night Ann and I had the mother of all graduation parties at our home at 307 Wesley Court in Chapel Hill. Although time had taken its toll of my parents' generation, many of those who were left showed up for the event: Mother, Aunt Eve, Rosa Parker, Betty Webb and Ray Veatch, Ann Brooks, Ann Redwine, and Uncle Vann and his bride Mary Douglas.

Most of my friends had to work, but Philip, home early from his post at Tulsa University and aware as always of the value of proximity in maintaining friendship, was on hand. So were Lil and John and their children Jim and Celeste, and Mary Cov and Bill with all four of their children, as well as Phil and Jane, David and Mindy, Molly and friend Alice Grainger, David's roommate John Collins, and most of the other Duke Sigma Chi's. Brack Craven, en route to court in Richmond, stopped by, as did Hill Wolfe and his fifth wife, Mary, up from Southern Pines.

Several of my students at UNC came over as well as colleagues from the School of Journalism. Even Terry Sanford, then president of Duke, dropped by, partly to pay his respects to David and me but mainly to see Lil, who taught school with his mother at Scotland High in Laurinburg.

I was particularly pleased, however, by the arrival of former Gov. Luther Hodges, who, as U.S. Secretary of Commerce, had been my over-all boss my first year with the Community Relations Service in Washington.

Luther in 1972 was still the best known public figure in North Carolina and its most celebrated and famous contemporary citizen. He had served as governor longer than any other, as governors were not then allowed to run for second terms. As lieutenant governor, he had assumed office in October 1954 when Governor William Umstead died and was easily re-elected in 1956, serving until January 1961 when President Kennedy named him U.S. Secretary of Commerce. I attended Hodges' inaugural. Sitting next to me was Terry Sanford. As Luther placed his hand on the Bible when he was sworn in, Terry whispered to me, "That's where I'm going to be four years from now." And sure enough, he was. Sanford became known as the education governor, even if he had to tax food and medicine to raise the money to achieve his goals.

The idea of a research center centrally located to draw upon the resources of Duke, UNC, and NC State originated in the mid-1950s during Hodges' second administration. He immediately recognized its potential and devoted his personal energy and political power to the enterprise. When the idea initially languished, Hodges breathed renewed life into it when he persuaded IBM and other major corporations to come to the area to further their basic research projects. If any one person earned the title, "Father of the RTP," it was Luther H. Hodges.

Never one to stay still, Hodges agreed to serve as president of Rotary International upon his retirement and used his influence there to further his state's economic development. During his years as governor, he also established the foundation for what became the N.C. Community College system.

Perhaps Luther's major achievement, however, for which he has never received recognition, lay in his steering a steady course of racial peace and reconciliation between 1954 and 1960. When most of the leaders of other states contiguous to North Carolina were in defiance or denial, Gov. Hodges backed a program known as the Pearsal Plan that, however dubious its constitutionality, was designed to provide time for a gradual but progressive compliance with the U.S. Supreme court's desegregation decisions. While some critics considered this too conservative, one can only be judged within the context of one's time.

Gov. Hodges' leadership in those early days stands head and shoulders above that of Virginia, South Carolina, Tennessee, and Georgia. I had placed his and Martha's names on the *Chronicle's* mailing list in 1954, and every now and again I'd receive a note of encouragement from Martha, saying in effect, "Keep up the good work. Luther and I are proud of you."

But no man is perfect, and Luther made a personal mistake when he married his secretary Louise Finlayson in 1970, nine months after Martha, his wife of 47 years, died of smoke inhalation when their new home on Battle Lane in Chapel Hill caught fire. Luther himself, confined to bed after cataract surgery, escaped only by jumping out of a second-story window, seriously injuring his feet, but, unbelievably, without damage to his eyes.

Everyone was pleased to see Luther at the party, even his sister-in-law Rosa Parker, who earlier had hotly denounced his hasty re-marriage as "an insult to my beautiful sister, who taught Luther many things he needed to know about manners and personal cultivation." The other guests also received Louise with civility.

Louise was a woman with flaws in her character. She had deserted her own family earlier. She had lied so often to herself that she probably had become unable to tell the difference between the truth and a lie. She palmed her daughter off as her sister. One never knew what to believe. She was intelligent, a competent secretary, apparently had a pleasant disposition. She was attractive. If she lacked expression in her face, it may have been because she lacked any inner convictions or clear set of personal standards or, perhaps, because of the nips and tucks she had done to make herself look more youthful.

She liked to drink but couldn't hold her liquor. Drink didn't stimulate her; it made her sleepy. Upon her and Luther's arrival at our party, she had a drink, sat down beside Mother, well now for two years and looking far younger than her age of 80, exchanged a few words, had another drink, and began to nod off. Soon her head came to rest on Lessie's shoulder, then if fell more comfortably upon her bosom. Mother just sat there, patting Louise's head gently and carrying on a conversation with others as if Louise weren't there.

Louise hadn't been asleep long before we heard a loud bang outside. Our across-the-street neighbor, also celebrating, had backed his car at high speed out of the driveway and straight into the side of Luther's limousine. Louise was awakened and pulled to her feet, as she and Luther had to leave, but the party rocked on until early morning.

Luther and Louise invited Ann and me over for a drink in early October 1974, at their home in The Oaks in Chapel Hill. Luther had to make the call, make the drinks, serve the hors d'oeuvres. Such social skills now appeared beyond Louise. But she was friendly as usual and soon sleepy. We stayed only a short time. Luther never made a critical remark about his wife. He was too much of a gentleman to do that. But it was painfully obvious that he was often embarrassed by Louise and was not happy living with her. He had indeed married in haste only to repent in leisure. Ann and I left the next day for the beach. A week later we heard on the radio that Luther had died suddenly while working in his garden.

In 1969 when Martha died, the news was headlined in every newspaper in North Carolina. In 1974 when Luther died, again the event was headline news. Thirty years later few people apparently remember much about Luther Hodges. He never really had a political machine. He was largely a one-man show. When he died, there was no organized group to carry on his name. Luther also believed one's legacy should speak for itself. He made it known that he wanted no roads, airports, or buildings named for him and no monuments erected in his honor.

Franklin D. Roosevelt had felt the same way. He said no monument that couldn't be accommodated on his desk should be built in his memory. Fifty years after his death, a monument in Washington was finally created. Maybe some day someone will rediscover Hodges and all that he did for his state and his country. And Louise will be long forgotten.

But she won't be the only one. The shelf-life of any individual, both in terms of mortality and human memory, is short. Except for those few people who, through a combination of genius and circumstance, achieve historical immortality, we "come and go as ripples on a stream," destined to become footnotes or erased entirely from memory. Life is short and fame is fleeting. . . dust to dust, ashes to ashes. Luther and FDR were right: Virtue is its own reward.

The years 1971-1976 passed rapidly, filled with many happy and stressful events. Dizzy Gillespie was performing at a couple of Raleigh clubs, The Purple Puddle and The Frog and Night Gown, when he called me one day in early 1972.

"Hey, man, how 'bout my coming over to Carolina and playing a little for your students? I heard you are teaching a course in popular culture. What do you think you know about bebop? You ain't never got that."

Gillespie, who could command thousands of dollars for a concert, came over to UNC for the mid-morning class the next day, pulled out his trumpet, puffed out his cheeks, and gave an upfront and personal demonstration of his technique to the enthusiastic reception of the fifty students. Howell Hall was jumping that morning, the bebop sound echoing through both floors and the basement. Between performances, he talked with the students, signed autographs, and never charged a penny.

Kay Kyser, a big band leader and former Hollywood star, was another matter. Kyser, a native of Rocky Mount, was a popular culture favorite for years. Bette Davis cites him as a regular at the Hollywood Canteen during the war years. The Andrews Sisters sang with him. Thirty-five years later when Maxeen Andrews performed at a one-woman show at Hotel Europa in Chapel Hill, Kyser made a rare public appearance to welcome her.

But in the years I was at UNC he kept a low profile. When I called his home to ask if he would talk to my class about show business, movies, early television and his music, I couldn't get past his secretary. He had become a recluse, though his wife Georgia remained active in community affairs. Kyser was then more interested in Christian Science than in students, in sharp contrast to Gillespie who not only remained involved in education and religion but also made a lasting contribution to the arts.

The new faculty in '71 included Richard Cole, a bright young Texan who would become dean of the School of Journalism in 1979 and serve for a record twenty-five years. As my colleague Stuart Sechriest put it, "I've never seen a better dean. He just knows what to do and when and how to do it. And how to raise money!" Cole has the knack of making a hard job look easy. A recent report ranks UNC among the very best journalism programs in the country.

Vermont Connecticut Royster also joined the faculty that year, having retired as editor of the *Wall Street Journal* and having won two Pulitzer Prizes. Royster, a native of Raleigh and a UNC graduate, came from a large, prominent family that operated a candy company. Royster's candy, especially the hard sour "jaw breaker" kind, filled Christmas stockings all across North Carolina from the latter part of the nineteenth century. All of the Royster children were named for states in the Union. V.C.'s and my maternal great grandparents were Wake County neighbors and friends.

Vermont not only won two Pulitzer prizes for editorial writing, he also helped build the *Journal* from a narrowly focused financial sheet with a circulation of fewer than 40,000 to a huge general circulation newspaper, including both national and international editions, with a combined circulation of well over one million. Despite being a huge journalistic success, he was a modest, decent, friendly man without a self-important bone in his body.

George Bernard Shaw once discerned, "Those who can, do. Those who can't, teach." That aphorism, barbed, witty and largely untrue, can be reversed. Often those who do, can't teach. Vermont was liked by his students and respected by his colleagues, but he couldn't teach. We shared a classroom. On the blackboard his first day on the job he wrote in huge letters, "What is the question and what is the answer?"

The message was not erased that entire year. Neither was the question answered. Vermont just sat down, often with his feet on the table, and talked about whatever came into his mind. He didn't bother with a syllabus, never used a text, and didn't pay much attention to papers or grades. Nothing was ever quantified. Maybe that's the way to do it.

Early in that first semester, Vermont said, laughingly, to me, "That first day in class was the easiest and most fun I've ever had. I just opened up my mouth and shared with my students what I'd learned in my life. The minutes flew by. The students appeared to hang on to my every word. The next class started off the same way, but before the bell rang I suddenly ran out. I realized that I had expended the full range of my knowledge and wisdom in less than two hours!"

I had had much the same experience earlier and knew just how helpless he felt. Of course he exaggerated, as do I, but classroom exposure can be a humbling experience and give one a new respect for "those who teach." But Vermont got the hang of it and in any event, with his journalistic track record, he had nothing to worry about.

Mark Ethridge, former editor of the *Louisville Courier-Journal*, to whom Aunt Sue introduced me in 1937 the summer I spent with the Fowler family, also had a tenuous connection with the School of Journalism in 1971-72. The Ethridges had moved to the area to be near their daughter Willie Snow, who was living in Pittsboro and had been a Duke classmate of mine a generation earlier.

Tom Bowers, now associate dean, was another newcomer. I also felt comfortable in the company of old friends Sechriest and Spearman, whom I'd known since 1949, and with Jim Mullen, with whom I had been at Harvard at Naval O.C.S in 1944.

A year later Jim Shumaker joined the faculty, bringing experience he had earned as editor of both the *Durham Morning Herald* and later the *Chapel Hill Weekly*. Shumaker had never received his AB degree from UNC because he had refused to take a physical education class. Dean Jack Adams and President Bill Friday arranged to have the University grant him that one hour of credit he lacked, give him his degree thirty years later, and put him on the payroll. Shumaker, despite occasional self-granted sabbaticals, remained on the faculty nearly thirty years, a perfect example of those "who can and do."

In 1975 I asked Dean Adams not to consider me for reappointment and promotion. He shouldn't have anyway, as I had already indicated that I wasn't going to abide by clearly understood rules of the game. Phil's recent death, my niece's health, and now Mother's renewed problems associated with a recently broken hip precluded any practical move toward tenure. Even if I had been willing, there wasn't enough time between Phil's death and the end of my contract to research, write and publish anything.

Besides, I had lost interest in the publish-or-perish academic game. It wasn't for me—not at my age of fifty-one and at my level of professional achievement. Research in a non-scientific field such as journalism no longer attracted me. I had no wish to prove the obvious, to discover the already known or to publish dry-as-dust articles about education in journalism for professional periodicals. Better to perish. I had already been offered a job at North Carolina Central University in Durham setting up a journalism curriculum. I somehow felt that I could make a useful contribution at a predominantly Black university now under a mandate to become more racially diversified. My professional experience between 1953 and 1968 and my personal involvement with civil rights had, I believed, prepared me for the job. I liked UNC and the School of Journalism, admired its faculty and would leave the following year with upbeat feelings. But it was time to move on. I may have changed jobs but not my address. Ann and I continued to make Chapel Hill home.

Dr. Charles Ray was chairman of the English Dept. at NCCU. He was a talented, gifted man and an excellent administrator. He had some personal problems, but racism was not one of them. One Saturday morning I went over to the University to show my son David around. Expecting no one else there, we took David's 180-pound solid black Great Dane along with us.

As we approached the chairman's office we found Dr. Ray there. Also expecting no one, he had brought his huge all-white German shepherd with him. When we came face to face, Ray broke out into a big laugh. "Secrest," he declared, "I don't know what it is, but there must be something Freudian about this scene!" No, Ray was no racist, and he had a keen sense of humor.

His successor was Dr. Patsy Perry, a fine scholar, a good chairman, a woman who had a way with people. Later she became an assistant chancellor as her administrative skills became known campus-wide. Dr. Ray and Dr. Perry had assembled an excellent group of professors in their department.

NCCU has been unfairly criticized. An editor of the *Raleigh News and Observer* once called the university an "academic slum." It was no such thing. It had a good faculty, some good students, a strong law school. Harry Groves, a distinguished educator, was once dean. Later Julius Chambers, a nationally known civil rights leader and educator, served as University president. I had known him a long time. Dr. John Hope Franklin, a prominent Black scholar now at Duke and formerly at the University of Chicago, was a product first of NCCU. It was, however, treated poorly by the greater University of North Carolina, underfunded, neglected, its dormitory facilities run down. It was often treated, like all of the predominantly black universities in the state system, as the proverbial "red-headed step-child," only its personnel mostly had black hair.

I enjoyed my nine years there, was always treated fairly and never felt I had any cause to complain, although being who I am, I am sure that I did do so often. I was unbelievably lucky to have two wonderful young men as my assistants, Tom Scheft and Tom Evans. I could not have functioned without them. They understood the new computer newsroom we set up. But like Rodney Dangerfield, I got no respect. "Don't let Dr. Secrest near these machines," they warned the students. "He'll really screw them up."

# 54. The Simmons Curse

In May 1973, nearly two years before I told the dean of my intention to leave UNC, my niece was well and ready to come home from NIH. I drove up to Bethesda to get her, just two months after Phil had died. While there I met with the director of the National Institute of Mental Health and suggested a research team do a study of our family—both immediate and extended. I told him of the genealogical research I had done and of my own personal knowledge. Episodes of mental and emotional dysfunction, far more than one might expect from a random sampling of the general population, had occurred in the Simmons line, extending as far back as my great-great-great grandfather Benjamin Simmons and his wife Anne Alexander. Most of these antecedents had been unusually intelligent and had led successful lives. But far too many had also suffered from periods of depression and irrationality. Others were conspicuously odd.

Ann and I, with David, Phil and Molly, had taken a trip to Troy, North Carolina, one Sunday afternoon ten years earlier to see if we could locate the original Simmons homestead. We found the site, along the banks of the Pee Dee River, but the house had long since burned.

Benjamin Simmons had come to North Carolina from Pennsylvania after the Revolutionary War, married Anne Alexander from Cross Creek, near where Fayetteville stands today, and settled in Montgomery County. Known as buckskins, the Simmons grew rich from their tannery and leather business. Ben and Anne had two sons, Lockey and Benjamin Whitfield, and two daughters, Anna and Deborah. Lockey was the line from which I came.

Soon we were joined by an old man who lived in a shack just up the road. "Whatcha lookin' for?" the old man asked.

"The family cemetery," I replied. "The Simmons family plot. They had to be buried somewhere."

"Naw, they h'aint. Old Dr. Alex just told his folks to plow up his remains in that field o'yonder. Used him as fertilizer. That's what they done. But there's a headstone around here, someplace," the old man added. He poked through overgrown weeds and underbrush until he found a small stone marker. We wiped dirt and dust away from the engraved letters.

Here lies Mary Lundy Pennington
1809-1834
Wife of Lockey Simmons

Mother of Nancy Anne, 1828
Calvin Jones, 1829
William Gaston, 1830
Walter Alexander, 1831
Benjamin Franklin, 1834

"Yew'unses related to these here folk?" the old man asked. "Well, they was pretty famous around these parts. Smart, and rich too. When old man Frank died back around 1924, people from all around came. Later broke into the house and ransacked the place, looking for money said hidden in there but nobody never found nuthin'."

"Did you actually know any of these people?" I asked the old fellow who must have been nearly ninety years old himself.

"Know 'em? Sure, I knowed 'em all. They lived a long time. I used to work for Dr. Alex and Colonel Frank."

I understood one of my great-great uncles was kind of crazy. I said, "Somebody told me Uncle Calvin would sometimes go off his rocker and needed to be confined. Do you remember that?"

"Oh, yes, Calvin was peculiar, but, you know, he wasn't much crazier than the rest of them," the old fellow said with a sly chuckle, as if he remembered other things he had yet to share. "Dr. Alex was an educated man. Went off to medical school in Pennsylvania and then came back to take care of all these people around here. He once took up with some woman named Mary Ann. Promised to marry her when they got home, but he never got around to it. He were so qu'ar, though, people called him Dr. Odd behind his back. Your great-great Uncle Franklin was a famous lawyer and a colonel in the Confederate Army. He went to a university somewhere up north, too. He never married. Just lived at home with his brothers Alex and Calvin. Nancy and Lockey were the only ones to get married and leave home."

The old man then told me about Calvin. "He was one of the first patients in the insane asylum they opened up in Raleigh back around 1858. He didn't like it none too well, so one day he jumped into a locomotive and drove that engine till the track done run out, and then walked on home. They say he was the smartest one of the bunch."

The old man must have been referring to the Dorothea Dix Hospital, named after the reformer and advocate for the insane, Dorothea Dix, in the mid-19th century. But he may have meant Morganton, N.C., also home of a state hospital. "But unpredictable and easy to upset. One day he got into a fight with Dr. Odd and choked him so bad that Dr. Odd could speak only in a raspy whisper after that. Course that wuz before my time, but that's what they say.

"After Calvin done left Raleigh, they wouldn't take him back. Then the Civil War come along and the hospital closed up fer a spell. After that, whenever Mr. Calvin got to acting strange, they'd chain him out in the backyard with the dawgs and the hawgs.

"Your great-great grandfather Lockey, now, he was a smart one. He was a fool for education. They say he set on the board that started Wake Forest College in 1834. When Alex and Calvin got too much for him, he moved to Wake Forest to live with his son, Gaston, who taught school there. Lockey said he wanted to live up there, within the sound of the school bells, so he could still hear them once he'd died. That's what he done, too."

Later on I asked Mother's second cousin Maude Coppedge in Rockingham about all that. She didn't say much about Dr. Alexander, after whom her brother was named, and nothing about Calvin, but she spoke most favorably about her own grandmother, Nancy Anne, her great-uncles Franklin and Gaston and our illustrious common ancestors, Benjamin and Lockey.

Benjamin was born on October 4, 1751, in Philadelphia. His wife Anne Alexander was ten years younger. Her parents, James Alexander and Elizabeth Carruthers, were from Fayetteville. According to Maude, Lockey was educated, wealthy, a public benefactor and, indeed, "a fool for education." He was also a handsome devil. His daughter Nancy Anne, Maude's grandmother, was equally blessed. A graduate of Salem Colege in

1848, she married a handsome Scot named Duncan Campbell, had several children but died early in poverty and from tuberculosis in Wilmington as a consequence of the Civil War.

Son Benjamin Franklin was a lawyer of renown, mentor to a young Walter Hines Page, journalist from Aberdeen who was later active in the movement to get the United States into the war against Germany. Page was appointed ambassador to the Court of St. James by President Woodrow Wilson. William Gaston, my great-grandfather, took after his father, a teacher, a lawyer, and a scientist at Wake Forest. There was nothing crazy about any of them, as far as Maude was concerned.

But I knew better. Descendants of Nancy Anne Simmons Campbell, and William Gaston Simmons, even some from the earlier generation of Anna, Benjamin and Debby Simmons—Lockey's sisters and brothers— had trouble down through the generations. Weren't seven generations enough? With new developments in the field of genetic testing, new drugs for treatment, promising expectations from research with RNA and DNA, wouldn't a genealogical investigation be worthwhile?

I sold the idea to NIH. Dr. Bell, a geneticist, came to see us in Chapel Hill. He made visits elsewhere. He drew blood. He took family histories, examined medical records, looked into our genealogy—some documented, much anecdotal. Back he went to NIH. Eventually I received a letter. Dr. Bell had enjoyed meeting "your charming, delightful family." He had completed his work. He could find nothing wrong with any of us and no underlying genetic reason why there should be.

Then how to explain great-great-uncle Calvin, Dr. Odd, grandmother Mary Foote Simmons Covington; my own mother's breakdowns, and others to follow, as well as those affecting Great Aunt Ada, her son Edgar Timberlake, a law professor at Wake Forest; cousin Betty Webb's brother Edwin; Sis Nannie's sons, Clarence and Willie, and her daughter Nan Poe—all first cousins of Lessie—and some of Nan's descendants?

While "The Simmons Curse" skipped Nan's sister Ada, it descended upon Ada's son and a grandson by her daughter. It didn't stop there. One of Great Uncle Henry's sons had taken his own life. Uncle Henry's son Tom's family didn't escape scot-free. Descendants from Nancy Simmons Campbell, some of Mother's second cousins, were affected, including Congressman Walter Lambeth from Thomasville who never married and later committed suicide. Even Betty Webb, when she was a sophomore at college, became obsessed with the corner of her eye, became hysterically blind, unable to read for the rest of the year. She made the Dean's List anyhow with the help of a tutor who read to her. But that certainly was unusual, wasn't it? But Betty recovered spontaneously and never had a recurrence.

Maybe it has all been nurture rather than nature. Maybe it has been largely the luck of the draw. But I am not so sure. I'm still pinning my hopes on medical progress and scientific advance and on the slow process of evolutionary change.

# 55. Freud and Psychoanalysis

Fifty-five years after I had my inoculation against the 'Simmons Curse' in Saranac Lake, what do I think of Freudian psychology and the effort to understand history better through psychiatric interpretations of world leaders?

Mary Cov several years after her experience with Dr. Herold concluded that Sigmund Freud was a fraud and that psychoanalysis was a cult. Yet for the rest of her life she suffered from "psychoanalosis" and continued to use Freudian language and models to define people and explain their behavior. Two generations later some people in the medical profession, especially pharmacology, while less openly hostile, seem to agree, concluding that Freud is passé and that traditional analysis, with patients lying prone on a couch for years, is not recommended procedure.

The idea that one can psychoanalyze historical figures one has never met or fictional characters that never existed seems far-fetched if not absurd. I never found much practical use for such knowledge in the classroom. It seemed more like a parlor game than academic research.

Freud made enormous contributions to the understanding of behavior and personality development but his therapy is of limited use. His greatest contributions lay elsewhere. The value of his concentration on the subconscious mind and his insistence on the importance of early childhood experience in the formation of adult personality cannot be overstated. His revelation of irrational, primordial impulses lurking just below the surface of what was accepted in the late 19th century as normal behavior had a significant impact on cultural change.

Freud had an intuitive understanding of the biological structure of the brain. While he did not have access to the tools of modern biology and chemistry, his descriptions of the mind and its component parts, which he described as the Id, the Ego and the Super Ego, correspond closely to what science has since confirmed.

Freud borrowed from many others. He stood on the shoulders of giants. He was raised in a Catholic society that understood if the Church had control of the child for the first six years of life, it could influence him forever. Many people instinctively understood that "As the twig is bent, so the tree inclines." Poet Robert Browning had already affirmed that "the child is father to the man."

Freud, like Karl Marx, was also widely misunderstood. He might well have said about himself what Marx later declared: "But I am not a Marxist!" A little knowledge can become a silly as well as a dangerous thing. By the 1920s, Freudian theories had become the subject of smart, trivial chatter at New York cocktail parties. His theory of patient and doctor transference and counter-transference had been distorted into the titillating notion that the patient always fell in love with the therapist.

Anyone who made a casual slip of the tongue was accused of having committed "a Freudian slip." People spoke of others as having a "psychological complex." Thus Freud—outside the medical profession—became popularized, degraded, and part of a kitsch culture. Inside the profession for many years his ideas were regarded with skepticism. That Freud was a non-religious Jew didn't help matters much.

The entertainment world, however, embraced Freud. Shallow but entertaining shows, such as "Lady in the Dark," first a Broadway musical starring Gertrude Lawrence and later a movie featuring Ginger Rogers, were big hits and further popularized Freudian theories. Later films such as *Spellbound* (1946), an MGM movie starring Gregory Peck and Ingrid Bergman, and *Rage in Heaven* (1941), another MGM movie featuring Robert Montgomery and Ingrid Bergman (again) relied heavily on Freudian symbolism to unravel mystery, murder and intrigue.

The 1934 and 1941 screen versions of Robert Louis Stevenson's *Dr. Jeckel and Mr. Hyde*, the latter interpretation an MGM production starring Spencer Tracy, Lana Turner and Ingrid Bergman (again) were far better shows because they ignored Freudian theory but skillfully revealed the reality and the reasons behind schizophrenia, then known as split personality. As good as the MGM remake was, I preferred the original film, starring Frederic March and Miriam Hopkins.

Despite popular culture's use and abuse of Freud, the doctor's contributions to a better understanding of early childhood training and of primary and elementary education are important. So was his insistence on the importance of the sex drive and the dangers of guilt and repression which a puritanical Victorian culture and many religions had fostered. Yet Freud violated his own concept when he subjected his daughter to psychoanalysis conducted by himself. That surely constituted child abuse if not psychological incest.

Jung, an early student of Freud, was also right. Freud did over-emphasize the role of sex in the evolution of personality. Hegel's emphasis on the power of ideas is closer to the mark. Freud couldn't let well enough alone. Like many theorists before him, he couldn't abide intellectual loose ends. Everything had to be neatly tied up and all contradictions reconciled. Hence he arrived at some conclusions that seriously weakened his concepts of the treatment of neuroses and the origins of psychoses. Too often common sense and everyday observations offering plausible explanations were sacrificed to theory. Emerson was right in his observations about "a foolish consistency."

Freud gained, however, growing acceptance throughout the first half of the twentieth century. Despite some later defection, he remains one of the strongest voices in psychiatry, a man who has led to a general acceptance of the need for emotional ventilation through talk. Today a therapist need not be a physician, a person with years of psychoanalytic study and a product of analysis himself. Social workers will do. So will ministers. Maybe even strangers on a park bench.

The mass media—press, talk TV, and radio—are full of such therapists. Traditional analysis, employing free association, dream interpretation, and other Freudian trappings, is not for popular consumption in the 21st century. The need for therapy is too great; the supply of analysts too small; the techniques too time-consuming, the cost prohibitive. Today psychoanalysis is for overpaid, self-centered celebrities. Woody Allen comes to mind. Perhaps Freud and the creative mind need each other. The rest of us can manage without him. As Freud himself suspected, the future of brain management lies in biology.

But Freud cannot be dismissed. His was one of the great creative minds of the 19th and early 20th centuries. He ranks along with others of that time, from Hegel, to Marx, to Darwin, and he owes much to each of them. While he paid homage to the romanticism of the 19th century, Freud remained basically a child of the 18th century—a rationalist who believed everything had an explanation and if one set out to find it, every problem had a solution. He was a true creature of the Enlightenment.

As for the power of analysis to change behavior, some may conclude that it doesn't have much. Its value lies in the understanding of the origins of behavior and the best ways to develop it properly. The human personality is formed by early childhood, largely so by ages six to twelve. Change occurs throughout life but it happens as result of experience, accident, conditioning, self-will and behavior modification. Change is unlikely to occur simply through talk and self-understanding.

Psychoanalysis also is subject to indictment on the charge of negative thinking. While a foolish optimism that leads to denial is not helpful, the power of positive thinking is too often overlooked. Psychiatry needs to focus more on mental health than mental illness. Just as bad art drives out good, and weak money drives out strong, so negative thoughts drive out positive ones. What's wrong with the decision to "Put on a Happy Face?" It is better to appreciate "Blue Skies" and walk on "The Sunny Side of the Street" than to wallow in self-pity on "Gloomy Sunday." A life filled with negative thoughts, fear, and pessimism is not a happy one. And psychoanalysis often fails to "accentuate the positive," satisfied with a conviction that bringing negative emotions to the level of consciousness is in itself sufficient.

Human beings are gregarious creatures. We need social interaction, we require outreach, we do not need to be locked within, obsessively concerned with ourselves. I can think of no worse fate than to be permanently occupied by the self. While psychoanalysis professes to free its practitioners from such an obsession, often it manages to foster it, thus providing a cure worse than the disease. The phenomenon of transference and counter-transference is supposed to solve the problem of self-obsession and patient dependence upon the doctor. But it doesn't necessarily work out that way. These are labels Freud and his disciples invented to tie up loose ends and to square the circle. A therapist's job is to listen, to suggest, to lend direction. He cannot collect a client's emotions, place them in a box and hand them back, labeled free by way of counter-transference. The real work must be done by the patient himself, often long after the analytic transaction has been completed.

# 56. God and the Church

Throughout these pages I have often referred to religion and faith. The words Providence, Fate and Nature appear, but there is infrequent use of the word God. The name of Jesus Christ seldom appears, although lessons derived from his teachings are implied and Biblical quotations cited. I have aligned myself with Albert Einstein who once described himself as a "devout disbeliever," that is, one who devoutly respects the philosophy of the prophet without believing in personal immortality. I have described myself as a Doubting Thomas.

Although human beings appear to be genetically wired to ask questions, they are, I suspect, incapable of finding answers to questions basic to spirituality. "Seek and ye shall find. Knock and the door shall be opened," Jesus tells us. But the words to a tune in the opera *Porgy and Bess* echo in my mind: "It ain't necessarily so." The lyrics in Jerome Kern's tune, "Why was I born, why am I living?" have never been answered to my satisfaction. I've never met anyone who could explain to me the meaning of being.

Is there a grand design for the universe, conceived by a supreme presence and erected by a master builder, who not only created our planet and all the people who have ever lived on it but who also keeps his eye on every sparrow? And beyond that, a master architect who also developed our solar system, and all the other stars and galaxies, as well as the atoms and sub-particles, gravity, matter and anti-matter, quasars, pulsars, galactic nuclei, X-ray binary stars and that other clutter that swirl around in constant motion, traveling at unimaginable speed throughout a forever expanding universe?

505

What ultimately happens? Does the universe finally reach its destination and bump into a wall? Or does it contract within itself and self-implode, thus starting the whole process over again? If the universe as we picture it started with the Big Bang fifteen billion years ago, what was there before that? Can you picture a void—nothing but unreality?

The Hubble telescope records pictures that are supposed to go back to the origins of time, thereby upsetting the beliefs of fundamental dogmatists who are clearly unwilling to believe in evolution, much less relativity, physical or moral. Yet can one rely upon the conclusion of the scientists and rationalists? The more answers they supply, the more questions arise. If one were to accept the Big Bang theory as a plausible explanation of the origins of the universe—and I do—one still knows no more about the reason for its creation or the purpose of the life that developed within it.

Perhaps there was no original intent. Creation may have been just an accident of the natural world—impersonal physical forces colliding and exploding and aimlessly moving about until things solidified and clarified and cooled down. That makes a kind of sense but says nothing about the creation of life evolving from some enzyme or pre-cell amylases to a self-conscious, complex, full-blown human being. Even if evolution explains such gradual development, it doesn't explain the why or wherefore of it all. The Book of Genesis says about as much and does it in more poetic form than Stephen Hawking.

If there is no intellectual or spiritual power behind our physical existence, if everything is accidental and happenstance, then how could something come out of nothing? Yet something did. Few people, except perhaps existential philosophers, dispute the existence of good and evil in the world.

No one can deny the evidence of science, let alone one's own sense and sensibility, that people exist, they laugh and cry, learn and work, eat and make love, live and die, sometimes leaving great monuments and achievements in the arts and sciences behind them. How can something as exciting and meaningful, sad and burdensome, noble and petty as human existence arise from nothing—without any original design or purpose? That is the question that scientists and philosophers, poets and thinkers always ask and fail to answer.

What is the nature of human beings? Are we born good—created in the image of God? Not likely. Are we born bad, conceived in sin, capable of goodness only through salvation? Not likely. Or are we a combination of both, or neither, just blank slates at birth whose fate is determined largely through nurture rather the nature? Little in experience or trained observation supports that view. It has been argued that if God had not existed, man would have had to invent Him. Maybe he did.

I think, like Anne Frank, that people are basically good. But only so long as they do not believe themselves in danger and hence become fearful and insecure. Then they can get aggressive, punitive and bloody-minded. History is replete with human heroism and selflessness as well as unworthiness. If individuals are not ruined early by unwise or cruel nurture, or damaged later by over-indulgence and a sense of unearned entitlement, or handicapped by genetic flaws over which they have little control, chances are they will be good, solid, substantial people who, with a little bit of luck, can behave with great humanity, courage and self-sacrifice in league with the angels. It is the purpose of religion, as taught by the church, to bring out the best in people and make their salvation on earth possible.

Is it really self-evident that all people are born equal, as our Declaration of Independence declares? Are we born with free will? One would be hard-pressed to prove that. The challenge every generation faces is to develop a political and social system that seeks to level the playing field so that every person has a better chance at equality and individual success.

But "born equal" with free will? People are born with unequal capabilities. They are born into unequal circumstances. Some are born with silver spoons in their mouths; others are born behind the eight ball. But if an individual is given tender, loving care from an early age, and is taught well, his chances of reaching a time when he is able to exercise a degree of free will and make personal choices are greatly enhanced. Again it is the burden of organized society to provide optimum opportunity for all—especially for the least of us.

So how does one explain the appearance of something good out of nothing? People of faith of course have the answer. God did it... a universal God by any name you choose to call him. For Jews, Muslims and Christians, God's word is to be found in the Bible (Old and New Testaments) and the Koran. Billions of other people find explanations that are not to be found in any text but which are still anchored in faith and mysticism rather than rationality.

"You'll never find the answer in Reason," friend Catherine Johnson Jackson once warned me. "You have to rely upon faith and truth as revealed by God and his son, our savior, Jesus Christ. Throw your think-box away and believe. Trust in the Lord."

Well, hallelujah! Now I know everything. I wish. I envy true believers. They're happier than Doubting Thomases. Why wouldn't they be? To them death has no sting. Billy Graham once said he could hardly wait to die and go to live with his heavenly father. To him it is so simple. Just believe. Have faith. Be good and you'll be rewarded in heaven. I wish.

To some Christian fundamentalists, you needn't have had to be especially good for very long. Just repent and gain faith, and God, whose only son gave his life and took on all the sins of the world for you, will grant you grace and provide a passport into heaven and eternal life. Does that sound self-serving? No wonder there are "no atheists in foxholes." And so many deathbed confessions.

Why give God so much credit for giving up his only begotten son? Many of us mere mortals lose sons and daughters, too. God got his back. We humans never do. Death of one's children isn't unusual. Five of my best friends have also lost sons and daughters: Bill Price, Bob Allen, Whit Bartley, Jim Crawford, and Ed Pepper.

The similarities among all religions, but especially the prevailing European and Middle Eastern ones, and mythology are evident. Why should one be given divine credence and the others not?

I have never understood, and hence cannot accept, the idea that at the sacraments wine (or if you're a Methodist, grape juice) turns into blood and bread into flesh. And how is it possible for God's son Jesus Christ to take on the sins of the world and thus free mankind of these burdens? The scapegoat theory, so prevalent in western faiths, was never a convincing one to me. How can there be a Holy Trinity—and inseparable God, Son and Holy Ghost? The Bible cannot offer unchallenged truths. It has been written and rewritten and edited so many times— not to mention re-interpretations, schisms and reformations—one cannot know its original text. The cutting room floor is littered with discarded material that once was considered holy writ.

I believe in the wisdom of Solomon and appreciate the beauty and truth in many Old Testament passages. I believe society would be better off if people learned and obeyed the Ten Commandments—well, at least most of them. So where does this leave me? Not alone, for sure, and not lonely or afraid. Just interested.

I favor the work of the community church and local parish. I believe the church (of any religion) stands for the best that is in human nature. I admire the teachings of Jesus Christ as expressed in the Golden Rule, the

Sermon on the Mount, and in his parables. Jesus had more common sense than Freud and understood human nature better, although he expected too much of us, given all our inherent moral limitations.

At times, however, Jesus sounds like a politician and an equivocator, urging people to "Render unto Caesar that which is Caesar's and unto God that which is God's." At others he sounds like a cult leader, urging young people to leave their homes and their parents, forsaking all others to follow him. He says he comes "not to bring peace, but a sword." He talks out of both sides of his mouth.

Psychologists have raised questions about his sanity and personality structure. Here's a young man, counter-culture to the core—proclaiming himself the son of God, a baby of immaculate conception, his only bride his creed and church. He died a martyr's death and in so doing saved all mankind. Now what would they say about a member of my family were he or she to make such claims? We would all say: victim of the Simmons Curse! Or bipolar disorder.

Some of my fondest memories are of the Central Methodist Church in Monroe. I enjoyed Sunday school, attended church regularly, participated in youth fellowship activities. In an earlier day families even occasionally went to evening services and Wednesday night prayer meetings. It was basically the same for members of the Baptist, Presbyterian, Episcopal and Lutheran churches, as well as the more fundamental Anabaptist congregations.

The church was dedicated to doing good. I have always believed that faith without good works was dead. There may have been many secular humanists among us who weren't really religious but found the church the best means by which to fulfill their wish to do good. I also believed that the Democratic Party was the closest political expression of the religious goal to realize the Brotherhood of Man under the Fatherhood of God. What more did I really need than to "do good, love mercy and walk humbly with my" fellow man, to paraphrase Micah?

Sunday was the Lord's day. Monroe had blue laws. No movies, no card playing, no dancing, no drinking on the seventh day. It was a time for contemplation. People cannot live by bread alone. We all need to believe in something beyond ourselves. Adolescents particularly need to have faith and a purpose in life. The community church often provided the idealism that led young people in the right direction. The annual daffodil luncheon at Easter in Pfeiffer Hall in the basement of Central Methodist Church remains one of my fondest childhood memories and a symbol of the positive Christian outreach to people in need. Hallelujah! Amen!

While blue laws have long since been repealed, I still think a day of quiet contemplation is better than what Sunday has become—a television night of programs dedicated to murder, drugs, sex and violence... a convenient afternoon of card playing... a fun day at the beach or shopping at the mall. It is hard to find piety anywhere. And above all, sports on television all day and all night long.

It is difficult to overestimate the historical significance of religion in every society from the earliest days of recorded history. The universal church has been in the forefront of movements to promote the progress of civilization, even as it has been a root cause of wars and revolutions, and a source of corruption and confusion. On balance, it has been a positive and powerful force, demonstrating that love is stronger than hate, that good ultimately wins out over bad. One can believe this and still recognize that religion, like patriotism, can also sometimes be the last refuge of scoundrels and the opiate of the masses.

The Marx-Engel-Lenin dogma that religion was the great enemy of progress led to the communist effort to substitute faith in God with faith in the state. During World War II, when Allied leaders raised the question of the Catholic Church with Josef Stalin, the Soviet dictator asked contemptuously, "How many divisions has the Pope?"

Stalin did not live long enough to get the answer. After seventy years of religious repression in the Soviet Union, the secular government collapsed in 1990, but the Russian Orthodox and Universal Catholic Church remained. If the church is in trouble today, it is due to its own corruption and internal contradictions. Without voluntary reforms, it will have done itself in. Personal faith cannot be regulated by political processes.

Religious toleration is not an easy thing to come by. Witness conflicts in Northern Ireland, the Middle East, Tibet and Africa today, not to mention the religious wars and persecutions that have been part of the history of nearly every society at one time or another. The only way to achieve such toleration is separation of church and state and the education of people to accept religious and cultural differences. One can only hope, however, that such separation can be achieved with a modicum of common sense and realism. I have never been persuaded that prayers said voluntarily in public schools or Christmas decorations on public property constitute much of a clear and present danger to the Republic.

While the First Amendment does protect one's rights to freedom of and freedom from religion, it is a constitutional stretch, in my opinion, to argue that Congress is establishing religion or depriving one of religious freedom when an individual or group seeks to express its religious beliefs, whatever they may be. The United States functioned as well before 1965 when the U.S. Supreme Court decided to intervene in religious issues as it has since. Maybe better. In its zeal to separate church and state, the ACLU seems willing to limit freedom of speech and worship.

I sprang from religious folk on all sides of my family. We've had Catholics, Protestants—-Baptists, Methodists, Congregationalists—-and Jews. No Muslims yet, but maybe someday soon. I welcome them all, but I do not subscribe to any of their theological doctrines. I am thankful that I live in a country where I can raise questions about faith without someone issuing a fatwa on me.

If God is Love; if God is Nature; if God is Goodness, Mercy, Truth and Justice; if He is Fate, Providence, Destiny, Karma; If He is Evolution and Reality—the way things are and are going to become, then of course I am a Believer.

But if He is the judgemental God as conventionally depicted in the Bible, and touted by Christian fundamentalists and the Religious Right, then I guess I'll have to remain a "Doubting Thomas."

The early Victorian home that my great-grandparents built at the end of South Main Street in Monroe is today the site of the First Baptist Church. Broadacre, the late Victorian home my grandfather built for his family in 1889, today is the site on which stands the Central Methodist Church. The Footes, the Pitchfords, the Simmonses, the Lundys, the Penningtons, the Covingtons, the Alexanders, the Gathings, the Secrests, the Jacksons, the Prices, the Robesons, the Pressons and the Winchesters were all devout Christian believers. As their direct descendant, I'm a devout disbeliever, a secular humanist. I believe we will all get to heaven—if there is one.

# 57. Issues and Answers

In the Foreword I described myself as a social historian who had lived through four-fifths of the twentieth century and who would look at major events I experienced and observed as we moved into the next millennium. Human conflict leads the list.

The issues Americans face today are a legacy from that past. A search for causes and solutions involves examining events rooted in this earlier era. Perhaps some historical perspective will help generations in the twenty-first century do a better job than their predecessors and leave a more peaceful legacy to their descendants.

Tom Brokaw, NBC anchorman, came upon a good phrase but a poor idea with "the greatest generation" to describe the young men and women who allegedly faced up to and triumphed over the Great Depression, World War II and the Cold War. That gives my generation far too much credit. We did what we had to do, just as other generations have done and future generations will do. We all had help, standing on the shoulders of those who came before. Furthermore, the people he honors were all born between 1905 and 1925, far too young to claim credit for victory in either the Great Depression or World War II.

The leaders of the two democracies that helped Joseph Stalin and the Soviet Union defeat Nazism—Franklin D. Roosevelt and Winston S. Churchill—were of an earlier generation. The allied military commanders and the industrial and labor leaders who mobilized the economy and sent it off to war were products of the nineteenth century, as were the scientists who developed the first weapons of mass destruction.

I was six years old when the stock market crashed in 1929, presaging worldwide economic collapse. No one mentioned in Brokaw's book was old enough to shoulder the responsibility for Roosevelt's New Deal. The men and women who bore the burden of the Great Depression were all born before the turn of the century . . . our parents.

An understanding of history cannot be achieved by a generational approach, as generations overlap, one blending into another. Although my generation did accept its responsibilities during the Cold War, we hardly stood alone. That war lasted nearly fifty years, stretching across several generations, involving people of different political perspectives, as well as foreign allies. As for World War II, the "greatest generation" were just "grunts," doing the scut work for the older men and women who were the real architects of victory.

When one examines the technological and scientific advances of the latter part of the twentieth century, he will discern roots that go back to earlier generations, some preceding World War I.

The greatest challenge facing the Boomer generation and their successors, Gen X and Next, is to avoid war and establish peace with justice. It is a test every generation has faced and, so far, failed. Time is no longer on our side. Science and technology enable mankind to destroy the environment, the human species, indeed the entire planet. Weapons of mass destruction—thermonuclear, biological, chemical—do exist, now easily attainable on the black market, even if they no longer are to be found in Iraq.

Although conventional wars between nations, which could escalate into a nuclear exchange, remain possible, a more likely scenario is an ideological and religious conflict, waged by zealots and terrorists, immune to the restraints of mutual assured destruction (MAD). Such wars must be waged by new methods, dependent upon reliable intelligence and an ability to win the hearts and minds of potential enemies who come from different cultures, customs, faiths, and philosophies. The challenge is aggravated by past grievances, Ottoman domination followed by Western colonialism, rising nationalism and racial and ethnic pride, capped by access to advanced technologies easily weaponized.

If terrorists managed to get a nuclear bomb or some other weapon of mass destruction and released it in a major metropolitan area, leaving no fingerprint as to its origin, what would be an appropriate response from a grievously wounded America?

If such a scenario seemed probable, would people question the morality of a pre-emptive strike? Winston Churchill had no qualms about pre-emption in the 1930s. He said World War II should have been named "the unnecessary war," as a pre-emptive attack on Nazi Germany as late as 1937, fully justified by Hitler's re-armament, professed plans of aggression and contempt for the League of Nations, would have removed the basic cause of that war and saved the world from such a holocaust.

Terrorism, now emanating from a militant branch of Islam, but not necessarily limited to it at some future time, may not be negotiable. A war against it may not be winnable in the way traditional wars have been. It may require an American presence in the Middle East for a long time. There is precedent for that. We have had troops in Europe and Asia for more than fifty years after the end of World War II and the Korean War.

If public opinion will not support such a commitment and the costs it will exact, the consequences could be a unilateral withdrawal from the Middle East, abandonment of Israel, the collapse of a traditional association with Europe, including NATO and the U.N, and a growing vulnerability to future attacks on the homeland.

The United Nations, with no independent military capability, withdrew its humanitarian mission in Iraq as soon as its personnel came in harm's way. The U.N. itself requires reorganization as it cannot long endure domination by five nations with veto power in the Security Council. The world has changed since 1945. Three of five permanent members are no longer superpowers qualified to make all the basic decisions about war and peace. The General Assembly, moreover, has come under the domination of some nations unacquainted with democratic institutions and hostile to civil liberties, human rights and racial justice, even as their autocratic leaders chair committees to oversee such rights.

Lessons the United States learned in 1940 may not universally apply in 2004. Roosevelt placed the nation's frontiers on the Rhine and the Sea of Japan. The war moved them east to the Elbe and the East China Sea. Truman placed them on the Yalu River in Korea, on the Eastern Mediterranean and Black Sea around Turkey, and on the River Jordan in the Middle East. Eisenhower placed our frontiers in the South China Sea to protect offshore islands and Taiwan from Communist China. Kennedy reaffirmed them all and extended them in the Caribbean. Lyndon Johnson moved them farther east and south until the Bay of Tonkin and the Mekong River in Vietnam marked their limits. After the terrorist attacks on New York and Washington on September 11, 2001, Bush moved our frontiers again, to the Hindu Kush mountains in Afghanistan. In April, 2003, he moved them to the Tigris and Euphrates Rivers in Iraq. As to South America, especially Colombia and Venezuela, I won't even go there, although the U.S. has, with new frontiers among the Andes mountains.

The time may have come for a redefinition of collective security. Roosevelt's vision of 1940, right then and well expressed by Wendell Wilkie's book, *One World*, may need modification. While few people believe in isolationism and Fortress America, more are beginning to believe in new interpretations of old ideas.

What applies in international politics may also apply to an international economy. High tariffs—Smoot Hawley of 1929 and economic nationalism—have been blamed for contributing to the worldwide depression of the 1930s, a decisive factor in the descent to World War II. In 2004 free trade and a global economy are causing economic dislocation, unemployment and domestic political disharmony. Is protectionism today the *bête noir* it was in 1929?

Do we really believe, as we did after World War II, that "peace is indivisible"? Can the United States become the policeman of the world? Should we seek to remake other nations in our image? Can we really make the whole world "safe for democracy"? Will our effort to establish democracy in every nation work any better than the efforts of the Third Internationale, backed by the Soviet Union, to convert all democratic societies into communist ones?

Empires and superpowers don't last long. The Roman and British empires enjoyed a long run but didn't last forever. The Holy Roman Empire lasted a long time too but was misnamed, as it was never really holy, Roman, or an empire.The Soviet Union collapsed after seventy years. Hitler's Third Reich, designed to last one thousand years, lasted only twelve. American superpower status, if over-extended, will soon be expended.

People, regardless of party affiliation, can differ on the decision by the Bush Administration to attack Iraq to achieve regime change. Sharply defined differences argued in the political arena during war time? Yes, we did that in 1940 and in 1944, during World War II and in 1952 during the Korean War. When we failed to do that in 1964, look what happened: an enlarged involvement that led to the Vietnam debacle.

It is apparent to me that President Bush, not unlike presidents before him, equivocated, lied, and misled the American people in order to lead the nation in a direction he believed it should go. The President, persuaded by hawks personified by Paul Wolfowitz and Richard Perle (backed by Vice President Dick Cheney and Defense Secretary Donald Rumsfeld) made a geo-political decision to intervene directly and massively in the Middle East to confront terrorism at its roots. Bush chose Afghanistan because that is where Usama bin Ladin had organized al-Qaida and Iraq because of its strategic importance and because we could gain a quick and easy initial military victory there.

By establishing a military presence in those two countries, the United States had in effect acquired common borders with states identified as sponsors of terrorism or home to radical Islamists fomenting it: Syria, Iran, Saudi Arabia, Pakistan, and several adjacent Emirates. He also sent warnings to other nations known to harbor terrorists.

George W. Bush borrowed a page out of the 1940-41 foreign policy ledger of Franklin D. Roosevelt . . . lend-lease, waging an undeclared naval war against Germany, saying "again and again and again" that American boys would "never be sent abroad to fight in foreign wars" when he knew better.

He took another from Lyndon B. Johnson, who lied to Congress and the American people in order to secure the Bay of Tonkin Resolution, thereby opening the door to military intervention in Vietnam. Roosevelt was on the right side of history, so he was vindicated. Johnson was on the wrong side and was condemned. Which side of history Bush will land on and whether he will be vindicated remains to be seen. Presidential lying often has good intentions and is not unusual. Sandy Vanocur, respected commentator once with NPR and PBS, observed thirty years ago that "presidents lie all the time" and proceeded to document that allegation.

Nine-eleven made the difference. It not only lent President Bush conviction, it gave him an opportunity to lance the boil of Middle Eastern terrorism at its center: Israel and Palestine. His decision to combat terrorism pro-actively was based on the belief that it was in the nation's interest to fight terrorism over there now rather than over here later. This intervention and the related issue of an enlarged American military, economic, and cultural presence in the Islamic world will determine foreign policy for the foreseeable future.

A passionate national debate, similar to the one between isolationists and interventionists in 1940 and 1941 is inevitable and appropriate. Whether one opposed the war in Iraq—as I did—or approved of it, the need now is to succeed. Defeat is not an option. It is not a matter to kick around for political advantage. National security trumps partisanship. "Politics stops at the water's edge."

The nation has been through this before. After Pearl Harbor, there were devotees of conspiracy theories. Die-hard isolationists believed President Roosevelt had knowledge of Japanese plans to bomb the Hawaiian naval base and deliberately concealed it so that the country would be propelled into war and unified by a surprise attack. Gen. George Marshall was accused of disappearing on a horseback ride Sunday morning, December 7, so he could not receive and relay intelligence of the looming attack to military authorities in Honolulu. These accusations, and worse, resurfaced with the emergence of McCarthyism in 1947 and the loss of the Chinese mainland to the communists in 1949.

There are those who believe President Bush knew in advance of the attack on the World Trade Center. Vermont Governor Howard Dean, an early contender for the Democratic presidential nomination, declared in 2004 that such a theory was "one of the more interesting reports" he had heard, while parenthetically inserting a mild disclaimer. Joe McCarthy would have had a hard time topping that. Winston Churchill warned British partisans in 1940 who wanted Neville Chamberlain' scalp for the horrible crisis he had led them to, "If we waste the present seeking victims from the past, we will squander the future." Indulge in fantasies and scapegoating later. There's a time and a season for everything.

### Political Transition

True to the observation that one grows more conservative as one grows older, I have moved further away from my Yellow Dawg Democrat days. I am impatient with an intellectual left that occupies increasingly large chunks of turf on campuses and in the mass media. It is disappointing that academia, traditional sanctuary for freedom of expression and all kinds of ideas, has allowed itself to become vulnerable to the charge that it is open to every sort of diversity except intellectual and political thought. Surveys indicate that academics are more than ninety percent housed in the Democratic camp. Intellectual arrogance shows in the often expressed view that those who disagree are "too dumb" to be granted a hearing. This state of mind leads to intellectual pandering and indoctrination, not to freedom of inquiry and education. The liberalism of Woodrow Wilson, FDR, Harry Truman, JFK and LBJ has faint echoes in the Democratic Party of 2004.

But then, the CEOs of corporations who are mostly Republican don't appeal to me either, even those who aren't crooks. Neither does a "compassionate conservatism" that favors tax advantages for those who need them the least. Doesn't "compassion" suggest an interest in controlling health costs and providing insurance for the millions who don't have it and can't afford it? The radical right, the religious fundamentalists, the National Rifle Association and Libertarian Know Nothings hold no attraction.

Yet I am uneasy with what I perceive to be a growing mood of appeasement and isolationism in my ancestral political home. Isolationism today takes the position of leaving decisions to a United Nations ill equipped to make or to enforce them. Such sentiments are willing to leave opinion on matters of military and foreign policy to ill-defined international law and a world court unable to render even-handed justice. While the sovereignty of international law remains the ideal, the practice is still far from a political reality. Are the Democrats now to swap places with the Republicans of 1940 who confused peace with military weakness? If so, is the Democratic Party capable of leading a unified national effort to combat global terrorism and create a better, safer world, based on security, peace and justice? Not that I am yet convinced that today's new Republicans have all the answers. Maybe nobody does.

*Civil Liberties*

On September 11, 2001, Americans learned again how vulnerable open, democratic societies are to attack. They may always have to absorb the first blow, prepared to respond only in retaliation. To mitigate such danger is why Congress passed the Patriot Act which provides tools with which the nation can better and more quickly respond to future assaults, or, better yet, prevent them altogether. National security, personal safety, even fear and anger will prevail initially over legitimate concerns about erosion of civil liberties.

Most Americans have not yet personally experienced any such erosion and are inclined to discount concerns about it. If illegal aliens or terrorist suspects, regardless of citizenship, have, that is the price an injured majority exacts under the circumstances. Fortunately democratic societies have built-in safeguards against prolonged injustices and self-correcting mechanisms that ultimately adjust the imbalance. That process is already underway, utilizing political, judicial and legislative resources.

When Americans feel threatened, they react. In 1796 they responded to foreign threats by passage of Alien and Sedition Acts which were used during John Adams' administration to seek to silence political dissent. He was a one-term president.

During the Civil War President Lincoln suspended habeas corpus and turned thousands of citizens over to military tribunals, bypassing the civilian judicial process. Southerners were deprived of their civil rights during the First Reconstruction but regained them seven years later. In 1876, after a disputed election, the Republicans, in a deal with the Democrats to throw the election to Republican Rutherford B. Hayes, agreed to end in every former Confederate state military occupation and readmit them to the

Union, all rights restored. As a result, the federal government abandoned its effort to protect the civil rights and liberties of recently freed slaves. The nation paid a high price for that cynical deal.

At the end of World War One the nation was swept by a wave of xenophobia and a fear of Communists, anarchists, and assorted radicals, not entirely without reason. But emotions careened out of control. Domestic terrorism was countered by governmental excess and vigilantism. The Boston police strike in 1919 was broken by the Massachusetts National Guard. U. S. Attorney General A. Mitchell Palmer conducted raids that resulted in thousands of arrests, with many deportations in violation of law and individual rights.

Two immigrants, Sacco and Vanzetti, were arrested in 1920 after two men were killed in a holdup. They may or may not have been guilty, but they were tried, convicted and executed, ultimately to have their convictions set aside fifty years later by Massachusetts Governor Michael Dukakis. The case, first dramatized on Broadway in 1935 by the play *Winterset*, is still a liberal cause célèbre. The situation was aggravated later in 1920 when a bomb exploded in Wall Street in New York City, killing thirty, injuring more than one hundred, and causing damage estimated in excess of two million dollars. No one was ever arrested.

The post-war unrest and disillusion led not only to Congressional disavowal of the League of Nations but also to the resurgence of a reconstituted Ku Klux Klan which targeted Catholics in the Northeast and Midwest in 1921. That same year Congress passed a discriminatory immigration bill, setting ethnic quotas aimed at Central and Southern Europeans. During World War One the nation mistreated recently naturalized German-Americans, calling them derogatory names and renaming sauerkraut "liberty cabbage."

Twenty years later there was little of that against American citizens of German descent and Italo-Americans even though we were locked in a far more dangerous war against a far more vicious enemy. This time American wrath was turned on Japanese-Americans, when fear and anxiety about national security arose after the Japanese attack on Pearl Harbor, a day that FDR declared would live forever "in infamy."

Both Japanese-Americans and Japanese aliens were interned, some in what could only be called concentration camps. Yet within two years steps were taken to free them, although restoration of property rights could never be fully made. The courts some years later settled lawsuits from these arrests at about ten cents on the dollar. Earle Warren, later chief justice of the U.S. Supreme Court who engineered the unanimous decision outlawing segregation in public schools in 1954, was the governor of California, and our great wartime president was, of course, FDR, when the Japanese-American "solution" was reached.

Reaction to the onset of the Cold War with the Soviet Union fueled another Red Scare in 1947 that led to investigations by the Committee on Un-American Activities in the U.S. House of Representatives which resulted in the blacklisting of actual or suspected Communists and fellow-travelers. Soon U.S. Senator Joseph McCarthy of Wisconsin conducted his own political witch hunts. But the hysteria passed, worn out not only by McCarthy's excess but also by the democratic process, aided and abetted by the press and television, as personified by Edward R. Murrow.

Even Great Britain, usually sensitive to human rights, arrested thousands of people, some British citizens, whom the government thought might be fifth columnists during the invasion threat in the summer of 1940. Most were released only a few months after the immediate danger had passed. Many of those arrested were later found to be refugees from Germany, some Jews and friends of England.

After the attack on the World Trade Center buildings in New York, Muslim clerics and Arab-American spokesmen were slow to denounce terrorism but quick to express fear and outrage at a persecution and a deprivation of civil liberties that basically never materialized. Had Islam denounced the violence practiced by extremists, disassociated themselves from radical clerics, and vowed to work for religious reform, Muslims would have earned respect and trust. They would have had less reason to be concerned about ethnic or racial profiling.

How successful moderate Islam is in controlling and ultimately reforming radical elements within its religion, governments, schools, the media, and throughout its societies will help determine how far American military reaction will go and how long this new kind of war will last. It will also have much to say about the Patriot Act, its successor, and future suspension of civil liberties, and how long such deprivations continue.

### The Dismal Science

Few people understand economics, domestic or global. If they did, there would have been fewer wars, cyclical depressions, recessions and panics throughout history. In politics it is nearly always "the economy, stupid." The experts are nearly as bad at predicting the economy as meteorologists are the weather. The late Louis Lyons, legendary curator of the Nieman Foundation, understood this. In his commentary on Boston's public television channel in the 1960s, he would give the weather report by going to the studio window, looking outside, and telling you what was really happening.

The economic experts ought to use a similar reality check. Most disagree among themselves and change about as often as the New England weather. Take Paul Volker, Alan Greenspan, John Maynard Keynes (deficits don't matter) and Milton Friedman (yes, they do) with a grain of salt.

No one understands annual U.S. government budgets, now weighing in at over ten pounds and in excess of two trillion dollars, even those who compile them. They are as arcane as the U.S. Tax Code, now beyond the comprehension even of the director of the Internal Revenue Service and the Secretary of the Treasury.

One can understand, however, anxiety about the loss of jobs in the American economy and the flight of capital overseas in search of off-shore tax havens. There is legitimate concern about NAFTA, unfair as opposed to free trade, and the selling of America, piece by piece, a process accelerated by corporate greed and a global economy partly driven by the World Trade Organization. Some observers are concerned that the United States could become a third world nation, unable to manufacture much at home anymore. The loss of jobs and that great "sucking sound" Ross Perot heard in 1992 invite political debate. "Outsourcing" is the word one hears the most today.

There is a limit to a service and information economy. This is a problem confronting all leading industrial nations but felt most sharply in the United States. It is aggravated by challenges from third world nations, emerging from their former agrarianism and unrestrained by labor laws, environmental regulations and other legal impediments to their revolution of rising expectations. The American economy is also threatened by the emergence of the European Union, surely a good thing but a complicating factor in the new economic equation of the twenty-first century.

Even American productivity, another good thing, carries with it additional problems for the job market. As technology becomes a substitute for human labor, unemployment may become chronic. Organized labor becomes increasingly irrelevant. The standard work week may be revised from forty to twenty hours a week. Or, in a worst case scenario, a handful of workers will labor fifty or sixty hours a week and everybody else will join the ranks of the unemployed. More people will work from home. Workers will be hired on time-limited contracts. They may have to forget about company pensions and corporate health care benefits, let alone social security. But does the answer lie in economic protectionism and high tariffs which could lead to international trade wars? Does the American consumer really want higher prices and fewer choices? It is easier to define the problem than to solve it.

But economic predictions are usually wrong. These dire consequences as the world adjusts to the new economy may never come to pass. They may be as unreliable as tomorrow's weather forecast. The economy may simply have to be redefined, as the American family has been. They will both survive, changed forever but somehow intact.

### Race Relations

The impact of slavery, segregation and racial discrimination on American society remained firmly in play throughout the twentieth century, affecting nearly every aspect of civic and political life. The civil rights struggle has, however, undergone many changes since the Brown decision of 1954.

Great changes have occurred over the past fifty years. Progress continues. The playing field gradually is being leveled. Black participation in the political process grows. Affirmative action has lent support to an expanding middle class and given new meaning to the hope expressed nearly a century ago by W.E.B. DuBois that an educated "talented tenth" would lead black people to freedom and self-realization in America.

While few people, black or white, support the idea of cash payments to right past wrongs, a domestic Marshall Plan to improve the lives of people, regardless of race, who seem otherwise fated to become part of a permanent American underclass, may prove a viable option. Poverty does not build character or add to the health of the nation. Contrary to the popular view, President Johnson's War on Poverty during the 1960s was not a total failure, nor is deficit spending always the worst alternative. Some of the nation's most prosperous times and productive periods have occurred with unbalanced budgets. Just look at FDR, Democrat, and Ronald Reagan, Republican.

Black leaders, now mostly from the Congressional Black Caucus, need to address the larger issues that most immediately affect their constituents: poverty, failing schools, out of wedlock babies borne by underage mothers, and the implosion of family life in the projects and ghettos, often both a cause and an effect of unemployment, drugs, gangs and crime. Black youths also need role models other than professional athletes, hip-hop musicians, and other celebrities. Every problem black people face in America today is not race-based or the fault of history dominated by white people.

## Church and State

Separation of Church and State is no longer a debatable issue. Everyone agrees that religion and politics don't mix. But God is different from Jesus, and God has been in the American political tradition since 1607. Reference to a divine Providence is present in the Declaration and the Preamble to the Constitution. The word God is engraved on the coin of the realm and on many public buildings and monuments. His name is invoked in ecumenical prayers at public functions. America is blessed by God every time a politician opens his mouth.

Christians, Jews and Muslims worship the same God. We secularists and Doubting Thomases shouldn't be so easily offended when a majority of God-fearing Americans want to honor His name in public places. Respect for a Deity and His words (whoever wrote them) shouldn't be so lightly set aside.

Why shouldn't a "community standards" test work as well with religion as it does with the arts? The message that calls for "peace on earth, good will to men" is one the world would do well to heed. I doubt the peace and security of the Republic is endangered by such sentiments, even when expressed by displays on government property. It is a question that involves history and heritage as much as religion. Let custom and tradition, as they are practiced from place to place, and freedom of expression decide such questions as a prayer in school assembly or before a football game. The government should occupy itself with larger issues.

The nation also has something better to do than to become involved with relatively trivial matters as whether "under God" remains a part of the Pledge of Allegiance. The phrase wasn't included until the mid-1950s, as one response in the Cold War against "Godless Communism." At the time I opposed its inclusion, not out of any political conviction but because it interrupted the flow and rhythm of the Pledge, making it even more difficult to say than it already was. The insistence on its inclusion was not President Eisenhower's finest hour, especially as he was not known for regular church attendance until he reached the White House.

## The Courts and Judicial Restraint

While judicial activism can be good and at times unavoidable, it is not a satisfactory substitute for legislative and executive leadership in enacting and administering law. A unanimous Court deciding school segregation unlawful was a good thing. But it would have been even better if integration could have resulted from laws passed by Congress, signed by the president, and affirmed by the courts. The Civil Rights Act of 1963 won quick acceptance, as did the Voting Rights Acts of 1965 and 1966, because they had behind them the will of the legislative bodies elected by the people.

The question of abortion (Roe v. Wade) is another example of a right social decision made by a split Court that would have resulted in greater national consensus if lawmakers had debated the issue and done the right thing. Today the question of judicial activism and lack of restraint is causing stress upon the concept of the separation of powers. The predictable five to four vote from a divided U.S. Supreme Court leads to public confusion and an erosion of respect for the Court and the rule of law.

### Denial of History

Sectional hostility, aligned with racial self-consciousness, is another national problem. Should the Georgia flag include a part of the Confederate flag? Should South Carolina display the Bonnie Blue Flag over the Columbia state house? Is its present location on the grounds of the Capitol an acceptable compromise? Would its removal offend white people who may regard the flag as a part of state history and heritage and a show of respect for their grandfathers, many of whom died in the Civil War?

Nearer home, should Silent Sam, the statue of the Confederate soldier standing in McCorkle Place near the Davie poplar under which the nation's first state university's charter was signed, be removed? Should historic campus buildings named after antebellum university leaders be re-identified, the offending names scrubbed because these men once owned slaves or, if they didn't, tolerated the existence of the South's "Peculiar Institution"? Is Cornelia Phillips Spencer, dead for over a hundred years and renowned as a UNC supporter who "rang the bell" to proclaim the University's re-opening after the Civil War, now to be dug up and pilloried as a segregationist?

All that smacks of Stalinism to me and the Kremlin's habit of rewriting history to suit the occasion, removing portraits and statues of disgraced leaders and making them non-persons. Let the historic record stand and judge people within the context of their times. Duke University succumbed to a similar form of political correctness when it removed a portrait of President Nixon in 1974 from the law school and hid it in a basement, as if such a move could deny the fact that Nixon took his degree at Duke.

*Civil Union and Gay Marriage*

The U.S. Congress and the federal courts would be wise to practice self-restraint in another personal matter that typifies the cultural divide in America: marriage for gay and lesbian couples. The nation continues to move in the right direction: equal rights, full access, fair treatment. Both federal and state governments will act to protect civil unions and to provide benefits to partners of the same sex that married couples get. But the states and the church may have to decide about gay marriage. The difference between civil union and marriage has become legally so narrow, it is now largely a matter of semantics. But no constitutional amendment is needed to answer this question. President Bush, the Congress, and the courts should hold their fire. Time, custom, and public acceptance will answer the question as people come to acknowledge and accept change.

To pass a constitutional amendment to forbid gay marriage is to play politics with an issue that doesn't merit that level of attention. And what's wrong with letting people do what they want to do if they hurt no one else? But what a contrast the earlier part of the twentieth century holds with the present. Then the question of homosexuality and lesbianism would never have been raised. The subject was taboo. If homosexuals were portrayed in the movies or the arts, it was always with a negative connotation. Raymond Chandler's tough guy private eye might on occasion rough up a queer but that was about it.

Young straight men might occasionally submit to service by a gay or a drag queen but usually for money. It never occurred to them they themselves were acting like prostitutes. If they rolled the guy or beat him up, even killed him, the crime was seldom reported, let alone prosecuted. The idea of a federal "hate crime" law would have been dismissed out of hand. So much for claiming the high moral ground for "the greatest generation."

Hollywood, always on the cutting edge, had its "lavender marriages," and its coterie of lesbian lovers, led by such glamour queens as Greta Garbo, Marlene Dietrich, Talulah Bankhead, Nazimova, and Miriam Hopkins, but it was all *sotto voce* and discreet. No fans knew about Charles Laughton, except his wife Elsa Lancaster who later said indulgently, "Of course I knew about his boys." Few suspected Tyrone Power, Cary Grant, or Randolph Scott, macho men of the Silver Screen who later were reputed to have swung both ways. By the 1980s, however, the veil had lifted and no one was surprised by Rock Hudson or Liberace.

As for dominatrix Madonna and her televised French kiss of the virginally seductive Britney Spears, they would have been arrested on the spot in 1950 and blacklisted. "Times," as Bob Dylan sang in 1963, "they are achangin'." Personal morals, the double standard, and the American family during the twentieth century have evolved and been redefined.

*Science, Faith and Ethics*

One would think the matter of teaching evolution in schools would have been settled by the Scopes Trial in 1924. Although the prosecutor William Jennings Bryan won the battle, he lost the war. No one challenged such teaching in the 1940s and '50s. Yet here we are in a new millennium feuding, fussing, and fighting about teaching evolution and creationism in the classroom.

Evolution is a theory with a body of research and evidence behind it. It is something that can be taught, whether you choose to accept it or not. Creationism is just a few lines from Genesis. It is faith-based. You can't teach faith as a scientific theory. There's nothing to teach. Either you have it or you don't. We may never have discovered the missing link, but evolution, in almost every aspect of life, is too important to be dismissed from public education. I like Jerry Falwell and Pat Robertson. They have done some constructive things. They are good citizens. But as leaders of the fundamentalist religious right, they also have a lot to answer for. They are examples of individuals who typified the twentieth century (along with Billy Graham and the whole evangelical movement) and have carried over intact into the twenty-first. I cannot imagine why.

In regard to scientific research and development, here's a law to consider: if the scientific community can do it, it will. Scientists transcend national boundaries. The U.S. government should encourage stem cell research. If we don't, someone else will. If it is possible to use embryonic cells and pre-natal tissue to prevent or to cure systemic diseases heretofore resistant to medical method, it is immoral not to do so. The government, working with scientists, ethical foundations and law enforcement agencies, can surely provide protection from misuses and abuses of such knowledge. The "slippery slope" argument, used so often to prevent progress, is not a convincing one.

The technological revolution admittedly can divide as well as unite. But whatever its dangers, if it can happen, it will. So I understand that technology is not only inevitable but more good than bad. It is here to stay. As entertainer Al Jolson said when talking pictures came to Warner Brothers in 1927, "You ain't seen nothin' yet."

# 58. New Branches from the Family Tree

Life is never static. The human story never ends. Good times, more numerous than bad, mingle. But there are always bumps ahead, old ones for us, new ones for the next generation. One surmounts them and moves on. The Boomer Generation began a baby boomlet themselves. Ann and I became grandparents in 1984.

David and Mindy married on my fiftieth birthday, September 15, 1973. They now have three children, Richard Phillips, born September 5, 1984; and twin girls, Mary Elizabeth and Catherine Ann, born January 9, 1986. Both are redheads. Ann certainly left her mark on the family. David is an editor at *The Atlanta Journal-Constitution*. Mindy, a graduate of Emory Law School, is an attorney. At first I was a bossy and buttinsky grandfather but eventually learned better.

Phil is a sophomore at Georgia State University in Atlanta. Elizabeth is a freshman at Appalachian State University at Boone, and Catherine is a freshman at Tulane University in New Orleans.

Molly married Lawrence Katz in April, 1981. Larry, a graduate of Brandeis University, received an M.A. in computer science. Molly graduated from Hamilton College, earned a graduate degree in speech pathology from Portland State University in Oregon, and practices in Westborough, Massachusetts. She and Larry have two children, Marion, 19, a sophomore at Brandeis University, and Abraham Alexander, 15, whose interests and talents lie in music.

Mary Cov's and Bill's eldest daughter, Mary Anita, born June 6, 1949, married John Clark in September, 1990. John, an Englishman, is a graduate of Cambridge University. John is retired. Mary Ann earned her

Ph.D. in education and teaches at the University of Florida in Gainesville. She earned her BA at Wake Forest and MA at UNC, Chapel Hill. Their son Christopher was born February 17, 1993.

Susan Vanessa was born on February 27, 1951. She graduated from Wake Forest University, received a master's degree from the School of Social Work at UNC-Chapel Hill and works in McLean, Virginia, where she lives with her husband Douglas Hall. Doug graduated from UNC-Chapel Hill, went to Stanford for an MBA, and has been involved both in politics and business related to the protection of the environment. Doug served as Assistant Secretary of Commerce in the first Clinton administration and later was president of the Nature Conservancy. Sue and Doug have two daughters, Katy, a graduate of Princeton and Lori, a junior at Duke.

Isabel and Andy are twins, born August 27, 1953. Bella is a UNC-Chapel Hill graduate, received her MA from Columbia University School of Journalism and studied journalism law at Yale. She worked as a reporter for *The New York Daily News* and is presently a writer for the *Boston Globe*. She married Francis Bailey, a graduate of Georgia Tech and of the School of Business Administration at UNC-Chapel Hill. He has also studied at Columbia and Harvard. He is a stock broker and financial advisor. Fran and Bella live in Milton, Massachusetts with their daughter Megan, 18, a freshman at Duke, and son Nick, 12.

Andy is a graduate of Wake Forest and is sports editor of the High Point Enterprise.

Lil's and John's eldest daughter Kathy, born December 5, 1943, graduated from UNC-Greensboro. She married John Vance of Kernersville, a graduate of North Carolina State University. John is retired from the State Forestry Service. He and Kathy live near Gainesville, Florida, where Kathy teaches in the public schools. They have two children. Eve is a graduate of Florida State and married to Mark Fleischman. They live in Boston.. Ted is married to Michelle Jones. They live in Margate, Florida.

Ann Buie, born August 3, 1945, is a graduate of UNC-Greensboro and later earned an M.A. in English. She is a writer and teacher, a specialist in Myers-Briggs psychological profiling and a student of Jungian thought. She is married to Robert Loomis, a graduate of Gettysburg College and of the Duke School of Forestry. He is retired from the U.S. Forestry Service, and they live in Chapel Hill. Ann and Bob have two sons. Dan, a graduate of West Virginia University, is married to Jennifer Becco, also a graduate of West Virginia University, of Laurel, Maryland. Dan and Jen have two daughters, Mackenzie, four and Olivia, two, with a third child on the way, the first members of a new generation of the extended family. They live in

Raleigh. Greg, born in December, 1972, is a graduate of James Madison University in Harrisonburg, Virginia, and works in sales in northern Virginia.

Mary Celeste Buie graduated from UNC-Charlotte. She has taught in North Carolina public schools with a degree in primary and elementary education. She has also worked as a librarian in a private school. Celeste married John Lewis of Atlanta in June, 1995. They live in Wagram, North Carolina near Laurinburg, where John works with the Department of Social Services.

Jim Buie is a graduate of UNC-Chapel Hill. He has worked for newspapers in Fayetteville, Durham, and Raleigh, and later was public relations director for the National Alliance for the Mentally Ill in Bethesda, Maryland. He has also been active in Maryland politics and is now a freelance writer. He is married to Lucia Holliday, a native of Indiana. Jim has a son Matthew, born December 1983, from an earlier marriage. Jim and Lucia have a son, Alexander, born in St. Petersburg, Russia, in 1999. Lucia is a teacher in Tacoma Park, Maryland.

When David married, we didn't lose a son, we gained a daughter. The cliché holds. When Molly married, we didn't lose a daughter, we gained a son. And between the two marriages we received a huge dividend—five grandchildren. The same holds true for nieces and nephews. There are no in-laws. They are all in the family.

All told: nine Secrests, twelve Englishes, and twenty Buies with others of this new generation yet to appear, about whom Ann and I will know nothing. But 41 isn't bad, with not a single clinker in the bunch.

*Great grandfather William Gaston Simmons (1830-89), Wake Forest professor and progenitor of the Simmons Curse.*

*Duchess, Delilah and Mac at the cabin, 1976.*

*Molly's wedding to Sam Katz, 1981.*

*Our Secrest grandchildren: Elizabeth, Phil, and Catherine 1989.*

531

*Outside our home at Carolina Meadows retirement community, Chapel Hill 1997.*

*Our final folly, Camilla Parker Bowles (Cammy), from 1998.*

*Larry, Marion, Molly and Abe Katz, 1998.*

*Cousin Vann, nephew John Clark, and Vann's daughter Martha Jane at Mary Cov's last rites, 2001.*

*My Buie nieces Celeste, Ann and Kathy, and nephew Jim, at my 80th birthday party, 2003.*

*My English nephew Andy and nieces Mary Ann, Bella and Sue at my 80th birthday party, 2003.*

# *Afterword*

Ann and I sold our house in Chapel Hill and bought a smaller place in Carrboro in 1977, now that David and Molly were out on their own. Only our boxer Dilly and cat Delilah moved with us. I retired from teaching in 1985 at sixty-two, having survived a prostate cancer operation in 1979 and a mild heart attack in 1983 in Cambridge, England, where I had been studying for the summer.

Twelve years later we moved again—to the retirement community of Carolina Meadows. Like everything else I've done, I have enjoyed retirement, even if I remain restless and sometimes dissatisfied. That's my nature. Since I can't get over it, I have gotten used to it. I have spent time reading, writing, traveling, with summers in the mountains and at the beach, and cultivating neglected interests such as classical music and an ever-changing popular culture.

I spend many afternoons walking our most recent boxer, Camilla Parker-Bowles, on campus and holding spontaneous seminars with students from whom I learn more than I teach. Richard Cole, dean of the School of Journalism, called me out of retirement in 2000 to take classes taught by an ailing Jim Shumaker, old friend and former colleague who died later that year. But it was a one-time revival not to last at my age of seventy-seven.

I have remained introspective but still do not really know myself. My life has certainly been self-examined, but has it been worth living? When I consider the happiness and joy, the sorrow and sadness, as well as the pleasure and pain, fun and excitement I have experienced, and the contributions I sometimes believe I have made, the answer is yes. One may not, in any event, lightly regard the gift of life, from whatever source it may have come.

If one has trouble knowing oneself, how can anybody understand others, especially those closest to us? People are complex and contradictory. And they change. Mary Cov remembered Mother differently from the way Lil and I do. Both she and Lil judged our father more benevolently than I. We were probably all off the mark.

Just as I failed to understand my parents, my children may misunderstand me. One hopes they don't even try, opting for acceptance over analysis. Unlike Lessie and Dowd, who forced their children to try to figure them out, Ann and I have given ours no reason to do so. We freed them early on to live their own lives, all the while generously sharing themselves and their friends with us. But they escaped prolonged preoccupation with parents and an obligation to live vicarious lives.

Even if others don't really know me, here are some traits I have observed that provide insight. I use an intrusive, extroverted personality to mask diffidence and insecurity. Having learned to dissemble early, it is second nature to me now. Those who see me as self-possessed and assured cannot know that I have rushed through life breathless, with set jaw, white knuckles and clenched teeth. Yet there is another side: calm in a crisis, reserved, a confident man, skeptical but never cynical, with an ironic, sardonic view of life, softened, I hope, by a sense of humor. I am satisfied with that self-portrait, itself perhaps a delusion.

One can sometimes feel sorry for oneself as one gets old. Every week brings news of the death of a friend. As I write, I read that Sara Justice, "Choo-choo's" wife, has died, joining her husband, my old Glen Lennox neighbor, who passed away only months earlier. When you look in the mirror and realize you are no longer that handsome fellow you once thought you were, it can be depressing. Bald head, crow's feet, loose thin skin, neck wattle, flat chest, fat stomach, wasting hips, skinny legs and flat feet. What's to be cheerful about?

Every day I look more and more like an aging Curly in the Three Stooges. The other day my wife told me, now an octogenarian, that I was smart and handsome. And Ann, at eighty-four, looks to me about the same as she did at twenty-four. How lucky that love is blind.

I wish I had the soul of an artist, able to see beauty in gnarled hands, lined, worn faces, twisted bodies. But every day in retirement at Carolina Meadows I do see something far more gratifying: incredible courage, faith and generosity and a nobility of spirit. I envy most of the elders here, as I fear I lack the kind of beauty they possess.

536

If one is lucky and still has his memory, and beyond that, sometimes feels young at heart, a young man trapped in an old man's body, the frustration can be especially sharp. Recently when the phone rang—some woman on the line to take a survey about life in general—I had my feelings hurt when she told me, having learned my age, that her focus group wasn't interested in my views.

In other words, I'm too ugly. I'm too old. "Nobody listens. Nobody cares." But then I thought a little clearer. That just isn't true. Several things have occurred in recent years to indicate just the opposite.

In 1994, when I had finally achieved the Biblical expectation of "three score and ten," the Cheraw chapter of the NAACP asked me to be speaker and guest of honor at the annual banquet of the Greater Pee Dee Association of the NAACP. I had been away for more than twenty-five years. Why ask me? Because race relations had been good in Cheraw, and the leaders of the NAACP believed a lot of the credit belonged to the *Cheraw Chronicle* and its editorial leadership between 1953 and 1968. The dinner was held in the National Guard Armory. The place was filled, the audience polkadotted by white and black faces, some old friends, some old adversaries, now all united in an enthusiastic welcome. It was a rare moment of going home again.

On May 31, 1998, family and friends gathered in Boston to honor Ann and me on our fiftieth wedding anniversary. Nearly everybody I would have expected who was still alive showed up. It was an unforgettable tribute to be remembered as a husband, father, grandfather, brother, uncle, cousin and friend to so many people whose names have frequented these pages. Ann felt equally gratified.

On October 11, 2003, David and Molly planned a party for my 80th birthday, and once again the family, now representing four generations, and friends gathered around. It was no doubt my last hurrah, but what an event it was. No, I can hardly claim that people "don't listen, don't care, and don't remember."

I have had a varied and interesting career. I'm satisfied with life's results. But nothing I have done professionally even remotely compares with the satisfaction of family life. I have had a lot to say about family dysfunction, occasioned largely by recurring illness and parental incompatibility.

But there's good as well as bad news about dysfunctional families. The good news is that they do function, often productively, even if somewhat differently. United by adversity, children from such families grow closer together. And their own children, because the feeling is fostered, seem more like siblings than first cousins. Consequently, instead of two children and five grandchildren, I feel as if Ann and I have ten children and fifteen grandchildren. My sisters have had reason to feel the same way.

The other good news is that dysfunctional families don't have to stay that way. Once problems are solved and troubles dissolve, life returns to normal (whatever that is) and people move on. The longer I live, the more I see that few families escape occasional dysfunction. If they do, they just don't understand the situation! Our family, given our set of circumstances, handled its episodes successfully. We never gave up and ended on top. I have replaced concern about the Simmons Curse with gratitude for Family Blessings.

# *Epilogue*

Unexpectedly this memoir turned into a *Sturm und Drang* tale of a turbulent childhood and a stormy adolescence that morphed into a contradictory life in the twentieth century South. I was surprised when the story I intended to tell assumed a life of its own and took me unexpectedly, sometimes unwillingly, in directions and places I never intended to go. Perhaps this result is basic to the creative impulse and unconscious imagination. Memories can be seductive and beguiling. I followed them to their natural conclusion, far removed from their original destination.

So what do I make of Locke's Final Judgment? I think he was right. Mother married the right man. Daddy married the right woman. Each supplied to the other what each lacked separately. All things considered, their children turned out all right. They did the best they could and their best proved good enough.

What about any final judgment my children may make of Ann and me, and any that my nieces and nephews may have about Lil and John, and Mary C. and Bill?

Like Lessie and Dowd, we too supplied to our mates, and they to us, things we needed. Ann lent stability. She has never had a nervous breakdown, and for me, that observation is not damning with faint praise. She accepted my family lovingly, perhaps finding in it freedom and permissiveness that she missed in her own. I drew her out of herself and into a stimulating life. As she once put it, "I pressed her talk button."

Bill gave Mary C. security and reliability, and a free rein to go and do what she wanted. She gave Bill sociability and encouragement to leave the pathology lab and reside among the living.

John gave Lil loving dependence, allowing her to raise their children as she wished, to make the basic decisions of family life and to rule the roost. She gave him security and self-acceptance, providing him with a tender, tolerant care that enabled him to live life beyond the walls of custodial care.

Marriage can be difficult. It becomes more so when all parties bring along additional baggage. You have to work at it. Love and commitment help.

Lessie's and Dowd's legacy (in Locke's own words, "three fine children and thirteen grandchildren,") which later morphed into sixteen great grandchildren and, so far, two great great ones, is good enough. And never mind "compatibility."

# *Index*

Oral Sex  480

# W

# Y

# *About the Author*

Andrew M. Secrest was born September 15, 1923, in Monroe, NC. Both a journalist and an educator, he received three degrees in history from Duke University and studied at Harvard as a Nieman Fellow.

A veteran of World War II, he served in the U.S. Navy for three years in both the Atlantic and the Pacific theatres.

Secrest was editor-publisher of the *Cheraw Chronicle* 1953-1968. Thereafter he taught at the School of Journalism at the University of North Carolina at Chapel Hill and established a journalism curriculum at North Carolina Central University in Durham, N.C.

Secrest now lives in a retirement community near Chapel Hill with his wife Ann, boxer Camilla Parker-Bowles and cats May and June. He and Ann are also blessed with a son, a daughter, and five grandchildren.

David Lide  p. 370

Printed in the United States
22957LVS00002B/28-279